The Complete Off-Premise Caterer

The Complete Off-Premise Caterer

Leopold K. Schaeli, C.M.C.

Judy Serra Lieberman

VNR VAN NOSTRAND REINHOLD
New York

Copyright © 1991 by Van Nostrand Reinhold

Library of Congress Catalog Number 90–12130
ISBN 0–442–31858–8

Printed in the United States of America

Van Nostrand Reinhold
115 Fifth Avenue
New York, New York 10003

Chapman and Hall
2–6 Boundary Row
London, SE1 8HN, England

Thomas Nelson Australia
102 Dodds Street
South Melbourne 3205
Victoria, Australia

Nelson Canada
1120 Birchmount Road
Scarborough, Ontario M1K 5G4, Canada

16 15 14 13 12 11 10 9 8 7 6 5 4 3 2 1

Library of Congress Cataloging-in-Publication Data
Lieberman, Judy Serra.
    The complete off-premise caterer/Judy Serra Lieberman.
        p. cm.
    ISBN 0–442–31858–8
    1. Caterers and catering—Handbooks, manuals, etc.   I. Title.
TX921.L54   1991
642'.4—dc20
                                                                    90–12130
                                                                    CIP

To Sal
who seasons my life with love,
patience, and laughter

Contents

Part One: BUSINESS BASICS   1

Chapter 14   The Buffet Meal   121

Chapter 15   The Seated Formal Meal   130

Chapter 16   Traditional Ceremonies and Celebrations   140

Chapter 17   The Working Lunch   145

Chapter 18   The Tea Party   149

Chapter 19   Theme Parties   156

List of Figures

Preface

Off-premise catering, a foodservice specialty that involves the preparation and delivery of food, service, and amenities to a site other than the caterer's own, is a fast-growing segment of the hospitality industry, both in the United States and abroad. This book is useful for those already in the business and essential for those planning a career in this lucrative field because it addresses the specific problems and potential of this specialty in a practical and detailed manner.

The successful off-premise caterer must have many strong qualities: he or she must be an astute business owner, a persuasive salesperson, a skilled chef, a calm supervisor, a sensitive psychologist, and a forceful manager. In addition, he or she must possess artistic flair, unlimited patience, physical stamina, a great sense of fun, and an acute eye for details. Does this superhuman exist? Remarkably, in many small catering operations the answer is yes, and for the purpose of clarity, this book addresses that single individual. In most cases, however, and especially as catering businesses expand, these multifaceted roles are played by partners, well-trained employees, and skilled specialists and consultants. Nonetheless, the primary business owner needs a thorough comprehension of the importance of these skills in order to fully exploit the potential of this enjoyable and financially rewarding career.

This book begins with an overview of the market and the procedures for setting up, organizing, and expanding an off-premise catering business, making it useful to both the aspiring and established off-premise caterer. Part II explores the varied party sites, functions, and styles of events that an off-premise caterer may be called upon to handle in the course of business and offers concrete advice for menu planning, staffing, and stylish presentation. Part III provides a selection of kitchen-tested recipes, specifically geared for off-premise catering, with many suitable variations that can lend diversity and distinction to a caterer's basic repertoire. An appendix, listing organizations and associations relative to the field, books for reference and ideas, and other resources for information, materials, and foodstuffs, should prove helpful, particularly to those located outside major metropolitan centers.

Off-premise catering is a happy, if hectic, business, and the ability to provide food with flair to satisfy the public is a well-respected achievement. While no text, course, or degree can guarantee success, the goal of this book is to advise and inspire: to warn of pitfalls, provide sensible guidelines, encourage ambition, and foster creativity in the hope that the talented professional will flourish in this fascinating, challenging, and rewarding field.

Acknowledgments

Acknowledgments, like Academy Award acceptance speeches, are always regarded from two points of view: The listener or, in this case, the reader hopes they will be informative and interesting, but certainly brief; the author, overwhelmed by the triumph of the moment (the book is, after all, *done*), is eager to express appreciation to anyone and everyone who has helped, contributed, or, at the least, continued to speak to her during the writing process.

I will say at the outset that I consider myself fortunate to be associated with Van Nostrand Reinhold, and the first among my thank-you's to people there must go to Judith Joseph, who inspired this project and helped shape the concept of the book. Thanks also to Pam Chirls, who provided encouragement and guidance throughout the project; to Lynette Ditz, who was always generous with her time and good humor; to Bob O'Brien, whose artistic skills made this book look so good; and to Leeann Graham for her hard work in getting the book manufactured. And thank you to Bernice Pettinato, of Beehive Production Services, who made the editing process seem easy.

I cannot give too much praise to Jim Smith, the talented photographer responsible for all of the photos in this book. Their creation was a truly collaborative effort, and working together with Jim, his wife Anne, and his hardworking assistants, Kelley O'Connor and Matthew Gillis, was both rewarding and fun. Other people contributed time, talent, prepared food and other props to make the photos possible, and so additional thanks go out to

Dan and Maggie Smith, The Thymes restaurant, Kingston, New York
Deising's Bakery and Coffee Shop, Kingston, New York

Carol, of Carol's Incredible Edibles, Rosendale, New York
The resourceful and cooperative staff of Grand Union in Kingston, New York
Amy at Genesis Flowers in Stone Ridge, New York
John Novi at the Depuy Canal House in High Falls, New York
The Banker's Daughter in Stone Ridge, New York
Bruce Scott, Scott Flowers, East Orange, New Jersey

And for permission to use two of the photos, thanks to

Hotel Thayer, West Point (located on the grounds of the U.S. Military Academy)—
Darlene Drechsler, Director of Catering Sales, and Ernst Meier, General
Manager
Stacy Gerber, of Total Party Concepts, Ltd., Nyack, New York

Special thanks to Judith Benn Hurley, who not only lent support, counsel, and
encouragement as a friend and colleague, but who contributed generously to the
appendix of this book.

I must express heartfelt appreciation for all my generous and understanding
friends, neighbors, and family who supported, consoled, and cajoled me throughout
the project; for my past clients, who challenged and inspired me; and for the late
Nathalie Martin, who worked beside me in the trenches in the early years and always
encouraged new projects.

These acknowledgments would not be complete if they did not include a thank-
you to my husband, Sal, who has been a working partner throughout my career. And,
finally, a special and well-deserved thank-you to my parents, Frances and Charlie
Serra, who have always been in my corner, and who donated long hours of shopping,
measuring, mixing, timing, and counting, as they assisted in testing and retesting many
of the recipes in this book.

The Complete
Off-Premise
Caterer

Part One

BUSINESS BASICS

*E*very business has its nuts-and-bolts side, and off-premise catering is no exception. There is a great deal of preliminary planning and work involved before answering the first phone call or baking the first pastry. The chapters in this section build a basic framework for a successful off-premise catering business, using a step-by-step approach starting with the very first moments when you chose catering as a career.

This part takes you through market analysis and positioning; setting up a proper legal and financial groundwork; acquiring the necessary skills, resources, equipment, and staff; and dealing with the basic concepts of costing, pricing, and salesmanship. Good management and careful documentation are essential to this business, so various approaches, policies, guidelines, and sample forms are provided to assist the caterer on a day-to-day basis, both behind the scenes and on the front lines.

Chapter 1

Preparing to Enter the Market

What is off-premise catering? This specialty of the hospitality industry can be defined as the preparation and delivery of food, service staff, and all amenities to a site other than the caterer's own. Off-premise caterers are challenged with creating a restaurant in a remote location for the purpose of serving a meal to a particular clientele. This logistical exercise is repeated daily, and the imagination, organizational skills, and culinary talents of a competent off-premise caterer are in increasing demand in today's society.

Who is the off-premise caterer? Unlike the on-premise caterer, whose business is run in his or her own building containing a banquet hall or function or party rooms, kitchens, preparation, and storage areas, the off-premise caterer is a traveling practitioner with the ability to provide complete entertaining concepts customized to a client's needs, transporting fine foods efficiently and safely, and serving them with ease and style.

Certain skills and abilities, as well as specific physical property and financial assets, are required for success in any business. If you are planning to enter the field of off-premise catering (or are already in the business and seek to expand), it is best to begin by taking a look at some of the building blocks of a successful business. Later chapters explore the importance of good legal and financial advice, but the owner or potential owner of a catering service should have an understanding of basic business practices; some aptitude for mathematics; an appreciation of the importance of sound planning and good record keeping; some familiarity with payrolls, taxes, budgets, and banking; and some sophistication in the areas of marketing, promotion, and advertising.

CULINARY SKILLS

It is essential for any caterer to have an understanding and appreciation of food preparation, basic culinary techniques, menu planning, and types and styles of

3

service. If you are a culinary student, working food professional, trained chef, or talented amateur cook, expand your talents by taking courses and jobs that will expose you to quantity cooking, purchasing, costing and pricing, staff management, wine and beverage service, buffet presentation, and banquet service.

Even if you are a trained and experienced food professional, you must make an ongoing effort to keep up to date. As a start, every off-premise caterer should build a basic reference library (see the Appendix). In addition to professional culinary texts, select one or two basic domestic cookbooks (e.g., *Fannie Farmer* or *Joy of Cooking*), at least one culinary encyclopedia (such as *Larousse Gastronomique*), a few books that deal with ethnic cuisines, and some books on specialty work (such as baking, garde-manger, and quantity cooking). You also should have ready access to sources of current information on safe food handling, nutritional information, and religious dietary rules. The Government Printing Office, religious organizations, and embassies of foreign countries provide easy and inexpensive access to this sort of information. Since clients expect a caterer to be knowledgable in all aspects of entertaining, add books on modern etiquette, fine wines, bartending, and table settings. Keep abreast of food trends and garner recipe and presentation ideas from both trade and consumer magazines.

SOUND BODY/SOUND MIND

Physical stamina is a prime requirement for anyone who has considered the food trade as a career. Off-premise catering is hard work. It involves hours of client meetings, planning, bookkeeping, shopping, heavy lifting and packing, setup, breakdown, and, in between, the whole day on your feet. You need to keep in good shape, maintain a high energy level, and have the resilience to bounce back from exhaustion to start work fresh and alert the next day. Your personality should be equally resilient: you should possess a genuine fondness for people, be comfortable with crowds, and feel confident about face-to-face dealings with persons from all walks of life. You should be cool-headed in a crisis and be able to give direction clearly and firmly, without resorting to threats or shouts. Patience, in this business, is indeed a virtue, and physical fitness is a prime requirement.

CATERING EXPERIENCE

If you are just entering the field, give serious consideration to working for an established caterer, even at low pay, to gain valuable hands-on experience. Seek employment in your weakest area: if you are a good manager, work in the kitchen; if you are skilled in the kitchen, work as a waiter or maître d'. Whether you work as a bartender or in a kitchen tent preparing hors d'oeuvre trays, you will see the catering operation firsthand and understand what it means to run such a business on a day-to-day basis.

Freelance Accommodators

If you plan a career in off-premise catering but are not on sound enough financial footing to begin your own business, consider working as an accommodator. An accommodator performs the services of a private chef, preparing, cooking, and sometimes serving food on the client's premises. Since the client provides all the food, equipment, working space, and serving area, the accommodator does not need a licensed commissary and expensive food and equipment inventory and is not burdened by board of health licensing, sales tax requirements, or insurance costs.

While some people make a full-time career as accommodators, it is an excellent means to gain experience, establish a reputation, and build a client base while accumulating savings that can be invested in a future catering business.

As an accommodator, you simply charge for your time and services, either a flat fee or an hourly rate. Be certain that you arrange to prepare all food on the client's premises, not in your own home, which may be both illegal and unsafe because of the possibility of spoilage. You would consult with the client beforehand, plan a menu and make suggestions on amounts and types of foods to be ordered, give advice on where certain specialty items may be purchased, and recommend types and amounts of beverages. In addition, you would visit the client's home (or other party site) to discuss the layout of tables, bar area, and buffet stations; to check out the cooking and serving equipment; and to ensure that the client's linens, china, glassware, and cutlery meet the needs of the planned function. If any party goods need to be rented, you may recommend one or two reliable sources to your client. If extra staff is required and you know responsible serving and kitchen help, arrange to put your client in touch with them.

It is always best to have your client do all the ordering, purchasing, hiring, and paying of bills, which frees you from bookkeeping and paperwork and removes you from any possible suspicion of padding bills or receiving illegal kickbacks. Your only legal responsibility is to perform your services well, charge fairly for your time, and report your earnings to the IRS.

FINANCIAL STATUS

Before embarking on this or any other business venture, it is important to have sufficient financial reserves to provide amply for start-up costs and to pay both business and living expenses for at least six months to a year. As you will see in the chapters that follow, the costs of going into business mount up, with licenses, fees, insurance premiums, and hefty deposits for rent and utilities. In addition, it will take you several months to establish lines of credit with purveyors and suppliers. It is important to allow a business to reach a comfortable level of profitability with a solid client base and dependable cash flow over a period of time. Sufficient capital will allow you to nurture a growing business without courting imminent bankruptcy and disaster with every slow week or cancelled event.

THE WORKPLACE

Having a place to do business is, of course, a basic requirement. An off-premise caterer must have a licensed kitchen or commissary in which to prepare food, a storage area for supplies, a truck or van (leased or owned) for transport and deliveries, and an office space for telephone and paperwork. Chapter 4 provides more detailed information on setting up a commissary, but if you are just starting out you might arrange to use a licensed kitchen on a time-share or rental basis and do the paperwork at home.

IMAGE

Off-premise catering is basically a sales business, and the product you are selling is, surprisingly, not your food but yourself. It is therefore essential that you analyze this specialized product—you, the capable and creative caterer—to define what image will make you successful in the market.

Make yourself special and unique to your public, and you will find yourself in demand. Explore your strengths in terms of skill and style. For example, if you have talent as a fabulous baker, you might offer breakfasts featuring muffins, scones, croissants, and danish; create an innovative selection of filled breads and sandwiches for luncheons and teas; or specialize in extraordinary dessert buffets. If you have an affinity for ethnic cuisines, offer paella parties, dim sum brunches, pasta buffets, or authentic Indonesian rijsttafel. The talented seafood or grill master might specialize in clambakes or barbecues. If your skill lies in elaborate garnishing and dramatic presentation, make your trademark jewellike canapés and stunning buffets.

SPECIALIZATION AND EXPANSION

If you have an ongoing catering business, analyze your past successes and failures and examine your recent bookings for trends among your clientele. Is your business moving in a new direction? Are you receiving more requests for business lunches than weddings? If so, you might explore the possibility of servicing the local business community in a more focused way: prepare sample menus for stylish breakfasts, buffet lunches, or coffee and juice breaks that can be delivered on short notice, and send letters to your corporate accounts announcing your new "Executive Express" service. If you enjoy providing the romantic flourishes and handling the complex logistics of lavish weddings, increase your exposure in that market by advertising your services to wedding consultants, or host a "Sweet Dreams" dessert buffet one weekend at a local bridal salon. In these ways, you can increase the profitability of your business by defining yourself as a specialist.

In some situations the opposite approach is worth exploring. Caterers in a small community might increase business by expanding their services to include more varied types of functions to fully serve their clientele. The successful gourmet takeout shop, restaurant, or specialty butcher would do well to capitalize on its popularity by offering off-premise catering to its customers. A school, hospital, or other public institution, with a fully equipped and staffed commissary, might look to an off-premise catering business to utilize its installation fully and gain additional revenues. In these cases, the smart move would be from a specialized service to a more general approach to build a broader business base.

Chapter 2

Understanding the Marketplace

The market for off-premise catering services is broad, diversified, ever-changing, and expandable and is affected by changes in living trends and taste on national, regional, and local levels. The professional who is planning to invest time and money in developing a business must be aware and sensitive to those trends that will affect and influence potential clients. It may be hard to believe that national or even international events and movements can affect a modest business in a small town, but in fact, with the instantaneous relay of information in today's media-oriented society, almost nothing happens in the world that doesn't ultimately have an effect that is felt in all but the most isolated communities. It is thus important for the ambitious off-premise caterer to keep informed of changes in demographics, life-style, and the economy.

DEMOGRAPHIC TRENDS

Demographics, which is the study of statistical data relating to births, deaths, marriages, mortality, and living patterns of a given population, seems like a dry subject indeed for a caterer. But consider these bits of information that can be found in even a cursory reading of national news magazines.

Many couples are marrying later in life, usually after both have become established in their careers. Their income is greater, their tastes are more expensive and sophisticated, and their dependence on prepared goods—from convenience foods to catered meals—is greater than in the past. Once these couples begin their families, they tend to move to suburbs and exurbs of large metropolitan areas, taking their habits and tastes with them. Such growing communities are fertile ground for new catering establishments. These couples are having children later in life and tend to indulge them more. Youngsters, constantly exposed to media in a high-tech world, are raised to a more sophisticated level of taste.

7

Other data show an increase in our nation's life expectancy; for example, seniors now make up the fastest growing segment of our population. At the low end of the economic spectrum, there is a greater demand for group feeding at senior citizen centers and group residences. More affluent seniors may relocate to retirement communities. Others may sell their suburban homes and move to city apartments. Those with extra income and leisure time tend to enjoy entertaining and are not hesitant to pay someone to do the work.

Changes in business and industry sometimes dictate shifts in population from one geographic region to another. Foreign investments in a city may bring an influx of new residents who will change the cultural makeup of a given population. Ethnic populations bring their particular food tastes with them to their new homes, and a familiarity with their cuisines usually spills over into the larger community. As a businessperson, you will be affected by either growth, decline, or change in your area, and by being aware of such changes, you can adjust your business plans accordingly.

LIFE-STYLE TRENDS

The intelligent businessperson watches for news of all kinds, particularly for items that deal with food, entertaining, and fashion and tries to interpret how those changes can be translated into additional business. One example is the current health and fitness consciousness. Food professionals everywhere quickly developed menus that are low in fat, cholesterol, and sodium content.

You might contact local runners' and bikers' clubs and solicit business for a pre-marathon supper; submit a quote for the service of nutritious juices and snacks for race participants, judges, and spectators; and offer a menu for the awards banquet. To further exploit this trend, explore your local area for attractive and spacious health clubs and meet with the manager of the facility to suggest the possibility of holding pool parties, barbecues, and the like on the premises.

Reading consumer food magazines and the life-style sections of newspapers keeps you abreast of food trends and changes in tastes. Ethnic and regional cuisines rise and fall in popularity, and many of your clients read these publications and want to serve and be served whatever is new and popular at the moment. Notice which restaurants are flourishing in your area, and be prepared to satisfy any new tastes in food or style that you see developing.

Keep in touch with the life of your own community as well. Dates and events of local importance (e.g., a town centennial, the renovation of a museum, the grand opening of a new shopping mall, political campaigns, and local cultural and charitable undertakings) should become as much a part of a caterer's calendar as the dates of traditional holidays. If you are mindful of these new business opportunities, you will be prepared to offer proposals to cater such events to potential clients.

ECONOMIC TRENDS

Changes in the economy, whether on a global or local scale, also have an impact on your business. Issues that affect the way both personal and public income are disbursed and taxed affect spending.

In business areas, upswings and downturns in industry cause corporations to change the way they decide what spending profile to maintain. In boom years, companies invest in promotional parties for new products, are lavish in entertaining their associates, and generous in rewarding and entertaining their employees. In tight budget years, layoffs and cutbacks dictate a more restrained and discreet entertaining style. In the late 1980s, changes in the tax laws made restaurant lunch deductions a tricky area for businesses. As the restaurant business lunch began to lose favor, many companies turned to the working in-office lunch as both efficient and more easily defensible to the IRS. This change created a new lucrative market for the off-premise caterer.

On the personal level, the portion of the family budget that might be spent on catered events is part of what is called discretionary income, money set aside for the extras or luxuries of life, not the necessities, including football tickets, restaurant meals, nights at the opera, jewelry, and so forth. When income levels are up, your clients clearly will be more disposed to entertain more frequently and on a grander scale. In leaner times, be prepared to offer more economical alternatives, perhaps proposing less expensive ethnic themes, which generally feature more pasta, grains, and vegetables and less meat, rather than luxury items on your menus. Staying in tune with such trends will help you retain and satisfy your client base.

MARKET SECTORS

For the purposes of simplification, the market can be divided into three sectors: private, corporate, and public. There is naturally some blurring of these lines, but for the most part, a caterer's clients fall into these three categories, and each group has special characteristics, needs, and goals that the caterer should understand.

The Private Sector

The private sector concerns itself with traditional family celebrations such as engagements, weddings, anniversaries, birthdays, bas and bar mitzvahs and general social entertaining that is often done at home. Society, in general, has shown a renewed interest in traditional entertaining. For example, large formal weddings, unfashionable during the sixties and seventies, have become popular again, and often the bride and groom are older and more well-established in their careers when they marry than they were in the past. This longer period of professional single life has exposed couples to a higher standard in terms of life-style and sophistication of taste. They often pay for their own wedding celebrations, and while they are prepared to spend more, they expect high quality, an original menu, and stylish presentation. Some clients will be concerned with adhering to a budget, especially if they have not had extensive exposure to the business of catering, and they may be under the misconception that catering done at home is less expensive than dining at a restaurant. Take pains to offer these clients a selection of menus that suits both their needs and their pocketbooks.

Clients from the private sector want their personal tastes and values to be respected. Their guest list often covers a broad age range, from children to seniors, and menu choices must be diverse enough to please such guests. Remember also that home entertaining (see Chapter 11) is the most intimate form of entertaining, and as a caterer you must understand a client's pride in his or her home.

Private clients may be quite inexperienced at large-scale social entertaining. They need to be handled with great patience and understanding. Especially for major functions, bear in mind that these events mark momentous occasions in the lives of your clients, and are truly once-in-a-lifetime events. Be prepared to exude confidence and caring, to counsel and advise an anxious host or hostess, to calm and reassure a nervous bride, in short, to guarantee that a special event will live up to your client's expectations.

The Corporate Sector

The corporate sector embraces all aspects of the business world's catering needs, including general business entertaining, employee meals, and serving during advertising or promotional events. In the corporate sphere, it is especially important to behave in a businesslike manner. You may be dealing directly with a small business owner, with a board chairperson or company president, with a secretary or administrative assistant, or with the meeting and events planner of an international corporation. It is important to remember that business clients are performance and bottom-line oriented. They are straightforward and clear cut as to purpose, style, and budget; in return, they expect professional execution of a project with no hassles. They often give short notice so have ready several simple menus and arrangements that can be offered quickly and efficiently.

Corporate catering needs are varied, and one of the most popular among them is the working lunch (see Chapter 17). In some cases, this lunch business can lead to a caterer's providing in-house staff to operate an employee cafeteria and/or executive dining room. Many successful caterers devote a separate branch of their businesses to providing such services to one or more companies.

Some prominent New York City Wall Street firms recently decided that time taken from the international trading day to eat out is too valuable and have set up an arrangement where caterers collect orders (chosen from a limited menu) each morning and deliver boxed or bagged lunches to employees at their desks at an appointed time. In this way, the company receives efficient and orderly delivery and the caterer is assured a fixed volume each day.

If you intend to cultivate corporate business, become sensitive to the needs of business. Different industries have their own calendars and cycles: the fashion industry, for instance, has regular showings of new collections several times a year and offers hospitality to an influx of buyers. Publishers promote books for spring and fall lists. Film and video production companies frequently work through the day and night, often on city streets. Architectural and construction firms celebrate the topping off of new buildings, and manufacturers plan major promotional parties to launch new products. Investigate the industries around you to gain a foothold with this clientele.

The corporate market can be the core of a caterer's business because it provides good repeat business and is consistent all year. A few corporate clients can ensure a steady cash flow, and a satisfied corporate client can provide good referrals to other companies that often results in spillover into the private and public sector.

The Public Sector

The public sector includes institutions; charities; civic, political, and fraternal organizations; religious and community groups; labor unions; museums; and schools. In this sphere, it is not unusual for a committee to be a client. There are often preproposal meetings, which may include tastings of sample menus, and the caterer should be prepared to listen to a chorus of opinions and requests. It is important to cultivate a presence that projects confidence and authority, to listen to a variety of ideas, and to help the committee reach a consensus regarding the menu and details of the event. Often the caterer will be expected to arrange for or coordinate a range of extra services such as tables and equipment for raffles, door prizes, table favors, ramps and lighting for fashion shows, microphones, podiums, and audio-visual equipment for slides and films, drums for ticket drawings, and so on.

In pricing for charity events, the caterer should never agree to do things "on the cheap" in order to meet budget demands. Yielding to the temptation to secure an influential account by providing a low bid and then lowering professional standards to protect a profit margin can be most damaging to a caterer's long-term business. The quality of a caterer's food and a professional level of performance are the best advertising, and any effort to cut corners that results in an inferior job reflects poorly on the caterer, not on the organization. Remember that the guests present at such a function (and their wider social circle) are all potential future clients.

It is wiser to donate an extra such as an occasion cake, a cheese course, after-dinner chocolates, or an elaborate ice carving free of charge than to severely discount the overall price. Choose this one-time gift so it is appropriate to the event, but you control its cost in terms of your time and money. In addition, it is clearly defined as a charitable contribution and therefore deductible at tax time. It establishes your generosity in the eyes of the organization and may help you clinch the deal. In contrast, an unprofitable bargain price lives on after the event and compromises your ability to negotiate future contracts with this and other similar organizations.

GAINING YOUR SHARE OF THE MARKET

By observing and analyzing market trends and by understanding the characteristics and special needs of the three market sectors, you can enhance the possibilities of expanding your business. In order to gain your market share, you should examine your competition, increase your business exposure, explore the possibilities of advertising and publicity, and take every opportunity to promote yourself and your business.

Examine the Competition

Begin your examination by doing a quick survey of the established catering businesses operating in your area. Check listings in local newspapers and magazines, contact the chamber of commerce, and talk with friends and acquaintances, professional groups, and fraternal organizations to find out who are the prominent caterers.

What sort of business do they do? Do they handle large or small volume jobs? Do they specialize in weddings and formal banquets? Do they cover one market sector for all types of functions, or do they specialize in one type of event for all sectors? Have they saturated a particular market or slot, or is there ample clientele for you to share? Have they neglected to offer a service that might provide you with a market niche? These types of questions help you decide how viable your business plans are. In an area with a large population of potential clients, many similar businesses can compete successfully. In a smaller, less affluent, or less densely populated area, you might choose to direct your efforts toward an untapped market to increase your chances of success.

Make some calls or inquiries to find out what menus your competition offers and at what prices. As you will see in Chapter 7, you must ultimately decide on a pricing structure that provides you with a satisfactory profit margin, but comparative pricing is useful in defining the going price for a given service in your area. Bear in mind that while it is true that people will pay more for perceived quality and excellence, there is almost always a certain price range that clients will find acceptable.

Increase Your Exposure

Join a local organization to network with other caterers or food professionals in your area. Search out local chapters of national food service organizations, whose meetings, bulletins, and seminars can be a great source of support and information (see Appendix). You thus make yourself and your ambitions known and can discuss common problems and share information. Most successful businesspersons welcome healthy competition in a free market, and if you conduct yourself graciously and ethically, you will be welcomed. You may be pleasantly surprised to find that some of your culinary colleagues can be very supportive and helpful to someone just starting out. If you're viewed as a threat, take it as a compliment and forge ahead!

Explore Advertising, Promotion, and Publicity

At the outset decide on the name of your company. It may be trendy, formal, informal, or simply your own name. The name you choose for your business should clearly and strongly project the image you have chosen: for example, The Crazy Italian Caterers, American Heartland (featuring American foods), Bayou Blues, or the Alpine Catering Company (specializing in Bavarian cuisine), all of which indicate the type of food served. Other names might indicate a style or target market—for example, Gourmet Bouquet, Affair of the Heart, Food for Lovers Only, for those specializing in romantic weddings; or Blue Chip Foods or The Gray Flannel Lunch for those pursuing a corporate clientele. In establishing a name that defines your service, avoid names that might be restricting or become quickly outdated.

A stylish logo, created by you or an artist, enhances your image. Make an initial investment in business cards, letterheads, and envelopes. If you have a truck or van, have your name or logo painted on its side; this traveling billboard will increase your visibility. Paid advertising can be expensive, and it is best to start small, with a listing in the *Yellow Pages*, and perhaps a line or two in a catering guide or party services listing in the town guide, a local newspaper, or a popular magazine. As your business grows, you will be able to increase your advertising budget, and you might choose to hire an advertising agency to help you create promotional brochures, sample menus, and more sophisticated advertising copy.

In the catering business, the very best advertising is word of mouth. As you first start out, your initial business will likely come from relatives, neighbors, friends, and business acquaintances. In this circle you've already established your reputation as a fabulous cook, and if you perform well, it is only a matter of time before you will have your first paying clients. They, in turn, will refer you to their friends and associates, and you'll be in business, but it is up to you to keep spreading the word.

Make it a habit to follow up with clients after every event with a simple thank-you call or letter that offers to serve them again in the future. Some caterers send attractive postcards to clients as reminders to plan for holiday parties. Others send occasional announcements of new services or the introduction of a new menu to a client mailing list. Still another possibility is to solicit new clients by sending letters, sample menus, or brochures to local businesspeople, new area residents, newly engaged couples, and local organizations. With today's computers and rapid printing services, it is simple to personalize letters; if you do so, make sure you spell the recipient's name correctly and use the proper title, if any. A small detail like this can make a most favorable impression.

In addition to joining professional food or trade groups, make yourself known to the larger community by becoming a member of one or two civic, fraternal, or cultural organizations, such as the local chamber of commerce or the visitor convention bureau. The camaraderie and contacts are rewarding and useful. Most organizations welcome speakers and events that are of interest to their membership. Offer to teach a holiday baking or table-setting class; give a demonstration on food garnishing or chocolate dipping; participate in or help organize a charity cook-off or chili festival. If you are just establishing yourself in the community, offer to provide refreshments free of charge at the next meeting.

Foster publicity whenever you can. When you cater an important function, encourage the host, company, or charity group to get a mention in the press. Drop a note or photo (with the host's permission) to the society or style editor of the local paper, including some newsworthy details about the menu, guest list, or staging of the party. Contact your local radio station and offer to participate in a call-in show about food trends, nutrition, or wedding planning.

If you have talent as a writer, submit an occasional article to a food magazine or the food section of your newspaper. Try to make yourself the focus of an article by offering distinctive recipes or entertaining pointers that represent your style to the food or life-style editor. If your company has a signature item such as a special dip, petits fours, jams, or cheese sticks, send or bring samples to your local newsroom, including a short release about your service and the specialty item. Undertake these approaches with some restraint: don't be a nuisance, but don't be shy. Blowing your own horn, provided it is done in good taste, is perfectly acceptable in this business.

Chapter 3

Structuring and Protecting the Business

It may be fair to say that every off-premise caterer enters into business with at least one partner—the government; should take on two more—an attorney and an accountant; and has the option of adding one more—a working business partner if it suits his or her business needs and temperament.

THE GOVERNMENT

As in any other business enterprise, the off-premise caterer is responsible to a variety of public institutions and under the jurisdiction of a network of regulatory agencies from the federal to the local level. First, you must obtain the necessary licenses and permits to conduct business. Second, since you are involved in financial transactions, you must collect and pay taxes to the government. And finally, to protect yourself, your business, your assets, and your employees, you must obtain appropriate and sufficient insurance coverage. The material that follows is, of necessity, somewhat generalized.

Licensing

Regulations vary from state to state and within towns and municipalities. It is imperative that you thoroughly research your specific licensing situation by checking with the local chamber of commerce, county seat, or city or town hall. To neglect to do so could surely result in problems that would cause you unwelcome expense, delay, and frustration.

Health Regulations   The board of health is a regulatory body whose function is to protect the health of the public it serves. Since you are in the business of serving food to that public, inspectors from the board of health regularly examine your premises and methods to see that they meet certain specifications and guidelines, which they provide, that ensure that the food items you produce are fit for consumption and do not pose a threat of illness. There's good sense behind these requirements: the government keeps a watchful eye on the whole food chain, from farm to feedlot to table. When you enter the catering business, you become part of that chain, and the regulations involved are a means of reassuring and protecting the public. You purchase the raw food from an approved or inspected source, and you should store it and prepare it in such a way that it is not contaminated or made unsafe for consumption. In addition, your employees must be trained and supervised in proper sanitation methods, and they should be in good health, with no infections that they might transmit to food, each other, or the public.

These rules are based on good common sense and are not intended to impede the operation of your business. Indeed, following board of health guidelines for proper sanitation and food handling protects your operation from waste, inefficiency, accidents caused by food spills, food spoilage, and illness and injury to your employees and saves your reputation from the grave damage that would result from an outbreak of illness that might be traced to your food. Specific regulations may vary from one area to another, but, in general, these are the areas of concern to health inspectors: food purchase, storage, and handling; conditions of the commissary and on-site facilities; and health and hygiene of employees.

FOOD PURCHASE, STORAGE, AND HANDLING   You should purchase your foods from approved or inspected sources. Meats, poultry, game, and fish should be properly stamped or tagged, and other products packaged and produced to ensure their wholesomeness. Then you must store and handle them properly:

- Keep dry and canned goods in a clean, dry, well-ventilated area and raise them off the floor as a protection from rodents and pests. Inspect cans for bulges or leaks.

- Be vigilant about broken packaging of dry goods, inspecting them for any contamination or tampering.

- Use first in/first out rule for all perishables to protect against spoilage and waste.

- Store dairy products in their original containers under appropriate refrigeration, and honor freshness dating. Check eggs for cracks to avoid salmonella.

- Wash produce well and/or peel to remove potentially harmful chemical sprays. Store all produce carefully, either in ventilated bins or under refrigeration to protect against spoilage. Never store produce, especially items to be consumed raw, under or near raw meat or poultry.

- Store meats, game, and poultry at proper temperatures (see Figure 3–1): keep refrigerated until used; keep frozen if received frozen, thaw under refrigeration (or under cold running water in an emergency). Use frozen items that have

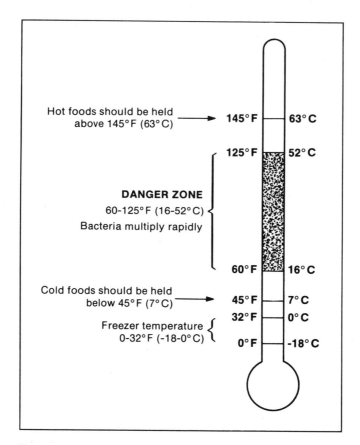

Figure 3–1
Safe food storage and handling temperatures.

partially thawed in transit or receiving as soon as possible. Refreezing not only affects quality but also can foster bacterial growth.

- Purchase fish and shellfish from a reliable source. Shellfish especially must be tagged to indicate its harvest from safe waters. Store at proper temperatures and in such a way as to prevent odor transfer or contamination of other foods. Storing fish improperly not only risks spoilage but also severely affects its texture and flavor.

- During food preparation, maintain proper temperature (see Figure 3–1) as much as is feasible; keep handling to a minimum, and cover prepared or partially prepared foods to protect them from contamination.

- Following the handling of raw meats and poultry, thoroughly wash all work surfaces and utensils, and make sure all employees wash their hands before handling any other food item or utensil.

- Maintain partially prepared foods at safe temperatures (45° F or below, 140° F or above; see Figure 3–1) during storage and transport, and tightly wrap or package them to preserve their quality and wholesomeness.

- Be sure perishable cooked foods (especially pastry creams, custards, egg-based dressings—are consumed within their allotted safe holding period. Never combine leftovers with fresh products.

COMMISSARY FACILITIES   The goal of the regulations governing commissary facilities is to ensure cleanliness and safety. Executing the regulations, however, can be complicated, and as we will see in Chapter 4, a good kitchen consultant who is expert in meeting these requirements can be a good ally. You can find reputable kitchen consultants through local restaurant equipment dealers, equipment manufacturer's representatives, or a culinary arts or restaurant management program at a local community college or university. In general, however, the following guidelines apply when planning a commissary.

- Ventilation should be sufficient to promote safety and comfort, maintain temperature, prevent grease buildup, remove unhealthy and unpleasant smoke, and provide a flow of fresh air with a minimum of dust, debris, and insect invasion.

- Lighting should be sufficient for good and safe working conditions: that is, bright enough to allow for ease in food preparation and thorough cleaning as well as to prevent falls and breakage.

- Refrigeration should be maintained at proper temperatures (see Figure 3–1), have thermometers, be properly installed and drained, and be easy to keep clean.

- Cooking equipment and appliances should be National Sanitation Foundation (NSF) approved and properly installed, vented, and maintained. These and other working surfaces should be well constructed, made of nonporous materials, and easy to clean and disinfect thoroughly. They should have no unnecessary moldings or crevices that could harbor dirt or contaminated matter.

- Plumbing should be adequate to provide fresh and clean water for cooking and washing, with no possible backflow or contamination from sewage.

- Dish- and/or pot-washing facilities should be separate from food prep or hand-washing activities, and have water hot enough (or chemically adjusted) to provide sterilization.

- Utensils should be properly sanitized and stored for safety and cleanliness.

- Cleaning equipment and products should be properly labeled and stored away from foods.

- Floors, walls, and ceilings should be properly cleaned on a regular schedule. Floors should be properly drained and mopped regularly to prevent falls and spills.

- Garbage should be handled, stored, and disposed of in an approved manner.

- A regular program of extermination and rodent control should be followed.

- Proper and separate storage should be provided for soiled and clean linens.

- Restrooms and lockers should be adequate for staff use and kept clean and in good repair.

- Materials, equipment, and vehicles used to transport food should be well maintained, cleaned, and stored in such a way as to keep them sanitary and vermin free. Disposable packaging or individual serving containers or utensils should not be reused.

ON-SITE FACILITIES   Off-premise caterers must maintain the same high standards at each party and function site that they expect in their own commissary. While on-site settings are often far from ideal, the principles of good sanitation and safety should apply wherever possible. You often have less than adequate facilities in which to work, but can strive to preserve correct conditions with the use of temperature-controlled vans and portable units. We discuss these items in more detail in Chapter 4, but bear in mind that this is a responsibility not to be taken lightly. Health inspectors have the right to inspect off-premise catering sites, as well as permanent facilities, and expect overall conditions and staff performance to reflect safe and proper handling of foods for public consumption.

EMPLOYEES   In addition to following your (or your chef's) instructions on safe and sanitary food-handling procedures, employees are expected to attend to their own personal hygiene. They should be provided with clean uniforms, wear hair or head coverings if needed for long hair, exercise care and cleanliness when handling food or utensils, observe no smoking or eating rules, and wash their hands frequently between tasks and visits to restrooms or lounge areas. If they suffer any cuts or burns on the job, they should be treated and bandaged appropriately and return to work only with the permission of their supervisor. They should not work with food if ill with a communicable disease, severe cold, or fever. In most operations, one or two persons are charged with the responsibility of inspecting or cleaning food storage and prep areas, but all employees should be aware of proper procedures and do their part on an everyday basis.

Zoning, Fire, Building, and Safety Codes   Zoning boards exist to maintain a certain quality of life in a given neighborhood. They take into account considerations such as noise, pollution, traffic congestion, community aesthetics, street and building lighting, signage, facility size and design, truck access, parking, garbage storage and collection, and public safety. They exercise the public consensus of what is pleasing and appropriate and what is construed as a nuisance or a detriment. In some areas, a maze of overlapping ordinances that define the zoning for a specific plot of land (or an already existing building) exists, and you are encouraged to take the advice of an experienced realtor and a knowledgeable attorney to help you understand the code and obtain the proper zoning board clearances to set up your operation.

Do not even consider signing a rental lease, buying a property, or contracting for any construction or renovation of your proposed business space until you have secured these zoning clearances. While it is true that zoning variances are sometimes granted and zoning codes changed, it is unwise to invest time and money until you are sure that you can proceed to set up your business.

Once you have filed for and received your zoning clearances and are aware of the requirements necessary to obtain your license to do business from the board of health, you will find yourself subject to further inspections and ordinances. In most areas, expect to meet fire safety codes and to have your plumbing, electrical, and gas installations, along with other building alterations, approved by local authorities. Again, check with your chamber of commerce in advance to be sure you are not planning anything that will violate local codes. As better reassurance, use licensed contractors to perform such work, and have your expert kitchen consultant jump the hurdles for you.

Alcohol Service Regulations   The legal sale and service of alcoholic beverages to the public is an area closely monitored by the government. As an off-premise caterer you are not involved in the sale of alcohol but must honor local regulations for beverage service, especially those regarding legal drinking age, and be aware of the responsibility involved in serving alcohol to someone already under the influence. We discuss proper procedures involving alcohol in other chapters (particularly Chapters 5, 6, 10, and 13), but research the rules of your state liquor authority to be properly informed.

Off-premise caterers often advise clients about alcohol purchase, perhaps referring them to a trusted wine or liquor shop for advice. You may even place orders for your clients, but under no circumstances should you sell or resell any alcoholic beverage without a license. In some special circumstances, such as when catering a fund raiser, you will be asked to operate a cash bar; in most areas, you can secure a one-time-only license for that event. Consult with a knowledgeable attorney.

In terms of licensing, one final note: some areas classify caterers under surprising categories, for example, as a simple commissary, a restaurant, or a food packager or processing plant, not specifically as on off-premise caterer. If possible, file at the outset for the most comprehensive license or licenses, so that future expansion (perhaps to include over-the-counter sale of desserts or specialty food baskets) will not be limited by a restrictive license. It is less expensive, in terms of both time and money, to file and qualify for comprehensive licensing than to make a number of changes, arrange for filings and inspections, and pay additional fees at later intervals.

Taxes

It is a fact of life that whenever you earn money or receive payment for goods or services, the government gets its share. And the more the government "simplifies" tax forms, the more complicated they get. Your best line of defense is to hire a good accountant. The fee or retainer you pay for accountancy services is money well spent. A sharp accountant not only sees that you pay the taxes required by law but also points out all the legitimate deductions to which you are entitled as a business owner. While local details may vary, in general you are required to pay personal income tax on your earnings—whether you are a member of a partnership, an officer of a corporation, or self-employed. Such taxes are often paid on a quarterly basis, and an accountant can set up the appropriate payment schedule for your situation.

Some areas require you to collect sales tax on your business transactions; your accountant can help you file for a tax identification number and guide you in proper collection and payment procedures. In addition, you are expected to pay and record payroll taxes for your salaried employees. Serving staff usually work sporadically on a freelance basis and are officially termed independent contractors. An independent contractor is responsible for paying his or her own taxes, and you should make this clear when you contract them for work. Should you find yourself employing the services of a few of these people on a regular, continuing basis, your accountant or attorney may advise you to alter their status in order to protect your business from any infringement of the tax laws.

Insurance

Protection of yourself, your assets, your property, and your employees is vitally important to your business and your future. Consult with one or two reputable insurance agents, and with the advice of both your attorney and accountant, decide on the coverage that is both required and desirable for your particular situation.

Comprehensive general liability insurance and/or products liability insurance cover you against claims from clients or guests in the event that illness or injury is a result of the food you serve or of careless or faulty performance by you or your staff. Products liability protects you in the event that a product you buy from another manufacturer and serve to your guests proves to be defective or causes harm.

Additional types of business and property insurance can offer protection in areas such as general business, mortgage and partnership, building and contents, fire, theft and burglary, and equipment damage and loss. The off-premise caterer is wise to invest in a floater policy that covers valuable equipment, whether in the commissary, in transport, or on a job site. In addition, any vehicles you own must be properly insured. Since policies and coverage sometimes overlap, and your needs change as your business develops, review your situation periodically. Insurance premiums can be expensive but are well worth the expense in terms of peace of mind.

Some insurance for employees is required by law and is tied in to payroll taxes: Social Security (FICA), Worker's Compensation, disability, and unemployment insurance. In addition, as your business increases you might find it possible and favorable to offer other plans to your employees, such as group medical or dental, retirement, and even profit-sharing plans. Discuss these options with your accountant and insurance agent.

ATTORNEY AND ACCOUNTANT

One of the wisest and most rewarding investments you can make in your business are the fees you will pay to a good attorney and accountant. Since you plan to be expert in the catering field, seek out and pay for expert advice outside your field. Find professionals who have some experience in the food field, are knowledgeable about business in general, are conversant with tax laws, and are established in the community in which you intend to do business. You should be comfortable with both their competence and their manner because they should be your most trusted advisors. You must find it easy to confide in them, seek their advice, and be confident that they will assist you in routine matters or in difficulties.

A good attorney walks you through the myriad procedures necessary to obtain licenses, permits, and zoning clearances. He or she guides you in setting up your business, handling lease negotiations, drawing up contracts, defending you in any legal actions, and keeping you on the smooth side of the law. An attorney with good business experience can discuss the pros and cons of your business structure: should you take on a partner? form a corporation? operate as a sole proprietorship?

Working hand in hand with you and your attorney is a skilled accountant to help you protect the money you earn. In addition to handling your taxes and helping you set up books and records for payroll, bills, and invoices, he or she can set up a clear and precise bookkeeping system. Such a system makes it easier for you to run your business, to take full advantage of tax deductions, and to see, via profit-and-loss statements, where and how you are making profit or incurring losses. Your accountant assists you in setting up a budget and prepares financial projections to help you keep your company growing. Such records will be a distinct asset should you decide to seek a bank loan to expand your business. Loan officers lend money much more readily to someone who can present well-kept records and professional business plans and projections.

PARTNERSHIP

A good working partnership can be the ideal structure for an off-premise catering operation. The nature of the business lends itself to a fairly simple division of responsibilities, with sales and management areas on one side, and culinary and design skills on the other. Two parties who work well together and share the same goals often form a team at the outset, developing the business between them. Sometimes, one principal begins the operation as a solo venture and, as the volume and burden of responsibility grows, takes on a partner to help the business expand and develop. Other owners are more comfortable being in complete control and prefer to cultivate and promote qualified staff to whom they delegate a good portion of responsibility and authority. Only you can decide what structure suits you best; your personality and skills (or lack of them) dictate the proper course for you. Should you decide on a partnership, seek good legal counsel in making such an arrangement; even good friends work together more smoothly with a fair and binding agreement between them.

Chapter 4

Equipping Yourself for Preparation, Transportation, and Service

If you are going to be in the business of off-premise catering, one everyday aspect of your operation will be devoted to providing food for the various events you are hired to handle. You will need a properly equipped kitchen in which to prepare food, whether it be your own commissary or a space leased for that purpose; you will need the means to transport it, packing material, containers, and/or vehicles in which to carry your food safely to the party site; and, once there, you must have the materials and utensils to serve the food properly, whether silverware or serving trays.

DO IT THE RIGHT WAY

Many off-premise caterers begin their careers cooking foods in their own home kitchens, and selling, delivering, and serving them without proper licensing. While in almost every area of the country this practice is illegal, it happens often enough to bear mention here. Their motives are usually benign rather than criminal: people just starting out often find the idea and the cost of setting up a professional kitchen overwhelming. They cater one event for a friend, then others for a few neighbors, and find themselves with a boomlet of business. Before they realize it, their business has grown, and they are burdened with a lack of space and equipment and the anxiety of being outside the law. If you find yourself tempted to take this route, think again. You would do far better to begin to develop your talents and clientele as an accommodator (see Chapter 1) and in the process earn the money to invest in a licensed kitchen.

There are other options. In most areas, well-outfitted and licensed kitchens are unused (or underutilized) for certain portions of the day or week: churches, schools, and community halls (such as VFW and Knights of Columbus) often have splendid kitchens that are used only occasionally or at fixed times. Such organizations might be willing to rent you their space during slow times. If they are properly licensed, and you carefully work out all the details of your access and use, the arrangement could be positive for both parties. The organization would gain welcome revenue, and you would have the proper equipment, space, and legal umbrella under which to develop your growing business.

Further possibilities exist. Explore your local area for other food operations. A baker or specialty food producer might welcome another food professional to share overhead costs and expenses in a licensed food facility. The relationship might also yield the extra benefits of mutual business referrals and a shared labor force.

EQUIPMENT FOR PREPARATION

The Commissary

Analyze your operation. When you have the opportunity and the financial where-withal to set up your own shop, it is imperative that you plan carefully. Try to estimate your space and equipment needs by analyzing your menus and guest counts from prior, current, and future bookings. If you do not have an ongoing business, give some thought to the types of foods and sizes of parties with which you plan to be involved. This preanalysis is not foolproof since every business changes as it grows, but some educated guesses as to the shape you think your business will take can be helpful in thinking through your setup. Whenever possible, allow room for change and expansion within reason: if you can afford a bit of extra square footage where you might later place another range or cooler, fine, but don't carry too much overhead in unnecessary space and underutilized equipment, or you will cripple your business from the start.

Unless you are fortunate enough to find a commissary that is ready for immediate start-up, do seek expert advice. You can hire kitchen design consultants to help you plan your space most efficiently. Many equipment supply houses have such experts on staff, and often their design service comes with the purchase of a certain dollar amount of equipment. Another advantage to using these professionals is that they provide or recommend qualified persons to install your equipment properly and according to code. They typically oversee the whole kitchen installation with respect to your pending licensing and protect you from the expense of having to undo or redo unsatisfactory or substandard work.

Space While most off-premise caterers can adapt to almost any working setup (remember, that's one of your special skills), some of your most important needs are ample refrigeration space and a comfortable amount of room in which to store bulky transporting equipment. Unlike an on-premise banquet operation or a restaurant kitchen, you can do without an extensive battery of ranges and broilers, but you do need extra space and sturdy work tables for packing your foods for an event. Clear and easy access to the street or driveway is important too: deliveries—incoming from suppliers and outgoing to events—are a big part of your business. Try to find a space that can accommodate a small private office area for you and your staff, and possibly even a modest dining table for tastings and client meetings.

Location   Location for street traffic or customer access is a low priority for an off-premise caterer. Instead, when you search out a location, think of its suitability to your needs: Will your suppliers' large delivery trucks have an easy approach? Will it be easy to load and unload your own delivery truck or van? Is there an elevator or ramp for heavy items and equipment? Are you reasonably close to major highways or main streets so you don't incur extensive travel time to your usual client base? Can your employees reach you by public transportation? If not, is there sufficient parking space for them? You may not be able to satisfy all these points, but use them as a framework when shopping for a business location. Of course, it may happen that you find a suitable and affordable space that does have a good street location. In that case, you can use your visibility to your advantage by creating an attractive window display or incorporating some takeout business into your operation. Allowing potential patrons to see and taste some of your food is a great form of business exposure.

Lease, Buy, or Build?   A reasonable long-term lease, with a fixed schedule of increases and an option to renew or buy, might be more advantageous to you than the outright purchase of a property or a structure that you will have to invest in heavily. If the available rentals are inadequate, however, you might be ill-advised to invest a great deal of money in alterations and renovations that you might lose if a lease is terminated or rent increased to an amount beyond your means. Consult with a trusted realtor, your attorney, and your accountant to select the situation that suits you best.

Outfitting the Commissary

You may have to compromise or begin small when outfitting your kitchen (most caterers do), so consider what you will most need and best use among the following general items. Have your basic major appliances installed at first, with the possibility of adding more later, as you need them. A good consultant provides the appropriate venting, wiring, power lines, plumbing, and drainage and waste disposal arrangements for your present setup, with the contingency for add-ons later. Explore the option of purchasing used equipment: provided the item is in good condition and really fits your needs, the savings can be substantial and worthwhile.

Major Equipment and Appliances   Based on your analysis of your needs, you should consider the following list as a general guideline for outfitting your commissary.

Refrigerators, walk-in and/or reach-in coolers. There never seems to be enough refrigeration space in a catering operation, so purchase the best and most you can. A walk-in is a real boon, since you can easily store large buffet pieces, aspics, and so forth, but try to have a smaller cooler near your cooking area for frequently used items to save time and energy.

A freezer (actually a frozen food storage cabinet). This appliance can be very useful in catering, not only for storing frozen foods, but for holding certain pastries, doughs, stocks, and hors d'oeuvre made in advance for an event. If you become involved in a frozen food takeout business, a blast freezer provides best results.

Sinks, at least one double sink (deep and heavy duty), preferably another for the chef/cook. Some locations require a separate sink for pot washing and a separate sink for hand washing as well.

A dishwasher, usually engineered by the manufacturer or your consultant to suit your needs and sanitation requirements.

Work tables (or usable counter space). Space is always at a premium for production line prep of foods and packaging. Work tables can be purchased with overhead racks, undershelves, or equipment drawers to save space and for working convenience.

A four- to six-burner open range top, preferably professional, heavy duty. Professional ranges not only are constructed to withstand the additional weight of large cooking utensils but also provide greater heat, which decreases cooking times. Shelves or a salamander are often placed above a range top.

A closed or flat-top range. If space and your budget allow, a flat top can greatly enhance your commissary's production. Various sized pots and pans can share space on a flat top and can be easily moved around on the surface for adjustable heat, as opposed to an open range on which you can place only four or six pieces of cookware. However, unless you really utilize a flat top, you can waste energy and space.

One or two conventional ovens, usually placed under your range tops. You can purchase stack ovens if they better suit your layout. Note that the size of your ovens dictates your choice of the size of your roasting and baking pans.

A salamander. This tool will probably satisfy most of your broiling or top-browning needs. Off-premise caterers seldom need heavy-duty broilers in the commissary.

A convection oven. This is an excellent addition to a kitchen. Its circulating heat promotes faster and more even cooking with no hot spots on any of its many shelves. It is particularly good for baking, because several trays of pastries, hors d'oeuvre, and cookies emerge perfectly browned. However, the drier heat results in more meat shrinkage than with a conventional oven. For job-site cooking and heating, domestic-sized convection ovens (not very expensive) are useful.

Steam-cooking appliances, ovens, tilting skillets, and trunion kettles. These items cook food quickly and evenly, with little loss of color and nutrients. Explore the various types and models with your equipment supplier to decide whether they are applicable to your needs. Since most items are now available with self-generated steam (rather than a steam-line hookup), they are becoming more popular in production kitchens.

A microwave oven. This is an option in a commissary, but it can be very useful at the job site, quickly thawing and heating small amounts of food, or reheating dense casseroles slowly without heating up a cramped cooking space. Since so many private homes (and many offices) now have microwaves, check beforehand.

Built-in deep fryer (some items can be fried then frozen and reheated successfully). A few domestic-sized deep fryers can work very nicely on a job site to prepare quick-cooking fried items just before service. They are lightweight, use household current, and have good thermostatic control. Be sure your staff uses them safely, and always pack their cords with them.

Food processor, preferably two, with extra work bowls. They are useful for chopping, pureeing, and blending. Heavy-duty models are available with greater capacity, large feed tubes, and optional attachments for grinding and so forth. Depending on your menu, they can be useful at the job site (check to see if a home client has one).

Food chopper (Buffalo chopper), a powerful, fast, and useful machine that can handle volume chopping. A slicer attachment makes short work of slaw and french fries; another attachment is a meat grinder.

A separate gravity-feed slicer. This item is a good investment if you plan to slice cold cuts or roast meats in volume. It can also produce paper-thin even slices of vegetables for fancy garnishes (e.g., turnip or potato lilies), chips, or raw meat slices for carpaccio, sukiyaki, sates, and the like.

A heavy-duty mixer. Such a mixer is invaluable. Have at least one 5-quart size and another larger one (probably not more than 20 quarts, unless you do enormous volume and quantity baking). Whatever size you have, buy several extra bowls to maximize machine usage. They come with a variety of attachments, including whips, paddles, and dough hooks. You can further utilize the heavy-duty motor with an attachment such as a grinder.

An immersion blender or power whisk. This appliance is handy in both the kitchen and on the job site. It mixes, blends, and purees foods right in the cooking utensil, eliminating the inconvenience of transferring food to another appliance or container.

Hand mixers. Hand mixers have limited use in the commissary but are very useful on the job site. Buy a few when they are on sale in your local department store; always store them with their cords and beaters to avoid loss and inconvenience.

Can openers. If you can, have a sturdy mechanical or electric one installed in the commissary. Have extra small (but easily operated) hand models to take on every job.

Cooking Equipment and Utensils   It is best to buy quality equipment at the outset. Cheaply made pots and pans do not cook very well and do not have the durability to withstand the wear and tear of heavy use. Professional-grade cookware is now widely available in domestic sizes suitable for use in home-sized ovens, which is a great advantage in off-premise catering.

Sauté pans, straight and slope-sided, a few in varying sizes, some with nonstick surfaces, some *cast iron fry pans,* and a *griddle,* if applicable, usually for job-site use.

Sauce pots, sauce pans, stock pot, and *brazier,* in applicable sizes.

Roast pans of varying sizes. Purchase some with locking lids, or squareheads, for ease in stacking for storage and transport.

Bake pans, in varied sizes. Some pans are available with slide tops, good for stacking in coolers and for transport.

Sheet pans, full and half-size. These are not only useful for cooking but also invaluable for prep and transport. Several half-size sheets should be taken along for job-site use because they fit into domestic ovens for reheating items, and are versatile for prep and plating.

Cake pans, in graduated sizes, *springforms, muffin tins, flan rings, and quiche pans*, if doing baking.

Loaf, pâté and en croute pans, if applicable.

An assortment of molds for gelatins, mousses, ice creams, and ice. These may be heavy-duty plastic or metal.

An assortment of ramekins, soufflé dishes, and casseroles, suitable for both baking and service.

Stainless steel mixing bowls, several in various sizes. Eminently versatile, unbreakable, and with good properties of temperature conduction. Use glass or ceramic bowls for serving only, not for kitchen work.

Colanders, strainers, sieves, food mill, china cap, chinois.

An assortment of hotel pans (full and half-size) and bain-marie liners, to be used for cooking, storage, and transport.

Cutting boards, several large and a few small sized (for job site). In most areas, health regulations permit the use of wood only in bakery; use composition plastic elsewhere.

Knives, good quality, several in most useful sizes, with a sharpening stone and steel. Some caterers keep a few knife rolls ready for job-site use, with a slicer or carving knife, an eight- or ten-inch chef's knife, a utility knife, a serrated knife, and several paring knives.

Assorted utensils, including solid and perforated stainless steel spoons, wooden spoons, metal spatulas, heavy-duty rubber spatulas, whisks (heavy and balloon), tongs, funnels, vegetable scrapers, some garnish tools (strippers, zesters, apple corers), cheesecloth, kitchen twine, pastry brushes, pastry bags with assorted tips, bench scrapers.

Thermometers, instant read, meat, candy, and fat.

Kitchen scales, preferably a receiving scale to weigh incoming goods, and at least one other tabletop scale for weighing portions and ingredients.

Measuring spoons, cups (plastic or metal), and graduated scoops and ladles.

Cleaning equipment and supplies.

EQUIPMENT FOR TRANSPORTATION

As an off-premise caterer you are concerned not with the rhythm of cooking to order and serving to an adjacent dining room but of prepping and pre- or partially cooking items to be finished, plated, and served in another location. Thus, your focus is on the equipment, materials, and means necessary to hold and transport food and equipment in the safest and most efficient manner possible. The items you purchase, whether for transport or service, are valuable and should be marked with your company name for identification.

The following is a general overview.

Vehicles

A vehicle, such as a truck or van, may be a worthwhile investment. Because of the nature of their business, some caterers can manage using taxis or cars, but most find a mid-sized van (which can hold food, supplies, and some staff) a good choice. Unless you do a great number of large-volume jobs, it is probably more useful to rent a large truck occasionally than to carry the costs of loan payments, maintenance, and insurance year round. Refrigerated trucks or vans are, understandably, more expensive to buy and operate. In some business formats, a refrigerated truck may be a better choice than individual cold-keeping containers and can be well utilized at a remote outdoor event as well. A dolly or hand truck is very useful for loading and unloading any truck or van.

Packaging

Transport containers for temperature control are of two types: either insulated to hold a food item at its current temperature for a fixed period of time or with heating or cooling units that can be set to hold or restore food to a chosen thermostat setting. Both types of food carriers come in a variety of sizes, and many are fitted with tracks to hold stacks of sheet or hotel pans; some have carrying handles, others have wheels or dolly bases for ease in moving. Such items are now so well designed that they eliminate the need for refrigerated trucks.

Enclosed food carriers, tray trucks, and tote boxes of various sizes are excellent for transporting items that are not temperature sensitive. They are sturdy, easy to clean and pack, and completely enclosed. They can also be used in refrigerated trucks.

Packing boxes of other types are also useful. Cardboard cartons, fitted (with permanent or removable separators) or plain, can be ordered in sizes to suit your needs. Household moving and truck rental companies are a good source for sturdy packing boxes of varying sizes. They are best used for serving equipment. If they are used for food items, they should not be reused for sanitary reasons. Be careful that they are not exposed to moisture, or they will collapse. Inexpensive cake boxes are useful for cakes, pies, pastry hors d'oeuvre, and delicate garnishes. Tape them closed and label clearly; do not stack them beyond their ability to bear weight. Plywood boxes can be fabricated to safely transport fragile or valuable serving pieces. They can be fitted with foam to protect contents and with padlocks for security.

Plastic film, aluminum foil, waxed or treated paper, plastic bags (both twist-tie and strip seal), and paper towels are, of course, useful in the kitchen, but essential for food transport. Purchase in bulk where feasible. Buy large food service sizes in general, but purchase some small rolls of plastic film and aluminum foil for job-site use as well. Heavy-duty garbage bags are needed for rubbish in both the commissary and on the job site and can be useful to overwrap items for transport, to carry clean and soiled linens, and to protect boxes from moisture. Plastic bubble wrap and/or thin, flexible foam are handy for cushioning packed items.

Plastic containers with lids, for both storage and transport, are useful in the commissary and on the job site. They are available in a wide variety of sizes and styles, from individual-portion condiment sizes to large-volume tubs for soups, salads, and so on. Flexible plastic is preferable to clear rigid plastic, which cracks easily.

Miscellaneous

An emergency kit, containing scissors, hammer, pliers, screwdriver, staple gun, safety pins, needle and thread, masking tape, gaffer's (duct) tape, pocket knife, extra can and bottle openers, extra twist ties, twine, extension cords (both domestic and heavy duty), first-aid kit, rubber bands, fuses, and thumbtacks should be taken to every job site.

Circumstances vary from business to business and from event to event. Your menu, and the type and volume of food to be served, determine what you need. Since a vast array of equipment is available, do some research in this area by visiting your local equipment supplier. Local rental companies have many such items in stock as well, and only you can decide, based on your business needs, which items to purchase and which to rent.

EQUIPMENT FOR SERVICE

The items you may need for service run the gamut from portable dance floors to salt and pepper shakers, and the quantities required can vary from one to one thousand. Each event dictates its own requirements. Virtually every item can be rented in most areas of the country, and only you can decide what items you wish to purchase, based on frequent need, available storage space, and significant elements of style and taste that are important to the overall image of your business.

Tableware

For the most part, it is impractical for the off-premise caterer to stock china, silverware, and glassware in sufficient variety and quantity to cover all events. In addition to the expense, such an inventory requires a great deal of storage space and burdens the caterer with the task of packing, unpacking, washing, and sanitizing these items for every use. Loss and breakage are inevitable, and continual replacement is expensive and a chore. Unless you are in an area where such rentals are scarce, and you could benefit by making china rental a secondary business, it is best to rent such basics for each event.

Disposables

The variety of disposable items available for tableware, service, and packaging is broad. The quality ranges from inexpensive paper plates to coated plates and tumblers to more expensive plastics that are durable and stylish. Disposable cutlery, dishes, drinking cups, glasses, tablecloths and napkins, serving platters and trays are now widely available, as well as an assortment of interesting containers and materials to package portions or whole meals, such as tote bags, boxes, meal trays, and fitted food containers with lids.

Explore the items that are available in the catalogs and showrooms of paper goods suppliers to make the selections that are most useful to your business. You may be pleasantly surprised to find that the use of disposables for many events is not only practical and cost efficient but also can lend a special touch to your tables. Many of these products are made in a variety of colors and attractive designs. You can even arrange to have some items customized with your business logo or in a distinctive pattern or design that enhances your presentation. Depending on the nature of your business, it may make sense for you to purchase some disposables in bulk quantities. White paper cocktail napkins are one good example: no caterer can have too many of these on hand.

Serving Pieces

Every catered event requires a specific list of serving pieces, but the likely items include chafers; tureens; serving bowls and platters; trays for beverages, canapés, meat, and display; coffee and tea pots, samovars, and urns; pitchers; cold beverage dispensers; cake stands; cake knives, serving spoons, forks, and ladles; gravy boats; candelabra; ash trays; and sugar and creamers. These and many other items are available in stainless steel, silver, ceramic, pottery, or glass, and you should choose the type and style most appropriate to the event you are serving.

Since all of these items can be rented, you may choose to do so rather than attempt to purchase such a broad and expensive inventory. However, owning certain of these items could be a good investment either because you would use them frequently or because they would lend a certain unique style to your service. Many caterers rent standard items and supplement serving pieces with unusual lacquer trays, woven baskets, copper items, or ornate antiquelike trays and dishes for their own trademark look. You decide which method is best for your business.

Linens

Attractive and colorful table linens, skirting, and napkins enhance the presentation of any menu. Here again, rental agencies and linen services can satisfy most of your needs. If you are located in an area where linen rentals are meager, and you have the space for inventory and laundry facilities, then purchase a supply of your own.

In some cases, customized linens can give you the competitive edge: You might specialize in down-home cooking for informal events; plaid or patchwork quilt linens might set you a cut above other such services. Or you might choose to serve your afternoon teas on flowered English chintz or thrift-shop lace. Such distinctive items, of course, are part of your own stock, and you can rely on rentals to provide you with basic supplies.

Chapter 5

Developing a Supplier Resource and Referral Network

An off-premise caterer is often called upon to provide clients not only with excellent food attractively served but also with a wide range of other items from chairs to pony carts that may be necessary to provide the total entertaining concept the client envisions. Some of these requests are routine, such as food, ice, tableware rentals, and floral centerpieces, and you are in regular and frequent contact with the suppliers of such products. At other times, clients ask for assistance and advice on functions that may be quite elaborate and require extensive equipment, construction, and planning. Whatever the case, having a reliable resource network is an invaluable aid in completely servicing your clientele.

INTERPROFESSIONAL REFERRALS

The resources used by a caterer can form the basis of a rewarding referral network, wherein client referrals are made from caterer to supplier and/or vice versa, resulting in an expanded client base for both parties. In addition to this desirable increase in business, a well-developed resource network provides expanded exposure for your company.

Understanding the resource and referral network is an asset to a caterer. Making referrals back and forth between resources is a valuable way to enhance business and lay the groundwork for future relationships throughout the hospitality industry. These reciprocal arrangements are not coercive or manipulative. Indeed, if any situation does seem negatively exploitative, avoid it if possible. Luckily, in most cases, aggressive networking is mutually beneficial to all parties. It is preferential, but that preferred status is honestly earned by all players.

The following examples demonstrate some of the ways such networking might occur:

A caterer uses a paper distributor frequently. As in all business, such a volume of business warrants a discount. The discounted prices, in turn, influence the caterer to use the distributor exclusively.

A specialty produce purveyor, eager to expand his business, offers the caterer (a pleasant, prompt-paying customer) the first wild mushrooms or berries of the season; the caterer, happy with this special service, increases her orders to the purveyor and recommends another food professional to this source. The purveyor, making rounds to his restaurant customers, meets a talented young cook looking for a better job and, knowing that the caterer is planning to expand her business, arranges a meeting between the two.

A bridal consultant, researching floral designers for a client, hears high praise from one respected designer about XYZ Caterers, a new establishment in the next town. She arranges a meeting with the owner of XYZ, and they work out a referral agreement.

A caterer arranges a lavish wedding for a client. The groom's family supplies a photographer who produces an exciting video presentation. The caterer admires the quality of the video work and the professional demeanor of the photographer and his crew and believes this would be an appealing service to offer to his other clients, including two major corporate accounts. The photographer, eager to expand his business to corporate clients, agrees to join in a referral arrangement with the caterer.

A caterer's clientele frequently requires printing services for announcements, invitations, raffle tickets, and the like. The caterer has used a local printer for her own printing needs, and is satisfied with the quality of the work and prompt delivery. The caterer passes on significant orders from her clients to the printer. The printer, grateful for the increased business, now prints the caterer's menus, fliers, and business cards free of charge or at a substantial discount.

Referral Fees

Sometimes, these transactions involve a finder's fee or commission paid for each successful referral. For example, a caterer may develop a relationship with a florist or floral designer, using that resource on a regular basis for buffet arrangements, table greens, and tray garnish. Because of frequent business, the florist may offer the caterer a discount on purchases, or both parties may display the other's business cards or brochures in their establishments. If the caterer has an established specialty business—for example, weddings—the florist's services may be offered as part of a package or the client may be referred to the caterer's "exclusive" florist. In return for this guaranteed (or, at the very least, increased) business, the florist agrees to pay the caterer a referral fee (either an agreed fixed amount or, more likely, a percentage of the value of the floral order). Conversely, that caterer, seeking an expanded wedding clientele, may establish a relationship with a wedding planner or bridal consultant, who has primary contact with prospective wedding couples. The wedding planner refers the couple to one (or more) of her preferred or recommended caterers, and if the client and caterer come to an agreement, the consultant receives a referral fee from the caterer.

There is sometimes confusion over the payment of referral fees because it appears, to the uninformed, that the client is paying extra for these peripheral services. In one sense this is true, since operating within a referral network is a cost of doing business to all parties involved, and is as much a part of overhead as advertising, rent, or utilities costs. In that same sense we all, as consumers, pay extra when we purchase a well-known brand of corn flakes. When we buy that particular brand, we pay a premium price for the name, and in return, we receive the freshness, quality, and flavor we expect from a known product. In a similar way, the caterer, by making a referral, is offering the client a known and established service that lives up to the standards of taste, quality, and reliability that his or her reputation stands for. In addition, an all-inclusive event is composed of many separate parts and the client is, in effect, paying the caterer, floral designer, or other resource for the time and skills involved in executing a well-coordinated event. It also often happens that the overall price turns out to be less expensive in both time and money than if the client had sought out individual services independent of any referrals.

RESOURCES FOR SUPPLIERS AND SERVICES

The following discussion of resources begins with the basics—those products and services almost every caterer needs on a regular basis—and then highlights some of the possible other sources of peripheral products and special effects that can assist a caterer in producing the most extravagant and unusual events.

Suppliers and Purveyors

With an imaginary shopping list in mind, explore your local area for sources for those items you need on a daily basis, as well as wide-ranging peripheral services, getting references from fellow food professionals whenever possible. Make contact with these sources, either by phone, letter, or in person, to begin to establish a relationship with them. Local or regional trade shows (publicized in newspapers, trade publications, or hospitality association mailings) offer the opportunity to explore many available resources and can be an efficient way of meeting suppliers and sampling their wares. National, international, and regional companies are the backbone of such trade shows, using them to display and advertise their merchandise and introduce new products and equipment. A caterer, visiting such a show, not only has the opportunity to handle and/or taste the item but also makes his or her name known to the food brokers, distributors, and representatives of such companies. Food brokers, who often handle a dizzying array of goods from equipment to fresh and frozen foods, are always eager for new business, and soon after a visit to a trade show, a caterer begins to receive mailers, catalogs, and calls from local salespeople.

Pursue any possibly useful contacts by introducing yourself to each source as a potential customer, explain the nature and scope of your business, and ask for information about product line, price lists, and delivery procedures. Some suppliers of specialty food products send samples to prospective customers. Visit rental companies to inspect china and glassware, linen samples, tenting, chairs, and tables. Ask for references and sample photos from photographers, florists, and special effects designers. Assemble brochures, price lists, and your notes into resource files that will grow along with your business.

Most suppliers and purveyors require that you operate on a C.O.D. basis with them for a short period of time, but once you have become a known customer, you may establish a line of credit. The best way to set the tone for a productive relationship with any supplier is to be specific about your needs, organized about ordering and scheduling deliveries or pickups, and prompt in paying your bills. Even if the orders you place are not huge or frequent at the outset, a courteous and professional manner marks you as a valued customer.

Guidelines for Food Purchasing   Good food sources and suppliers are vitally important to the success of any off-premise caterer. Each caterer's business and the economic bracket and style level of his or her clientele determine the quantity and types of food supplies that are needed. Good, consistent quality, however, is always important and comes at all price levels.

Bear in mind that each caterer's menus and volume of business vary seasonally and reflect the nature of each business. Unlike the needs of a restaurant with a fixed menu and predictable usage, a caterer's business flow may dictate that some items are better bought in domestic sizes than from bulk purveyors. Institutional sizes are not a bargain if they result in waste and spoilage or require too much valuable storage space or too great an outlay of cash. Sometimes, a wholesale purveyor will be willing to sell split or mixed master cases of goods to accommodate a caterer's smaller or more eclectic needs. It can be helpful to offer to pick up smaller orders or accept delivery at the convenience of the purveyor, perhaps when his or her truck is en route to a major customer.

Food brokers, since they represent so many products, can be a good solution to a caterer's supply problems. They often base their minimum delivery order on total dollar amount rather than bulk purchase. In addition, a food broker can provide a caterer in a remote geographical location access to a myriad of widespread suppliers, and keeps that caterer informed of new product development in the industry.

A caterer who is just starting out, or who has a small volume of business, may find better values in supermarkets and local stores rather than through wholesalers. A supermarket butcher can sometimes be cajoled into charging next week's sale price on a whole box of chickens; a gourmet shop may offer a loyal customer a reduced price on a case of balsamic vinegar. Provided that these bargains do not cost a disproportionate waste of time and fuel, such shopping can be a boon to a caterer's budget. A word of caution on "bargain" prices: in pricing menus (discussed in detail in Chapter 7), it is important to use average and current food costs, not occasional sale prices, for accuracy. This is the reason why most experienced caterers use their wholesalers' current price lists when costing out jobs.

STAPLES, DRY GOODS, AND PACKAGED AND CANNED GOODS   Many grocery purveyors have different types and varieties of items they carry. Some carry a wide assortment of staples (from flours to cooking oils) in a variety of brands, sizes, and price ranges. Others are more specialty oriented, carrying top-of-the-line imported and domestic regional goods, such as vinegars, mustards, truffles, cornichons, blue corn flour, dried chilis, basmati rice, and premium preserves. Whenever possible, order regularly from one or two suppliers of both everyday and specialty goods to establish a working relationship and to increase the efficiency of your ordering.

In some areas, caterers purchase flours and sugars from bakery suppliers; others buy them from grocery wholesalers or food brokers. Large metropolitan areas tend to have more suppliers of specialized items such as phyllo dough, feta cheese, brine-cured olives, and carp roe from a Greek house; pastas, olive oils, dried mushrooms, semolina flour from an Italian house; rice paper, wonton wrappers, lemongrass, tamarind paste, and coconut milk from an Oriental supply house; and nuts, seeds, dried fruits, candies, and chocolate from a confectionery or bakery supplier. Many specialty products and supplies are also available from a growing number of mail order suppliers (see Appendix).

DAIRY PRODUCTS   Quality is very important in the dairy products area. In many regions, the finest sweet butter and high-butterfat cream, bulk brick cream cheese, and tubs of cultured sour cream can be purchased only through commercial suppliers. Where large volume or special characteristics (such as non-ultrapasteurized cream, individual-portion creamers, and butter pats) are not required, bargains do exist at local supermarkets.

CHEESES   A good cheese supplier is essential to a caterer because good quality in cheeses is vital to their enjoyment. A knowledgeable and reliable cheese supplier offers cheeses that have been purchased from varied reputable regional and international sources; stores, ages, and cuts them properly; and is able to offer expert advice on quality, cooking properties, proper service, appropriate combinations and serving quantities, and compatibility with other foods and wines. Specialty cheese making is currently quite popular, and some of these handmade cheeses are sold through the small producers or local farmers' markets. A source for such unusual cheese can provide a caterer with some distinctive offerings as well.

PRODUCE   Finding a purveyor who can be relied upon to deliver produce of consistent quality—that is, fresh, unblemished, and of the maturity, ripeness, size, and quantity ordered—may take a bit of time and effort, but it is well worth it. From your very first orders, make your needs and expectations clear, and don't hesitate to refuse items of inferior quality. A good purveyor makes every effort to keep your business, and together you can develop an effective business relationship. It is not unusual for a purveyor, once he or she knows a client, to alert a good customer to the first arrival of exotic mushrooms, fiddlehead ferns, or stemmed strawberries in the market.

Remember that, as with all live and growing things, produce prices fluctuate according to season and climate conditions. A regular purveyor eventually recognizes your needs and flexibility and gives you a fair price or offers to make appropriate substitutions when necessary.

Caterers who are located in farming areas can sometimes cultivate contacts with small farmers individually or through cooperatives to gain access to organic produce, wild foods (especially mushrooms, berries, herbs, edible flowers, and specialty greens), miniature vegetables, and the like. A source of such unique or exotic produce can give a caterer's menus a competitive edge.

POULTRY AND MEAT   When choosing a butcher or meat wholesaler as a supplier, a caterer must consider not only the reputation and reliability of the supplier but also the format of his or her business, kitchen staff, and space. The supplier must be able to provide consistently good meats (federally inspected, of course) of the quality, grade, and cuts that are most suitable to the caterer's business.

Wholesale cuts can be economical if the caterer's kitchen staff has the ability to cut meats properly, if the kitchen has sufficient refrigeration and freezer storage, and if that particular week's or month's menus guarantee full usage of the cut.

Fabricated cuts, which provide oven-ready meats needing little trimming or prep, are often used by caterers, since they cost little in time or effort and provide minimal waste. They are of course, more expensive.

The most expensive cuts (and the easiest to use) are portion-controlled meats, such as precut, specific-weight steaks and chops and beef patties. Each caterer needs to decide which manner of purchasing is most efficient for his or her operation or a particular event.

FISH   The best guarantee of fresh, good quality fish and seafood is a reliable and reputable fishmonger. As of this writing, there is no standard of federal inspection for fresh fish, although there seems to be an inclination toward such a system within the industry. Facilities that process fish, however, can voluntarily request government inspection that insures cleanliness and proper handling. Governmental agencies, however, do monitor the waters from which shellfish is taken, and wholesale markets tag such items to indicate that they have been taken from safe waters and beds. For the present, the caterer must rely on his or her eyes and nose and the relationship he or she cultivates with a fish purveyor to ensure serving a wholesome quality product.

FROZEN AND PREPARED FOODS   There is an abundant supply of frozen, preportioned, prepared, and partially cooked food items available through specialty suppliers, food brokers, and other wholesalers. A caterer may take advantage of the convenience of such products if they are suitable to his or her particular needs, provided that the finished food product meets the standard of quality that the caterer's clients have come to expect.

CUSTOM PREPARED FOODS   In many areas, food professionals specialize in items that can supplement a caterer's menu: for example, intricate pastry hors d'oeuvre, pâtés, chutneys, and cheese straws. Usually, these operators produce too small a volume to sell through food brokers and are eager for the individual caterer's business.

They are often willing to prepare customized items to suit a particular menu or event. As with all prepared products, they should first be tested to ensure that they are wholesome and of excellent quality.

BREADS AND BAKED GOODS   It is essential for a caterer to have one or more suppliers of varied and tasty breads and rolls. Most catering operations have neither the staff nor equipment to do large-scale bakery production, and if they do bake, they focus their efforts and attention on items such as muffins, biscuits, loaf cakes, crepes, and cookies. While most caterers prepare some desserts (mousses, puddings, small-scale cakes, and tarts), they usually rely on outside producers for items such as Danish or Viennese pastries, croissants, and brioches, especially when they need these items in volume. In the case of elaborate special occasion cakes and multitiered wedding cakes, most caterers find it practical and desirable to subcontract these orders to specialists who have the equipment and know-how to prepare, transport, and assemble such cakes at the party site.

BEVERAGES   Beverage suppliers stock not only a wide variety of sodas and beer (in bottles, cans, and kegs for tapping) but also an assortment of juices, mineral waters, and fruit punch. Their inventory usually includes complete bar supplies such as drink mixes, maraschino cherries, olives, stirrers, straws, drink novelties and decorations, siphon bottles for soda, and flavored syrups for alcoholic drinks, egg creams, and ice cream sodas. Some beverage dealers also stock disposable drink glasses and other plastic goods, as well as ice.

ICE   Ice dealers can provide cubes of various sizes and shapes, chipped and shaved ice, as well as large blocks to serve any purpose. The smaller sizes are usually available in bags or reusable metal drums. The drums are slightly more expensive but can be used as attractive serving containers and are also convenient for chilling wines and champagnes. The empty containers are often reused as packing or storage containers.

The dealers are also able to offer advice on types and quantities of ice needed for specific functions. A note on ordering ice: when in doubt, always order more. It is relatively inexpensive to have extra; it is embarrassing or disastrous to run short.

Guidelines for Peripherals and Special Effects

RENTALS   It is not an exaggeration to say that almost everything any caterer might need can be rented. Most caterers have an ongoing need for glassware, china, silverware, table linens, serving trays and utensils, tables, and chairs. In addition, as the need arises, it is possible to rent everything from coat racks to candelabra. Since rental companies sometimes differ in the style of equipment they carry (some feature fine bone china and delicate crystal; others offer more utilitarian tableware), a caterer typically does business regularly with two rental resources. Always try to work with companies that are dependable in their delivery time and accuracy of orders (proper count, items clean and in good repair), and respect that professionalism by placing orders in an organized manner (ordering well in advance during busy seasons), carefully repacking according to spec (glasses rinsed, trays wiped clean, etc.), and reporting breakage or damage. These simple tactics guarantee satisfaction to all parties.

Some full-service rental companies also carry equipment for outdoor events: tenting (for both guests and cooking staff), space heaters and air conditioning, dance floors, podiums, portable ranges, outdoor grills, and so on. Some rental companies specialize in outdoor equipment exclusively. Note that for outdoor tenting situations, it is essential to hire an experienced firm with good references from other caterers: proper and efficient setup of a sturdy, weatherproof enclosure is imperative for the comfort and safety of guests.

PAPER GOODS AND PACKAGING   Every caterer needs some paper products: paper cocktail napkins, paper toweling for kitchen use, as well as waxed paper, foil, plastic wrap, and disposable foil pans for cooking, baking, and transporting.

While disposables were discussed in Chapter 4, it bears repeating that the quality and variety of paper and plastic servingware now available are very impressive. Since many such items are least expensive when purchased in bulk quantities, you need some storage space, but a supply of some good quality basic items is a great convenience for a caterer. Specialty items, in unusual shapes, colors, and patterns, are best purchased for individual jobs as needed. Many paper goods distributors also carry a variety of food packaging items similar to those used by fast-food enterprises, such as beverage, sandwich, salad, and main or side dish containers with fitted lids that can be very useful for box lunches, office lunches, and picnics.

Paper or party goods specialists can often assist a caterer with other needs, such as party favors, printed matches, ribbons, colored tissue, crepe or mylar streamers, colored foils or cellophanes, papier-mâché piñatas, noisemakers, party hats, confetti, and so on. Even though most caterers might choose to subcontract an extensive decorating project to a designer, it is helpful to have such a resource on tap.

Box and bag distributors can be very useful to a caterer. Cake boxes in varied sizes are ideal for packing hors d'oeuvre and small pastry items; bags or small boxes, imprinted with a caterer's logo, are handy for box lunches, client's leftovers, and take-home favors. In addition, sturdy reinforced cardboard boxes, in suitable ready-made or custom-cut sizes, are very efficient for transporting baking pans, serving platters, glass bowls, and silver chafers to party sites. Movers can supply sturdy knock-down packing cartons, bubble wrap, even portable cardboard closets.

FLORISTS   While a simple florist can satisfy routine requests for table centerpieces or buffet showpieces, today's catering client often requests more elaborate productions. Floral designers combine the skills of both florist and architect and are capable of creating wisteria arbors, pine forests, flower-decked chandeliers, rose gardens, or jungles—whatever effect a client can imagine.

WINE AND LIQUOR   Because of the alcohol laws in most regions, caterers and/or clients purchase wine and liquor from retailers. It is best to search out a retailer who offers a wide selection, fair prices, good delivery, and a helpful staff, to whom you can confidently refer clients. The retailer, in turn, often refers his or her party-giving clients to you.

This chosen retailer can serve as a consultant, suggesting kinds and amounts of liquor required for functions; advising on appropriate wines and vintages; keeping you and your clients informed on new trends, fashionable cocktails, and serving suggestions. A knowledgeable retailer can teach you and your staff about wine service and can arrange wine tastings for you or your clients. Because of the relationship retailers have with distillers and vintners, they often have available many recipe books, mixing guides, and serving ideas that can provide both information and inspiration. Bear in mind that, in general, according to law (check local statutes), such a relationship should involve the exchange of good will, service, and referrals, not cash.

PRINTERS   Most caterers require the services of a printer for business cards, menus, office stationery, flyers, bulk mail, and the like. A reliable and imaginative printer who does quality work is also a good reference for clients for invitations, place cards, matches, programs, raffle and sweepstakes tickets—in short, any corporate or personal printing need.

LIMOUSINES   Some catering clients desire cars with luxury appointments, vintage models, or superstretches. Others are content with "basic black." A caterer should have the ability to refer clients to a reputable firm: one with clean and well-running cars and safe and courteous drivers who know the territory.

MUSICIANS AND ENTERTAINERS   Today it is commonplace for catering clients to request background music for cocktail parties and receptions. Even a modest wedding requires at least a three-piece band for dancing; every bar mitzvah or sweet sixteen party seems incomplete without the service of a disc jockey. Caterers should thus cultivate contacts with sources of music to satisfy their client's needs. It is often possible for either potential clients or caterers to audition musicians, either in person or, more commonly, by means of audio or videotapes of performances. Such information, along with price guidelines, should be in a caterer's resource file.

Other entertainment is often requested, and the possibilities are numerous: singers, dancers, comedians, mimes, magicians, jugglers, acrobats, caricaturists, palm readers, celebrity lookalikes, expert guest speakers, models, and trained animal acts, to name just a few. Barring personal references, good sources for such performers are universities, theatrical agents, drama schools, music conservatories, art institutes, speakers' bureaus, and performers' unions. While all such unusual entertainment requests are not routine for most caterers, it is good to have such ideas and contacts ready for reference.

LIGHTING   Lighting technicians and designers possess both creative talents and the solid technical knowledge necessary to achieve the desired lighting effects with efficiency and safety. Sometimes a caterer's lighting needs are practical: for example, safety lights for hallways, runways, parking areas, or stairways. For outdoor events, a caterer requires adequate lighting for loading areas, cooking tents, and loading and staging areas, as well as more decorative lighting for dining and dance tents.

For decorative effects, lighting designers, who usually have stage or theatrical experience, are capable of producing extraordinary settings. They can provide klieg lights for showy entrances, laser light shows coordinated with music, and special effects such as meteor showers, starry nights, or dramatic sunsets to dazzle and enchant guests.

SPECIAL EFFECTS   Today's parties have taken on theatrical proportions. People expect drama, unique decor, and peripherals that are beyond the average caterer's time and ability. Specialists can and should be called upon to satisfy client's needs.

It is impossible to list all of the various special effects a caterer and his or her resources can conjure for a client; in fact, it is safe to say that whatever a client can imagine, it can be produced (given the requisite time and money, of course). Special decor can range from bunches, arches, or releases of balloons; special audiovisual equipment can provide the sights and sounds of a distant planet; backlit scrims and stage sets can transport guests to Broadway or Bangkok; camels, silken tents, and belly dancers can evoke an Arabian Nights theme. A team of skilled special effects people can transform a barren space into Versailles, Superman's Metropolis, or a Moroccan bazaar. While such events are not an everyday occurrence for most caterers, a resource list of such talented specialists can enhance even more modest events, and such capabilities can greatly enhance a caterer's reputation and business.

PARTY PLANNERS   Sometimes called events managers, party planners act as coordinators for elaborate events. They usually work directly for clients, and are paid a consulting fee or a percentage of the overall cost of the event. They have primary contact with clients and, in their role as consultant, recommend specialists to produce the necessary components of an event. They oversee every detail of a function, coordinate all the various parts, and can conceptualize and produce a theme party from invitations to take-home favors.

Wedding planners, or bridal consultants, are subspecialists in this field. They perform all the functions of party planners but also take on other responsibilities, advising on the selection of gowns for the bride and bridal party, cataloging wedding gifts, shopping for the trousseau, and booking the honeymoon travel.

A caterer's relationship with such party planners and bridal consultants can be a valuable source of referral business. In addition, a caterer can benefit from the services of such a professional, particularly if he or she has neither the experience nor the time to coordinate a particularly complex event. Caterers who do a volume of such events often have a party planner on staff or retainer to insure the satisfaction of his clients.

Chapter 6

Managing a Superior Staff

No business can succeed and grow without good employees, and off-premise catering is no exception to that rule. At the outset, when your business is small and your events few and far between, you may be able to handle all functions pretty much on your own, hiring just a bartender and one or two serving people to staff a party. However, as the volume of your business increases, you need more helping hands in all aspects of the business: business management; sales; events planning; food prep, cooking, and baking; service; and stocking, packing, delivery, and cleanup. Each caterer's needs are different, and based on the scope and growth of your business, you ultimately decide on the type of organization that best suits your needs. What follows are some overall guidelines for selecting, training, and developing a staff that enhances your business.

If you have a working business partner, you have already defined your separate areas of responsibility. For example, your partner may be handling sales and office management, while you focus primarily on creating recipes, planning menus, and cooking. In this instance, each of you covers different areas of decision making, and you hire staff to supplement your business needs. If you are running the business as a sole proprietorship, you will make all the important policy and planning decisions and you need well-trained staff to whom you can delegate the responsibility of execution and follow-up.

BUSINESS STAFF

Sales Personnel

We examine the art and craft of sales in more detail in Chapter 8, but for now, let it suffice to say that the presentation and sale of your catering services is pivotal to your business and is a skill that demands both intelligence and sensitivity. If you choose to hire salespeople in your business, screen them carefully and train them thoroughly so that, as much as humanly possible, they become an extension of yourself and project the personality and image you have chosen for your business. Even if you hire people with prior sales experience in the catering business, it is a good idea for you or your partner to accompany them on their first few calls, until they become comfortable with your style and you are satisfied that they accurately represent you.

Events Managers or Party Coordinators

In many catering operations, the preferred policy is for the owner (or one of the owners) to handle the first client meeting personally and then assign an events manager to work through all the follow-up details with the client. Using this method, you have control over the initial contact and overall scope of the event, yet are protected from the overwhelming day-to-day detail on every job.

Whether you use the title events manager, party coordinator, or banquet manager, a person well trained in this role can be invaluable to an organization. Once initial negotiations with a client are completed and the contract signed, the events manager can take over the routine operation, generating work plans, menus, staff requirements; coordinating all peripheral needs; following up on ordering details and the like up to and including being on site to manage the function in your stead. You act as overall supervisor, available for advice or consultation when needed, devoting your time and energy to the especially difficult or challenging questions. While you may be able to hire someone with such experience, it is more often the case that you can find a particularly bright, organized, and eager individual among your other employees, be they office clerks, waitstaff, or prep cooks. As a matter of fact, the best candidates for this position are often those who have worked in many roles in your business, been promoted from within, and come to the job with a well-rounded understanding of how all the parts of catering form a satisfying whole.

Office Staff

As your business expands, so does the paperwork, and you will likely need a few competent and efficient people to perform such tasks as telephone answering, filing, correspondence, and bookkeeping. Sometimes, one person, acting as an administrative assistant, can perform all of these duties. With the aid of a personal computer, which today has a place in almost every business, many formerly tedious tasks—issuing contracts, forming work schedules, preparing payrolls, factoring menus, and ordering supplies—can be handled expeditiously. In some cases, part-time or flex-time help, utilizing students, seniors, or parents of school-age children, can take care of your office needs. Whoever you hire, make it clear that they must always be prompt and courteous in answering the telephone and that they understand the importance of accuracy in details regarding your work.

WAITSTAFF

A reliable roster of capable party service personnel is essential to a smoothly running catering operation. Few caterers have the luxury of a full-time staff until they are very well established and have a volume of business that dictates several parties each day throughout the year. In average circumstances, business fluctuates, with hectic and slow seasons, from several parties in one week to only one or two the following. How do you staff a business that requires four employees one week and forty the next? Most caterers find that the solution to this dilemma evolves along with their business growth.

In the very early stages of your work, you may find yourself hiring friends or acquaintances or freelance serving staff from agencies to fill your irregular needs. You may eventually be selecting a handful of these temporary employees repeatedly, either for their agreeable personalities, work skills, or supervisory potential. This reliable core group becomes your permanent (albeit part-time) staff. By repeated exposure, they learn your work habits and absorb your style; you, in turn, rely on them to do a good job for you.

Since many freelancers work part-time for several employers, they come in contact with a great number of waitstaff personnel and can help you expand your staff. They are usually pleased to recommend others with whom they have worked to help staff your business. This can be both convenient and beneficial to you because a waitress or waiter whose work habits you admire chooses co-workers who share similar performance standards. People enjoy working alongside others who carry their share of the load. And people who work together frequently develop a harmony and rhythm that make an event run smoothly.

To supplement such referrals, some caterers place imaginative advertisements for employees in local newspapers, community journals, and magazines, making their ads sound enticing by mentioning benefits such as flexible hours, good pay, working with people in glamorous surroundings. These benefits do exist, in spite of the hard work involved. Other good sources of waitstaff personnel are students (either full or part-time); aspiring actors, singers, or dancers (they have a stage presence that can add a certain sparkle to a party); culinary students (who are always eager for experience in the food field); health-care workers and teachers (they are usually underpaid, work irregular hours, have good people skills, are used to routine and following orders, and have developed stamina and the ability to think on their feet).

You should personally interview all prospective employees, offer a clear description of the job, and ask for and check references. An employee manual, specifying duties, work requirements, and behavior expected of any staff members, is a good way to clarify both job descriptions and responsibilities. The caterer must follow all the accepted procedures of fair hiring and employee management practices.

BARTENDERS AND WINE STEWARDS   When hiring bartenders, you must be very selective. It is perfectly acceptable to have one of your regular waitstaff handle a simple wine or champagne bar. With a little bit of instruction, any serving person can master pouring wine at table carefully and neatly. If, however, you are staffing a full-service bar, you need an experienced bartender, capable of stocking and setting up a bar, mixing and serving a variety of standard drinks, and handling a drinking crowd courteously and quickly. In addition, a bartender should be an honest and responsible person who understands that he or she is to give a fair bottle count to you or your client, does not drink on the job, and does not serve drinks to other employees. A knowledge of wines and the protocol of wine service is an added asset in a bartender, as is the ability to serve and garnish exotic drinks, decant rare ports, and so forth when called upon to do so.

Since most off-premise caterers are never involved in the actual sale of wine or liquor, the need for a wine steward, in the traditional sense of maintaining a cellar, is limited. However, someone in your organization should be capable of selecting appropriate wines for formal dinners and have the knowledge to properly handle, chill, and serve them. If you have connections in one or two good wine shops, much of this advice is easily available to you, and you can be sure that your clients receive expert wine service at any function.

KITCHEN STAFF

Just as you cannot expect to personally file every letter, set every table, and pour every glass of wine, you cannot plan to chop every onion. Good kitchen staffing is a must for a successful catering operation, and your own skills and areas of specialization, or lack of them, dictate your needs. If you are not a talented chef and don't plan to devote most of your energies to creating dishes, planning menus, and preparing sauces, then hire a working chef or experienced cook to supervise your kitchen. Even if you do have good food skills, you should be prepared to act as overall manager of the kitchen and train others to perform most of the cooking tasks. As your business becomes more established, you prepare similar items repeatedly in fairly large volume. You may add variations to the basics to keep your menus interesting, but the process of revolutionary creation does not take place daily. A catering kitchen is really a little food factory, with orders to be completed, packaged, and sent out every day. Wherever possible, you should employ production techniques that yield a good product in the most efficient way.

You may choose to hire one or two experienced food professionals as part of your kitchen staff. You, or one of your staff, should be well versed in food handling and sanitation, and you must obtain certification to that effect from the board of health or other local agency. Someone in your kitchen should also be charged with the responsibility of ordering and keeping inventory; this person must take that responsibility seriously, or your business profits might be spoiled, wasted, or stolen before you have a chance to earn them.

In the kitchen, efficiency, safety, and cleanliness must be scrupulously adhered to. Food preparation must be done efficiently to minimize waste of product, energy, or time. Great care must be taken in packing prepared and raw foods for transport at safe temperatures to preserve their taste and quality. Your kitchen staff must be able to understand and follow precise instructions for reheating, finishing, and garnishing dishes at the party site, and they must have enough knowledge of food to correct problems or improvise if necessary in order to present a wholesome, delicious, and attractive dish.

In addition, there are certain rules that apply to waitstaff. In terms of appearance, make it clear that employees must report to work freshly bathed and well groomed. They must be conscious of body odor and apply a good deodorant/antiperspirant.

Fresh breath is important in the close quarters of party service: keep a mouthwash in the employees' bathroom at the commissary and breath spray or mints on the job. Strong perfumes, after shaves, or colognes can be equally offensive and interfere with guests' enjoyment of their food. Men should be clean shaven. If mustaches and/or beards are acceptable to the employer, they should be well trimmed. Women should wear subtle makeup. Hair should appear healthy and clean and be neatly arranged. On the serving floor, long hair is not a problem provided it is attractively arranged and pinned up or back so that it may not dangle on or near food or open flame. Hands should be impeccably clean, and fingernails clean and well manicured.

Jewelry must be simple; a wristwatch and simple, tasteful earrings are fine. Employees should avoid wearing large-stoned rings or dangling jewelry of any kind as they may snag guests' clothing or table linens, create distracting noise, and in the case of employees working near heat, inflict burns. Anyone who has ever reached into a hot oven or over a cooktop wearing a metal bracelet or neck chain can attest to this danger.

Don't overlook the fact that your commissary, no matter how small, has to be cleaned regularly, and that, while dish and pot washing do not approach the magnitude of that required in a banquet hall or restaurant, it still must be done. Some establishments employ both a dishwasher and a porter to cover these tasks, but you might explore the possibility of creating a position that covers both jobs in addition to a myriad of other functions: the cleaning and occasional maintenance of small kitchen appliances; cleaning, polishing, sorting, and storing of serving and transporting equipment and utensils; maintaining sanitary conditions in walk-in units, refrigerators, and freezers; and tending to drains, grease traps, and fryer wells. These are not menial tasks; maintaining a clean and orderly kitchen and properly stored equipment is an important job in a catering operation. One reliable and capable person, well paid and given proper responsibility (and an assistant, if needed), is a valued member of your team.

Other kitchen positions may be filled by part-timers or apprentices from culinary or vocational schools. People with some skills and an interest in the field are eager to learn and easy to train in your methods. Check with local job opportunity programs in your area, who seek placement and training for troubled youth, the impoverished, or the handicapped. While performing a community service, you gain a valued employee and have the satisfaction of knowing that you have given someone a chance at a career in the food field. Retirees are also an excellent choice for part-time employees for both kitchen and office. They are usually reliable and stable and generally have a good track record for hard work and dependability. The local senior center or a chapter of the American Association of Retired Persons could provide some referrals.

Even unskilled workers can easily be trained for simple packing and prep procedures at an entry level and moved up as they become familiar with your kitchen procedures. Promoting from within is an especially good idea in kitchen positions because you eventually have a staff that is comfortable working together and trained in all areas. Since moving from job to job and employer to employer is a given in the food trade, building your own staff from within protects you not only from temporary absences due to illness and vacations but also from the inevitable departure of some of your more skilled employees moving on to other opportunities.

PRODUCTIVE MANAGEMENT GUIDELINES

There are no magical rules for running a perfect business, or for being a perfect boss, but there are some guidelines or methods that may help you to cultivate a well-informed, promotable, and reliable staff. At the outset, make it clear that you (or you and your partner) are the boss. This does not mean being arrogant and abusive. The successful off-premise caterer is a take-charge person, not a bully. When you are sure of yourself and understand the work that needs to be accomplished, it is simple to give orders and delegate authority firmly and clearly.

Communication and Attitude

Employees, whether at the senior level or at the lowest rank, appreciate and work better under well-defined areas of responsibility. Define the chains of command, whether in the office, kitchen, or party site. When each person knows what he or she is expected to do, who reports to whom, who gives the orders and who follows them, then the work can be accomplished without friction and resentment. Orientation programs for new employees and periodic training sessions for all staff can be helpful in setting and maintaining performance standards.

It is a good idea to let your employees understand how their jobs fit into the overall picture by involving them in the party process. Party plans and schedules posted in employee areas, menus for events posted in the kitchen, worksheets clearly outlining duties, occasional staff meetings, and food and wine tastings all make individual employees feel like valued members of a team rather than just workers.

It is equally important to let your employees know that they are a valuable asset to the business. Remember to congratulate them after successful jobs, provide small bonuses when possible, send treats home with them for their family and friends, or provide long-term employees with business cards imprinted with their names (and perhaps a title where applicable).

Employees who take pride in their work and are treated with respect perform their job better and seek to improve themselves. Pay your employees a competitive wage. Protect the interests of your waitstaff by discussing gratuities frankly with clients, so that your employees feel rewarded for their hard work. Make an effort to provide pleasant staff meals and snacks for workers and an occasional break for them even on very busy days. You may find yourself feeling frantic at times, but a temper outburst only makes things worse. Unavoidable crises develop even in the most well-planned catered event, and employees whom you treat well pitch in willingly when the going gets rough.

Uniforms and Work Clothes

Plan on a simple uniform for your waitstaff that suits the image of your company and is relatively easy for the employees to provide for themselves. Many caterers choose to have their waitstaff dress in tuxedos or in black slacks or skirts and simple white shirts or blouses. You might choose gray or navy slacks or skirts, pin-stripe shirts or oxford blue button-downs. If you want a more distinctive look, add a striped tie, ascot, suspenders, neckerchief, or chef's apron with your company logo; these extras should be at your expense. In the event that a particular party has a theme, you might want your waitstaff to dress in costume—for example, Hawaiian shirts, togas, cowboy outfits, or medieval garb. You, of course, arrange for these outfits, charging the cost to your client. Costumes can add a great look to a theme party and can be lots of fun for your staff, provided the costumes are in good taste and cause them no physical discomfort or embarrassment.

You should provide kitchen staff with clean work clothes. Be sure that fresh chef's whites, extra clean aprons and side towels are always available for party site cooking: guests often wander into kitchens and food tents, and you want your staff to present a clean and tidy appearance.

Rules of Behavior

There are certain rules of behavior that you must make clear to your employees. In the office, courtesy, promptness, and precision are a must. Carelessness in regard to details can be a caterer's worst internal enemy.

On-Site Responsibility

Employees are to arrive promptly for an assigned function. If they are responsible for their own uniforms, those items should be freshly laundered, ironed, or cleaned; shoes should be polished; and accessories (bow tie, belt, etc.) neat and in place.

Employees are responsible for reading party work plans, menu, and the like before the event. If they are unsure of their duties or of any detail, they should confer with the maître d', supervisor, or event manager before the function. They are to check their stations at the party site to see if any utensils are missing, and either correct the situation or bring it to the attention of someone in charge. In the same vein, if they are given, for example, a tray of hors d'oeuvre to pass, they should check to see that they have the needed garnish or dipping sauce, picks, and sufficient cocktail napkins in hand before they leave the kitchen.

During the function, they are to perform their duties efficiently and cheerfully, always being polite to guests and cooperative to their co-workers. They should be careful not to touch their hands to their hair, face, or mouth. No eating, drinking, gum chewing, or smoking is ever permitted on the serving floor. Such activities are confined to behind the scenes, at appointed break times. No alcohol or drug use is ever tolerated among employees. They are to appear respectful and dignified at all times. If idle on the serving floor, they should stand on the sidelines, ready to perform if needed, maintaining an upright and alert posture. The image of a waitperson slouched against a wall or of two employees chatting and laughing while ignoring guests is a very negative one indeed.

The Difficult Guest

While we are discussing issues relating to staff management, we must also discuss guest management, particularly when it involves a difficult, rude, or intoxicated guest.

In the usual course of events, one of your staff members is the first line of defense against such problems, but you will be called upon to handle them. As a matter of fact, unless a situation calls for split-second action, it is the best policy to instruct your waitstaff to report a potential problem to a superior (a maître d' or yourself) rather than to attempt to handle the problem themselves.

Handling the intoxicated guest is, unfortunately, a necessary skill. In small home entertaining situations, trouble is usually averted by the host or guests, but they may call on the caterer or staff for assistance. Remember that as the caterer, you are ultimately responsible for the party going smoothly for the benefit of your client's comforts and your future business. Legal responsibility must be considered as well: in many states, the person serving (even if not selling) alcohol to a person already under the influence can be held responsible for that person's subsequent dangerous or illegal behavior.

You can employ certain preventive measures when planning the party: encourage your client to provide some nonalcoholic beverages such as fruit punch, mineral waters, and sparkling cider and to foster wine service over only hard drinks; at cocktail parties, structure your menu so that the first hors d'oeuvre are protein rich and substantial so guests have something solid in their stomachs to help absorb their first drinks.

If, despite these strategies, you notice that a guest is beyond his or her limit, you must act. Discreetly inform your host: "Mr. Brown's first drinks seem to have gone to his head. Would one of his friends like to take him for some air, or shall I serve him some coffee in the kitchen?" Usually your host offers to assist you in avoiding a scene. If Mr. Brown is staggering or out of control, your host may need assistance from one or two of your staff to escort him to another room or send him home in a taxi or with a friend. Whatever action you must take, try to do it quickly and with minimal commotion so it doesn't disturb other guests or embarrass your client.

Sometimes, a guest is difficult in regard to food choices or preferences, insisting that a server bring something else, or complaining about the portion, for example. Whenever possible, have your server, maître d', or captain employ the customer-is-always-right approach, and quickly and discreetly try to satisfy the guest. If possible, your kitchen staff should cooperate, serving an impromptu salad or vegetable plate to a vegetarian or regrilling beef to ultra well-done, if that is the request.

Very rarely (but it does happen), a guest is rude or obnoxious to a server, perhaps making unwelcome advances or belligerent remarks, and your server cannot seem to handle it gracefully. You can't scold a guest or engage in an argument, but once it has been brought to your attention, try to abort the whole process. For example, you walk over to the scene, take the canapé tray from the server, and say, "Excuse me, Christine, but Richard needs you in the kitchen right away." Then you turn to the guests, smile, and offer another caviar toast. Usually, this action, or simply reassigning Christine to another table or station, changes the dynamics of the situation enough to avoid any confrontation. It is a polite way of taking charge without causing an awkward scene. Tricky situations like these do not come up often, but it's important to give them some thought so that you can always keep your cool and strive for your ultimate goal, which is to keep things running smoothly and happily along.

Chapter 7

Pricing for Profit

Catering products and services must be sold at a price that will be accepted by clients and still make a reasonable profit for the caterer. Arriving at the right selling price for a job may seem complicated, and, indeed, many factors are involved, but a reliable system of price structuring is necessary to place a business on a sound footing.

FIGURE COST

Before a price can be established for any item, its cost—in raw materials and labor, packaging, and delivery—must be considered. Since the off-premise catering business is filled with variables as to where and in what setting a prepared food will be consumed, it is helpful to begin by establishing food-only prices.

A food-only price reflects the cost of the food and its preparation, plus a business profit. This includes the raw food cost, plus the dollar value of the labor required to prepare it, an additional factor (usually a percentage) to cover overhead or operating costs, and finally, a reasonable profit. In addition, if the item requires a special nonfood item—for example, a basket for crudités or skewers for kabobs—this cost may be included as well.

Raw Food Cost

The first step in pricing is determining the raw food cost per portion of any given recipe. Proceed as follows:

1. List all the ingredients, in appropriate amounts, for a chosen recipe, and record the actual dollar cost of each item. For instance, the total cost of the broccoli used is included even if only the florets are used and the stems discarded (a wasteful practice).

49

RAW FOOD COST SHEET

Item   <u>Vegetable Cheese Squares</u>

Yield   <u>75 pieces</u>

Portion size   <u>1" × 2"</u>

Ingredient	Measure	Unit Cost	Actual Cost
margarine	5 oz	$1.00/lb	$0.30
onion	8 oz	$0.39/lb	$0.20
sandwich bread	4 slices	$1.15/loaf	$0.38
milk	4 fl oz	$1.00/qt	$0.13
frozen French-style green beans	20 oz	$0.79/10 oz	$1.58
whipped cream cheese	12 oz	$1.75	$1.75
whole large eggs	4	$0.99/doz	$0.33
salt and pepper	to taste	–	$0.03
dry bread crumbs	2 tbls	$0.69/lb	$0.05

Total raw food cost $4.75

Cost/piece $0.07 (rounded)

Figure 7–1
Raw food cost sheet.

If ten ducks are boned for their breasts for one recipe, and the balance of the duck meat is used for a pâté, charge appropriate amounts off to each recipe. Be certain to use average current prices, not a one-time sale price, for accuracy. Double check all ingredients to be sure nothing has been omitted. Items used for garnish and materials that are recipe specific (the crudité basket mentioned earlier, e.g.) should be included here.

Remember that even small amounts of staple ingredients bear some cost. For example, the shortening and flour used to grease one muffin tin seems insignificant, but after preparing thirty dozen muffins, you have used a good deal of both materials. Salt and pepper fall into a similar category, and some caterers simplify their costing by figuring a cost of $0.05 or $0.10 for seasonings for every twenty or twenty-five portions of a prepared dish. This averages out well for everyday herbs and spices; however, if, for example, saffron, an expensive item, is one of the seasonings in a dish, this cost would be entered separately. Use common sense to make educated guesses for small amounts of staple items. When all the entries are complete, add the costs to arrive at the total raw food cost for the recipe.

2. Determine the exact yield of the prepared recipe, by actual volume, weight, or count. For example, if the end slices of the roast beef or bread loaf are not used in your sandwich, they cannot be counted as part of the yield. Conversely, five pounds of chicken breast yield more than five pounds of chicken salad once the celery, apples, nuts, and dressing have been added. Measure and weigh (allowing for some serving loss and spillage), to get an accurate yield.

3. Establish an appropriate portion size, and divide this measurement into the total yield to arrive at the number of portions that can be served from the recipe. Note that this figure may vary depending on planned usage—that is, a smaller appetizer portion versus a luncheon plate or the larger portion for a single entrée at dinner versus one of three entrée selections at a buffet.

4. Divide the total raw food cost of the entire recipe by the number of portions to arrive at the per-portion raw food cost (Figure 7–1).

Labor Costs

Part of the cost of any recipe is the time the kitchen staff must spend in prepping and cooking the item. If it takes a cook one and one-half hours to fry a batch of chicken, account for the cook's wages for that time in the selling price. Of course, the oven roasting time for the prime rib may require only ten minutes of hands-on tending by the cook, and that person probably would be occupied during that time preparing another dish, so apply a relatively low labor cost to the prime rib. If, as a beginner, you start out doing most of your cooking yourself, always factor a fair wage into your prices for your own time. In the event that you are unable to perform for any reason, and in the future when your cooking is done by staff, the cook's wages (yours or someone else's) must be allowed for if your selling price is to be valid.

Overhead or Operating Expenses

Every dish prepared in a caterer's kitchen entails other less obvious costs, including, for example, disposable baking pans, waxed paper, foil, and paper toweling. Unless they are recipe specific (as mentioned earlier), these items are part of a caterer's everyday operating expenses. In addition, each food item prepared adds to the ongoing expenses of the business such as rent, utilities, insurance, office salaries, laundry, cleaning and housekeeping, lawyer's and attorney's fees, stationery, and advertising. These are overhead or operating expenses, and every item sold by a business must help to defray these costs. In an ongoing business, simply average out such expenses over a three- or six-month period to find out how much it costs to keep the business running by the day, week, or month. An accountant can help a beginning caterer to project these figures.

Profit Margin

When all of these cost factors have been totaled, you must decide how to earn an appropriate net profit on the item sold. One establishes a profit margin by estimating what dollar amount (or, more generally, percentage of the selling price) should return to the business as a result of any successful transaction. Your accountant, in developing your business plan, can assist you in arriving at a percentage that insures the solvency and growth of your enterprise.

Summary

One arrives at a *food-only selling price* by totaling *raw food costs*, *labor costs*, and *overhead costs*, and then factoring by a profit percentage. As we shall discuss later, *food-only prices* may not always be used when arriving at a total party price, but they can be useful for brochures, menus, and as a response to telephone inquiries about price ranges. Remember that since overall catering jobs vary greatly depending on site selection, rentals, staffing, and other peripherals, it is essential that a caterer's menus, brochures, and sales staff specify clearly that these prices are for *food only*. Make it clear that only after a consultation or meeting between client and caterer can an accurate estimate be given for a total party.

USE STANDARDIZED RECIPES

In order to make any food-pricing system valid and to improve the efficiency of a catering kitchen, it is important to use standardized recipes. Every caterer finds recipes from a variety of sources, including his or her imagination and experimentation. Eventually, the recipes you use are those you have customized to your business, taking into account the capabilities of kitchen staff, equipment, and the tastes of your clientele. At this point you create a standardized recipe, one that specifies the exact ingredients, procedures, portioning, serving, and garnishing instructions that suit your purposes. It is this recipe that is costed out as described.

The use of this standardized recipe ensures that a menu item is properly prepared, of consistent quality, and of predictable yield and cost each time it is made. Keep one copy of this recipe in a master recipe file and another copy (preferably either laminated or in a plastic sleeve) for the use of the kitchen staff. Figure 7–2 is an example of a standardized recipe.

REGULARLY REVIEW COSTS

Preparing an itemized cost breakdown for every single menu item is often impractical. What you can do, even with a hectic schedule and often-varying menus, is a close cost analysis of representative items to establish a profitable and acceptable selling price, and then review and update those figures periodically—perhaps quarterly, or when a significant change has occurred, say, in food cost, monthly rent, staff salaries, or insurance premiums—to insure that the prices are still viable and that the profit margin remains intact.

Item Vegetable Cheese Squares		Category Hors d' Oeuvre
Yield 75 pieces		
Portion size 1" × 2"		

Ingredient	Amount	Procedure
margarine	5 oz	1. Saute onion in margarine.
chopped onion	8 oz	
sandwich bread	4 slices	2. Soak bread in milk.
milk	½ cup	3. Beat cream cheese with eggs, add onions, bread, and green beans. Mix well and season to taste.
frozen French-style green beans, thawed and drained	20 oz	
whipped cream cheese	12 oz	
whole large eggs, beaten	4	4. Pan, sprinkle with dry bread crumbs.
salt and pepper	to taste	5. Bake at 350° until set, about 25 minutes.
dry bread crumbs	2 tbls	6. Cool before cutting.

Pan: 15" × 10" × 1" greased, dusted with dry bread crumbs
Store: Wrap, refrigerate 3 days, or freeze, thaw wrapped
To portion: cut 15 × 5

Figure 7–2
Standardized recipe card.

As an example, a whole group of veal scallop dishes, whatever the sauces, can be priced similarly; the same preparations, substituting chicken or turkey breast slices, can be offered at a lesser price. The following is a different example: You know that to prepare several of your meat or seafood salads, you use three pounds of primary ingredient (whether turkey, ham, or shrimp), one and one-half pounds of secondary ingredients (celery, apple, onion), and a fixed amount of similar mayonnaise dressing for twenty-five portions. Since you know that the cost (in both dollars and labor) are the same except for the primary ingredient, you can simply factor the cost by the difference in the price of turkey to shrimp per pound. When the cost of turkey breast or shrimp changes significantly, so does a whole group of your selling prices.

With experience, you learn to make these transitions easily when preparing menus or discussing budget limits with clients. Having a knowledge of some sound representative prices allows the caterer to have ballpark prices for substitutions and menu variations.

DETERMINE SELLING PRICE

Once you have worked your way through these procedures, you should have a price that you feel is mathematically correct for a certain food item or menu. Then you have to add the costs of all the extras such as rentals, flowers, and serving staff and either charge a markup or consultation fee: a percentage or dollar amount for the time and effort involved in coordinating all those details. Having now done all this paper accounting, how do you know that you have arrived at the right price? This might seem a really tough question for a caterer who is just starting out, but finding a valid answer is important: prices that are too high deny you any business; prices that are too low put you out of business. Even experienced caterers reevaluate and change their pricing structures from time to time to accommodate changes in their business, clientele, or the economy.

While no book can state absolutely that there is only one way for any individual business to operate, it is helpful to examine the methods commonly used in the industry, understand their advantages and drawbacks, and see how they interact with each other. Within the industry, there are three common approaches to pricing:

1. Pricing based on competition: Useful for analyzing one's place in the market, but risky if used indiscriminately.

2. Pricing based on a multiplier: Accurate for food-only costs for average dishes; useful in balancing overall menu costs.

3. Pricing based on a total cost breakdown: Detailed and time consuming, but the most accurate.

You should understand and consider all these methods when defining your selling prices. Each lends its own perspective that can act as a triple-check system when they are compared to each other.

Pricing Based on Competition

Every caterer should be aware of the prices charged by the competition, provided that those competitors are operating in a comparable market—that is, providing the same level of service, similar quality, and complexity of menu and sharing a common client base. Each local area has its own pricing standards: what the public perceives as a reasonable price in the midtown areas of Washington, D.C., New York, or San Francisco would be high for the suburbs or outlying areas of those cities and exorbitant in smaller cities and towns in other parts of the country. Some comparison shopping among caterers in a given area helps you to define fairly accurate price ranges. However, meeting or beating the price of the competition should never be the only reason for settling on a given price; the correct selling price offered by any caterer should be the one that yields an acceptable profit, job by job. If, in exploring competitors' prices, you find that yours are far out of line, a bit of self-examination is in order.

Are the food items and levels of service truly equal? Do you use organic fresh vegetables, while the competition uses frozen? Are you preparing cheese dip with Roquefort while another caterer uses domestic blue? Do you staff your silver-laden buffet with tuxedoed waiters while the competition offers self-serve from stainless steel?

Are you underselling menu items? Name your foods accurately but dramatically: your Roquefort Calvados Dip is worth more and should command a higher price than Blue Cheese Dip. Often, when you emphasize the quality and value you are offering, a client is willing to pay more.

Are you offering more than you need to in a given situation? If your client is happy with (and only willing to pay for) green beans, don't use haricots verts.

Are you wasting time or money? Are you sure your staff is following your standardized recipe, using the most efficient prep methods, carefully observing portion control? Instead of chopping small shrimp, would tiny salad shrimp be more economical (and just as tasty) in your dilled shrimp salad? Would frozen, chopped spinach be more efficient to prepare than fresh (and work just as well) in your spinach-stuffed mushrooms? Remember that you can maintain quality and reduce labor by using convenience foods wisely.

Is there an unknown factor? Your competition may have an advantage you're not aware of: she may be working out of her home with little overhead; family members may be recruited as unpaid staff; she may do enormous volume in a particular specialty and so offer reduced prices. As a matter of fact, she may be losing money because of underpricing.

After reviewing these points, you may find that you can lower your price and still make a profit. Remember that when you are just starting out, you may not be efficient enough or have adequate business volume to make great profits. Sometimes it is worth working on a narrow profit margin to build a reputation and clientele. Basing your prices solely on your competition can be risky, but knowing your competitors' prices and analyzing your own in comparison to theirs can help keep you in the running.

Pricing Based on a Multiplier

A common practice used in the food industry in determining the selling price of a food item or menu is to multiply the raw food cost times three. Recently, as costs of labor and overhead have increased, particularly in urban areas, this multiplier has been revised to "times four" to ensure a reasonable profit. This method can be useful in arriving at food-only prices for a particular menu, since the multiplier yields a dollar amount three or four times above the cost of the food, and that dollar amount should cover labor, overhead, and profit. Given the variables of catering, other costs (serving staff, rentals, etc.) are not considered and would have to be added on as extras.

This method of establishing a selling price can be quite effective, especially when dealing with an average menu. When exotic, expensive, or labor-intensive items come into play, however, the multiplier method may be far from accurate.

When raw food costs for a particular menu item are either very low or very high, further analysis is needed. Some items have a very high cost but require little or no labor; employing the standard multiplier might make the menu item exorbitantly expensive. In these cases, it is best to balance a menu based on all the parts of the meal, so that the overall selling price for the full menu stays within the appropriate multiplier range. In other words, the basic raw cost of the lobster, salmon, or veal chop main course item may be multiplied by only 1.5 or 2, while the cost of ingredients for the elegant-looking but inexpensive garnished consommé may be multiplied by 5 or 6. In this way the overall selling price for the meal is acceptable to the client and still yields a profit.

Pricing Based on Total Cost Breakdown

This method for determining the correct selling price for a whole catering job may seem complicated, but it really is the simplest, relying less on formulas, factoring, and percentages and much more on a clear, step-by-step procedure. Since it itemizes every aspect of the job, it is very useful for both estimated and final pricing of a complex or unusual event, since it really amounts to a straightforward list of every item or service, each bearing its own cost.

It has special advantages to the beginner. Its detail and completeness comprise a powerful tool toward organization. With every bit of minutiae laid out in black and white, it is less likely that some costly item or service gets overlooked. It is also reassuring to a beginner to see a whole job, which might seem overwhelmingly complex, transformed into a manageable, one-page outline. In addition, since its framework is similar to a profit-and-loss statement, it is simple to do such an accounting after a job has been completed. Then, if the profit from the job is not what you expected, if something has gone wrong in the pricing procedure, this detailed breakdown makes the error easy to spot and easy to avoid the next time around.

To prepare such a breakdown, the following categories must be included:

1. Raw food costs

2. Labor costs for food preparation

3. Overhead costs and operating expenses

4. Labor costs at the site: kitchen and serving staff, delivery personnel, dishwashers, and so on, including travel, setup, and breakdown time

5. Transportation or delivery charges

6. Consultation or events management fees

7. All peripherals: rentals, flowers, decor, photography, entertainment, and the like

8. Markups on peripherals, if not charged off as consultation fees

9. Profit margin

Note that items 1, 2, 3, and all or part of item 9, may be absorbed into a single entry as the food-only selling price for the planned menu, if those have already been worked out by the caterer. The results are equally valid.

BALANCE THE MENU

Throughout Part II, menu balance is discussed from the point of view of tastes, textures, food harmony, and serving ease, but menu balance can also be viewed from the point of view of overall price. Most clients have a budget limit in mind when they book a party, and an understanding of menu balance helps a caterer plan a menu that satisfies the clients' needs at an overall price they are willing to pay. While an overall selling price (as we have seen earlier) must cover a number of costs plus a reasonable profit, it must still fall within a range that the customer perceives as suitable for the value received. At the same time, for practical purposes of efficiency and manageable preparation, it is to the caterer's advantage to structure a menu that combines complicated, labor-intensive dishes with dishes that are easy to prepare. A balanced menu can honor both points of view.

To understand menu balance, give some thought to analyzing the real cost of prepared items by looking at them from different points of view: their actual cost to prepare (in labor, time, and materials) and the perceived value that they display to a customer. For the most part, it is true that more expensive items require less fuss (steamed lobster), more economical dishes (seafood mousse) require more work. For example, beef tenderloin begins with a high raw food cost. Trimming the tenderloin results in a high proportion of waste to useful meat (usually, about two- to one-third). However, it is easy to portion, extraordinarily simple and quick to prepare, and results in no plate waste. In addition, it is perceived as a luxury item by both clients and guests and can be priced accordingly.

Compare these two menu items: A roast turkey with sausage and herb dressing is simple and economical to prepare. While it can be quite delicious and popular, it presents a "homey" appearance and thus cannot be priced too high. A galantine of turkey, boned and stuffed with sausage and spinach, is relatively more complicated and time consuming to prepare. It requires similar inexpensive ingredients, but makes a far more striking and elegant presentation. Since it is thus perceived as special by the customer, it warrants a more expensive selling price than the first dish that more than makes up for its preparation time.

Consider the case of luxury items: There is no question that a side of smoked salmon or a large tin of the finest caviar makes a statement of luxury. Clients understand that these items are expensive and are willing to pay the price for them. If they are served in the classic manner, there is virtually no preparation involved, save for attractive display garnish such as an ice mold to hold the caviar tin or a silver-trimmed fish board for the salmon. However, most guests indulge themselves in such items with abandon, and the caterer needs to charge a high price per person for such a lavish display.

If the client balks at the estimated price for such generous servings of a luxury item, there is still room to maneuver. Place a server at the salmon board to exert portion (and thereby cost) control or garnish tiny new potatoes or warm blini with caviar to pass as hors d'oeuvre, which limits consumption and reduces the price per head. The same expensive ingredients can get even more mileage if you create an appetizer of salmon cornets filled with herbed cream cheese and topped with a dab of caviar. True, you've added more labor and still need expensive ingredients, but the ingredients go farther and your client has the satisfaction of serving guests luxury items at a more moderate price.

In contrast, some menu items that utilize inexpensive ingredients in a simple preparation are very favorably received by clients and guests. Soups, imaginative vegetable preparations, colorful salads, pastas, puddings, and fruit-sauced ice cream desserts are a few examples of such items. Including such dishes in a menu with an expensive, but simply prepared, entrée can help you achieve an overall cost balance that is acceptable to a client and profitable to you.

Prepare sample menus, in a variety of price ranges, that are balanced between fancy and plain dishes, expensive and inexpensive ingredients, and complex and simple preparations. Menus prepared within this framework enhance efficiency, protect profits, and promote customer satisfaction.

Chapter 8

Selling Your Service:
From Client Contact to Contract

Contact with a client is the caterer's primary access to business. The foundation for this salesmanship process has been built through all the procedures undertaken to go into business; it has been enhanced with the caterer's establishment and promotion of an image, can be expanded by networking, and is backed up by the sample menus, brochures, advertising, and word-of-mouth that define and publicize the caterer's service to a chosen market.

These preliminaries are most important to the development of a business profile, but it is in the interface between caterer and client that active salesmanship begins. It is also in this one-to-one setting that the event is defined, details are worked out, price is negotiated and agreed upon, and the ultimate contractual arrangement between caterer and client—the sale—is finalized. This chapter shows that the potential sale often begins with a casual inquiry, either in person or by mail or phone, and that each step taken from that point should be directed toward the ultimate goal: a signed contract for a scheduled event and the promise of future repeat business.

TELEPHONE TECHNIQUE

Most often, the initial contact is made when a client calls a caterer, and thus, the proper handling of such a telephone call is essential. A caterer's telephone should be answered promptly, courteously, and professionally. During especially hectic periods of the workday or when no one is available to answer, a service or answering machine should be used and the calls returned as soon as possible. This is both a courtesy and an indication to the caller that the caterer's business is professionally and conscientiously run.

Keep a booking request form (Figure 8–1) near the phone for initial phone calls,

59

BOOKING REQUEST FORM

Today's date _____ Rec'd by _____

Client name _____ Event day/date _____

Company _____ Time _____AM/PM

Address _____ Number of guests _____

  Apt/Flr _____ City _____ Event _____

Phone (biz) _____ Type of function _____

  home _____ Referred by _____

Concept/theme _____ Location _____

_____

Tentative menu/likes, dislikes _____

_____

_____

Beverage _____

_____

Service _____ Ice _____

_____ Decor _____

Rentals _____ Other _____

Budget range _____ Follow-up date _____

Notes _____ Client meeting date _____

Figure 8–1
Booking request form.

and fill it in during the conversation, which is helpful in focusing the conversation and recording details for future reference. Both client and caterer use an initial phone call to see if they feel compatible and to gather knowledge. It is up to the caterer to elicit as many specifics from the client as possible in a gracious manner, while giving the client responses that sell the caterer's service for the event.

If promotional brochures or sample menus are available, you may, of course, offer to send them to callers, but since the ultimate goal of the telephone conversation is to set up a planning meeting with the client, emphasize the fact that these printed materials offer suggested menus and approximate price ranges. Tell the client that you would be happy to meet with him or her to customize a menu for the upcoming event and to discuss the planning of the total party concept. This method intrigues and tantalizes the client without either party's becoming locked in to a fixed plan or price. Remember that the more information that can be gained from an initial telephone call, the more likely the caterer's face-to-face meeting with the client results in a successful sale.

PRICE QUOTATION

A caterer should never quote a firm price for an event over the phone because there are too many variables, such as service, rentals, party site, and other peripherals, that could drastically affect the final price of the event. The only exceptions that can be made are to long-established repeat customers (where all the variables are known) or in the case of a straight delivery of prepared party platters, trays of hors d'oeuvre, and so on where a food-only selling price (plus delivery charge, if warranted) can be accurately quoted.

CAREFUL BOOKING

If you happen to be overbooked for a particular date, try to lead the client to a more available time. Be certain, however, that the other bookings are firm. If they are not, indicate only that you have other tentative bookings for that date, and continue your sales pitch. (Before plans get too far along, recheck on the tentative bookings so you do not offer the new client a false promise of performance.) Of course, the client often has an immovable date in mind, and then you must decide whether to adjust (by taking on more staff, e.g.) or subcontracting some of your work to another caterer. Whatever you decide, be sure that one client does not benefit at the expense of another. Behave ethically—that is, don't give short shrift to a "less important" client so you can take on a big party for a VIP. Make it your policy to do your best for every client and event you commit to, large or small.

There may be other instances where it becomes necessary or advisable to refer a client to another caterer. While no one likes to give away business, if a caterer truly cannot satisfy a client's needs, it is wiser to admit this rather than to attempt something and fail. If, for example, a client requests an authentic clambake, it may be preferable for a caterer to subcontract the project to a specialist, perhaps retaining control of the overall project by acting as party planner or playing a minor role by providing only hors d'oeuvre, beverage service, and desserts. While the lion's share of the profits might go out to subcontract, the caterer retains the goodwill of a satisfied client.

SHOPPERS

Caterers get a certain percentage of phone calls from shoppers—people who are simply surveying a number of caterers to compare prices and services. While some of these calls may result in actual client meetings and successful sales, most do not. Every call should be handled with courtesy, but it is unwise to spend too much time on such calls. If you have the time and inclination, you might offer to make a competitive tentative bid; if not, make it a polite, but short, call. Offer to send sample menus, or respond to a request for a price quote in an oblique manner: "Well, Mrs. Shopper, I can't give you a complete price for the menu you describe, but I can tell you that we offer a chicken luncheon for $17.50 per person, exclusive of service, wine and other extras." or "Our cocktail parties range from $14.00 to $35.00 per person." Experience gives caterers a sixth sense that alerts them to callers who are shoppers, and they deal with these people politely but expeditiously.

CONSULTATION FEES

Try not to be lured into offering too much free party-planning advice over the phone. It is a sad fact that some clients take advantage of the enthusiasm of caterers (especially novices), pick their brains for detailed menus and decor ideas, then go sailing merrily off with their ideas, never to be heard from again. One of the ways of reducing such incidents is by charging a consultation fee for a planning meeting with certain clients.

As we explained in Chapter 7, a caterer must be paid for the time and effort spent conceptualizing, planning, coordinating, and executing an event, either by adding a consultation fee or by markup. It is equally legitimate for a caterer to be paid for preparty planning. The fee charged can be by the hour ($25 to $35) or a flat rate ($75) for a meeting and proposal or bid. The charge is applicable to the deposit (which is usually 50%), so if a function goes through to contract, the client has lost no money. Clients who are interested in reviewing detailed and extensive bids prior to selecting a caterer or who are truly in the market for thorough planning advice do not object to this method. Casual shoppers either get serious or go elsewhere for their free party planning. Note, however, that this device must be used with great restraint and good judgment. It should not be a regular policy, just a protective device to ward off unscrupulous clients.

THE CLIENT MEETING

Since few caterers have the luxury of elaborate office meeting space, most client meetings take place either at the client's home, office, or planned party site. If the plans are for a home party, a home visit is essential (see Chapter 11). If the meeting is at the party site, take along a site inspection checklist (see Figure 10–1) to ensure that no detail of logistics or equipment is overlooked.

It is important to set a competent and positive image in a first meeting with a client. Arrive promptly and well prepared. Prior to the meeting, review the particulars noted on the booking request form. Based on that information, think through some menu ideas that take into account the theme of the event, the size and style of the party, and the price range the client has in mind. Have some copies of suggested menu plans and creative concepts ready to offer the client.

In addition, many caterers find it useful to take along a small photo portfolio to illustrate the presentation of certain dishes and the style of table settings, floral arrangements, and so forth that might apply. Copies of pretty menus (in calligraphy or specially decorated) can be good selling tools. Some caterers even bring clients treats (zucchini muffins for a morning meeting or delicate cookies later in the day).

If extensive peripherals are likely to be involved in the event, it is helpful to have rental brochures, color charts for linens, and approximate price lists for party favors, tenting, and so on and to be ready to make referrals from within your resource network. Of course, some caterers prefer to subcontract extensive decor and other extras, and in that case, you should arrange a separate meeting with the client and the subcontractor (with or without the caterer present) to finalize those details. Other caterers, once they have worked successfully with certain suppliers, feel comfortable in presenting full-service coordination at the outset.

Whatever the case, the caterer should come prepared to discuss all the aspects of an event intelligently with the client, providing the client with enough information to arrive at a relatively complete plan within the space of this one meeting. Repeated meetings and phone calls are an inefficient use of both the caterer's and the client's time, can lead to confusion, and might leave the client with the impression that the caterer is disorganized or careless.

The best results come when the caterer is well prepared and able to direct the flow of the meeting. Using a guide or form (Figure 8–2) is helpful, since it acts both as a reminder of details and an aid in note taking. Remember that good meeting notes are the basis of all subsequent party planning and should be as complete as possible.

Be efficient, but try not to overwhelm or intimidate a client with too many questions, lists, and charts. Listen to the client, watch for reactions to certain suggestions, and try to read between the lines to pick up clues about food preferences, style of service, and budget. Especially when dealing with a new client, or one who has little experience in catered affairs, be gentle and sympathetic to the client's concerns and taste. If, however, you feel that the client is making a mistake, either in choices of foods or protocol, you, as the expert advisor, are obliged to discreetly but firmly lead the way.

The Hidden Agenda

While every catered function has a stated and obvious purpose, such as wedding, birthday celebration, product promotion, or a simple gathering of friends, many also

---

MEETING NOTES

Today's date: _____ By _____

Client name _____ Event day/date _____

Bill to _____ Time _____AM/PM

_____ Number of guests _____

Type of function _____ Event _____

_____

Concept/theme _____ Location _____

_____

Menu _____

_____

_____

Beverage _____ Ice _____

_____

Service _____ Rentals _____

_____

_____

Floral _____ Decor _____

Music _____ Photo _____ Other _____

Site inspection/visit? _____ When? _____

Estimated price/budget _____

Booking confirmed? _____ Proposal/letter of agreement? _____

Figure 8-2
Meeting notes form.

have an unstated and more subtle hidden agenda, which should be honored if the function is to be truly successful. If the client is trying to please or impress a prospective employer or business associate, he might be very specific about menu choices, or the selection of a wine. Sometimes employers host a party for staff and want to go all out to thank them for struggling through a tough year. A company executive might want to appear frugal and conservative when she entertains members of her board of directors, lest her extravagance contrast with poor last quarter profits. Or the situation might be simpler: a new wife might be nervous about meeting her husband's business associates for the first time; or a host may want the staff to be particularly solicitous of his prospective mother-in-law. Whatever the case, be sensitive to such hints or signals, and do all you can to see that the unspoken goal is achieved.

THE CLIENT'S BUDGET

It is important for the caterer to encourage the client to reveal what budget limits he or she may have set for a particular function and to stay within those guidelines as much as possible. If the initial telephone call has yielded some budget information, then the caterer can come to the meeting prepared to honor them. If not, the caterer should initiate the discussion, possibly by suggesting a menu, and then quoting an approximate price. If the client flinches at the price or says, "That's very nice, but a bit more lavish than I would like," then the caterer should suggest a less expensive variation. If that price yields a request for "something simpler," it might be time for the caterer to ask directly what the client's budget restrictions are. This can be done tactfully: "Why don't you tell me what you were thinking of spending, Mrs. Trask? Then we can plan a very nice party that you will be comfortable with." Remember that even small jobs yield profit, and building a clientele requires cultivating repeat business.

Don't be afraid of creative selling, but don't oversell or pressure clients into spending over their limits. If you make clients uncomfortable, or if they feel taken advantage of, they will never use your service again. Of course, in some situations a client's expectations are completely out of line with reality, and if that's the case, you must say so. Back away from "suicide" bids, but do so nicely and leave the door open for future contact.

THE MEETING REVIEW

When most of the preliminary discussion has been completed, and the party has begun to take shape, review all the areas one more time:

Balance the menu for price and taste, and be sure that it can be accomplished at the site.

Make recommendations on rentals and equipment and give the client an approximate idea of those costs, if possible. Point out what you need from the client: for example, cleared shelves in the refrigerator, confirmed time of access, seating plans, guests lists. If the client is providing any serving pieces, beverages, or paper goods, make sure they are adequate and available at the time of the party.

Discuss the plans for staffing the party. Let the client know how many will be in service, for what time period, and how they will dress. Explain hourly rates, party minimums (usually no less than four hours), and overtime rates, if applicable. Mention gratuities for staff, and decide whether they will be included in your fee or distributed by the client.

Discuss any other peripheral services, such as flowers, music, and photographers, and either make referrals or discuss tentative arrangements to the client's satisfaction.

After reviewing all the details you have discussed, one by one, explain that you will send a letter of agreement (or contract) to the client, so that both parties are clear on all details. If you feel comfortable, give the client an approximate price estimate. Explain that you expect a deposit (usually 50% of the total price) along with a signed copy of the letter of agreement.

At this time, also explain your cancellation policy. Some states and regions have guidelines for cancellations: in general, they are based on the premise of protecting the consumer from unfair policies, while allowing caterers to recoup costs for actual monies laid out and loss of business. Have your attorney check these out for you.

Explain what you mean by a guaranteed minimum and at what date before the party (usually three to ten days) you need the final number of guests. When discussing minimums, be sure the client understands that a per person price usually rises as the number of guests decreases. A lot of clients get last-minute pangs of pocketbook and think they can save money by cutting their guest lists, so give a client parameters for a per person price.

If the party is particularly complex, or if your meeting has resulted in a menu or plan far different from the original concept, if prices must be obtained for many peripherals, or if a site inspection has not been done, it is best to tell the client that you will call in (or send) an itemized estimate for approval. Follow that up with a contract or letter of agreement when you have finalized all the particulars.

LETTER OF AGREEMENT OR CONTRACT

In most cases, the client meeting results in a fairly complete party plan, with both parties in agreement as to all the details and approximate costs involved. The next step, then, is to formalize this understanding in writing, secure a deposit, and begin to plan the party. Many caterers are quite comfortable with a detailed letter of agreement (Figure 8–3 on pages 68–69). Signed by both parties and confirmed by the submission and acceptance of a deposit, it is a binding document in most areas. While its form is proper, it is more easily read and understood (and less intimidating) to a client than a multi-page contract. In some cases, however, especially where a party is extensive, complex, and costly, a more formal and lengthy contract is used. Always consult with an attorney for approval of whatever form or forms you decide to use because local statutes vary as to what constitutes a binding contract. Whatever method of confirmation you use, be sure that you have a signed piece of paper and a deposit before you proceed one step further. Without it, you don't have a sale, all you have is the potential for misunderstanding, wasted time, and lost revenue.

FOLLOW-UP

Following an event, of course, there may be practical reasons for a caterer to make contact with the client. There may be some late billing for overtime or delayed payment for unexpected peripherals or other loose ends to tie up. However, even if all business matters are completed at the moment the event ends, it is imperative that the caterer make one more contact with the client. At the minimum, a thank-you letter or personal note expressing the caterer's pleasure in serving the client is essential. Typically, a client experiences an "afterglow" following a successful party, and the caterer, with a thoughtful note of gratitude, builds a bond with the client by sharing that pleasant experience. As a further step, in addition to the immediate follow-up, the caterer should develop a plan to contact such clients periodically.

If the completed event was one of a sporadic nature—an at-home cocktail party, dinner party, or business lunch—place the clients on a seasonal mailing list, and send out mailers announcing ideas such as a new Spring Menu, Hors D'oeuvre Ideas, Lo-Cal Lunches, Budget Buffets, or Ethnic Theme Party Menus. This device reminds satisfied clients of the caterer's creativity, availability, and interest in their business.

If the event was one of a repeatable nature—for example, a birthday, anniversary, annual awards banquet, holiday dance—send a reminder letter at the appropriate time each year. Most sales-oriented businesses establish a "tickler" file, usually a monthly review of prospective upcoming business. Friendly calls are made or letters are sent to such prospects (incorporating sufficient lead time for planning), reminding the clients of the firm's eagerness and readiness to serve them again. A caterer with an ongoing business need only review the past year's bookings to create such a tickler file.

NEW BUSINESS PROSPECTS

A newly established caterer should begin to build a tickler file at the outset, and make good use of it, since future bookings are money in the bank to a growing business. Lacking the long history of past bookings, the beginning caterer can create a file of prospects by watching for annual events that are publicized in the local media. The cultural and society pages might mention a recent charity ball or fund raiser for the local art society, and a letter could be sent to the chairperson, expressing interest in submitting a proposal for the group's next event. A sample menu or brochure should be included, along with the information that the caterer (or the salesperson who sends the letter) will telephone in the near future to discuss the event. Then the follow-up phone call should be made.

If the call results in a routine response such as, "We won't be meeting to plan the dance until next March," then the caterer should insert a note into the tickler file for March as follows: "Call Mrs. Klein, Art Society, re Harvest Dance, 525-1234." If the phone call yields the information that the group has an ongoing relationship with another caterer for this event, then the caller may choose either to drop out of the running or compete.

Esprit Caterers, Inc.
340 West 18th Street
New York, New York 10011

September 4, 19xx

Ms. Allison Brown
263 East 71st Street
New York, New York 10021

Dear Ms. Brown:

This letter will serve to confirm our mutual agreement on the following arrangements for your upcoming cocktail party:

Guarantee: 60 persons at $27.00 each, inclusive of all arrangements as specified below. The final number of guests must be confirmed no later than October 13.

Deposit and Payment: Of the total $1620.00, one-half, or $810, is due as a nonrefundable deposit upon signing of this agreement. Final payment, with possible overtime charges, will be due upon completion of the party. Gratuities are not included.

Overall Description: A Cocktail Party for 60 guests, to be held at your home on Thursday, October 19, 19xx, from 6 to 8 P.M. The party will take place on the ground floor only, in the foyer, front parlor, and dining room. The staff will work out of the ground floor kitchen and maid's room adjacent to the service entrance. One bar will be set in the far corner of the front parlor. A server will butler-pass wine as well.

Bar Service: Wine and mineral water only. I have placed a wine order with Gladstone Liquors on your behalf for the following: 18 bottles sauvignon blanc, 6 bottles white zinfandel, 6 bottles red zinfandel. Peter, at Gladstone, will call one week before the party to discuss final selections and confirm delivery time. The order will be charged to your account at the shop. You have agreed to provide additional beverages as follows: 1 case mineral water and 6 liters club soda.

Ice: Will be delivered by 4:30 P.M.

Figure 8–3
Sample letter of agreement.

Menu: Crudite Arrangement in Harvest Basket   Red Caviar Dip
French Cheese Assortment with Autumn Leaves
Crackers, Grapes, and Roasted Nuts

Passed hors d'oeuvre:
Hot: Mini Empanadas   Miniature Reubens
     Escargots in Mushroom Caps   Chicken Sate
Cold:Ginger Poached Shrimp   Smoked Salmon Roulades
     Assorted Vegetable Cheese Squares

Service: 1 bartender, 3 servers, 1 cook.

Rentals: 8 dozen all-purpose balloon wine glasses have been
ordered along with a table for the bar, white linens, ashtrays,
trays for passing, and a coatrack with hangers for the
entryway. Delivery will be made before 3 P.M. on the day of the
party, by Party Rent-All; they will pick up before 11 A.M. the
following day.

Flowers: Les Fleurs has been contacted and awaits your order.
They will bill you directly.

Access: At the service entrance, no later than 4 P.M., on the
day of the party. Please have counter and refrigerator space
available as we discussed.

Maintenance: General cleanup only. All rentals will be
packed for pickup; trash removed to curb. All leftovers will
be wrapped and stored for your use. Empty wine bottles (and
remaining full bottles) will be placed in the pantry.

Any changes to be made in the above agreement will be
finalized before October 1. If all of the above meets with
your understanding and approval, please sign below and
return one copy, along with your deposit, in the enclosed
envelope. Please retain one copy for your records.

Agreed   Agreed

_____   _____
                                (for Esprit Caterers, Inc.)

Dated _____ 19xx   Dated _____ 19xx

Figure 8-3
Continued.

Proposals and Bids

If the business of a company or association appears to be a worthwhile pursuit, the caterer should courteously suggest submitting a competitive bid, to see if he or she can arouse any interest. If so, prepare and submit a bid proposal, with the understanding that there is no obligation on the part of the receiving client or organization. In general, a low-key approach is best; high-pressure sales tactics may injure a caterer's chances for future or referral business if the approach is pushy or annoying. If a client strongly resists, it may be better to retreat graciously, making a note to try again at a more favorable time. Bear in mind that preparing proposals or bids takes a certain amount of time and effort: if done efficiently and judiciously, such efforts can reap rewards, but each caterer must decide whether the timing, the potential client's attitude, and the possibility of success make the effort worthwhile.

Some caterers have developed bids and proposals into a fine art. They have decided that such efforts should be an ongoing part of their business development plans and thus submit their bids in amazingly creative and successful ways. Proposals, rather than being prepared on ordinary stationery and sent through the mail, can be delivered in a much more exciting fashion. The proposal for an Elizabethan gala can be done on a parchment scroll and delivered by a liveried messenger. A party with a tropical island theme can be bid by a beachcomber bearing a conch shell or a note in a bottle. A basket of teas, jams, and crumpets, with a serious proposal tucked inside, can be sent to the committee planning an art society's Victorian tea. A recent column in *Restaurant Exchange News* ("Covering Catering," by Janet Lee, November, 1989) describes more imaginative approaches. A planned celebration for Ellis Island was bid in dramatic fashion: a steamer trunk, filled with symbols of our melting pot culture, was sent on a trip around the world before it arrived at the government office in charge of the event. A Mexican fiesta was bid via a sombrero, bearing the proposal and a bottle of tequila, all wrapped in colored cellophane and decked with a profusion of ribbon streamers.

Local Opportunities

Many caterers gather information from local papers and organizations about upcoming events and potential clients. Read engagement and birth announcements as notices of forthcoming weddings and christenings. News items about business expansion could mean a party to celebrate the opening of a new showroom or introduction of a new product. The chamber of commerce is a source for new businesses entering the area, and realtors or a community's Welcome Wagon (or new neighbor group) can provide access to new residents. Send all these prospects an appropriate letter or fliers introducing the caterer's service. A good system of follow-up on present customers can turn one-time clients into full-time clients, and the aggressive pursuit of new potential business can increase a caterer's visibility and help expand a business base.

Chapter 9

Organizing and Executing a Successful Event

Organization is the key to flawless performance in catering and a great insurance policy against frayed nerves, missed cues, and irate clients. Precise attention to detail and the blending of these details into a smooth, flowing whole mark a successful catered event. This total organization is found in a master job file compiled for each function. Simply put, lists are made; details are checked and double-checked; orders are placed; foods are prepared; materials are received, counted, and packed; staff is hired and duties assigned; general instructions are given and explained; and on the day of the event, these pieces and plans come together to stage the perfect party.

While there are no hard and fast rules for the components of a master job file, this chapter analyzes all the pieces of data (and, indeed, all the pieces of paper) that define the concept and scope of a catered event in a logical sequence. It presents suggested forms and worksheets to make the organization of these pieces more manageable for the off-premise caterer. Each individual or organization devises a personal working style and method most suitable for his or her particular business, but the following material provides hints and guidelines that are useful to any working caterer.

Please bear in mind that these organizational steps and forms are offered in what may be an artificial straight line approach. Real life tends to take a more serpentine route, so in practice, many of the steps are taken concurrently, with overlaps and alterations in sequence. As a matter of fact, at a point in the planning process, the route divides into two paths, one to the kitchen and one to the dining room; then the paths converge to produce the final event. Figure 9–1 shows a schematic overview of the possible sequence of planning steps in organizing an event.

71

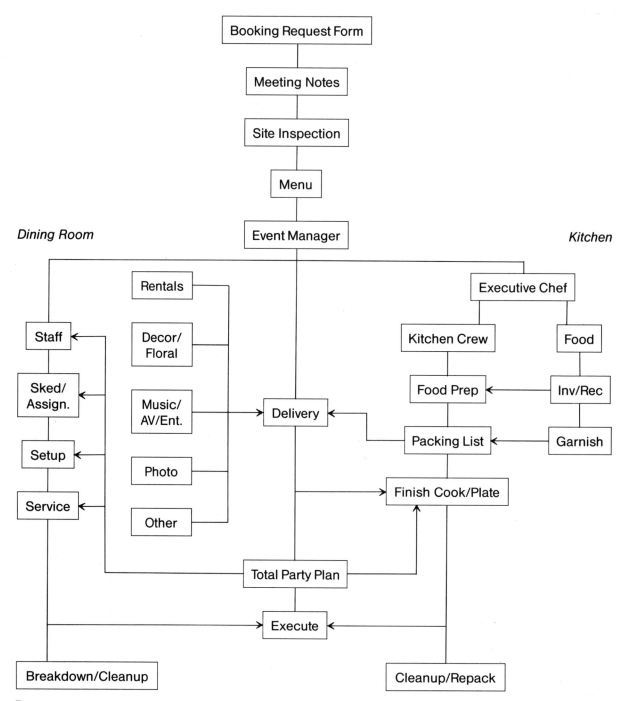

Figure 9–1
Event management flow chart.

STRATEGIES AND FORMS FOR OVERALL PLANNING

Initial Forms

The booking request form is the very first record of a client's contact with the caterer and provides the bare framework for a potential event (see Figure 8–1). It should be filled out thoroughly during the first phone call from the client. The meeting notes form (see Figure 8–2) serves as a record of the client meeting, the next step in the event planning process, in which more details are discussed and refined, resulting in a fairly complete project outline. Usually, a site inspection (see Chapter 10) is conducted at this point or soon thereafter, with notations made on a site inspection checklist (see Figure 10–1) as to the particulars of the chosen site.

Menu

A few suggested or tentative menus may be presented at a client meeting, often with varying prices, and the pros and cons of the menu choices are discussed. In most cases, a fairly detailed finalized menu is agreed upon, and this becomes the operative menu that is entered into the master job file. In other cases, a menu may remain tentative pending the confirmation of other details, such as the availability or market price of certain foods, the need for extra crew or cooking equipment, a final decision on type of service, and so forth. In either case, the menu is made as complete as possible so that work on the other aspects of the job can begin. A menu (with notes as to options) should be placed in the master job file. All the orders and assignments to both kitchen and dining room flow from this complete menu.

Event Manager

An event manager is now assigned, assuming the caterer is not handling all the details and follow-through him- or herself, and becomes the total coordinator for the entire job. By analyzing both the menu and the collected meeting notes, the event manager is able to generate directives to both the front and back of the house.

Rentals and Other Peripherals

A discussion of needed rentals and other peripherals, such as flowers or other decor, photography, music, or printing, should take place either at the client meeting or soon after. Either appropriate referrals are made or orders placed for these extras by the event manager. The event manager also remains in contact with the various vendors or services to ensure that all production details, performance, and deliveries are made in a timely manner. When these orders are made or the details finalized, this information becomes part of the master job file, either as copies of the orders themselves or with entries made on vendor breakout orders (Figure 9–2) detailing the particulars.

For rentals, in particular, most caterers find it convenient to make multiple copies of their rental company's order form and then check off or quantify the list of rental

---

VENDOR BREAKOUT ORDER

Vendor _____   Client _____

Address _____   Event date _____

_____   Event time _____

Phone _____   Deliver by (*time*) _____

Contact _____   Location _____

Product/service _____   Address _____

Order _____   Phone at site _____

_____   Event manager _____

_____

_____

_____

_____

_____

_____

Order placed (*date*) _____ By _____ Confirmed (*date*) _____

Payment/billing _____

Notes _____

_____

Figure 9–2
Vendor breakout order.

items as needed for a particular job. Since the prices are usually listed on an order form, further accounting is simplified, and it is easy for a caterer to give a quick estimate of the cost of the rentals to the client during a planning meeting. The same list can then be used to call the order in to the rental company, confirm availability and delivery times, and finalize amount and time of deposit and payment.

An overview of all the event's peripherals is noted on a peripherals summary sheet (Figure 9–3), which is handy for quick reference during the final planning stages of the job. (This summary sheet is also a useful point of reference when informing a superintendent at a rental site of the comings and goings of vendors for a planned function.) When most of the details are finalized either at the client meeting or in

PERIPHERALS SUMMARY SHEET

Function _____ Client _____

Location _____ Event date _____

Address _____ Event time _____

_____ Event mgr _____

Service entrance _____ Phone at site _____

Rentals (*company*) _____ Contact _____ Phone _____

Order placed (*date*) _____ Sched. delivery (*date/time*) _____

Payment (*circle one*)   bill to client   bill caterer   C.O.D.   on account

Notes _____

Floral (*company*) _____ Contact _____ Phone _____

Order placed (*date*) _____ Sched. delivery (*date/time*) _____

Payment (*circle one*)   bill to client   bill caterer   C.O.D.   on account

Notes _____

Decor (*company*) _____ Contact _____ Phone _____

Order placed (*date*) _____ Sched. delivery (*date/time*) _____

Payment (*circle one*)   bill to client   bill caterer   C.O.D.   on account

Notes _____

Music (*company*) _____ Contact _____ Phone _____

Plans confirmed (*date*) _____ Sched. arrival (*time*) _____

Payment (*circle one*)   bill to client   bill caterer   C.O.D.   on account

Photography (*company*) _____ Contact _____ Phone _____

Plans confirmed (*date*) _____ Sched. arrival (*time*) _____

Printing (*company*) _____ Contact _____ Phone _____

Order placed (*date*) _____ Delivery (*date/time*) _____

Payment (*circle one*)   bill to client   bill caterer   C.O.D.   on account

Other _____

Figure 9–3
Peripherals summary sheet.

follow-up correspondence, then the final price is established, a letter of agreement (see Figure 8–3) or contract is signed, and the job is underway.

Planning Meeting

Once the event manager has a relatively firm menu and party plan in hand, he or she holds a planning meeting with the executive chef (or whoever is in charge of food supplies, preparations, and kitchen staff) to review the menu, party format, and style and timing of service. The chef indicates needs for tableware, silverware, serving platters, and so forth to the event manager to be sure that no possible need has been overlooked. The event manager informs the chef of any aspect of party planning that may affect or interrupt kitchen production—for example, the need for buffet carvers, demo cooking at stations, speeches, or musical cues. Both the chef and the event manager (along with a serving staff supervisor or permanent maître d', if there is one) give opinions on the number of floor staff needed and other front-of-the-house details if such comment is warranted.

The Kitchen

For kitchen use, the final menu for a function is more detailed. Where the client's menu (as on a letter of agreement, i.e.) might read:

Tarragon Chicken Salad

the working menu, detailed by the event manager and chef, would appear as follows:

4 quarts Tarragon Chicken Salad
(use pecans, red delicious apple, celery, *no* bell peppers)

As another example, where a client's menu might read:

Assorted Vegetable Cheese Squares

the working menu would be more specific:

6 dozen Assorted Vegetable Cheese Squares
(see recipe variations, prepare ⅓ each carrot, string bean, mushroom. Store uncut.)

The chef analyzes this working menu and summarizes the foods needed to execute it. He or she checks the recipe file for correct amounts, cuts, and portion sizes and makes note of reheating techniques, garnishes, sauces, skewers, and on-site equipment and utensils. From this information, the chef inventories the current stock of supplies and places orders for items needed. He or she then follows through by scheduling kitchen help for both the commissary and job site, distributes the appropriate standardized recipes to the kitchen crew, and issues detailed instructions for both prep and on-site kitchen duties to ensure that each food item is properly prepared, stored, packed, finished, plated, and garnished as specified in the menu.

Multiple Jobs

In an ongoing catering operation, it is not unusual for more than one job to be underway on the same day, and certainly several during the same week. In this case, the chef combines the foods and prep time needed to prepare the foods for several events, placing bulk orders where possible, and fully utilizing the kitchen staff, so that many items are prepared either in larger quantities or in variations for several functions. In these cases, good organization requires precise labeling, so that food items are clearly marked for their appropriate destination. For example,

Brown Party 10/19

Sesame Chicken (1 of 2 pans)

or

Chutney Sauce (Smith Party, 4/17)

Careful labeling, even if an operation is handling only a single party, is always important. Pertinent information about handling and serving can be listed on a label to save time and confusion during service. For safety's sake, always affix the label to the container, not the lid, as lids can magically rearrange themselves during transport and on-site prep. Some examples of labels follow:

Chutney Sauce/room temp.
for Fruit Fritters:
serve in ramekin on serving tray

Spicy Tomato Sauce/hot:
serve with Mozzarella Sticks

Chocolate Rum Sauce (1 of 2):
reheat carefully,
serve 2 oz. ladle each ice cream coupe

Packing List

A packing list, which typically involves only the kitchen equipment, foods, and accessories, is prepared, itemizing all the foods, materials, and equipment necessary for a particular job. This list should be very detailed, specifying the number of items or portions of each food:

Four dozen eggrolls (frozen)
1 pt sour cream
2 sides smoked salmon (sliced)
2 bunches chives

along with other requirements:

48 6-in. bamboo skewers
2 6-qt stainless mixing bowls
1 whisk
3 aprons
8 side towels

so that no possible item can be overlooked. In some operations, where serving items such as baskets, silver trays, and coffee urns belong to the caterer rather than being rentals, itemize these items in the packing list as well. This final packing list is revised or updated as needed before the event and used as a checklist as the party is being prepared, as it is packed out of the commissary, and as it is unloaded at the job site, reducing the possibility of error, and allowing last-minute slip-ups to be caught in time.

Delivery

In some cases, caterers can use cars or taxicabs to deliver small jobs. Such operations are usually small scale, and an event manager or key staff member may be assigned to manage the transport and delivery. In most cases, however, a delivery truck or van is used, often to deliver more than one job on a given day or evening.

The truck should be packed in a first-in, last-out sequence to make the trucker's job easier, and each item, box, or container should be appropriately marked. A routing slip may be prepared for the trucker, with the timing and sequence of deliveries specified, or the trucker may prepare a route based on his or her knowledge of the area. Provide the driver with a delivery instruction sheet (Figure 9–4), which contains precise directions to each job and necessary specifics, such as "delivery to service entrance, corner of 83rd & Madison" or "narrow, steep driveway, loading dock at back; Jeff and Pam will meet you at loading dock to off-load." In addition, when multiple jobs are packed in one truck or van, give the trucker helpful information such as: "Brown Party, 6 boxes, 2 coolers," and mark the containers "Brown Party/1 of 6, 2 of 6," and so forth.

A trucker or driver should always be given petty cash to cover tolls or emergencies, the number of a local garage for repairs or towing, and the name and phone number (or beeper number) of the event manager, both in the office and at the party site. If any mishap or delay occurs, the driver can then keep the event manager informed. If your operation can afford it, a mobile phone in your delivery truck is a great asset.

Staff Scheduling and Assignments

The event manager (or whoever is in charge of hiring and assigning staff) decides on the serving staff requirements for a particular party and hires them, making specific assignments. As the date of the event approaches, more detailed assignments are worked out and specific instructions prepared for serving staff.

Where complex functions are involved (a banquet, wedding, large cocktail party with satellite kitchens, or huge outdoor event, complete staff assignment sheets are prepared and copies posted and distributed to all concerned parties (Figure 9–5). These can be overall assignments for all staff or categorized: bartenders, wine stewards, captains, waiters, busboys or -girls, depending on the complexity of the job. For the event manager and maître d', such lists are a great aid in planning; for staff, they are a foolproof guide to specific duties and details that assist them in doing their jobs well.

Plans for Setup and Seating

For any seated event, the table setting arrangement is specifically planned so that the entire room is correctly and uniformly laid out. Of course, the event manager has a

DELIVERY INSTRUCTION SHEET

Deliver to _____   Client _____

Address _____   Event date _____

_____   Event time _____

Service entrance _____   Event mgr _____

Elevator/loading dock: _____   Phone at site _____

Contact _____   Beeper no. _____

Drop off/unload (*circle one*)   Route stop # ____   # of units _____

Time depart: _____ AM/PM Arrive: _____ AM/PM Pick-up: _____ AM/PM

Directions: _____

_____

_____

_____

_____

Packed by (*signature*) _____ Driver (*signature*) _____

For emergency/repair call _____

Received petty cash $_____ Tolls/expenses $_____ Att. receipts _____

Driver: Place copies of all delivery sheets and remaining cash in Route Envelope and return to office with van keys at end of shift. See Event Manager for overtime or other charges.

Figure 9–4
Delivery instruction sheet.

STAFF ASSIGNMENT SHEET

Event   Brown Cocktail Party   Date/time   Oct. 19, 6—8 PM
Event Mgr.   Mary Klein

Set-up and prep: See Party Plan for overall instructions.

Matt and Rick: On arrival, check rentals, set up party rooms,
     coatrack, and bar.

Matt: Do ice. Chill 12 bottles sauvignon, 6 white
     zin to start. At 5:30, open 3 whites, 2 white zin, 1 red.
     Open others as needed. Chill extra whites later on if
     needed. Francine has ice bucket, tongs, mineral water,
     and soda.

Lisa: Arrange cheese trays as you did for Wallace
     party. Get cheese knives from Mary. Place floral arrange-
     ment on dining room table, place cheeses at either ends,
     then add garnishes, etc. All can be placed on table by 5
     or 5:30, except slice breads and place just before 6.
     When finished arranging cheeses, assist Harold with prep
     for reubens. As party winds down, Mary may signal you to
     begin cleanup and repack in kitchen.

Claire: Assist Mary with finishing and arranging
     crudites. Keep dip in fridge until just before guests
     arrive. Remember that crudites are placed in front of
     mirror, so make sure back looks good.
          When first crowd of guests arrive, go to bar for
     gallery tray of wines to pass. Matt will let you know if
     he needs you for more wine passing later on. Otherwise,
     pass hors d' per Mary.

Harold: Set up kitchen and staging to your liking.
     Francine will show you sockets for fryers (two separate
     lines). Show Lisa how to prep reubens.
          Remember to advance heat oil for empanadas (fryers
     have thermostats). Cut veg squares early, let them come
     to room temp. Mary will oversee garnish and timing for
     serving rotation. Everyone will help you clean up and
     repack; Rick will return to commissary with you to help
     you unload.

Figure 9–5
Staff assignment sheet.

Breakdown: Rick is in charge, will check rentals, etc. Claire will assist. Matt will break down bar, inventory wine, store all bottles in pantry as per party plan. Remember that trash must be brought out to curb for morning pick-up.

ALL STAFF: Bus and cleanup throughout party, especially skewers, napkins, and ashtrays. By 5:30, everyone should be dressed for service. Harold has snacks and cold drinks. At 5:45, Mary will run through plan.

Note: Francine (Mrs. Brown's maid) is a sweetheart, very cooperative and helpful, but if you need her for anything, catch her before 5. After that, Mrs. Brown will keep her busy. When guests arrive and leave, Francine will be doing coats, etc.

Figure 9–5
Continued.

master room and seating plan and also is aware of the need for the placement of the dais, microphones, place cards, and so on.

For large events, the room may be broken down into sections and each captain assigned responsibility for a certain number of tables. In other cases, where a smaller room is involved, the waitstaff or buspeople can be given a room and seating plan, attached to their assignment sheets, and do the setup accordingly. In all cases, one person in charge (either the event manager, maître d', or senior staff person) lays one place, and all the others are laid to duplicate it.

Different caterers use different methods for room setups: some have one person handle all the glasses, another all the place plates (or chargers), and so on. Others have each section of the dining room laid by teams of staff. Whatever method is used, it is important that each table have the correct number of covers, each setting be identical to the next, each cloth overhang be exact, and each napkin folded and placed correctly so that the entire room looks perfect.

Total Party Plan

These lists, orders, assignments, and details define the scope and final execution of a function. A total party plan should be prepared that incorporates all the details of both service and menu (Figure 9–6). One copy is placed in the master job file as a permanent record of the event. The event manager and/or maître d' should have another copy at the site, and at least one other should be posted, either in the on-site kitchen or at the

---

TOTAL PARTY PLAN

Event ___Cocktail Party___   Date ___October 19, 19xx___

Client ___Mrs. Allison Brown___   Time ___6 to 8 PM___

Location ___263 East 71st Street___   Event Mgr ___Mary Klein___

___New York, New York 10021___   Phone/site ___288—1111___

Access ___No later than 4 PM for ALL staff___

Use service entrance at right side of building, black iron

gate   Mrs. Brown's maid will let us in

Staff   1 bartender: Matt Smith

    3 servers: Rick Wilson

                  Claire Freyer

                  Lisa Perez

    1 cook: Harold Clark

    (Mary will supervise and assist with plating in

    kitchen)

Dress ___All black pants, white shirts, paisley vests, black___

    tie for waitstaff; Harold in kitchen whites (extra clean

    apron).

Overall Description: Elegant setting for all-wine cocktail party
with substantial hors d'oeuvre. Guests will probably all
arrive fairly promptly and stay on to end. Mrs. Brown's maid
(Francine) will greet and take coats and wraps to store in
foyer closet and one entryway rack (rented from Party
Rent-All—we set up).

     Party will take place on the ground floor only: the large
entry foyer, front parlor, and dining room are fairly open so

---

Figure 9–6
Total party plan.

guests will move around easily in this area. The upstairs is off limits to staff. The powder room off the foyer is for guests (Francine will monitor); bathroom off back maid's room is for our use.

Work Space: We have complete use of ground floor kitchen and maid's room adjacent to service entrance. Kitchen has rear door to garden, which can be opened for ventilation if needed. Tub in back bathroom to be filled with ice for chilling white wine and white zin. Extra space for rental storage or trash just outside back kitchen door if needed. Hold tin of ice cubes there as well. Good kitchen: Large fridge, open counters, good broiler. We need to bring 2 electric fryers, 3 paring knives, 1 narrow slicer for salmon, bread knife, stripper for bar, along with regular kit. Bring 6 extra baking sheets and parchment.

Setup:
> Bar: Rental table double-draped with white linen to be
>   set in far corner of parlor.
> In foyer: Crudite arrangement set on console below large
>   mirror.
> Dining room: Mrs. Brown's table should have all leaves
>   removed (store in back closet) to reduce to small oval.
>   Chairs will have been removed. Cover table with
>   protective pad, double white linens. Les Fleurs is
>   providing centerpiece arrangement of gourds, flowers,
>   vines, bittersweet. We will prepare two French willow
>   cheese trays to set at each end of arrangement,
>   garnished with autumn leaves (Les Fleurs will provide
>   in kitchen), with crackers, sliced baguettes, seed-
>   less grapes, roasted nuts.

All other items will be butler-passed. Spot stacks of cocktail napkins and ashtrays here and there in all three rooms.

Bar: Sauvignon blanc, white zinfandel, red zinfandel, mineral
>   water. Club soda for spritzers, lemon twists. Have one
>   bottle of each wine on bar, labels showing, for guests
>   to view. Mrs. Brown may have two guests who drink

Figure 9–6
Continued.

single-malt scotch; if so, she will provide and inform Matt just before party. Claire will pass wine at beginning of party or as needed by Matt. Use gallery trays. All-purpose balloons for all drinks.

Menu:

Crudite arrangement: Arranged on site in foyer in harvest basket, red caviar dip in glass bowl nested in flowering kale.

2 French cheese trays: Duplicate cheeses have been ordered. Arrange and place as above. Each cheese to have its own knife (see Mary). Cut grapes into small bunches, reassemble.

All the following are butler-passed (Harold and Mary will time rotation).

Hot:

Mini-Empanadas—Fresh-fried in kitchen, serve on linen-lined tray, garnish with orange fiji mum. Warn guests these are both spicy and hot.

Miniature Reubens—prepped and broiled in kitchen, serve on silver tray, no garnish. These can be a bit drippy, offer extra napkins.

Escargots in Mushroom Caps—Broiled in kitchen, garnish with fresh cress in one corner of silver tray.

Chicken Sate—Broiled just before service. Plate on square bamboo tray, red lotus bowl with peanut sauce. Have all skewer ends pointing out for easy service.

Cold:

Ginger-Poached Shrimp—Completely ready from commissary. Plate on red lacquer, lined with ti leaves, garnish with bird of paradise (Mary will arrange).

Smoked Salmon Roulades—Harold will slice, must be served cold. Arrange on round silver tray, garnish with fresh dill sprig and lemon twist each pass. Tray must be washed and dried before each use.

Vegetable Cheese Squares—Carrot, string bean, and mushroom, pass assortment on rectangular silver tray, small bouquet of vegetable flowers in center of tray.

Logistics: Rentals will have been delivered before 3 PM. Check on arrival against Mary's sheet; if anything short, call Fred at

Figure 9–6
Continued.

once; they are just a few blocks away. Rentals will be held at service entrance. Repack and leave there for pick-up next day. To Repack: wet-wipe and dry trays and ashtrays, wipe glasses dry, repack carefully in cartons. Shake linens, recount napkins, store in garbage bag for pick-up (mark clearly PARTY-RENT-ALL). Fold up table and coat rack, replace hangers in box.

Les Fleurs will deliver arrangements by 3 PM; will place our garnish flowers and leaves in kitchen fridge, or in vase.

Mary and Harold will arrive at 4 PM with our delivery. All staff must be on time. You may come in casual clothes, dress at Mrs. Brown's. Mary will distribute prep and setup assignments on arrival. All waitstaff should bus party rooms throughout, keep an eye on crudite and cheese arrangements, tidy up, replace napkins as needed. Party may run overtime, but not later than 8:30 or 9 PM. We can begin cleanup then, even if few stragglers remain. Do not break down rooms until Mrs. Brown or Mary gives o.k.

Kitchen must be left very clean and neat. Trash should be removed to curb. All leftovers wrapped and stored. Matt will place wine empties and full bottles back in cases in pantry. Empty soda bottles should be placed in pantry, not in trash. Harold and Rick will handle return to commissary, all staff to assist with packing and loading.

Figure 9–6
Continued.

staging area, so that all crew can refer to it before, during, and after service. (Some caterers distribute one to each staff member, especially for complex jobs.) This total party plan can be used as the focus of the preparty meeting, which should take place at the site, when all crew has assembled and before the party begins. This meeting allows the event manager to run through the party plan, pointing out unusual or complicated points, and allows the staff to ask any questions they may have in regard to their duties.

This meeting also serves as a pep rally, allowing all the staff members to feel part of an enthusiastic, well-informed team. If time and space allow, this is a good time for a few minutes of relaxation, when all the tables are set, and most items are ready for finishing and plating, before the guests have arrived. Allow time for a last cold drink, cup of coffee, bathroom or cigarette break, or snack. If the staff has a few minutes to relax before plunging into the party frenzy, they will begin work refreshed and in good spirits, confident and ready to do a good job.

IT AIN'T OVER TILL IT'S OVER

As can be seen on the flow chart (see Figure 9–1), after the last guests depart, the crew must break down the party room, clean up the function rooms and kitchen, and repack both rental and commissary equipment. The truck or van must be repacked and unloaded at the commissary. The event manager, after summing up with the client (clarifying overtime, tips, final payment, etc.), should make whatever post mortem notes are necessary and enter them in the master job file. The event manager also does a final inspection of the premises and oversees or gives instructions for the return and storage of items to the commissary. It is a good idea to hold a brief meeting the following day (or soon after the party) to review the entire job. Problems or possible improvements should be noted for future reference. In most cases, the review affirms the good results of careful planning—the job was a great success—and after a follow-up call or note to the satisfied client, planning for the next event gets underway.

Part Two

SITES, FUNCTIONS, AND MENUS

The site or location of a party, the type of function planned, and the theme or menu of an event are closely interrelated. Part Two deals first with general rules for analyzing and handling different types of party sites with a view toward strategic planning, specific logistics, menu planning, staffing, and serving. After discussing the three general types of party sites, several categories of events are walked through, with detailed advice on logistics, service, decor, and suggestions for menu planning, food preparation, and presentation techniques to suit each one.

In reading through this section, notice how various themes and functions can overlap and how the menu suggestions and food ideas are interchangeable from event to event, exhibiting the diversity that is inherent in off-premise catering and encouraging a caterer to develop a flexible and diverse repertoire that can make food preparation efficient and many recipes multipurpose.

Chapter 10

Sites and Spaces

A discussion of the various party sites that may be rented or loaned to a client or organization for a particular function includes a wide range of possible options. Museums, mansions, yachts, and boardrooms are only the beginning. A caterer may be called upon to arrange gracious meals for guests in art galleries, theatres and rehearsal halls, department stores and judge's chambers, book stores, subway tunnels, or manufacturing plants.

Each of these sites has various features that can enhance an event, as well as restrictions that could make the execution of the job more difficult. In the present situation, a new factor surfaces: unlike the home party, where planning and negotiation take place between caterer and client in the client's own space, a third party is now involved. The owner or lessor of the space has the right to impose rules and restrictions on both the client and the caterer.

Understand at the outset that these factors do not automatically predict an adversarial relationship. Most lessor's rules and regulations are based on common sense, physical limitations, and past experience (both good and bad) with other caterers and types of functions. The lessor or rental agent, having entered into this arrangement for a fee, donation, or publicity and prestige, can offer sound advice and cooperation, but also is concerned with the protection of the space and its furnishings. The client has chosen this site for reasons such as ample space, reasonable cost, convenient location, spectacular view, elegant furnishings, suitability to a theme, or the panache of a unique locale. The caterer is charged with understanding and satisfying both parties' desires and requirements, all the while maintaining his or her high standards of performance. This task does not seem so formidable if the caterer remembers that all three parties involved—the lessor, the client, and the caterer—share the same ultimate goal, a successful event.

Going in to a new space and performing well provides the caterer with an excellent opportunity to enhance his or her business. This chapter provides an overview of the special challenges presented to the off-premise caterer working in such a space, along with strategy suggestions for overcoming obstacles and arranging a successful event. In planning any event, the key factors in mastering any location are a thorough site inspection, the completion of a detailed checklist, and the formation of a solid work plan that reconciles the event concept with practical limitations and results in a satisfactory outcome for both the client and the caterer (see Chapter 9).

THE SITE INSPECTION

It would be wonderful if all special locations had many factors in common, but in truth, few generalizations can be made. Certain facilities, such as dining halls in country clubs, schools, churches, temples, factories, and corporate headquarters, usually have reasonably adequate kitchen facilities. A restored mansion or historically preserved city townhouse usually has a kitchen (although it may be antiquated or three flights away from the party site); a yacht, however spacious, most likely has an efficient but cramped galley; and a library or office lobby may leave the caterer not only without a kitchen but also with only a single source of running water, and that in a remote utility closet. These are just a few of the considerations to be dealt with in planning a function, and these deal only with food! All of these possibilities make a thorough site inspection imperative, and such a tour and analysis must be completed before the caterer finalizes either menu or price.

This outlook should not be intimidating and is not negative, only realistic, since in catering, an unknown factor can become an unpleasant surprise. The anticipation of every possible complication, using a complete checklist (see Figure 10–1), will ensure smooth execution.

The decision whether or not to take the client along on the initial site visit must be based on several factors. If the caterer is dealing with a new client on a particularly complicated project, or if the client is unfamiliar with the site or unsure of the final structure of the event, a personal visit and walk-through is useful to the caterer and reassuring to the client. If, in contrast, this is a client of long standing and the caterer fully understands the client's sense of taste and style and how the client sees the function, he or she can avoid taking the client on the tour. Now the caterer can go into exhaustive detail with the superintendent or rental agent, without involving the client in the humdrum mechanics of the catering process. The caterer may also decide on a compromise solution: a front-of-the-house aesthetic tour with the client and a separate working tour with the superintendent or rental agent.

Role of the Superintendent

In most cases, the inspection tour is conducted by a representative of the lessor or building owner, who shows the caterer around the premises and answers questions of policy and usage. For the purposes of this discussion, the term *superintendent* indicates the person in charge. In fact, the caterer may deal first with the rental agent or building manager, and then complete the tour with a custodian or other members of

SITE INSPECTION CHECKLIST

Today's date _____ By _____ Client _____

Location _____ Event date _____

Address _____ Function time _____ AM/PM

City _____ Fee/client? _____ Fee/caterer? _____

Room(s) _____ Cocktails _____ Dinner _____ Other _____

Contact _____ Service entrance? _____

Day phone _____ Elevator? _____

Emergency # _____ Loading dock? _____

Access/deliveries _____ AM/PM Where? _____ By? _____

Access/kitchen _____ AM/PM | Function rooms _____ AM/PM

Burners? _____ Fryers? _____ | Floor Plan? _____

Ovens? _____ Broiler? _____ | Bar? _____ License? _____

Gas/power? _____ Fuse box? _____ | Tables? _____ Chairs? _____

Water/sinks? _____ D'wshr? _____ | Serving equip.? _____

Reefers? _____ Walk-in? _____ | Other _____

Urns? _____ Racks? _____ | Dance floor? _____ Stage? _____

Icemaker? _____ Micro? _____ | Podium? _____ Lectern? _____

Work space? _____ Tables? _____ | A/V? _____ Lighting? _____

Other? _____ | Guest parking? _____ Valet? _____

Cleanup? _____ | Directions? _____ Map? _____

Trash? _____ Bags? _____ | Checkrooms? ___ Attendant? ___

Decor/floral/special setup? _____ | Restroom? _____ Attendant? _____

Music/band/other? _____ In-house staff? _____

Lockers/restroom for staff? _____

Rental pick-up arrangements _____

Notes _____

_____

_____

Follow-up meeting notes to contact _____ Copy attached ____

Call to reconfirm by _____ (date, 1 wk prior to event)

Figure 10–1
Site inspection checklist.

the house staff. It is important that the caterer establish who is in charge of what and make notes of names and phone numbers on a checklist.

Establishing a good rapport with the superintendent is essential. Even though the superintendent is a salaried employee of the owner, a gratuity in advance of the function is a gracious and productive gesture that helps to ensure a good working relationship. In addition, the caterer should:

- Act professionally and with courtesy.

- Listen attentively as policy and procedures are explained.

- Ask pertinent questions related to the planned event, using a checklist as a guide.

- Make notes: a written record of the details is invaluable later on.

FEES

As a rule, the rental or usage fee for a site is handled directly between the lessor and the client. Sometimes a separate fee is charged to the caterer for the use of kitchen facilities, storage space, cooking or serving equipment, and other such amenities. It is important for the caterer to discuss all the details of the upcoming event with the superintendent. If, for instance, the client has requested special audiovisual equipment for the event, the superintendent may be able to provide it in-house or make a referral. If the client has requested special decor that may require advance setup, additional electrical power, or special holding conditions (e.g., refrigeration for elaborate floral displays), the caterer should seek the superintendent's approval and cooperation during these arrangements. Additional fees may be charged to accommodate these requests, and both the caterer and the superintendent should agree on the amount of such fees and the dates on which deposits and payments are due.

RENTALS AND DELIVERIES

In almost all cases, the caterer has to rent some equipment for a function; in almost every case, these deliveries are made well before she or her staff arrive on location, so arrangements must be made for their safe delivery and storage. Working from a checklist (see Figure 10–1), gather the following information:

- Where and during what hours can deliveries be made?

- Is there a separate service ramp, loading dock, entrance, or elevator?

- Who will receive and be responsible for checking in the items?

- Where will they be stored? will they be secured, and if so, who holds the keys to the storage area?

The answers to these questions can be relayed to the rental company, florist, and others involved, and efficient follow-up made with the superintendent in advance of the event to ensure that all is in order.

ACCESS

The next issue is access to the kitchen and function room(s) for working staff. Most sites allow access for a few hours before the function is scheduled to begin. In some cases, a caterer may have use of the kitchen for a longer time, perhaps even for the whole day. In that case, it is possible to have purveyors deliver raw materials directly to the site and have members of the prep and cook staff prepare most of the food on site, scheduling the service staff to arrive two hours before the event to set up tables, bar, and so forth. At a popular site, another event may be scheduled earlier in the day, resulting in less time for the caterer's crew to ready both function rooms and food. Establishing these usage hours during this site inspection allows the caterer to adjust the menu and staffing needs with efficiency and organize the planned event for the smoothest possible execution.

The second consideration for access involves the guests. The caterer must consider the following questions:

- Is there adequate parking?

- Does the site provide valet parking or must the caterer arrange such a service?

- Does the client need to arrange for prepaid parking fees or gratuities?

- Is there a special waiting space for limousines or buses?

- Is there a car or cab service in the area for departing guests' needs?

- Is the guest entrance clearly marked?

- Does the facility provide printed maps or directions?

- In case of inclement weather, does the superintendent handle ice and snow removal?

- Is there a marquee or canopy to provide rain protection at the entrance?

If the space is located on a public street, and a large crowd is expected, either the caterer or the superintendent should inform the local police of possible traffic congestion.

THE ON-SITE KITCHEN

The amount of space and type of equipment available in the on-site kitchen has an important bearing on the final plans for the function's menu and staging. You should bring a tentative menu while checking the kitchen for the following points:

- How many and what size ovens are available?

- How many top burners?

- Is there a flat top? a deep fryer? a broiler or salamander?

- Is the equipment in working order and reasonably clean?

- Are there any mechanical idiosyncracies to be noted?

- If the units are gas powered, are there any special techniques for lighting pilots?

- If electric, are they on separate lines?

- Are there other heavy-duty lines available for supplementary appliances?

- Where are the circuit breakers or fuse boxes?

- Where is the fire extinguisher? the first aid kit?

- Is there adequate venting?

- Is there sufficient working space for packing and unpacking?

- Is there ample counter or table surface available for food prep, plating, and arranging of hors d'oeuvre trays?

- Is there room in the kitchen or an adjacent room to set up folding tables to provide a staging area?

- What about sinks for prep and pot washing?

- Is there a dishwasher?

- Are cleaning materials and equipment available for your use?

- Is there a mop and bucket for emergency spills?

- How is trash removal to be handled?

Assess the amount of refrigeration and freezer space and decide whether you need supplementary cold boxes. Decide what other equipment and utensils are needed. While some on-site kitchens come completely equipped with everything from garbage bags to serving platters, it is still vital that the caterer verbally confirm with the superintendent what items he expects to use. It would be a serious mistake for the caterer to assume that the coffee urns and saucepans seen on the initial visit are there for his or her use. They may actually belong to another caterer or may have been allotted to another function being held the same day in another function room. The caterer should not count on using items seen during inspection unless the superintendent guarantees they will be available to him or her on the date of the planned event.

THE INADEQUATE OR NONEXISTENT KITCHEN

In some spaces, the off-premise caterer may find himself faced with either very limited kitchen facilities or none at all. Improvisation and organization are his best course of action. The menu should be streamlined to make cooking or finishing the least troublesome. Whatever cooking equipment is available may be supplemented with portable units. It may be possible, for instance, in a business office, to set aside an enclosed space (a mailroom or back office) as a prep pantry, setting up sturdy work tables, and bringing in small portable electric convection or microwave ovens. It is helpful to be near a source of water, to see that the room has good ventilation, and to make sure that the available wiring is sufficient to withstand the planned usage.

In the case of an unwieldy, sprawling, or multilevel space, with its kitchen facility in a remote part of the building, some variation on the above theme may be advisable — that is, creating staging areas or minipantries in different locations to facilitate serving. This technique works especially well with large-scale cocktail parties, where major preparation of hors d'oeuvre can be done in a central location and butler trays finished and arranged in the staging areas. Whatever means the caterer decides to use to circumvent the difficulties of space or lack of facilities, he should review these plans with the superintendent to be certain that he has his cooperation and approval.

FUNCTION ROOMS

As the caterer and the superintendent tour the function rooms or party space, both parties must visualize the planned event taking place within that space. Following are some of the points to be considered:

- Does the facility have a printed floor plan?

- Is a floor plan needed to arrange table seating?

- How does traffic flow for guests and staff work best in this space?

- Is there a fixed bar or bars? If not, where would portable bars be set up?

- Is there a dance floor? If not, can a portable one be brought in?

- Is there a stage, podium, or elevated dais platform, or is one needed?

- Does the room have a fireplace, terrace, or windowed or mirrored wall that creates a natural focal point?

If tables and chairs are included in the site rental, it is important to check on their condition, style, and size to be sure that they suit the client's needs. The caterer should confirm with the superintendent and note on his checklist the exact number of items he will expect to be ready for use.

He must observe the other furnishings throughout the function rooms. Are they needed for the event, or should they be moved? The off-premise caterer often finds himself working in a historic space, museum, or gallery, where there may be decorative items that need to be protected or removed. He must establish whether his staff or house staff is charged with this responsibility.

Arrangements must be made for the room and its furnishings to be clean and ready for use on the day of the event, as well as cleaned and restored to its original condition after use. The caterer should ask the superintendent what procedures are to be followed in this regard and make appropriate entries on his checklist.

LIQUOR ARRANGEMENTS

As discussed in Chapter 3, liquor laws vary from area to area. Many rental sites have an on-premise liquor license that may not allow any liquor to be brought in from outside. In this case, the rental agent or lessor agrees to provide liquor for the event in one of several ways:

An unlimited bar, where guests order drinks as they choose and the client pays for the amount consumed, usually at a predetermined charge per bottle, or sometimes at a fixed charge per drink, with the bartender keeping a running count or bottle inventory at the bar.

A limited bar, where the client presents tickets or chits to each guest who then gives the chit to the bartender in exchange for a drink. Sometimes, the liquor is controlled by allotting bottles of liquor or wine to each table for the guests to self-pour.

A cash bar, where guests pay for their drinks individually as they would in a public bar or cocktail lounge.

In some cases, the lessor allows liquor to be brought in and provides mixers and setups for a fee. In the case of wine-tasting societies, for example, the lessor allows various wines to be brought in under his license and charges a corkage fee, either per bottle or per guest.

If the site does not have an on-premise bar, the caterer has to arrange for beverage service. The client purchases the liquor, and the caterer provides the bartenders, mixers, bars, glasses, and ice, usually for a fixed hourly rate.

IN-HOUSE STAFF

In some situations, the caterer may find that certain house staff members must also be part of her kitchen or serving staff. These persons may have specific assigned duties, such as coat check or dishwasher, or they may be incorporated into the serving staff. Such personnel can work to the caterer's advantage since these persons may be skilled in the use of particular house equipment. The caterer should accept these workers into her work plan, partner them with her experienced help if possible, and be prepared to tip them appropriately and provide them with meals and other courtesies as she would her own staff.

MISCELLANEOUS ITEMS

Restroom facilities should be sufficient for the number of guests, clean, well kept, and lighted. Does the house provide an attendant? Is one needed?

Cloakroom facilities and an attendant are usually provided by the owner, whose insurance covers the security of the items. If lockers are not available, a changing area should be set aside for the staff, preferably one where their personal belongings can be secured.

If musicians or other entertainment is planned, check to see if approval or clearance is needed from the superintendent, and arrange for the payment of any fees and the delivery, storage, and power supply for equipment. Make suitable arrangements for these persons to change, and plan to provide them with meals or snacks.

If the caterer and his staff are in a rented premises alone before and during a function, he must be certain that he has all the necessary keys; that he is comfortable with the operation of lighting, heating, and air-conditioning systems; that he knows the location of circuit breakers and fuse boxes; and that he has the phone number of a person in charge in case of any emergency.

If catering is to take place on a boat of some kind, the caterer should be especially precise in discussing arrangements with the boat captain or rental agent, since restrictions involving safety are stringently monitored by the Coast Guard or local marine authorities. The packing of supplies and equipment must be scrupulously detailed because once a vessel has set sail, there is no going back for any missing item. Another consideration in yacht catering is the dock master, who may charge a fee per person for access to a marina or pier. This charge is sometimes paid directly by the caterer, the yacht charter company, or the client. In addition, the caterer should obtain permission from the dock master for advance access to the marina or boat, and find out whether marina storage facilities are available for holding rentals or other equipment and whether any additional fees are due for this service.

FOLLOW-UP

Upon the caterer's return to her office (or as soon as possible after the site visit), she should carefully review her checklist, making additional notes if necessary while all the details are fresh in her mind. She should then proceed with the following steps:

1. Make a preliminary work plan, incorporating all the requirements for the event, such as rentals, staffing, food, and so forth, and arrive at an estimated cost. This cost should include any additional fees incurred by the use of the space and a charge for the additional time involved in planning and coordinating the event.

2. Consult with the client about any changes or alterations that need to be made in the menu or staging of the function. Explain additional fees and charges, and get the client's approval of these changes and of the estimated price. Confirm this conversation in writing.

3. When the caterer has gained her client's approval, she should write a confirming letter to the lessor or superintendent, expressing appreciation for his cooperation and detailing any special arrangements that have been agreed upon.

4. Make a note of the time or times close to the date of the event when calls confirming all the finalized details should be made to the superintendent.

With these items complete, the caterer now has the essential documents necessary for the master job file for the planned event. In the many months that may precede the scheduled date, she thus has ready reference to all the details needed to execute a successful and smoothly running function.

Chapter 11

The Home Party

When an off-premise caterer contracts for an entertainment event to take place in a client's home, the role of the caterer changes subtly. The party site is now a private space, bearing the stamp of the host's personality, and lending a special touch of intimacy to even the most formal event. The caterer, entering a person's home to do business, should be aware of both the practical and psychological aspects that present themselves in this special circumstance.

RESETTING THE STAGE

A home, whether a lavish estate, a townhouse, a split-level suburban home, or a city apartment, provides a special setting for a party. Furnishings, decor, and available partyware, such as china, crystal, and silver, all reflect the host's taste and personal style. The client meeting, whenever possible, should take place in the client's home, so that the setting can be considered firsthand during the discussion of the tone and flow of the party. A caterer must perform the same type of thorough site inspection that would take place in a rented space, but the caterer's manner must, of necessity, be more gracious and thoughtful.

Room Arrangement

Many caterers have entered a home or apartment that is as cluttered as an antique shop or so overgrown with vegetation that palm fronds, tree branches, and trailing ivy are everywhere. While these homes may be stunningly attractive viewed as they are and, indeed, make a statement about their owners, the caterer imagines forty guests milling around during a cocktail party and envisions disaster. Such problems must be handled

98

with great tact, but with practical forthrightness, as the following examples illustrate: Mrs. Jones may be justly proud of her collection of antique English teacups, but perhaps, for the evening of the party, they might be attractively arranged on the cleared shelves of a bookcase rather than on the many small tables scattered about the room. Could most of the plants be massed in one corner of the room to create a dramatic backdrop for the bar or buffet? All such suggestions should be made gently, in the interest of keeping guests comfortable, providing service easily, and protecting the client's possessions from harm, while still keeping them in view. Remember that while Mrs. Jones takes personal satisfaction in her collection, part of her pleasure is to have these special objects viewed and admired by her friends.

Sometimes, the arrangement or nature of furnishings in a room may make service or traffic flow difficult. No hostess appreciates having her home decor completely altered for the sake of a party (after all, she may have expended a great deal of money and time designing the room to her liking), but most understand and accept some minor changes for practical reasons. Again, the caterer must act with courtesy and restraint. A frank and friendly discussion can result in an agreement to reposition some pieces to improve traffic patterns, to provide protective pads for a table or sideboard, or to remove the client's six large dining room chairs to another room, and instead rent ten ballroom chairs to give seating for the dinner party a consistent look.

Sometimes, the basic design of a home or apartment presents built-in problems. For some reason (known only, it seems, to architects and designers), home bars are always situated either in the entry foyer or adjacent to the doorway of the kitchen or living room, greatly increasing the possibilities for congestion. If this is a permanent installation (and most are), the caterer might suggest using it as a service bar only, to eliminate the expected congestion during arrivals and predinner cocktails. Later in the party, when all the guests have arrived, it may revert to its use as a guest bar, or at a buffet, it may be used to offer after-dinner drinks and fancy coffees. In this way, traffic congestion is eased, and the hostess can still show off her beautiful mirrored or wood-panelled bar.

Both client and caterer must discuss the setup of secondary rooms to be used by guests during a party. Small tables and chairs can be arranged for buffet seating in an adjacent den or guest room, so rentals may have to be arranged or flowers ordered for those rooms as well. Check the lighting in the rooms to see if it needs to be adjusted or enhanced, and use the same people-proofing procedures as in the main party room. Tactfully remind the hostess that valuables should be secured as well. While both client and caterer may trust their guests and staff, it is foolish to leave cash or jewelry out on a dressing table. The caterer (and staff) should also know which rooms are considered off limits for both guests and staff.

Establish which powder room(s) is to be used for guests and which for staff. Make sure the guest bathroom is well stocked with toilet paper, tissues, and other necessities. Have someone on staff check it over during a long party to see that things are in order. It is a nice touch, especially at a large party, to leave items such as aspirin, safety pins, hair spray, and an emery board out in a guest bathroom, so that guests have everything they may need without troubling the hostess. The caterer, of course, carries a first aid or emergency kit along to every function to tend to staff needs.

Coatrooms

Arrangements should be discussed for guests' coats or wraps and especially for foul weather gear. Unless you assign one staff member to handle checkroom duties throughout the party, it is a better idea, for both convenience and security, to let guests (or a member of the hostess's own household) handle their personal belongings. Remember that, in the legal sense, if anyone from the caterer's staff take these personal items from guests, the caterer becomes responsible for their security, and unless one particular staffer is assigned to watch these items, the caterer is held accountable if something is missing.

Decor and Flowers

Discuss the details of decor or floral arrangements with the client, and make what referrals are necessary. Be sure both parties are clear as to what is planned to avoid misjudgments: the caterer may prepare a large arrangement of crudités or cheeses for the handsome sideboard, while the hostess orders a stunning floral bouquet for the same space.

SERVICEWARE AND RENTALS

It is often the case in a home setting that serving pieces belonging to the hostess may be used in combination with rentals and some pieces that belong to the caterer. If such items are used for the party, examine them (count and measure as well), to avoid misunderstandings or last-minute surprises such as a too-short tablecloth, not enough forks, or a chipped wine glass. The use of personal items can give a dinner party or buffet a special charm, provided the pieces work together and are not so fragile or rare that an accident by either staff or guest becomes a catastrophe. The caterer is obliged to warn a client of such possibilities, emphasizing that the serving staff will exercise the greatest care in handling her Baccarat but that, even in the best circumstances, accidents can happen.

Even though most clients carry insurance to cover just such mishaps, it may be wise for the caterer to take additional precautions. Staff should be especially warned about the breakables, and some protective measures planned: for example, all the used stemware should be set aside in the back pantry and carefully hand washed after the event; the hostess's silver platters should be sponged off with warm soapy water, rubbed dry with a soft cloth, and stacked on a particular shelf in a cupboard. In all catering situations, careful inventories for both packing and repacking a job are important, but in the home setting, where items are combined (the client's, the caterer's, and rentals), such an inventory and sorting are essential. Special care should be taken to double-check lists when repacking a party, lest one of the hostess's platters be inadvertently included in a rental carton.

In addition, if the client suggests using particular serving pieces for a party, the caterer should be certain that the item is of appropriate size and style and can sustain the use it is assigned. Metal finishes, for example, can be badly discolored by acid ingredients; some finishes impart an unpleasant taste to foods; and the extreme heat of a boiling sauce or sizzling roast can shatter antique (or previously repaired) china. These problems can be avoided if both client and caterer make a detailed party plan and discuss in advance just how pieces are to be used and washed.

Finalize the details for all other needed rentals, and find out to what building entrance they must be delivered, who will receive them (and provide for their pick-up the following day), and where they will be stored. If a wine or liquor order is placed for the client, go over the details in advance. If the client handles the ordering personally, give advice on sufficient amounts and types if needed. Make clear who provides mixers, and arrange for ice or other deliveries.

THE MENU AND THE HOME KITCHEN

Naturally, as with any event, the menu for a home party is chosen based on a variety of criteria, including style and mood of the party, number and type of guests, host's preferences and dislikes, appropriateness to setting and season, budget, and the usual considerations of menu balance for flavor, color, and texture. The home kitchen's equipment, venting, size, and location also influence menu choices.

The usual site inspection defines the capabilities of the kitchen, but bear in mind the fact that domestic appliances are smaller than professional ones, so the caterer's baking pans and sheets, large pots, and roasting pans may not fit inside the client's ovens or may be too large or heavy for a domestic stove top. Venting is an important factor as well, since in many home settings, especially city apartments, the kitchen may be quite close or even open to the party site. This means the caterer must eliminate items that may cause smoking or overwhelming odors.

Space in a home kitchen may be limited. To compensate, the caterer should ask the client to clear the work counters as much as possible and to leave some refrigerator space clear. If your staff is planning to use tools such as blenders, processors, knives, and ice makers, be sure they are in working order, and make a reminder list for the client enumerating the items and space needs. If there is a back pantry, service entrance hall, or maid's or storage room in the back of the house, ask if it can be commandeered as a staging area for the party. The tub or shower stall of a back bathroom, for instance, can play party duty as a chilling tub for wine and champagne; a table or dresser top in a back room can be used to set up trays for hors d'oeuvre or desserts. If you use such a room for food prep, cover the furniture with protective drop cloths, and be sure it is restored to order at the end of the party. Inquire about trash disposal in the client's area or building: items may need to be sorted for recycling, or there may be rules and hours that pertain to disposal in a garbage room or compactor area.

If the kitchen is not separate from the party space, you can do one of two things. If the kitchen is an integral part of the entertaining space, such as one might encounter in a loft setting, the kitchen can be made part of the entertainment by planning a menu that involves some demonstration cooking or by serving some items from a cooking island or counter. In this case, staff must be informed that they will be "onstage" while working and to behave accordingly. If a view of the kitchen infringes on the style of the event, some provision should be made to conceal the kitchen operations. For example, folding screens can be rented and set up to block off the view, or a mass of plants or another decor device can be constructed to provide screening. In this case, remind the staff that while they may not be seen, they can probably be heard, so voices and other noise should be kept at as low a level as possible.

IN-HOUSE STAFF, CHILDREN, AND PETS

It is not unusual for clients with resident staff to hire caterers for large parties, formal dinners, or other events. In some cases, the staff is dismissed for the evening; in others, they stay on to supplement the caterer's crew. The client defines the situation, but the caterer must make it work. A well-trained house staff can be of great assistance to a caterer. Usually, they are quite happy to be relieved of the major burden of preparing for a party and welcome the additional help. Sometimes, however, they are not thrilled with having their space invaded by strangers, so a friendly and cooperative attitude on the part of the caterer and staff (particularly for a first-time encounter) goes a long way in easing any tensions. Crack household staff can be a caterer's best ally: they know where everything in the kitchen is and how it works, and they are familiar with the mood and tone of the household and conversant with any idiosyncracies of the host and hostess. Always befriend house staff; have your own staff treat them with courtesy and respect, provide them with meals as you would your own staff, and if possible, extend them a small gratuity (or send a little personal gift or treat after the party) if they have been especially helpful.

Children and pets can be an aspect of the home party as well. No caterer should be expected to perform with a great dane, three toddlers, and a cat in residence in the kitchen before and during a party, however. Be polite but firm with the client on this account, since these elements are not only inconvenient but also unsanitary and dangerous. Most hostesses are considerate and provide a sitter or companion for the small members of the household (human and otherwise). However, the caterer should know in advance whether the client expects a meal or snacks to be provided for children and sitters and plan accordingly. In fact, in situations where some of the guests are youngsters, it is often a simple solution to provide a separate area and menu for the children as part of the overall party plan.

THE UPSTAIRS-DOWNSTAIRS PHENOMENON

It may seem frivolous to refer to this long-running TV series, but the message conveyed by the program was that a staffed household had two separate lives: one above stairs, that of the prominent wealthy family, and that below stairs, of the varied staff, from houseman to chauffeur. These lives ran parallel, and while both were filled with dramas of their own, it was only rarely that the two lives crossed. Whatever upheaval might be going on in the kitchen was never felt in the tranquil dining room; conversely, when ill fortune or shocking goings-on occurred above stairs, the staff went about their business, discreetly avoiding any embarrassment of the master and mistress. The same principle applies to the catered home party. Chaos may erupt in the kitchen, but guests and host should feel not the slightest ripple. This, of course, should be true in any catered event, but the intimacy and close quarters of the home setting make it even more important.

In terms of tone and style, the staff takes their cue from a host or hostess, whether the mood be one of reserved courtesy or smiling friendliness. Guests at a home party know that they are being hosted in a very special and personal way so, as much as possible, a caterer's staff should be an extension of the client's own personality, reflecting warmth and welcome, but never crossing the line to improper or intrusive intimacy. Some clients prefer that home entertaining be relaxed and informal, but the caterer must make certain that casual never descends to laxity, or the hoped-for effect will be ruined.

Clients who entertain regularly at home can become long-term repeat clients for caterers. A professional who performs well is a great treasure to a host, who always feels secure that whatever event he or she plans will be a social success. The caterer gains the advantage of a familiar setting for him- or herself and staff. As the bond between caterer and client develops, both can enjoy the creative process of planning wonderful parties together, in a setting in which all the participants, including guests, feel at home.

Chapter 12

The Great Outdoors

Outdoor entertaining can be as simple as a garden party served from a hostess's kitchen or as complex as a bicentennial celebration complete with fireworks, but in all cases outdoor remote events present unique challenges to the off-premise caterer. A caterer planning any outdoor event must be mindful of the variety of special problems, strategies, and equipment requirements that go into executing such a function.

Literally any event may take place outdoors, with any scope or level of formality. The reasons that a client may request, or a caterer may suggest, that an event take place out of doors are varied, but generally fall into these three categories:

1. An outdoor setting may be embedded in the nature of an event: a company picnic, a school's field day, a spectacular public celebration (like the Statue of Liberty's birthday or the dedication of a park or government building), the opening of a new zoo exhibit or shopping mall, or the groundbreaking for a new factory or theatre.

2. An outdoor setting may provide the proper atmosphere for a particular menu or theme: a Texas barbecue, a clambake, a street or country fair, a hunt breakfast, or a winter carnival.

3. A site is chosen for an event, but the indoor space is not sufficient for the number of guests involved. This last notion may seem like the result of poor planning or appear impractical, but it is not. What of the bride, who dreams of being married in her parents' home, or the committee planning a dance to celebrate the recent renovation of the town's most prized historical home? The basic location is already fixed, and the caterer must adapt and expand the space (usually by tenting) to accommodate the client's needs.

PLANNING OVERALL LOGISTICS

The first consideration is an analysis of just how out-of-doors the event shall be. In some cases, you may be only a few steps away from a structure, and therefore have relatively easy access to light, power, and water. In other cases, the event may take place near enough to a permanent structure or outbuilding so that a combination of indoor and field facilities satisfies the needs of both staff and guests. Sometimes, the event is literally in the great outdoors, and a base of operations has to be constructed from scratch.

All types of outdoor events have factors in common: some arrangements are fairly simple, some are the equivalent of feeding an army on maneuvers (the term "field kitchen" has real meaning here). Each event has the basic requirements common to any catered event, thus all the guidelines and checklists used in planning and executing a catered affair are still useful. The particulars of the chosen outdoor setting, however, force the caterer to find a variety of different ways to perform what in other circumstances are routine tasks. What follows is an outline of major problems and suggested solutions to this most off-premise facet of the off-premise catering business.

The Indoor-Outdoor Event

When an event takes place just outside a permanent structure (as in the case of a garden party, backyard barbecue, or wedding at home, e.g.), it is often possible that the indoor kitchen suffices as the cooking facility for the party. Other staff space requirements might be met by commandeering an adjacent room or garage. In this case, the fabricated structure (usually a tent or tents) provides guest space for buffets, serving, seating, and /or dancing. In most cases, restrooms and cloakrooms, sources of water, and storage space for rentals and equipment are provided within the existing structure. In some cases, even the party space is part indoors and part outdoors (with perhaps the wedding ceremony being held in a parlor, or cocktails being served in the reception foyer of a large home, followed by dinner in a glamorously tented terrace).

Outdoors/Outbuilding Arrangement

Sometimes the event takes place outside but close to a permanent structure, which provides power, water, and some shelter for the working operations of the party. This structure can be a garage, barn, or other outbuilding on a home property, or may be the office of the beach patrol or the maintenance shed in a public park. This sort of event may require full tenting for the party space, but the field kitchen may be set up either in a commodious outbuilding or connected to the water and power lines of that building. Kitchen or prep tents may still be needed, along with an auxiliary refrigerated truck, temperature-controlled food units, or a secondary generator for additional power, but overall this setup is easier than having no building nearby. In some cases, even restrooms for guests are available within the standing structure.

The True Remote

Sometimes the caterer has to do a true remote, with nothing more than the scenery as a backdrop. Such an operation may require generators and fuel tanks for power and water tank trucks. All the usual available buildings have to be fabricated using tents, trucks, or trailers. Portable toilet facilities have to be rented for guests as well, parking or transportation needs to be arranged for arriving guests and staff, and it might be necessary to shuttle guests to the actual entertainment area by jitney, bus, jeep, or horse-drawn carriages. Anything is possible, based on the scope of the event and extent of the budget, and a good relationship with a full-service rental agency and an expert special events planner can solve the most difficult logistical problems.

PREPARATIONS FOR INCLEMENT WEATHER

Unlike ball games, catered parties are seldom "called on account of rain"; only in the most severe weather—a blizzard or hurricane warning, for example—does a party contract allow for such a cancellation. In ordinary circumstances, both caterers and clients hope for the best and are prepared for the worst, with a well-thought-out foul weather plan ready if needed. Both client and caterer should discuss such a plan and the client be informed of what changes in service, menu, or expense might occur in case the weather is uncooperative.

Tents

When an outdoor party is planned, a weatherproof tent or canopy is good insurance against inclement weather. Unless the chosen setting has adequate indoor space to provide emergency shelter (or an alternate setup for party space; for example, a large garage, finished basement, or gymnasium), it is far safer to plan on tenting, even in the most delightful climates and seasons of the year. Many tent companies allow a caterer to reserve a tent in advance on a contingency basis, confirming the order closer to the chosen date. The expense of a tent reservation or cancellation fee is a bargain compared to the trouble of reorganizing an event at the last minute.

Tenting is also often arranged to provide space as well as shelter. In a historic homesite, for example, cocktails might be served as guests tour the restored rooms, and then enter a tented ballroom for the banquet or dinner-dance. There may also be settings where a tent is erected indoors to transform a warehouse or gymnasium into an elegant room for a party.

Whatever the planned usage of tenting, it cannot be overemphasized that the design, provision, and erection of tents is a technical specialty. Tents must be secured from and erected by experienced professionals for both the comfort and safety of guests and staff. (Caterers who have a tent or tents in their inventory should train their own crew to do the task.) Caterers should acquaint themselves with the professionals in their area, using those who exhibit the most expertise and who have references from other caterers. An experienced tent rental company can offer advice on the proper type of tent for a particular event, the various styles and capacities, and ideal placement and can provide a skilled crew for setup and breakdown. Many of these firms also rent an array of outdoor cooking and serving equipment and are happy to provide advice on planning for safety and logistics.

Tents are available in a wide variety of colors, shapes, and styles. Poleless tents (an open-span design minus center poles) are much more convenient for table placement than those with poles because they provide more usable inside space if dance floors, dais platforms, and so on are to be erected. Tents can be open pavilions or canopies or have solid or roll-down sides for wind and weather protection. They can be heated, air conditioned, or rigged with lighting.

Tents can be provided for both guest and work areas and can provide cosmetic sheathing for portable toilet facilities. Connections between building and tent or tent and tent can be created by canopied walkways or marquees. Complex layout and decor should be thoroughly analyzed by the caterer, decor specialist, or tent rental agent for best results.

Keep the following pointers in mind in regard to tents:

- Tents should usually be set up a day ahead (to allow time for decor, lighting, and table setup) or at least early on the day of the event.

- Tents can be erected over level paved, dirt, or sodded surfaces, or they can be floored and/or carpeted. Solid floors are the best plan for formal seating, since soil can be soft or become muddy so that leveling the tables and chairs presents problems.

- Safety clearance and protective decor should be positioned around outside pegs and tent lines to prevent accidents or tripping by either guests or staff.

LIGHTING AND DECOR

Lighting is usually a practical necessity in an enclosed tent or in the evening for any outdoor party. Lighting can serve a decorative purpose as well: decor specialists can provide fabulous atmospheric effects with lighting to add drama and dimension to the setting. Exterior areas, around tents or from a building to a tent, should be well lighted for safety's sake. Any paths that staff or guests might take should be well and attractively lighted. Cables, tent lines, gas lines, and the like should be out of traffic patterns, if possible; if not, they must be clearly marked to prevent accidents. All lighting used outdoors must be UL (Underwriters Laboratories) approved for such use, and sufficient power or generators must be provided to safely supply current without danger of overloading any building circuits involved. Remember to provide lighting at the driveway, building entrance, or parking valet station as well.

Sometimes an outdoor setting provides splendid decor of its own, and the floral designer can take inspiration from the setting. A blooming garden, for example, might be the perfect setting for an outdoor wedding ceremony, with only the addition of stanchions and ribbon garlands to frame an altar or chuppah. Other natural settings, such as a stand of pine trees, a hedge, or a vine-covered trellis, might provide the perfect backdrop for a bar or buffet. The caterer should consult not only with the floral designer but also with the client (and his or her gardener or landscaper as well) to see that the grounds are in good order for the event. Bugs and pests can be effectively prevented by advance spraying or placement of smoke torches or citronella smudge sticks or pots. Be aware of possible changes in wind direction when placing such smoke devices, so that the guests are not overwhelmed with smoke.

Tents for field kitchens, while provided for practical purposes, should be as attractive as possible if they are in guests' view. Potted plants or trees might be used to provide screening of unsightly areas such as garbage cans, generators, and trucks.

THE MENU AND THE FIELD KITCHEN

The menu you choose for an outdoor event naturally dictates cooking needs, and in some sense, the limits of the cooking facilities constrain the menu choices. Of course, for something like a barbecue or clambake, most of the menu is predetermined by the theme. The bake pit or steamers need to be properly constructed and placed, and the barbecues must be rented and fueled to accommodate the choice of grilled foods and the number of guests involved. For a more general menu, the cooking procedures required to prepare and finish each item should be listed, then appliances and vessels chosen to fill these requirements. Try to construct the menu as efficiently as possible, so that you are not forced to rent a portable appliance that you barely use. Some rental companies (many of those who also rent tents) specialize in outdoor or portable cooking equipment. Other large rental firms carry some items and can refer you to sources for other needs.

Depending on the amount of cooking that needs to be done, and the remoteness of the location, it may be necessary or desirable to rent or arrange for a large cooking truck or semi-trailer, completely outfitted with the needed stoves and refrigeration, generators and water tanks. In large metropolitan areas, truck and trailer rentals, as well as rental services and equipment specialists, can either provide or customize such vehicles for outdoor events. Some caterers who do many remote events find that having a completely outfitted "road kitchen" is an investment that earns back its cost in a short period of time. (If one caterer cannot make full use of such a vehicle, renting it out to other caterers in the area can be a good source of income as well.)

In other situations, cook tents, near or attached to the guest tents, may be outfitted with portable stoves and ranges, rolling proofing cabinets, refrigerators or coolers, work tables, dollied racks, temperature-controlled food storage containers, hot and cold beverage dispensers, and thermal carriers to create a very workable field kitchen. Facilities for pot and dish washing can be as primitive as a garden hose and wash tubs, or a water tank truck may be brought in to supply water for all purposes. Fuel for the appliances may be bottled gas. Some smaller heating and heat-maintaining units use solid fuel. Generators may be rented to supply power for lighting and for smaller cooking appliances (like fryers, microwaves, hot trays, and electric skillets).

SAFETY PRECAUTIONS AND PERMITS

Every precaution must be taken in planning and using the field kitchen, and for the outdoor setting as a whole, to prevent any accidents or mishaps. In general, all equipment for both guests and staff should be placed and secured in such a way that they do not cause accidents: for example, tables and chairs should be sturdy and set level, and all wires, lighting, decor, and surrounding grounds should be walked through to spot possible hazards. Lighting, to repeat, must be sufficient for its purpose. Kitchen staff, working with packaged fuels, open fires, hot coals, and bottled fuels, should be extra certain to follow instructions and safety regulations. The field kitchen should be maintained in a sanitary fashion.

If an outdoor event is on public grounds, has the public as its guests, or infringes in any way on public streets, the local authorities may have to issue special permits, temporary licenses, or permits of access. Moving or parking large vans in a residential area may require clearance with local authorities as well. Either the homeowner, site rental agent, or caterer should contact local agencies to acquire the proper permissions. The local police, state police, or sheriff's office should be informed of any possible traffic tie-ups so traffic can be routed expeditiously in and around the area. It may also be necessary for the caterer to hire an approved (by the facility [park, museum, school] and/or properly licensed by local law enforcement officials if weapons are to be carried) parking or security force for very large events. Check with the local fire department for ordinances or safety regulations covering the transport and use of bottled gas or other fuels. Safety regulations must also be followed in regard to tenting, but an established tent company is usually conversant with these rules.

STAFFING

First, prepare staffing guidelines based on the type of party, menu, service, and number of guests. Then, take into account the extra personnel required to perform ordinary tasks under extraordinary conditions: for example, drivers and trucks for additional equipment; extra porters or maintenance crew to assist with water, light, and power hookup and monitoring; and extra crew required for setup and breakdown of tents, tables, and so on. In addition, the distance from the field kitchen to the dining room, or guest tent, may add time and difficulty to service, so extra serving personnel or runners should be available to help in this area. A supplemented kitchen staff may be needed as well since most field kitchens are not as efficient because appliance and work space placement are less convenient than in ordinary circumstances. Remember to add any personnel that may be needed to assist arriving and departing guests, to park cars, to retrieve supplies from one tent to another, and to assist in breakdown and cleanup.

SERVICE AND TABLEWARE

There are no restrictions on the types of events that can be held outdoors. With proper planning and materials, the most formal banquet can take place as though it were being held in a hotel ballroom. Once the style and tone of the function have been established, the usual procedures for ordering or procuring serving equipment and tableware are followed, whether the event is a cocktail party, seated dinner, picnic, or buffet.

One style that can work particularly well for a large outdoor event is the station-to-station buffet. Sometimes this is easier and more efficient as well: instead of setting up one large field kitchen, cooking and serving equipment is positioned at each station, either in a large tent or a combination of tents and canopies spread throughout an area—for example, barbecue pit, raw bar, fish-fry station, bakery, or ice cream stand. Another form of service that can work well without making great demands on either cooking or serving staff is a prepackaged meal, given to each guest or set at each place (see Chapter 20).

Whatever form the menu and event take, choose serving ware and utensils that are appropriate to the nature of the function. Allow extra serving equipment (more butler and bus trays, more chafer liners, platters, etc.) to compensate for a less efficient kitchen.

In some cases, for reasons of safety, convenience, cost or theme, disposables become the preferred choice. As discussed in Chapter 4, disposable dinnerware, serving platters, and other paper and plastic goods are now available in enormous variety, so making a suitable and practical choice is not difficult. When factoring amounts, however, remember that for any sort of walkabout affair, in an outdoor setting, guests use and discard disposables with abandon, so provide generous amounts of items, particularly glasses, accordingly.

Chapter 13

The Cocktail Party

For decades, the cocktail party—a gathering of guests, the offering of (usually alcoholic) beverages, and some form of sustenance, typically light finger food, has been a favored format of both hosts and caterers. It has also been much maligned, often by etiquette authorities, and sometimes by guests, as an impersonal, chaotic mob scene, and scorned as the easy way out for a host or hostess to repay a long list of social obligations with one fell swoop. A poorly planned and badly managed cocktail "bash" deserves such criticism, but a well arranged and graciously executed cocktail event can be enjoyed by both hosts and guests.

Clients like the more informal, less structured atmosphere of a cocktail party, where a large group can be entertained without the need for extensive rentals of tables, chairs, dishes, and silverware. Clients also perceive the cocktail party as less expensive than other forms of entertaining. In ordinary circumstances, it is true that a modestly presented cocktail party, with an interesting (but not overly lavish) menu, is less expensive than an elegant seated dinner, but situations vary so, as with any catered event, both client and caterer should have a clear understanding of budget and selling price based on the detailed plans for a particular event. Cost factors aside, the cocktail party is a good solution for entertaining in an awkward space, where formal seating would be impossible, and it does allow for a broad mix of guests, whose only common link may be that they know or are known to the hostess, do business with a company, or are involved in a common interest or cause.

Guests enjoy cocktail parties because they provide an opportunity to mix and mingle with an assortment of people, perhaps providing business or social contacts that might not occur in a more structured setting. The form also allows a guest mobility (no endless evening seated next to a deadly bore) and the flexibility of time since it is acceptable to drop in to a cocktail party and leave, after socializing for awhile, without offending either one's host or other guests.

111

The services of an off-premise caterer are often solicited for such events, and a successful performance can yield solid repeat business and be financially rewarding. A caterer with imagination and style can create an atmosphere and menu that makes such an event much more than "just another cocktail party." An off-premise caterer with good management skills and a well-trained staff can master the techniques of timing, traffic flow, and crowd control to avoid the mob scene cliché and produce a party with a lively and exciting pace.

There is no set formula for a cocktail party, which can be arranged for as few as, say, six to more than a thousand. A cocktail party has a flexible style, allowing for almost any setting, theme, or menu. It can be the appropriate form for events that range from solemn to silly, in every conceivable setting, at any season of the year. Over the years, tastes in food and drinking habits have altered, but the cocktail party has remained viable.

TYPES OF COCKTAIL PARTIES

While there are many variations, most events that can be labeled with the term *cocktail party* fit into one of the following formats: the simple cocktail party, the expanded cocktail party, the simple reception, or the lavish cocktail reception.

The Simple Cocktail Party

This is the old-fashioned kind of cocktail party. Its timing is dictated by an era in which Dinner At Eight was the standard, and such gatherings were scheduled for an hour or two sometime between 5 and 8 P.M. Guests, who might come straight from work or be on their way to another event or formal dinner, either alone or in a group, convene to share a few drinks, good conversation, and some interesting tidbits of food. In earlier days, the nibbles might be as simple as salted nuts or crackers, possibly some garnished canapés. Today, the menu is expanded somewhat, with at least an offering of cheese, cold shrimp, crudités with a dip, perhaps a selection of olives or pickled mushrooms, a pâté, and crackers or breadsticks. The food selection may be expanded to include as many interesting and exotic morsels as desired, but it should serve merely as an accompaniment to drinks and not be so filling and substantial that it becomes a meal. Rather, the menu comprises an appetizer.

The Expanded Cocktail Party

This type of gathering effectively takes the place of a meal. The format is the same as for a simple cocktail party, with no real need for tables and seating, but with enough hors d'oeuvre passed and offered on a sideboard or cocktail table to keep guests happily fed for a few hours. Since such an event is planned to run longer than a simple cocktail party, many clients schedule the party for an entire afternoon or evening.

The menu can include a broad selection of hors d'oeuvre, some of a substantial nature, and usually includes one or two cocktail centerpiece items, such as an iced seafood bar, an arrangement of sausages and pâtés, a lavish crudité display with choices of dips, a generous cheese board, or other similar self-serve items. Some caterers have found that clients and guests enjoy such an event when the menu is conceived as a full meal, eaten morsel by morsel, and ending with fruits, tiny desserts, and coffee. This type of event comes close to being a buffet meal, but only sometimes requires small plates and forks for the foods served. Guests have the option of dropping in at any time (in a sort of open-house style), but the majority of guests comes at the start and stays for the duration.

The Simple Cocktail Reception

This type of party is sometimes called a champagne reception. It is usually a very elegant and refined prelude to a formal seated multicourse dinner. Typically, only champagne (or perhaps wine, sherry, or simple aperitifs) are served. The menu may be very luxurious, but spare: iced beluga, smoked salmon, cheese straws, items delicate in both size and taste. The duration of such a reception may be as little as thirty minutes, usually no more than an hour. It serves as an elegant welcome to guests as they assemble for dinner, and the menu is designed to merely pique the appetite, not to sate guests or to overwhelm the palate.

The Lavish Cocktail Reception

This type of party is of a very different nature indeed. This event also precedes an important event—a wedding or banquet, for example—but it is also an event in itself. Guests arrive and are feted with a lavish and substantial array of both food and drink. Some of the foods may be hot, buffetlike foods, served from chafers. Plates, forks, and small cocktail table seating is often provided.

The expansive and highly decorative displays of foods serve a dual purpose. One, of course, is symbolic, to mark the importance of the event or occasion by a festive display of abundance, particularly of traditional and celebratory foods. The other reason is a more practical one, that of sufficiently feeding guests who may have traveled a distance from a lengthy ceremony or who may have a long wait before the actual banquet begins (because of long receiving lines at a diplomatic reception or because the bridal party is delayed at a photographic session, e.g.). In some settings, where an event takes place between cocktails and dinner (e.g., a wedding ceremony at the site; a long seige of invocations, ritual blessings, toasts, introductions, or award presentations that may precede dinner; or an opening night ballet or other performance to be followed by supper or a ball), the extensive and substantial nature of the menu serves the purpose of staving off hunger.

MENU PLANNING

As with all catered events, the first planning steps involve an understanding of the nature of the function, the number and type of guests, and a thorough site inspection. With this information, a menu is devised that is suitable to the occasion and manageable in the kitchen and serving areas available on site.

An enormous variety of foods can be served at a cocktail party. (The recipe section of this book contains about seventy-five recipes with variations suitable for cocktail parties, and that is merely scratching the surface.) During a meeting with a client, the caterer can determine the theme, style, and budget of the party, and make a preliminary selection of hors d'oeuvre. The kitchen facilities (or lack of them) is an important determining factor.

While it would be impossible to dictate the actual selection of hors d'oeuvre for any event, certain guidelines can be helpful. For example, there should be a proper balance of hot and cold butler-passed items (unless no warming facilities are available), and a similar balance between subtle and spicy, pastry-wrapped and plain, and crisp and creamy foods. Usually, one tries to offer at least one meat, one seafood, one cheese, and one vegetable selection, all prepared and seasoned differently, for a satisfactory variety. Working to achieve such a balance not only provides choices and different taste sensations for guests but also allows the caterer to balance costly and less expensive ingredients as well as simple and labor-intensive items.

When making a final selection of hors d'oeuvre, add these considerations: contrast the colors and shapes of the items, as well as their flavor and texture, and make adjustments for the tastes and ages of guests—that is, older guests tend to prefer milder flavored items, and may also have more health and diet restrictions, and younger guests often have a taste for more highly spiced, exotic, or hearty items. If including a cocktail centerpiece item, such as a display of crudités, a fish terrine, or pâté, include these items when assessing menu choices as well. When cocktails are served prior to a meal, take the total menu into consideration to avoid monotony by repeating items and to respect the flavors of dinner items that follow.

Once the cocktail menu has been determined, think about the order of the menu and the pacing of service. Always offer something substantial and popular at the outset for two reasons: it immediately involves all the guests in the party, and it protects guests from feeling the effects of their first drinks too quickly. Pace other items according to their character, alternating hot with cold, spicy with bland, and so on. This service rhythm allows guests to enjoy each item separately and also gives the kitchen or pantry staff proper time for heating, frying, and plating. It is a nice idea to introduce a new passed item midway during service or to reserve a second round of an especially popular or costly item (such as shrimp, smoked salmon, or beef tenderloin canapés) for later in the party. This surprise or reprise renews guests' interest and creates a feeling of luxury and abundance.

The question of how many items to include and how many of each to serve is somewhat a matter of preference and experience with certain groups, but in general, for a small group (from eight to twenty guests), two hot and two cold butler-passed items and one cocktail centerpiece selection provide a satisfactory variety. For a larger crowd (up to forty guests), add one or two each hot and cold items and one or two additional centerpiece items. For much larger groups (or for parties that extend for more than ninety minutes), the choices can be expanded somewhat, but in most cases, the selection of passed items does not need to exceed more than five or six each of hot and cold choices, even for the largest crowd. Extending the choices beyond this number can overtax the kitchen and serving staff, and with a very large crowd in a large space, the hoped-for effect of abundance is lost on guests. It is far better, even with a lavish reception, to increase the number of centerpiece items or chafing-dish foods (doubling or tripling up on the items to spread the display throughout the space) so that guests appreciate the bounty and can partake of all the offerings with ease.

As a rule, most guests consume from eight to twelve pieces or bites of hors d'oeuvre for every hour to ninety minutes of a cocktail party. Portions of centerpiece items should be included in this count. This estimate is good as an average, but bear in mind that when a larger variety of items is offered, guests are likely to eat more than the average, since they are tempted to taste at least one piece of each item available. The pace of eating is enthusiastic at the outset, then subsides somewhat, and as the party passes the hour mark and guests become more relaxed and have had more to drink, it increases again. When cocktails precede dinner, the cocktail party food consumption is at the lesser end of the average; when the party spans a meal hour, more is consumed. Items that are especially popular or luxurious (cocktail shrimp is a prime example) are always outside the average, since guests devour such items with abandon. For such selections, provide as much as the client's budget will allow, and supervise passing so that all guests get a fair share.

When the cocktail party is conceived as a full meal, the presentation of finger desserts later in the event should be considered as a separate minimenu. For the presentation to be effective, a variety of sweets must be offered (at least three or four, even for a small group), and guests (no matter how many hors d'oeuvre they have consumed before) can be counted on to take at least one taste of each item.

Suggested Menus

Simple Cocktail Party

Crudites with Artichoke Dip

Basket of Sweet Potato and Parsnip Chips

Assorted Cheese Truffles

Spiced Hush Puppies   Toasted Asparagus Rolls

Cocktail Shrimp with Caper Mayonnaise

Skewered Apple and Turkey with Chutney Dipping Sauce

Expanded Cocktail Party

Crudite with Taramasalata

Skewered Seviche   Leek-Glazed Oysters

Endive Rosettes with Goat Cheese   Coconut Shrimp

Szechuan Chicken Chunks   Mini Empanadas

Stuffed Tuscan Loaf

Assortment of Cheeses, Crackers, and Breads

Bowl of Fresh Cherries or Stemmed Strawberries

Rugelach   Swirled Brownies   Lime Curd Tarts

Simple Cocktail Reception

Fans of Asparagus and Endive with Red Caviar Dip
Gravlax with Sweet Mustard Dill Sauce
Phyllo Kisses filled with Brie

Lavish Cocktail Reception

Golden Caviar Layer Cake
Crab Claws, Cocktail Shrimp, and Raw Oysters
on Ice Sculpture
Choice of Sauces
Elaborate Crudite Display   Herbed Mayonnaise Dip
Assortment of Skewered and Wrapped Fruits
Assortment of Meat and Vegetable Pâtés Garni
Breads and Crackers
Wild Rice Stuffed Mushrooms   Shrimp and Feta Turnovers
Miniature Spring Rolls   Miniature Reubens
Fish Brochettes   Grilled Baby Lamb Chops

LOGISTICS

Analyze traffic flow for both staff and guests, and plan, especially with larger groups in small or awkward spaces, to keep the party area as open as possible. In this way, guests can circulate easily, and servers can pass hors d'oeuvre without constantly breaking through conversational groups. If cocktail centerpieces are offered, they should be strategically placed, either along the sides of a room or centered, so that guests may easily enjoy the display and serve themselves or be served with ease. Use the same sensible approach with floral arrangements, large plants, decorative sculptures, or candles: such items should enhance the atmosphere of a room, not create inconvenience or danger. The bar or bars should be positioned away from the entrance, doorways, or other narrow passageways to allow for the inevitable clustering of guests at a bar. Wherever possible, space any food tables and bars separately from each other, to even out the traffic flow. Keep the main traffic lanes open as well: that is, the routes for servers to and from kitchen or staging areas and the routes to restrooms or cloakrooms.

In addition to decorative trays, bowls, and baskets to display centerpiece items, a good supply of passing trays of silver or other decorative metal, wood, woven straw, lacquer, china, or glass should be on hand, with the trays chosen to suit the foods being passed. Paper doilies have long been a standard for lining trays, since they are inexpensive, but they lack imagination and become tattered and greasy looking quite easily. A better choice for greasy items is starched and ironed, heavy-duty napkins of linen or other fabric, which stay fresh looking longer. Depending on each item's color and texture, many hors d'oeuvre look attractive on lemon, fern, and lettuce leaves or other greens. In addition, trays can be garnished with fresh flower blossoms, fancy cut vegetables, or fruit. Just be certain that the garnish enhances the platter and is not unwieldy for service. When dipping sauces are offered on trays, seafood shells, tiny porcelain ramekins, or oriental lotus bowls work very well. Be sure to keep them refilled and tidy looking for each repeat use. If toothpicks are used with hors d'oeuvre, a small receptacle on each tray for used picks is a good idea. Other items, such as ice buckets, folding tables, table linens, or chairs, can be rented as the menu and room require.

Seating is an option at cocktail parties. As a matter of fact, too much seating can make an event static, eliminating the mingling that is essential for a lively party. At large receptions in rented or public spaces, positioning some chairs or small tables and chairs along the sides of a room is nice if space allows. This is a consideration particularly appreciated by older or disabled guests. At a home party (see Chapter 11), some seating occurs naturally, with adjustments made for comfort and ease of movement wherever possible. Remember that whenever you are serving any item that requires plates and forks, you must provide some surface for guests to rest at least a glass, or it is impossible for them to eat. Remember as well that if you don't provide such resting places, guests find their own, using the edges of bookcases, windowsills, serving tables, or the floor. Ashtrays present a similar problem, and some arrangement should be made for their placement (and frequent bussing) to avoid accidents.

STOCKING THE BAR

The first consideration is the type of bar service appropriate to the occasion. Do the client and guests appreciate a full liquor bar? Or is the decision made to serve only wine or, in the case of a formal reception, only champagne? With today's changing tastes, less hard liquor is being consumed, especially by younger guests. The drinking preferences of the nation in general are tending toward wines and white liquors (vodka, gin, rum) and away from the dark liquors. Naturally, every group has its own tastes, and the client often can inform the caterer of guests' preferences. If the guests are known to be hard drinkers, if they prefer single malt scotches, bourbon, dacquiris, or margaritas, such tastes must be accommodated. A particular season or time of day may dictate other choices: eggnog or hot toddies for a holiday party or Bloody Marys, screwdrivers, or mimosas for a brunch.

It is usually best to keep the bar simple, so that service for a large number of guests can be efficient. Remember that a party bar is set up to serve guests with ease and graciousness. It is not a public bar, so requests for mai tais, sloe gin fizzes, and brandy Alexanders need not be planned for unless the facility has a full cash bar or a client insists on custom-mixed cocktails. If that is the case, a staff of crack bartenders and a fully stocked bar need to be arranged and paid for.

Under ordinary circumstances, however, it is wise for a caterer to advise a client that there is no obligation on the part of a host or hostess to provide a full-service bar for a party. Aside from providing for the known eccentricities of particular guests (preparing a sour mix, having the vermouths for martinis and manhattans, e.g.), a basic liquor and wine bar serves the needs of most parties.

With any service of hard liquor, mixers are necessary (more club soda and ginger ale in winter, more tonic in summer), along with appropriate garnishes, including lemon twists, lime wedges, and orange slices. Beer is generally included in a full bar, depending on tastes in a given area and on the age of guests: a premium or imported beer is a nice touch. Plain mineral water, club soda, seltzer, or other nonalcoholic beverages (like diet colas) should be available. Iced tea can be a nice addition for a summer party; a dry, nonalcoholic sparkling cider or white grape juice is also much appreciated by nondrinkers.

Once it has been decided what to serve, the quantities needed must be determined, using the following guidelines:

Mixed drinks: Most guests consume two to three mixed drinks each in the first hour to hour and a half of a party; during additional hours, it's about two drinks per hour. The standard mixed drink contains 1½ oz. of liquor to 4 oz. of mixer.

Wine Bar: If serving only wine, allow at least half a bottle of wine per person for a one-hour party. If serving both red and white wine, plan on at least twice as much white as red. Blush wines are also very popular with cocktails and can be incorporated in a wine bar: allot about three-quarters of the total wine to white and blush combined, the balance red.

Champagne: For a reception, which usually lasts less than an hour, one bottle for every two to three people is sufficient. For a toast, one case of champagne should be allotted for every fifty people.

Note that in almost all cases, the client purchases alcohol directly from a liquor store, with the caterer acting as a consultant if necessary. (Note: in most localities, unopened bottles of liquor, and unopened and unchilled wines and champagnes are accepted for return, so buying extra supplies is not a problem.) It is difficult to dictate the stocking of a bar since tastes vary, but in the most general terms, a wine and liquor bar for about twenty-five to thirty people for a two- to three-hour period should contain the following:

2 liters scotch
1 liter bourbon
1 liter rye or Canadian blend
2 liters vodka (more in summer)
1 liter gin (more in summer)
1 liter white rum
6–8 bottles dry white wine (or blush)
3–5 bottles dry red wine
12–24 bottles beer

In addition, to provide for some special tastes, you need the following:

½-size bottles sweet and dry vermouth
1 fifth campari or dubonnet
1 fifth tequila
1 fifth brandy

For other beverages and mixers:

12 liters mineral water
8 liters club soda or seltzer
6 liters tonic (more in summer)
3 liters ginger ale
6 liters other soda (colas, diet, 7-Up)
2 quarts orange or tomato juice, if needed

And some oranges, lemons, limes, olives, onions, and cherries as garnishes for drinks.

For most parties where mixed drinks or soft drinks are to be served, purchase about one pound of ice per person, with 10 percent overage for melting and waste. For chilling wine or champagne, order an extra twenty pounds of ice for each twelve to eighteen bottles to be chilled.

Allow about one and one-half glasses per person for an event lasting an hour to ninety minutes. Three glasses per person should be provided for longer events, with some provision for washing and reuse. In general, the larger the event, the more likely guests will lose their glasses, so more need to be provided. As a backup for any event, good-quality disposable glasses should always be on hand: in a glass crisis, they can be used, especially for soft drinks or mineral waters, and the glasses reserved for hard drinks and wine.

Plenty of cocktail napkins must be available to servers, guests, and bartenders alike. It is not unusual for a guest to use twenty to thirty napkins during the course of a party. Small paper napkins are inexpensive, so a generous supply should be in every caterer's stock of basics.

STAFFING

Bartenders

In most cases, a bartender is able to service about thirty-five to fifty guests, depending on how complicated the drinks and setup are. If all the guests arrive at one time, or if a crunch develops, one member of the serving staff should be prepared to pitch in. If only a simple wine bar is planned, one person can easily pour for fifty. For a large party, if space allows, separate bars staffed by individual bartenders are more efficient and keep crowding down. Remember that for wine- or champagne-only service, it is perfectly acceptable, and may be far more efficient, to butler-pass filled glasses among the guests. In that case, only a service bar (which need not be in public view) is necessary. Butler service for other drinks is also possible, and can lend an elegant touch to a smaller or home party, with a server taking orders from guests and delivering prepared drinks from the service bar.

Serving Staff

For butler-passing of hors d'oeuvre, one server can handle about twenty-five to thirty people. If centerpieces are self-serve, one serving person can handle thirty-five to forty guests. If centerpiece foods or chafing dish items are served, one server per table is required. In all cases, where a party exceeds fifty guests, one extra server to act as an expeditor for trays from the kitchen, as well as to replenish and freshen centerpiece items, should be added to the staff; for one hundred guests, two extra server/expeditors, and so on. Although all servers should be in the habit of picking up empty glasses, used napkins, ashtrays, and so forth whenever possible on their return to the kitchen, for large parties in sprawling rooms or multilevel spaces, buspersons are very helpful to retrieve used glasses and empty ashtrays and to help replenish the bar and buffets.

Kitchen Staff

If hors d'oeuvre are prepared ahead, simply to be baked, fried, or reheated on site during service, one kitchen or pantry person can handle forty to fifty guests. If the menu requires more last-minute cooking and more complex plating and garnishing, a second cook or helper is needed. With good kitchen refrigeration, counter space, and oven space, two in staff in a kitchen can feed one hundred people. In sites where separate satellite kitchens or staging areas are required, add one pantry person for each staging area and one runner (from main kitchen to staging area) for each three satellites. Naturally, where much food prep is done on site in the hours before a party, extra help is needed, either cook's helpers or serving staff brought on early to help with prep. In addition, to help in cleanup throughout and following the party, a busperson or dishwasher is helpful to rinse glasses for reuse, clean trays, and repack equipment. Plan this help according to the size and logistics of the party and the space available in the kitchen.

As with all large parties, particularly those in vast or awkward spaces, either the caterer, events manager, or a maître d' of some sort should have the ongoing responsibility of overseeing the general timing and flow of the event. For very large parties, some caterers use several such managers, who communicate with one another either with hand signals or walkie-talkies to keep the party flowing smoothly.

While the information contained here refers primarily to the cocktail party, much of it is referred to in the following chapters, which provide specific guidelines based on many of the principles here.

Chapter 14

The Buffet Meal

The buffet meal is an extraordinarily popular form of dining, suitable for any time of day, and especially preferred for large groups of people, unwieldy spaces, and mixed crowds. In a sense, it has a lot in common with the extended cocktail party, in that a larger number of people can be entertained than would be possible at a sit-down dinner, in a more relaxed manner. The format lends itself to many occasions, both grand and intimate, and is as suitable to a casual lunch, brunch, or outdoor theme party as it is to a luxury fund raiser, a gala dinner-dance, or an intimate and elegant midnight supper for just a few very special guests.

Many hosts and caterers favor a buffet over a seated dinner because it provides the opportunity for lavish spectacle and highly decorative display. Enticing presentation of buffet foods, whether simple, unpretentious dishes or elaborately displayed luxury items, is essential to the enjoyment of the event. It is interesting to note that in the hospitality trade, *buffet* refers to a style of service, while in the mind of the public, the same word generates the expectation of an abundant spread and party atmosphere. Showmanship, always a key to a caterer's success, takes center stage here and can truly enhance a caterer's reputation and increase business.

TYPES OF BUFFETS

The Simple Buffet

The simple buffet has a casual approach, very suitable to an open house, a brunch, business breakfast or luncheon, or a home party. The menu is composed of dishes that are both visually attractive and able to be served either at room temperature or to tolerate standing in chafing dishes. The buffet is typically completely set up and open throughout the party, being replenished and refreshed as needed. It may be served or self-serve.

121

The Grand Buffet

This type of buffet is an elegant affair, which might be preceded by a reception or cocktails and some hors d'oeuvre. Such an event can be associated with a wedding or other ceremonial celebration, a dinner dance, a ball, or a late supper following a gala opening night. The presentation of the buffet can be the highlight of the party. Whenever possible, have the guests first see the buffet in all its glory when the announcement "Dinner is served" is heard. This is best managed when cocktails take place in a separate anteroom, then the spectacle of the opening of the buffet takes on theatrical proportions.

This sort of buffet often involves serving, especially carving stations, or prepared-to-order foods: omelets being prepared, crepes flamed, pastas sauced and tossed, and in an outdoor setting, meats and fish being grilled to order. In this sort of format, servers portion and prepare foods as guests move along the buffet line (or lines).

The Station-to-Station Buffet

This format is great fun for guests and allows for the management of a large group of people in either a large or awkward space. Each food being offered is served from its own station, and guests can wander from point to point, choosing as much of whatever they like, and at the same time be entertained by the drama of each station.

Caterers can take great advantage of this format by having the staff at each station dress the part (sushi chefs, bakers, cowhands, street vendors, soda jerks, etc.). The foods presented can comprise one overall theme (e.g., A Salute to American Regional Foods) or a variety of ethnic foods, so that guests can visit Chinatown, Little Italy, the fish market, the beefsteak corral, for example, or travel through the capitals of the world à la Disney. In a sense, this sort of buffet is a glorified cocktail party (as a matter of fact, if desired, you could serve only finger foods, so that the event is a cocktail party), since guests do a great deal of mingling. It takes good staffing and strong organization, but it has the advantage of spreading a crowd throughout a space and eliminating or reducing buffet lines.

Group Functional Feeding

Group functional feeding is not a very glamorous name, admittedly, but there are some situations in which a caterer is called upon to provide buffet meals in a setting that is not geared for entertaining but for the practical purpose of feeding people. For caterers with clients from the corporate and public sector, this can mean providing meals for the volunteer staffers of a large charity auction; setting up coffee breaks or dinner for work crews handling the preparations for a parade, sporting event, or city street fair; setting up a cafeteria for the staff of a telethon or election-night media team; or trucking in the midnight lunch break for a television commercial or movie film crew on a downtown street or other remote location.

Theatrical presentation and pretty touches are not a primary requirement here (although food, even hearty sandwiches, should always be presented in an appetizing fashion). Instead, practical methods and efficient serving techniques are most important. (Note that in some instances, especially those involving union personnel, some menu requirements must be met—e.g., a hot entrée, two vegetables, choice of meat or fish, etc.). This sort of work can be good business for a caterer: the logistics are practical, not atmospheric; the food is basic and less fussy than for parties; and while staffing and transport can be unusual, the needs can be met in a straightforward manner. Another great advantage is that such business tends to occur at off-hours and throughout the year, filling out a caterer's calendar to great financial advantage.

MENU PLANNING AND LOGISTICS

A thorough site inspection with an understanding of the style and concept of the function is a first step in planning a buffet. The number and age of guests, the time of day, and the relative formality or informality of the event should be determined at a client meeting. A thorough review of kitchen and prep facilities, an analysis of public space, and consideration of all of the factors mentioned in the last section dictate menu choices.

Menu Balance

Buffet foods, in general, in addition to being decorative and somewhat durable, should be easily served and eaten. A decision can be made to serve fork-only foods or foods that require both knife and fork. As with any menu, a balance of tastes and textures is important (see Chapter 13). In addition, since buffet foods, unlike hors d'oeuvre, are usually presented and eaten together as a meal, compatibility of all the elements is a special consideration. Although in a station-to-station buffet different foods are eaten separately, for most other buffet forms, the foods should look and taste harmonious on the same plate. Imagine how each item will look both arranged on the buffet table and served on a guest's plate; this little trick quickly points out the error of serving three foods in creamed sauces or every dish doused in wine sauce or vinaigrette. Of course, the more extensive and lavish the buffet, the more latitude in menu planning, since guests may make several forays to the buffet or buffets and select different items. As a matter of fact, one of the advantages of the buffet menu is that a wide enough selection of foods can be offered to please both plain and fancy tastes. Conversely, if the client desires, a strong theme menu can be planned to very good effect.

There are no absolute rules for a buffet menu: a breakfast or brunch held in an office or home has a distinctly different menu and style than an elegant buffet for a bar mitzvah. There are some guidelines, however. Most buffets are composed as a meal with choices: at least one fish or seafood item along with a meat, poultry, or vegetarian entrée; one or two starches; and several vegetables, salads, or side dishes. Usually an assortment of breads, biscuits, or rolls is offered and, when appropriate, a beautiful display of fruits and cheeses. Desserts or sweets are offered separately, usually also in a buffet style, although in some instances an occasion cake (such as wedding or birthday) can be the only dessert.

Amounts to Serve

The question of how much to serve is determined by the type of menu, the number of choices, and whether the buffet is staff-served or self-serve. In the case of a one-entrée menu, portions should be measured as you would do for a dinner, with each guest consuming about one-half to three-quarters of a pound (225 g to 350 g) of meat or main course item. For more than one entrée (meat, fish, or poultry), guests take some of two or more, but the total consumption of main course remains about the same. Thus, for sixty people, if only roast beef is served, prepare sixty six- to eight-ounce (180 g to 225 g) portions; if roast beef and chicken are offered, prepare about thirty full-size portions of each choice; if a third choice is offered, prepare twenty to twenty-five full-size portions of each, and so on.

Tastes may vary from dish to dish, and some things are inherently more popular than others (roast beef and shrimp will probably have more takers than lamb curry or sausage), but unless the crowd is strongly weighted by age or distinct taste, the averages hold. For side dishes or starches, guests usually take a two-ounce (60 g) portion of each, or one serving spoon's worth, whichever is less. A sauced or filled pasta or a fancy rice with vegetables is more popular than plain buttered noodles or steamed rice, but more filling. For salad, plan on about a handful (less than a cup [¼ L]) per person, with three to four tablespoons of dressing. Most guests consume two to three rolls, biscuits, or slices of bread. For an assortment of desserts, allow at least a taste of each per person, with extras on such items as whole strawberries, brownies, or cookies.

When planning food amounts, take these other factors into consideration: in general, in a large crowd, slightly less than the average is consumed. The time of day often affects food consumption as well: people eat slightly less of main courses or heavier foods at breakfast buffets but consume more fruit, bread and pastries, coffee and juice. At brunches, the later the hour and the more alcohol served, the more food consumed. Lunch buffets usually have a shorter time span, guests have less time to eat, so they may make only one trip to the buffet. At dinner buffets, guests consume their full share, especially since they have time for return trips, and especially as wine or liquor is consumed over the span of the party. Women and older guests tend to consume slightly smaller portions of meat and hearty entrées; if many of the guests are young men, plan on higher-than-average portions.

Suggested Menus

Mediterranean Buffet (suitable for Station-to-Station)

Parmigiano, Taleggio, Feta

Mozzarella and Roasted Red Peppers

Assorted Marinated Olives

Baugettes, Focaccia, Breadsticks, Toasted Pita Strips

Lemony Grilled Chicken   Assorted Grilled Sausages

Grilled Butterfly of Lamb

Pasta Primavera Salad   Lentil and White Bean Salad

Tabbouleh   Vegetables Provencale   Sauteed Polenta

Ripe Figs, Melons, Peaches and Apricots

Fruit Galettes   Zuppa Inglese

Assorted Italian Pastries

Dinner Buffet (for Group Functional Feeding)

Lentil and Carrot Soup
Hero Sandwiches of Roast Beef with Vegetable Sauce
Chunk of Jarlsberg Cheese   Stuffed Eggs
Mixed Green Salad
Triple Chocolate Brownies   Sour Cream Bourbon Cake
Fresh Fruit: Apples, Pears, Oranges or Tangerines

Late Supper Buffet

Watercress, Endive, and Mushroom Salad (plattered)
Turkey Crepes Gratinee   Broccoli Mimosa
Raspberry Strawberry Mousse in Brown Sugar Tuiles

SETTING THE STAGE

Seating is the most important consideration for a buffet. No matter how casual the event or where it takes place, it is inconsiderate to offer guests plates of food and not provide a setting where they can comfortably enjoy the offering. If there is one universal criticism of buffets, it is that guests are sometimes expected to have three hands, one for a glass, one for a fork, and one for a plate. Whatever the setting or the client's request, no caterer should agree to serve a buffet without adequate seating; discomfort can quickly turn a pleasant event into an ordeal.

In a home setting, where there is not adequate space for a large number of rented tables and chairs, arrangements must be made so that guests have an eating surface and some place to sit. Card tables, snack tables, lap trays, desks, and cocktail tables can be used, as well as some folding chairs, floor cushions, hassocks, and so on. Other parts of the house or apartment can be utilized: bedrooms, dens, and foyers (and in fine weather, a patio or terrace) provide secondary seating areas. Guests do not object to such makeshift arrangements in the informality of a home setting: a seat on a staircase, with a sturdy lap tray, oversized napkin, and good company can add up to a good time for relaxed guests.

In an office, the conference room, the executive suite, library, reception area, or a space created by clearing a few rows of desks can be converted into adequate seating. Even at the most informal outdoor event, picnic tables, wooden planks laid across sawhorses, benches, even sturdy crates or bales of hay, can do the job. Sometimes, such rough-and-tumble arrangements add to the atmosphere of the party.

In a more formal setting, seating should be provided at regular dining tables, set with linens, possibly with cutlery and glasses at each place, and usually with a small centerpiece or flower vase at each table. In a room (or tent) large enough to accommodate the entire party, tables are usually arranged as they would be for a banquet or around a dance floor. Tables can accommodate from four to twelve guests, depending on the space available and client preference. A seating plan and place cards can be used as they would for a seated dinner. In all cases, the buffet table(s) and bar(s) may be set in the same room or in a convenient anteroom.

Traffic flow is also important to the success of a buffet. Guests should have easy access to the buffet, to their seats, and to the bar, if they will be going after their own drinks. The staff should have an unobstructed route from the kitchen to the buffet table or tables, so that foods can be easily replenished and trays refreshed as needed. If a dance floor is part of the setting, then alternate routes for both guests and staff should be available, to avoid any possible accidents. As with a cocktail party, the bar should be set separately from buffet traffic.

THE BUFFET TABLE

Showpieces, including ice and tallow sculptures, beautifully garnished platters, highly polished silver chafers, elegant linens, and carefully placed flowers and candles, can play a part in making a buffet look spectacular and inviting (see Culinary Showmanship in Chapter 15). Ease of service is an equally important consideration. The number and/or position of buffet tables is determined by the size of the crowd, the scope of the menu, and the type of service involved.

For a small and casual event, one table set with buffet foods can be arranged against one wall of a room. In a home setting, a kitchen buffet can be arranged, with guests being served directly from the stove top or counters. Dinner plates should be available at the beginning of the line, and each item with its serving utensil should be laid out attractively down the length of the table, with cold or room-temperature foods first, then hot. Individual cutlery (perhaps wrapped in a large napkin), butter, and bread or rolls should be at the other end or at a separate side table. As an alternate and more elegant method, where proper tables are available, each place setting can be laid with cutlery, napkins and glasses and the tables set with butter, salt and pepper, and so on.

For a larger group, two identical buffets can be set in different parts of the room to expedite service. Or a double buffet, with matching platters of foods set from both ends to the middle, allows two lines of guests to approach the buffet from either end. If the room allows, a double buffet can be set in the center of the room, and guests can approach from either side. These methods help to alleviate waiting lines.

When setting up and replenishing a buffet, the goal is to have food taste and appear at its best and be served at optimum temperature. To accomplish this, plan on replacing trays and chafer liners at regular intervals as food is consumed, rather than putting the total food quantities out at one time, whenever possible. This lets all the guests enjoy the abundance and freshness of a fully laid buffet, even when large crowds are involved. Guests who come along later in a buffet line should not face the dispiriting sight of devastated trays and almost-empty chafers. Appetizing refills or replacement trays are much more attractive, and also promote food safety.

SERVING STAFF

Service at the buffet is preferred by many caterers, since it lends an extra air of graciousness, provides for greater efficiency and order during service, helps to maintain a neater buffet, and is a great aid in portion control. Servers should be instructed to serve small or average-size portions (more, of course, at a guest's request), not to be stingy, but to help eliminate waste, make plates more attractive, and allow guests to sample all the offerings. One service person can usually handle serving two to three items. One carver at a carving board can serve two to three meats. For a station-to-station buffet, each station requires its own staff. For a self-serve buffet, one or two in the staff should be required to oversee the buffet, keep things tidy, and replenish dishes as needed.

Additional staff needs depend on the size of the crowd, the formality of the event, and the size of the room. Even for the smallest party, one staff person should retrieve used plates and be available to guests. In addition, where table seating is involved, one staff person per twenty-five to thirty guests (or two to three tables) should be assigned not only to clear plates, debris, and ashtrays but also to fill water glasses, replenish beverages, and tend to the comfort of the guests. For very large parties, especially when waitstaff is involved in serving wine or other beverages, one busperson should act as assistant to every two staffers. In addition, even though timing for buffet service is less hectic than for a cocktail party, and less precise than for a sit-down dinner, a party of any significant size should always have a maître d' or some sort of floor manager to oversee the party flow. The larger the crowd and the more complex the service, the more management is needed.

The number of kitchen staff is dictated by the size and complexity of the menu and the anticipated number of refills required. As with all large events, where facilities permit, a kitchen helper, to clear and either wash or repack used trays, plates, cutlery, and glasses, is a useful addition.

THE BAR AND BEVERAGE SERVICE

At the outset, a decision must be made as to the type of beverages offered at a buffet. In some cases, only coffee, juice, or soft drinks are needed. In others, cocktails may precede the buffet, which may involve only wine or champagne or a particular prepared drink or drinks (mimosas or Bloody Marys at a brunch, e.g.). Other clients prefer a full open bar for an entire event, while others choose to offer only select wines and soft drinks (or mineral water or iced tea). Review the guidelines in Chapter 13 for wine and liquor service, bearing in mind that at a buffet, people prefer to drink wine or soft drinks with a meal. Thus, the amounts of hard liquor can be reduced, the supplies of wine and other beverages increased.

If possible, ice water should be available to guests, preferably at their tables, and servers or buspersons should refill as needed throughout the event, especially in a warm room or if dancing is involved. It is rude to leave guests panting with thirst, and refreshing options, other than alcohol, are a good idea from both a practical and legal standpoint.

Where the seating is structured, beverage service can be handled butler-style, rather than having guests constantly going to the bar for their drinks. When wines have been selected for dinner service, a server (or bartenders or wine stewards) can circulate and pour white or red wine to guests at each table. In general, one such staff member can pour for four tables (or about thirty-five to forty people), since groups seat themselves at different times.

Some clients opt for a rolling bar service, which works well if the room allows sufficient space for easy movement. Another option, which reduces the need for staff, is to place bottles of wine and pitchers of ice water on each table for guests to serve themselves. In casual settings, even carafes or pitchers of soft drinks can be placed on large tables. In some regions and settings, the placement of bottles of liquor and setups on tables, along with pitchers of beer, is acceptable. If this practice is used, be certain that ice is replenished and that beer is ice cold and not allowed to go flat.

In some instances, especially at holiday or summer parties, punches, with or without alcohol, are offered. Most of these can seem too sweet with a full meal, so other options should certainly be available to guests. In rustic or outdoor settings, it can be fun to offer beer tapped from kegs or bottles or cans of beer and soft drinks in tubs of ice. For breakfast and brunches, coffee, tea, and juice may be the beverages of choice, and a sufficient amount should be available to guests, either self-serve or served at tables.

Coffee and tea should be served whenever desserts are offered or when the dessert buffet is opened. This service can be made more special by offering specialty coffees, as well as after-dinner cognacs and cordials. This presentation is especially effective as the finish to a gala evening or a festive winter brunch. Whatever specialty glasses are needed for this service should be included in equipment lists.

EQUIPMENT

Of primary importance is the selection of the buffet table or tables. Whether rented or the client's own, they must be long or large enough to accommodate the planned buffet, but most important, they must be sturdy and able to safely sustain the weight of all the filled dishes, trays, chafers, and decorative pieces. This seems obvious, but a fragile table or one weak table leg or leaf can spell absolute disaster to a buffet. In addition, the table must stand rigid, and items placed on it must be secured, since both guests and servers may bump into and lean against a fully loaded table.

Serving plates, trays, and bowls should be attractive and sufficiently large and deep to be well filled without spillage. Chafers, hot trays, heat lamps, demonstration cooking apparatus, or other temperature-controlled serving pieces must be placed for both safety and convenience.

Replacement fuel must be in good supply, readily available, and handled with care. Servers should be reminded that fuel containers are very hot, even when almost empty, so caution should be used in replacing and discarding them. If electric wiring is used for heating appliances, it should first be secured to the table, and the remainder of the wire, which extends from the table to the power source, must be well secured: wide gaffer's tape works well to protect and secure electrical cords along floors or baseboards. Wires should never be run in guests' traffic lanes, and staff should be made aware of the placement of wires to avoid accidents. Advance planning should define the needs for power and determine whether or not the circuits are adequate to cover your needs. If cold foods are placed on beds of ice (or if ice sculptures are part of a display), assign a staff member to drain melting ice periodically to prevent dripping and spills.

Dinner plates provided for guests should be adequately sized and attractive. China, glass, or good-quality sturdy disposables may be used. When costing out a job, however, remember that top-of-the-line disposables can cost almost as much as rentals; still, they may be the appropriate choice for an outdoor setting, on a boat, or where the storage of bulk rentals presents a problem. For most buffets, allow 125 plates for each 100 guests; if multiple trips to the buffet are expected, and guests do not reuse their plates, provide at least 160 plates, more or less depending on dishwashing facilities and timing of the event. Cutlery follows the same amounts, unless tables are preset with silverware; in that case allow a 10 percent overage for replacements. If guests serve themselves or a cocktail hour is involved, one and one-half to two glasses per person should be provided; if tables are set, only 10 to 15 percent overage is needed. For dessert service, small plates, dessert forks, and spoons may be needed, along with cups and saucers (or only mugs) for hot beverage service, and additional snifters or pony glasses for cognacs and cordials, if these are offered.

At station-to-station buffets, some caterers prefer to supply each station with small plates for that station's foods, while others prefer to provide guests with large plates to fill as they move from station to station. The latter requires more repeat trips, so more plates must be provided.

Extra-large good-quality napkins are best for buffets, at least two per person for fabric, three to four per person for substantial paper goods. In a home setting, or one where full table seating is not provided, extra lap napkins for guests are a nice addition. Linens for guest tables, along with cloths (and skirting if desired) for buffet tables and bars, are needed. A few extra small cloths or replacement cloths for buffet tables should be on hand to recover tables or cover spills. Remember that servers at buffets need extra linens to cover drips or to handle hot chafers or trays. In addition, check the menu and be sure to include coffee urns or pots, sugars and creamers, gravy and sauceboats, carafes or pitchers, bus trays, salt and pepper shakers, ashtrays, and serving pieces such as ladles, spoons, meat forks, and tongs.

Chapter 15

The Seated Formal Meal

The seated meal, formally served, can take range from an intimate multicourse dinner for two to a banquet for hundreds of guests. The rhythm and pageantry of the service, the carefully orchestrated selection of both foods and wines, the glamorous room setting, and the specially chosen and arranged table appointments can raise such an event to the highest level of social entertainment.

While a seated formal meal is not inherently difficult to cater, it does require careful preplanning and timing, a well-balanced and executed menu, and the services of a well-trained staff. The menu does not necessarily have to be lavish and expensive, but it should be prepared and served with grace and style. Many other catering functions may be more complex and difficult to manage, but a seated formal meal is more carefully planned and closely scrutinized and so, in a sense, must be more perfect.

Banquet service is really just another term for the formal seated dinner, but it has come to mean a large event, like a wedding, bar mitzvah, dinner dance, or other function, especially those with ceremonies or speeches built into the evening. As a matter of fact, the American banquet has earned a sorry reputation for itself: public personalities and politicians have dubbed such functions the rubber-chicken circuit, often with good reason. Carelessly prepared and flavorless food, sloppy plating, and perfunctory service have no place in professional food service, and the off-premise caterer who can handle such functions with professionalism, care, and style garners ample rewards from this part of the business.

TYPES OF SERVICE

American Service

American, or preplated, service is the type wherein foods for each course are finished, portioned, and arranged on individual diner's plates in the kitchen and brought to the

130

table complete. A finished plate is placed before each guest, and sauces may be passed or served by a waiter, busperson, or captain, who spoons sauce at each guest's request.

This service is efficient for large groups but is the one most subject to the criticism mentioned earlier. Care must be taken to ensure that both guests and clients feel that it was chosen for its positive aspects rather than as the easy route. It is most effective when plates are of the proper temperature and when service in both kitchen and dining room is sufficient to deliver plates at optimum temperature to guests. American service guarantees that every plate is exactly the same, and beautifully arranged, and is much preferred for nouvelle-style cuisine.

Russian Service

Russian, or platter, service means that foods for each table (or a specified number of guests) is arranged on platters (or in bowls, tureens, etc.) in the kitchen. The platters can be artfully garnished—for example, slices of roast surrounded by fluted duchesse potatoes and clusters of turned vegetables. The platter is first presented to the table so guests can appreciate its beauty, then each diner is served portions onto his or her individual plate. This type of service requires skilled servers: the platters can be hot and heavy, and staff must be skilled in manipulating serving utensils gracefully so that service takes place without any drips or spills. The kitchen must prepare platters so that portions are easily defined and served, and items must be served so that each finished plate has a handsome and similar appearance. Sometimes, a second server follows the first with vegetables or other accompaniments. Again, sauces, if any, are brought around by another server as plates are completed.

French Service

French, tableside, or gueridon service is that in which foods are presented on hot carts or platters in a whole form (an entire roast, poached fish, etc.) and carved and portioned tableside. In some instances, foods are finished in the dining room (crepes are flamed, pasta sauces are finished over burners and tossed tableside). Plates may be sauced or otherwise garnished before service, or sauce may be passed as described for Russian service. This service can be quite showy, but it requires additional personnel and equipment and is often deemed too impractical or slow for many functions. It is more often used in restaurants or catering facilities than by the off-premise caterer.

This style can have a very grand impact, however, and may be effective for a smaller gourmet banquet or a formal home dinner. As an example, a whole saddle of lamb en croute may be presented to table, taken to a sideboard, and carved in view of guests. Whatever the case, one server (usually a skilled captain) handles the carving or tableside cooking, and servers assist and present a completed plate to each diner.

It is interesting to recall that a version of this service (sometimes called English Service) was the norm in earlier times in a home setting, where the maid brought the Sunday roast to the head of the table, and the man of the house carved and filled the plates, which were then served round the table. In many families, this is still a feature of holiday dinners.

Service Variations

For all types of service, it is acceptable practice to serve from the guest's left side and to clear from the guest's right. Service proceeds around a table in a counterclockwise motion; clearing is clockwise. European custom dictates both service and clearing from the guest's right, and this is sometimes requested by clients. All beverages are poured, and glasses placed and cleared, from the right. It is a consistent style and the ease and comfort of guests that make any service effective. Staff should be well trained to follow the prescribed method, but should exercise common sense and courtesy if awkward or cramped table placement requires some bending of the rules. Caution servers that the guests' convenience and comfort take priority over their own.

Both caterer and client should discuss the varying types of service, emphasizing the expense, complications, and time involved in each, and then determine which is appropriate. Remember that it is acceptable to combine types of service, if desired, perhaps serving a salad course preplated, an entrée with Russian service, and tableside service for the cheese or dessert course.

In some settings, especially at a large banquet or dinner-dance, it can be acceptable to have a first or appetizer course already at table when guests are seated. This is not strictly formal service, but it has come to be expected at certain functions. From the caterer's point of view, it is a time and labor saver, but to be effective, the item must look attractive and be at proper temperature. In most cases, this item is served in an ice coupe or is a room-temperature item that does not suffer on standing. Under no circumstances should a caterer jeopardize his or her reputation by serving a tepid soup or limp, lukewarm salad just to help a client economize on either time or labor.

Timing the Service

The timing of a formal dinner should be such that all guests are presented with each course at the same time or within minutes of each other. Naturally, in a vast dining room, with many tables, there must be some variance. However, guests at each table should be served at one time, each section of a large room should be very close in timing, the whole room as close as possible. Usually, this is accomplished by appointing captains to sections of the room, with a squad of servers who deliver trays or plates in unison to their appointed tables. (This procedure can become more complicated when there is a choice of entrée, as there often is at banquets. In this case, captains should plan a strategy for a section by having one waiter pick up the poultry orders for several tables while the other servers in the section pick up and serve the beef.)

A well-functioning kitchen, alert captain, and skilled servers can ensure that no table in any section is left abandoned and neglected, with guests still facing empty appetizer plates while all those around them are halfway through their next course. In very large rooms, or in sites where the kitchen is a trek from the dining room, enclosed hot or cold carts, holding racks of prepared plates, expedite service. Floor managers and/or kitchen runners can be very helpful in cueing both the kitchen and captains at a large function to keep service flowing smoothly.

Timing of the courses, in addition to being dependent on the kitchen and on the rate at which each course is consumed at table, should be coordinated with the formal proceedings of the function. Toasts, invocations, introductions, speeches, and such all have a planned schedule, which should be integrated into the course of an evening, so that neither interferes with the other. For example, before the scheduled speeches, all used dinner plates should be cleared and all water glasses filled, so staff is not working the room, distracting guests and speakers. A brief coordination meeting or notes transmitted between caterer and master of ceremonies guarantees that the entire evening flows gracefully.

Music, as well, should set a proper pace. Arrange with the orchestra leader or other musicians, after consultation with the client, to be certain that dance music is played between courses, rather than just when a hot entrée is served. Weddings and other ceremonial functions also require the services of the bandleader to introduce the bride and groom and their families, the cake-cutting ceremony, and the like. Such procedures require coordination between the caterer and bandleader (and usually the photographer) so that everything runs on schedule.

Another timing factor integral to formal service is the pouring of selected wines just before each appropriate course. This is sometimes handled by a sommelier, but may also be properly handled by a captain or server. The proper size and placement of glasses and the stylish pouring of fine wines should be skills mastered by the staff people assigned. Wines are most often poured from the bottles, with care taken so that guests can see the label; glasses are filled one-half full, and servers refill if necessary.

Unlike a restaurant setting, no cork and tasting procedure takes place, since the wines have been preselected by the client or host and uncorked by a wine steward before pouring. Sometimes, at wine tastings, or epicurean events, rare bottles are presented to the host, then uncorked, and the cork placed at table for other connoisseurs to inspect. When such rare wines are decanted, the procedure can also take place in view of guests since it is an event in itself. In most cases, however, if decanting of a wine is desirable, because of its age and sediment, that procedure is handled by a sommelier, usually off-stage. (Having an excellent wine shop or expert as a resource can be invaluable to a caterer by providing information and guidance on wine selection, as well as instruction in handling wines.) If other alcoholic beverages are served to guests during dinner (in some circles, this is expected), then either butler service from a service bar or rolling bars should be arranged.

MENU PLANNING

As in all other cases, the final selection of the menu depends on the expected variables, including budget, style, client preference, age and number of guests, and kitchen facilities. Moreover, for a seated formal meal, the balance of menu items and the sequence of courses are key to the success and enjoyment of the meal. Unlike a cocktail party or buffet, where guests may choose items at will, a seated meal must be planned so that each course pleases the palate in such a way that, while each item is enjoyed, the next can be anticipated and savored in its turn. A well-prepared formal meal builds to a crescendo with the main course, then tapers gently off to a sweet finish at the end of the meal. Guests should feel beautifully fed, not overstuffed or glutted with too many rich courses. Neither should they feel bored by repetition or confused by a series of intense and conflicting tastes. For the client and caterer who share the same appreciation for food and glamour, planning a harmonious menu can bring as much pleasure as that experienced by the guests who enjoy it.

While every possible banquet menu cannot be discussed here, certain pitfalls can be mentioned. In general, do not repeat a major ingredient from course to course—for example, no mushroom soup if mushrooms are one of the accompaniments to a main course. Do not repeat a prominent texture or method of preparation—that is, do not follow a cream soup with a crab in cream sauce or serve an appetizer en croute and a puff pastry dessert. Do not serve course after course dominated by the same look or form of plating—for example, fanned slices of melon, followed by slices of scallops or beef, and a dessert tart topped with sliced pears. In the same vein, the colors of the prepared foods, both within and among courses, should vary. As always, there are exceptions to these rules: sometimes a client has a theme in mind, such as an all-seafood dinner, a mushroom feast, or sometimes, in a whimsical vein, an all-golden dinner, in which case, all the rules are broken and special effort is made to reinforce a given notion or theme in every course.

Portions

Once the menu has been determined, certain guidelines may be used to judge portion amounts. The suggested amounts for each course in a multicourse meal are given below, with the understanding that variations can occur, depending on whether a preparation is particularly rich or lean (foie gras as compared to an ethereal seafood timbale) and whether an item has a unit size of its own, for example, a whole artichoke, squab, half-melon, or trout.

Appetizer: such as fruit cup or juice, 6 to 8 oz. (⅓ to ¼ L)

Soup: 6 to 8 oz. (⅓ to ¼ L)

Small or Fish Course: 3 to 6 oz. (100 to 200 g) depending on sauce or presentation

Pasta as a Small Course: 6 to 8 portions per dry pound (or per 450 g pkg.)

Intermezzo or Palate Refresher: 2 to 3 oz. scoop or ⅓ cup (80 ml)

Main Course or Entrée: 4 to 8 oz. (125 to 250 g) boneless meat or fish, depending on richness, or by units or parts of units, especially birds

Sauce for Entrée: 1 to 2 fl oz. (30 to 60 ml) per portion

Side Dishes: 2 oz. (60 ml) cooked starch, 4 fl oz. or ½ cup (60 g or ⅛ L) vegetable

Salad Course: 1 handful, less than 1 cup (¼ L), 2 oz. (60 ml) dressing. If plated or arranged, salad will vary

Cheese Course: about 3 oz. (100 g) total, of one or a selection, depending on type, with 1 tbls butter, bread or crackers if desired

For *desserts*, use the following guidelines for portions: one quart of mousse serves eight. An 8- to 10-inch cake serves eight to twelve people, depending on richness and composition (e.g., a cheesecake or dense chocolate torte might yield up to fourteen portions). A fragile fruit tart or galette of the same dimensions may serve only six to eight portions. Other desserts are served by unit—for example, one poached pear, one pastry swan, or one parfait. If secondary sweets, friandises, petit fours, or dessert truffles are served to the table after coffee, allow at least two per person.

Variations of Courses

Note that not all of the courses are served at every dinner or always in the above sequence. It is proper, from the classical standpoint, and the appreciation of wine, to defer salad service until the end of the meal because the acid component (vinegar, lemon) of many salad dressings conflicts with wine. However, in some regions of the United States, local practice dictates salad as an earlier or intermediate course.

The intermezzo, usually a granite or sorbet flavored with fruit or herbs, sometimes topped with a liqueur, has a practical purpose: that of relieving or cleansing the palate after two or more courses in preparation for the next wine and main course. Moreover, it has an air of glamour and luxury that is most appreciated by clients and guests alike. It is inexpensive to prepare and serve, so it is a simple way to add profit to a meal.

Suggested Menu

Following is a suggested menu for a formal seated winter dinner. This dinner is to be preceded by a thirty-minute champagne reception where caviar toasts and cheese straws have been served.

Game Consommé   Carrot and Leek Julienne
   (served from tureens into double-handled bouillon cups with liners)
                                                    Manzanilla Sherry

Field Greens with Hot Goat Cheese
   (a lukewarm salad, preplated in kitchen onto black salad plates)
                                                    White Burgundy or
                                                    California Chardonnay

Intermezzo of Grapefruit Sorbet   Crème de Cassis
   (one small scoop in champagne saucer, drizzled with cassis, mint leaf garnish, served on liner)

                                                    No Wine Service

Venison Scallops   Wild Game Sauce
      Root Vegetable Purée in Zucchini Boat
      Sautéed Forest Mushrooms
      (all preplated on hot dinner plate, sauce passed)

                                                    California Cabernet or
                                                    Estate-bottled Bordeaux

Cheese Board   L'Explorateur, Stilton, Chèvre
(Russian service, sweet butter and sliced sourdough baguette passed)
Continuation of red wine

Short pause in service, requested by client, who wishes to make a brief speech to guests

Vanilla Poached Pear   Chocolate Rum Sauce
(Pear preplated in kitchen, cold, on bed of crème anglaise, each pear garnished
with chocolate leaf, warm sauce passed at table)
Late-bottled Vintage Port

Café Filtre (regular and decaf)
Sweets: Chocolate Truffles   Tiny Palmiers
Crystallized Ginger   Stemmed Strawberries
(placed on table)
Port, Cognacs, Liqueurs

CULINARY SHOWMANSHIP

Banquets and formal dinners rank high in importance to clients, and caterers take the opportunity not only to promote future business but also to merchandise extras within a banquet by providing special culinary effects and flourishes. Unlike a buffet, where grand and sweeping gestures are called for, in towering showpieces, ice sculptures and the like, the formal dinner is the place for delicate and intricate detail that can be appreciated up close. Fine vegetable carving, detailed pastry shapes, delicate items in pulled and blown sugar, molded chocolate, and striated sauces all make an excellent impression at the dining table. Do not overdo in any one course, but take advantage of the chance to show off your skills or those of your staff.

In some areas, and especially for events such as weddings and bar mitzvahs, it has become the practice to serve certain courses of a banquet with great theatrical fanfare. A parade of waiters bearing skewers of flaming shashlik into a dim room, the flaming of crepes suzette by a chef in the center of the dance floor, or the presentation of the Viennese table (a grand buffet of desserts, sweets, and liqueurs) toward the end of an affair have all earned a place in certain circles. If they can be accomplished with polish (and safety), such additions to a banquet are welcomed by many clients.

BASIC REQUIREMENTS

Along with many possible extras, such as flowers and other decor, lighting, photography, music, and other audiovisual equipment, a seated dinner has the following basic requirements.

Tables and Chairs   Round tables (for eight to ten) provide the most comfortable and gracious seating, allow for easy conversation, and give a room its prettiest look. Oval or rectangular tables are sometimes chosen for space efficiency or used because they are available in a rented site. As always, tables should be checked to see that they are sturdy and level. Table pads or cushions let cloths hang better and reduce noise.

Chairs should be comfortable and sturdy; the cushioned ballroom type are most elegant, but are more expensive and take up a lot of storage space when rentals are delivered ahead. Very nice-quality folding chairs can be rented. Some facilities have stacking chairs, which are not quite so comfortable but are space efficient. Beware of chairs with splayed legs, as they can trip up serving staff and guests.

Linens For a formal dinner, the finest quality linens should always be used. They may be white or off-white, but they are also available in a wide range of colors to suit a client's taste or particular theme. Decor specialists are often consulted for unusual tablecloths, overcloths, or overdrapes available in a variety of special fabrics, patterns, and colors to produce particular effects. Napkins, to match or coordinate with cloths, can be folded in a decorative manner to lend interest to table settings.

China and Flatware Supplies should be double-checked against the final menu to be certain that the proper number and types of plates are available or have been ordered for rental. Remember that show or place plates are expected at a formal dinner (a place setting should never be bare) and that many courses may require liners as well. For flatware, a formal dinner requires fresh utensils for each course. In some cases, these are set all at once; in others, fresh utensils are placed by servers just before each course, so the number required has to be allotted accordingly. Check the menu to be certain that appropriate pieces are ordered (e.g., fish knives, steak knives, and soup and sauce spoons).

Crystal The finest quality colorless crystal should be used (unless, of course, a hostess has her own heirloom glasses, which may very well be tinted, etched, or rimmed), and fresh and appropriately sized glasses should be selected for each wine (don't forget water goblets). Glasses are always set out fully before dinner (unless table space absolutely prevents this, or for a wine tasting, which requires duplicate glasses for each course). A properly and fully set table, incidentally, traditionally serves as a clue to guests, who can read the items to determine the number and types of expected courses and wines and thus pace their dining.

Serving Utensils Review the menu, floor plan, and predetermined style of service to determine the number and type of silver serving trays, platters, bowls, sauceboats, coffee pots, pitchers, and so on that is required at each station or for each table. Provide the proper serving utensils as well. A side buffet or other service station should always hold additional napkins and some extras in both guest silver and serving pieces in case something is dropped or misplaced. Bus, cocktail, or butler trays should also be ordered as needed.

Smoking and Ashtrays In many gourmet circles, as well as in the general population, guests normally refrain from smoking during a formal dinner. Following dinner, or with the service of coffee and after-dinner drinks, smoking (and sometimes the offering of fine cigars) is more acceptable. Of course, the caterer must take direction in this regard from both the client and local custom (and, of course, the safety regulations of a rented facility) and should pack or rent sufficient ashtrays so that tables can be serviced frequently and neatly.

Centerpieces Whether floral or otherwise, centerpieces should be shaped and positioned to enhance the overall look of the room and table but not to interfere with table settings, guests' comfort, or conversation. Experienced floral designers can achieve spectacular effects for table settings and are usually aware of these considerations. Bear in mind also that the enjoyment of delicately sauced foods and fine wines can be tainted if floral fragrance is overwhelming. Candles add particular charm to table settings, but they should be positioned so that their flames are well above eye level (tall tapers) or well below (multiple votive-type candles); in no case should candles ever be scented. Servers or buspersons should be cautioned to watch the condition of candles: sometimes air currents cause them to burn too rapidly, and they may threaten to ignite part of a centerpiece.

Special Printing Menus, place cards, and book or box matches can be printed to good effect, in calligraphy, for example. Table numbers, used to assist in banquet seating, should be removed as soon as all guests find their places and before any wine or food is served.

STAFF

The menu, the number and complexity of courses, and the chosen type of service determine the needs for kitchen staff for a formal meal. Remember the overriding consideration that, as much as possible, every guest should receive each course in prime and timely condition, so plan staff accordingly. As mentioned earlier, temperature-controlled carts and runners, an expeditor, and captains can assist the kitchen as well as the dining room in achieving flawless service.

For the dining room, use the following guidelines:

- American service: One server for every two tables, to a maximum of twenty guests total.

- Russian service: One server for every ten guests or a team of two servers for every two to three tables, depending on the complexity of items to be served.

- French service: Two servers for every two to three tables, to a maximum of thirty guests. This assumes a captain to carve.

In all cases, where the number of guests exceeds thirty or the number of tables is more than six (or in any case where the dining room is difficult to view as a whole), assign one captain for every four to six tables. This provision allows for the experience and skill of the waitstaff and for the type of service involved.

A busperson should be able to adequately assist in service for two to three tables, depending on the number of guests and on whether he or she is also involved in passing any sauces. Also take into account the physical distance from the tables to the kitchen or used-plate area. A sommelier can pour for every two to three tables, or up to thirty guests.

Dressing the Staff   The more formal the event, the more dignified the dress required. Some caterers require staff to wear black tie at all times; others have some version of a formal uniform. There are some who favor distinctive uniforms for each level of staff, to differentiate one from the other. This is not absolutely necessary but is useful, especially at very large banquets. Many caterers have all serving staff wear white gloves; this not only has an elegant and pristine look but also protects servers' hands from the heat of trays. Have extra sets of gloves on hand, and be certain that staff is comfortable using serving utensils with gloved hands.

Chapter 16

Traditional Ceremonies and Celebrations

Weddings, bar and bas mitzvahs, anniversary celebrations, and other religious and family holidays are associated with traditional foods and honored rituals that underline their importance to a family, religious, or ethnic group. Other ceremonial or official events, such as debutante cotillions, diplomatic receptions, and awards banquets or government inaugurals, may all require some level of formal staging, seating, timing, and knowledge of tradition and protocol. While these functions may take the form of any of the general categories of events discussed so far, there may be special matters of etiquette and certain required or expected menu items, ceremonial foods, or procedures that a caterer must observe or provide to properly serve clients.

So many fine points are involved in all of these functions that a mere chapter cannot provide detailed information. As mentioned earlier, however, the off-premise caterer is expected to be an expert on all forms of entertaining. To achieve this expertise, begin with one or two complete etiquette books. Many books have been written about weddings alone, and they are excellent sources of information and ideas. A temple, rabbi, diocesan headquarters, member of the clergy, or mosque can provide guidance on religious ceremonies and traditions. For the fine points of protocol, our own government or foreign embassies are happy to provide information to the interested professional (see Appendix for recommended readings). This chapter provides an overview of such functions and some guidelines for handling such events.

WEDDINGS

Styles have changed over the years, and probably will continue to do so. In the 1960s and 1970s, weddings took place underwater, in the air, in forest groves, and on water skis, but the most recent trend appears to be a return to the more traditional and

140

romantic style of wedding. Since the late 1980s, as a matter of fact, some modern couples have become so nostalgic in planning their weddings that they have been more old-fashioned than their parents were. Remember that wedding consultants, who specialize only in the planning of these events, are tuned in to the latest trends and touches and can be an invaluable aid to a caterer.

Some wedding details to be mindful of are as follows:

- Be aware when planning the wedding that such items as specially designed invitations, place cards done in calligraphy, engraved or novel wedding favors, or boxes of groom's cake may be among the extras requested by a bride.

- Determine whether the ceremony will take place on site, either in a chapel or under a chuppah, or be a simple civil ceremony. Or will guests come from a church or temple directly to the reception?

- Many brides envision fantasy decor, best referred to a designer.

- The plain white wedding cake has lost favor: chocolate, carrot, or other unusual flavor may be preferred, usually frosted in white or a pastel shade and often garnished with fresh or intricate pastillage flowers.

- Will there be a receiving line? If so, confirm the proper order with a good etiquette book (see the Appendix), especially where divorced and remarried parents or children from prior marriages are concerned.

- Some planned ceremonies require coordination with the band or orchestra, especially for the introduction of the bridal party, the couple's first dance, dance of bride with father, groom with mother, and so on.

- Will there be a bridal table or special family tables?

- Schedule the best man's toast. Will there be any other toasts?

- Coordinate the cake-cutting ceremony with both the photographer and the band. Will the bride throw her bouquet? Do the bride and groom want to have a garter throwing?

- Will there be any videotaping (or viewing) or photography session that might interfere with timing of service?

ANNIVERSARIES

Significant wedding anniversaries (usually the twenty-fifth, fortieth, or fiftieth) are quite often celebrated with the same extravagance as weddings. A caterer can add extra interest by suggesting some of the following:

- Hold a ceremony for the anniversary couple to renew their vows or to receive a blessing by their clergyman.

- A bridal table with members of the original bridal party or the immediate family, along with special toasts, tributes, and speeches by these people, can lend a special touch.

- The orchestra should be informed in advance of the couple's wedding song or favorite tunes, and the couple may dance to the "Anniversary Waltz" or to a medley of tunes from the year of their marriage.

- Old wedding photos, a wedding album, or a video collage of the key events in their married life can be presented, perhaps narrated by one of the couple's children or grandchildren.

- A cake ceremony and nostalgic favors should be offered, perhaps as a gift from the caterer.

- The decor and linens can duplicate the couple's original wedding colors or celebrate the particular milestone (silver, gold, ruby, etc.) involved.

BAR AND BAS MITZVAHS

A nontraditional, or more casual, celebration of a bar or bas mitzvah is described in Chapter 19, and these events can take any form the client desires, but certain factors are constant:

- The menu and setting are lavish and extravagant, as this is a most important event in a young Jewish person's life and a time of great joy and pride for the family.

- Emphasis is placed on the celebrant's tastes in entertainment and food, since young friends make up part of the guest list. Usually, a separate table or area is devoted solely to the enjoyment and entertainment of the youngsters.

- A ceremonial blessing and sharing of the challah bread officially signals the start of the banquet. In most cases, a grandparent or cherished elder relative or friend takes part in this ceremony with the celebrant.

- A candle-lighting ceremony takes place, with honored relatives and friends being called up individually or in couples or groups to light one of the fourteen candles on the cake. This is a token of great respect to those so honored and captivates the attention of the room. Finally, the celebrant lights the fourteenth candle to much applause. Then the cake is cut and distributed to guests.

- The menu usually includes some special favorites of the young guest of honor, as well as traditional Jewish foods such as gefilte fish, lox, sturgeon, potato pancakes, chopped liver, stuffed derma, or other favorites.

FAMILY AND RELIGIOUS HOLIDAYS

In today's busy world, it is not unusual for a caterer to prepare and serve buffets or dinners for family holidays. Special menus and decor should be developed for Thanksgiving, Christmas, Easter, Passover, Rosh Hashanah, and Chanukah. Some other ethnic groups have the following food traditions for holidays: Italians and Greeks, for example, celebrate Christmas Eve with an all-seafood feast; the French always feature their bûche de Nöel for Christmas and pancakes for Mardi Gras; Hispanics celebrate

Twelfth Night or Three Kings every January 6; the British celebrate Boxing Day December 26.

For regular clients, a caterer might research and develop special holiday menus, such as a Dickens Christmas, Scandinavian Yule, or Russian Easter, to add new interest. A look through ethnic and regional cookbooks brings more ideas to light and provides a caterer with that something different to offer clients. Innovation is fun, but do bear in mind that family celebrations can involve guests of a variety of ages and tastes, so some comforting, traditional foods should also be included.

DEBUTANTE COTILLIONS

These are formal dances or balls, usually preceded by cocktails or a champagne reception and/or followed by a late supper or dessert buffet. The highlight of the evening is the presentation of a group of young women to society. The ceremony varies depending on the traditions of the organization hosting the event. This is often a religious, fraternal, or civic association, but may involve a member or representative of a royal family or a member of the diplomatic corps—in effect, whatever circle of society the young woman is about to enter.

The details may vary, but generally, each of the young women (usually wearing elaborate white ball gowns) is introduced and makes her entrance to a stage, runway, or spotlit point on the dance floor or descending a staircase. She may be carrying or be presented with flowers and is met by a bachelor escort, an acquaintance, a military officer, or a junior member of the given organization. She then executes a deep curtsy, either to the assemblage or to the honored host—perhaps the Cardinal, a member of a royal family, or some other dignitary.

Sometimes, the entire group of young women then participates in a group ceremony, either reciting a verse or pledge, singing a hymn, or taking part in a candlelight procession. Once the ceremony has taken place and all the debutantes have been presented, the function proceeds with dancing, dining, or whatever is planned.

DIPLOMATIC RECEPTIONS, INAUGURALS, AND AWARDS BANQUETS

These events may take any form, from champagne reception, tea, buffet, to banquet. The watchpoints, however, are the protocol and staged ceremonies involved. Receiving lines must be structured with strict attention to protocol; seating also follows status and rank to the finest degree. If awards, swearing-ins, speeches, presentations, initiations, or inductions are involved, the timing and staging should be well coordinated will all participants so that the proceedings are flawless. Close consultation with the client or the officiating body, embassy, or society representative clarifies all details and ensures that the proper regimen is followed.

KOSHER AND KOSHER-STYLE CATERING

These are two different entities. Kosher-style catering can be undertaken by any caterer who wishes to cultivate a Jewish (but not strictly religious) clientele. It merely involves the preparation and serving of traditional Jewish foods and an understanding of the holidays and ceremonies celebrated by this group of clients.

True kosher catering, however, is a very specialized field. It requires the setup and maintenance of a strictly kosher kitchen, in which all equipment, utensils, and serviceware are maintained separate and apart from any other use. The presence of a rabbi (or rabbinical authority) is required to maintain the strictest supervision over all food purchasing, preparation, and handling, as well as to oversee the maintenance of the premises according to Jewish dietary law.

If an off-premise caterer wishes to specialize in kosher catering, he should do so with the knowledge that this is a serious responsibility that involves a real commitment of resources (multiple sets of china and silverware, for instance, must be purchased and maintained). He should be prepared to conscientiously and scrupulously adhere to all the requirements of such an endeavor (see the Appendix for books to refer to for kosher catering).

OTHER CUSTOMS AND DIETARY RULES

Various cultures have strong cultural traditions and proscriptions surrounding food and dining, and if a caterer does business in an international community, she may have occasion to serve such a clientele. Muslims, for example, eschew not only all pork products but also alcohol. Other cultures have taboos against certain foods or the handling of foods. Before planning a function for any group whose customs are unfamiliar, contact the embassy or legation of the country involved to be briefed on proper menus and procedures. The state department, department of protocol, or the United Nations can provide information or advice as well.

Chapter 17

The Working Lunch

Many corporate clients are beginning to favor the concept of the in-house working lunch. It provides convenience, efficiency, the comfort of one's own turf, and security, allowing businesses to feed staff or host clients and associates in an office setting, without interrupting the flow of a meeting or unduly disrupting the business day. Since the IRS began to look more closely at expense accounts that reflected expensive restaurant lunches, companies have found the catered business lunch, and its easier acceptance by tax authorities, appealing. In addition to these advantages is the added benefit of controlling both the tone and cost of such a meeting and the convenience of having access to one's own staff and equipment should a need for those services arise during a meeting.

Many caterers have successfully exploited this phenomenon and made it a core of their business; others have found that the corporate clientele they cultivate for other events (such as company banquets and holiday parties) have made the in-office business lunch a necessary part of their service. Whether this meal is boxed, plattered, self-serve, or course-served, it has some built-in requirements: delivery and timing must be exact; efficiency in proposal, planning, and service is expected; and an appropriate mood and style, usually a neutral one of restraint and good taste, must be maintained so that the food and its service does not intrude on the business being conducted during the meal.

The working lunch presents other challenges to the off-premise caterer as well: an office setting usually offers little in the way of food preparation facilities; delivery can be difficult, either to a remote plant or to a congested downtown area at midday, for example; and the whole catering process must be managed in a discreet and unobtrusive way, so that the lunch in the chairman's suite does not cause upheaval of the entire office staff. General strategies for planning and conducting the working lunch are offered here, along with some possible scenarios and suggested solutions.

145

THE BUSINESS CLIENT MEETING

This meeting may take place with the executive in charge or with a secretary, office manager, or other administrator. Such meetings may be conducted over the phone if it is repeat business following a previous office visit. When dealing with corporate clientele, it is especially important to maintain an efficient tone and businesslike attitude. Unlike a client planning a home entertainment event or an organization or business planning a large-scale function, the functions under discussion here are requests for simple and practical feeding needs and should be met directly and in a straightforward manner. Businesses have a budget amount in mind for such events, and the caterer cultivating a corporate lunch business should be careful to adhere to it as closely as possible.

It may be possible for a caterer to lay the groundwork for continuing repeat business by bringing along several menus for meals that can be ordered only a day (or a few hours) ahead to provide the client with an easy answer to last-minute feeding crises. Once the caterer has visited and inspected the premises, she can set a fixed price for execution and delivery, adding on the food-only price of the selected menu. The caterer is thus assured of her expected profit, and the client can control his expenditure by selecting a particular meal. If the off-premise caterer makes the process this simple and convenient, she can be assured of frequent business.

In many cases, such a steady relationship develops between a company and caterer that the company does not look to the competition for any of its catering needs. The caterer may find herself not only handling executive lunches but also employee entertainments, staff feeding, and the private functions of company officers as well.

LOGISTICS AND OVERALL PLANNING

A complete site inspection (see Figure 10–1) is an important starting point in planning a working lunch, since office buildings can have an unpredictable range of food facilities, ranging from the completely equipped executive dining room/kitchen to nothing more than a coffee machine in a corridor and a water source in a janitor's closet or restroom. Once a good inspection is complete, you know the job is either as easy as cooking lunch in your own kitchen or filled with seemingly insurmountable inconveniences. Make special note of power sources, circuits, and such: most modern offices have ample power, but they are also filled with a variety of business machines that may draw heavily on that source. Be especially cautious of computer, modem, and FAX areas, which can be interconnected to various other networks and may be dependent on uninterrupted power flow. If the office manager is not conversant with the system, check with the building manager or superintendent as you make your inspection or soon after.

First, establish where the meal will be served and to whom and what menu items require either cooking, chilling, or reheating. Then go about scouting a suitable location for a prep area and kitchen setup if no permanent facility exists. Depending on the client's request, the meal may involve a simple drop-off of prepared platters or individual meals (see Chapter 20 for suggestions on boxed meals). Or a client may request a formally served seated lunch for important board members, and a caterer may be asked to pull out all the stops, even if this means cooking a meal with no kitchen.

THE TEMPORARY, BORROWED, OR NONEXISTENT KITCHEN

In some instances, a caterer may have no choice but to create a temporary kitchen, perhaps in a mail room or back office, bringing in work tables, appliances, coffeemakers, and so on to create a workable cooking setting. In other cases, a kitchen (or approximation of a kitchen) may exist elsewhere in the office or building, and the caterer may arrange to borrow all or part of the facility as a work space. This may be part of a company cafeteria located on another floor or an employee lunchroom, equipped with a coffee machine, microwave, and hot plate or toaster oven. In another possible situation, not only will no kitchen exist but also cooking (other than a coffee machine or microwave) will not be permitted. (In such circumstances you will have to plan a menu of chilled or room-temperature items [a Cold Knife and Fork Lunch or Light Elegant Buffet require no on-site cooking], or reheat one or two items in the microwave.)

MENU PLANNING

Whatever the available facilities, the caterer must draw upon his imagination and versatility to plan an attractive menu that works within the restrictions of the setting. Other factors should also be considered when devising corporate luncheon menus. For instance, be sure to determine just how much and what kind of work will take place during the meal. If a true working lunch is planned, with spreadsheets, files, and lap-tops on the table along with the plates, plan food choices that are easy to eat, nongreasy or drippy, and require only the hand or a fork. If the meal is a relaxing break in the middle of a monthly meeting or seminar, then an attractive buffet, which allows guests to move around, socialize, and be amused and distracted by the activity of making food selections, is a good choice. If, however, this is to be a talking lunch — negotiating a deal or pitching an account — then a served seated meal would be most impressive and appropriate. When the menu is selected with these factors in mind, then the amount of service, type of serviceware, and other embellishments become obvious.

Remember that food preferences among many of today's executives run to healthful low-cholesterol, low-salt choices, so a variety of light, attractive meals should be part of the corporate caterer's repertoire. Usually, little or no alcohol is served at working lunches, possibly only a glass of wine or a prelunch dry sherry. Some businesspeople prefer to serve basic and traditional foods, with no exotic items or fancy touches. Others, especially those involved in glamour industries, share very current or avant garde food tastes with their associates and want the latest trends in foods.

A wide selection of menus offered to a client at an initial meeting illustrates the caterer's diversity and flexibility. Sometimes executives customize a menu to the expected tastes of their guests; others may order the same meal, changing only with the seasons, and even then very little. Determine whether there should be choices within a menu, or whether a single, predetermined plate should be served. Once the facilities and client's needs, tastes, and budget have been determined, a menu can be successfully agreed upon.

Suggested Menus

Some suggested menus, of varying cost, formality, and style appear below. Most require very little in the way of last-minute heating or cooking, and in almost all cases, a good cooler, a coffee maker, and a microwave are sufficient.

Cold Knife and Fork Lunch: Can be dropped off, plattered, and ready to be self-served buffet style.

Barbecued or Lemony Grilled Chicken Breasts
Carrot and Celeriac Salad/Six-Bean Salad
Pumpkin Cloverleaf Rolls/Butter
Lemon Cheesecake Squares/Applesauce Cookies
Sodas/Coffee/Milk

Cold Boxed Lunch/No Utensils: Can be dropped off.

Assorted Small Sandwiches/Deviled Eggs
Cherry Tomatoes/Vegetable Sticks
Bourbon Cake/Brownie/Tangerine
(Office provides soft drinks and coffee)

Light, Elegant Buffet/Full Table Setting: Server sets up, assists, serves beverages.

Chilled Summer Pea Soup
Cold Poached Salmon Fillets/Dilled Cucumbers
Whole-grain Rolls
Lemon Sorbet/Fresh Fruit Sauce
Iced Tea/Mineral Water/Coffee

Plated, Served Hot Lunch: Needs some cooking.

Papaya and Honeydew Slices/Prosciutto
Baby Florentine Lamb Chops
Roasted Peppers, Broccoli Florets
Grapes/Strawberries/Assorted Cookies
White or Red Wine/Espresso

Chapter 18

The Tea Party

The tea party is an old-fashioned idea that is currently very popular. A tea is a British tradition, wherein a late afternoon minimeal of dainty sandwiches and fancy cakes provides refreshment after a day's activities, restores good humor, and appeases the appetite until later dinner or the evening's social whirl.

Teas are held in the late afternoon, between the hours of 3 P.M. and 6 P.M. They can be served as the refreshment for a committee meeting, gallery opening, fashion show, or following a matinee performance of a cultural event. A tea is often an economical and charming way to celebrate a special event such as a small family wedding, a christening, a birthday, or a class or club reunion. In addition, since teas have an old-fashioned and elegant flavor, signaling good breeding and appreciation of social niceties, teas are often the entertaining form of choice in diplomatic and political circles. Tea dances, traditionally held on Sunday afternoons, may extend a bit longer and usually comprise more than tea as a beverage, perhaps a punch, sparkling wine, sherries, or a hard liquor bar.

The format for a tea is similar to that for a cocktail party since the food served is almost always of the finger variety, seating can be spotty and casual, and much mingling and socializing takes place. The needs for service are about the same, even less if items are arranged for self-service on a buffet rather than passed.

THE TEA SERVICE

Well-made, steeped tea or a variety of different teas must be properly served. The role of pouring tea was traditionally held by the hostess, sometimes with a friend chosen to assist. Today, some hostesses still choose to pour, but that role is often taken over by a server. In some instances, at very large, public events, large urns or samovars are set out at a tea table, with cups and saucers, sugar, milk, and lemon provided, so that guests can serve themselves. This method is quite workable if care is taken that the brew remains hot and delicious, and the table is easily accessible and kept well stocked and neat in appearance.

If possible, arrangements should be made for tea to be poured. It is a far more elegant method, and can be accomplished as follows.

Traditional Service   This service works well for small groups, less than twenty-five or thirty, or supplementary tea tables can be set up to serve parts of a larger group. Strong tea is prepared in the kitchen, allowed to steep, covered, in its pot, then brought to the tea table along with an additional pot of scalding hot water (to dilute the tea for those who prefer a weaker brew). Tea is poured for each guest, who is then offered cold milk, sugar, and paper-thin slices of seeded lemon (and sometimes honey). The pots are successively replaced as needed, so each guest receives fresh, hot tea.

Russian Method   Workable for either a small or large crowd, this service requires preparing a very strong tea essence in advance. Some of this essence is poured into the teacup, followed by boiling water from the samovar, resulting in delicious, fresh-tasting tea.

Coffee

Coffee, while not traditional, is popular, so it is not uncommon to serve freshly brewed coffee, again from elegant silver pots (these are replenished from an urn in the kitchen) or from a handsome urn in the dining room. Half and half, or light cream, should be offered, along with sugars and sweeteners.

MAKING TEA

Loose tea leaves should be used whenever possible, either one generally popular type or another more exotic choice. Some caterers find it worthwhile to consult a good specialty tea shop to sample different brews, so they can offer appropriate choices to clients. Tea should be made in a pot and steeped for three to five minutes for best flavor.

First, warm the pot with boiling or very hot water. Add the leaves (one teaspoon per cup, one more for the pot), and then add fresh, boiling water. Cover, wrap in a cozy (or a thick cloth), and allow to steep. While the tea leaves naturally settle to the bottom of the pot, and a few in the cup are not offensive to true tea lovers, for catering service it is best to strain the steeped tea into a heated pot for pouring at table.

To prepare a tea essence, follow the same method, but use half again as much tea to water. The essence can be prepared ahead, strained, and allowed to cool until ready to use. Never boil or reheat tea because it will taste flat and bitter.

SETTING THE STAGE

A tea evokes feelings of elegance and a nostalgia for a more pampered, leisurely life, so it is an appropriate occasion to use highly polished silver, fine china teacups, linens, and lace. Rental agencies have handsome urns and samovars, along with silver teapots, sugars, creamers, and trays that give the setting an elegant look. If the tea is held at home, the host might have some heirloom pieces that should be shown off for the occasion. Pretty glass and china trays, cake stands, and pedestallike cookie servers all work very well.

Cups and saucers for tea should be bone china if possible (mixing patterns is fine), although Russians and eastern Europeans drink their tea from glasses, and that certainly is acceptable, if the style of the tea has that accent. Teaspoons are needed, along with small plates and forks, if some of the sweets served require them. Plates are convenient for finger foods, since guests can help themselves to a variety at one time. If a punch is to be served, a punch bowl and cups should be set out, preferably on a separate table. For other drink service, provide appropriate glassware and ice, if needed.

Table linens should be as pretty and elegant looking as possible. Rental companies are a good source, but additions, like lace overlays, embroidered cloths, flowery chintzes or pastel plaids or stripes can add interest to table settings. Antique linens are marvelous, as are embroidered or cutwork mats and runners on highly polished wood. For a simple tea, paper cocktail napkins are fine, but it is nicer to use larger linen napkins if the budget allows. Guests appreciate having lap napkins as well, especially if a wide and rich assortment of food is served.

Flowers, as always, add a special touch to the setting. For teas, many designers favor garden bouquets or romantic nosegays to further enhance the old-fashioned theme. Candles provide a lovely atmosphere after sunset. A victorian theme is especially suited to teas, and a designer could be consulted for authentic touches of the era. Serving staff could be dressed as English butlers and maids.

At least one sturdy table is needed for tea service. For a small group, tea can be served from one end of the table, with sufficient space for the service and for cups and saucers. The rest of the table can be used for the display of foods, and small plates, forks, and napkins should be conveniently placed. If this table can be placed so guests can circulate around it, all the better. In a home setting, the dining room, with its table and accompanying sideboard or buffet, makes an ideal arrangement. Guests can then move into the living room or other rooms to socialize and enjoy their tea.

For a large group, it is sometimes more convenient to place the tea (and coffee) table separately, using one or more buffet tables for food service. As mentioned before, a punch, if served, is ideally placed on its own table, where guests can easily help themselves. If liquor or other beverages are served, either set up a bar or use butler service.

It is perfectly acceptable to pass some of the foods, butler-style, among the guests. This works very well with sandwiches, which stay fresher if passed from the kitchen or pantry rather than standing on a buffet a long time.

For a tea dance, the placement of food and beverages can be the same as discussed. The dance floor can be either in the same room, if large enough, or in an adjacent room. Music can be provided by a band or orchestra. In a small home setting, tapes can be used. For a tea that is not a dance, other music is optional—for example, subtle background music by a harpist, a string quartet, or pianist.

MENU PLANNING

The menu for a tea may be as simple or lavish as desired. The simplest tea should have at least three varieties of finger sandwiches and three to four cakes or hot breads, like crumpets or muffins. The cakes may be frosted or plain, layered or loaf types, or small pastries, tarts, and cookies may take the place of whole cakes. Berries or cut fruits are always welcome. For the crumpets, muffins, or tea breads, butter, honey, jams, and preserves should be served. Bowls of cream, custard, or fruit sauces may be served as topping for plain cakes or berries. All items should be arranged so that they look pretty and delicate.

Sandwiches may be very simple, just herb or compound butters spread on thin crustless bread, or they may contain heartier or more complex fillings. They may be simply arranged on trays or presented in a more spectacular way. In general, all breads should be thin sliced and of excellent quality. Most sandwiches keep well if they are first buttered before adding fillings. Prepared sandwiches stay fresher if covered with damp towels and then with plastic wrap. Refrigerate if the filling is perishable, or keep in a cool place. Some sandwiches can be made ahead, well wrapped, and frozen, but not those containing egg, raw tomato, cucumber, or watercress sprigs.

Check the recipe section (or your own collection) for bread or toast-based canapés that might supplement the following ideas.

Sandwiches

Some suggestions and instructions for tea party sandwiches follow:

Finely minced egg, tuna, chicken, or shrimp salad, spread on buttered white or whole wheat breads, crusts trimmed, cut into fingers or triangles.

Thin slices of ripe tomato, spread with a bit of avocado cream, on buttered whole wheat bread, crust trimmed, cut into triangles.

Wheat bread, spread with cream cheese, topped with wafers of salted and drained cucumber.

Herb butter, spread on thin slices of crustless white bread, rolled around a sprig of watercress, packed together tightly in a shallow pan. As they chill, they will hold their shape.

Party rye, spread with sweet mustard dill sauce, topped with a slice or curl of smoked salmon or gravlax, served open face.

Softened goat cheese, spread on thin-sliced rye or baguette, topped with nasturtium petals, capers, or olive slices.

Shrimp or shellfish butter, spread on thin slices of white bread, rolled, chilled, and sliced into pinwheels.

Tiny biscuits made with pumpkin bread dough, split and filled with cranberry chutney, onion jam, or smoked trout mousse.

Tiny buttermilk biscuits, split, buttered, filled with thin slices of ham or smoked turkey (or minced ham), heated, and served warm.

Cream cheese, blended with pesto, spread on baguette slices.

Very thin slices of rare roast beef or filet, placed either on buttered baguette slices or pumpernickel rounds, topped with horseradish cream and a dab of caviar.

Red caviar mousse, spread on crustless triangles of limpa bread.

Rye or pumpernickel squares, spread thickly with salted butter, thin slices of red radish arranged on top, cut into fingers, served open face.

Thin slices of fruit breads—banana, cranberry, or carrot—spread with honey or fruit butter. These breads can also be toasted and passed hot to guests, if desired.

Triple-decker sandwiches using alternating thin slices of white and wheat bread, spread with compatible fillings, crusts trimmed, cut into triangles, and served standing on end on tray.

Tiny croissants, split partway, filled with chicken or shrimp salad, and piled into a napkin-lined silver or vermeil basket, tucking a few flowers or leaves among them.

Sandwich Loaves

One- or two-pound pullman loaves, at least one day old, are thin-sliced horizontally, with the slices kept in order. The loaf is then reassembled, spreading each layer with complementary fillings, preferably of contrasting colors. The whole loaf is wrapped tightly and chilled. Trim the crusts and discard. Vertical slices can then be made and those slices either halved and served as is or cross-stacked and sliced into checkerboard squares. Alternately, the filled and trimmed loaf may be frosted with thinned, softened cream cheese and garnished and sliced like a cake.

Trim the crust from a fat, round loaf of dense bread. Cut horizontally into several layers. Fill and reassemble as above, using harmonious fillings. If using rye or other attractive grain bread, the loaf may be left plain. Otherwise, frost as above, garnishing with herbs, olives, or other choice, and slice as a layer cake.

Hollow out long, round baguette-type loaves, using a sharpening steel or end of a wooden spoon. Remove as much of the inside as possible, leaving the crust intact. For very long loaves, cut into sections. Pack the insides either with pâté, seasoned liverwurst, or deviled ham. Wrap tightly and chill, then cut into thin, straight or diagonal slices.

Select small- or medium-sized brioche or pannetone. Starting from the bottom, make thin crosswise slices almost to the top (leave the crowns uncut). Spread the slices with compatible butters (caviar butter for the brioche, apricot or brandied butter for the pannetone). Reassemble and chill. Serve several of each together, leaving one or two whole, cutting the others into quarters or sixths.

Bread Baskets and Containers

Select an attractive pullman-type loaf, mark off a central basket handle, and cut down on either side of the handle, then across the top to either end to form a basket shape. Hollow out the insides of the bread, leaving an intact shell. The edges of the basket can be carved into points or scallops, if desired. This basket may be made permanent by spraying with several coats of lacquer or varnish (ask the advice of a craft shop or hardware store). Or it may be used as is within a few days (kept longer it may mold, or become so stale that it is brittle). When ready to serve, fill with finger sandwiches (not runny ones). It may be lined with a fancy napkin, or fresh herbs may be tucked along the sides for garnish.

To make a treasure chest, slice the top from a pullman loaf, hollow out the insides of both the bottom and the top. Lacquer or shellac the outsides of both parts. Using thin strips of gold lamé ribbon, glue on bands (like a pirate's chest), and use gold dragées to simulate studs or nails. Before serving, fill the chest to overflowing with an assortment of sandwiches (rolled, pinwheels, etc.). Attach the top to the base of the chest with skewers, leaving it in a partly open position. If you like you may use ropes of cheap pearls or gold chains hanging out of the chest here and there, or add gold foil-covered chocolates to enhance the look. The treasure chest can also be filled to the brim with ripe strawberries.

Select one rye and one pumpernickel loaf of similar size and shape. Slice a lid off the top of each. Carefully cut down to, but not through, the bottom crust, using the lid opening as a guide. Insert a very sharp long knife into the side of the loaf, just above the bottom crust, and swivel the knife back and forth to free the inner section of bread. Slice this bread thinly, and make sandwiches: shrimp or smoked salmon butter on the rye, herb butter or caper mayonnaise on the pumpernickel. Fill each hollowed bread case with the mixed sandwiches. To display, set on a wreath of greens, dill weed, or smilax.

Order or bake an extra-large topknot brioche. Cut around the rim of the top, following the scallops carefully, to remove a lid. Remove the insides, fill with sandwiches, one kind or an assortment, made on brioche bread. Close the lid to store. To serve, prop the lid off to the side of the filled brioches.

Other Finger Foods

Prepare bread croustades (if frozen, freshen in warm oven), fill with finely chopped salads, garnish each with tiny herb leaves.

Make choux paste, and form small round cream-puff or oblong eclair shapes. Fill with caviar mousse, chicken salad, deviled ham, and so forth. The tops of puffs may be coated with aspic, mayonnaise collé, or dark meat glaze to simulate the look of an icing on the puffs. These should be eaten within two hours of preparing if the filling is very moist.

Tiny choux puffs can be filled with foie gras mousse or a creamed mushroom or spinach filling (like that used for spanokopita; see recipe section). Poke a hole in the side of the puff and pipe in the filling. Heat before serving.

Stuffed eggs are popular. They may be the traditional deviled eggs, or the yolks may be blended or seasoned with any of the following: deviled ham, smoked salmon, finely minced herbs and mayonnaise, curry mayonnaise, or sour cream topped with a dab of caviar.

A caviar layer cake (see Recipe Index) is a very special centerpiece offering at a tea, especially for an important occasion like a wedding or other reception.

For more serious food, at the end of a tea dance, or when a hostess wants to provide something more like a meal, select one item, such as a baked sliced ham, smoked turkey, or one casserole dish. Offer an assortment of breads and spreads (or in the case of a casserole, steamed rice or bouchées). Whatever the food selection, it should be easily eaten with a fork only or as a sandwich.

Chapter 19

Theme Parties

Structuring entertaining around themes or concepts is always popular. It allows clients and caterers to turn any function into an extraordinary event. The theme can be manifested by simple strokes: a menu that evokes a particular cuisine or era, for example, a tempura party or a Victorian tea, or a setting such as a beach, sailing yacht, barnyard, or historic mansion. In many cases, the theme is carried through to every facet of the event, with the invitations, locale, decor, music, and a specially designed menu served by appropriately costumed waitstaff all reinforcing the selected fantasy.

Guests of all ages enjoy theme parties: The most sophisticated partygoers perk up when a charity organization announces a masked ball or safari adventure; business clients are intrigued when the introduction of a new product is celebrated with a space odyssey theme; guests at home parties are charmed and delighted when a hostess presents a Nutcracker Christmas or a backyard clambake; and children and youngsters are best entertained when everything from the napkins, food, entertainment, and take-home favors feature their favorite cartoon characters, sports activity, or rock stars and music.

Many off-premise caterers have made such party extravaganzas a specialty and have developed a resource network and events-planning skills that provide total party concepts and execution of the most detailed theme events to eager clients who are always looking for something different to impress and entertain their guests.

Themes are limited only by the imagination, and execution of the most outstanding events is restricted only by the budget, space, and capabilities of the caterer and staff. While every off-premise caterer does not undertake such events with the same frequency and scope as others, every caterer should understand the basics of theme entertaining, since it is a concept very much in popular demand.

This chapter discusses some suggestions for theme parties and offers general guidelines and ideas for their execution, with the hope that each caterer uses them only as a springboard for many successful events.

THEME: TROPICAL ISLANDS

Event:	Bar Mitzvah
Setting:	Swim Club Lounge, Deck, and Pool
Time:	Late Afternoon, Early Evening
Guests:	75 (55 adults; 20 children, Aged 6 to 17)
Format:	Expanded Cocktail Party/Station-to-Station Buffet

Overall Concept and Logistics

The client meeting establishes that the overall style of the party is informal, a very modern and lively nontraditional party with a special focus, naturally, on the bar mitzvah and his younger guests. Comfort, and some tradition, are to be upheld for the sake of the older guests and grandparents.

The layout of the club is a good one: There is an adequate lounge room that can be set with small tables and chairs to provide adequate seating for all of the adults and some of the children. The outdoor pool area is visible from the lounge, connected by sliding glass doors, and adjacent is a large deck or patio area with two built-in gas barbecues. Even though it is late summer, it is decided to tent part of the deck area in case of inclement weather and to install a large dance floor; some additional seating will be provided there as well. The kitchen of the club is small, but adequate, with an equipment room that can be used as a food pantry or work area for kitchen staff. Power supplies are good, and the club has built-in outdoor lighting.

Staff Three people from the pool staff have been retained to work the party. They will lifeguard the children during the water games and generally see to their comfort and safety throughout. In addition, one senior member will be available to the caterer's staff for any technical or superintendent functions. The caterer will provide a total of ten in staff, including two bartenders for the adults and one for the children's beverage service. The cook will supervise food prep both in the kitchen and at the cooking stations, assisted by two cook's helpers. The caterer will supervise the remaining servers, who will rotate positions from service of hors d'oeuvre, to buffet service and barbecue, to dessert buffet and ice cream hut.

Music Music will be provided by a disc jockey, who will bring in his own equipment and amplifiers; music for the cocktail period will be background tropical-island-type music; for the balance of the party, both rock and reggae for the kids interspersed with some oldies and some traditional music for the adults. The disc jockey will also handle announcements, such as the introduction of the guest of honor, provide a microphone for other speeches and blessings, and handle the cake ceremony introductions. A photographer will be hired to videotape highlights of the party and will do some posed portraits as well as candid stills.

Decor A decor designer is coordinating the theme, augmenting the many large plants in the club with potted palms, arrangements of tropical flowers, and a floating floral piece in a wading pool. The designer is also providing a few thatched-roof pieces for the bars, one or two food stations, and a large balloon arch over the pool; colored gels will be placed over some of the lights for a more festive effect. Hawaiian torches will be lit around the pool, both for effect and to ward off insects.

Dress To further enhance the theme, staff will wear Hawaiian shirts and white shorts or slacks; some of the women will wear sarong-type wraps, others opt for grass skirts; all will wear paper leis. Women will have flowers in their hair, while the men will have island straw hats. Lifeguards will wear the club's bright blue T-shirts so they can be easily identified. (Remind the hostess that the lifeguards and other club staff on duty, along with disc jockey and photographer, are to be provided with a meal.)

Brightly colored T-shirts (logoed [child's name]'s Wild Tribe) will be provided for all the youngsters. Fake coconut shells, filled with coconut candies, will be take-home favors. In addition, printed matches and paper napkins will be ordered.

Ceremony The general plan is to have all the guests, youngsters included, arrive from temple at one time and assemble in the main lounge area of the swim club. A large challah will be positioned on a decorated table in the center of the room. The young guests of the bar mitzvah are lined up behind the table, and each is presented with a flower lei by one of the servers. The grandparents and special honored guests are also assembled and all of the ladies given corsages of vanya orchids. Then, the bar mitzvah and his parents will enter with a flourish, and the ceremonial blessing and sharing of the challah will take place at that time.

Following this formal ceremony, the youngsters will change in the locker rooms and swim under the supervision of club staff, who have been retained as lifeguards for the event. The kids will participate in races, water balloon polo, and other swimming games for the duration of the cocktail period (about ninety minutes). Separate food and beverage service will be arranged in the kids' area as well.

The menu will begin with passed items, then progress to more substantial buffet station foods, including barbecued items. Near the end of the event, there will be the ceremonial candle lighting of the bar mitzvah cake, followed by a dessert buffet. Weather permitting, the cake ceremony will take place under the balloon arch near the pool, in full view of all guests; in inclement weather, the lounge will be used.

The Menu

The menu is planned with some concessions both to tradition and to the tastes of the kids. The hostess wants shrimp served as a choice for her non-Jewish guests.

Butler-passed:

Salmon Cornucopias   Ginger Poached Shrimp

Smoked Trout Canapés   Steamed Dumplings   Potato Pancakes

For the kids: Mini-pizzas, Beef Franks in Blankets

Cocktail centerpieces:

> Crudites with avocado cream and garlic herb dip
> Chicken Liver Mousse Mold, garnished with apple and onion slices

At one station (with server, carver):

> Smoked Fish Bar: Salmon, whitefish, sturgeon

At second station (with two fryers):

Lacy Bean Sprout Cakes	Coconut Shrimp	Chicken Wings
Tempura Vegetables	Fried Wontons	Beer Batter Fish Sticks

At third buffet station (after cocktails):

Szechuan Chicken	Sesame Noodles	Curried Rice Salad
Stir-fried Beef with Vegetables		Corned Beef with Pineapple

At barbecue (after cocktails):

> Chicken Sates   Sliced Steak   Fish Brochettes
> Barbecued Lamb Riblets   Mini-Burgers for the kids

Dessert buffet (served after cake ceremony and service):

Coconut Cookies	Chocolate Macadamia Tartlets	Fruit Mousse

> Tropical Fruit Display, with cut pineapple, papayas,
> mangoes, honeydew, canteloupe, watermelon, fresh coconut
> chunks, strawberries, kiwi, and star fruit,
> all lavishly arranged

There will be an ice cream hut, where ice creams and sherbets are served along with choices of fruit sauces, chocolate rum sauce, shredded coconut, and chopped macadamias. Guests make their own sundaes, with one or two servers to assist.

Beverages The adults will be served drinks from bars in both the lounge area of the club and at one end of the tented deck. These bars will offer choices of hard liquors, along with a semisweet white wine, piña coladas, mai tais, and pineapple juice and vodka offered as specialty drinks. Garnish fancy drinks with little umbrellas and skewered fruits.

The kids will have their own juice and soda bar, and their drinks can also be garnished with fruit and fancy umbrellas. (Some caterers serve kids mock cocktails, but today, with the elevated awareness of substance abuse, some people object to this practice on the grounds that it encourages a negative behavior; check with a client before planning such a feature.)

When the cake ceremony is completed, glasses of champagne (or an asti spumante) will be passed to all guests, so the bar mitzvah can be toasted for his birthday. At that point, he will make a thank-you speech to his family and guests. Coffee, tea, and after-dinner drinks will be offered to guests at dessert and through the end of the evening.

THEME: PLANTATION BRUNCH

Event:	Social Gathering of Committee
Setting:	Suburban Home of Committee Chair
Time:	10:30 A.M.–1 P.M., Early March
Guests:	32 Adults (Members and Spouses)
Format:	Simple Buffet, Some Service

Overall Concept and Logistics

The chair of the Winter Dance Committee hosts a brunch in her home to thank committee members for their time, congratulate them on success, and encourage participation for next year's event. The menu is hearty and a bit showy, as the group is very sociable and in a celebratory mood. The Southern Plantation theme is a preview of the theme planned for next year. Not incidentally, the caterer handling the event is proposing for that event as well.

While no actual meeting will take place during the event, the hostess will make an informal speech, and the treasurer will report on the proceeds of the past event. Guests will arrive promptly, probably between 10:30 and 10:45, and be offered drinks and a few nibbles. The buffet will be partly served, and seating at preset small tables will be in the family room and adjacent garden room.

Staff   One bartender and three staff to cover the dining room and kitchen will be needed. Caterer will attend in the kitchen to oversee the event. Only simple cooking is required: baking the eggs and the cornbread batter that has been prepared ahead and heating the stuffed mushrooms, biscuits, and croissants. The bartender will serve from the bar and then pour wine at tables as needed. One server will attend the buffet; one will attend guests and clear tables in each of the seating areas. At dessert, the buffet server will transfer to the dessert buffet, and one server (or bartender) will assist with coffee service at that time.

Decor   The hostess's garden room has pots of forced spring bulbs expected to bloom, which a florist will supplement if nature does not cooperate. Tiny vases of spring flowers will be placed on each set table, along with three small arrangements of spring flowers; one for the entrance foyer, one on the buffet, and one on the dessert table. Lighting, either natural or artificial, is sufficient as is. No photography or music is needed.

Bar and Beverages   White wine, mimosas, bellinis, planter's punch cocktails, and mint juleps will be offered for tastings, as samples for the next year's event. Mineral water should also be available along with plain orange juice. Coffee and tea will be available from the outset, as well as with dessert.

The Menu

As guests first arrive, cheese pennies and benne wafers are available for nibbles along with drinks.

Brunch Buffet

Eggs Baked in Tomatoes   Sherried Crab and Shrimp Bouchées

Wild Rice–Stuffed Mushrooms   Blanched Asparagus

Country Ham with Honey Mustard

Smoked Turkey with Cranberry Chutney

Creamy Souf*léd Cornbread

Hot Buttermilk Biscuits   Small Croissants   Sweet Butter

Dessert Buffet

Bourbon Bread Pudding   Blueberry Brunch Cake

Fresh Strawberries   Tiny Pecan Tarts   Poached Peaches

THEME: SCANDINAVIAN MIDWINTER PARTY

Event: Skating Party

Setting: Client's City Apartment

Time: Late afternoon through evening

Guests: 8 young couples

Format: Cocktail Buffet/Late Night Supper

Overall Concepts and Logistics

Friends will gather at the host's home late on a winter weekend afternoon. After cocktails and a hearty self-serve cocktail buffet, guests will depart to a local skating rink for about two hours of skating. When they return to the apartment, they will be greeted with hot drinks and enjoy a seated buffet supper. The dress is distinctly casual, but the setting for the room will be elegant. Provision must be made for snowy boots and other winter outerwear. The guests are all good close friends, so spirits will be high, and good food and cheerful service will be more appropriate than stiff, formal service.

Staff

Three staff will attend, one to serve drinks and wine as needed, one to assist in the kitchen with setup during cocktails and dinner, and one to handle the dining room during dinner, assisted as needed by other server. (When guests are gone skating, the staff will be able to reset the room to complete the preparations for supper.)

Decor

Birch branches, evergreens, plaid ribbons, bunches of dried juniper berries, and lots of candles set a cozy wintry scene. Lighting should be bright for cocktails, dimmed for supper.

Bar and Beverage

Cocktails include iced vodka, beer, and nonalcoholic dry cider. When guests return from skating, mulled wine, hot cider, and cups of game consommé with vegetable stick stirrers will be offered. For dinner, a red bordeaux, cabernet sauvignon, or zinfandel will be selected for service.

The Menu

For Cocktail Buffet

Gravlax with Sweet Mustard Dill Sauce

Smoked Trout Mousse   Herring and Beet Salad

Open-Face Sandwiches: Egg Salad and Onion,
Roast Beef with Horseradish Butter

Pumpernickel, Limpa, and Lefse Breads

For Supper Buffet

Norwegian Pot Roast   Sweet and Sour Red Cabbage

Roast Potatoes   Sautéed Brussels Sprouts

For Dessert

Chocolate Tart   Cherry Torte   Apple Galette

Gingered Pear Mousse

Coffee and Cognac

CHILDREN'S PARTIES

We live in a very child-oriented society. Parents who have delayed having their children until later in life have more money to spend on them and are willing to do it. Children who enjoy the parties they attend are good salespeople since they report to their parents and provide recommendations for their own upcoming events. In a sense, children are also a caterer's future clientele, so they comprise a market worth pursuing.

There are some special techniques involved in entertaining youngsters, and the word *entertain* plays a key role. Kids are not big on conversation, and they take little pleasure in just sitting around eating, no matter how wonderful the food. In general, young people need to be actively entertained and amused. The younger they are, the shorter their attention span, so the distractions and activities planned for them should come in short, exciting bursts.

As mentioned before, kids respond well to themes: they enjoy settings that feature familiar or favorite characters, things that are part of their world. They have the same standards for foods: familiar favorites, in sizes that are manageable and shapes that are funny or interesting, have the greatest appeal. Kids follow and exhaust trends with amazing speed, so keep current of what is "hot" in your area at a given time. In almost all cases, your client is a parent or family member, but be sure to get input from the young guest of honor or host if possible.

As far as entertainment and activities are concerned, remember that in addition to watching things like puppet shows, jugglers, and movies or videos, young kids enjoy funny surprises (clowns and magicians), being safely scared (a mock house of horrors), making noise (games and songs that include shouting, stomping, clapping), running around (outdoor games, races, sports), learning new things (face painting, card tricks, balloon sculpture, designing glitter T-shirts), and making a mess (food play, tie-dying, slime wars). Pre- and early adolescents like participation sports, playing video games, dancing (or watching each other dance), treasure or scavenger hunts, and living out fantasies (dressing in costumes, play-acting, making their own music video). The older the children, the more definite cues you receive: older adolescents know absolutely what they like and don't like.

Selecting food for a kid's party can easily go to an all-junk menu. This is all right with some parents (and with most kids), but you can sometimes add some healthful items, like vegetable sticks, peanut butter, tiny fruit muffins, frozen yogurt, pizza, raisins, trail mix, chicken wings, and fresh fruit.

Settings can run the gamut for such parties, with the following watchpoints:

- In an outdoor area, near a pool, lake, or beach, be certain to hire trained lifeguards and some babysitters to tend to kids' safety.

- In rented spaces, be sure that the lessor is prepared for kids and that the space utilized is free of hazards or damageable goods.

- In the home setting, use an area, like a family room or playroom if possible, and kid-proof it by removing breakables and generally clearing the area of things kids can trip on or over.

Young children especially need to burn off energy periodically, so physical activity, preferably outdoors, helps to defuse them.

What follows are two scenarios for young people's parties that might suit a caterer's needs.

Theme: Circus Fair

Event:	Family Birthday for Five-Year-Old
Setting:	Home with Patio, Lawn
Time:	12 Noon to 3:30 P.M.
Guests:	30 Children (aged 4 to 7), 25 Adults
Format:	Stationary Buffet for Adults, Station-to-Station Buffet for Kids

Overall Concept and Logistics

This is to be a lavish, showy party not only for the birthday child, her friends, and cousins but also for family members, neighbors, and friends. The parents have a large home, suitable for entertaining, with large patio and surrounding grounds. They are very liberal with the budget for the event. The caterer is told to "go all out." Grown-ups and kids will arrive at about the same time. Even though it is late springtime and the climate is balmy, a striped tent (with roll-down clear plastic sides, if needed) will be erected over the patio area.

Assuming the weather will be pleasant, the surrounding lawn will be used for games such as tag and sack races for the children (and probably some of the adults as well), a trampoline setup, and two tumblers who will put on a show and then teach the little ones simple tumbles.

The tent is to have fair booths (built at children's height) with games and refreshments. One corner of the tent is set with some chairs and floor cushions for adult and kids to watch a magic act, a juggler, and a clown show. A disc jockey will provide tapes of circus music, Americana, and children's sing-along songs. The children will all win prizes at the various booths and games and will be given loot bags when they leave.

The family room adjacent to the patio will have an adult bar (beer, wine spritzers, iced tea) and a buffet. A few cocktail-sized tables with chairs will be added to the room to supplement seating.

For the children's seating, patio furniture will be cleared to the garage. Permanent benches remain under the tent, for kids' seating if needed.

A videographer will be hired for the whole event. An uncle will take instant photos of all the kids to take home.

Disposables will be used throughout, with sturdy plastics for the adults, who will also use real cutlery. The kids need little more than tons of napkins, paper dishes or holders for their hot dogs and burgers, and paper cups. All should be ordered in bright colors or special circus motif.

Staff   For the adults, in the family room, one bartender and one server are needed to lay out the buffet, assist guests, and clear. Both are to be dressed in striped blazers, bow ties, and straw boaters.

Four teenagers have been hired (they are known to the caterer and client) to act as supervisors and/or babysitters. They are to wear red T-shirts and shorts or jeans, socks and sneakers. Two older cousins will tend the game booths.

Five more staff members will be needed to tend the various refreshment stands, and two more will be floaters to help with setup and cleanup. The caterer's event manager will be the ringmaster, appropriately dressed; other staff will wear various carnival or circus costumes or hats. A mime has been hired to greet guests and then circulate in both areas, doing his act improvisationally.

The Menu

For the adults, there will be the following self-serve buffet:

Chunky Tarragon Chicken Salad

Thin-Sliced Honey Baked Ham   Sliced Ripe Tomatoes

Old-Fashioned Potato and Egg Salad   Six-Bean Salad

Croissants   Rye Rolls   Mustards   Butter

For the kids, the food stands will be as follows:

> McSusy's: Serving small hot dogs and burgers, with fries and fixings
>
> The Melon Man: Serving small wedges of watermelon, paper cups filled with semifrozen grapes
>
> A Cotton Candy and Popcorn Machine
>
> A Soft-Freeze Ice Cream and/or Frozen Yogurt Machine (small cones, with sprinkles or dips)
>
> A Juice and Soda Bar

Birthday cake will be served to all.

Theme: Chef for the Day

Event:	Tenth Birthday
Setting:	Caterer's Kitchen or Large Home Kitchen
Time:	Saturday or Sunday Morning
Guests:	6 Nine-Year-Old Boys, 2 Sisters
Format:	A Cooking Class

Overall Concept and Logistics

Since Michael, the birthday boy, and many boys and girls his age, like to cook, plans are made for a cooking class. One or two cooks plus one extra staff person will be needed to help keep order and clean up. If the caterer's schedule allows, her kitchen will be used. If not, the mother has a large enough home kitchen to manage the event. The plan is to have all the kids arrive in the kitchen early. They will cook, have lunch and cake, and then go to a movie or sporting event, accompanied by another volunteer parent.

In preparation for the event, chef's hats are bought for each of the kids, and aprons, printed with their names, are ordered. In addition, cooking supplies are checked and extras set aside, so each chef will have the working materials needed. The night before (or several hours ahead), pizza dough is prepared and cold-proofed, so it will be ready to use. The kids will make a large batch of bread dough (egg or pumpkin are good choices) using quick-rising yeast. They will also learn to decorate a cake, using icing spatulas and pastry bags and tubes (a basic white buttercream will be made ahead). Then the plan calls for them each to shape their own pizzas and top them as they like. These will be baked for lunch. Soda will be their beverage.

For cooking, one or two work counters or tables and two ovens are needed. For eating, you need one table with chairs, a tablecloth (optional), paper plates and cups, knives and forks, and napkins. Provide extra side or hand towels for the kids to use while they work, extra pastry bags and tips (disposable bags are fine), a large mixing bowl for bread dough, and several small bowls for other ingredients.

The Cooking Class

When the kids arrive, they will be shown around the kitchen, given their hats and aprons, instructed to wash their hands, and assigned to work groups or places at their work tables. Michael will be the chief assistant chef, so he gets to read the recipes (all the kids can be given copies to take home).

The bread dough will be prepared first. It is all mixed in one large bowl, then divided into segments for the kids to knead. While the bread is being made, the cook can give instructions in breaking eggs, sifting flour, and weighing and mixing ingredients. The dough is set to rise, and the kids clean their work area.

While they wait for the dough to rise, they will discuss their cake-decorating ideas, tinting icing and selecting candy decorations. They can decorate one large sheet cake together or, better, small squares or layers individually. The cook first demonstrates how to frost the cake in plain white (or chocolate) icing, and the kids follow suit. Next the pastry bag is demonstrated, and the kids get help filling their own, then decorate their cakes. This will be hectic, but fun; some of the colors and decorations will be amazing. When the decorating is done, the cakes are set aside, and the work area and the kids are cleaned up.

The risen bread dough will be divided among all the guests, who are shown various ways to shape and braid dough. They glaze or egg wash the breads, sprinkling them with poppy, caraway, or sesame seeds. The breads are set aside for a short rise and then baked. Each guest gets to take home a completed bread, but a few extras should be made for immediate taste tests.

Pizza production will begin with the preparation of chosen toppings. The kids learn how to grate cheese and to use scissors to snip herbs and olives, and salami slices, for example. Then the pizza dough will be portioned out and instructions given in shaping and stretching the dough (there will surely be some flying dough during this session). Then everyone will finish their pizza with the sauce and toppings of their choice. While the pizzas bake, general cleanup takes place. As a finale, everyone will be seated at the table for pizza, soda, and birthday cake.

Chapter 20

Meals in a Box

The box lunch, brown bag meal, or lunch box has been with us for a long time. People from office workers to schoolchildren are expert consumers of this specialty, and the family picnic basket, taken to the beach or the park, is just a larger version of the same concept.

Takeout shops, delis, and fast-food restaurants base their business on supplying meals to go, and some off-premise caterers develop a secondary business with packaged meals, providing bulk orders from limited menus for delivery to offices, construction sites, film and video crews, schools, and other businesses. In addition to the additional revenue made by fully using your already operating kitchen and staff, developing a line of boxed meals has other advantages. Packaging either a simple sandwich or several courses of a meal in a portable container can provide a workable solution to feeding large groups in unwieldy or remote locations.

Boxed meals can range in style and complexity from a simple sandwich, piece of fruit, and a brownie to a multicourse meal, as beautifully packaged as the most luxurious gift basket, offered to formally clad guests at an elegant midnight supper. Whatever the style or setting, some basics are common to all.

CREATIVE PACKAGING

One of the beneficial results of the burgeoning of the fast-food industry is the enormous variety of individual or single-portion containers available from paper and packaging suppliers. It would be difficult to include a complete list, but such containers might include the following:

- Soup, coffee, or hot-drink containers with lids

- One-piece square or round hinged containers, in varying sizes for salads, sandwiches, or main dishes

167

- Shallow bowl-like containers with lids, for soups, pastas, puddings, side dishes, or salads
- Tiny lidded containers for sauces and condiments
- Foil dishes in varying sizes with crimped edges to secure clear plastic lids
- Classic Chinese food cardboard containers (usually with wire metal handles)
- Cake, pie, and cookie boxes

Paper suppliers also have a large array of boxes, bags, small shopping bags, and decorative boxes and meal containers in a variety of materials and colors. Available as well are rolled or precut foil or waxed wraps, cellophanes, stirrers, plastic utensils, and portioned spices and condiments, all of which are useful in completing a planned packaged meal.

Possibilities for containers are endless: glass and ceramic jars and bottles, such as those sold for canning, cosmetics, candy, jellies, etc.; tins and cans that might otherwise hold cookies, mints, crayons, or nuts; cardboard attaché cases; jewelry boxes or trays; baskets of varying shapes and sizes; plastic shoe and closet storage boxes; children's lunch boxes; old-fashioned worker's lunch pails; small vintage suitcases and train cases; small wooden crates; even coffee cans, cigar boxes, and shoe boxes can be recycled, painted, wrapped in paper or fabric, and made into innovative food packages. If you have trouble thinking of ideas, take a stroll through the local five and dime, novelty store, hardware store, notions department, toy store, and stationery and party goods store to get your imagination rolling.

Lest the term *meal in a box* seem too limiting, remember that the same meal can be packaged in a basket, sombrero, cowboy hat, calico bonnet, miniature trash can, corsage box, old-fashioned doctor's bag, tool box, sewing basket, hobo pouch, knapsack, dishpan, bicycle bag or baskets, fisherman's creel, briefcase, ice bucket, toiletries or cosmetic bag, bamboo steamer, saddlebag, duffel, flowerpot, colander, salad spinner, or sand pail. Fabric, ribbon, and notion stores can provide decorative or interesting wrapping in everything from plaid flannel to satin, chiffon, and lace. Buy (or have made) inexpensive hand and lap napkins in matching or coordinating colors and fabrics. Tie bunches of cookies, chocolate truffles, salted nuts, or silverware (real or otherwise) in cellophane, mylar, fabric, handkerchiefs, or scarves, and tie with ribbons, leather thongs, shoelaces, yarn, bandanas, measuring tapes, string ties, extension cords, licorice whips, upholstery trim, sweat bands, or elastic scrunchies (ponytail holders).

Naturally, such elaborate packaging can be time consuming to put together, but for the client who wants a special effect, it is well worth the added cost. The packaging may be relatively inexpensive or more luxurious items that guests may take with them as favors. Many corporations find that this keepsake aspect can serve as a marketing or advertising tool, if the item is emblazoned with a company logo or is, in fact, a product they manufacture or represent.

MENU PLANNING

The off-premise caterer has an advantage in the boxed-meal area, since so much of the food prepared for catering must be of the durable variety, whether for wholesome transport, easy eating, or holding quality for a buffet. It isn't even always necessary to think of fork-only or finger food (although that is the more common tack), since there are times when boxed or packaged meals are served to diners at fully set dining tables.

Meals may be conceived so that each package is totally self-contained, or the package may contain certain more durable food items, with the balance of the meal, perhaps a hot soup, ice cream, or beverage, served or passed.

Of course, hot items can be packed as well, either in insulated styrofoam-type containers soon before serving, or in reusable thermos-style containers. Chemical hot packs can be placed in the lining of the meal container to keep the contents warm. To keep foods cool in a package, you can use a tried-and-true mother's trick for chilling the contents of a child's lunch box: freeze a container of juice, pudding, or chilled soup, which provides proper chilling while it thaws in time for the meal. Or you can use frozen gel packs.

PRODUCTION METHODS

While every situation varies depending on the setting, menu, complexity of packaging, and delivery, the assembly of boxed meals is really nothing more than a standard production line. Work through the assembly of one package with your staff, itemizing all the contents, how each is packaged, in what order each is placed within the container, the overwrap, if any, and decoration or other embellishment, and set up an assembly line. Pack the prepared boxed meals in appropriate cartons or transport containers, and send the job on its way. There may even be settings in which assembly can take place behind the scenes on site, eliminating the need for bulk packaging, sorting, and transporting already decorated meals. Whatever the framework or volume, once the prototype is successfully designed, the work goes smoothly.

SOME THEMES AND IDEAS

Every caterer's imagination and every client's request generate a different approach to meal-in-a-box entertainments. A few ideas and suggestions follow.

A Night in Hong Kong

Overall Description   A chartered junk, anchored in a marina, provides the decor and atmosphere for guests at this summertime evening cocktail party. Seating is random, both below and above deck; brightly colored cushions provide additional seating on deck; and some small low tables are placed wherever possible for guests' comfort.

Menu and Service   The meal is served in stages by costumed waitstaff: first, bento boxes with sushi (just prepared in the junk's galley), then a series of small bamboo steamers with finger-sized dim sum (some cold or room temperature, some freshly steamed and fried). Then, as guests wander about, sates are grilled and served. Finally, as guests depart, each receives a colorful paper Chinese food container filled with candied fruits and fortune cookies. Beverages, passed on trays, consist of wine, mineral water, and jasmine or black tea.

A Murder Mystery Train Ride

Overall Description   A vintage train, with parlor car, baggage car, and bar car, is rented for the evening, and an entertainment company provides the murderous goings-on. Guests are asked to dress as their favorite detective, villain, "Orient Express" or "Clue" character. As guests board, they receive baggage claim checks and champagne. Then a ruckus ensues, a "body" is discovered in the baggage car, and the game proceeds as the party continues.

Menu and Service   Soon after the discovery of the "murder," guests are asked to present their baggage checks and identify themselves to the "detective." At this point, each is presented with his or her luggage, an old-fashioned train case, filled with a cold supper of cheese truffles, cold sliced beef filet, baguette, curried rice salad, and blanched pea pods. Guests seat themselves for dinner and find "clues," "weapons," or "evidence" tucked into their cases as well. The entertainment continues with guests participating in the investigation of the crime, and staff passes more champagne or wine. When the "mystery" is solved, dessert and coffee are served in the parlor car. As guests depart, they take their emptied train cases, each marked with engraved luggage tags, courtesy of their host.

Barnyard Auction

Overall Description   This event is an actual fund-raising auction, with an auctioneer conducting the proceedings just after the meal is served. A large warehouse is decorated as a barnyard, with bales of hay, farm equipment, a farmhouse with porch, a lemonade stand that serves as a bar, and assorted wooden, metal, and ceramic farm animals positioned around the barnyard. Items to be auctioned are displayed in corrals or gardens. Tables are set for guests, with red- and blue-checked cloths.

Menu and Service   The lemonade stand serves drinks when guests arrive, servers pass baskets of hush puppies, sweet potato chips, and vegetable squares, while guests circulate and inspect the auction items. After about forty minutes, the auctioneer calls the bidders to their tables, where a calico-lined basket at each place holds a meal of fried chicken, watermelon pickles, and vegetable slaw. At the center of each table, a straw farmer's hat holds biscuits and corn bread, and small mason jars contain plain, herb, and honey butter. Servers pour wine, beer, soda, or iced tea. When the meal is winding down, the auction takes place. Following the auction, guests can approach the front porch of the farm house for ice cream and brownies.

Part Three

RECIPES

This section presents an assortment of kitchen-tested recipes, with precise instructions for preparation, procedure, storage, and presentation. Most menu items mentioned in Part Two, along with many others, are included. Since so many catered food items must be partially prepared in one kitchen and then completed on site, special attention is given to advance preparation, storage, finishing techniques, plating, and garnishing. Wherever practical, test quantities, as well as larger yields, are given. The test quantities will be appreciated not only by the small producer, but also by volume caterers who wish to taste-test and personalize a recipe before preparing it in a larger quantity. In some recipes, specific quantities of ingredients are given for large volume, in others, instructions are given for increasing the yield of the preparation.

In addition, any recipes that lend themselves to additional variations are followed by notes to that effect. The notes are meant to encourage the reader to think in terms of variations on a theme, rather then reinventing the wheel, when faced with the challenge of creating a menu or devising a new food idea.

For example, the recipe for Pesto alla Genovese can be used as-is to sauce pasta; in addition, it is added to Creamy Zucchini Rice Soup and Peasant Chicken Ragout as an enrichment; it can be blended with goat cheese, spread

171

on baguette rounds, and grilled to create herbed chèvre toasts; and it can be mixed with cream cheese as a savory filling for cherry tomatoes. In the same vein, many of the substantial salad recipes that are offered as main dish entrees or the vegetable side dishes may be prepared using finely chopped or minced ingredients and become hors d'oeuvre when used to fill croustades, barquettes, or vegetables such as tiny beets, cucumber cups, or mushroom caps. Some of these same minced salads also make excellent fillings for tea sandwiches. In a similar fashion, some of the appetizers or hors d'oeuvre recipes (for example, Spinach Phyllo Triangles or Stuffed Pizza Slices) can be served in larger portions to become a side dish or luncheon entrée.

Whenever possible, suggestions for substitutions and variations are mentioned to encourage the reader to improvise. It is important to remember that from the caterer's point of view, the more routine and standardized the repertoire, the more efficient and cost-effective the menu; however, from the client's point of view, the more imaginative and current the menu items, the more enticing and special the function seems. While every catering business is expected to deliver certain basics to its clientele, no caterer should offer dated or limited choices. By continually improvising on standard recipe concepts and varying basic menu items, a caterer develops a repertoire that provides clients with customized menus to suit every occasion, taste, and budget.

About the Ingredients: *It will become obvious in reading the recipes that there is a great preference for the use of fresh, rather than processed ingredients whenever possible, with some exceptions made to offer convenience without a significant sacrifice in quality. One of the main reasons for offering variations and possible substitutions in the recipes is to allow the individual caterer to make intelligent judgments at his or her own home base, subject to market fluctuations and seasonal variations in products. The hoped-for final outcome is an excellent finished product that will increase customer appreciation. At the same time, this flexibility allows the caterer to control the waste of both time and money, while enjoying the creativity inspired by a bouquet of fresh herbs or a flat of golden raspberries. Ultimately, the success of any recipe depends on the active participation of the cook: do touch, smell, and taste, whether in the market or at the stove, and good results are guaranteed.*

About the Measurements: *Measurements of ingredients have been provided in both U.S. and metric units for the convenience of all readers. The conversions are approximate, generally based on 1 lb = 450 g and 1 qt = 1 L.*

While these are not exact mathematical equivalents, this system has been chosen to provide the greatest convenience and ease for the users of either method. A metric user should not be expected to measure 237 ml of a liquid any more than an American user would appreciate having to measure ¹⁵/₁₆ of a cup. The proportion within each set of measured ingredients, however, is valid. In baking recipes where more precision is required, some metric measures have been rounded up or down. In addition, a decision was made to use teaspoon and tablespoon measurements (or parts thereof) for both systems, to make the recipes easier to use for all readers.

In the same way, the yields indicated in the recipes are geared toward practical application. Individual caterers may make changes in suggested portion sizes to suit an overall menu, time of day, or clientele. In many cases, notes accompanying individual recipes give advice on such changes. Since off-premise catering often involves transfer from a transport container to a cooking vessel, allowances have been made in some preparations for a certain amount of unavoidable waste.

About the Recipes: *The overall selection of the recipes may seem unusual, but there is a practical philosophy behind it. First in importance is that a recipe works for off-premise catering in a variety of circumstances. Second, the recipes must have both taste and visual appeal. Third, they should satisfy basic tastes as well as current trends (or as current as possible given the realities of publishing). The reader will immediately notice that a large number of the recipes deal with hors d'oeuvre: These items are requested so frequently that no caterer can have too many. Among the meats, chicken has the lion's share of recipes because of its versatility, economy, and popularity. Beef, while still popular for catered affairs, is commonly requested in one of only a few forms: filet, roast beef or prime rib, or some version of sliced steak, chili, or stews. Baked goods and desserts are weighted heavily toward recipes that require no extraordinary pastry skills, but yield products that are delicious, transport easily, and keep well.*

Ethnic foods, particularly in the area of hors d'oeuvre, are extraordinarily popular, but in some cases their traditional or authentic ingredients or preparations might make them impractical for the off-premise caterer. Thus, certain liberties have been taken with ethnic cuisines to adapt their preparation to the usual off-premise catering situation. For instance, adaptations have been made in some oriental dishes to make them suitable for buffet service because, unless a caterer were operating in a facility equipped with ranges with wok wells and had a battery of cooks as staff, stir frying for a multitude would be impossible. In spite of this concession to practical reality, these recipes have been devised so that significant flavors, textures, and visual appeal are retained.

Although more than three hundred recipes appear in this section, the selection barely begins to answer the needs of every off-premise caterer. This book, however, is not intended to be a culinary text, or even an all-purpose cookbook. The Appendix contains a list of excellent books, both general texts and specialty publications, that provide recipes for such useful items as puff pastry, choux paste, pâtés, and traditional sauces, as well as detailed explanations of basic·culinary techniques that are not included here. This recipe collection is a good starting point, however, and, supplemented by the caterer's own recipe file and knowhow, offers a variety of techniques, ideas, and suggestions that will allow even the novice to assemble a "starter set" of workable menus, combining both traditional foods and unusual items.

Hors d'Oeuvre, Canapés, and Appetizers

Gravlax (Dill-Cured Salmon)

Yield: 5 lb		2 kg 250 g

Ingredients:

5 lb	center cut salmon fillets	2 kg 250 g
⅓ cup	kosher salt	78 ml
2 oz	granulated sugar	56 g
2 or 3	large bunches fresh dill	2 or 3
3 tbls	cognac	45 ml
2 tbls	pepper-flavored vodka	30 ml
2 tbls	cracked white peppercorns	2 tbls

Garnish: fresh dill, Sweet Mustard Dill Sauce (see in recipe index), thinly
   sliced pumpernickel, or multigrain bread

The fish should be perfectly fresh. The center cut is preferred for its even thickness, but you can manage with nice end cuts if you position the fillets thick end to thin and concentrate more of the cure on the thicker ends. The fillets should have their skin intact.

1. Select a glass or ceramic pan or deep dish just large enough to hold the fish.
2. Run your fingers carefully over the whole surface of both fillets to detect any fine bones. Remove them with needle-nose pliers or tweezers.
3. Combine the salt and sugar and rub gently over the flesh side of the fillets. Sprinkle with the cracked pepper. Drizzle the cognac and vodka evenly over the fillets.

4. Place a layer of dill sprigs in the bottom of the chosen dish. Lay in one salmon fillet, skin side down. Chop a bunch of dill into two or three lengths, and use to cover the first fillet. Place the second fillet, flesh side down over the first, so that the thick part of one rests on the thin part of the other. Cover with the balance of the dill. Wrap the dish well with two layers of plastic wrap.

5. Place a board or plate on top of the wrapped fish and place about 5 lb (2 kg) of weight on top of the board.

6. Refrigerate to cure for 3 to 4 days. Twice a day, turn the "fish sandwich" over in the juices. Be sure to rewrap carefully and replace the weights. After 3 days, taste a bit of the fish to check on the cure. You may adjust the flavor with more cognac, sugar, or salt. When the fish is done it will have a subtle flavor and silky texture.

7. Remove from the dish, remove and discard the dill, and scrape off any residue of the cure. Discard the accumulated juices. Wrap the fillets separately, first in plastic wrap, then in aluminum foil. The cured fish may be held refrigerated for 1 week. It may be frozen for about a month.

8. To serve, place the fillet skin side down on a serving board. Slice thinly on the diagonal, as for smoked salmon. Serve with Sweet Mustard Dill Sauce and thinly sliced bread. Garnish with fresh dill, if desired.

Note: Gravlax (or Gravad Lax) has always been a favorite salmon preparation in Scandinavia; its popularity is spreading to the rest of the world. It is a good alternative to smoked salmon; some people prefer it. It is generally less expensive to serve, but, since it is custom prepared, still connotes luxury.

Salmon Mousse Canapés

Yield: 24 canapés

	Ingredients:	
24 slices	seedless cucumber or zucchini, about ¼-in. (¾ cm) thick	24 slices
	or	
24 leaves	Belgian endive	24 leaves
8 oz	smoked salmon, ends and trim	224 g
4 oz	whipped cream cheese	112 g
2 oz	sour cream	56 g
1 tbls	lemon juice	15 ml
	salt and white pepper (to taste)	
	Garnish: salmon caviar or red lumpfish caviar	

1. Chop the salmon into pieces. Use a food processor to combine with the cream cheese and sour cream until a smooth paste forms. Season with salt, pepper, and lemon juice to taste.

2. Use a pastry bag fitted with an open rosette tip to pipe a bit of mousse in the center of each vegetable slice. For the endive you may pipe a rosette at the wide end of the blade or you can use a spoon.

3. The cucumber and zucchini slices can be piped ahead and held, covered and refrigerated, for a few hours. Do not attempt to hold the endive for more than an hour or the leaf edges may begin to brown.
4. Just before serving, garnish each canapé with a single egg of the salmon caviar or a dab of the lumpfish. Serve very cold.

Note: You may also pipe this filling onto crackers, bread, or toast rounds. Or use as a filling for croustades, tiny tart shells, pea pods, cherry tomatoes, or raw mushroom caps. It also makes a nice filling for tea sandwiches.

Smoked Salmon Roulades

Yield: 30 roulades

Ingredients:

6 or 8 slices	smoked salmon	6 or 8 slices
6 oz	whipped cream cheese	168 g
2 oz	sour cream	56 g
2 tbls	grated onion	2 tbls
3 tbls	minced dill	3 tbls
	ground white pepper (to taste)	

1. Place two salmon slices, short end to short end and slightly overlapping, on a piece of waxed paper. You should have an oblong about 4 in. (10 cm) wide. Trim the short ends straight and use the pieces to patch any gaps on the long side. Repeat with the other slices to form neat rectangles about 4 in. (10 cm) wide. They may not be all the same length, depending on the size and shape of the slices.
2. Grate the onion onto a paper towel and pat to remove excess juice. Combine with the cream cheese, sour cream, dill, salt, and pepper.
3. Spread the mixture evenly over the slices. Roll the coated slices firmly, jellyroll style, starting from one of the long sides. The salmon should seal to itself and stay rolled. Wrap tightly in plastic wrap and refrigerate for several hours or overnight.
4. To serve, use a very sharp knife to slice the rolls into 1-in. (2½ cm) pinwheels. Arrange on an attractive serving plate, garnish each slice with a feather of dill if desired. If not serving immediately, store wrapped and refrigerated for a few hours. Serve very cold.

Note: You may place each slice on a round of dark-grain or pumpernickel bread if you like.

Crab Claws and Chilled Crab

Yield: about 80 large crab claws

	Ingredients:	
5 lb	frozen snow crab claws	2 kg
	For cocktail sauce:	
½ cup	tomato ketchup	125 ml
½ cup	bottled chili sauce	125 ml
2 tbls	lemon juice	2 tbls
3 tbls	strong prepared horseradish	3 tbls
dash	hot pepper sauce, if desired	dash

1. Thaw the crab claws under refrigeration. Keep cold at all times because these are very perishable. The claws tend to be wet so gently pat each one dry with paper towel, squeezing lightly. Combine sauce ingredients and serve claws with sauce for dipping.

Note: Tiny crab claws are also available: They are not as luxurious but a great abundance can be served for effect. Chunks of crab legs can also be served in the same manner.

Stuffed Crab Claws

Yield: 12 claws

	Ingredients:	
1 recipe	Chinese Shrimp Paste (see in recipe index)	1 recipe
12	frozen crab claws	12
	oil for frying	

Fish suppliers carry crab claws suitable for this recipe. They have been shelled except for the pincers. The main cartilage remains intact, holding a good portion of meat. Their size may vary, but the shrimp paste is sufficient to generously coat at least twelve 3- to 4-in. (8 to 10 cm) claws.

1. Thaw the crab claws refrigerated. Pat or squeeze gently to remove excess moisture. Use the shrimp paste to surround the flesh of the claw completely. Leave the pincers exposed. Hold, refrigerated, until ready to fry.
2. Heat oil for frying. Fry claws a few at a time until puffed and golden. Serve as soon as possible after frying for best texture and flavor. Serve with Spicy Plum Sauce (see in recipe index), with a prepared sweet and sour sauce, or with Sesame Soy Dipping Sauce (see in recipe index).

Note: These can be prepared for frying and held refrigerated for one day, or frozen, uncooked, for later use.

Golden Caviar Layer Cake

Yield: 15 cups, serving about 40 people		*3 L 750 ml*

Ingredients:

1	medium sweet onion	1
6 tbls	minced dill	6 tbls
24	eggs, hard-cooked and peeled	24
1 pt	sour cream, divided	500 ml
4 fl oz	mayonnaise	120 ml
2 tbls	Dijon mustard	2 tbls
2 tbls	dry mustard	2 tbls
¼ tsp	ground white pepper	¼ tsp
2 envelopes	unflavored gelatin (¼ oz or 7 g ea)	2 envelopes
	water	
3 lb	whipped cream cheese	1 kg 350 g
10 oz	golden whitefish caviar	280 g

Optional garnish: watercress, parsley, carved vegetable flowers,
   pumpernickel bread, water crackers, toast points

This recipe was created at the request of Romanoff International, Inc., for a gala celebration in 1986. At the time, I developed this new recipe (inspired by one in a Romanoff Caviar brochure) to create a six-foot-long sheet cake, garnished with garlands of carved vegetable flowers. The recipe that follows is of more reasonable size, but can be easily multiplied or divided and chilled in shapes that suit your creativity and needs.

1. Prepare a pan or mold with a 15-cup (3¾ L) capacity by spraying with an un-flavored nonstick spray.
2. Grate the onion onto a piece of cheesecloth. Wring out vigorously to remove the juice. Spread the grated onion onto clean absorbent paper to drain for 30 minutes. Measure out a scant cup (¼ L) of the drained, grated onion for use in the recipe. Set aside.
3. Put the eggs through a ricer or food mill. Set aside, covered.
4. In a separate bowl, combine ½ cup (125 ml) of sour cream with the mayonnaise, both mustards, and the white pepper. When well mixed, gently fold in the eggs.
5. Soften one package of gelatin in 1 tbls warm water. Add a scant ½ cup (125 ml) boiling water and stir to dissolve. Allow to cool for a few minutes, then stir into the egg mixture. Set aside.
6. Combine the cream cheese with the remaining sour cream, beating well to combine. Prepare the second envelope of gelatin as in step 5 and beat into the cream cheese mixture. Set aside.
7. Pour cream cheese mixture into prepared pan in an even layer. Thump the pan on the work surface to release any trapped air pockets. Scatter the prepared onion evenly over the surface. Top the onion with a layer of the minced dill, concentrating the herb toward the pan edges. Spoon on the egg mixture, again banging the pan to level the filling. Cover tightly with plastic wrap and refrigerate for at least 12 hours or up to 3 days.

8. Just before serving, spread the caviar out on several thicknesses of paper towel to drain. Unmold the cake onto a serving platter and "frost" with the drained caviar. Garnish the edges of the cake with herbs and/or carved vegetable flowers. Slice into small "cake" portions, serve with bread, crackers, or toast, if desired.

Note: Although the golden caviar is particularly delicate in color and flavor, other varieties may be used to suit your taste, for example a checkerboard of red and black lumpfish. The cake unmolds easily, but if you use a springform pan, reverse the layering since the cake will not be inverted. Ring molds are pretty, centered with more caviar or a tiny vase of flowers.

Cocktail Shrimp Variations

Yield: 75 to 125 shrimp, depending on size

Ingredients:

5 lb	shrimp, either U-15, 16–20, or 21–25 count	2 kg
2	lemons	2
	few peppercorns, if desired	

1. If shrimp are block frozen, partially thaw under refrigeration, just enough to loosen from block, so the shrimp will cook evenly.
2. Add a halved lemon and peppercorns to water in a pot and bring to boil. Add the shrimp and stir. Lower heat and simmer just until shrimp turn pink.
3. Drain immediately. Rinse under cold running water to wash off scum and cool down.
4. Shell and remove sandy intestinal vein that runs down outside curve of shrimp. Pack into plastic bags with a few slices of lemon. Seal tightly. Chill and keep very cold while transporting. Serve with choice of sauce, as below:

Cocktail Sauce: Combine ½ cup (125 ml) tomato ketchup, ½ cup (125 ml) bottled chili sauce, 2 tbls lemon juice, 3 tbls strong prepared horseradish (or to taste), salt and pepper if needed.
Horseradish Mustard Sauce: Combine 1 cup (250 ml) basic mayonnaise, 2 tbls strong prepared horseradish, 2 tbls Pommery mustard, pinch of sugar, dash of white vinegar.
  Or serve with the following dipping sauces: Hot Peanut Sauce (see in recipe index), Sesame Soy Dipping Sauce (see in recipe index), Sweet Mustard Dill Sauce (see in recipe index), or Lemon-Caper Mayonnaise (see Mayonnaise and Variations in recipe index).

Variation: **Marinated Shrimp Wrapped in Pea Pods:** Marinate shrimp in either Herb and Caper Vinaigrette (see in recipe index) or Orange Vinaigrette (see Vinaigrette Basics in recipe index). Split barely blanched pea pods, wrap one half around each drained shrimp and secure with pick.

Ginger-Poached Shrimp Oriental

Yield: 100 shrimp

Ingredients:

5 lb	shrimp (16–20 count), thawed	2 kg 250 g
2	lemons	2
4 oz	gingerroot, in two pieces	115 g
6 fl oz	soy sauce	180 ml
2 fl oz	sesame oil	60 ml
dash	Oriental chili oil	dash
2	garlic cloves, smashed	2
	Optional Garnish: scallion brushes, lemon twists	

This recipe yields approximately 100 shrimp of a nice size for cocktails. Since 5 lb (2 kg 250g) block-frozen shrimp are generally available, their use has been assumed.

1. Rinse the shrimp under cold running water to complete thawing and separate. Drain and set aside.
2. Grate or zest the whole lemons. If you use a hand zester, you will get nice little threads, but regular grating is fine. Set the zest aside, well wrapped to prevent drying out. Juice the lemons and reserve the juice. Reserve the lemon shells.
3. Cut the pieces of the gingerroot in half lengthwise and smash with the side of a cleaver or heavy knife.
4. Combine two pieces of the smashed ginger, the lemon juice, lemon zest, soy sauce, sesame oil, Oriental chili oil, and garlic in a container large enough to hold the cooked shrimp. Set aside.
5. Place the shrimp, lemon shells, and smashed ginger in a large pot. Add water to cover. Heat until water comes to the simmer and shrimp are pink and just tender. Do not overcook or they will toughen. Remove from heat and drain immediately. Rinse briefly to remove any scum.
6. As soon as the shrimp can be handled, peel and devein.
7. Place the still-warm cleaned shrimp in the prepared dressing mixture and toss to coat thoroughly. Let stand, refrigerated and covered, for several hours or overnight.
8. To serve: Remove the smashed gingerroot and garlic and discard. Drain the excess dressing from the shrimp. Some of the lemon zest will remain on the shrimp; this is perfectly acceptable. For buffet service: Heap the shrimp into an attractive serving dish or shell. For passed hors d'oeuvre, arrange individual shrimp, well drained, on serving trays (red or black lacquer works well). They are especially handsome laid on ti leaves or flat fern. Use scallion brushes or twisted lemon slices for garnish if desired.

Coconut Shrimp I

Yield: about 30 shrimp

	Ingredients:	
1 lb	shrimp (26–30 count)	450 g
1 tbls	soy sauce	15 ml
1 tbls	rum	15 ml
	Batter:	
4 oz	all-purpose flour	112 g
6 fl oz	milk	180 ml
1 tbls	honey	15 ml
1	whole egg, beaten	1
½ tsp	salt	½ tsp
1 tsp	ground black pepper	1 tsp
14 oz	shredded coconut (approx.)	400 g
	oil for frying	

1. Peel, devein, and butterfly the shrimp. Place the shrimp in a bowl with soy sauce and rum and toss to coat. Marinate, refrigerated and covered, for a few hours.
2. Prepare the batter: Combine the flour, milk, honey, beaten egg, salt, and pepper. Stir until smooth. Refrigerate for several hours to rest the batter.
3. Remove the shrimp from the marinade and pat dry. Coat the shrimp with the batter and roll in the shredded coconut. Pat the coconut on well. If possible, let the coated shrimp stand refrigerated to set.
4. Heat the oil for frying. Cooking hint: Since some coconut tends to fall off into the oil, this residue will burn with repeated frying. It is best to skim or strain the oil after a few batches have been fried to eliminate this problem. Adjust the heat while frying so that shrimp cook quickly but do not burn.
5. Drain well on clean absorbent paper. May be held in a warm oven for about half an hour and still remain crisp. These may be prepared ahead, if necessary, and reheated at 375°F (190°C) for 15 to 20 minutes. They will still be quite good. They can be frozen, after they are well drained and cooled, and then reheated. There will be some loss in quality. If advance preparation and freezing is absolutely necessary, the batter for Coconut Shrimp II (see following recipe) yields far better results.

Note: Shrimp of other size may be used. However, the butterflying and coconut coating gives the finished shrimp a very large appearance, so in this case, less is more. Smaller shrimp will still make an attractive, generous appearance. On the other hand, shrimp that are too large will not cook through without the coconut burning.

Variations: **Coconut Chicken:** substitute pieces or fingers of raw chicken for the shrimp.
Coconut Fruit Puffs: substitute peeled and cored wedges of apple or firm pear for the shrimp. Eliminate the marinade: Instead, sprinkle the raw fruit with a bit of cinnamon before batter dipping. The Fruit Puffs do not freeze and reheat successfully.

Coconut Shrimp II

Yield: about 30 shrimp

Ingredients:

1 lb	shrimp (26–30 count)	450 g
5 oz	mochiko*	140 g
10 fl oz	coconut milk†	300 ml
2 tsp	curry powder (more to taste)	2 tsp
1 tsp	ground ginger	1 tsp
1 tsp	each salt and pepper	1 tsp
2 dashes	hot pepper sauce	2 dashes
14 oz	shredded coconut (approx.)	400 g
	oil for frying	

*Mochiko, also called sweet rice flour or glutinous rice starch, is similar to cornstarch. However, it does not get gluey or separate out from liquids and provides an extra crisp coating when used in a batter. It is available from Japanese or other Oriental sources.

†This is coconut milk, not the sweetened coconut cream that is sold for use in desserts and piña coladas. It is available where Oriental, Indonesian, and Indian food products are sold.

1. Shell, devein, and butterfly the shrimp. Refrigerate, covered.
2. Mix together the mochiko, coconut milk, and spices. The seasonings should be assertive, or they will not come through the coconut. This batter is very thick. It does not require resting time, however, it may be made ahead and stored refrigerated. Let come to room temperature before using, as it will thicken when very cold.
3. Coat the shrimp with batter and roll in coconut (prepare as for Coconut Shrimp I, previous recipe).
4. Heat the oil for frying. See Cooking Hint in Coconut Shrimp I.
5. Drain on clean absorbent paper. These may be held for up to an hour in a warm oven. They reheat very successfully, and will freeze and reheat with very little loss in quality.

Variations: See Coconut Shrimp I.

Since this batter is so highly flavored, it is quite good used as a batter alone without the shredded coconut. Raw chicken that has been previously marinated in coconut milk and smashed garlic, and then batter-fried, is especially good prepared this way.

Scampi Croustades

Yield: 24 appetizers

Ingredients:

24	croustades made with French or Italian bread (see Bread Croustades in recipe index)	24
1 lb	shrimp, any size	450 g
2 tbls	sweet butter	30 g
2 tbls	olive oil	30 ml
3 oz	minced shallots	84 g
2 tbls	minced garlic	2 tbls
2 tbls	dry white wine	30 ml
2 tbls	lemon juice	30 ml
½ cup	minced parsley	125 ml
	salt and pepper to taste	
	seasoned dry breadcrumbs (as needed)	

1. Wash, shell, and devein the shrimp. Chop coarsely and set aside.
2. Heat the butter and olive oil in a sauté pan; add the shallots and garlic. Sauté until just softened. Do not let the garlic brown or it will be bitter.
3. Quickly deglaze the pan with wine and lemon juice, add the shrimp and sauté until just pink. Remove from heat and toss in most of the parsley. Season with salt and pepper to taste.
4. Arrange the croustades on a shallow baking pan. Spoon some of the shrimp into each croustade. Sprinkle a tiny pinch of bread crumb and parsley on top of each and drizzle with any butter or juices remaining in the pan.
5. Place in a 350°F (180°C) oven just to heat through. Serve hot. Hold covered in a warm oven for about 30 minutes if necessary, but it is preferable to heat in batches just before serving.

Note: You can use small whole shrimp if you like rather than chopping the shrimp into pieces.

Variation: **Seafood in Garlic Butter:** Combine even amounts of shrimp, crab legs, poached calamari, firm-fleshed fish chunks, shucked mussels. Increase the sauce ingredients accordingly. Sauté each ingredient until just tender and heated through. Serve in a chafer with small dishes for portions. Serve crusty bread alongside.

Bread Croustades

Yield: 24 croustades

Ingredients:

1	2 lb (1 kg) loaf sandwich bread, white or wheat	1
	or	
2	loaves French or Italian bread, each 12-in. (30 cm) long	2
	melted butter, seasoned or plain	

1. Season the melted butter with a bit of paprika or Worcestershire sauce if desired.
2. To prepare sandwich bread croustades: Prepare two miniature muffin tins by greasing lightly or brushing with melted butter. Place bread slices on a board, cover with waxed paper, and roll lightly with a rolling pin to flatten slightly. Using a 2- or 2½-in. (6 cm) cutter, cut rounds from the slices. Reserve the trimmings for another use. Brush the bread rounds with butter on both sides and ease into muffin tins to form little cups. Lightly toast in a 325°F (165°C) oven. When cool, remove from tins. Store airtight or freeze.
3. To prepare croustades from French or Italian bread: Slice the loaves into 1-in. (2½ cm) slices. Use a sharp knife or serrated spoon to hollow out a cup in the center of the slice. Trim the crust to make an attractive shape. Reserve the bread trimmings for another use. Brush the cups on all sides with melted butter and toast in a 325°F (165°C) oven until golden on all sides. Cool and store as above.

Note: These croustades provide a visual and textural change from pastry tart shells. Each will hold a scant tablespoon of filling. They may be filled and then baked for hot hors d'oeuvre. If serving with a cold filling, refresh in a hot oven, let cool, and then fill as desired. Since they keep well, they can be prepared in bulk in advance and then frozen, well wrapped, for later use. They are more sturdy than fragile pastry shells, so they are easy to transport and handle.

Variations: Experiment with different types of bread, for example, rye or pumpernickel. Sturdy corn bread, prepared as for French or Italian bread, makes a delicious casing for chili, topped with a bit of shredded cheese, and heated until the cheese bubbles.

Shrimp and Feta Turnovers

Yield: 36 turnovers

Ingredients:

1 recipe	Flaky Cream Cheese Pastry (see in recipe index)	1 recipe
1 lb	shrimp, any size	450 g
2 fl oz	ouzo (or anise liqueur)	60 ml
2 tbls	olive oil	30 ml
6 oz	scallions, minced	180 g
1 tsp	minced garlic	1 tsp
4 oz	bulb fennel, finely chopped	112 g
4 oz	whipped cream cheese	112 g
8 oz	feta cheese, crumbled	224 g
2 tbls	chopped dill	2 tbls
2 tbls	chopped parsley	2 tbls
dash	hot pepper sauce	dash
	salt and pepper (to taste)	
	egg wash	

1. Shell and devein the shrimp. Chop coarsely. Pour on ouzo and toss to coat. Set aside.
2. Sweat the scallions, garlic, and fennel in olive oil until wilted. Add the shrimp and ouzo, raise the heat, and flame or cook off the ouzo, stirring. As soon as the shrimp are just turning pink, remove from heat.
3. Transfer the mixture to a mixing bowl and add the cream cheese, feta, dill, and parsley. Mix well to combine all the ingredients. Add the seasonings, mix again, and adjust to taste. Set aside, refrigerated, while preparing the dough.
4. On a lightly floured board, roll out the pastry about ⅛ in. (½ cm) thick, cut into 3-in. (8 cm) squares or rounds. Place a spoonful of the prepared filling on each round, brush the edges with egg wash, fold over, and seal. Place the completed pastries on a greased baking sheet. They may be prepared to this point and held, refrigerated, for a day, if desired.
5. Preheat the oven to 425°F (220°C). Brush the turnovers with egg wash and bake for about 15 minutes, until golden brown. If time requires that you freeze after baking, partially bake, cool and freeze, then complete baking in a moderate oven just before serving. They are at their best, however, when baked just before serving.

Note: Other fillings bake, freeze, and reheat more successfully. In this recipe, however, the shrimp may toughen with repeated baking, so the partial baking is preferred.

Shrimp Toast

Yield: **24 appetizers**

Ingredients:

1 recipe	**Chinese Shrimp Paste (see in recipe index)**	1 recipe
6 slices	**white sandwich bread**	6 slices
	oil for frying	

1. Spread the shrimp paste evenly over the bread slices. Trim the crusts and cut the slices into four triangles or fingers. Chill until ready to fry.
2. Heat oil for frying. Place the shrimp toasts, filling side down in the hot oil. Turn to brown other side. Drain on clean absorbent paper.
3. These may be held in a warm oven for up to one half hour, or prepare ahead, freeze, and reheat for service.

Note: Test fry one or two to adjust the oil temperature to the thickness of the paste and bread to be sure that the mixture cooks through before the toast becomes too dark. These are delicious served plain or serve with an appropriate dipping sauce.

Prickly Shrimp Balls

Yield: **about 40 appetizers**

Ingredients:

1 recipe	**Chinese Shrimp Paste (see in recipe index)**	1 recipe
¼ lb	**cellophane noodles***	125 g
	cornstarch as needed	
1	**egg white**	1
	oil for blanching and frying	

*Cellophane noodles are also called glass noodles or bean thread noodles. They are translucent and sold dried, usually in one pound bags, in Oriental food stores.

1. Roll the shrimp paste into balls of desired size (approx. 1 to 2 in. [2½ to 6 cm]). Dust hands with cornstarch or wet with cold water to prevent sticking. Set on a wet work tray and keep refrigerated until ready to fry.
2. Blanch the cellophane noodles as follows: Heat some oil to frying temperature, drop in a batch of noodles. They will sizzle and puff into a nest and rise to the top of the oil almost immediately. Remove with a skimmer and drain thoroughly on clean absorbent paper. When they are cool and brittle, crush into pieces. Set aside on a flat tray.

3. Heat the frying oil. Beat the egg white until just frothy.
4. Brush the prepared shrimp balls with a bit of egg white and roll in the crushed noodles. Fry a batch at a time in moderately hot oil until the shrimp balls are light and fluffy. The noodles will sizzle again but should barely color. Test fry to gauge exact time and temperature so that the balls cook through. Drain on clean absorbent paper and serve. Hold for 15 to 20 minutes in a warm oven.

Note: Plain shrimp balls can be prepared by the same method without rolling in noodles. This preparation can be fried, frozen, and reheated. Serve either preparation with a thin dipping sauce if desired.

Chinese Shrimp Paste

Yield: 3 cups   *500 g*

	Ingredients:	
1 lb	shrimp, any size, shelled and deveined	450 g
1½	egg whites	1½
2 tbls	soy sauce	30 ml
2 tbls	dry sherry	30 ml
2 tsp	sesame oil	10 ml
3	dried Chinese mushrooms	3
1 tsp	minced garlic	1 tsp
2 tbls	grated gingerroot	2 tbls
2 tbls	cornstarch	15 g
1½ tsp	salt	1½ tsp
1 tsp	ground white pepper	1 tsp

1. Soak the dried mushrooms in water until rehydrated. Drain, rinse well, and squeeze dry. Trim stems and any hard parts away. Mince.
2. Mince the shrimp to a pulp with a sharp knife or use a food processor.
3. Combine the shrimp pulp with the remaining ingredients and beat well to form a paste.
4. Refrigerate until ice cold before using.

Note: Chinese Shrimp Paste is used in several recipes: Shrimp Toast, Stuffed Crab Claws, and Prickly Shrimp Balls. It can also be used as a filling for wontons, dumplings, or other dim sum. It should be used within 24 hours or frozen.

Scallop Timbales with Salmon and Caviar

Serves: 10–12

Ingredients:

1 lb	sea scallops	450 g
2 tbls	lemon juice	30 ml
2 tbls	aquavit	30 ml
2 tbls	minced shallots	2 tbls
1 tsp	salt	1 tsp
½ tsp	white pepper	½ tsp
pinch	nutmeg	pinch
pinch	sugar	pinch
3 cups	heavy cream	¾ L
1 cup	dry white wine	¼ L
1 cup	fish or mussel stock	¼ L
4 tbls	minced shallots	4 tbls
pinch	dry mustard	pinch
1 cup	heavy cream	¼ L
2	egg yolks	2
	salt and white pepper (to taste)	
	softened butter (as needed)	
6–8 slices	smoked salmon or gravlax	6–8 slices
4 oz	salmon caviar	115 g

1. Rinse the scallops, pat dry, remove the tiny side muscle and discard. Keep well chilled.
2. Prepare timbale molds or custard cups with a 4- or 5-ounce (115–140 g) capacity by buttering thoroughly. Select a baking pan large enough to hold them to use as a water bath. Preheat the oven to 350°F (180°C).
3. Place the scallops, lemon juice, aquavit, shallots, and seasonings in the bowl of a food processor. Puree until the mixture is smooth and fine textured. Add almost all of the 3 cups (¾ L) of cream and pulse until the mixture is smooth and just holds its shape in a spoon. You may not need all the cream. Taste and adjust seasonings if needed.
4. Spoon the mousse into the molds, thumping them once or twice to release air pockets. Spread smooth over the tops. Place in the outer pan and gently lay a sheet of buttered parchment over the top. Place in the oven and pour water in the outer pan to come at least halfway up the timbale molds. Cover the pan with foil, sealing the edges, but allowing some slack for the timbales to rise. Bake for about 20 to 25 minutes until they are puffed and somewhat firm. Remove from the pan and set aside.
5. While the timbales are baking, prepare the sauce. Combine the wine and the fish stock in a saucepan with the shallots. Boil down to reduce by half. In a separate bowl, combine the 1 cup (¼ L) of cream with the yolks, add some of the reduced stock, stir to blend, then return to the saucepan. Simmer for 1 to 2 minutes to thicken the sauce. Add the dry mustard and additional salt and white pepper to taste. Set aside.

6. Unmold the timbales onto individual serving plates. Cut the salmon into length-wise strips and wrap around the timbales like a collar or ribbon. Pour some of the sauce around each timbale, and place a few eggs of salmon caviar on top of each timbale and a few on the sauce as garnish. Serve hot.

Note: The timbales may be prepared ahead and held refrigerated for several hours or overnight, then baked before service. They may be baked ahead (bake only for 20 minutes), allowed to cool, and then reheated in their molds before serving. If necessary, they may be baked and unmolded. To reheat, place in a buttered pan, add a little wine, cover and steam hot. In all cases, garnish and sauce just before serving.

Smoked Trout with Horseradish Cream

Serves: 12

	Ingredients:	
6	whole smoked trout	6
½ cup	whipping cream	125 ml
4 oz	sour cream	115 g
4 oz	grated fresh horseradish (or more to taste)	115 g
1 tbls	white wine vinegar	1 tbls
1 tsp	salt	1 tsp
	ground white pepper (to taste)	

Fresh horseradish should be washed and peeled. It is best grated in a food processor. Use caution: The fumes can really sting the eyes. Mix into sauce as soon as grated or it will lose its flavor.

1. Carefully cut the heads from the trout, peel off the skin, gently removing any fins and tail. Separate the fillets from the skeletons; you will have four half fillets. Examine each piece for stray bones and remove, taking care to keep the fillets intact.
2. Whip the cream until stiff and fold in the sour cream and seasonings. Fresh horseradish varies in strength; add as much as needed for desired flavor.
3. Keep trout and sauce refrigerated until ready to serve.
4. To serve place two half fillets attractively on each plate, serve portion of sauce at side of plate or in a separate ramekin. Garnish with a lemon twist or sprig of watercress if desired.

Variation: To serve as hors d'oeuvre: Break the trout flesh into bite-size portions; the flesh has natural V-shaped separations. One trout will yield about 30 pieces. Lay trout on loose-leaf lettuce. Use a large, curved leaf of radicchio as a sauce cup, set at one corner of tray.

Smoked mackerel or bluefish fillets, in appropriate size portions, are also delicious with this sauce.

Leek-Glazed Oysters on the Half Shell

Yield: **24 oysters**

	Ingredients:	
24	oysters	24
3 oz	butter	84 g
24 oz	washed and chopped leeks	674 g
3 tbls	All-Purpose Demi-glace (see in recipe index)	45 ml
2 tbls	all-purpose flour	15 g
½ cup	light cream	125 ml
6 oz	grated Gruyère cheese	168 g

1. Scrub and rinse off the oysters to remove exterior grit. Set aside, refrigerated.
2. Heat the butter in a sauté pan, add the leeks and cook until soft and lightly colored. Add the demi-glace and cook for 1 minute to melt.
3. Sprinkle flour over and cook stirring for 1 or 2 minutes. Add the cream and stir until mixture has thickened. Lower heat and add half the cheese. Stir until cheese melts. Remove from heat and season to taste with salt and pepper.
4. Just before serving, open the oysters, free the connecting muscle but leave each oyster in its presentation half shell. Pick off bits of shell, if any.
5. Heat the oven to 350°F (180°C). Set the oysters on a shallow pan, place a generous tablespoon of filling on each oyster. Sprinkle remaining cheese on top. Bake in the oven until heated through and slightly glazed. You may cook under a broiler or salamander if you watch carefully. It is important not to overcook the oysters or they will become tough. As soon as the edges of the oysters curl, they are done. Serve immediately: These should not be reheated.

Note: If you can serve on a bed of hot rock salt, do so, as it will conserve the oysters' heat. These should be served or passed on small plates with forks at a cocktail party or buffet. If serving as a dinner appetizer, serve three to six per person, depending on the size of the oysters and the overall balance of the meal.

Variations: The leek filling, which yields about 1½ cups (350 ml) can be used as a filling for baked pastry tarts, mushrooms, or artichoke bottoms. It may also be used alone, or with chopped poultry or seafood as a filling for turnovers or phyllo triangles. It is wonderful as a topping for baked eggs as a brunch dish or as an omelet filling, especially when combined with sautéed mushrooms.
Leek-Glazed Clams: Simply substitute half-shell clams for the oysters.
Leek-Glazed Mussels: Steam mussels open in wine or broth, then proceed as per recipe. Mussels require less cooking time; just heat through.
Leek-Glazed Escargots: Marinate snails in brandy or wine, drain, and place in mushroom caps or bouchées. Top with filling and heat through.

Crisp Calamari (Squid)

Serves: 8

Ingredients:

2 lb	squid, cleaned	900 g
4 oz	all-purpose flour	112 g
4 oz	cornmeal	112 g
pinch	cayenne pepper	pinch
	salt and pepper	
	oil for frying	
	Optional garnish: fried parsley	

Some fishmongers will clean and prepare squid. However, many offer squid block frozen, some cleaned, some not. To clean squid: First, remove the head portion (or tentacles) from the body. Usually attached to the tentacles is the ink sac and stomach. Remove and discard, being sure the body tube is clean and free of grit. If the bodies are not skinned, rub off the thin grey skin by rubbing with salt and running under water. Be sure to remove the quill bone, or feathery cartilage, and discard. To clean the head, press on the center of tentacle ring to pop out the beak (a hard bony little piece). Rinse the tentacles well to remove grit and set aside.

1. Slice the body tubes of the squid into rings, rinse, and set aside in a colander to drain. If the tentacles are small, they should be left whole; if large, cut in half. Rinse and set aside in a colander to drain.
2. Combine the flour, cornmeal, cayenne, salt, and pepper.
3. Heat the oil for frying. You may use a deep fryer but 2 to 3 in. (6 to 8 cm) of oil in a frying pan is sufficient.
4. Prepare squid in batches just before frying by dredging in flour mixture. Fry the rings and tentacles separately since cooking time varies. Thoroughly shake off any excess flour and fry until crisp and golden (about 2 to 3 minutes is usually sufficient).
5. Drain on clean absorbent paper. Serve immediately or hold in a warm oven. Do not cover or they will steam and lose their crispness.
6. Serve on a tray lined with a fresh linen napkin to absorb any grease. Cluster the tentacles in the center or in one section of the serving tray and place the rings around. Since people have a tendency to prefer one to the other, this prevents guests from picking through a tray for their favorite.
7. To prepare optional fried parsley garnish: Wash and spin dry attractive short sprigs of curly parsley. Fry in hot fat until crisp. Be careful: They will pop and spatter. Use immediately as garnish.

Note: The calamari are very good served plain or with lemon wedges. They are also delicious served with either Spicy Tomato Sauce (see in recipe index) or Lemon-Caper Mayonnaise (see Mayonnaise and Variations in recipe index).

Fish Brochettes

Yield: 24 skewers

Ingredients:

24	**bamboo skewers**	24
2 lb	**raw tuna or swordfish**	1 k
¼ cup	**lemon juice**	60 ml
1½ tbls	**soy or teriyaki sauce**	25 ml
1	**garlic clove, smashed**	1
pinch	**granulated sugar**	pinch
	ground black pepper	

If grilling on skewers, soak the skewers in water several hours ahead to prevent them from burning. If not, grill the fish pieces and serve with picks and dipping sauce.

1. Trim the fish of all skin, fat, and bone. Remove the dark muscle meat, if desired, because some people do not care for its looks or stronger flavor.
2. Cut the fish into 1-in. (2½ cm) cubes, or two-bite-thick slices.
3. Combine the other ingredients, pour over fish, and toss to coat the pieces. Marinate for at least 1 hour, covered and refrigerated.
4. Heat a grill, broiler, or salamander. If using skewers, spear fish pieces, one or two to a skewer, depending on size. Grill, turning to brown all sides. Swordfish requires about 10 minutes. Tuna is delicious rare; about 5 minutes should do. Serve hot or cold, with Sesame Soy Dipping Sauce or Hot Peanut Sauce (see in recipe index). To hold for a short time, wrap closely to preserve moisture and keep in a warm oven. If a longer holding period is necessary, only sear or partially cook on grill and complete cooking when reheating. Remember that raw or partly cooked fish is very perishable so do not leave at room temperature for any length of time.

Variations: **Spiced Butter Fish Brochettes:** Substitute sherry, white wine, or tequila for soy sauce, season with salt and pepper. Baste with butter flavored with paprika and hot pepper sauce.

Herbed Fish Brochettes: Use white wine for marinade, baste and serve with your choice of seasoned butter (see recipe for Compound or Flavored Butters for ideas). These variations are good served hot. If serving cold offer a compatible mayonnaise as a dipping sauce.

Fish and Vegetable Brochettes: Add shrimp if you like or just skewer fish along with pieces of onion and red and green bell pepper.

Brie-Glazed Escargots

Yield: 20

Ingredients:

20	mushroom caps (about 2-in. [6 cm] diam.)	20
20	canned escargots	20
6 oz	Brie	180 g
2 oz	sweet butter	56 g
2 oz	garlic butter (see in recipe index)	56 g
	butter for sautéing	

1. Clean or wash the mushroom caps. Drain the escargots.
2. Sauté the mushroom caps in a bit of butter for a minute or two just until golden. Remove and set aside. Place the escargots in the same pan, heat for one minute, remove from heat, and let rest in warm butter.
3. Trim the rind from the Brie. Put in a food processor with the sweet butter and process until smooth and combined.
4. Place the caps in a shallow baking pan. Place a dab of garlic butter in each. Put one escargot in each cap. Spread the Brie and butter mixture over each escargot, rounding the mixture so each cap is sealed with Brie butter. They may be prepared to this point and held, refrigerated and covered, for a day. Let them come to room temperature before baking.
5. Bake at 375°F (190°C) for 8 to 10 minutes until heated through. The cheese mixture should be bubbly. Preferably, they should be browned for the final cooking minute under a broiler or salamander. Serve hot.

Note: This is a good use for leftover cheese, provided that it is wholesome, if not attractive. Camembert may be substituted for the Brie.

Herbed Escargots in Mushroom Caps

Yield: 20

Ingredients:

20	mushroom caps (about 2-in. [6 cm] diam.)	20
20	canned escargots	20
2 oz	cognac	60 ml
4 oz	Herb and Shallot Butter (see Compound or Flavored Butters in recipe index)	112 g
	Garnish: minced parsley, dry bread crumbs	

1. Drain the escargots and marinate in cognac for a few hours. Keep refrigerated until an hour before baking.
2. Wash or clean the mushroom caps and place on a baking sheet.
3. Place a bit of herb butter in the bottom of each cap, then a drained escargot, then press on more butter.
4. Combine the parsley with the bread crumbs and place some of this mixture on each filled cap. Refrigerate for up to one day. Let come to room temperature before baking.
5. Preheat the oven to 350° F (180° C). Bake the mushroom caps until heated through, about 10 minutes. Serve soon after baking. Do not reheat or the escargots will toughen.

Foie Gras Stuffed Mushrooms

Yield: 20

Ingredients:

20	mushroom caps (1½-in. [4 cm] diam.)	20
2 oz	butter	56 g
1 tbls	brandy	15 ml
	salt and pepper	
5 to 6 oz	pate de foie gras mousse*	140 to 180 g
	Optional garnish: bits of preserved black truffle	

*Many varieties of packaged foie gras mousse exist, along with other canned pâtés. Any will work in this recipe but please choose one that has a good flavor to stand on its own. Some of the pork-liver combinations can be quite harsh tasting.

1. Clean the mushroom caps and sauté just until golden colored. Add the brandy and flame or burn off. Season with salt and pepper and set aside to cool in their pan.
2. When the caps are cool enough to handle, use a small spoon to mound each cap with pâté. Set on a baking sheet and brush with remaining pan butter. Keep refrigerated until one half hour before baking.
3. Bake in a 375° F (190° C) oven just until the pâté softens and is heated through. Serve soon after baking. May be stuffed one day ahead.
4. If using the optional garnish, dot each cap with a bit of truffle slice just before serving.

Note: Larger mushrooms may be used and the filling adjusted accordingly. Do not use very large caps, as they will splay out and not hold the filling.

Variation: If budget is a concern, rather than using a cheaper, inferior tasting pâté, make Chicken Liver Stuffed Mushrooms instead as follows: Substitute a flavorful chopped chicken liver mixture for the pâté. Proceed according to the recipe. Sprinkle the baked caps with minced parsley just before serving.

Wild Rice Stuffed Mushrooms

Yield: 48

Ingredients:

48	medium mushrooms (about 3-in. [8 cm] diam.)	48
4 oz	sweet butter	112 g
4 oz	wild rice	112 g
3 oz	golden raisins	84 g
4 fl oz	dry sherry	125 ml
6 oz	onion, finely chopped	168 g
2 oz	celery, finely chopped	56 g
2 tbls	all-purpose flour	15 g
4 fl oz	milk (or as needed)	120 ml
	salt and pepper (to taste)	
pinch	nutmeg	pinch

1. Clean or wash the mushrooms. Separate the stems from the caps. Cut the stems into fine mince, place in a clean towel, and wring out excess moisture.
2. Heat half the butter in a sauté pan, toss in the caps just to coat with butter and color slightly. Remove the caps and set aside.
3. Add the minced mushrooms (duxelles) to the pan and sauté until dark brown and dry. Set aside.
4. Cook the wild rice until tender and set aside. Soak the raisins in sherry.
5. Sauté the onions and celery in the remaining butter until tender, sprinkle with flour and cook, stirring for 2 minutes. Slowly add some of the milk, stirring and simmering until the mixture thickens. Set aside.
6. Drain the sherry from the raisins and stir into the thickened sauce. Chop the raisins coarsely and add to the sauce along with the duxelles.
7. Drain the wild rice in a colander to remove any excess moisture. Add to the stuffing mixture. Add seasonings, taste and adjust. The stuffing should be flavorful and nicely bound together.
8. Stuff each of the prepared mushroom caps with about 2 tbls of mixture, pressing the stuffing in firmly. Can be prepared ahead to this point and refrigerated for several hours or overnight.
9. To bake, place in a 375°F (190°C) oven for 15 to 20 minutes until heated through. Serve hot or warm. If holding, keep in a warm oven loosely covered.

Note: The yield will vary based on the variable size of mushrooms. Made with larger mushrooms, with the filling mounded high, these mushrooms make a very festive and luxurious side dish for turkey or game.

Variations: To make more economically, mix half white rice with the wild grain. The mixture can also be used to stuff game birds, Cornish hens, or rolled boneless chicken breasts. Add a beaten whole egg and a bit more sherry to moisten the mixture for this purpose.

Truffled Camembert

Serves: 12

Ingredients:

1	**wheel Camembert**	1
1	**small jar chopped truffles in juice**	1
2 tbls	**cognac**	30 ml

1. Split the Camembert in two horizontally. Leaving the rind and edges intact, prick the cut surfaces of the cheese all over with a fork.
2. Sprinkle with cognac. Distribute the truffles and their juice over the cut surfaces of the cheeses. Let stand about 10 minutes to soak in, then fit the two halves together, wrap and refrigerate for 1 to 2 days.
3. Cut into small wedges to serve.

Brie en Croute

Serves: 14

Ingredients:

½ lb	**Egg Bread dough (see in recipe index)***	225 g
2 oz	**herb butter**	60 g
1	**baby Brie (1 lb [500 g])**	1
	egg wash	

*Use the plain dough version, with only 1 tablespoon sugar.

1. Unwrap the Brie and chill for at least 2 hours. It should not be too ripe, and it should be chilled so it is not runny, for easy handling. Take care not to break the crust.
2. On a lightly floured surface, roll the dough out to a rough rectangle. Spread half the herb butter across the center of the rectangle. Fold dough one end over butter, spread that fold with remaining butter, and fold other end to close. (This technique is similar to the one used for puff pastry.) Chill for 15 minutes.
3. Return dough to board and roll out to a 15-in. (38 cm) circle. Brush whole surface with egg wash. Let rest 5 minutes. With a pastry wheel cut five 3-in. (8 cm) deep slashes at even intervals all around the perimeter of the circle.
4. Place the chilled Brie in the center of the pastry. Brush the top of the cheese with egg wash. Draw each of the cut sections of pastry up around the cheese in order, as though closing the petals of a flower. Use the palm of your hand to press each piece of dough to the side and top of the Brie, and overlap each petal, pressing to seal. You will probably have excess left at the top center. Pinch under the excess to seal and turn each point back to form a flower or star shape. Brush overall with egg wash, chill for 30 minutes, or up to 1 day. It may be frozen.

5. Preheat the oven to 350° F (180° C). Place wrapped Brie on a lightly greased baking sheet and bake for 25 to 30 minutes, until pastry is golden brown. Allow to rest for at least 30 minutes before cutting Brie.

Note: You may use a wrapping method of your own choice, using excess dough to make decorations, leaves, coils, and so forth on the pastry.

Variations: You may use this wrapping method with Camembert or other Brie-like cheeses, flavored or not: You may also use this method to wrap Roquefort-Stuffed Brie (see in recipe index).

Roquefort-Stuffed Brie

Serves: 10–12

	Ingredients:	
1	baby Brie (1 lb [500 g])	1
4 oz	Roquefort, crumbled	112 g
2 oz	sweet butter, softened	56 g
1 oz	walnuts, chopped	28 g
2 tbls	calvados	30 ml

1. Split the Brie in half crosswise. From both cut sides, scrape out a total of one cup of the center of the cheese, leaving the side walls intact.
2. Place the scooped Brie and the other ingredients in the bowl of a food processor. Pulse two or three times to combine into a rough mixture.
3. Pack this mixture into the hollows of the Brie halves, fit the two halves back together, and wrap the whole cheese in waxed paper. If you have the original box, repack the cheese in it. Store, refrigerated for at least 1 day or up to 3. Let come to room temperature to serve, cut into small wedges.

Note: The same treatment may be applied to Camembert or other Brie-like cheeses.

Assorted Cheese Truffles

Yield: 48 truffles

	Ingredients:	
12 oz	Brie or Camembert	340 g
6 oz	sweet butter	180 g
6 oz	cream cheese, softened	180 g
2 tbls	pear brandy	30 ml
	salt and pepper (to taste)	
about 1 cup	chopped blanched almonds	115 g

For this recipe and the variations that follow, the procedure remains the same. The ingredient proportions may vary slightly depending on the flavor and consistency of the cheese. You may serve only one kind, or an assortment, varying color, texture, and flavor. These recipes are a frugal use of leftover cheese that is still wholesome but no longer attractive for service. Each recipe makes about 4 dozen.

1. Combine the cheeses and butter in the bowl of a processor, add the seasonings and/or herbs or flavorings. Refrigerate until hard enough to scoop.
2. Using your hands or a melon baller, shape into rough rounds, roll in nuts, crumbs or seeds. Store refrigerated until about 30 minutes before service. Prepare up to one day ahead.

Variations: **Blue Cheese Truffles:** Use Stilton, Roquefort, or other blue, in place of the Brie or Camembert, use same amounts cream cheese and butter, season with 2 tbls Port and a dash of hot pepper sauce. Roll in finely chopped toasted pecans or walnuts.
Cheddar Truffles: Use sharp white cheddar, grated, instead of Brie or Camembert, same amount cream cheese and butter, season with 2 tbls grated onion, 2 tbls applejack or calvados. Roll in a mixture of dry bread crumbs and paprika.
Southwestern Truffles: Use shredded Monterey Jack instead of Brie, same amounts of cream cheese and butter, season with 2 tsp jalapeño or hot pepper jelly, 2 tbls tequila. Roll in minced chives.
Goat Cheese Truffles: Use 16 oz (500 g) Montrachet (herbed or plain), combine with only 4 oz (115 g) each of butter and whipped cream cheese; add 2 tbls minced sun-dried tomatoes or pitted minced oil-cured olives. Roll in poppy seeds.
Swiss Truffles: Use 6 oz (180 g) each grated Gruyère and Emmentaler, blend with 6 oz (180 g) each butter and cream cheese, season with 1 tsp Dijon mustard and 2 tbls kirsch. Roll in dry pumpernickel bread crumbs.

Phyllo Kisses

Yield: 48

	Ingredients:	
12 sheets	**phyllo dough**	12 sheets
	melted butter (as needed)	
48	**Cheese Truffles (see in recipe index)**	48
	or	
48	**1-in. (2 cm) cubes smoked mozzarella**	48
½ cup	**thick pesto (see Pesto Alla Genovese in recipe index)**	125 ml
	or	
2 lb	**mashed potato**	1 kg
4 tbls	**chopped scallions**	4 tbls
1 tsp	**minced garlic**	1 tsp
2 tsp	**curry powder (or to taste)**	2 tsp
1 tsp	**salt**	1 tsp
½ tsp	**ground pepper**	½ tsp
2 tbls	**peanut oil**	30 ml

Cheese Truffles provide a very easy way to make Cheese Phyllo Kisses. Prepare the truffles of your choice: Use each to make a kiss as directed below. You don't need to roll in nuts or crumbs, but if you have prepared truffles left over, use them as is—the crumbs or nuts lend an interesting texture.

1. Prepare any of the other fillings. Toss the mozzarella in the pesto, set aside until ready to use. For curried potato, sauté the scallion and garlic in oil, add curry, cook for one minute, season to taste. Mix thoroughly into potatoes and allow to cool.
2. To make kisses: If phyllo is frozen, thaw according to package directions. Then unroll as you would fresh phyllo, cover with plastic wrap and damp towel to protect from drying (see recipe for Spinach Phyllo Triangles for more information on handling phyllo dough).
3. Place one sheet of phyllo on work surface, brush with melted butter. Fold lengthwise into thirds, brush with butter, cut folded strip into four sections (you will have three 4-in. [10 cm] squares). Place a cheese truffle (or cube of mozzarella, or tablespoon of potato filling) on each square. Quickly pinch corners together and twist into kiss. Set on a buttered baking sheet and refrigerate until ready to bake.
4. Bake at 350°F (180°C) for about 10 minutes until golden brown. Serve at once. The baked phyllo can be held in a warm oven for about 30 minutes. Most filled kisses can be frozen unbaked, except for the potato, which loses texture upon freezing.

Note: Other fillings that one might use for turnovers of baked pastry tarts can be substituted as filling for kisses, provided they are not too runny. This can be a different and easier way to make Spinach Phyllo Triangles, for example.

Vegetable Cheese Squares

Yield: about 75 pieces

	Ingredients:	
4 oz	butter or margarine	115 g
8 oz	chopped onion	225 g
4 slices	white sandwich bread	4 slices
	milk for soaking	
20 oz	frozen French-style green beans	560 g
12 oz	whipped cream cheese	340 g
4	whole eggs	4
	salt and pepper (to taste)	
	dry bread crumbs (as needed)	

1. Preheat the oven to 350°F (180°C). Prepare 15 × 10 ×1 in. jelly roll or similar pan by greasing and dusting liberally with dry bread crumbs. Set aside.
2. Sauté the onion in butter until lightly browned. Set aside.

3. Soak the slices of bread in enough milk to cover and set aside.

4. Thaw the green beans under running hot tap water to separate and bring to room temperature. Drain thoroughly.

5. In a mixing bowl, beat the cream cheese with the eggs to combine. Add the onions with their butter, the soaked bread, and the green beans. Mix thoroughly and season highly with salt and pepper.

6. Turn into prepared pan, sprinkle top with a handful of dry bread crumbs, and bake for 20 to 30 minutes or until set.

7. Allow to cool completely until firm. Store refrigerated for up to 3 days. May be baked ahead and frozen. To thaw and serve: Thaw refrigerated, then bake about 5 minutes in a moderate oven to reduce moisture. Let cool before cutting. Serve at cool room temperature, not ice cold.

Note: The specified pan can be cut into 75 portions (each 1 × 2 in.—not really squares) by using a 5 × 15 cut. For tiny bites, cut each in half or portion as desired. The recipe may simply be multiplied for large batches.

Variations: **Carrot Squares:** Substitute grated carrots for green beans; add a bit of curry powder or ground ginger and some minced parsley.
Broccoli Cheddar Squares: Substitute chopped, blanched broccoli for the green beans, add a dash of hot pepper sauce and 2 oz (56 g) of grated sharp yellow cheddar.
Zucchini Squares: Substitute grated, drained, and sautéed zucchini for green beans, add 1 to 2 tsp dried basil and 1 oz (28 g) grated Italian cheese, or to taste.
Mexican Corn Squares: Substitute a combination of blanched corn kernels and sautéed diced red and green bell pepper for the same amount of green beans, add chili powder and hot pepper sauce to taste, and up to 2 oz (56 g) grated jack cheese or cheddar. Other blanched or sautéed vegetables of compatible colors and flavors can be combined to create more variations, for example broccoli and red peppers or carrot and zucchini.

Potato and Leek Torta

Yield: 24 pieces

	Ingredients:	
1 cup	olive oil	¼ L
2 lb	chopped leeks	900 g
1 lb	chopped onion	450 g
5 lbs	mealy potatoes	2 kg 250 g
1 oz	salt (or to taste)	28 g
	pepper (to taste)	
6 oz	grated Parmesan cheese	180 g
1 lb	phyllo pastry (strudel leaves)	450 g
4 oz	sweet butter, melted	112 g
2 fl oz	olive oil	60 ml

1. Heat the oil in a large pan or brazier and sweat the leeks and onions. Stir occasionally and adjust heat so that the vegetables soften and color lightly.
2. Meanwhile, boil the potatoes in salted water until tender. Drain, and when barely cool enough to handle, peel and put through a ricer or coarse sieve.
3. Add the cooked vegetables and their cooking oil to the potatoes. Both should still be warm. Mix thoroughly and gradually stir in the cheese, salt, and pepper to taste. Set mixture aside at room temperature while preparing the pastry.
4. Combine the melted butter and oil. Use some of the mixture to grease a suitable baking pan (18 × 13 × 2 in.).
5. Carefully unroll the phyllo onto a sheet of plastic wrap. Immediately cover with another sheet of plastic and with a damp towel. (Phyllo becomes very fragile when allowed to dry out. Work with a few sheets at a time, keep the remainder covered.) Transfer a few sheets to a board, brush with the melted butter and oil, and place in the baking pan. You will be placing the sheets in the pan as though lining a gift box with tissue paper. Position the sheets so that there is plenty of overhang. Brush each layer of sheets with additional butter and oil.
6. When the pan is completely lined, spoon in the potato filling, spreading it to the corners and making the filling fairly level.
7. Place a layer of phyllo over the top and brush with butter and oil.
8. Quickly bring up the overhanging sheets of pastry to cover the top (as though wrapping a package). Brush with a bit more of the butter and oil to seal.
9. Place the pan on a larger baking sheet or drip pan. Bake for about an hour. The pastry will be crisp and lightly browned; the filling will rise a bit and then sink. Don't be concerned about little cracks in the pastry. If the pastry appears to be browning too fast, cover loosely with a sheet of aluminum foil.
10. Remove to a rack to cool and set before cutting. May be served warm. Will keep covered and refrigerated for two or three days. May be reheated before serving.

Antipasto Crepe Torta

Serves: 16

Ingredients:

16	8-in. (20 cm) crepes (see Basic Crepes and Variations in recipe index)*	16
¼ lb	imported Swiss, thinly sliced	112 g
¼ lb	provolone, thinly sliced	112 g
¼ lb	boiled ham, thinly sliced	112 g
¼ lb	mortadella, thinly sliced	112 g
¼ lb	Genoa salami, thinly sliced	112 g
½ cup	Artichoke Dip (see in recipe index)†	125 ml

½ cup	**Lemon-Caper Mayonnaise (see Mayonnaise and Variations in recipe index)**	120 ml
¼ cup	**spicy or Dijon mustard**	60 ml
3 tbls	**pitted and chopped oil-cured black olives**	3 tbls
6 tbls	**chopped pimientos**	6 tbls
2 tbls	**minced yellow pepper**	2 tbls
2 tbls	**minced parsley**	2 tbls

*You may use plain crepes, or the variation for Parmesan Crepes or Confetti Crepes for added interest. Make them in an 8 or 9-in. (20 or 23 cm) pan.
†Make the variation using marinated artichokes and mayonnaise.

1. Prepare an 8-in. (20 cm) springform pan by spraying lightly with a nonstick spray. Place a waxed cake circle in the bottom of the pan for easy unmolding: or, line the bottom with a circle of waxed paper or parchment.

2. Trim the crepes, if necessary, so they are the exact diameter of the pan bottom. You will be layering crepes and filling with spreads used as "glue." The springform pan will keep the edges neat and also make the completed torta easy to transport. The pan, however, is not absolutely necessary, so if you don't object to a more rustic look, just stack freehand as neatly as possible. This recipe will make two tortas of eight crepes each.

3. Place first crepe in bottom on pan, spread with spicy mustard, lay in five or six slices of salami, top with about three slices of provolone, spread thinly with mustard. Top with next crepe, spread with Lemon-Caper Mayonnaise, layer with two or three slices boiled ham, then with two slices Swiss cheese. Spread with a bit more mayonnaise. Top with next crepe, press down lightly, spread with mustard, then slices of mortadella, a bit more mustard, and next crepe. Spread this crepe with artichoke dip, scatter with some pimientos and olives, cover with another crepe, press down firmly.

4. Repeat layers again, beginning with mustard, salami, and provolone and continuing as before until you place the final crepe.

5. Place top (or eighth) crepe best side up, press down. Spread top with artichoke dip, and garnish with some pimientos, olives, yellow pepper, and parsley. The dip is the "frosting" on the cake, so be sure it is attractive. Follow the same procedure with the remaining eight crepes until you have two completed tortas. Wrap well and refrigerate for several hours or overnight.

6. To unmold, release the sides of the spring mold pan, lift onto a serving plate, using the cake circle. Or slide off on paper liner, peel off paper, place on serving plate.

7. For hors d'oeuvre portions, cut into eight cake portions. As a plated appetizer, the portions may be larger. Serve with forks for easier and neater eating.

Note: You may alter the choice or order of ingredients as you like. However, be certain that the meat and cheeses are cut paper thin and that you layer evenly for most attractive results.

Lacy Bean Sprout Cakes

Yield: about 40 cakes

Ingredients:

14 oz	mung bean sprouts, drained	400 g
1½ tbls	soy sauce	20 ml
1	garlic clove, minced (optional)	1
2 oz	minced gingerroot	60 g
4 oz	finely chopped scallions	115 g
4 oz	finely chopped red pepper	115 g
4 oz	finely chopped water chestnuts	115 g
1 cup	Simple Beer Batter (see in recipe index)	250 ml
2 fl oz	water	60 ml
	oil for frying	
4 to 6 oz	Optional additions: diced cooked shrimp, chicken, or ham	115 to 180 g

1. Combine the bean sprouts with the flavorings and vegetables. Add your choice of the optional additions, if desired. Toss to mix.
2. Dilute Simple Beer Batter with water, add to the sprout mixture, and stir to combine.
3. Heat 1 to 2 in. (2½ to 6 cm) of oil in a frying pan. Have a mesh skimmer handy.
4. Drop the mixture by small spoonfuls into the hot oil. The batter should be thin enough to spread to a lacy pancake. Test fry one and adjust with a bit of water if needed. The pancake should crisp quickly. Turn once to brown other side and remove to clean absorbent paper to drain.
5. These are best served immediately after frying and draining, so cook in batches. Stir the mixture before cooking each new batch to redistribute the ingredients.

Note: These may be even more highly seasoned depending on taste. A bit of ketjap manis, Vietnamese fish sauce, sesame oil, or hot chili oil may be added (all available at Oriental markets). The recipe yield is approximate and depends on the size of each cake.

Variation: For more showy (and expensive) Shrimp and Sprout Cakes, proceed as follows: Have ready 40 to 50 small, whole cooked shrimp. Immediately after dropping the batter in the pan, place a whole shrimp in the center of the cake. The batter and hot oil will cause it to adhere. Continue as above and serve cakes shrimp side up.

Miniature Spring Rolls

Serves: 16

Ingredients:

4 oz	cooked chicken, shredded	112 g
1 tbls	rice wine vinegar	15 ml
2 tbls	minced gingerroot	2 tbls
¼ cup	minced scallions	60 ml
1 tbls	minced garlic	1 tbls
2 tbls	minced water chestnuts	2 tbls
3	dried Chinese mushroom caps, soaked, drained, and slivered	3
¼ cup	shredded carrot	60 ml
5 oz	drained bean sprouts	140 g
½ cup	softened cellophane noodles*	120 ml
1½ tbls	soy sauce	25 ml
1 tbls	bottled oyster sauce†	15 ml
dash	hot chili oil	dash
	salt and pepper (to taste)	
1 tbls	cornstarch	7 g
1 tbls	water	15 ml
4	8-in. (20 cm) square spring roll wrappers‡	4
	beaten egg to seal	
	peanut oil for frying	

*Cellophane (or bean thread or glass) noodles are available in Oriental markets. Soften in boiling water for a few minutes, then drain and snip into 2-in. (6 cm) lengths with a scissors.
†Oyster sauce is available in Oriental markets.
‡Spring roll wrappers (often called Lumpia wrappers) are thinner than egg roll skins. They are available fresh or frozen in Oriental markets.

1. Sprinkle the chicken with the vinegar. Set aside.
2. In a wok or skillet, heat a bit of peanut oil until hot but not smoking. Add the gingerroot, scallions, and garlic and stir fry for a few seconds. Add the water chestnuts, mushrooms, carrot, bean sprouts, and noodles. Stir fry for a minute.
3. Add the chicken, soy and oyster sauces, and chili oil. Stir fry to combine. Taste and add salt and pepper until highly seasoned.
4. Combine the cornstarch and water, add to the wok, and stir fry until the entire mixture is glossy and there is no excess moisture in the pan. Set aside to cool completely before preparing wrappers.
5. Prepare the wrappers. If frozen, defrost according to package directions. Remove 4 sheets from the package, place on work surface and cover immediately with a dampened towel. Reseal the package and return to refrigerator or freezer.

6. Use a sharp knife or scissors to cut the wrapper into four squares. Place one square before you diagonally, place a small cylinder of the cooled filling on the wrapper. Bring the bottom corner up over the filling, neatly fold in the sides, and roll tightly toward the far point, sealing all the joints with a bit of egg wash. Continue with the other three squares and the balance of the sheets, until all filling is used.

7. The filled rolls may be held refrigerated or frozen at this point.

8. To fry, heat about 2 in. (6 cm) of peanut oil in a wok or fryer to 350°F (180°C). Fry the spring rolls until golden brown on all sides. Transfer to clean absorbent paper to drain. Serve hot. They may be held in a warm oven for about half an hour. It is possible to fry, freeze, and reheat the spring rolls but the results will not be as crisp. It is better to freeze filled rolls and fry before service. To handle large quantities, it is possible to partially fry the rolls (until barely colored), drain, and hold at room temperature. Plunge into hot oil to finish cooking just before service.

Variations: Minced ham, Chinese roast pork, roast duck, shrimp, lobster, or crab may be substituted or combined with chicken. For a vegetarian version, substitute Chinese cabbage and dried soybean cake for the meat.

Spinach Phyllo Triangles (Spanokopita)

Yield: 90

	Ingredients:	
24 oz	frozen chopped spinach	674 g
2	scallions, minced	2
1 oz	butter or margarine	28 g
4 tbls	chopped dill	4 tbls
1 tbls	chopped mint	1 tbls
1 lb	feta cheese, crumbled	450 g
3	eggs, beaten	3
1 lb	phyllo leaves	450 g
4 oz	sweet butter, melted	115 g
3 tbls	olive oil	45 ml
	soft pastry brush	

1. Blanch the spinach just to thaw. Drain and squeeze dry. Set aside.

2. Sauté the scallions in a small amount of butter until wilted. Drain excess butter. Add scallions to spinach.

3. Add the herbs and crumbled feta cheese to the spinach and scallions. Mix thoroughly so that all the ingredients are evenly distributed. Mash any large lumps of feta.

4. Add the beaten eggs and mix until well combined. The filling should be fairly dry, not runny. If needed, sprinkle with a bit of dry bread crumbs to bind. Set aside.

5. Combine the melted butter and the olive oil. This will be used to brush on the phyllo sheets.

6. When working with phyllo, it is important to keep the dough from drying out and becoming brittle. If purchased frozen, follow package directions for thawing under refrigeration. If purchased fresh (refrigerated), unroll the sheets gently onto plastic wrap, cover with more plastic wrap and then with a damp towel. Work with one sheet at a time, keeping the rest covered.

7. For these triangles, the pastry sheets should be cut into strips about 2-in. (6 cm) wide. Place a strip on work surface and brush with melted butter and oil. Place a scant tablespoon of filling about 1 in. (2½ cm) from one end, lift one corner of the dough over to the opposite side of the strip to form a triangle. Turn that triangle over on itself (like point-folding a flag). Brush with a bit of the butter mixture. Continue to the end of the strip, brushing lightly with butter between every two or three turns as you go. Continue with the rest of the strips until all the filling is used. Place the completed triangles on a baking sheet brushed with melted butter. Hint: You may freeze the pastries at this point for later baking.

8. Preheat the oven to 375° F (190° C). Brush the tops of the filled pastries with more melted butter and bake for about 20 minutes until puffed and golden brown. Serve hot or at room temperature. The pastries may be reheated in a warm oven if desired. They may also be baked and frozen, but the results are better if frozen uncooked and baked before serving.

Note: Most packages of phyllo (filo or strudel leaves) contain about 24 sheets per pound. Some breakage may occur in use, so allowing for variations and loss, this recipe yields about 90 triangles.

Variations: Other fillings, such as spiced ground meat with onions, or mushrooms and cheese, may be substituted, provided the filling is not runny. Also, this recipe may be prepared in a baking pan and cut in squares for a luncheon or side dish. See recipe for Potato and Leek Torta.

Lefse Pinwheels

Yield: 40 appetizers

Ingredients:

4	sheets of dried lefse bread*	4
20–24	paper thin slices of boiled or Virginia ham, or smoked turkey	20–24
20	paper-thin slices Swiss cheese	20
	spicy brown or deli mustard, as needed	

*Lefse bread, a Scandinavian unleavened crackerlike bread, is available in ethnic markets. It looks very much like matzoh, and is usually prepared in sheets about 10 inches (25 cm) square.

1. Prepare the lefse: Wet thoroughly under running water, lay on a piece of plastic wrap. Stack one on top of the other, with waxed paper in between sheets. Cover with a damp towel and more plastic wrap. Let stand until softened and easy to roll.
2. Spread each softened lefse square with some mustard, covering the whole surface except for a thin strip along one edge. Arrange the meat slices evenly over the mustard, follow with the slices of cheese.
3. With the plain uncoated edge away from you, roll the layered lefse into a tight pinwheel, sealing the uncoated edge to the roll with a bit more water and pressing to make it stick.
4. Wrap each roll tightly in plastic wrap. Seal the completed rolls in an airtight plastic bag, and store for one or two days, until ready to serve.
5. To serve, slice the rolls into pinwheels about 1-in. (2½ cm) thick and serve immediately. If you wish to slice and arrange the pinwheels ahead of time, cover with a dampened paper towel and seal the tray with plastic wrap. They can be held refrigerated for a few hours.

Variation: **Norwegian Goat Cheese Lefse:** Combine 6 oz (180 g) of gjetost (a dark rust-colored cheese, sometimes called "chocolate cheese," available in many supermarkets and specialty stores) with 2 oz (60 g) of sweet butter. A food processor will turn this into a spread. Spread this mixture on the softened lefse and proceed as above. This mixture has a unique taste—a bit tangy, a bit sweet.

Other filling variations of your own choosing can be devised. The lefse is fairly neutral in flavor, so any thin sliced cold-cuts, cheese spreads, or flavored butters will work quite well.

Miniature Reubens

Yield: 30 appetizers

	Ingredients:	
30 slices	**small (party) rye bread***	30 slices
2 oz	**softened butter**	60 g
6 oz	**lean corned beef (12 slices)**	180 g
1 pt	**Russian dressing**	½ L
10 oz	**sauerkraut (drained)**	280 g
6 oz	**thin-sliced Swiss cheese (about 15 slices)**	180 g

*The small sliced loaves have ovals about 2½ in. (6 cm) in diameter and are handy for this recipe. Otherwise, cut rye or pumpernickel into small, attractive pieces.

1. Spread the slices of bread with a thin layer of softened butter. Lay the slices out on baking sheets.
2. Divide the corned beef among the slices and top each with a scant tablespoon of Russian dressing.

3. Place a portion of sauerkraut on each canape and top with pieces of the cheese.
4. Just before serving, place in a hot oven for about 5 minutes, finish under a broiler until cheese melts and bubbles. Serve immediately.
5. These can be prepared ahead and kept refrigerated, well wrapped or at room temperature for about an hour.

Toasted Asparagus Rolls

Yield: 40

Ingredients:

20 slices	whole wheat sandwich bread	20 slices
15–20	asparagus spears*	15–20
8 oz	whipped cream cheese	225 g
1 tbls	Worcestershire sauce	15 ml
¼ tsp	cayenne pepper	¼ tsp
1 tbls	lemon juice	15 ml
1 tsp	Dijon mustard	1 tsp
4 oz	melted butter or margarine	120 ml

*You may use fresh or frozen asparagus, cooked tender, or canned asparagus. This recipe is a good use for stalks remaining from recipes where only asparagus tips have been used.

1. Combine the cream cheese, Worcestershire, cayenne, lemon juice, and mustard. Beat or whip to mix well.
2. Spread the cream cheese mixture evenly on the bread slices and trim the crusts.
3. Roll up each asparagus spear, trimmed to fit or pieced, if necessary, in the bread slices. Press to seal. Cut into two logs. May be prepared to this point and refrigerated, covered.
4. Preheat the oven to 350° F (180° C). Place the rolls on a baking sheet, brush with a bit of melted butter and bake until lightly toasted and heated through. Roll them around on the sheet once or twice during baking to color evenly. Serve soon after baking. May be held in a warm oven or gently reheated if necessary.

Variations: **Ham and Asparagus Rolls:** Substitute deviled ham spread for half the amount of cream cheese. Cream together and adjust other seasonings to taste.
Parmesan Asparagus Rolls: Eliminate the Worcestershire sauce, cayenne, and mustard and add 2 tbls each grated Parmesan cheese and seasoned bread crumbs to the cheese.
Curried Asparagus Rolls: Eliminate the cayenne, substitute curry powder and a dab of tomato paste to the cream cheese.

Mini Empanadas

Yield: 30

Ingredients:

1 recipe	Oil Pastry for Fried Pies (see in recipe index)	1 recipe
3 tbls	olive oil	45 ml
8 oz	chopped onion	224 g
2 tbls	minced garlic	2 tbls
1 lb	ground beef	450 g
3 tbls	red taco sauce*	45 ml
2 oz	golden raisins, chopped	56 g
6	pickled tabasco peppers, tipped and chopped	6
3 oz	pimento-stuffed olives, chopped	84 g
2 oz	slivered almonds, chopped	56 g
	oil for frying	

*A good brand of bottled red taco sauce has just the right balance of tomato, jalapeño, vinegar, and spices. You may use the degree of hotness you prefer. The empanada filling should be spicy but alter to suit the taste of your client. Remember that you can always spike the filling with a little hot pepper sauce or cayenne before preparing the turnovers.

1. Prepare the pastry and allow to rest as per recipe. If it has been frozen, thaw under refrigeration.
2. Sauté the onion and garlic in the olive oil until wilted and lightly colored. Add the ground beef and cook until the meat is barely pink. Set over a colander to drain most of the excess fat.
3. Return meat mixture to skillet and add the taco sauce, raisins, peppers, olives, and almonds. Stir over low heat for a minute or two. Remove from heat and set aside for about 30 minutes to mellow flavors. Taste and correct seasonings. Place in a food processor and pulse a few times so that the entire mixture is well combined and finely chopped. The filling may be refrigerated or frozen at this point for later use. Return to room temperature before filling turnovers.
4. Lightly flour a rolling pin and work surface and roll the dough out to about ⅛-in. (½ cm) thickness. Cut 3-in. (8 cm) circles from the dough, reroll the scraps, and cut out more circles. Roll the dough firmly, but do not stretch, as the dough is quite resilient and will distort the shape of the empanadas.
5. Place a scant spoonful of filling on each dough circle, moisten the edges with water, and press firmly to seal. Crimp with a fork or pinch the edges to create a ruffled effect.
6. Heat the oil (about 3 in. or 8 cm in depth) to 350°F (180°C). Fry the empanadas a batch at a time, allowing room for them to bob around in the oil. Turn to color on both sides. Adjust the oil temperature so that the dough puffs and blisters but does not color too quickly. The empanadas should be crisp and golden, the filling heated through.

7. Drain on clean absorbent paper. They may be served immediately but will hold in a warm oven for about 45 minutes. Or hold at room temperature and reheat in a 350°F (180°C) oven. If they darken too quickly, tent (but do not cover) with foil. Fried empanadas freeze and reheat perfectly. Thaw uncovered at room temperature and reheat as above.

Miniature Calzone

Yield: 30

Ingredients:

1 recipe	**Oil Pastry for Fried Pies (see in recipe index)**	1 recipe
1 lb	**ricotta cheese**	450 g
½ lb	**mozzarella in tiny dice**	225 g
½ cup	**minced parsley**	120 ml
3 oz	**Pecorino Romano cheese, grated**	84 g
8 oz	**pepperoni, thinly sliced**	224 g
	salt and pepper (to taste)	
	oil for frying	

1. Prepare the pastry and allow to rest as per recipe. If it has been frozen, thaw under refrigeration. If cold, allow to stand covered at room temperature while preparing filling.
2. Turn the ricotta into a colander to drain any excess moisture. If the mozzarella is freshly made or water packed, press to release water and pat dry. Cut the pepperoni slices into small bits.
3. Combine the ricotta, mozzarella, parsley, grated cheese, and pepperoni. Mix vigorously to distribute all ingredients evenly in the mixture. Add a generous amount of ground black pepper and salt if needed. The mixture should be highly spiced, however, Pecorino Romano cheese is sharp and salty, so add salt only after tasting. Set aside.
4. Lightly flour a rolling pin and work surface and roll the dough out to about ⅛-in. (½ cm) thickness. Cut out circles about 3 in. (8 cm) and reserve the scraps, covered. When all the circles have been cut from the sheet of dough, reroll the scraps and cut as many more circles as possible. Roll the dough firmly, but do not stretch, as the dough is quite resilient and will distort the shape of the calzone.
5. Place a scant spoonful of filling on the center of each circle, moisten the edges with water, fold over into a half-moon shape and press firmly to seal. Use a floured fork to crimp the edges of the calzone.
6. Heat the oil (about 3 in. or 8 cm in depth) to 350°F (180°C).

7. Place the calzone into the oil a batch at a time so they have room to bob around. Turn to color both sides. Adjust the oil temperature so that the dough puffs and blisters, but does not color too quickly. The calzone should be crisp and a light golden color; the filling will be very hot and melted.
8. Drain on clean absorbent paper. The calzone may be served immediately or held in a warm oven for about 45 minutes or held at room temperature and reheated in a 350°F (180°C) oven. If they darken too quickly, tent (but do not cover) with foil. Fried calzone freeze and reheat perfectly. Thaw uncovered at room temperature, then reheat as above.

Variations: **Other Meats:** Substitute genoa salami or cooked and crumbled Italian sausage for the pepperoni, adjust seasonings to taste.
Vegetable Calzone: Add minced red and green pepper, onion, and cooked broccoli.
Prosciutto and Cheese Calzone: Substitute prosciutto for pepperoni and Parmesan for the Romano.
Basil and Cheese Calzone: Eliminate meat, add ⅓ (80 ml) cup pesto to cheeses.
Spinach Calzone: Add chopped spinach sautéed with garlic, drain excess oil; eliminate Romano, add a bit of Parmesan.

Oil Pastry For Fried Pies

Yield: 1½ lb		*674 g*
	Ingredients:	
8 oz	all-purpose flour	224 g
4 oz	bread flour*	112 g
1½ tsp	salt	1½ tsp
	Optional: pinch cayenne, turmeric, annato seed	
1 oz	lard or solid shortening	28 g
3 tbls	flavorful olive oil	45 ml
8 fl oz	water (approx.)	250 ml

*High-gluten, bleached, bromated, enriched bread flour is available through baker's suppliers but is also widely available in supermarkets.

1. Combine the dry ingredients in the bowl of a food processor (or mixer with dough hook for large quantities). See Note below for optional seasoning.
2. Place the lard or shortening and the olive oil in a saucepan and heat just until the lard melts.
3. With the machine motor running, add the heated fat, then add water just until dough begins to form a mass. (You may need a spoonful more or less of water.) Remove the dough to a lightly floured piece of waxed paper or plastic wrap, shape into a ball or disk, wrap in paper and then in a plastic bag. Let the dough rest for 1 to 2 hours at room temperature or in the refrigerator overnight or up to 3 days. For longer storage, freeze. Thaw wrapped, under refrigeration.

Note: This recipe is sufficient to make 30 to 34 small turnovers or eight 3-in. (8 cm) circles or squares of dough. Scraps can be rerolled if prevented from drying out. This dough is more substantial than the other flaky doughs, with a crisp, yet slightly chewy, breadlike consistency that makes it ideal for hearty turnovers such as calzone, empanadas, meat pies, or pasties. Such turnovers must be fried; they will not bake satisfactorily. Once fried, the turnovers may be held at room temperature or frozen and reheated very successfully.

About optional seasonings: Empanadas, Jamaican meat pies, and other Latin turnovers can be enhanced with a seasoned dough. Either add a pinch of cayenne or turmeric to the dry ingredients, or simmer one or two annato seeds in the oil until the reddish-orange color is released. Proceed with the recipe as written.

Stuffed Devils on Horseback

Yield: 50 appetizers

	Ingredients:	
50	pitted prunes*	50
½ cup	dry red or white wine	120 ml
2 fl oz	brandy	60 ml
1 fl oz	lemon juice	30 ml
pinch	quatre epices (or nutmeg and ginger)	pinch
1 tsp	ground black pepper	1 tsp
5 oz	can water chestnuts	140 g
1 lb	bacon (about 25 slices)	450 g

*Depending on the size of the fruit, a 12-oz (360 g) package of ready to eat pitted prunes contains 30 to 40 prunes.

1. Combine the wine, brandy, lemon juice, spices, and pepper in a bowl. Add the prunes and marinate at room temperature for 2 to 4 hours.
2. Cut each water chestnut into four or five pieces or slices, one piece for each prune. Cut the bacon slices in half.
3. Remove the prunes from the marinade, stuff each with a piece of water chestnut, wrap with a half slice bacon and secure with a wooden tooth pick that has been soaked in water (this prevents the picks from charring).
4. Just before serving, preheat the oven to 350° F (180° C). Place the prepared stuffed prunes on a baking pan and bake until the bacon is cooked but not too crisp. Remove to clean absorbent paper to drain grease.
5. These become very hot inside, so arrange on a tray, and wait a minute before serving so guests will not burn themselves. These can be partially cooked, held, and then reheated to speed service of large quantities.

Prunes with Bacon and Orange

Yield: 50

Ingredients:

50	pitted prunes*	50
1	orange, juice and zest	1
2 fl oz	rye or bourbon	60 ml
1 lb	bacon (about 25 slices)	450 g
	oil for frying	
	Garnish: oranges, strip of orange peel, crisp greens	

*Depending on the size of the fruit, a 12-oz (360 g) package of ready to eat pitted prunes contains 30 to 40 prunes.

1. Marinate the prunes in the juice, zest, and whiskey. Let stand 2 to 4 hours at room temperature. Remove and drain well.
2. Heat oil for frying. Use a basket or mesh skimmer.
3. Wrap each prune in one half slice bacon and secure with previously soaked toothpicks.
4. Plunge into hot fat (be careful of spatters) and cook until the bacon is cooked but not too crisp. Drain on clean absorbent paper.
5. These may be served on a bed of crisp greens or stuck into an orange (remove an inch slice from one end of the orange for stability). Garnish the tray with strips of orange zest.

Skewered and Wrapped Fruits

Yield: 100 skewers

Ingredients:

25	honeydew melon balls	25
1	large ripe papaya	1
12	ripe figs, halved	12
3	Granny Smith apples or Asian pears	3
¼ lb each	Westphalian ham, prosciutto, and braesola (air-dried beef), thinly sliced	115 g each
½ lb	smoked turkey breast, cubed	225 g
	lemon juice as needed	
	ground black pepper	
	skewers or picks as needed	
	Garnish: lemon or lime	

1. Prepare the fruits and set aside separately, refrigerated: Halve the papaya, remove the seeds and fiber, peel and cut into bite-size pieces. Cut the apples or Asian pears into six wedges, core. Cut each wedge in half. Dip the apples in lemon juice. The Asian pear will not discolor on standing.
2. Cut the turkey into chunks and skewer with the apple or pear.
3. Wrap the melon balls in pieces of Westphalian ham, the papaya pieces in strips of prosciutto, and the halved figs in the braesola. Grind black pepper over some or all of the prepared fruits. Arrange attractively on separate or mixed trays. Garnish with fresh watercress or use a carved or hollowed-out fruit as a buffet tray garnish. Lemon or lime wedges can be offered along with the fruit.

Note: This is such a simple preparation that it really requires no recipe. What is offered here is a suggestion that you can vary according to your own taste. Almost any sweet fresh fruit is complimented by smoked or cured meat. Choose your own combinations, and make the shapes and wrapping attractive to the eye and easy to pick up and eat.

Reminder: Don't forget the appeal of whole fresh fruit at a cocktail party or tea. Bowls of fresh tart or bing cherries, whole ripe strawberries, clusters of grapes, small lady apples, tiny pears, or clementines, all to be eaten out of hand, are always refreshing. They provide respite from rich and spicy cocktail offerings and to dieters or health-conscious guests, they are a welcome sight.

Szechuan Chicken Chunks

Yield: about 80 pieces

	Ingredients:	
5 lb	skinless, boneless chicken breasts*	2½ kg
3 oz	cornstarch	85 g
2 tbls	ground ginger	2 tbls
1 tbls	dry mustard	1 tbls
	oil for frying	
	Optional sauce:	
6 cups	Szechuan Chili Sauce (see in recipe index) or	1½ L
2 cups	Spicy Plum Sauce (see in recipe index)	½ L

*The recipe yield, although approximate, is based on cutting each half chicken breast into about eight generous 1-in. (2½ cm) cubes. Obviously, the size of the chunk can be altered to adjust the yield.

1. Trim the chicken breasts of fat and any cartilage or bits of bone that might be present. Cut into generous 1-in. (2½ cm) cubes.
2. Heat the frying oil. You may deep or shallow fry as convenient.
3. Combine the cornstarch with the dry spices. Sprinkle over chicken chunks and toss to combine.
4. Fry the chicken in small batches, just until they have colored and are slightly crisp on all sides. Remove to dry absorbent paper to drain.
5. If serving immediately, fry a bit longer but do not burn or overcook. The chicken should be moist and juicy inside.
6. To hold briefly, keep in a warm oven for no more than 30 minutes. If holding longer, refrigerate and reheat.
7. To prepare a day or more ahead, combine with Szechuan Chili Sauce to coat and refrigerate or freeze. The pieces can then be reheated for service without drying out. Handle carefully when reheating, as vigorous stirring will break the pieces into bits.
8. If serving dry, use either sauce as a dip when passing.

Note: This chicken preparation, along with the Szechuan Chili Sauce, can be made into a buffet dish to be served over rice, as follows: Prepare the chicken, lightly browning the pieces and add to prepared sauce. Just before serving (or before placing in chafer), add 1 lb (450 g) red and green bell pepper cut into bite-size triangles, 2 cups (500 ml) of pineapple chunks, 1 cup (¼ L) sliced water chestnuts, and 1 bunch of scallions chopped. Combine some of this into the chicken and sauce, reserve some as garnish for top. All of these additions will need very little further cooking. Usually, the heat of the sauce and the warming tray or chafer is sufficient. This expanded dish will serve 20 or more generously at a buffet.

Italian Cocktail Meatballs

Yield: 300 meatballs

	Ingredients:	
1½ lb	ground beef	700 g
1½ lb	ground pork	700 g
6 oz	stale Italian or French bread	180 g
	water for soaking bread	
8	eggs, beaten	8
3 tbls	chopped Italian parsley	3 tbls
4 oz	Italian grated cheese	115 g
	salt and pepper (to taste)	
	dry bread crumbs (as needed)	
	oil for frying	

Have the butcher grind the two meats together so they are well combined. You can alter the proportions if you like but this mixture yields a moist and flavorful meatball.

1. Soak the bread in water until soft. Squeeze out the moisture by hand, drain, and add to meat.
2. Work the soaked bread thoroughly into the meat, so that no obvious pieces of bread remain. Try not to compress the mixture; work with the hands or a large kitchen fork for best results.
3. Add the beaten egg, the parsley, the cheese, and generous seasoning. Mix as above until the mixture is well combined and fluffy.
4. If you are unsure of the seasonings, test fry a bit and taste.
5. Dust your hands with bread crumbs and roll the mixture into balls the size of large marbles.
6. Heat the oil for frying (a combination of vegetable and olive oil is preferred) in a frying pan or cast-iron skillet. Fry the meatballs, a batch at a time over moderate heat, turning to brown on all sides. They should be crusty and cooked through but not dry. Adjust the heat so that the interior cooks without the crust burning. Drain on clean absorbent paper.
7. Serve soon after frying or hold at room temperature or in a warm oven. Do not overheat or they will dry out. To hold for a day or two, refrigerate. They may be cooked ahead and frozen. Let come to room temperature before reheating gently.

Note: These meatballs are very good served plain, especially when freshly fried. You may also serve with a spicy tomato sauce if desired. They are quite tasty at room temperature and a good choice for a plain, unsauced hors d'oeuvre. Children love them because of their small size and uncomplicated taste.

Variation: Obviously, these may be made in a larger size to be served with spaghetti or in a hero. This recipe yields about 50 2½-in. meatballs. The tiny meatballs may be poached in broth rather than fried, as they are in Escarole and Meatball Soup (see in recipe index).

Chicken Sate

Yield: *36 skewers*

Ingredients:

36	bamboo skewers	36
2	chicken breasts, boned and skinned (about 2 lb [900 g])	2
3 tbls	lime juice	45 ml
2 tbls	soy sauce	30 ml
1 tbls	sesame oil	15 ml
1	whole garlic clove	1
dash	hot pepper sauce	dash
few slices	gingerroot	few slices

1. Soak the bamboo skewers in water for a few hours to protect them from burning on the grill or broiler.
2. Trim the chicken breasts of any fat or cartilage, cut into ribbonlike slices or strips. Combine the remaining ingredients and pour over the chicken, tossing to coat. Marinate, covered and refrigerated, for at least one hour.
3. Remove the chicken from the marinade, discard the ginger and garlic. Thread the strips of chicken on the bamboo skewers. Do not crowd the meat, but concentrate the meat toward one end of the skewer so it can be eaten easily.
4. Just before serving, heat a grill, broiler, or salamander. Cook the meat about 3 in. (8 cm) from the flame or heat source, turning to brown evenly. Do not overcook or the chicken will be dried out. Serve immediately or wrap in foil and hold in a warm oven for about 30 minutes. Serve with lime wedges, Hot Peanut Sauce (see in recipe index), or a dipping sauce of your choice.

Note: The sates can be prepared for broiling several hours ahead. To pack for transport, bunch together, wrap the meat ends in foil, wrap wet paper towel and foil over the skewer ends, pinch the foil to close tightly and place the whole bunch in a plastic bag. Keep cold.

Pork Sate

Yield: 30 skewers

Ingredients:

30	bamboo skewers	30
2 lb	boneless pork butt	900 g
3 tbls	peanut oil	45 ml
1	garlic clove, smashed	1
1 tbls	minced gingerroot	1 tbls
1 tbls	hot red pepper flakes (to taste)	1 tbls
4 tbls	orange juice	60 ml

1. Soak the bamboo skewers in water for a few hours to protect them from burning on the grill or broiler.
2. Trim the meat of all visible fat. Cut across the grain into ½-in. (1½ cm) slices. Cut the slices into squares about the size of postage stamps.
3. Combine the other ingredients, pour over the pork, mixing well to coat the meat. Marinate, covered and refrigerated, for at least two hours.
4. Thread three or four pieces of meat on the end of each skewer, keeping them close together.

5. Heat a grill, broiler, or salamander. Cook at least 4 in. (10 cm) from flame so the meat cooks through without burning. Turn to brown on all sides. The cooking should take about 10 to 12 minutes. The pork should be crisp on the outside and show no trace of pink when tested. Serve immediately or wrap in foil and hold in a warm oven for about 45 minutes. Serve hot with Hot Peanut Sauce (see in recipe index) for dipping. Or to serve without sauce, sprinkle with toasted sesame seeds just as you remove from the broiler.

Note: See recipe for Chicken Sate for advance preparation, storage, and transport.

Beef Sate

Yield: 24 skewers

Ingredients:

24	bamboo skewers	24
1½ lb	boneless sirloin	675 g
1	garlic clove, smashed	1
1 tbls	soy sauce	15 ml
1 tsp	Worcestershire sauce	5 ml
1 tbls	dry sherry	15 ml
1 tsp	brown sugar	5 g
1 tsp	cracked black pepper	1 tsp
1 tbls	peanut or vegetable oil	15 ml

You may use any tender broiling cut. This recipe is an excellent use for the tip (or tail end) of whole tenderloins. You may use lesser cuts as well—the filet of chuck or rump—but marinate those meats for at least 3 hours.

1. Soak the bamboo skewers in water for a few hours to protect them from burning on the grill or broiler.
2. Trim the meat of all visible fat and cut into 1-in. (2½ cm) cubes. You should have about 48 pieces.
3. Combine the other ingredients, pour over the meat, and massage in for a minute or two. Marinate for 15 minutes.
4. Thread two pieces of meat on each skewer. Or serve one to a skewer for double yield if you like. Obviously, you will need double the amount of skewers.
5. Heat a grill, broiler, or salamander. Cook, turning to sear all sides. These will cook very quickly and should be served very rare. These are good served hot or at room temperature. If serving hot, use Hot Peanut Sauce or Barbecue Sauce (see in recipe index). If serving at room temperature, select a horseradish dip or seasoned mayonnaise.

Note: See recipe for Chicken Sate for advance preparation, storage, and transport.

Curried Lamb Sate

Yield: 24 skewers

	Ingredients:	
24	bamboo skewers	24
2 lb	boneless leg of lamb	900 g
2	whole garlic cloves	2
1 tsp	salt	1 tsp
few sprigs	cilantro (leaf coriander)	few sprigs
1 tbls	hot curry powder	1 tbls
¼ tsp	cumin	¼ tsp
1 cup	coconut milk*	¼ L

*This is coconut milk, used in curries and Far Eastern dishes, not the canned sweetened coconut cream used for making piña coladas.

1. Soak the bamboo skewers in water for a few hours to protect them from burning on the grill or broiler.
2. Carefully trim the meat of all visible fat, especially the interior fat glands between the muscle segments, as this has a particularly unpleasant odor and taste. Cut the trimmed meat into ½-in. (1½ cm) cubes.
3. Place the garlic cloves on a cutting board, smash with the side of a knife, and sprinkle salt over. Roll garlic in the salt and chop with the salt. Rinse the cilantro and chop coarsely. Include the stem and root (if attached). Add to the garlic and salt and mince all together to a paste. Transfer the paste to a small bowl and mix in curry powder and cumin. Stir in the coconut milk.
4. Add the lamb cubes to the marinade and stir well to coat. Marinate for about 30 minutes at cool room temperature or refrigerated for 1 or 2 hours.
5. Thread three or four cubes of meat on one end of each skewer, keeping the pieces fairly close together.
6. Heat a grill, broiler, or salamander. Broil the pieces about 4 in. (10 cm) from the heat, turning to brown evenly. Cook about 5 minutes for medium rare. Serve immediately or wrap in foil and keep warm in a moderate oven for about 30 minutes. Serve with Hot Peanut Sauce (see in recipe index) or the dipping sauce of your choice. They are also delicious plain or sprinkled with chopped peanuts just as you take them from the broiler.

Note: See recipe for Chicken Sate for advance preparation, storage, and transport.

Curried Potato Balls

Yield: 24–30 appetizers

Ingredients:

3 cups	mashed potatoes	¾ L
2 tbls	olive oil or butter	30 ml or 30 g
2	scallions, minced	2
1 tsp	minced garlic	1 tsp
1 tsp	minced coriander	1 tsp
1 tbls	minced parsley	1 tbls
½ tsp	curry powder (or to taste)	½ tsp
	salt and pepper (to taste)	
1	egg, lightly beaten	1
	flour, egg wash, and bread crumbs for coating	
	oil for frying	

1. Heat the oil or butter in a sauté pan or skillet, add the scallion and garlic, and sauté until wilted and lightly colored. Add the fresh herbs and the curry powder and stir over low heat for about 30 seconds. Remove from heat.
2. Add the sautéed mixture to the mashed potatoes, stirring to mix well. Season with salt and pepper. Add only enough of the beaten egg to moisten; the mixture should not be loose. Chill for at least 1 hour.
3. With well-floured hands, roll the mixture into balls. Dip into egg wash then roll in bread crumbs. Fry in hot oil.

Zucchini Basil Pancakes

Serves: 24

Ingredients:

2 lb	zucchini	900 g
4	eggs, beaten	4
1 oz	all-purpose flour (approx.)	28 g
4 tbls	grated Parmesan cheese	4 tbls
2 tbls	minced basil leaves	2 tbls
2 tbls	minced parsley	2 tbls
	salt and pepper (to taste)	
	clarified butter or olive oil to grease skillet	

1. Scrub the zucchini to remove all surface grit. Trim and grate, preferably into long shreds. If you are using very large zucchini, remove the seedy centers and add a bit more zucchini to make up for the loss.
2. Place the zucchini in a cheesecloth-lined colander to drain. Gently squeeze the cloth to remove excess moisture.
3. Place the zucchini in a bowl, add the eggs, flour, cheese, herbs, and seasonings.
4. Heat a nonstick skillet. Wipe with a paper towel or brush dipped in either the clarified butter or oil to grease surface. Test-fry 1 tbls (15 ml) of the batter to check consistency. The pancake should be small and lacy and brown quickly on both sides. If the batter seems too runny, add a sprinkle more flour. If too thick, add drops of water.
5. Fry all the pancakes, removing them to clean absorbent paper to drain any grease. Place on a shallow pan in a moderate oven to keep warm. Brush skillet with fat occasionally if the pancakes stick.
6. Serve soon after frying with either Pesto Alla Genovese or Spicy Tomato Sauce (see in recipe index).

Note: Pesto sauce may be thinned to dipping consistency by blending in a bit more either olive oil or warm water. The yield for this recipe is approximate, based on the size of the pancake: For hors d'oeuvre, pancakes can be made from 1 to 3 in. (2½ to 8 cm).

Variation: **Multicolored Pancakes:** You may substitute shredded yellow summer squash for half the amount of zucchini, eliminate the basil and Parmesan, substitute grated cheddar and 2 tbls finely minced red bell pepper. Serve these pancakes at room temperature with an herb mayonnaise for dipping.

Savory Fruit Fritters

Yield: *about 30 fritters*

	Ingredients:	
6 oz	all-purpose flour	180 g
1 tsp	baking powder	1 tsp
2	egg yolks	2
½ tsp	each salt and pepper	½ tsp
½ tsp	paprika	½ tsp
	cinnamon, curry, or other spice (to taste)	
1 cup	beer	¼ L
1 lb	fruit pieces (approx.)	450 g
	oil for frying	

Chunks of banana, coarsely chopped apples or pears, canned and drained peaches, apricots, or pineapple chunks (or rings), or halved seedless grapes can all be used. The amount is approximate because of the size of the cuts and the relative weights of the fruit. However, as a guideline, this amount of batter is sufficient to coat 2 cups (500 ml) of pineapple chunks. The batter can be made in larger batches but should be used within 24 to 36 hours.

1. Combine the flour, baking powder, egg yolks, and spices. Mix well.
2. Mix in the beer, stirring until the foam subsides (or use flat beer). Beat a minute or two.
3. Let the batter stand, refrigerated, at least several hours or overnight to relax the gluten.
4. When ready to cook, prepare the fruit. Apples, pears, and bananas can be sprinkled with lemon or orange juice to prevent discoloration if prepared ahead. Drain before using. Canned fruits are best drained on absorbent paper before adding to batter.
5. Heat oil for frying (350° F) (175° C). Do not use a basket.
6. Stir fruit into batter or dip larger pieces such as pineapple rings or banana chunks, if desired. Drop into fat and fry until golden and crisp. Drain well on absorbent paper. Serve soon after frying or hold, uncovered in a warm oven.

Note: These may be served plain or sprinkled with salt and pepper, if desired. They are also very good served with a dipping sauce, such as Spicy Plum Sauce or Chutney Dipping Sauce (see in recipe index).

Variations: Use the spices listed or others to enhance the various fruits: cinnamon with apple, pear, or banana; curry with banana, apple, or grapes; peaches and apricots with cinnamon, cloves, and nutmeg.

Sweet Fruit Fritters: Eliminate all the spices except ¼ tsp salt, then add sweet spices, especially cinnamon. Add about a tablespoon of sugar to the batter and a teaspoon of vanilla, rum, brandy, or other liqueur. Before serving, sprinkle with a dusting of confectioner's sugar. These fritters make a very nice addition to a dessert buffet or a tea.

Simple Beer Batter

Yield: 1 cup   *250 ml*

Ingredients:

4 oz	**all-purpose flour**	112 g
8 fl oz	**beer**	¼ L
	salt, pepper and/or other seasonings (to taste)	

1. Combine the beer with the flour, stirring until the foam subsides. Season according to use, with either savory or sweet spices. You may add up to 2 tsp of liquid flavoring, such as soy sauce, brandy, sherry, or vanilla. For sweet frying, add 1 tablespoon of sugar to batter.
2. Let the batter rest, refrigerated, for several hours or overnight to complete fermentation and relax gluten.

Note: Use as a frying batter for fruits, vegetables, shrimp, fish, or meats. One item should be test fried and the batter thinned with a bit of water to achieve the desired crust, if the coating seems a bit too thick. Be certain that the items to be dipped in batter are well drained of excess moisture.

Sweet Potato and Other Chips and Fries

Serves: 25

Ingredients:

5 lb	sweet potatoes	2½ kg
	oil for deep frying	
	salt, pepper, or other seasonings (as desired)	

1. Peel the sweet potatoes, removing deep blemishes or soft spots. Trim one end flat.
2. Heat the oil in a deep fryer with a basket or have a mesh skimmer handy.
3. Using a mandoline or electric slicer, slice the potatoes wafer thin.
4. Separate the slices if they have stuck together and fry in hot oil until lightly browned and crisp. Do not burn. Some of the irregular or extra-thin slices will curl up. Drain on clean absorbent paper.
5. Salt or season if desired, although they are delicious unsalted. The salt may be mixed with pepper or seasoned with a bit of curry or chili powder if desired.
6. When completely drained and cool, transfer to sturdy containers for transport. Cookie tins or cake boxes lined with waxed paper work well. These chips will stay fresh for at least a week.

Note: It's hard to specify a yield for this recipe but a batch this size will do as chips for a cocktail party along with other nibbles.

Variations: Parsnips and/or yellow turnips (rutabagas) can be handled in the same manner. They also make interesting chips.

Sweet potatoes and the other root vegetables can be prepared as shoestring fries as well. These preparations, however, do not hold and must be served as soon as possible after frying. Try mixing the vegetables for an interesting side dish.

Spiced Hush Puppies

Yield: about 40

Ingredients:

7 oz	cornmeal	200 g
2 oz	all purpose flour	60 g
2 tsp	baking powder	2 tsp
½ tsp	cayenne pepper (or to taste)	½ tsp
1 tsp	salt	1 tsp
½ tsp	ground black pepper	½ tsp
½ tsp	dry mustard	½ tsp

pinch	**thyme**	pinch
1	**whole egg, beaten**	1
6 fl oz	**buttermilk**	180 ml
4 oz	**onion, chopped fine**	115 g
4 oz	**scallions, chopped fine**	115 g
	oil for frying	

1. Heat oil for frying. You may shallow or deep fry, but do not use a basket.
2. Combine the cornmeal, flour, baking powder, and dry spices. Set aside. Combine the egg with the buttermilk, mix and add to the dry ingredients. Stir to mix.
3. Stir in the scallion and onions, stir to distribute.
4. Drop by spoonfuls into hot fat. Test-fry one or two to determine desired size and cooking temperature. Usually, a soup spoon used as a measure and oil at about 375°F (190°C) is best. If they are too large, they will not cook through without burning; if too small, they will be dry and hard. Do not overcrowd the pan because they puff up and need room to bob around to cook evenly.
5. Drain on absorbent paper. They are best made in batches just before service. To hold for a short time, place in a flat, shallow pan, uncovered, in a warm oven.

Note: These are spicy, but not unbearably so. Adjust the seasonings to suit the tastes of guests and the overall menu.

Variations: **Filled Hush Puppies:** Diced ham, crumbled bacon, diced red and green bell pepper, diced cooked shrimp, cooked or smoked fish, and minced parsley or chives may be added to the batter. Choose a single ingredient or an appropriate combination, adding about 1 cup (6 to 8 oz or 200 g) to the batter and mixing to combine. Adjust the seasonings accordingly. Cooked or canned whole-kernel corn may also be added, but because of the weight and density, the batter will need adjustment: Add a bit more cornmeal or buttermilk for consistency, and another ½ tsp baking powder to lighten.

Mozzarella Puffs

Yield: 36 appetizers

	Ingredients:	
8 oz	**mozzarella cheese,* grated**	250 g
1 oz	**grated Romano cheese**	28 g
½ tsp	**ground white pepper**	½ tsp
3	**egg whites**	3
8 oz	**dry seasoned bread crumbs**	250 g
	oil for frying	

*Use the packaged dry mozzarella for this recipe, not the freshly made or water-packed.

1. Combine the mozzarella, Romano cheese, and pepper. Set aside.
2. Whip the egg whites until stiff, but not dry and grainy, or they will break down.
3. Fold the whites into the cheese just to combine. Try not to deflate the whites.
4. Drop the mixture by spoonfuls into the bread crumbs and roll into round balls. Set out on a work surface or tray to dry for about 20 minutes.
5. Heat the oil for frying. Fry the balls until golden brown and crusty. Do not overcook or the cheese will melt and leak out. They are done very quickly. Drain on clean absorbent paper. Serve soon after frying. Keep warm for about 30 minutes in a very slow oven.
6. To prepare ahead, fry, drain, and cool. Freeze on flat trays until hard, then place in plastic bags. Reheat in a 350° (180° C) oven before serving. Do not overheat or they will collapse.

Variations: Smoked Mozzarella Puffs can be made as follows: Eliminate the Romano cheese, add some minced sun-dried tomatoes and substitute dry smoked mozzarella. Proceed as above.

Ham and Swiss Puffs

Yield: 36 appetizers

	Ingredients:	
6 oz	Swiss cheese, grated	180 g
4 oz	minced cooked ham	115 g
2 tbls	minced chives	2 tbls
1 tbls	mustard, brown or Dijon	1 tbls
1 dash	hot pepper sauce	1 dash
3	egg whites	3
8 oz	dry bread crumbs	225 g
	oil for frying	

1. Combine the Swiss cheese with the ham and scallions, add the mustard and hot pepper sauce, and stir to combine the seasonings.
2. Whip the egg whites until stiff, but not dry and grainy, or they will break down.
3. Stir a large spoonful of the egg whites into the ham and cheese mixture to lighten the texture. Fold in the remaining egg whites just to combine. Try not to deflate.
4. Drop the mixture by spoonfuls into bread crumbs and roll into round balls. Set out on a work surface or tray to dry for about 20 minutes.
5. Heat the oil for frying. Fry the balls until golden and crusty. Do not overcook or the cheese will melt and leak out. They cook quickly. Drain on clean absorbent paper. Serve soon after frying. They may be held for about 30 minutes in a very slow oven.
6. To prepare ahead, fry, drain, and cool. Freeze on flat trays until hard. Then store in plastic bags. Reheat in a 350° F (180° C) oven before serving. Do not overheat or they will collapse.

Celery or Endive Rosettes

Yield: 40 appetizers

Ingredients:

2	celery hearts	2
4–5	Belgian endive	4–5
1½ cups	of any of the following:	350 ml
	Roquefort Calvados Dip (see in recipe index)	
	Pesto Cream (see in recipe index)	
	Herb Butter (see Compound or Flavored Butters in recipe index)	
	Goat Cheese Butter (see Compound or Flavored Butters in recipe index)	
	lemon juice (as needed)	

1. Allow the chosen butter or dip to soften slightly at room temperature.
2. Wash the celery hearts: Trim off and discard about an inch from the end and enough of the root to release the outer stalks. Dismantle the celery heart, stalk by stalk, keeping the stalks in order so they can be reassembled. Spread or pipe the chosen filling into the tiny center stalks and reshape. Continue with the next layer of stalks, adding more filling as you go, until the heart is reshaped. Place on a sheet of plastic wrap and wrap tightly to hold into shape. Overwrap with more plastic wrap and refrigerate at least overnight or for 2 or 3 days.
3. Follow the same procedure with each head of Belgian endive but be a bit more gentle, since the leaves are easily bruised. Sprinkle the outer leaves of the reshaped endive with a bit of lemon juice to protect it from discoloration. Wrap tightly as above. Refrigerate for several hours or overnight.
4. When ready to serve, use a sharp knife to cut the stuffed vegetables into crosswise slices to form "rosettes" and arrange on serving trays. Keep refrigerated until about 20 minutes before serving. In very hot weather, keep well chilled and replenish trays often or the rosettes will soften too much and fall apart.

Salami Cornucopias

Yield: 25 appetizers

Ingredients:

1 lb	Genoa salami, diagonally thin sliced (about 25 slices)	450 g
8 oz	pot cheese, drained	224 g
8 oz	ricotta, drained	224 g
2 tbls	Parmesan cheese	2 tbls

2 tbls	minced parsley or chives	2 tbls
	salt and pepper (to taste)	
	Optional garnish: Minced parsley or chives	

1. Shape each salami slice into a cone, pressing the overlapped portion firmly. It should stick together and hold its shape; if not, secure with a toothpick and refrigerate covered.
2. When the pot cheese and ricotta have been drained of excess moisture, mash together with a fork, stir in the Parmesan cheese, either the minced parsley or chives, and salt and pepper to taste. Stir well to distribute all the ingredients.
3. Fill each cornucopia with a generous tablespoon of cheese mixture. Or use a pastry bag with an open tube to fill. Store, covered and refrigerated, until ready to serve. They may be held, filled for several hours. Just before serving, sprinkle with a bit of herb, if desired.

Note: These can be prepared up to 36 hours ahead, if kept well covered and chilled. However, they could be messy to transport, so it is probably easier (in the catering sense) to fill on site.

Stuffed Tuscan Loaf

Yield: about 75 pieces

Ingredients:

1	large round crusty loaf of Italian bread (12–14-in. [30–35 cm] diam.)	1
10 thin slices	Virginia or boiled ham	10 thin slices
30	thin asparagus spears	30
25 thin slices	Genoa salami	25 thin slices
25	sesame bread sticks	25
4 oz	whipped cream cheese	115 g
1 tbls	brown mustard	15 ml
10 stalks	hearts of palm	10 stalks
10 slices	prosciutto	10 slices
	curly endive or kale	

My local bakery prepares a brick oven bread, called a Tuscan Loaf, with a magnificent raised pattern of crust centered on its top. Any sturdy, handsome rustic loaf will work as well.

1. Prepare the bread by cutting an attractive round or square lid about 1 in. (2½ cm) deep. Set the lid aside and hollow out some of the inside dough to form a container for the following rolled hors d'oeuvre.
2. Trim the asparagus, plunge in boiling salted water for less than a minute (just to color), shock in ice water, and drain. If the asparagus are very thin and tender, you may use them raw; simply wash and trim well.

3. Cut the ham into three lengthwise strips. Roll each strip in a spiral fashion around each asparagus spear. Set aside.
4. Combine the cream cheese with the mustard. Spread thinly on each salami slice and wrap the coated slices, cheese side in around the bread sticks.
5. Drain the hearts of palm and cut into three sections each. Some of the stalks may be thick enough to split lengthwise. You should have at least 30 pieces, each about 2-in (5 cm) long. Cut the prosciutto to appropriate size and wrap around the pieces of palm. If the prosciutto does not stick to itself, use a pick to secure.
6. Trim, wash, and drain the curly endive or kale.
7. To assemble the loaf on site: Place some greens in the bread cavity. Begin to place the bread sticks and the asparagus in a random pattern in the cavity of the bread container, as though arranging a bouquet. Use pieces of green in between for color and support. Gently tuck in some of the hearts of palm among the other hors d'oeuvre. You may use picks to secure some pieces of palm here and there around the edge of the cavity.
8. Place the filled bread on a board or appropriate serving piece and lay the balance of the rolled hors d'oeuvre around the bread. Fill in with extra unwrapped breadsticks if needed.
9. While assembly is best done just before service begins, the palm and prosciutto can be prepared a few hours ahead and kept covered and refrigerated. The asparagus and the salami can be wrapped about an hour ahead and kept at cool room temperature. If held and refrigerated too long, the bread sticks will get soggy and the asparagus begin to wilt. The whole assembly can be complete about 45 minutes before guests are served, provided the room is not too hot. Drape with plastic wrap.

Note: To adjust yield, choose a smaller loaf and prepare fewer pieces. To serve a very large crowd, prepare the loaf as directed but have additional rolled pieces ready to refresh the buffet.

Chewy Crust Pizza

Yield: 3 lb		1 kg 360 g

	Ingredients:	
	Dough:	
1¾ lb	bread flour	800 g
3 tsp	salt	3 tsp
1 tbls	granulated sugar	15 g
1 pt	warm water, 115°F (46°C)	½ L
1 oz	dry yeast (3 pkg)	30 g
3 tbls	olive oil	45 ml

Toppings: 1 cup (¼ L) plum tomatoes or Spicy Tomato Sauce (see in recipe index), basil, 2 cups (500 ml) shredded mozzarella; 1 cup (¼ L) ricotta, 1 cup (¼ L) shredded mozzarella, basil, parsley; 1 cup (¼ L) Spicy Tomato Sauce (see in recipe index), ½ cup (125 ml) grated Romano cheese, 1½ cups (375 ml) shredded mozzarella, ½ cup (125 ml) sliced pepperoni

olive oil (as needed)
flour or cornmeal for dusting pans

Since this recipe makes enough dough for three pizzas, each approximately 15-in. (38 cm) round or 10 × 15 in. (25 × 38 cm) rectangles, the ingredients for three different pizza toppings are included: a plain tomato and cheese (or Margherita); a white pizza (bianco) with just herbs and cheese, no tomatoes; and an old-fashioned spicy pepperoni, pizzeria style. Of course, you may choose the toppings you like to create your own. This dough, stretched a bit thinner, is very good for new-wave pizzas, with ingredients ranging from sun-dried tomato and goat cheese to cajun-spiced shrimp. For Chicago-style deep dish pizza, leave the dough a bit thicker and place in a rimmed pan.

1. Combine the bread flour, salt, and sugar in a large bowl.
2. Dissolve the yeast in the water, let stand a few minutes.
3. Add the dissolved yeast and olive oil to the flour, mix into a rough dough. Knead on a floured board for at least 10 minutes (or in the mixer with a dough hook for at least 5 minutes, until the dough is firm, resilient, and smooth. If the dough is a bit too dry, sprinkle with a few drops more water.
4. When kneading is complete, rub the dough ball with a bit of olive oil to coat the surface, place in an oiled bowl, and allow to rise, covered, for about an hour, until doubled in size.
5. Punch down the raised dough, shape into a fat roll, and divide into three portions.
6. Working with one portion at a time, roll and stretch into desired shape. It will be very resistant at first but will soon yield to gentle stretching and coaxing. When each piece is the shape and size you want, place on a pan or peel (if you have a baking stone and peel, the pizza will be that much better, but it is still very good using metal pans or heavy-duty baking sheets). Dust the peel and the pans with flour or cornmeal before placing dough.
7. Preheat the oven to 450°F (230°C). Prepare the pizzas: Use your fingertips to make little depressions all over the dough except for the rim. Sprinkle generously with olive oil, rubbing it all over the dough. Brush oil on the thicker edges as well. Spread tomato sauce (or ideally, raw or canned plum tomatoes, peeled, seeded, and chopped) over one pizza. Sprinkle with minced fresh basil, scatter with mozzarella, sprinkle with salt and pepper if you have not used prepared sauce. For White Pizza, combine the ricotta, mozzarella, and grated cheese. Oil the dough lightly as above. Spread cheese mixture over pizza, sprinkle with minced herbs, and a bit of ground pepper to taste. Sprinkle more olive oil over top. For third pizza, oil dough liberally as in first pizza, spread tomato sauce, sprinkle with Romano, scatter slices of pepperoni, top with mozzarella.

8. Place the completed pizzas in the oven to bake for a total of 20 to 25 minutes. After the first 10 minutes, when the dough bottom has browned, lower the heat to about 400°F (205°C) to allow the pizzas to bake through without burning. It is especially important for the white pizza; very high heat can make the cheese rubbery.

9. Remove the pizzas and cut into wedges or squares to serve. Pizza can be held in a warm oven for about 45 minutes, and even gently reheated, but it is at its best freshly baked.

10. Preparing ahead: Pizza dough can be refrigerated, either while rising to retard growth, or after rising, for a few hours. Or, you can prepare the discs of dough ahead and freeze, topping just before baking. Pizzas made with prepared sauce can be topped and frozen if necessary with pretty good results. Partially baked pizza may be frozen if necessary (do not overbrown) and baking completed before serving. There will be a small, but acceptable, loss in quality.

Note: This dough is easy to make and particularly chewy and yeasty. You may, of course, use a good-quality prepared pizza dough. Test bake a pizza to be sure it yields the results you desire. Adjust treatment and cooking times to suit the dough you use. This dough has other uses: See recipes for Focaccia and Stuffed Pizza Slices (see in recipe index).

Variations: A Pissaladière, a pizzalike specialty of the south of France, can be prepared using this dough. Roll a bit thinner, spread with olive oil. The usual topping for pissaladière is sautéed onion and garlic, sprinkled with herbs, and topped with nicoise olives and strips of anchovies. It is traditionally baked in a rectangle and cut into squares.

Focaccia

Yield: about 60 3-inch squares

Ingredients:

1 recipe	**Chewy Crust Pizza dough (see in preceding recipe)**	1 recipe
12 fl oz	**flavorful olive oil**	350 ml

Toppings: coarse salt, freshly ground pepper; herbs, such as basil, sage, rosemary, oregano; canned plum tomatoes; Italian grated cheeses

flour or cornmeal for dusting pans

1. Prepare the pizza dough according to the recipe up to first rising. Punch down the dough and shape into rectangles or rounds.

2. Select pans or dishes large enough to accommodate the shaped pieces of dough. Pour in some olive oil, place the dough in the pan and pour more oil over the top. Allow the dough to soak in the oil for about 20 minutes.

3. Preheat the oven to 375° F (190° C).

4. Remove the dough to a floured baking pan (or peel, if you are using one). Press with fingertips to form depressions all over the dough. Sprinkle liberally with some of the oil from the soaking dishes, sprinkle with toppings of your choice. You may use only liberal salt and pepper or add bits of fresh (or even dried herbs). If you choose to use tomatoes, carefully seed them, drain their juice, and crumble with your fingers. Smear the tomato on the dough to make a thin coating.

5. Bake for about 15 minutes, then lower oven to 350° F (180° C) for 5 minutes to complete cooking. Focaccia may be served hot or warm cut into wedges or squares. It is traditionally eaten at room temperature as a snack. As it stands, the oil redistributes through the dough making it even more delicious, so it is recommended that these be made ahead. They can be kept at room temperature for a day, refrigerated for about 3 days, or frozen for longer storage. Let come to room temperature and reheat for just a few minutes to freshen.

Note: Remember that focaccias are never loaded down with toppings like pizzas but flavored by rubbed-in toppings that season the dough so they can be served like bread, in small pieces to be eaten out of hand, either as an accompaniment to other foods or as tasty snacks. Because they are salty and chewy, they are good served with drinks.

Variations: If you like the softer, oilier consistency of the focaccia, instead of the crisper pizza, you may use the same oil-rising technique and lower baking temperatures here used for preparing Chewy Crust Pizza (see preceding recipe). It is best to make these small individual pizzas to be served on a plate with knife and fork for easier eating.

Stuffed Pizza Slices

Yield: 45 slices

Ingredients:

1 recipe	Chewy Crust Pizza dough (see in recipe index)	1 recipe
4 tbls	flavorful olive oil	60 ml
	egg wash	
	flour for pans	

Fillings: 1 cup (¼ L) thick pesto, 2 cups (500 ml) shredded mozzarella; 12 slices Genoa salami, 12 thin slices provolone; 1 cup (¼ L) chopped and drained roasted peppers, garlic clove, 8 anchovies, ¼ cup (60 ml) pitted and minced oil-cured olives

sesame and/or poppy seeds, if desired for garnish

Three fillings are suggested here to make three different stuffed pizzas. The long shape makes them easy to slice into portions as hearty hors d'oeuvre or part of an Italian buffet. Each roll provides about 15 slices. You may invent fillings of your own, selecting from other sliced meats, cheeses, and flavorful spreads, provided the fillings are not too runny and thin enough to fold nicely and cook through.

1. Prepare the pizza dough as per recipe. Divide the raised dough into three portions.
2. On a lightly floured board, roll each piece into a rectangle no wider than 6 in. (15 cm). Be patient and make the dough very thin.
3. Rub a sheet of dough with a bit of olive oil, spread with pesto, and sprinkle with cheese, leaving a 1-in. (2½ cm) border on all but one long side. Brush the border with egg wash, and fold over twice, beginning at the filled long edge. Pinch the edges and the long seam to seal tightly. Place seam side down on a floured baking sheet.
4. Prepare the second sheet of dough by rubbing with a bit of oil and layering with salami and provolone. Egg wash, fold, and seal as above.
5. Prepare the third sheet as follows: Put the garlic through a press, add the puree to a bit of oil, and mix with the roasted peppers. Spread this mixture over the dough sheet. Distribute the anchovies and olives over the filling. Egg wash, fold, and seal as above.
6. Preheat the oven to 400°F (205°C). Let the rolls rest, covered, for about 15 minutes.
7. After the rolls have rested and risen slightly, brush all over with egg wash, sprinkle with sesame or poppy seeds if desired, or sprinkle with salt and pepper. Double-pan to prevent burning the bottoms.
8. Bake for 15 minutes at 400°F (205°C), lower oven to 350°F (180°C) and bake an additional 5 to 10 minutes, until golden brown. Remove from oven to a rack and let cool for about 15 minutes before slicing. These are good served warm or at room temperature. They may be made ahead and reheated, or partially baked, frozen and reheated to brown before serving. Do not slice until ready to serve.

Note: These pizzas may be made into individual portions (about the size of club rolls) to serve as a luncheon main course.

Variation: You may also make Sfincione, the Sicilian stuffed pizza. Shape dough into rounds, fill, and top with another round of dough. Egg wash the edges, seal well, and bake. In Palermo, these are filled with tomato, onions, and anchovies or sardines, but you may use fillings of your own choosing.

Dressings, Dips, and Sauces

Mayonnaise and Variations

Yield: 1 qt   *1 L*

	Ingredients:	
2	eggs	2
4	egg yolks	4
1 tbls	Dijon mustard	1 tbls
2 tbls	lemon juice or vinegar	2 tbls
½ tsp	salt (or to taste)	½ tsp
1 tsp	ground white pepper	1 tsp
2 cups	oil	½ L

Lemon juice can almost always be used. Some cooks choose a vinegar or oil for its particular flavor, for example, tarragon vinegar or olive oil. Whatever you choose, be sure it is first quality, since mayonnaise can only be as good as its few simple ingredients.

1. Prepare in a blender or processor as follows: Combine the eggs, yolks, mustard, salt and some white pepper, process about 30 seconds. Add the lemon juice or vinegar, again process 30 seconds.
2. With the machine running, slowly add oil in a thin stream. As the mayonnaise takes shape, you can add the balance of the oil more quickly. Add oil until the mixture is

the desired consistency. Taste for seasoning. You may add more salt and pepper, or more lemon juice or vinegar.

3. Store, covered and refrigerated, for no more than 1 week.

Note: For some purposes, a thinner or thicker mayonnaise is desirable. Beat in a bit more oil to thicken or a few spoons of warm water to thin.

Variations: **Green Mayonnaise:** Add the following with the lemon juice: a pinch of fresh chervil, few leaves of tarragon, 2 tbls parsley, ½ cup (125 ml) watercress leaves, three or four leaves fresh spinach. Process the greens, then proceed with mayonnaise, or add the pureed leaves to already prepared mayonnaise.
Herb Mayonnaise: Add 2 to 3 tbls of one selected herb or a complimentary mixture. Choose from cilantro, dill, parsley, tarragon, or basil, for example.
Lemon-Caper Mayonnaise: Increase the lemon to taste, fold in 3 tbls chopped capers, add ground pepper for a piquant flavor.
Grainy Mustard Mayonnaise: Begin mayonnaise with 2 tbls Pommery mustard, soften flavor with a bit of apple or orange juice.
Avocado Mayonnaise: Begin recipe as directed, using 3 tbls of lemon juice. Add a small amount of oil just to form the emulsion, then add a chopped, ripe avocado. Puree and add only enough oil to bring to desired consistency.

Other variations may be easily achieved by adding flavorings to finished mayonnaise, such as curry powder, garlic, pureed pimientos, or saffron.

Herbed Tartar Sauce

Yield: 1 qt		1 L
	Ingredients:	
1 qt	basic Mayonnaise (see Mayonnaise and Variations) or prepared mayonnaise	1 L
3 tbls	minced sour gherkins	3 tbls
2 tbls	grated onion	2 tbls
3 tbls	chopped capers	3 tbls
3 tbls	minced parsley	3 tbls
1 tbls	minced dill	1 tbls
1 tbls	minced fresh tarragon	1 tbls
½ tsp	dry mustard (or to taste)	½ tsp
dash	hot pepper sauce	dash

1. Combine all ingredients. Store refrigerated and covered for up to 5 days.

Vinaigrette Basics

Yield: *1 qt*   **1 L**

	Ingredients:	
6–8 fl oz	**acid, such as lemon juice, fruit juice, or vinegar**	160–240 ml
1 tsp	**salt**	1 tsp
½ tsp	**ground black or white pepper**	½ tsp
¼ tsp	**dry or Dijon mustard (optional)**	¼ tsp
3–4 cups	**vegetable, olive, or peanut oil**	¾–1 L

This is a simple guideline rather than a precise recipe, since vinaigrette-type dressings are so frequently used and can have so many personal variations. The usual proportion is ⅓ to ¼ acid to oil, but these can be varied to suit your taste and the nature of the item to be dressed. As a general rule, the denser and more bland the item, the sharper and more vigorous in flavor the vinaigrette. The basic plain vinaigrette can be stored refrigerated for a few weeks. Once you have added other items, like fresh herbs, vegetables, etc., the sauce will be at its best for only a few days. It can be prepared in a bowl with a fork, whisk or mixer, or in a blender or food processor. The machines both aerate and emulsify the dressing, so it holds longer without separating.

1. Combine the acid, salt, pepper, and mustard, blend well. Continue to beat while adding the oil until the whole is well mixed. Taste and adjust seasonings.

Variations: Herbs (in combination, or one chosen herb alone) can be added, either at the outset, so they are blended in, or stirred in after mixing the vinaigrette. Minced shallots can be blended along with the acid and seasonings. If you desire garlic flavoring, however, it is better to soak a cut clove in the dressing for a few hours to flavor the vinaigrette. Thickened vinaigrettes are prepared by the addition of any of the following: an egg, egg white, or yolk; cream or sour cream; or a puree, such as roasted peppers, tomato pulp, mashed avocado, peeled and seeded cucumber, chutney, tuna, anchovy, capers, etc.

All of these additions yield a better product if made in the processor or blender and should not be stored for more than a few days to be at their peak of flavor or wholesomeness.

Orange Vinaigrette

Yield: *1 qt*   **1 L**

	Ingredients:	
1 oz	**shallots, minced**	30 g
2 tbls	**Dijon mustard**	2 tbls
8 fl oz	**orange juice**	250 ml
1 tbls	**sugar**	1 tbls

16 fl oz	**vegetable oil**	500 ml
6 fl oz	**olive oil**	180 ml
pinch	**salt**	pinch
to taste	**white pepper, ground**	to taste

1. Using a mixer, whisk, or processor, combine the shallots, mustard, orange juice, and sugar.
2. With the mixer running, slowly add first the vegetable oil and then the olive oil. Add the seasonings to taste. Mix or whip at high speed for one minute to stabilize the suspension.

Note: The mixture keeps well at cool room temperature or if refrigerated.

Herb and Caper Vinaigrette

Yield: 1 qt   *1 L*

Ingredients:

6 oz	**combined: 1 bunch watercress, 1 bunch Italian parsley, few sprigs dill, chives**	168 g
2 oz	**Pommery mustard**	56 g
4 fl oz	**red wine vinegar**	125 ml
1 tsp	**salt**	1 tsp
½ tsp	**ground black pepper**	½ tsp
3 cups	**olive or vegetable oil**	750 ml
3 oz	**capers**	84 g

1. Pick over and clean or wash the herbs, shake or spin dry. Trim most of the stems from the watercress, parsley, and dill. Weigh out the herbs; the weight can be approximate. It's fine to leave some of the stems in—they will be pulverized in the processor.
2. Place the herbs in the processor, add the mustard, and process until the mixture is reduced to a paste. Add the vinegar, salt and pepper, and pulse once or twice to combine.
3. With the motor running, add the oil in a stream. The mixture will emulsify. Add the capers and pulse a few times until the capers are chopped and the mixture is well combined. Keeps refrigerated for a week.

Note: This very highly seasoned vinaigrette is sharp, briny, and peppery. It is obviously too strong for a salad of delicate greens, but makes an excellent dressing for bland items, such as rice salads, steamed new potatoes, hearty tuna niçoise, or pasta and grain salads.

Compound or Flavored Butters

Yield: 2 lb		1 kg

	Ingredients:	
2 lb	sweet butter, softened	1 kg
4 oz	flavoring agent as described below	115 g

1. Whip the butter smooth in a processor or mixer with paddle.
2. Prepare the flavoring agent, sieve or puree as necessary.
3. Beat the flavoring agent into the softened butter until well combined.
4. Shape the completed butter into a cylinder and wrap well in wax paper or parchment, or pack in small container. Refrigerate or freeze until ready to use.

Note: A good culinary text will provide more ideas for compound or seasoned butters than can be given here. Also, see Mayonnaise and Variations (see in recipe index) for more possibilities.

Variations: **Herb Butter:** one or several fresh herbs, 2 tbls lemon juice, salt and white pepper. Pulverize in processor, add to butter.
Shallot and Herb Butter: As above, add two large shallots.
Garlic Butter: Raw garlic (or elephant garlic for mellow flavor), pulverized, add salt and white pepper.
Roasted Garlic Butter: Bake a whole head of garlic (skins and all) until softened. Press through a sieve to puree. Add the puree and 1 tbls highly flavored olive oil, salt and white pepper to the butter.
Mustard Shallot Butter: Saute four chopped shallots until soft and lightly colored, deglaze the pan with 2 tbls white wine vinegar, add to butter along with 2 tbls Dijon (or Pommery) mustard. Add salt and pepper to taste.
Goat Cheese Butter: Use plain or herbed Montrachet, beat into softened butter. Add softened and minced sun-dried tomatoes if desired.
Olive or Caper Butter: Use pitted and minced oil-cured olives or minced capers. Stir into butter. Do not puree or the mixture will have an unattractive color.
Shellfish Butter: Cook 2 tbls shrimp, and chopped shrimp and/or lobster shells in a bit of fish or mussel stock. Puree and press through a sieve to remove shells. Add to butter and season with salt, pepper and a pinch of cayenne.
Chili Butter: Add pureed fresh or roasted chili peppers to taste, add 2 tbls pimiento, puree into butter, add salt to taste.
Orange Butter: Add grated orange rind, 3 tbls each orange juice and orange liqueur, and some superfine sugar, if desired. Blend into butter.
Honey Butter: Blend in honey of choice.
Fruit Butters: Blend in pureed strawberries or peaches in syrup. Add pureed poached or syrup-packed pears, add cinnamon, ground cloves, and nutmeg to taste.

Barbecue Sauce

Yield: 2 qt		2 L

	Ingredients:	
1 qt	tomato ketchup	1 L
10 fl oz	bottled chili sauce	310 ml
1 cup	cider vinegar	250 ml
1 cup	soy sauce	250 ml
6 fl oz	molasses	180 ml
8 oz	brown sugar	224 g
2	garlic cloves, smashed	2
dash	hot pepper sauce (to taste)	dash
dash	liquid smoke (optional)	dash

1. Combine all the ingredients except the hot pepper sauce and the liquid smoke in a heavy saucepan. Place over medium heat and stir to dissolve the sugar and molasses. Let simmer, stirring occasionally for at least half an hour.
2. Remove the garlic cloves and season to taste with hot sauce and liquid smoke. Store refrigerated for up to 3 months.

Note: This can be used as a basting sauce when grilling or barbecuing chicken or ribs. Apply only during the last 5 or 10 minutes of cooking to prevent charring. It can be served as a dipping sauce for the above and is also good served with sliced flank steak, burgers, or London broil. Heat before serving. It is best to season this mildly in bulk; you can add more hot pepper sauce for spicier versions as needed.

Chutney Dipping Sauce

Yield: 1 qt		1 L

	Ingredients:	
1 lb	prepared chutney	450 g
10 oz	apple or currant jelly	280 g
2 fl oz	vinegar or lemon juice	60 ml
2 tbls	Pommery mustard	2 tbls
	gin, vermouth, or white wine (as needed)	

1. Combine the chutney, jelly, vinegar or lemon juice, and mustard in a food processor. Pulse a few times to combine and chop the large chunks of chutney. Add a bit of either gin, vermouth, or white wine and process until the sauce is of desired consistency. If warmed before serving, it will be thinner; if served at room temperature, it will thicken slightly. Adjust accordingly.

Note: This sauce is good as an accompaniment to Savory Fruit Fritters (see in recipe index), as well as to some vegetable fritters or pancakes, fried fish, shrimp, or chicken.

Hot Peanut Sauce

Yield: 1 qt		1 L
	Ingredients:	
10 oz	chunky peanut butter	280 g
1 cup	soy sauce	250 ml
¾ cup	rice wine vinegar	180 ml
½ cup	honey	125 ml
½ cup	sesame oil	125 ml
1 tbls	hot chili oil (or to taste)	15 ml
2 oz	grated gingerroot	56 g

1. Combine all the ingredients in a food processor or blender. Taste and adjust chili oil to desired hotness. Store refrigerated for several weeks.

Note: This sauce makes an excellent dipping sauce for satays, grilled chicken wings, boiled shrimp, or crudités. It is also used as the dressing for Thai Noodle Salad (see in recipe index).

Lime Dipping Sauce

Yield: 2 cups		500 ml
	Ingredients:	
1 lb	lime marmalade (good quality)	450 g
¼ cup	prepared horseradish (hot)	60 ml
¼ cup	Dijon mustard	60 ml
2 tsp	Worcestershire sauce	10 ml
	water and cornstarch (as needed)	

1. Combine the marmalade, horseradish, mustard, and Worcestershire in a blender or processor. Blend to liquify, adding a bit of water if needed.
2. Heat for 1 or 2 minutes, taste for seasoning, and adjust. The lime taste may vary according to the marmalade. The sauce should not be cloyingly sweet; use more seasonings if needed. If sauce is too thin for planned use, thicken with a tiny bit of cornstarch paste and bring to boil to thicken. Serve warm or at room temperature. Store refrigerated for a few weeks.

Variation: **Spicy Lime Mayo:** Combine the sauce in roughly equal proportions with prepared mayonnaise, add some ground pepper to taste and a bit of grated lime zest for color and flavor.

Mint and Mustard Sauce

Yield: 1 pt   ½ *L*

Ingredients:

1 cup	each mint jelly and honey mustard	240 ml
4 tbls	chopped mint leaves	4 tbls
1 tbls	white vinegar	1 tbls

1. Combine the jelly and honey mustard, heat until smoothly combined. Add mint leaves and vinegar, simmer 2 minutes. Remove from heat and store refrigerated for 1 week.
2. To serve, bring to room temperature, stir to mix. You may heat to serve if desired.

This sauce is nice to serve with roast or grilled lamb. Also, use it as a basting glaze for Cornish hens or roast or grilled chicken.

Sesame Soy Dipping Sauce

Yield: 1 qt   1 *L*

Ingredients:

1 qt	soy sauce	1 L
½ cup	sesame oil	125 ml
2 or 3 tbls	hot chili oil (or to taste)	2 or 3 tbls
4 oz	minced scallions	115 g
4 oz	minced gingerroot	115 g

1. Combine all the ingredients. Allow to stand to mellow flavors. To store longer than 2 weeks, strain. Refrigerate.
2. If desired, the sauce can be garnished for service with fresh bits of scallion and gingerroot.

A good dipping sauce for fried or steamed Oriental hors d'oeuvre.

Spicy Plum Sauce

Yield: 1 qt		1 L

	Ingredients:	
3 cups	plum preserves	750 ml
2 oz	brown sugar	60 g
½ cup	cider vinegar	120 ml
¼ cup	soy sauce	60 ml
¼ cup	chili sauce	60 ml
to taste	hot pepper sauce	to taste
to taste	minced garlic (optional)	to taste
to taste	grated gingerroot (optional)	to taste

1. Puree the preserves in the food processor. Add the remaining ingredients and simmer 5 minutes.
2. Taste for seasoning. Add ginger for more Oriental flavor; add garlic if desired. If additions are made, simmer few minutes more.
3. Keeps refrigerated for several weeks.

Note: Serve hot or at room temperature as a dipping sauce for hors d'oeuvre such as fried shrimp, chicken nuggets, fritters, and so forth. To make a glaze or sauce for roast poultry, game, or pork, thin with pan juices or appropriate stock.

Sweet Mustard Dill Sauce

Yield: 1 pt		500 mL

	Ingredients:	
⅓ cup	Pommery mustard	80 ml
⅓ cup	Dijon mustard	80 ml
2½ tsp	dry mustard	2½ tsp
⅓ cup	light brown sugar	70 g
⅓ cup	white wine vinegar	80 ml
1 cup	vegetable oil	¼ L
⅔ cup	minced dill	1½ dl

1. Place the mustards, brown sugar, and vinegar in the workbowl of a food processor. Pulse to form a paste. With the machine motor running, slowly add the oil to emulsify the sauce. Add the minced dill and process until well blended. Store, refrigerated and covered for up to one week.

Note: If you wish to prepare the sauce in larger quantity and store longer, prepare the emulsion and store. Add fresh minced dill a few hours before using. This sauce is traditionally served with Gravlax (see in recipe index), but is also excellent as a dip or sauce for cocktail shrimp, crab claws, cold steamed or smoked mussels, smoked trout, mackerel, or bluefish. Use as a dip for raw vegetables, such as broccoli, celery, endive, or daikon. It is very good with grilled or poached tuna or swordfish. A bit of the sauce spread on thin pumpernickel, whole grain, or limpa bread, and topped with wafer-thin slices of cucumber, makes a refreshing canapé or open-face tea sandwich.

Szechuan Chili Sauce

Yield: 6 cups		*1½ L*

Ingredients:

1 cup	soy sauce	¼ L
1½ cups	cider vinegar	350 ml
12 oz	light brown sugar	340 g
10 fl oz	bottled chili sauce	300 ml
2 cups	crushed pineapple and juice	500 ml
3 fl oz	Worcestershire sauce	90 ml
3 fl oz	sherry	90 ml
	Szechuan hot bean paste (to taste)	

1. Combine all ingredients except hot bean paste in pan over low heat, stirring and simmering for 5 to 10 minutes. Adjust sweet sour taste with a bit more sugar or vinegar.
2. Add a bit of bean paste, stir well, and taste. Some varieties are much hotter than others, so cautiously add more bit by bit to taste. This sauce is enjoyed by the largest number of people when piquant with a slight sting, not searingly hot. You can always add more later.
3. This sauce keeps very well, covered and refrigerated, for a few weeks. Store in small containers as this is often used as a dipping sauce. It can be frozen, but may need flavor adjustment when thawed. Serve at room temperature or heated, depending on use.

Note: This dipping sauce is good for fried fish, shrimp, chicken, or fruit or vegetable fritters. It is also the sauce component for Szechuan Chicken Chunks (see recipe index).

Artichoke Dip

Yield: 1 qt		1 L
	Ingredients:	
16 oz	canned artichoke hearts, drained	450 g
4 oz	drained chopped spinach*	112 g
8 oz	drained part-skim ricotta, pot cheese, or cottage cheese	224 g
½ cup	chopped parsley	125 ml
½ tsp	Dijon mustard	½ tsp
pinch	nutmeg	pinch
½ tsp	ground black pepper	½ tsp
2 tbls	sour cream or plain yogurt (or as needed)	2 tbls
	salt (if needed)	

*You may use thawed frozen spinach or fresh spinach, blanched and finely chopped. In either case, squeeze dry thoroughly before weighing out.

1. Use a food processor to thoroughly chop the artichoke hearts, add the spinach and puree. Add the ricotta and pot cheese, the chopped parsley, mustard, nutmeg, and pepper. Process until well blended.
2. Add sour cream to the mixture until desired consistency is achieved. Taste and add salt or more pepper to taste. Store, refrigerated, for 2 to 3 days. Does not freeze.

Note: Canned plain artichoke hearts are used since processing makes them softer. If you use frozen artichoke hearts, cook until soft and drain very well before using. Since canned artichoke hearts are processed with salt, you may need to add more salt if you use frozen. This dip is lower in calories and fat than those made with mayonnaise or cream cheese as a base. It is flavorful and provides a more healthful choice for guests.

Variations: You may substitute mayonnaise for the ricotta for a dip with a different taste and consistency.

You may substitute well drained marinated artichoke hearts. Since these are spiced, adjust seasonings to taste.

Red Caviar Dip

Yield: 2 cups		½ L
	Ingredients:	
12 oz	whipped cream cheese	340 g
2 oz	sour cream	60 g
1 tsp	lemon juice	1 tsp
2 tbls	grated onion	2 tbls
4 oz	red lumpish caviar	115 g

1. Combine the cream cheese, sour cream, and lemon juice. Beat together until smooth.
2. Put the grated onion in a square of cheesecloth, rinse, and squeeze dry.
3. Gently fold the onion into the cheese mixture. Fold in most of the caviar.
4. Place the mixture in a serving bowl or container (such as a hollowed brioche or carved vegetable). Just before serving, dot the remaining caviar over the top of the dip. Serve with plain crackers or pumpernickel fingers.

Note: This dip can also be used as a filling for delicate crepes, either rolled, or tied up as "beggar's purses" (little pouches fastened with lengths of chives or scallion strips).

Variations: If desired, this mixture can be molded. Simply dissolve a packet of gelatin according to directions, stir into finished mixture, place in a rinsed or oiled decorative mold, and chill until firm. For a pretty effect, use a ring mold or one fitted with a central well, and fill the hollow with additional lumpfish caviar.

Roquefort Calvados Dip

Yield: 2 cups		500 ml
	Ingredients:	
6 oz	crumbled Roquefort	168 g
4 oz	pot cheese	112 g
4 oz	whipped cream cheese	112 g
2 tbls	apple juice	2 tbls
4 tbls	calvados or applejack	60 ml
dash	hot pepper sauce	dash
4 oz	coarsely chopped walnuts	112 g

1. In a food processor, combine half the roquefort, and all of the pot cheese and cream cheese until well blended. Add the juice, calvados and hot pepper sauce, pulse once or twice to mix, and transfer to a large bowl.
2. Stir in the remaining Roquefort and the nuts and mix or fold only enough to evenly distribute the ingredients. The mixture should be slightly lumpy.

Note: This dip is good for most vegetables, but especially for broccoli, cauliflower, and celery. Good as a filling for raw mushrooms or endive spears. Or serve with bland unsalted crackers or toasts.

Taramosalata (Greek Carp Roe Dip)

Yield: 3 cups   *750 ml*

	Ingredients:	
8 slices	**crustless white bread**	8 slices
3	**garlic cloves**	3
10 oz	**tarama (carp roe)***	285 g
4 tbls	**fresh lemon juice**	60 ml
1 tsp	**ground white pepper**	1 tsp
1 cup	**flavorful olive oil, Greek if possible**	¼ L

*Tarama, an orange-colored dense paste of carp roe, is available in ethnic markets.

1. Soak the bread in a little water until wet through. Drain and squeeze as dry as possible. Shred the bread pulp into the bowl of a food processor.
2. Use a garlic press to puree the cloves into the bowl of the processor as well. Add the tarama and pulse the machine once or twice to combine. Add the lemon juice and the seasonings and run the machine until the mixture is well combined and the bread is no longer visible.
3. With the motor still running, add the olive oil through the feed tube, a little at a time at first, as one would for mayonnaise. Add enough oil to make a smooth but somewhat stiff mixture. You may not need all the oil. Taste and adjust seasonings, adding a bit more lemon juice or pepper if desired.
4. Refrigerate covered. Traditionally, this dip is served with pita for dipping, but it makes an excellent dip for vegetables as well.

Note: If using as a dip, you may like the mixture softer. However, this is very good piped into or on raw vegetables, such as hollowed-out cherry tomatoes, raw mushroom caps, cucumber or zucchini cups or rounds, or used as a topping for tiny steamed new potatoes. In this case, you should keep the mixture stiff enough to pipe nicely.

Avocado Cream

Yield: 1 pt   *½ L*

	Ingredients:	
2	**ripe avocados**	2
4 tbls	**mayonnaise**	4 tbls
3 tbls	**lemon juice**	3 tbls
1 tbls	**Dijon mustard**	1 tbls
3 tbls	**minced parsley**	3 tbls
	salt and pepper (to taste)	

1. Halve, pit, and scoop the flesh from the avocados, retaining a couple of the prettiest shells as containers for the dip if desired.
2. Place the avocado flesh in a bowl and mash together with all the other ingredients. Taste and adjust seasonings.
3. Cover closely with plastic wrap. This is best served the day it is made. To hold longer and protect from discoloration, some cooks use the trick of submerging one of the pits in the dip. Or, you can pack into a container and film the top surface with lemon juice and olive oil.
4. If planning to use the avocado shells for containers, rub the insides with oil or lemon juice and keep refrigerated and well wrapped until ready to use. Serve with vegetables or crackers for dipping.

Note: This mixture can be used as a sandwich spread: It is delicious with sliced chicken, bacon, and tomato. It can be used as a filling for stuffed eggs: Simply mash the yolks with the avocado mixture and restuff whites. To make a salad dressing for a hearty chef's salad, simply thin with herb vinaigrette to dressing consistency.

Pesto Cream

Yield: 1 pt		½ L

	Ingredients:	
8 oz	whipped cream cheese	225 g
6 oz	boursin-type herbed cheese	180 g
4–6 tbls	Pesto Alla Genovese (see in recipe index)	60–90 ml

1. With a food processor, blend the cream cheese with the boursin until light and fluffy. Turn it into a bowl and stir in most of the pesto by hand until the mixture is streaked with the green of the pesto. Place in a serving bowl and make a small depression in the top of the mound. Put a spoonful of the pesto in the hollow. Keeps well wrapped and refrigerated for a few days. Let soften at room temperature before serving.

Note: This mixture is very good served with rustic genoa toasts or toasted baguette slices brushed with olive oil. It can be smoothly processed and piped as a filling into raw vegetables, such as cherry tomatoes, mushroom caps, and pea pods.

Spicy Tomato Sauce

Yield: 2 qt		2 L

Ingredients:

2 cans	Italian plum tomatoes, 28 oz (8 dl) each can	2 cans
½ cup	flavorful olive oil	125 ml
2	garlic cloves, smashed	2
4 tbls	minced onion	4 tbls
1 tsp	salt	1 tsp
1 tsp	ground black pepper (or to taste)	1 tsp
pinch	sugar	pinch
2 tbls	minced parsley	2 tbls
1 tsp	oregano	1 tsp
4 tbls	minced basil leaves	4 tbls
½ tsp	hot red pepper flakes (or more to taste)	½ tsp

1. Drain the tomatoes, reserving the juice. Remove the hard cores and seeds from the tomato flesh. Add the flesh to the drained juice and set aside.
2. In a heavy gauge saucepan or large cast-iron skillet, heat the oil and add the garlic and onion. Adjust the heat so the vegetables soften and brown lightly but do not burn.
3. Add the tomatoes (be careful of spatters), raise the heat and stir with a wooden spoon, breaking the tomato into chunks. Add the salt, black pepper, sugar, parsley, and oregano, and simmer for about 40 minutes or until the tomatoes have lost any raw or very acid taste.
4. Remove the garlic cloves and discard. Stir in the basil and as much hot pepper as desired. Store refrigerated for 2 to 3 days. Freeze for longer storage.

Note: This makes a chunky, rustic sauce. If you want a bit more refinement, chop the tomato flesh fine before cooking.

Variations: **Plain Marinara:** Eliminate the onion, the oregano, and the hot pepper flakes.
Seafood Marinara: Add raw shelled shrimp or mussels or clams in their shell for the last few minutes of cooking time. Cook until the shrimp are pink and the shells have opened. Cleaned, cut, and blanched squid may also be added. Serve over spaghetti or linguine.
Prosciutto Sauce: Prepare the recipe as given except eliminate one clove garlic and all the oregano. In a separate skillet, sauté 1 cup diced prosciutto with one minced shallot in a bit of butter until shallots have softened. Add 3 tbls cognac and flame or cook off. Add to finished tomato sauce. Add about 1½ cups (375 ml) reduced light cream to the mixture to obtain a rosy color and mellow flavor. Serve over fresh egg fettucine, rigatoni, or ziti.

Christmas Eve Lobster Sauce

Yield: *3 qt*		*3 L*
	Ingredients:	
3½ qt	canned imported plum tomatoes	3½ L
1 cup	mild olive oil	¼ L
1	garlic clove	1
3 oz	pignoli	84 g
pinch	sugar (if needed)	pinch
1 tsp	salt	1 tsp
1½ tsp	ground black pepper (to taste)	1½ tsp
2	1½-pound (675 g) lobsters, live	2
3 fl oz	brandy	90 ml

This recipe is a family favorite. My grandmother, who is 94, still prepares it as the highlight of the traditional Italian all-seafood feast on Christmas Eve.

1. Crush the tomatoes in a food mill to remove the seeds and hard cores. Set aside.
2. Heat the olive oil in a large, heavy gauge pot. Add the garlic clove and cook until barely colored. Add the pignoli, stir for a minute, and add the tomatoes. Use caution: They will spatter. Reduce the heat to medium and simmer for about 1 hour, stirring occasionally and adjusting the heat so the tomatoes cook down but do not scorch.
3. Add the salt, pepper, and pinch of sugar if the tomatoes seem acid. You can adjust the seasonings again later on. Continue to simmer for another hour.
4. Prepare the lobsters. Pierce the heads with a sharp knife, letting the juices run into a small bowl. Lay each lobster on its back and use a heavy knife to split in half. Remove and discard the stomach sac from the head and the attached intestinal vein that runs down the center of the lobster to the tail. Continue to collect all the juices you can in the small bowl. Use a mallet or the back of a cleaver or heavy knife to crack the claws.
5. Carefully examine the prepared lobsters for any tiny bits of shell that may come off in the sauce. Pick off and discard.
6. Put the lobsters and the collected juices into the simmering sauce. Add the brandy and simmer for at least another hour. Taste and adjust seasoning. The sauce should be peppery with a pronounced lobster flavor. If acid, add a pinch more sugar and continue to simmer until thickened and mellow.
7. If you like, after the first half hour's cooking, you may retrieve the tails and/or claws, dice the meat, and return meat and shells to the sauce. This is not absolutely necessary since some of the meat will crumble into the sauce naturally.
8. When the sauce is done, remove from heat and let cool. Leave the lobsters in the sauce until ready to serve or freeze. The sauce can be held, refrigerated and covered, for up to 3 days or frozen for longer storage.

Note: Serve with a string pasta: spaghetti, perciatelli, or angel hair.

Variations: **Seafood in Lobster Sauce:** Shelled and cleaned shrimp, scrubbed mussels and clams, cleaned and cut squid, chunks of crabmeat (or sealegs), or scallops (any or all), may be cooked or heated in the sauce. Serve as an entree as is or over spaghetti. Traditionally, this sauce is highly spiced with hot pepper flakes.
Crab Sauce: Prepare recipe with cleaned blue crabs.

Italian Meat Sauce

Yield: 8 qt		8 L
	Ingredients:	
10	28 oz (794 g) cans imported plum tomatoes	10
½ lb	round steak (2 thin slices)	224 g
4 tbls	minced parsley	4 tbls
4 tbls	pignoli	4 tbls
4 tbls	golden raisins	4 tbls
	salt and pepper (to taste)	
4 tbls	mild olive oil	60 ml
4 links	Italian sausage*	4 links
1 lb	boneless beef (chuck, in one or two pieces)	450 g
1	clove garlic, minced	1
6 oz	tomato paste	168 g
2 fl oz	rye or bourbon	60 ml
1 cup	minced parsley	¼ L
¼ cup	minced fresh basil	60 ml
	Optional: pinch oregano	

Italian Meatballs (see in recipe index) to be added to sauce during last
  half hour cooking time

*You may use hot or sweet, or those flavored with fennel seed, according to taste, but using a well-flavored sweet sausage provides most versatility for use of the sauce.

1. Crush the tomatoes, with their juice, in a food mill to remove seeds and hard cores. Set aside.
2. Prepare beef braciole as follows: Use a mallet or meat pounder to flatten the round steaks and cut into four or eight equal portions, depending on size. Sprinkle each piece liberally with salt and pepper. Divide the 4 tbls parsley, pignoli, and raisins among the pieces. Roll up and tie into secure bundles with kitchen string.
3. Heat the oil in a heavy gauge pot, brown the sausage, pricking here and there with a fork to release some of the fat. Add the chuck and brown on all sides. Add the braciole (if necessary remove some of the other meat to avoid overcrowding the pot) and brown on all sides. Keep the flame at moderate heat so the meat sears but does not burn.

4. Add the garlic to the pan and cook until softened and barely colored. If you have removed any meat from the pot, return it. Add the tomatoes. Use caution, it will spatter. Reduce the heat so the sauce simmers for one hour.

5. Add the tomato paste, whiskey, ½ cup (125 ml) parsley, and oregano, if you choose to use it. Simmer for 2 to 3 more hours, stirring occasionally and adjusting the heat so no scorching occurs.

6. Taste the sauce and add salt and pepper. If the tomatoes were very acid, adjust flavor with a pinch of sugar. The sauce should be thick and meaty tasting. If sausage was very fatty, skim excess fat from the surface.

7. When the sauce flavor and consistency seems right, add the balance of the parsley and the fresh basil. Remove from heat, cool, and hold refrigerated for at least one day for best flavor. Leave the meat in the sauce until ready to serve or freeze. The sauce will hold refrigerated and covered for 3 to 4 days. Freeze for longer storage.

Note: While this sauce is popular served over spaghetti (with or without meatballs), it is traditionally served over dried tubular pasta, such as ziti, rigatoni, or mostaccioli. It can be served over meat- or cheese-filled ravioli and is used in preparing lasagne and manicotti. Fresh egg pasta, such as fettucine or tagliatelle, are too delicate for this sauce. When they are served with a meat sauce, it is usually Ragu Bolognese (see in recipe index).

About the meat used to make the sauce: Served family style, this is a treat. Braciole and sausage are particularly prized. Make extra and remove from sauce when tender. Remove the string and serve whole or sliced.

Pesto Alla Genovese

Yield: 3 cups		750 ml
	Ingredients:	
3 cups	packed basil leaves	750 ml
2	garlic cloves	2
3 oz	pignoli and/or walnuts	90 g
pinch	salt	pinch
2 oz	Parmesan cheese, grated	60 g
12 fl oz	olive oil	370 ml

Basil is often gritty or covered with a film of fine soil. Carefully pick off the leaves and wash them in several changes of cold water until no trace of dirt remains. Dry thoroughly (a salad spinner works well for this). The classic pesto is made only with fresh basil, imported Italian pignoli, and the finest Parmesan cheese. Pignoli, however, are very expensive, so substituting some walnuts is more economical and still produces a flavorful pesto. Do use mostly Parmesan cheese, however, as other grated cheeses, like Romano, are much saltier and sharper in taste.

1. Place the basil, garlic, nuts, and salt in a food processor or blender and puree to a paste.
2. Add some of the cheese, blend, and taste, adding more according to your taste. A good pesto will have a balance of flavor; neither the garlic nor cheese should overwhelm the basil.
3. Add the oil while blending or processing until the pesto is of the desired consistency.
4. If not using within a few days, pack in small containers and freeze.

Note: Some cooks contend that on long storage, the nuts and/or cheese acquire an off taste. I have never found this to be true, however, I make and use pesto frequently. If you are concerned about this, or if you have a great quantity of fresh basil available but not the other ingredients or time available to make pesto, prepare pureed basil as follows: Process the cleaned basil leaves with a pinch of salt and enough olive oil to make a paste. Store this mixture in the freezer and use to prepare pesto at another time. This basil puree is good to have on hand as a seasoning for sauces, soups, and stews.

Ragu Bolognese

Yield: 2 qt		2 L
	Ingredients:	
2 oz	dried Italian mushrooms	56 g
4 tbls	sweet butter	60 g
4 tbls	olive oil	60 ml
1 lb	finely chopped onion	450 g
10 oz	finely chopped carrot	280 g
8 oz	finely chopped celery	224 g
3½ lb	lean ground beef	1 kg 600 g
1 cup	dry white wine	250 ml
1 cup	milk or cream (optional)*	250 ml
1 cup	canned plum tomatoes, cored, seeded, and chopped	250 ml
4 tbls	tomato paste	4 tbls
pinch	nutmeg	pinch
½ tsp	salt	½ tsp
	pepper (if desired)	

*Many classic cook books call for cream in the sauce, many traditional family recipes do not. My own family recipe does not include cream but always includes dried mushrooms. I have tried the cream, and it lends a more mellow flavor to the sauce.

1. Soak the dried mushrooms in water, and, when they have softened, drain, reserving the liquid, rinse, and chop. Strain the liquid through a fine cloth and add to the sauce when you add the wine.
2. Heat the butter and oil in a heavy-bottom pot, add the onion, carrot, and celery and sweat until the carrots and celery are just tender and lightly colored.

Flowers, delicate china, dainty sandwiches, and finger desserts create an inviting atmosphere for an intimate, at-home tea.

An elegant menu and sophisticated accessories lend a sleek, black-tie air to this New Year's Eve celebration.

A wedding cake, decorated with fresh flowers, is the centerpiece for a romantic champagne reception. The bridal party's bouquets enhance the elegant table setting.

Nautical props add interest to a rawbar/seafood station at a casual buffet.

A tower of artichokes, lemons, and herbs lends drama to a free-form arrangement of crudites.

Bright ribbons, evergreens, and candles set a holiday tone for a lavish dessert buffet.

Opulent fabrics and gleaming table accessories provide a dramatic backdrop for a buffet of curry, condiments, and an assortment of Indian breads.

A craggy stone wall and rough-hewn table provide the perfect outdoor setting for rustic Italian antipasto.

Patriotic colors, a "flag" fruit tart, and all-American barbecue foods make a festive yet easy-to-manage 4th of July celebration.

Meals in boxes (in this case, napkin-lined baskets) provide easy and attractive service at this casual "hoedown" seated buffet. Note that relishes and beverages are already at each table.

A banquet room set for a formal event. Note the table draping and color coordination of the centerpieces, napkins, and ribbon table trim. *(Courtesy of Hotel Thayer, West Point, New York)*

Bold colors and dramatic tableware set an unusual Southwestern holiday theme.

Whether as a continental breakfast, coffee break, or sideboard to a brunch, pastries, muffins, and assorted baked goods have extra appeal when displayed in baskets and with bright, crisp linens.

A simple cheese tray becomes a stunning still life with the addition of some autumn leaves, nuts, and fruits.

A menu of Pan-Asian foods, vibrant fabrics, jungle plants, exotic flowers, and tropical fruits combine to create a South Sea Islands fantasy theme. A painted mural is used as a backdrop, but colorful travel posters would serve just as well.

Pretty pinks—from pale to vivid—provide a sweet setting for any special event in a young woman's life: a bas mitzvah, sweet-sixteen party, or a shower.

3. Add the beef, breaking up the lumps of meat, and cook until the meat just loses its pink color. Add the wine and mushroom liquid and cook over moderate heat, stirring, until most of the wine has cooked away. Add the cream (if you are using it), and cook down again.

4. Add the tomatoes and tomato paste. Stir well and cook over moderate heat for 2 to 3 minutes. Adjust the heat so that the mixture is barely simmering and continue to cook, stirring occasionally, for about 2 hours.

5. Add the mushrooms, the nutmeg, and a pinch of salt. Continue to simmer very gently for at least another hour, preferably two, stirring now and then to be certain the sauce is not sticking. Taste and add additional salt, if needed, and some freshly ground pepper, if desired. The completed sauce will have an intense but mellow earthy flavor.

6. The sauce can be held under refrigeration for 3 to 4 days, or frozen for longer storage. Reheat carefully before using. Often, a bit of cream or butter is used to finish the sauce just before serving.

Note: This sauce is traditionally used over the fresh egg pasta that is most often prepared and eaten in the north of Italy; typically, with trenette, fettucine, or tagliatelle, rather than a dried pasta such as spaghetti or fusili. It is also used over tortellini or cappelletti, used in preparing Bolognese lasagne, and in polenta dishes.

Cranberry Fruit Chutney

Yield: 1 qt

		1 L
	Ingredients:	
12 oz	fresh cranberries	340 g
½ cup	water	125 ml
2 oz	raisins	60 g
4	dried apricots, plumped	4
4 oz	chopped onion	115 g
8 oz	granulated sugar	224 g
2 oz	gingerroot, chopped	60 g
1 tsp	grated orange rind	1 tsp
¼ tsp	cinnamon	¼ tsp
¼ tsp	allspice	¼ tsp
pinch	salt	pinch
1 tsp	Worcestershire sauce	5 ml
1 lb	walnut meats, broken	450 g

1. Combine all the ingredients in a heavy-bottom saucepan. Cook over medium heat, stirring to combine and dissolve the sugar. Lower the heat and simmer, stirring occasionally, for an additional 30 minutes to an hour, until the flavors are well combined. Watch carefully toward the end of the cooking time, adjusting the heat to prevent scorching. Keeps refrigerated for several weeks.

Sweet and Sour Onion Jam

Yield: 3 qt		3 L

Ingredients:

10 lb	yellow onions	5 kg
6 oz	sweet butter	180 g
2 fl oz	balsamic vinegar (or to taste)	60 ml
2 oz	granulated sugar (or to taste)	60 g
	salt and pepper (to taste)	
12 oz	Optional additions: golden raisins, dried tart cherries, dried cranberries, or dried currants	400 g

1. Trim, peel, and thinly slice the onions. Select a heavy gauge saucepan or Dutch oven with a tight-fitting lid.
2. If using optional additions, plump the fruit in vermouth, scotch, or water. Set aside.
3. Heat the butter in the pan, add the onions, cover the pan and sweat over medium-low heat for 30 to 40 minutes, stirring once or twice.
4. After about 40 minutes, the onions should be translucent and just beginning to color. Adjust the heat so that they do not burn.
5. Once the onions have reduced in volume by at least half, remove the lid and continue cooking over low heat to evaporate most of the liquid and caramelize the onions (possibly another hour). Stir frequently to prevent sticking.
6. When the onions are well-reduced and nicely browned, add the vinegar and sugar a bit at a time, to achieve a piquant taste. Add salt and pepper if desired. If using the plumped fruits, drain them and add to the mixture. Continue to simmer until all excess moisture has cooked away and the mixture is spoonable. Refrigerate or freeze for storage. Reheat before serving.

Note: This jam makes an excellent accompaniment to game birds, pork, or venison. It also makes a delicious filling for tiny tartlets or biscuits as a canapé.

Variations: You may use one of the varieties of sweet onions: Vidalia, Maui, Walla Walla, or Texas Sweet, any of which will yield a more mellow version of the jam. Or make Red Onion Jam, using red or purple onions, adding a splash of vinegar at the outset to help keep the color. Make Onion Fruit Sauce by combining equal amounts of onion jam and plumped dried fruit, such as apricots, pears, or apples. Puree the mixture and thin with pan juices or appropriate stock to use as a gravy for game birds, pork, or venison.

Soups

Chunky Cream of Tomato Soup

Yield: 2 qt	8 qt		2 L	8 L
		Ingredients:		
8 oz	2 lb	finely chopped onion	224 g	900 g
6 cups	6 qt	strained tomatoes*	1½ L	6 L
¾ cup	3 cups	water	180 ml	720 ml
1	1	bay leaf	1	1
2	5	whole peppercorns	2	5
2	8	parsley stems	2	8
pinch	1 tsp	powdered thyme	pinch	1 tsp
1 lb	4 lb	ripe tomatoes	450 g	1 kg 800 g
3 cups	3 qt	medium white sauce	750 ml	3 L
		salt and pepper to taste		
		Optional garnish: sour cream or creme fraiche; minced parsley, dill, or chervil		

*I use the Pomi brand (Parmalat) vacuum-boxed strained tomatoes. If not available, use first-quality canned tomatoes and strain through a food mill. Reduce the water in the recipe by half.

1. Place the onion, strained tomato, and water in a heavy pot and simmer, stirring occasionally, for about 45 minutes. Keep the heat low enough to prevent any scorching. Cook until the onion is very soft.
2. Prepare a bouquet garni using the bay leaf, peppercorns, parsley stems, and thyme. Add to the tomato mixture.

3. Peel, seed, and finely dice the fresh tomatoes, add to the tomato mixture, and simmer for 30 minutes more. Remove from heat and let cool to lukewarm.
4. Remove the bouquet garni from the tomato mixture and discard.
5. Warm the white sauce and combine with the tomato mixture. Add gradually and stir to avoid lumping. Hold, covered and refrigerated, until ready to serve.
6. To serve, heat the soup, but do not boil. If desired, garnish each portion with a dollop of sour cream or creme fraiche and a sprinkle of chopped fresh herbs.

Creamy Zucchini Rice Soup

Yield: 3 qt	8 qt	Ingredients:	3 L	8 L
4 oz	10 oz	butter or margarine	115 g	300 g
1½ lb	4 lb	chopped onions	700 g	2 kg
1 cup	3 cup	cooked white rice	¼ L	¾ L
20 fl oz	6 cup	chicken broth	650 ml	1½ L
10 fl oz	3 cup	water	325 ml	¾ L
2 lb	5½ lb	zucchini	900 g	2½ kg
2 tbls	5 tbls	minced parsley	2 tbls	5 tbls
2 tbls	5 tbls	minced basil	2 tbls	5 tbls
		salt and pepper (to taste)		

1. Melt half the butter in a heavy pot, add the onion, and sweat until soft.
2. Add the cooked rice, the chicken broth, and water, and simmer until the rice and onions are very soft (about 1 hour). Remove from heat and let cool to lukewarm.
3. While the rice and onions are cooking, scrub, trim, and grate or shred the zucchini (if the zucchini are very large, remove seedy centers before grating). Drain excess moisture from zucchini using a colander.
4. When the rice and onion mixture has cooled sufficiently, puree in batches in a blender (or food mill with a fine disk). The result should be a creamy soup base.
5. Sauté the grated drained zucchini in the remaining butter until limp and tender. Do not brown or overcook.
6. Combine the zucchini with the creamed base, add the chopped herbs, and adjust the seasoning with salt and pepper. Keeps refrigerated for 3 to 5 days. Since the soup contains no cream, it can be reheated without fear of curdling.

Note: This soup can be further enhanced by garnishing with a swirl of pesto (see in recipe index) or a dollop of crème fraîche or sour cream.

Escarole and Meatball Soup

Yield: 2 qt		2 L

Ingredients:

2 heads	escarole	2 heads
3 tbls	butter	45 g
⅓ to ½	recipe for Italian Cocktail Meatballs (see in recipe index)	⅓ to ½
2 qt	flavorful chicken broth	2 L
	grated Parmesan cheese for passing	

1. Remove the tough outer leaves from the escarole. Separate the leaves, trimming the tough ribs from the larger leaves, and wash in several changes of clean water until no trace of grit remains. Chop the escarole, or cut into chiffonade (thin strips). Set aside.
2. Prepare the meatball mixture and roll into tiny balls, about the size of a marble.
3. Heat the butter in a large soup pot, add the escarole, lower the heat and sweat until tender.
4. In a smaller saucepan, heat some of the broth to a simmer, add the meatballs, and poach gently until cooked through. Remove with a skimmer and add to the escarole. Poach in batches if necessary.
5. Add the balance of the broth to the escarole and meatballs. Heat and serve with grated cheese on the side.

Note: To increase volume, multiply ingredients with no changes.

Five Onion Soup

Yield: 2 qt	8 qt		2 L	8 L

Ingredients:

8 oz	2 lb	butter or margarine	224 g	900 g
6 oz	1 lb 8 oz	onions, finely chopped	180 g	750 g
2 oz	8 oz	minced shallots	60 g	250 g
8 oz	2 lb	white of leeks, finely chopped	224 g	900 g
2 oz	8 oz	scallions, sliced very thin	60 g	250 g
3 oz	12 oz	all-purpose flour	90 g	360 g
6 cups	6 qt	beef or veal stock*	1½ L	6 L

2 cups	2 qt	hot milk (approx.)	½ L	2 L
		salt and white pepper (to taste)		
1 cup	1 qt	light or heavy cream	¼ L	1 L
		Garnish: fresh chives or chive flowers		

*If using canned beef stock or broth (most of which varieties are very salty) dilute by half with water.

1. In a large pot, heat the butter and sweat the onions until they begin to soften. Raise the heat and cook, stirring, until they take on some color.
2. Add the shallots and continue to cook over low heat until they begin to soften. Stir and check that the shallots do not burn.
3. Add the leeks and continue cooking, stirring frequently, until they begin to soften. They should color slightly. Add the scallions and cook for 1 minute.
4. Add the flour, and cook stirring, over low heat, for about 3 minutes.
5. While the vegetables are cooking, heat the stock.
6. Slowly add the hot stock to the pot, stirring as the roux thickens the soup.
7. Simmer the soup until all the vegetables are tender. Remove from heat.
8. For a smooth soup, puree through a food mill. This step is optional, as the soup is quite good with texture.
9. Add enough hot milk to achieve proper consistency. Season to taste.
10. To serve, heat the soup gently, adding some hot cream. Do not boil.
11. Garnish with a sprinkling of chopped chives or a chive flower.

Gingered Carrot Soup

Yield: 2 qt	8 qt		2 L	8 L
		Ingredients:		
3 oz	12 oz	butter or margarine	85 g	340 g
1 lb	4 lb	onion, chopped	500 g	2 kg
2 lb	8 lb	carrots, chopped	900 g	3½ kg
2	8	cloves of garlic	2	8
2 oz	8 oz	gingerroot, peeled	60 g	240 g
1 qt	1 gal	chicken stock (approx.)	1 L	4 L
16 fl oz	2 qt	water	½ L	2 L
		salt and white pepper (to taste)		
		Garnish: light cream, chopped parsley		

1. Heat the butter or margarine in a heavy pot, add the chopped onion and sweat 5 minutes. Add the carrots and garlic and stir to coat with butter.
2. Smash the gingerroot slightly to help it release flavor. Add to the pot with enough chicken stock diluted with water to cover.

3. Simmer, covered, adding more liquid as needed, for at least an hour until carrots are quite soft. Remove from heat and set aside to cool to lukewarm.
4. When the mixture is cool enough to handle, remove the gingerroot and puree the soup in batches, or pass through a food mill.
5. Taste the puree and add salt and pepper to taste. Thin to desired consistency with additional stock if desired. Refrigerate for a few days or freeze for longer storage.
6. To serve hot, garnish with a splash of cream or chopped parsley. To serve cold, thin with cream and stir or blend smooth. Adjust seasoning and garnish with chopped parsley and/or a dash of ground ginger.

Jackson Pollock Soup

Yield: 2 qt   **2 L**

	Ingredients:	
2 qt	recipe Chunky Cream of Tomato Soup (see in recipe index), less 1 cup (¼ L)	2 L
12 cup	pureed green split pea soup*	3 L
	heavy cream (if needed)	
	Garnish: whole chives cut in random lengths	

*You can make your own or use a good quality canned soup, provided it is pureed.

1. Puree the tomato soup in a blender. (If you make the tomato soup just for this recipe, do the following: substitute grated onion for chopped; eliminate the chopped fresh tomato and substitute about an ounce of tomato paste to taste.)
2. Heat the tomato soup to just below the simmer, adjust seasoning if needed. Do not boil or it will curdle.
3. Warm the pea soup and add enough cream to bring the consistency to the point where it is lighter than the tomato soup.
4. Portion the tomato soup into hot bowls and, using the pea soup as "paint," splash or dribble it on the surface of the tomato soup. Place two or three pieces of chive on the soup in a random pattern.

Note: The service of this soup is attention-getting, but the flavor combination is legitimate: Soup Mongole is a blend of tomato and pea soup. To make the painting easier and quicker, use a plastic squeeze bottle, with the nozzle tip cut to allow the soup to squeeze out easily.

Lentil and Carrot Soup

Yield: 2 qt	8 qt		2 L	8 L
		Ingredients:		
4 oz	1 lb	butter, margarine, or oil*	112 g	500 g
1 lb	4 lb	finely chopped onion	450 g	2 kg
8 oz	2 lb	finely chopped celery	224 g	900 g
1 lb	4 lb	diced carrots	450 g	2 kg
1	2	clove garlic	1	2
pinch	½ tsp	thyme (or to taste)	pinch	½ tsp
pinch	⅛ tsp	ground cloves (or to taste)	pinch	⅛ tsp
1 lb	4 lb	lentils, rinsed and drained	450 g	2 kg
2 qt	2 gal	water (or diluted stock) approx.*	2 L	8 L
4 oz	1 lb	chopped parsley	112 g	500 g
		salt and pepper (to taste)		

*For a vegetarian soup, choose margarine or vegetable oil for the fat and water or vegetable stock for the liquid. The soup is quite flavorful made that way. However, you may use salt pork and/or ham or meat stock if desired.

1. Sweat the onions, celery, carrots, and whole garlic clove until celery has softened. Remove the garlic and discard.
2. Add the thyme, cloves, lentils, and liquid. Simmer until lentils and carrot are tender, about 1 hour. Halfway through cooking time, add half the parsley.
3. Remove from heat. Transfer about one-fourth of the mixture to a blender, processor, or food mill and puree.
4. Return the puree to the soup, stir to combine, and season with salt and pepper to taste (lentils are enhanced by the liberal use of pepper). Cool, cover, and store refrigerated. If preparing in large quantity, cool quickly to prevent souring.
5. To serve, heat, adding most of the reserved parsley. Sprinkle a bit of parsley on each serving for color.

Minestrone

Yield: 2 qt	8 qt		2 L	8 L
		Ingredients:		
2 fl oz	8 fl oz	olive oil	60 ml	240 ml
1 oz	4 oz	sweet butter	28 g	112 g
6 oz	1½ lbs	chopped onions	168 g	672 g
6 oz	1½ lbs	scraped carrots, sliced	168 g	672 g

6 oz	1½ lbs	celery, coarsely chopped (Use tender inner leaves as well as stalks.)	168 g	672 g
12 oz	3 lbs	peeled and cubed potatoes	336 g	1 kg 344 g
1 qt	1 gal	chicken or vegetable stock*	1 L	4 L
1 qt	1 gal	water	1 L	4 L
7 fl oz	28 fl oz	canned tomatoes, chopped	210 ml	840 ml
⅜ tsp	1½ tsp	dried oregano	1 ml	4 ml
½ tsp	2 tsp	ground black pepper	2 ml	8 ml
6 oz	1½ lbs	frozen lima beans	168 g	672 g
6 oz	1½ lbs	frozen cut green beans	168 g	672 g
4¾ oz	1 lb 3 oz	canned cannellini†	112 g	448 g
4¾ oz	1 lb 3 oz	canned chick peas	112 g	448 g
6 oz	1½ lbs	zucchini, cubed	168 g	672 g
1 oz	4 oz	each chopped parsley and basil	28 g	112 g
¼ tsp	1 tsp	salt (or to taste)	1 ml	4 ml
		Garnish: grated Parmesan cheese, pesto (see in recipe index), or extra-virgin olive oil		

*If using canned stock, check for saltiness before adding additional salt included in recipe. Also, more stock may be added to thin the soup. This recipe yields a very thick and rich soup, almost a vegetable stew.

†Great Northern or any white bean. Canned, cooked beans and chick peas are used for time economy, with little change in quality result.

1. Heat half the olive oil and the butter in a heavy pot. Add the onions, carrots, and celery, and sweat until the onions are translucent and just beginning to color. Add additional olive oil as needed.
2. Add the potatoes, stock, water, canned tomatoes, oregano, and pepper. Simmer, covered, until the potatoes are just tender.
3. If the lima and green beans are block frozen, place in a colander and run under water to break up. Drain and add to the soup. Cook 5 to 10 minutes, just until the green beans are tender.
4. Drain the cannellini and chick peas and add to the soup. Cook five minutes.
5. Add the zucchini and chopped fresh herbs, stir to combine, and simmer for a few minutes.
6. Remove from heat, let stand for 15 to 20 minutes. The vegetables will continue to cook with residual heat. It is important not to overcook, especially if storing and reheating before service. If the vegetables are already losing texture (the zucchini breaks down first), you can preserve the quality by quickly turning the soup out into hotel pans to hasten cooling.
7. After standing time, taste and check for seasoning and consistency. Upon long standing, the mixture tends to thicken further. It can always be thinned to desired consistency with a bit of broth just before service.
8. Garnish if desired by serving each portion with a dollop of pesto or a drizzle of highly flavored good-quality olive oil. Pass grated cheese.

Note: Traditionally in the north of Italy, this soup is served at room temperature, generously laced with pesto, as a nourishing summer lunch.

Variations: Some versions of this soup also include shredded Savoy cabbage added after the aromatic vegetables and before the potatoes. Garlic also may be included with the aromatics unless pesto is used as a garnish. It is also possible to add cooked, drained pasta to a thinned version of the soup when reheating for service (use a small type such as elbows, shells, ditalini, or bowties). Obviously, such an addition will increase the recipe's yield.

Saffron Bisque

Yield: 2 qt	8 qt	Ingredients:	2 L	8 L
4	16	medium shrimp	4	16
3 cups	3 qt	mussel broth*	750 ml	3 L
3 cups	3 qt	fish stock or fumet	750 ml	3 L
2 cups	2 qt	dry white wine	500 ml	2 L
4 oz	1 lb	chopped shallots	115 g	450 g
4	16	parsley stems	4	16
1	1	bay leaf	1	1
pinch	¼ tsp	thyme	pinch	¼ tsp
1	2	whole clove	1	2
2 each	5 each	black and white peppercorns	2 each	5 each
4 oz	1 lb	sweet butter	115 g	450 g
4 oz	1 lb	all-purpose flour	115 g	450 g
1 cup	1 qt	hot milk	250 ml	1 L
2 cups	2 qt	heavy cream	500 ml	2 L
		salt and pepper (to taste)		
pinch	3 pinches	saffron threads	pinch	3 pinches
2 fl oz	1 cup	dry white wine	60 ml	250 ml
		Garnish:		
2 oz combined	8 oz	julienne of carrot, celery, and leek	80 g	225 g
4	16	large sea scallops	4	16

*The broth from steamed mussels (see Mussels in Saffron Cream in recipe index), if it is not served with the prepared dish, should be carefully strained and reserved for use in recipes such as this or other soups or fish sauces. Its flavor adds depth but does not overwhelm such preparations.

1. Wash and shell the shrimp, devein, and split lengthwise in two. Refrigerate the shrimp until ready to garnish the soup. (If holding the soup for more than several hours, lightly poach the shrimp, and refrigerate.)
2. Place the shrimp shells in a heavy pot along with the mussel broth, fish stock, white wine, shallots, herbs, and spices. Simmer for about 30 minutes, until the shallots are softened. Carefully strain the mixture into a clean saucepan, pressing on the solids to release the juices.
3. Boil the broth down to reduce by one-fourth. Set aside.
4. Meanwhile, prepare a roux with the butter and flour, and cook, stirring, for 3 to 5 minutes. Adjust the heat so the roux does not color. Set aside.
5. Gradually combine the broth and roux, whisking vigorously to avoid lumping. Simmer, stirring occasionally, for at least 15 to 20 minutes.
6. Add hot milk while cooking to adjust consistency.
7. Taste the soup to see that the taste of raw flour has been cooked away. Season with salt and pepper, strain again and set aside. Hold refrigerated.
8. Before serving, place the saffron threads and a small amount of white wine in a saucepan and simmer for a minute or two.
9. Gently reheat the soup, add the wine and saffron, and enough heavy cream to bring the soup to desired consistency. Do not boil or the soup will curdle. Adjust the seasoning if necessary.
10. Prepare the garnishes: Slice each scallop crosswise into four wafers. Lightly poach the halved shrimp, toss in the vegetable julienne, stir only for a minute, and remove from heat. Transfer to a strainer, drain thoroughly, and set aside.
11. Prepare hot soup bowls as follows: In the bottom of each bowl, place half a shrimp, two raw scallop slices, and a portion of the julienne. Ladle hot soup over and serve immediately.

Note: This soup should be velvety but not so thick that the garnishes are weighted down to the bottom of the bowl. When the soup is just the right thickness, some of the garnish will float toward the top. If staffing and number of guests allow, the presentation of this soup can be quite dramatic. Place heated, garnished bowls before each guest, then ladle soup from a tureen.

Summer Pea Soup

Yield: 2 qt   *2 L*

	Ingredients:	
1½ lb	frozen tiny peas, divided	675 g
3 tbls	sweet butter	3 tbls
1 bunch	scallions, trimmed and chopped	1 bunch
1 cup	chopped white of leek	240 ml

1 head	Boston lettuce, cored, washed, and chopped	1 head
2 tbls	all-purpose flour	2 tbls
6 cups	dilute chicken stock	1½ L
4 tbls each	minced parsley and dill	4 tbls each
2 tsp each	fresh mint leaves, chives, and tarragon leaves, minced	2 tsp each
1 cup	cream or half-and-half	¼ L
1 cup	buttermilk	¼ L
	salt and white pepper (to taste)	

1. Divide the peas, keep a third frozen, allow the remainder to thaw.
2. Heat the butter in a large pot, add the scallions and leeks and sweat for about 10 minutes until wilted but not colored. Add the lettuce and peas and sweat an additional 5 minutes.
3. Sprinkle the flour over the vegetables and cook, stirring, over very low heat for 2 minutes. Do not allow the roux to darken. Slowly add the stock, stirring to blend with the roux. Adjust the heat so the soup barely simmers for 10 minutes. Set aside to cool to lukewarm.
4. Puree in a blender or processor. At this point, the soup base may be stored, refrigerated or frozen until ready to use.
5. Just before finishing the soup for service, pass the frozen peas through a food mill to remove the skins. Add the bits of pulp to the soup, stir in the herbs, cream, and buttermilk. Add salt and white pepper to taste.

Note: This soup is delicious served cold. Add a dollop of sour cream or yogurt to the top of each portion and scatter with additional fresh herbs if desired. To serve hot, substitute an additional cup of half-and-half for the buttermilk. Heat but do not boil.
To increase volume, multiply all ingredients with no adjustments.

White and Wild Mushroom Soup

Yield: 2 qt	8 qt		2 L	8 L
		Ingredients:		
2 oz	6 oz	butter or margarine	56 g	224 g
10 oz	2½ lb	white mushrooms	250 g	1 kg 100 g
6 oz	1½ lb	exotic mushrooms	180 g	675 g
1 oz	4 oz	dried porcini, soaked	28 g	112 g
3 oz	10 oz	minced shallots	85 g	280 g
1½ cup	6 cups	medium white sauce	350 ml	1 L 500 ml
1 pt	2 qt	hot milk (approx.)	500 ml	2 L
¾ cup	1½ pt	heavy cream (approx.)	180 ml	750 ml
		salt and pepper (to taste)		
		Garnish:		
2 oz	6 oz	julienne of mushrooms, preferably exotic	56 g	180 g

The proportion and types of mushrooms can be varied according to availability, season, and cost. Taken at face value, this recipe is expensive, but it can be made more economical if it is made using the stems and trim of mushrooms and caps that have been used for another purpose. Many hors d'oeuvre call for mushroom caps, caps are peeled and/or fluted, and exotic types often require trim. Clean trimmings should be chopped and reduced to duxelles as indicated in the recipe then refrigerated or frozen until enough have accumulated to prepare the soup.

1. Clean and mince the fresh mushrooms. Place them in a linen towel and squeeze to remove excess moisture. Sauté in some of the butter until browned and dry. Set aside.
2. Drain the soaked dried mushrooms, reserving the soaking liquid. Strain the liquid through a fine linen handkerchief to remove all grit. Add to the sautéed mushrooms. Chop the soaked mushrooms and add to the mixture as well.
3. In a separate pan, sweat the shallots in the remaining butter until they are quite soft but only lightly colored. Do not burn.
4. Combine the mushroom mixture, shallots, and white sauce in a large pot and simmer, stirring occasionally, for about 30 minutes or until the mushroom flavor is blended throughout.
5. Add enough hot milk to bring the soup to desired consistency. Add salt and pepper to taste. If the mushrooms have been minced fine, the soup should not require straining. Of course, you may pass through a food mill if desired. Hold, refrigerated, for service.
6. When ready to serve prepare the garnish by sauteeing the julienne of mushroom. Heat the soup, add as much cream as desired, and correct seasoning if needed. Do not boil or the soup will curdle.
7. Serve in hot soup bowls, garnished with a few strips of sautéed mushroom.

Curried Apple Soup

Yield: 2 qt	8 qt		2L	8L
		Ingredients:		
2 oz	5 oz	sweet butter	56 g	140 g
8 oz	2 lb	minced onion	225 g	900 g
1 lb	4 lb	grated apple	450 g	2 kg
1 tbls	2 tbls	curry powder	1 tbls	2 tbls
2 oz	5 oz	all-purpose flour	56 g	140 g
4 cups	1 gal	chicken stock (approx.)	1 L	4 L
1½ cups	6 cups	apple cider or juice	370 ml	1½ L
1 cup	1 qt	milk	¼ L	1 L
		and/or		
1 cup	1 qt	light cream	¼ L	1 L
1	1	dash hot pepper sauce	1	1
		Possible garnishes: toasted slivered almonds; cooked chicken diced; toasted coconut		

1. Heat butter in a heavy pot, add onion, and sweat until translucent. Add apple and cook until soft.
2. Add curry powder and simmer, stirring, for 1 minute. Sprinkle flour over the contents of the pot and continue to stir and simmer for 2 minutes.
3. In another saucepan, heat the apple cider and half the chicken broth.
4. Slowly stir the broth mixture into the soup base and continue to cook until the soup thickens.
5. Add the milk and/or cream and some of the remaining broth to bring the soup to the desired consistency.
6. Add the dash of hot pepper sauce, and taste for seasoning. Adjust with salt and pepper, if desired. Refrigerate for storage.
7. To serve, carefully reheat the soup. Do not boil. Top each portion with one or more of the possible garnishes.

Chilled Fruit Soup

Yield: 2 qt	8 qt		2 L	8 L
		Ingredients:		
4 lb	16 lb	prepared fruit of choice	2 kg	8 kg
1 cup	1 qt	dry white wine	¼ L	1 L
1 cup	1 qt	semisweet white wine	¼ L	1 L
4 cups	1 gal	water and/or fruit juice	1 L	4 L
2 tsp	4 tsp	cinnamon or other spice	2 tsp	4 tsp
2 fl oz	1 cup	lemon juice (approx.)	60 ml	¼ L
4 oz	1 lb	sugar as needed	112 g	500 g
		heavy cream (as needed)		

Almost any fruit, fresh, canned, or dried can be used. Dried fruit, of course, should be plumped or rehydrated before weighing. Ripe, firm-fleshed melon is very good; some berries and grapes need to be sieved to remove seeds. Berries and melon should not be cooked, rather they are placed into the hot, seasoned liquid, stirred, and immediately pureed. Apples are a poor choice (the result is spiced applesauce); try Curried Apple Soup instead (see in recipe index). Nectarines, peaches, apricots, cherries, plums, even rhubarb (sieved), make delicious and pretty soups. Ripe bananas make a tropical, if somewhat sweet, soup: Spice well, eliminate all or most of the sugar and garnish with a splash of dark rum. Since this is a generic recipe, choose and adjust the seasonings, sugar, and spices to taste. Use the lemon juice to cut sweetness or enliven flavors. Be creative with garnishes: Use sliced or whole berries, fresh mint or other herbs, the petals or blossoms of edible flowers, or fortified wines, brandies, or liqueurs (a spoonful of good port in the center of a bowl of cantaloupe soup is fabulous).

1. Combine the wines, water and/or fruit juice, chosen spices, and some of the sugar in a large pot. Heat to the simmer.
2. Add the fruit (except berries and melon as above) and simmer for about 10 to 15 minutes until the fruit is soft enough to puree. It does not need to be fully cooked. Remove from heat.
3. Remove any flavoring agents such as cinnamon stick, cloves, peppercorns, or vanilla bean. These can be tied in a cheesecloth before adding to aid in removal.
4. Puree in a blender, processor, or food mill.
5. Taste the puree and adjust seasonings with sugar or lemon juice. Chill.
6. Before serving, add enough chilled cream to adjust flavor and consistency. Garnish as desired.

Game Consommé Garni

Yield: 8 qt		8 L
	Ingredients:	
10 lb	game bones or trim	5 kg
10 qt	poultry broth or stock	10 L
8 oz	chopped onion, carrot, leek, and celery	250 g
6	parsley stems	6
4	whole peppercorns	4
4	dried juniper berries	4
1	whole clove	1
1 each	sprig thyme and tarragon	1 each
6 oz	tomato puree	180 g
1 lb	lean ground chicken	500 g
8	egg whites	8
6 oz each	chopped onion, parsnip, leek, carrot, and celery	200 g
1	bay leaf	1
5	whole peppercorns	5
4 oz	tomato puree	115 g
2 cups	dry white wine	500 ml
1 cup	port or sherry	250 ml
1 lb	**Optional garnish: carrot, parsnip, leek, and parsley (combined)**	500 g

In the course of preparing "fancy," often boneless, dishes for catering, a good deal of waste (of game bird carcasses and bones and trim of game meats) can occur. This trim can be well utilized to make this luxurious consommé. Store trimmings in a wholesome manner (refrigerating or freezing) until enough is amassed to make this recipe. Remove excess fatty skin from duck and goose; always discard fat from venison and wild game meat as the flavor is most unpleasant. (Goose and duckling skin can be rendered for cracklings, reserving the fat for other uses.) If the bones are uncooked, first roast them, along with a halved large onion, until well browned.

1. In a large stock pot, combine the prepared bones with the broth and all the other ingredients up to, *but not including*, lean ground chicken.

2. Cook as for stock (see a good culinary text for more detail), skimming as needed, and simmering for at least 3 to 4 hours. Strain through a china cap or fine strainer lined with a few thicknesses of washed cheesecloth. You should have about 8 or 9 quarts (8 or 9 L) of game stock. Reduce if necessary. Cool rapidly and refrigerate (at least overnight).

3. To clarify the consommé: First, thoroughly degrease the cooled game stock by removing the congealed fat at the top and blotting the surface with clean paper.

4. In a large stock pot, combine the ground chicken with the egg whites, the chopped vegetables, spices, and tomato puree. Mix vigorously.

5. Gradually add the cold stock, mixing well. Add the white wine and heat, stirring, until the mixture just reaches the simmer. Now, stop stirring and adjust the heat so that the stock barely simmers for 1 to 2 hours. This is the clarifying process. The meat and egg white mixture will congeal into a raft and collect all the impurities, leaving behind a sparkling clear consommé. (For more detail, consult a culinary text.) Do not stir or disturb the raft in any way during the simmering time.

6. Line a fine strainer or china cap with several thicknesses of washed cheesecloth. Make a single opening in the raft and carefully ladle the simmered stock into the strainer. Let the mixture drain undisturbed into a clean vessel. Do not press on the contents of the strainer—let gravity do the work. When you get near the end, transfer the strainer to another clean vessel since the last few cups may be cloudy. Reserve any clouded liquid for use in other sauces or soups. Refrigerate the consommé until ready to serve.

7. To serve: Heat consommé to the simmer, add the port or sherry and adjust seasoning. Garnish with blanched slivers of vegetables and minced parsley or any classic consommé garnish (see a Larousse or culinary text.)

All-Purpose Demi-glace

Yield: 1 gal		4 L
	Ingredients:	
20 lb	beef and veal bones*	9 kg
3 lb	onions	1 kg 350 g
1 lb	chopped white of leek	450 g
1 lb	chopped carrot	450 g
1 lb	chopped celery	450 g
1	bouquet garni: bunch parsley stems, 3 cloves garlic, 2 bay leaves, 2 sprigs thyme, few cloves, 5 black and 5 white peppercorns	1
4 gal	water	16 L

*The more veal the better. Beef bones will give color and flavor but veal bones, particularly knuckle, will give body because of the large amount of collagen or gelatin contained in the cartilage.

1. Wash and crack the bones. Place in a large roasting pan along with one or two unpeeled onions, cut in half. Roast in a 425°F (220°C) oven for about two hours, until well browned. Turn the bones occasionally for even browning.

2. Peel and chop the balance of the onion and add to the other chopped vegetables. Add the onion skins. Prepare a bouquet garni by tying the herbs and spices into a cheesecloth bag.

3. When the bones have browned, transfer to a large stock pot. Pour off accumulated fat from pan, deglaze with some of the water, and add to the stock pot along with the vegetables and bouquet garni.

4. Place the stock pot over heat and bring to the simmer. If obvious scum appears on the surface during the first half hour, skim off. Continue to simmer to 10 to 12 hours.

5. Strain into clean container(s). Refrigerate overnight.

6. Remove fat from surface of cold stock. Transfer to a clean pot and simmer to reduce to 1 gal (4 L). While reduction proceeds, it is best to transfer the glace to progressively smaller saucepans. The result will be a dark, syrupy glace.

7. Transfer the glace to a clean roasting or hotel pan. Chill. The glace will set up to a jellylike substance. Cut this into small blocks and keep refrigerated or frozen for later use.

Note: For a fuller understanding of the classic preparation of demi-glace, see a good culinary text. While many culinary basics are not discussed in this book's recipe section, this recipe is included since demi-glace is so useful for enriching the flavor and consistency of so many dishes.

Salads and Vegetable Side Dishes

Watercress, Endive, and Mushroom Salad

Serves: 8

Ingredients:

½ lb	raw mushrooms	225 g
1 bunch	watercress	1 bunch
3	heads Belgian endive	3
1 cup	orange vinaigrette or basic vinaigrette made with lemon (see Vinaigrette Basics in recipe index)	¼ L

1. Chill salad plates. Clean, trim, and thinly slice the mushrooms. Moisten with some vinaigrette and set aside refrigerated.
2. Cut the tough stems from the watercress, rinse the remaining sprigs, trim into short sprigs, wrap, and chill.
3. Trim the root end from the endive, separate 16 outer leaves and set aside, cut the remaining endive into thin crosswise slices. Add the cut endive to the mushrooms.
4. To plate: Place a portion of the mushrooms and cut endive in the center of each plate, surround with a fringe of watercress, place two outer endive leaves at an angle on each plate. Drizzle the salads with a bit more dressing. These can be held for 1 or 2 hours, covered and refrigerated.

Field Greens with Hot Goat Cheese

Serves: 8

Ingredients:

1 qt	mesclun	1 L
6 tbls	sherry vinegar	6 tbls
½ cup	olive oil	125 ml
¼ cup	walnut oil	60 ml
	salt and pepper to taste	
8 oz	Montrachet or other goat cheese log	225 g
6 oz	broken pecan or walnut meats	180 g

Mesclun is a combination of tiny field greens, selected and combined by specialty produce purveyors. You may devise your own combination of tender baby lettuces, herbs, and edible flowers for this salad.

1. Trim and clean the lettuces for the salad. Wrap and crisp or arrange on chilled plates and hold for service.
2. Reserve 2 tbls of the olive oil. Combine the rest with the walnut oil, vinegar, and salt and pepper. Set the dressing aside.
3. Slice the cheese into equal slices and set aside.
4. Just before serving, sauté the nuts in the oil and either sauté or briefly grill the cheese until just at the point of melting.
5. Place the soft cheese in the center of the salad. Garnish with the hot sautéed nuts and serve.

Avocado and Papaya Salad

Serves: 6

Ingredients:

1	large ripe avocado	1
1	large ripe papaya	1
2 bunches	watercress	2 bunches
1 cup	orange vinaigrette (see in recipe index)	¼ L
	ground black pepper	

1. Chill six individual salad plates. Rinse the watercress, shaking off excess moisture, cut off most of the heavy stems, and discard. Wrap the remaining sprigs in paper towel and place in a plastic bag. Refrigerate until ready to garnish the salad.
2. Pour some of the vinaigrette into a shallow bowl. Halve both the papaya and the avocado. Discard the avocado pit, carefully peel the avocado and slice each half into six lengthwise crescent-shaped slices. Place the slices in the vinaigrette, turn to coat. Remove and reserve the papaya seeds; peel and slice the papaya as you did the avocado.

3. Set the salad plates on a tray or baking sheet. On each plate, place two slices each of papaya and avocado, in alternating colors. Fan them out from one edge of the plate with their curved sides facing in the same direction. Drizzle dressing over all, letting some run onto the plate. Place a few papaya seeds here and there on each plate. These can be held, well wrapped and refrigerated, for 1 to 2 hours.

4. Just before serving, place a small bunch of watercress sprigs at the point on the plate where the papaya and avocado meet. Drizzle with a bit of dressing, grind black pepper over all, and serve.

Sicilian Citrus Salad

Serves: 8

	Ingredients:	
3	large seedless oranges	3
2	large lemons	2
½ cup	flavorful olive oil	125 ml
1 tsp	salt	1 tsp
1 tsp	coarsely ground pepper	1 tsp
⅓ cup	oil-cured black olives	80 ml

1. Peel the oranges and lemons removing both the skin and the pith. Use a sharp knife to slice evenly. Pick any seeds out of the lemon leaving the slices intact.

2. Arrange the fruit slices in an attractive pattern on a serving dish. Drizzle with olive oil and sprinkle with salt and pepper. Garnish with olives. Let stand for 2 hours before serving.

Variation: Add thin sliced red onions to the salad, sprinkled with extra salt.

Sautéed Zucchini Salad

Serves: 8

	Ingredients:	
5 or 6	young narrow zucchini	5 or 6
	olive oil for frying	
5 tbls	balsamic vinegar	80 ml
¼ cup	minced parsley	60 ml
½ cup	chopped fresh mint	125 ml
	salt and pepper (to taste)	

1. Scrub the zucchini to remove external grit, trim the ends, and slice very thin. Lay the slices on paper towel for a few minutes to drain excess moisture.
2. Heat the olive oil in a skillet and fry the zucchini over high heat until they are well browned on both sides. As they are cooked, transfer to a bowl without draining.
3. Sprinkle the fried zucchini with most of the vinegar and the herbs. Season with salt and pepper and toss carefully but thoroughly. Taste and add as much more vinegar as is needed for a tangy, but not overly sharp flavor. This salad is best eaten within a day of being made. It should be served at room temperature.

Note: Small zucchini are desirable for this salad for their sweet taste and lack of large seeds.

Fruited Cabbage Slaw

Yield: 2 qt		2 L
	Ingredients:	
1 qt	commercial mayonnaise	1 L
16 oz	sour cream	450 g
12 fl oz	pear nectar	350 ml
12 fl oz	apricot nectar	350 ml
4 tsp	dry mustard	4 tsp
4 tsp	paprika	4 tsp
1½ tsp	turmeric	1½ tsp
1½ tsp	ground ginger	1½ tsp
1 tsp	salt	1 tsp
½ tsp	ground black pepper	½ tsp
pinch	cayenne	pinch
2 tbls	granulated sugar	2 tbls
1 large	cabbage (about 3 lb [1400 g])	1 large
1 small	red cabbage (about 1 lb [500 g])	1 small
2 lb	carrots	1 kg

1. Combine the mayonnaise with the sour cream, stir together, then whisk in the fruit nectars, the spices, and granulated sugar, mixing vigorously to combine all the seasonings and incorporate the fruit nectars. Set dressing aside, refrigerated.
2. Wash, trim, and core the cabbages. Shred by hand or use an electric slicer to produce fine threads of cabbage. Wash, scrape, and shred or grate the carrots. These can all be stored separately, well wrapped and refrigerated, for up to two days. Do not combine them or the red cabbage will stain the other vegetables.

3. About an hour before serving, combine the vegetables in a large bowl, toss dry to thoroughly blend the colors. Pour on some dressing, toss, and continue to add dressing until the slaw is well coated but not drippy. Taste and adjust seasonings, adding a bit more salt and pepper if needed. In warm weather, keep well chilled. Serve with tongs for easiest handling. If using in volume, dress each batch in sequence as needed, if you prefer a crisp textured slaw.

Variations: Grated or sliced onion, chopped apple, or drained crushed pineapple may be added to the slaw when adding dressing.

Mixed Vegetable Slaw: Add appropriate amounts of thin sliced onion, slivered red and green bell pepper, chopped celery, and grated zucchini to the slaw.

Broccoli and Cauliflower Mimosa

Serves: 10

	Ingredients:	
1 head	**cauliflower**	1 head
2 bunches	**broccoli**	2 bunches
	salted water	
1½ cups	**orange vinaigrette (see in recipe index)**	350 ml
2	**hard-boiled eggs**	2
½ cup	**minced parsley**	125 ml
4 tbls	**chopped capers**	4 tbls

1. Steam or boil the cauliflower until just tender. Drain, shock in ice water, and drain again. Remove the core, separate the head into florets.
2. Trim the tough stems from the broccoli, reserve for another use. Peel the balance of the stems up to the florets. Blanch in boiling salted water for 2 to 3 minutes, drain, shock, and drain thoroughly. Cut the stems into diagonal pieces, separate the florets and cut into even pieces.
3. Arrange the vegetables on a serving platter or dish, place paper towel over the top of the plate, and seal in plastic wrap. Hold at room temperature for 1 or 2 hours or refrigerate for up to 8 hours.
4. Mince the eggs or rub through a sieve. Cover and store refrigerated.
5. About 45 minutes before serving, spoon some of the dressing over the vegetables. Sprinkle with parsley, egg, and capers.

Carrot and Celery Root Salad

Serves: 12

Ingredients:

3 cups	shredded carrot	¾ L
2 cups	shredded celery root	½ L
2 cups	orange vinaigrette (see in recipe index)	½ L
½ cup	parsley	125 ml

1. Soak the shredded celery root in salted water for 30 minutes. Drain and squeeze dry.
2. Combine the celery root with the carrot, toss with dressing, and garnish with parsley. Let stand about an hour before serving.

Herbed Vegetable Julienne

Serves: 8

Ingredients:

2	large carrots	2
3	leeks	3
3	small zucchini	3
3	parsnips	3
4 tbls	shallot and herb butter (see Compound or Flavored Butters in recipe index)	56 g
	salt and pepper (to taste)	

1. The vegetables can all be prepared a day ahead. Scrape the carrots and parsnips, trim, and cut into fine julienne. Trim and wash the leeks, and, using only the white and tender green, cut into julienne. Scrub the zucchini, trim and cut into julienne, a bit thicker than the carrot. Wrap and store refrigerated until ready to cook.
2. Stem or blanch the vegetables only until their colors brighten. Drain well. Toss with herb butter and season with salt and pepper just before serving.

Haricot Verts with Hazelnuts

Serves: 10

Ingredients:

1½ lb	haricot verts, or tiny tender green beans	675 g
1 tbls	sweet butter	1 tbls
1 tbls	champagne vinegar	1 tbls
4 tbls	hazelnut oil	4 tbls
3 tbls	minced shallots	3 tbls
¼ tsp	ground white pepper	¼ tsp
6 oz	Toasted hazelnuts, chopped	180 g

1. Rinse the beans; tip and string if needed. Steam or blanch until brightly colored and barely tender. Drain immediately and turn into a shallow pan to stop cooking.
2. In a saucepan, melt the butter, quickly add vinegar, hazelnut oil, shallots, and pepper. Remove from heat after 15 seconds, toss with the beans and turn into a serving platter. Scatter the toasted nuts over the top and serve.

Note: These can be served warm, rather than piping hot. Avoid reheating to too high a temperature or all the components will be overcooked and the oil will lose its fresh flavor.

Variation: To prepare as a salad: Blanch the beans (not more than 2 hours ahead), wrap in moist paper towel and plastic, and refrigerate. Eliminate the butter from the recipe; instead combine the vinegar, shallots, hazelnut oil, and pepper with 1 cup (¼ L) of creme fraiche or drained sour cream or yogurt. Add salt, if desired. Either toss the beans and nuts in the dressing, or preferably, serve bunches of beans topped with a dab of dressing and chopped nuts.

Six-Bean Salad

Serves: 12–14

Ingredients:

½ lb	green beans	225 g
½ lb	yellow wax beans	225 g
10 oz	frozen lima beans	285 g
1 cup each	cooked and drained chick peas, kidney beans, cannellini	¼ L each
2 cups	minced onion	½ L
2 cups	orange vinaigrette (see in recipe index)	½ L
½ cup	lemon juice	125 ml
4 tbls each	minced parsley and chives	4 tbls each
	salt and pepper to taste	

1. Tip and string the green and yellow beans. Cut into two or three pieces. Blanch in salted water just until tender, drain. Cook the limas until just tender, drain.
2. Combine all the beans and the chopped onion with the dressing. Add lemon juice to taste. Let stand at room temperature for a few hours to mellow flavors.
3. Season with salt and pepper, stir in fresh herbs, and serve.

Note: A variety of other cooked beans of your choice may be substituted in the salad if desired. Chopped celery or diced red and green peppers may be added as well.

Glazed Carrots and Sugar Snaps

Serves: 6–8

	Ingredients:	
1 lb	sugar snap peas	450 g
1 lb	baby carrots*	450 g
3 tbls	butter	42 g
2 tbls	lemon juice	2 tbls
2 tbls	orange juice	2 tbls
1 tbls	granulated sugar	1 tbls
	salt and pepper (to taste)	
4 tbls	minced dill	4 tbls

*If miniature carrots are available, these should be used. Or use small Belgian carrots or tender young carrots, sliced diagonally into pieces smaller than the sugar snaps.

1. Tip and string the peas. Steam until barely tender. Boil or steam carrots separately until fork tender. Set both vegetables aside, well wrapped until just before serving.
2. Prepare the glaze by heating the butter and adding the juices and sugar. When ready to serve, toss in the vegetables to coat lightly. Season with salt and pepper and sprinkle with dill.

Frizzled Radicchio

Serves: 8

	Ingredients:	
3 or 4 heads	radicchio	3 or 4 heads
	oil for frying	
	salt and pepper (to taste)	

1. Trim the root end from the radicchio, open the leaves and rinse, and shake dry. Cut into fine chiffonade.
2. Heat oil in a deep fryer, plunge the radicchio into the oil for just a minute, then remove and drain on absorbent paper. Sprinkle with salt and pepper and serve as a garnish or vegetable.

Carrot and Broccoli Custards

Serves: 8

Ingredients:

12 oz	grated carrots	350 g
6 oz	broccoli florets, chopped	180 g
3	eggs, lightly beaten	3
1 cup	cream	¼ L
1 tsp	salt	1 tsp
½ tsp	white pepper	½ tsp
1 tbls	minced shallots	1 tbls
pinch	nutmeg	pinch
	softened butter (as needed)	

1. If the carrots are in long shreds, chop them a bit to make shorter pieces. Heat a bit of butter in a pan and sauté the carrots for 2 minutes. Add the broccoli, stir, and remove from heat.
2. Butter custard cups, timbale molds, or a ring or other suitable mold. Have ready a baking pan to serve as a water bath. Preheat the oven to 400° F (205° C).
3. Stir the cream into the eggs, add the seasonings and the shallots. Fold in the vegetables. Spoon the custard into molds, set in the outer pan, and place in the hot oven. Add hot water to the outer pan to come at least halfway up the sides of the mold. Bake for 15 to 20 minutes until set.
4. Unmold onto plates or serving platter.

Note: These timbales can be served as a vegetable side dish or can be used as a first course, served on a bed of buttered spinach or surrounded by sautéed mushrooms.

Variations: Other vegetables of harmonious flavors and colors can be substituted in the custard, or a puree of vegetable, such as cooked eggplant, red pepper, or zucchini, seasoned with appropriate herbs, can be used.

Cucumber and Fennel in Pernod Cream

Serves: 8–10

Ingredients:

5	cucumbers, peeled and seeded	5
2 or 3	bulbs fennel	2 or 3
4 tbls	butter	56 g
4 tbls	cream	60 ml

2 tbls	**pernod**	30 ml
2 tbls each	**minced dill, parsley, chives**	2 tbls each
	salt and pepper (to taste)	

1. Cut the halved peeled and seeded cucumbers into ½-in. (1½ cm) slices. Salt lightly and drain in a colander.
2. Trim the fennel bulbs, discarding the tough stems and outer leaves. Cut into quarters or sixths, depending on size, cut away the tough core, and slice the wedges as the cucumbers.
3. Place the fennel slices in a saucepan with a bit of water and simmer until the fennel begins to soften and the water evaporates. Add the butter and the cucumber and cook until the vegetables have absorbed most of the butter. May be set aside at this point and finished just before service.
4. Add the cream and the pernod, cook down until the vegetables are coated with sauce. Add a few grindings of pepper (salt should not be necessary), sprinkle with herbs and serve.

Note: Very good as an accompaniment to poached or grilled fish, or simple, unsauced veal or chicken dishes.

Variation: Tiny peas, blanched sugar snaps, or snow peas may be added to the dish just before serving.

Peas and Mushrooms with Cointreau

Serves: 8

Ingredients:

1 lb	**fresh mushrooms, sliced**	450 g
1½ lb	**frozen tiny peas**	675 g
3 tbls	**butter**	42 g
2 tbls	**minced shallots**	2 tbls
3 tbls	**Cointreau**	3 tbls
	salt and pepper (to taste)	

1. Thaw the peas by plunging into hot water for 20 seconds. Drain and set aside.
2. Heat the butter in a deep skillet, add the mushrooms and sauté until the mushroom liquid has reduced and the mushrooms are golden brown.
3. Add peas, and cook just to heat through, season with salt and pepper, add the Cointreau, and toss to coat all the vegetables. Serve hot.

Note: You may prepare up to one day ahead up to the point of adding the peas and Cointreau.

Variation: Sautéed chicken livers may be added to the vegetable mixture.

Root Vegetable Puree

Yield: *6 cups* 1½ L

Ingredients:

8 oz	butter or margarine	225 g
8 oz	onion, finely chopped	225 g
1 oz	minced shallot	28 g
16 oz	carrot, coarsely chopped	450 g
16 oz	turnip, coarsely chopped	450 g
16 oz	parsnip, coarsely chopped	450 g
8 fl oz	water	250 ml
1 tsp	salt	1 tsp
1 tsp	pepper	1 tsp

Optional: allspice and nutmeg and/or cinnamon (to taste)

1. Sweat onion and shallot in butter until translucent. Add vegetables and water and cook, covered, over moderate heat for about one and a half hours.
2. Stir, checking for tenderness and water level. The vegetables may need another 30 minutes of cooking time. When finished, the vegetables should be tender enough to break apart with a fork and almost all of the moisture should have evaporated. Check occasionally while cooking, especially during the last half hour, and add a bit of water if needed to prevent scorching.
3. Remove from the heat and pass through a food mill fitted with a coarse blade or process smooth in a food processor, depending on the texture you desire.
4. If the puree seems too wet to hold its shape in a spoon, place in a clean sauce pan and cook for a few minutes over high heat, stirring, to dry the mixture. Season according to taste and planned usage. This freezes very well.

Note: You may alter the proportions of the vegetables to suit, for example, more carrot for sweetness or rutabagas rather than turnips for a sharper flavor. You may add a bit of garlic puree if desired. Cooked riced potatoes may be added to the mixture either to soften flavor or to stiffen to a consistency suitable for piping.

This mixture can be used simply as a side dish or piped into vegetable cups or boats, such as zucchini, onions, pattypan squash, or tiny pumpkins. For cost efficiency, remember that the flexibility of this recipe makes it ideal as a use for trimmings of turned vegetables, crudités, and garnish preparations.

Sautéed Brussels Sprouts

Serves: 8

Ingredients:

2 lb	fresh brussels sprouts	1 kg
2 tbls	butter	28 g
1 oz	red onion, chopped	28 g
1 tbls	balsamic vinegar	1 tbls
2 tsp	sugar	2 tsp
3 tbls	orange juice	3 tbls
	salt and pepper (to taste)	

1. Trim the sprouts, removing any blemished outer leaves, and cut out the core. Drop the sprouts into water and peel off the leaves as much as possible. Drain well. Chop the centers but keep as many leaves as possible whole.
2. Heat the butter in a large pot, add the red onion, and toss a few times. Add the balsamic vinegar and continue to cook until the onion begins to soften.
3. Add the sugar, the orange juice, and the sprouts and toss until the leaves turn bright green and just begin to wilt. Season with salt and pepper and serve.

Note: May be prepared ahead as follows: Remove from heat after adding leaves. Hold for about an hour. Just before serving, place over high heat, cover and cook for about a minute. Then toss until done and serve.

Sautéed Forest Mushrooms

Serves: 8

Ingredients:

2 lb	chanterelles, morels, or other fresh wild mushrooms, alone or combined	1 kg
4 tbls	olive oil	60 ml
1 tbls	minced garlic	1 tbls
3 tbls	minced shallots	3 tbls
2 tbls each	minced parsley, chives, thyme, chervil, tarragon	2 tbls each
	salt and coarse black pepper	
	Optional: ½ pt (250 ml) reduced cream*	

*Reduced cream has been simmered to reduce its water content. Its use results in a smoother, more concentrated sauce.

1. Clean the mushrooms well, preferably by brushing thoroughly with a soft brush or damp cloth. Morels will need a few quick rinses in water to remove fine grit. Other mushrooms may be washed, but none should have prolonged soaking. Shake and pat dry. Leave whole wherever possible, breaking the chanterelles into branches if the clumps are very large. Portobellos, which can be very large, should be sliced into thick strips. In all cases, trim away tough stems or stem ends. Trimmings may be washed and used in soups and sauces.

2. Heat the oil in a sauté pan, add the mushrooms (if using a combination, add the heavy sturdier varieties first, the fragile ones later, and sauté until almost tender. Add the garlic and shallots, lower the heat and cook for about a minute. Add the garlic and shallots, lower the heat and cook for about a minute. Add the herbs and season with salt and pepper. If using the cream, add and simmer until it is almost completely absorbed by the mushrooms. Serve as soon as possible after cooking for best flavor and texture.

Spinach with Pears and Port

Serves: 6

Ingredients:

2 lb	fresh spinach, washed, stemmed, and crisped	1 kg
1	ripe pear	1
dash	nutmeg	dash
¼ tsp	cinnamon	¼ tsp
pinch	ground ginger	pinch
2 tbls	butter	28 g
2 tbls	port	2 tbls
	salt and pepper (to taste)	

1. About 10 minutes before cooking, peel and core the pear and cut into medium dice. Toss with the spices and port and set aside.

2. Immediately before serving, heat butter in a pot large enough to hold the spinach. Add half the pears, all the spinach, a sprinkle of water (about 2 tbls), some salt and pepper, and the balance of the pears and port. Cook over high heat for 30 seconds, tossing the spinach with tongs to coat all the leaves with butter and port. Lower the heat and cover the pot for about 30 seconds, but no more than a minute. The spinach should just begin to wilt.

3. Serve at once as a vegetable garnish or a separate side dish while the spinach is still somewhat crisp.

Note: To prepare ahead: Melt the butter, add the pears and port. Remove from heat and add the spinach, tossing to coat with liquid. Leave off the heat and uncovered while you plate the balance of the course. Just before the plates are to leave the kitchen, place the pot over high heat, toss a few times to heat through, and serve.

Stir-fried Asparagus with Mushrooms

Serves: 8

	Ingredients:	
2 lb	slim asparagus	1 kg
6 oz	oyster mushrooms	180 g
2 tbls	peanut oil	30 ml
1 tbls	minced garlic	1 tbls
2 tbls	minced gingerroot	2 tbls
1 tbls	soy sauce	1 tbls
1 tbls	oyster sauce	1 tbls
2 tsp	cornstarch dissolved in water	2 tsp

1. Snap the tough ends from the asparagus and cut into diagonal pieces.
2. Clean the mushrooms, trimming off tough stem ends.
3. Heat the oil in a wok or skillet, add the garlic and ginger and cook for 30 seconds until fragrant and lightly colored. Add the mushrooms and stir fry for about 1 minute. Add the asparagus, soy sauce, and oyster sauce, and stir fry until the asparagus turn bright green.
4. Push the vegetables up the side of the wok, add the stirred cornstarch paste, and stir into the sauce until glossy. Toss the vegetables in the sauce until coated and transfer to serving dish.

Note: You may prepare the mushrooms and sauce ahead. Blanch the asparagus separately and combine with the reheated mushrooms and sauce just before serving.

Stuffed Eggplant Marinara

Serves: 8

	Ingredients:	
2	medium-size eggplants	2
1 lb	well drained ricotta	450 g
½ lb	diced mozzarella	225 g
6 tbls	grated Romano cheese	6 tbls
4 tbls	minced parsley	4 tbls
½ cup	chopped eggplant trimmings	125 ml
½ cup	crumbled cooked sausage or minced prosciutto	125 ml
1	egg, beaten	1
	flour for dredging	
	oil for frying	
	salt and pepper	
2 cups	Marinara Sauce (see Spicy Tomato Sauce in recipe index)	½ L

1. Trim the eggplants; peel or not as preferred. Slice lengthwise into at least eight thin oval slices each. Salt the slices and place in a colander to extract bitter juice.
2. If using eggplant in filling, peel the trimmings and chop up the extra pieces. Salt and set aside separately from the slices to drain.
3. Prepare the cheese filling: Combine the ricotta, mozzarella, grated cheese, parsley, and egg. Add pepper to taste. If using eggplant, sauté for 1 or 2 minutes, drain and add to filling. Taste for salt and adjust seasonings. If using the meats, fold into cheese mixture. Set stuffing aside refrigerated.
4. Wipe the eggplant slices with a wet cloth to remove salt and juice. Pat dry with paper towels. Dredge in flour and fry in a bit of oil until golden. Drain on absorbent paper to remove excess grease. If you would rather not fry, you can cook the eggplant slices, brushed with melted margarine or oil, in a broiler until golden on both sides. Do not burn or overcook.
5. Spread the filling on the cooked and cooled eggplant slices. Starting at one short end, roll into little bundles.
6. Spoon a thin layer of marinara sauce in a shallow casserole or baking dish just large enough to hold the rolled eggplant. Place the rolls in the pan, seam side down. Spoon more sauce over the top of the rolls. Hold until ready to bake.
7. Bake in a 350° F (180° C) oven until heated through. Leave the pan uncovered while baking. Cover to hold for up to 1 hour in a warm oven. Hold refrigerated before or after baking but avoid freezing as the dish will become too watery. If reheating, use gentle heat.

Note: These will hold up well on a buffet and are good either piping hot or at warm room temperature. Since these are really a prettier version of an eggplant parmigiana, if you like, you may sprinkle extra shredded mozzarella and grated cheese over the top just before serving. Extra sauce may be served on the side or plates may be napped with sauce as a base for the stuffed eggplant.

Sweet and Sour Red Cabbage

Serves: 8

Ingredients:

2 heads	red cabbage (about 4 lbs or 2 kg)	2 heads
5 tbls	butter	70 g
1 cup	chopped onion	240 g
1 cup	chopped apple	240 g
½ tsp	salt	½ tsp
⅓ cup	red wine vinegar (or to taste)	80 ml
2 tbls	brown sugar (or to taste)	2 tbls
	pepper (to taste)	

1. Trim the wilted outer leaves from the cabbage, remove the cores, and finely shred cabbage. Soak in water for about 15 minutes.
2. Heat the butter in a pot large enough to hold the cabbage, add the onion, and cook until wilted. Life the cabbage from its soaking water and add to the pot. Cook and stir for about 5 minutes.
3. Add the apple, salt, and some of the vinegar, stir to combine, then cover the pot and simmer over low heat for 45 minutes to 1 hour, stirring once or twice.
4. Stir in some of the sugar and cook for another 15 to 20 minutes until the cabbage is well wilted and tender. Taste and add pepper to taste, adjust the sweet-sour flavor with more vinegar or sugar as desired.
5. If there is excess moisture in the pot, turn up the heat to reduce the liquid. Can be prepared ahead and reheated.

Vegetables Provencale

Serves: 8

	Ingredients:	
5	ripe plum tomatoes	5
5	tiny eggplants	5
3	young zucchini	3
3	yellow summer squash	3
6 tbls	flavorful olive oil	100 ml
2	garlic cloves	2
3 tbls	minced parsley	3 tbls
4 tbls	minced basil	4 tbls
pinch	thyme	pinch
	salt and pepper (to taste)	

If possible, all the vegetables should be approximately the same diameter.

1. Prepare the eggplant first. Trim the ends and cut into even ¼-in. (¾ cm) slices. Salt and place between paper towel on a baking sheet, top with another baking sheet, and a weight. Set aside to drain for about 30 minutes.
2. Place the olive oil in a bowl. Use a garlic press to add the garlic to the oil, add the herbs, and set aside to mellow flavors.
3. Scrub the zucchini to remove grit. Wash the yellow squash. Trim the ends of both and cut into slices the same as the eggplant. Trim the ends from the tomatoes and slice as the other vegetables.
4. Rub a shallow casserole or gratin dish with a bit of the oil. Place the vegetable slices in the pan on their edges, alternating the colors. Depending on the shape of the pan, either place them in rows or concentric circles. They can be fitted tightly together, they will shrink up when they bake. Drizzle the flavored oil all over the vegetables so they are evenly coated. Sprinkle with a bit of salt and generously with pepper.

5. Bake uncovered in a 350°F (180°C) oven for about 20 to 30 minutes until baked through and lightly browned.

Note: The vegetables can be prepared several hours ahead and baked before serving. They may also be baked about an hour or two ahead and reheated. They may exude moisture while standing, which can be drained off before reheating.

Zucchini Cups with Vegetable Fillings

Serves: 10–12

	Ingredients:	
3 or 4	large zucchini	3 or 4
3 cups	Root Vegetable Puree (see in recipe index)	¾ L
3 cups	Sweet and Sour Onion Jam (see in recipe index)	¾ L
	butter or margarine (as needed)	
	salt and pepper (to taste)	

1. Scrub the zucchini and trim the ends. Cut crosswise into three or four sections each to form little logs. Set each log on end and use a small spoon or melon baller to remove most of the pulp. If you like, you may notch or carve the upper edge into a decorative pattern.
2. Set the zucchini cups into a shallow baking pan, add a little water and dab a bit of butter or margarine into the hollow of each. Cover and bake for a few minutes until barely tender. Sprinkle the cups with salt and pepper.
3. You may fill the cups with your choice of filling beforehand, store, and heat through just before serving. Or, if more convenient, heat the cups and filling separately and fill just before serving.

Note: If you have tiny zucchini available, split them lengthwise in two, scoop out the centers, cook, fill, and heat as above. Either way, these are pretty and easy to portion and plate.

Roasted Peppers

Yield: 4 qt   *4 L*

	Ingredients:	
40–50	sweet red and/or yellow bell peppers	40–50
	plastic bags, storage jars, or freezer containers	

This is not so much a recipe as a method and a strong suggestion that you prepare these peppers in bulk and store in the freezer for use throughout the year. Your own broiled or barbecued roasted peppers are infinitely superior to jarred pimientos or commercially prepared roasted peppers and far less expensive. They take a little time but no special skills and are useful served alone on a buffet or as part of an antipasto, in salads, sauces, soups, or as parts of platters featuring fresh and smoked cheese or meats.

They can be prepared any time of the year, but, in the Northeast, autumn brings the thickest, most beautiful specimens to market in abundance. In my family, we prepare five crates or bushels once a year on the outdoor barbecue.

1. Remove the stem and core of the peppers, shaking and pulling out most of the seeds and ribs.
2. Grill in a broiler, salamander, or outdoor grill, turning the peppers until the skin is blistered and blackened on all sides. Immediately place a batch in a large plastic bag, twist closed and set aside for at least 15 minutes, until they are just cool enough to handle and the skins have steamed loose.
3. Rub and pull the blackened skin from the peppers, cleaning them as well as possible and place the cleaned peppers into jars or containers for freezing. This is a messy job but easy. It helps to keep a pan of water close by to rinse the charcoaled skin from your hands. Don't worry if little black flecks remain on the peppers, it is part of their charm. You can always pick it off later on if you need pristine peppers for a sauce or soup.
4. These can be used at once, stored in the refrigerator for a week, or in the freezer for a year. Season with salt, olive oil, garlic, or other herbs as desired when ready to use. They are delicious plain.

Note: If roasting both red and yellow (or orange) peppers, pack each color separately. Any peppers can be roasted in this manner, but use caution in handling hot or chili peppers: The seeds, flesh, and fumes can sting and irritate the eyes and skin. So far as esthetics are concerned, the reds are vibrant and evenly colored; yellow and orange peppers will have darker mottled patches but are still pretty. Green peppers are rather dull looking, and since they are not as sweet, have a different flavor. Since black or purple peppers lose their colored skins during peeling, your end product will be a very expensive roasted green pepper.

Tomato (or Roasted Pepper) and Basil Salad

Serves: 10–12

Ingredients:

3 or 4	ripe beefsteak tomatoes or other vine-ripened tomatoes	3 or 4
1 lb	fresh or water-packed unsalted mozzarella or smoked mozzarella	450 g
1	small bunch fresh basil	1
½ cup	fruity extra-virgin olive oil	125 ml

½ cup	Pesto Alla Genovese (see in recipe index)	125 ml
1	garlic clove (optional)	1

Optional garnishes: capers, oil-cured or nicoise olives, anchovies,
   or prosciutto

salt and optional pepper

1. Core and slice the tomatoes. Slice or cube the chosen mozzarella.
2. If you have sliced the cheese, place it on or between the sliced tomatoes in a shallow platter or serving plate. Cubed, it can be scattered over the top of the slices. Sprinkle the salad with salt.
3. For the simplest salad, top with strips of fresh basil leaves and coat with oil. Or add one of the following: anchovy strips, bits of prosciutto, olives, or capers. Any of these are suitable with either fresh or smoked mozzarella. In all cases, a garlic clove may be used to flavor the oil if desired. Some cooks chop garlic and sprinkle over the salad; if you do so, be absolutely certain guests will appreciate the strong taste. Grind black pepper over the salads, if desired.
4. For a tomato pesto salad, arrange tomatoes and fresh mozzarella, spoon pesto in a ribbon over the salad.

Note: For any of these salads, the sweetest, most perfectly ripe red tomatoes are essential. Pale, cottony, inferior tomatoes are a waste of money and time. If great tomatoes are not available, roasted peppers may be substituted in any of the versions except the pesto-dressed salad. The peppers are equally delicious and pretty.

Variation: **Sun-dried Tomato Salad:** Use oil-packed tomatoes that are sweet and plump, for best results. Chop them in bite-size pieces and scatter over either fresh or smoked mozzarella slices. Use any of the above dressing and garnishing suggestions, except for anchovies.

Tarragon Tomato Salad

Serves: 8

	Ingredients:	
3 or 4	large ripe tomatoes	3 or 4
1 tsp	salt	1 tsp
1 tbls	sugar	1 tbls
1 cup	basic vinaigrette made with tarragon vinegar and olive oil	¼ L
2 tbls	chopped fresh tarragon	2 tbls

1. Core and slice the tomatoes, arrange on a platter, sprinkle with salt and sugar. Drizzle dressing over and sprinkle with tarragon. Hold at least 1 hour before serving.

Steakhouse Tomatoes with Blue Cheese

Serves: 8–10

Ingredients:

4	ripe beefsteak tomatoes	4
2	large sweet onions, such as Vidalias, Mauis, Texas Sweets, or Walla Wallas	2
1 cup	basic vinaigrette made with balsamic vinegar or use orange vinaigrette (see in recipe index)	¼ L
6 oz	crumbled blue cheese	180 g
	salt and pepper (to taste)	

1. Core and thick-slice the tomatoes. Trim and peel the onions, slice half as thick as tomatoes. Arrange the slices in an attractive alternating pattern. Sprinkle with very little salt.
2. Drizzle dressing over the slices, grind black pepper over all. Let stand at room temperature for at least an hour.
3. Just before serving, scatter the crumbled blue cheese over the salad.

Note: It is not necessary to use the finest Roquefort, Stilton or Gorgonzola for this salad, but do select a good quality blue-veined cheese.

Variation: A fresh goat cheese, a feta or a Montrachet, is very good with tomatoes and onions. Use an herb vinaigrette made with olive oil and lemon juice as the dressing.

Fried Green Tomatoes

Serves: 8

Ingredients:

3 or 4	Large green tomatoes	3 or 4
	seasoned flour for dredging	
	egg wash	
	seasoned dry bread crumbs	
	vegetable oil for frying	

1. Core the tomatoes and cut into thick crosswise slices.
2. Dredge the slices in flour, then in egg, then bread crumbs, patting to help coating adhere. Let the slices rest on a rack at room temperature for about an hour.
3. Heat a shallow layer of oil in a skillet. Add the tomatoes and fry until golden brown on both sides. Take care when turning so as not to break the crust. Serve hot or at warm room temperature. May be held in a warm oven for about 1 hour, uncovered.

Potatoes, Pasta, Rice, and Grains

Spinach Crespelle with Prosciutto Sauce

Yield: 24

	Ingredients:	
24	**Spinach Crepes (see in recipe index)**	24
	For filling:	
4 tbls	**butter or margarine**	4 tbls
3 tbls	**minced shallots**	3 tbls
6 slices	**prosciutto, cut into bits**	6 slices
8 oz	**mushrooms, sliced**	225 g
1 oz	**all-purpose flour**	28 g
1 cup	**milk or half-and-half**	¼ L
4 oz	**ricotta**	112 g
2 oz	**grated Parmesan cheese**	56 g
1	**egg, lightly beaten**	1
	salt and pepper (to taste)	
	softened butter (as needed)	
1½ cups	**Prosciutto Sauce (see Spicy Tomato Sauce in recipe index)**	375 ml

1. Prepare the spinach crepes and set aside. If they have been frozen, allow to thaw. Keep covered to prevent drying out.
2. Heat the butter or margarine in a sauté pan, add the shallots, and cook until soft and lightly colored. Add the prosciutto, sauté for a few seconds, then add the mushrooms and continue to cook until the mushrooms have browned and the mixture begins to dry.

3. Sprinkle with the flour and cook over medium heat, stirring for 1 or 2 minutes. Add the milk or half-and-half gradually and cook until the mixture thickens. Remove from heat and allow to cool for 1 or 2 minutes.
4. Place the ricotta, Parmesan, and egg in a bowl and stir to mix. Add the somewhat cooled prosciutto mixture and mix thoroughly. Taste and season with salt and pepper.
5. Prepare an ovenproof baking dish by smearing with softened butter.
6. Lay the crepes out on a work surface. You may fill and fold in either of two ways. Method 1: Spread a spoon of filling on half of each crepe, fold in half, spread with more filling and fold into a triangle. Or, Method 2: Place about 2 tbls of filling in a strip along the center of each crepe, fold up two sides over the filling, and place seam-side down in the baking pan.
7. If you have shaped the crepes into triangles, arrange them in slightly overlapping rows in the baking pan.
8. At this point the filled crespelle may be stored, covered and refrigerated, for several hours or overnight. Bring to room temperature before baking.
9. To bake, preheat the oven to 350°F (180°C). Spoon the sauce over the crespelle, placing a thin film over the center of the pan, more at the edges. You may have sauce left over, which you can serve on the side. Bake, uncovered for about 10 minutes, just until the filling is heated through. Serve immediately or keep warm in a very low oven for about 20 minutes.

Note: For volume buffet service, heat pans in sequence so as not to dry out. Serve in chafers.

Spinach Crepes

Yield: 30

	Ingredients:	
2 oz	**drained chopped spinach***	56 g
6	**eggs**	6
14 fl oz	**milk**	430 ml
¼ tsp	**salt**	¼ tsp
pinch	**ground white pepper**	pinch
pinch	**nutmeg**	pinch
4½ oz	**instant-blending flour (Wondra)**	112 g
2–3 tbls	**melted butter**	2–3 tbls

*You may use thawed frozen spinach or fresh spinach, blanched and finely chopped. In both cases, squeeze dry thoroughly before weighing out.

1. Place the spinach, eggs, milk, and seasonings in a blender. Blend until completely liquified, scraping the blender container once or twice.
2. Add the flour and blend until smooth. Let the batter come to room temperature and add 2 tbls melted butter.

3. Following the crepe-making procedure in the recipe for Basic Crepes and Variations, test one crepe for consistency. Add additional melted butter and possibly a bit more milk until a thin crepe results. *Caution:* If the batter is too thin, the crepe will brown too much. The crepes should be thin and tender and have a lovely green color.
4. Prepare all the crepes. Stack and store, refrigerated or frozen, until needed.

Note: Instant-blending flour is most successful for this recipe. Also, a blender, rather than a food processor, produces the smooth batter needed for these crepes.

Penne with Broccoli, Bacon, and Mushrooms

Serves: 6

Ingredients:

1 lb	penne or cut ziti	450 g
3 slices	bacon	3 slices
1 lb	raw sliced mushrooms	450 g
6 tbls	minced shallots	6 tbls
½ cup	diced red pepper	125 ml
2 cups	diced broccoli florets, blanched	½ L
6 tbls	sweet butter	70 g
1 pt	heavy cream	½ L
5 oz	grated Parmesan cheese	140 g
	coarsely ground black pepper	

1. Cook the pasta in boiling salted water. It should take about 8 minutes, during which time you can prepare the sauce.
2. Fry the bacon until just crisp. Remove from pan, drain, and crumble or chop into pieces. Set aside.
3. Remove all but 2 tbls of bacon fat from the pan, add the mushrooms and shallots, and sauté until golden. Stir in the red pepper and broccoli just to coat. Set aside and keep warm.
4. While the mushrooms are sautéeing, heat the butter and cream in a saucepan until slightly thickened and reduced. Stir in the cheese and simmer for about 30 seconds to thicken.
5. Combine the cream sauce with the vegetables. Season the sauce with coarsely ground pepper.
6. When the pasta is cooked al dente, drain well, toss with the sauce, portion, and sprinkle bits of bacon on top. Serve hot.

Spaghetti Frittata

Yield: 6–10 appetizer portions

	Ingredients:	
2 oz	spaghetti, cooked*	56 g
2	eggs	2
3 oz	mozzarella, shredded	84 g
3 tbls	grated Romano cheese†	3 tbls
3 tbls	chopped parsley	3 tbls
3 tbls	minced red bell pepper	3 tbls
	salt and pepper (to taste)	
3 tbls	olive oil (or as needed)	3 tbls

*If preparing the spaghetti ahead, drain and toss with a bit of vegetable oil to prevent sticking. Store, covered and refrigerated, until ready to use.

†Any combination of Italian grated cheese may be used, just be sure the flavor is sharp enough to come through the bland pasta and egg.

1. Combine the eggs with the cheeses, parsley, and red bell pepper. Add salt and pepper to taste. Add the cooked spaghetti and mix well to distribute all the ingredients.
2. Heat an 8-in. (20 cm) diameter nonstick skillet. Add just enough olive oil to coat bottom of pan. Place the spaghetti mixture evenly in the pan. If any garnish or egg remains in the bowl, quickly add to the frittata where needed.
3. Lower the heat to medium to cook slowly without burning. Use a spatula to press on the frittata as it cooks. After 1 or 2 minutes, check to see if the bottom is beginning to brown. As soon as it has browned, flip or turn over to cook other side. The easiest way to turn the frittata is to invert on a flat plate and slide back into the pan. Just before sliding into the pan, add a bit more oil to film the surface again. Adjust the heat while cooking so the frittata cooks through without becoming too crusty or burned. It should have an attractive, golden brown color, with the spaghetti still tender enough to cut easily. Overcooking will make the spaghetti brittle and impossible to chew.
4. As soon as the frittata is done (a clue is that the oil begins to foam at the edges), remove to clean absorbent paper. Blot the surface to remove excess oil. Cut into wedges to serve.
5. May be served hot, warm, or at room temperature. Hold refrigerated and well wrapped for three days. Or freeze, wrapped in foil. Defrost at room temperature and reheat in a 375° F (190° C) oven for 10 to 15 minutes until heated through. Or reheat in a microwave, uncovered and laid on paper towel at low to medium power for a minute or two. Always blot on absorbent paper after reheating to remove any excess grease.

Note: This recipe calls for a higher proportion of egg to pasta than is usually seen. However, it yields a product that is far more tender, even after storage and reheating. Larger batches (or larger sizes) may be made, provided the thickness of the frittata remains about ½ in. (1½ cm) for even cooking.

Variations: Minced ham, salami, cooked and crumbled Italian sausage, pepperoni, sun-dried tomatoes, chopped basil, or scallions, may all be added alone or in combination to the frittata mixture for both flavor and color. Be cautious if adding raw minced garlic as it may burn.

Pasta with Fresh Tomato Salad

Serves: 4–6

	Ingredients:	
2 lb	red, ripe tomatoes	1 kg
½ cup	flavorful olive oil	125 ml
2 tsp	salt (or to taste)	2 tsp
	water if needed	
½ cup	chopped basil leaves	125 ml
1 lb	fresh mozzarella, diced	500 g
4 tbls	grated Parmesan cheese	4 tbls
	ground black pepper (to taste)	
1 lb	rigatoni, ziti, or mostaciolli	450 g

Use only vine-ripened, fragrant, and flavorful tomatoes for this dish. It is simply not worth making with anemic or inferior tomatoes. It is a very simple dish, dependent only on the raw flavor of its ingredients, so use the same care in selecting all the other ingredients as well.

1. A few hours before serving, wash and dry the tomatoes. Core and cut into rough 1-in. (2½ cm) chunks. Cut over a bowl or save all the juice you can. Sprinkle liberally with the salt, toss well, add all but 2 tbls of the olive oil and all the basil. Toss to combine and let stand at room temperature. The salt helps the tomatoes to release their juice. If they do not seem very juicy, you can add a few spoons of water (Italians preparing summer tomato salad at home often toss some ice chips over the salad while it stands to ensure that there will be extra juice to sop up with crusty bread).
2. Just before service, cook the pasta in salted water until al dente.
3. While the pasta is cooking, place the mozzarella and the remaining oil in the bottom of a large pasta bowl.
4. As soon as the pasta is cooked, drain, and add to the pasta bowl. Toss once or twice with the mozzarella and oil. Quickly add the tomato mixture and toss again. Sprinkle with half the Parmesan and serve while still lukewarm. Each portion can be topped with some ground black pepper and a bit more cheese, if desired, or guests can use their own to taste.

Note: Served lukewarm, this dish is especially delicious, with cool tomato, hot pasta, and slightly melted cheese creating an interesting texture. However, it is still very good as it cools to room temperature. Absolutely do not refrigerate if prepared as above. If you must prepare ahead, use the following procedure: Prepare the tomato mixture as above, cook the pasta, drain, and add to the tomato. This mixture can be held at room temperature for several hours or refrigerated for one or even two days. Just before serving, return to room temperature or warm slightly by placing the bowl over simmering water for 2 or 3 minutes. Just before serving add the mozzarella, toss, and drizzle on additional olive oil. Sprinkle with Parmesan and a few grindings of black pepper and serve. This method yields a delicious, somewhat different dish, since the cheese is not quite as melted, but it is far preferable to refrigerating the completed dish and having the cheese congeal into unattractive lumps.

Note on fresh mozzarella: Freshly made, soft mozzarella works best for this dish. However, the fresher it is, the more likely its milk will leak out into the sauce on long standing, giving the juices a cloudy look. Either pat it dry before using or serve in a shallow platter to correct the problem.

Variations: You may add any or all of the following to the salad: a garlic clove, added when preparing the tomato mixture and removed before serving; capers; chopped anchovies (eliminate Parmesan); or pitted and chopped oil-cured olives.

If you eliminate the pasta altogether, you will have a delicious tomato, basil, and mozzarella salad, which can be offered in lieu of the usual platter of the same ingredients when a visual variety is desired or when the chopped salad will provide for easier serving and eating. The salad, with or without the mozzarella, is also good served alongside or over freshly sautéed boneless chicken breasts or freshly fried breaded veal cutlets for an interesting summer main dish. The cool salad provides accompaniment and sauce for the hot meat.

Cheese-Stuffed Pasta Shells

Yield: 60 shells

	Ingredients:	
1 lb	jumbo pasta shells (about 60)	450 g
2 lb	ricotta, well drained	1 kg
1 lb	mozzarella, diced	450 g
½ cup	chopped parsley	125 ml
½ cup	grated Romano cheese	125 m
½ cup	grated Parmesan cheese	125 ml
1	egg	1
	ground pepper (to taste)	
5–6 cups	Italian Meat Sauce (see in recipe index)	1250–1500 ml

1. Cook the pasta shells in salted boiling water until barely tender. Drain, rinse, drain again, and cool.
2. Combine the ricotta with the mozzarella, grated cheeses, parsley, and egg. Mix thoroughly and season with pepper to taste.
3. Prepare ovenproof dishes or pans by rubbing with a little oil. Spoon a layer of Italian Meat Sauce into the pans.
4. Fill the shells with the ricotta mixture. Place the filled shells in neat, tight rows in the pans. Spoon more sauce over if desired or add additional sauce when ready to bake. The prepared shells may be refrigerated for up to 2 days before baking.
5. Bake, covered, in a 350°F (180°C) oven for 30 to 40 minutes until the filling is hot and melted. Serve with extra sauce on the side.

Note: These will hold up well on a buffet, but try not to overheat and reheat, or they will fall apart or dry out.

Variations: **Spinach-Filled Pasta Shells:** Reduce the ricotta to 20 oz (560 g), add 10 oz (285 g) well-drained chopped spinach and a pinch of nutmeg. Fill as above. Sauce with Spicy Tomato Sauce (see in recipe index), if preferred, rather than Italian Meat Sauce, for a meatless entree.
Meat and Cheese Stuffed Shells: Use fillings as for Miniature Calzone (see in recipe index), either with pepperoni or cooked, drained, and crumbled Italian sausage. Fill and bake as in basic recipe above.

Sausage Lasagne

Serves: 12

Ingredients:

1 lb	lasagne noodles*	450 g
3 lb	ricotta, well drained	1 kg 350 g
2 lb	mozzarella, diced small	900 g
4 oz	grated Italian cheese, a mixture of Parmesan and romano	112 g
2 qt	Italian Meat Sauce (see in recipe index)	2 L
1 lb	Italian sausage	450 g
1 lb	ground beef	450 g

*Most boxed dry lasagne noodles have about 18 strips to a pound, each about 10-in. (25 cm) long and about 2 to 3-in. (5 to 8 cm) wide. The curly-edged noodles look nice but are not essential. If you use sheets of pasta or other sized noodles, allow enough to make three layers.

1. Prepare the cheeses: Combine the well-drained ricotta with the mozzarella, stir in a few spoons of grated cheese. Set aside.
2. Remove the sausage from its casing and brown in a skillet until the meat loses its pink color. Add the ground beef, stirring to break up any lumps and cook until no longer pink. Drain in a colander and discard rendered fat. Combine the cooked meats with the sauce, and simmer for about 10 minutes. Set aside.
3. Prepare a half-size hotel pan or a disposable foil pan 12 × 9 × 2½ in. (30 × 23 × 7 cm) by rubbing with a little oil or spraying with a nonstick spray. If using disposable, double pan for extra strength.
4. Cook the lasagne in salted boiling water, to which a bit of oil or solid shortening has been added. When the pasta is al dente, drain, and turn into a pan of cold water to cool and separate the noodles. Carefully remove the noodles one by one from the water and lay on plastic wrap. Some may break, use those for the inside layers. Reserve five or six perfect noodles for the top.
5. Ladle a thin layer of sauce in the bottom of the prepared pan. Top with a layer of noodles (about five strips crosswise will do nicely). Spread sauce evenly over the pasta, distributing the meat as much as possible. Layer one third of the ricotta mixture over the sauce, as evenly as possible. Sprinkle with grated cheese, top with more sauce. Place the next layer of noodles, cover with sauce, then the next third of the ricotta mixture, more grated cheese and more sauce. Top with the final layer of noodles, and completely blanket with most of the remaining meat and sauce, tucking any noodle edges down into the sauce. (You may have some sauce left over.) Spoon the rest of the ricotta mixture evenly over the sauce and sprinkle with the grated cheese.
6. The lasagne may be baked at once or held, covered and refrigerated, for up to 2 days. Freeze for longer storage (see note below).
7. Bake in a preheated 350°F (180°C) oven for about 30 minutes or until heated through and bubbly. Do not overcook. If the lasagne has been refrigerated beforehand, let come to cool room temperature before baking, so the baking time will not have to be increased by too much. Cover with foil while reheating until the last 10 minutes. Let stand out of the oven for at least 30 minutes to set, before cutting into 3-in. (8 cm) squares. (Since this lasagne is very rich, this size portion is adequate for a serving.)
8. Lasagne may be held, covered in a warm oven for up to an hour or kept warm in a chafer or water bath.

Note: If planning to freeze prepared lasagne, it is essential to drain the ricotta and the mozzarella (if you are using freshly made or water-packed) of all excess moisture before using. Sometimes even with this precaution, some excess water accumulates when the lasagne is thawed. Use a bulb baster to drain off as much excess moisture as you can before baking. Then bake uncovered for part or all of the baking time to dry out a bit.

Note on Volume Preparation: This recipe may be multiplied as desired. The area of the baking pans can increase as needed but the depth should remain the same for best results.

Variation: **Vegetable Lasagne:** Use Spicy Tomato Sauce or Marinara (see Spicy Tomato Sauce in recipe index) instead of meat sauce. Mix about 1 cup (¼ L) well-drained chopped spinach into the ricotta mixture. Cube eggplant and/or zucchini, sauté with garlic, drain well, and add to sauce. Layer and bake as above. This does not freeze well.

Vegetable Lasagne with Mushroom Marinara

Serves: 8

	Ingredients:	
1 lb	lasagne noodles	450 g
	boiling water and salt	
2 tbls	butter or oil (or as needed)	2 tbls
1 lb	raw sliced mushrooms	450 g
l qt	Marinara sauce (see Spicy Tomato Sauce in recipe index)	1 L
	For filling:	
2 tbls	olive oil	2 tbls
2 tsp	minced garlic	2 tsp
2 tbls	chopped onion	2 tbls
½ cup	diced red pepper	125 ml
½ cup	chopped blanched broccoli	125 ml
10 oz	frozen chopped spinach, blanched and squeezed dry	285 g
2 cups	pot cheese	½ L
½ cup	grated Romano cheese	125 ml
1 cup	shredded mozzarella	¼ L
2	eggs, beaten	2

1. Cook the lasagne noodles until just tender, drain, rinse, and lay out on waxed paper on a work surface until ready to fill.
2. Sauté the mushrooms in butter until browned, add to marinara sauce, and simmer for about 15 minutes. Set aside.
3. Prepare the filling: Heat the olive oil in a sauté pan, add the garlic and onion and cook until wilted but not brown. Add the pepper and the broccoli, cook 30 seconds. Remove from heat.
4. Place the sautéed vegetables in a large bowl, add the spinach and the pot cheese, half each of the Romano and mozzarella, and the eggs. Mix to combine thoroughly.

5. Preheat the oven to 350°F (180°C). Spread some of the mushroom marinara sauce on the bottom of a 2-qt (2 L) shallow ovenproof dish.
6. Spread the filling on each lasagne noodle. Roll up and place seam side down in the prepared pan. Pour more sauce over the rolls (don't drown them), and sprinkle with the remaining grated and shredded cheese. Cover with oiled foil. Store for up to two days, refrigerated, if desired. Bring to room temperature before baking.
7. Bake covered for 20 minutes then uncover and bake an additional 15 to 20 minutes until heated through. Serve additional hot sauce on the side.

Note: This lasagne is best not frozen as the vegetables lose their texture. However, the sauce can be prepared ahead and frozen.

Variations: Spinach noodles may be used if desired. The vegetables may be varied according to taste. You may eliminate the pot cheese and use tofu instead. Buy fresh tofu and press between layers of paper towels to remove excess water before using in the mixture.

Manicotti

Serves: 12

Ingredients:

24	**Basic or Parmesan crepes (see Basic Crepes and Variations in recipe index)**	24
1 qt	**Italian Meat Sauce (see in recipe index) or Marinara Sauce (see Spicy Tomato Sauce in recipe index)**	1 L
2 lb	**ricotta, well drained**	1 kg
1 lb	**shredded mozzarella**	450 g
2	**egg yolks, lightly beaten**	2
4 oz	**grated Italian cheese**	115 g
4 tbls	**minced parsley**	4 tbls
	ground pepper (to taste)	

1. Prepare a shallow baking pan by rubbing with a bit of oil or spraying with a nonstick cooking spray. The pan(s) should be large enough to hold the filled, rolled crepes in one layer. Set aside.
2. Lay the crepes, most attractive side down, on waxed paper. Cover with plastic wrap while preparing filling.
3. Combine the ricotta, the mozzarella, half the grated cheese, the egg yolks, and the parsley. Stir vigorously to combine completely. Taste and add a bit of pepper if desired.
4. Spread about a cup of sauce on the bottom of the baking pan.

5. Place 2 to 3 tbls of filling in a strip down the center of each crepe. Roll up and place seam-side down in the baking pan. The filled crepes may touch each other, but do not overcrowd as they will swell slightly as they bake. Cover the crepes with thin layer of sauce, especially at the edges, sprinkle the remaining grated cheese evenly over the manicotti. They may be baked at once or held, covered and refrigerated for a day. The filled manicotti can be frozen ahead, but they are subject to the same "watering down" as is Sausage Lasagne (see Note for that recipe).

6. Bake in a preheated 350°F (180°C) oven for 15 to 20 minutes, just until heated through. They are best baked uncovered, provided they are carefully watched to prevent scorching or burning. If close attention cannot be paid to their baking, then cover with oiled or sprayed foil (to prevent sticking). Take care when removing the foil so that condensation does not run onto the manicotti.

7. The manicotti can be served at once, with additional sauce on the side if desired. They can be held, loosely covered, in a warm oven for about 30 minutes or in an open chafer or water bath. If making in volume (this recipe may be multiplied as desired) it is better to heat pans in sequence and bring each batch, freshly baked, to the buffet, rather than risk overheating.

Note: One or two manicotti per person is a portion, depending upon the balance of the meal. If they are offered as a main course or as a pasta course preceding a light meat or fish, you might choose to serve three per person.

Classic Risotto

Serves: 8

Ingredients:

1 lb	Italian Arborio rice	450 g
2 qt	diluted chicken or veal stock (or as needed)	2 L
4–5 oz	sweet butter	115–140 g
2 tbls	minced onion	30 ml
6–8 oz	grated Parmesan cheese	180–225 g
	salt and pepper (to taste)	

The preparation of a classic risotto requires Arborio rice, which is short or round grained, and cooks to the creamy, tender point that makes this dish unique. This preparation is intended for dinner party service, since it must be served at once to be truly enjoyed. Once mastered, the technique is simple, and an experienced cook can prepare 2 or even 3 pounds (2 to 2½ kg) of rice in this manner. For this larger volume, a wider, rather than deeper, pot makes it easier to keep the rice in motion. The cook, of course, must devote total attention to the risotto for the entire cooking time, and hot plates and servers must be ready to bring it to table at its peak goodness. To serve risotto to a larger group, use the recipe for Risotto Bolognese (see in recipe index), a different but still delicious compromise version using converted rice, unless you have a battery of burners, pots, cooks, and waiters at your disposal.

1. Pick over the rice to remove any debris but do not wash or rinse. Put the stock in a large pot, bring to the boil, and keep at a bare simmer while you prepare the rice. In another heavy-gauge pot or saucepan, sauté the onion in about 2 oz (60 g) butter until wilted but only lightly colored.
2. Add the rice and stir over medium heat for 2 or 3 minutes until the grains are all coated with butter, and the mixture begins to look dry. Immediately add a ladle of hot stock, and, stirring constantly, regulate the heat to maintain a vigorous simmer. As the rice cooks, it will absorb the stock and again appear dry. Add another ladle of stock and repeat as above. Continue this procedure for at least 20 minutes, stirring constantly and scraping the bottom and sides of the pan repeatedly. The point is to prevent the rice from sticking, all the while maintaining enough heat to cook the rice while it absorbs the stock.
3. After about 20 minutes, taste the rice to check on its cooking progress. If the center of the grain is still hard and brittle, you will need to cook for another 10 to 15 minutes. If it is beginning to reach tenderness, you have only 5 to 10 minutes to go. Continue adding the stock, cooking and stirring, until the rice is almost al dente, tender with just the slightest resistance to the bite. Then add just a bit more stock, about ½ cup (125 ml), cook for a few seconds, and stir in the cheese, a sprinkling of salt and pepper, and about 2 to 3 tbls of butter. Ladle into warm bowls or dishes and serve at once, while the risotto is still creamy.

Note: The total cooking time should be about 40 minutes. You may not need all the stock, or, if you use it all, may need a bit of water.

Variations: **Champagne Risotto with Truffles:** Proceed as with basic recipe except substitute 1 cup (¼ L) of champagne (or good quality dry white sparkling wine) for stock, close to the end of cooking time. Reduce the amount of Parmesan by half. At the very end, stir in bits of sliced preserved black truffles, or in season, top each portion with one or two shavings of fresh white truffle.

Saffron Risotto with Porcini: If using fresh porcini, sauté in butter and chop. If using dried, soak, drain, rinse, and chop. You should have at least ⅓ cup mushrooms per pound of rice. Proceed with basic recipe. About midway through cooking time, add mushrooms and 2 or 3 pinches of saffron threads. Continue to completion, using only enough Parmesan to flavor without overwhelming the saffron taste.

There are many other versions of risotto. Examine a good Italian cookbook (see Appendix) for other variations.

Risotto Bolognese

Serves: 8–10

Ingredients:

6 tbls	butter or olive oil	90 ml
1 lb	ground beef	450 g
10 oz	chopped onions	300 g
1 oz	dried Italian mushrooms	28 g
¼ cup	chopped Italian parsley	60 ml
14 oz	canned Italian plum tomatoes	392 g
	salt and pepper (to taste)	
3 pt	chicken broth	1 L 500 ml
3 cups	converted rice, raw*	750 ml
4 oz	grated Parmesan cheese (or as needed)	112 g

*For this risotto, which can stand holding and reheating, you must use converted rice. If you choose to prepare with Arborio rice, refer to the Classic Risotto recipe (see in recipe index), and observe all cooking and serving techniques included there.

1. Heat 2 tbls of the butter in a heavy-bottomed pot, add the ground beef and cook, stirring, until no pink color remains in the meat. Add the onions and continue to cook until they wilt and begin to color.
2. While the meat is browning, soak the dried mushrooms. When they have softened, remove from soaking water, rinse, and chop. Strain the soaking water through fine cloth and reserve.
3. Drain the tomatoes in a colander set over a bowl. Pick out the hard cores and the seeds and discard. Put the tomato pulp into the drained liquid and add to the browned meat and onions along with the parsley. Stir, breaking up the tomatoes with a wooden spoon. Stir in the mushrooms and their soaking water. Reduce heat to a simmer and cook, stirring occasionally, for about 40 minutes, or until the mushrooms are tender and the flavors have mellowed. The tomatoes should not have any acid taste. Add salt and pepper to taste.
4. Place the broth in a second saucepan and heat to boiling. Keep hot.
5. When the sauce is ready, add the rice, cooking and stirring for a few minutes to coat all the grains with sauce. Add a cup of broth, stir and adjust the heat to maintain a gentle simmer. When most of the broth has been absorbed into the mixture, add another cup of broth, again stirring a few times until the broth is absorbed. Continue in this manner until almost all the broth is used and the rice is tender. The rice should be cooked within a total cooking time of 40 minutes. However, you can stop or slow down the process at any time. Unlike the classic risotto, this mixture does not need constant stirring and flawless timing. You can stop midway and let the mixture rest covered off the heat for an hour if need be. During the waiting time the rice will absorb more liquid from the sauce, so when you resume cooking, less time and less broth will be needed to finish the risotto, but the results will be good.

6. When the rice is ready, stir in a bit of Parmesan cheese, taste, and adjust seasonings. Stir in a tablespoon or more of butter just before serving. Pass additional Parmesan on the side.
7. Unlike the classic risotto, this dish can be prepared ahead, carefully reheated, and served. It holds up well for buffet service and is hearty and richly flavored. If it seems dry when reheating, add a bit more marinara sauce or butter, not water, or the rice may become mushy.

Variation: To make the preparation of this dish even easier, you may use already prepared Ragu Bolognese as a base for the risotto. It is advisable to thin the sauce with some additional crushed tomato to provide enough liquid for the rice. That extra tomato should be cooked down for about 30 minutes before adding the rice.

Timbale di Risotto

Serves: 12

Ingredients:

1 recipe	**Classic Risotto (see in recipe index)**	1 recipe
1	**egg, beaten lightly**	1
6 oz	**shredded mozzarella**	180 g
2 cups	**Ragu Bolognese**	½ L
4 thin slices	**mozzarella**	
	butter and dry bread crumbs (as needed)	

1. Prepare a mold, souffle dish, or springform pan, with a capacity of about 2 qt (2 L), by greasing well with softened butter and dusting with dry bread crumbs. Set aside.
2. Prepare the risotto according to recipe, omitting the final addition of butter at the end. Let rest off heat for a few minutes.
3. When the risotto is still quite warm, but not piping hot, stir in the egg and the shredded mozzarella. Mix thoroughly.
4. Firmly pack half the risotto mixture in the prepared mold. Spread with a layer of ragu, then sliced mozzarella, then a bit more ragu. Top with the remaining risotto. Let stand to firm up. This can be held, well wrapped and refrigerated for a day or two, then reheated preferably in a water bath or in a microwave at medium power, just until heated through. Or, it can be served soon after being prepared, held in a warm oven, covered. Always allow the timbale to settle for 5 to 10 minutes before unmolding.
5. When unmolded, the risotto can be cut into slices like a layer cake. Serve additional hot ragu and grated Parmesan on the side.

Note: You can use a ring mold, filled with just the risotto, egg, and cheese mixture. Unmold and fill the center with hot ragu. Of course, you may fill larger molds or several to serve a crowd, but don't make the structure too high or unmolding and serving will be difficult. Individual timbales can also be prepared, which can be very pretty either for buffet service or as a plated appetizer at a seated dinner.

Variations: Cooked, crumbled sausage meat or sautéed chicken livers can be added to the ragu, if desired.

Other risottos, such as Risotto Bolognese, can be molded in the same manner, minus the layer of sauce. Layer instead with plain mozzarella, or, in the case of an asparagus or other vegetable risotto, with fontina and bits of prosciutto.

Rice Croquettes

Yield: 24–36 croquettes

Ingredients:

3 cups	cold cooked rice	¾ L
1	egg, beaten	1
½ cup	shredded mozzarella	125 ml
½ cup	Ragu Bolognese (see in recipe index)	125 ml
½ cup	tiny green peas, blanched	125 ml
	flour, egg, and dry bread crumbs for dredging and breading	
	oil for frying	

1. Combine the cooked rice with the beaten egg and shredded mozzarella.
2. Place the flour, egg wash, and bread crumbs in three bowls or plates.
3. Place a small amount of the rice mixture in the palm of one hand, in the center of the rice put a bit of sauce and one or two peas. Wrap the rice mixture around the filling to form a ball. Set on a plate and continue until all the rice balls are shaped.
4. Roll the balls first in flour, then in egg wash, and finally in bread crumbs. Set aside until all the croquettes are breaded.
5. Heat the frying oil, fry the rice balls until golden brown on all sides. Either serve at once, or cool and reheat, covered in a moderate oven.

Note: The mixture may be shaped larger and formed into cylinders or little peaked cones, if desired. The small balls are the most manageable for hors d'oeuvre.

Sautéed or Layered Polenta

Serves: 8–10 or more

Ingredients:

1 lb	coarse yellow cornmeal	450 g
10 cups	water (approx.)	2½ L
4 tsp	salt	4 tsp
4 oz	butter (if desired)	115 g

To sauté: butter, pepper

For layered polenta:

2 lb	mozzarella cheese	900 g
2 cups	grated Parmesan cheese	½ L
3 cups	Ragu Bolognese (see in recipe index)	¾ L
	softened butter	

1. The traditional method of preparing polenta (the Italian version of cornmeal mush) is to set the salted water to boiling and add the dry polenta grains in a trickling stream, stirring vigorously to prevent lumps. This technique is not difficult to master but is tedious. A more practical method is to first wet all the cornmeal with cold water (measured out from the total amount) in a large pot, then add the balance of the boiling salted water stirring to make a smooth mixture. Continue to simmer and stir, using a sturdy wooden spoon (preferably one with a pointed corner so you can get into the edges and bottom of the pan. The polenta is done when it becomes very thick and difficult to stir and begins to pull away from the sides of the pan. If using the optional butter, stir in at this point.

2. Turn the polenta out onto a wet surface (a cutting board, baking sheet, or into loaf pans, depending on how you plan to cut and use the polenta). It will set up almost immediately, but wait until it is completely cool before cutting.

3. To make Sautéed Polenta: Turn the hot polenta into baking sheets or loaf pans, then either slice or use a cookie cutter to cut rounds of the cold, hardened mush. These can be prepared and held up to three days ahead. Before serving, sauté in melted butter until golden brown and crisp on both sides. Use as a side dish instead of a potato or other starch. Sprinkle with pepper before serving, if desired. To serve at a buffet, place slices or rounds in a buttered baking dish, drizzle with melted butter, and bake until golden and heated through.

4. To make Layered Polenta: Cut into very thin slices from a loaf shape or, as traditional Italians do, let the polenta cool into a mound on a work surface. Use a strong thread or string to cut thin horizontal slabs from the mound. Butter a casserole or lasagne pan. Layer the polenta like lasagne, using sauce, slices of mozzarella and grated cheese between the layers. Use a rimless baking sheet to lift the layers into place. Bake to heat through. This dish can be assembled well ahead and refrigerated or even frozen. Bake until hot and bubbly. This preparation is very sturdy and stands very well on a buffet.

Variations: The sautéed polenta can be enriched by melting a slice of taleggio or fontina over the top of each round. Simply place on the pieces while they are in the sauté pan, cover the pan, and allow cheese to melt. Serve at once while the cheese is moist. Or simply sprinkle the plain sautéed rounds with grated Parmesan, either singly or in casserole for added flavor.

Yield will vary depending on use.

Herbed Noodle Pudding

Serves: 10–12

Ingredients:

1 lb	broad noodles, cooked	450 g
2	whole eggs	2
1	egg yolk	1
6 oz	melted butter	180 g
2 tbls each	minced parsley, dill, and chives	2 tbls each
3	scallions, thinly sliced	3
3 tbls	dry bread crumbs	3 tbls
	salt and pepper (to taste)	

1. Butter a 2-qt (2 L) baking dish. Preheat oven to 325°F (165°C).
2. Mix the eggs with the yolk, combine with all the other ingredients, including the noodles.
3. Turn into prepared pan. Bake for 35 to 45 minutes. Serve hot or at warm room temperature. Let rest at least 10 minutes before cutting into squares.

Creamy Souffléed Spoonbread

Serves: 8–10

Ingredients:

1 cup	buttermilk	¼ L
¼ tsp	salt	¼ tsp
1 cup	yellow or white cornmeal	¼ L
4 oz	sweet butter	115 g
17 oz	canned creamed corn	480 g
¾ cup	milk	180 ml
	salt and white pepper (to taste)	

¼ tsp	dry mustard	¼ tsp
pinch	cayenne	pinch
4 tbls	pure maple syrup	60 ml
3	eggs, separated	3
	butter and dry bread crumbs for pan	

1. Preheat the oven to 350°F (180°C). Prepare a 2-qt (2 L) soufflé dish or ovenproof casserole by greasing completely with softened butter and dusting with dry breadcrumbs.
2. Heat the buttermilk to a boil, lower the heat to a simmer and gradually add the cornmeal, stirring to blend smoothly. Cook for about 30 seconds, then add the creamed corn, remove from the heat and stir in the butter until melted.
3. Stir in the milk and all the seasonings. Beat the egg yolks lightly and stir into the corn mixture. Set aside.
4. Beat the egg whites until stiff but not grainy. Stir some of the beaten whites into the corn mixture to lighten, then fold the corn base and whites together.
5. Spoon the mixture into the prepared dish and bake for 35 to 45 minutes, until a crust has formed at the edges. The center of the spoonbread will not quite be firm. The spoonbread can be served hot as one would a soufflé or allowed to collapse and served at room temperature. The center will be creamy and a bit dense.

Note: Spoonbread may be baked in either a deep soufflé dish or a shallow casserole. The baking time will vary based on the dimensions of the dish.

Mashed Potato Gratin

Serves: 8–10

	Ingredients:	
4 lb	all-purpose potatoes	1800 g
6 oz	butter, cut into bits	180 g
1 tsp	salt	1 tsp
½ tsp	pepper	½ tsp
2	whole eggs, beaten	2
1 cup	grated Parmesan cheese	240 g
	dry bread crumbs (as needed)	
	softened butter (as needed)	

1. Boil or steam the potatoes until tender. As soon as they are cool enough to handle, peel and pass through a ricer or food mill into a bowl holding the bits of butter. Add the salt and pepper, mix thoroughly, and set aside until lukewarm.
2. Stir in the beaten egg until well combined and add all but 3 tbls of the grated cheese.

3. Turn into a well-buttered baking dish or casserole. Sprinkle the remaining cheese and some dry bread crumbs over the top. Dot the top with butter.
4. Before serving, bake in a moderately hot oven until heated through and browned on top.

Note: This mixture can be piped as duchesse on the border of plates or platter and can also be used as a topping for casseroles, such as shepherd's pie.

Variations: Diced cooked ham, minced sautéed scallions or onion, herbs, or crumbled cooked sausage can be added to the mixture.

Twice-Baked Potatoes

Serves: 6–8

Ingredients:

5	large Idaho potatoes	5
1 cup	combined melted margarine or butter and vegetable oil	¼ L
	salt and pepper (to taste)	
	Any of the following coatings: paprika, minced garlic, curry powder, rosemary, dry mustard	

1. Partially bake the potatoes, either in the oven for about 40 minutes or in a microwave for about 12 minutes (rotating halfway through cooking time).
2. Place the butter and oil in a saucepan and add your choice of coating. You can combine the seasonings according to taste, for example, rosemary and garlic, paprika and mustard, or use them separately. Warm the mixture just to blend flavors. Let stand until ready to use.
3. Preheat the oven to 350°F (180°C), or, if using the oven for another purpose, adjust baking time accordingly. As soon as you can handle the potatoes, cut them into neat chunks or long fingers, leaving the skin on.
4. Coat with the butter and seasonings, sprinkle with salt and pepper and roast, turning once or twice, until well browned and crusty. Serve hot.
5. Unlike fried or even baked potatoes, these potatoes can be held in a warm oven without loss in quality. They can be prepared ahead, held at room temperature, and reheated on site. Use a low oven and baste them occasionally with the accumulated butter in the pan or a bit more butter.

Note: If you prefer the more elegant look of peeled potatoes, steam or boil all-purpose potatoes until almost tender, then coat with seasoned butter and bake until browned. The skins, however, taste very good and give the potatoes a hearty rustic look.

Truffled Potato Cake

Serves: 4–6

Ingredients:

2 lb	all-purpose potatoes	1 kg
4 oz	clarified butter	180 g
1 oz	chopped preserved truffles	30 g
1 tbls	minced garlic	1 tbls
	salt and pepper	

1. Boil the potatoes until partially cooked, about 20 minutes. Drain and chill several hours or overnight.
2. Peel the potatoes and shred coarsely.
3. Heat 2 tbls of the butter with the garlic until soft but not browned. Add the garlic and butter to the potatoes and toss to coat. Stir in the drained chopped truffles, season with salt and pepper.
4. Heat the rest of the butter in a heavy 8- or 9-in. (20 or 23 cm) skillet. Add the potatoes, flatten them into a cake, and cook over moderate heat until browned on the bottom side. Shake the pan throughout to prevent sticking. Press down on the potatoes while cooking to form a cake.
5. When the potato cake is browned on one side, turn over (or transfer with a flat plate and invert) to cook other side. Serve hot, cut into wedges.

Note: This potato cake is best prepared just before serving but may be held in a warm oven for about 40 minutes. Or, cook the potatoes on one side, turn and finish browning in a moderate oven until crusty.

Variations: You may eliminate either the garlic or the truffles from the recipe. Or add sautéed onion instead of either. Shredded Swiss cheese may be combined with the potatoes, but be sure to use a well-seasoned pan and shake vigorously to prevent scorching and sticking.

Potatoes Raclette

Serves: 10

Ingredients:

3 lb	new potatoes	1 kg 350 g
12 oz	butter	336 g
1½ cups	tiny pickled onions	370 ml
24	cornichons (approx.)	24

	salt and pepper (to taste)	
1 lb	**raclette cheese, thinly sliced**	450 g

Traditionally, raclette (the name of a dish and a cheese) is prepared by facing the cut end of a cheese wedge to a heat source. When the surface has melted it is scraped off onto a hot plate and eaten with potato, pickled onion, and cornichon. A good cheese shop will have raclette or a suitable substitute from the Valais.

1. Steam the potatoes until tender. Butter a casserole or gratin dish large enough to hold the potatoes when they are sliced and slightly overlapped. Slice the potatoes, peeled or not, and arrange in the dish, sprinkle with a bit of salt and generous pepper.
2. Scatter the pickled onions over the potatoes. Reserve a few cornichons for garnish, finely chop the remainer and scatter over the potatoes.
3. Melt the remainder of the butter and pour enough over the potatoes so that they are all coated. You may have some left over. If you hold the dish for several hours before final heating, the potatoes may absorb much of the butter and need a bit more before baking.
4. No more than an hour before serving, cover the casserole and bake until the potatoes are piping hot. Just before serving, remove the foil or cover from the casserole and cover the potatoes with a layer of the sliced raclette. Place uncovered in the oven just until the cheese melts. Serve at once, garnished with fans of reserved cornichons or serve the cornichons on the side. Do not hold or reheat or the cheese will become overcooked.

Note: When preparing large quantities, use several dishes so they can be heated and served in succession for very best quality.

Hot Potato Salad

Serves: 12

	Ingredients:	
5 lb	**Idaho or baking potatoes**	2¼ kg
6 slices	**bacon, chopped**	6 slices
1 cup each	**onions, red and green bell pepper, and celery cut into small dice**	¼ L
½ cup	**red wine vinegar**	125 ml
1 cup	**olive oil**	¼ L
	salt and pepper (to taste)	
4 tbls	**minced parsley**	125 ml

1. Bake the potatoes in the oven or a microwave until tender. Leaving the skin on, cut into coarse chunks. Keep hot.
2. In a skillet, cook the bacon until it renders most of its fat and begins to crisp. Remove the bacon and keep warm.

3. To the bacon fat add the vegetables and cook over high heat, tossing, for a minute or two, just until the vegetables are colored and beginning to soften. Add the vinegar, cook for about 30 seconds, scraping the pan to loosen any browned bits. Remove from heat and stir in half the oil.
4. Pour the dressing over the hot potatoes, salt to taste, and add generous grindings of black pepper. Add more oil as needed to coat potatoes, but do not make too greasy. Either serve at once or hold, loosely covered, in a moderate oven. If serving immediately, toss with chives and parsley. If holding, sprinkle with herbs just before serving.

Note: If you have access to a microwave on site, this salad is easy to make just before serving, since the dressing only takes minutes to prepare. If not, prepare the dressing ahead. Bake the potatoes ahead, leave whole and pack them close together while hot in an insulated container, preferably one just large enough to hold them. Otherwise, pack closely, cover with a layer of foil and pack other hot food on top or around them. On site, cut into chunks and place in a lightly oiled roasting pan. Place in a hot oven until heated through. Reheat the dressing and pour over the hot potatoes. Prepared either way, this hot salad will hold up pretty well in an open chafer. Stir occasionally to prevent sticking. If the potatoes brown a bit either in the oven or the chafer, no harm is done. They are still quite tasty.

Sweet Potato Casserole

Serves: 10–12

Ingredients:

4 lb	orange-fleshed sweet potatoes	1800 g
10 oz	butter	285 g
10 oz	chopped onion	300 g
8 oz	crushed pineapple	225 g
1 tsp	salt	1 tsp
½ tsp	pepper	½ tsp
½ tsp	cinnamon	½ tsp
½ tsp	ground ginger	½ tsp
pinch	nutmeg	pinch
2 tbls	brown sugar	2 tbls
2	**Granny Smith or Golden Delicious apples**	2
6 oz	broken pecan meats	180 g

1. Bake the potatoes in their skins until tender.
2. While the potatoes are baking, sauté the onion in 2 tbls butter until soft and golden colored. Set aside.

3. Place all but 4 tbls of butter in a large bowl. When the potatoes are done, scoop their flesh into the bowl. Use a masher or wooden spoon to combine the potatoes with the butter, sautéed onion, pineapple, spices, and 1 tbls of the brown sugar. Mix well, taste, and adjust seasonings.

4. Peel and core the apples, halve and slice crosswise into thin slices. Heat the remaining butter in a sauté pan, add the brown sugar to melt, then add the apple slices and toss to coat. Remove from heat.

5. Place the sweet potato mixture in a buttered shallow casserole. Arrange the apple slices decoratively over the top. Scatter the pecans over the apple and spoon any remaining sugar butter mixture over the top of the casserole. May be prepared up to two days ahead and baked until heated through and crusty on top just before serving.

Note: If desired, this mixture may be baked in individual servings: Use hollowed out small patty-pan or acorn squash, orange-skin shells, pastry tart shells, zucchini boats, or even the potato skins as containers. The vegetable containers must be steamed tender before filling.

Variations: For a less sweet version, omit the pineapple and substitute either sautéed chopped celery or an equivalent amount of Sweet and Sour Onion Jam (see in recipe index). Use only 1 tbls of brown sugar for the topping. For Maple-Glazed Sweet Potatoes, omit the sugar and substitute pure maple syrup (not pancake syrup).

To create a dessert of Sweet Potato Pie from this recipe, omit the onion and pepper, add more sugar, syrup, or honey as desired, beat in three eggs, and 4 tbls cream. Turn into pie or tart shells and bake until the filling is set and the top golden brown.

Pasta Primavera Salad

Serves: 15	110–125	Ingredients:	15	110–125
1 lb	8 lbs	small pasta, such as rotini, cut fusilli, or radiatore	500 g	4 kg
3 stalks	4 heads	broccoli, peeled, blanched, and chopped into small pieces	3 stalks	4 heads
1 each	10 (total)	red, yellow, and green bell pepper, seeded and finely chopped	1 each	10 (total)
1	3	large red onion, finely chopped	1	3
1	3 or 4	zucchini or yellow summer squash, scrubbed and chopped	1	3 or 4
1 large	3 cups	carrot, scraped, finely chopped, and blanched tender	1 large	¾ L

1 cup	3 or 4 cups	**pitted black olives, sliced**	¼ L	¾–1 L
2 cups	1 gal	**Herb and Caper Vinaigrette (see in recipe index)**	½ L	4 L
		salt and pepper (to taste)		

1. Cook the pasta in boiling salted water, drain, rinse to cool, and drain thoroughly. Moisten the pasta with a little vegetable oil or a bit of the dressing to prevent it from sticking. Set aside, covered. Refrigerate if holding for more than 4 hours.
2. Prepare the vegetables as indicated. Fresh broccoli, rather than frozen, should be used. Use all of the tender stem. Blanch the florets and stems separately for best results. The carrot pieces will need a bit of blanching so they are tender to the bite. All the other vegetables should be used raw. Of course, you may vary the vegetables according to taste and availability but the ingredients listed make a tasty and colorful salad.
3. At least 1 hour before serving but preferably not more than one day, combine the pasta, the vegetables, and enough dressing to coat. Taste for seasoning: you will probably need to add more salt. After standing, the salad may need a little reseasoning, so taste just before serving. Use a splash of vinegar to sharpen the taste.

Note: The pasta types suggested are ideal for this salad since they have little curls and ridges that capture the dressing and vegetables and they are easy to serve and eat from a buffet. You may use multicolored varieties of these pastas if you choose.

Note on Yield: One pound of pasta, with the additional vegetables, will yield buffet portions for at least 15 people or even more if other side dish items are available.

New Potato Salad

Serves: 10–12

Ingredients:

3 lb	**small waxy (or new) potatoes**	1350 g
12 oz	**chopped red onion**	340 g
1½ cups	**Herb and Caper Vinaigrette (see in recipe index)**	350 ml
	additional salt, pepper, and balsamic vinegar (if needed)	

1. Wash the potatoes thoroughly to remove exterior grime. Steam until just tender. Drain. If tiny, leave whole or cut into halves or quarters. Immediately combine the hot potatoes with the dressing and the chopped onion. Let stand for at least an hour at room temperature to mellow flavors. Just before serving adjust seasonings if necessary.

Potato Pancakes

Yield: 48

Ingredients:

8 oz	grated onion	225 g
2	eggs, lightly beaten	2
3 slices	white sandwich bread, cubed	3 slices
3 tbls	minced parsley	3 tbls
4 lb	Idaho potatoes	2 kg
	salt and pepper (to taste)	
	fat for greasing skillet or griddle	

1. In a large bowl, combine the grated onion, eggs, bread cubes, and parsley.
2. Peel the potatoes, grate directly into the egg mixture. Season generously with salt and pepper. Mix thoroughly to coat all the potatoes with egg mixture and break up the bread pieces.
3. Heat a well-seasoned griddle or skillet (or use a nonstick pan). Brush or rub the surface with fat. You may use clarified butter, or solid shortening, or add extra flavor by using rendered fat from goose, duck, chicken, or bacon.
4. Drop potato mixture by spoonfuls onto griddle or skillet. Cook, turning to brown on both sides. Transfer to clean absorbent paper to drain and serve soon after frying. The pancakes may be kept warm in a slow oven for about 40 minutes. Serve plain or with applesauce or with sour cream mixed with minced chives.

Variation: **Potato-Zucchini Pancakes:** Substitute grated, drained zucchini for half the amount of potato. Add 2 tbls flour or potato starch to mixture. Proceed as above.

Lentil and White Bean Salad

Serves: 12–14

Ingredients:

½ lb	brown or pink lentils	225 g
½ lb	white navy beans	225 g
	salted water (as needed)	
1 cup	diced red pepper	¼ L
2 bunches	scallions, sliced thinly	2 bunches
1½ cups	red wine vinaigrette	355 ml
1 cup	minced parsley	¼ L

1. Pick over the beans, rinse, and soak overnight. Drain, rinse, and simmer until tender. When tender, drain and spread out in a hotel pan to cool.
2. Pick over the lentils, rinse, and simmer in 2 cups (500 ml) salted water until just tender, about 25 to 30 minutes. Drain, rinse, and cool to lukewarm.
3. Add most of the prepared vegetables to the vinaigrette, add the beans, and toss gently to combine. Season with salt and pepper to taste. They can be held for 3 days, refrigerated. Bring to cool room temperature before serving.
4. Just before serving, mix in the parsley, adjust seasoning if necessary. Garnish the top of the salad with the balance of the peppers and scallions.

Old-Fashioned Potato Egg Salad

Serves: 10–12

	Ingredients:	
3 lb	waxy boiling potatoes	1350 g
	salted water	
6	hard-boiled eggs	6
1 cup	minced onion	¼ L
1 cup	mayonnaise	¼ L
4 oz	drained sour cream	115 g
	salt and pepper (to taste)	
4 tbls	snipped chives	4 tbls

Try the reduced-calorie, no or low cholesterol commercial mayonnaise and sour cream products now on the market in this salad. In addition to their health benefits, they have a tangier flavor and lighter texture that lets the potato flavor come through. For true cholesterol watchers, you can prepare egg substitute according to package directions, chop and use in the salad as well with very good results. If using these dressing products, prepare the salad no more than 2 hours ahead for best consistency.

1. Cook the potatoes until just tender in boiling salted water. Drain, and when cool enough to handle, peel and cut into slices or large dice. Set aside.
2. Peel the eggs and chop coarsely. Set aside.
3. In a large bowl, stir the sour cream into the mayonnaise. Fold in the potatoes and eggs to coat with dressing. Season to taste with salt and pepper, and add half the chives. Stir gently to mix evenly. Hold chilled.
4. When ready to serve, sprinkle remaining snipped chives over the top of the salad.

Note: Finely chopped celery may be added to the salad.

Tabbouleh Salad

Yield: 10 cups		2 L 500 ml

Ingredients:

2 cups	bulgur (cracked wheat)	500 ml
1½ cups	boiling water	370 ml
1½ cups	fresh lemon juice	370 ml
1 cup	chopped onion	¼ L
1½ cups	ripe tomatoes, peeled, seeded, and chopped	370 ml
1 bunch	scallions, sliced thinly	1 bunch
1–2 tsp	salt (or to taste)	1–2 tsp
1 tsp	black pepper (or to taste)	1 tsp
1 cup	chopped parsley	¼ L
1 cup	chopped fresh mint	¼ L
6 fl oz	flavorful olive oil	180 ml

1. Place the bulgur in a large bowl. Combine the boiling water with ½ cup (125 ml) lemon juice and pour over bulgur. Let stand until absorbed. Drain the bulgur into a cheesecloth-lined sieve. Wrap the grain in the cloth and press gently to extract any extra soaking water. Turn into a clean bowl.
2. Pour the remaining lemon juice over the grains, then add the onion, tomato, scallions, and salt and pepper. Toss to coat completely.
3. Add most of the parsley and mint and about half the olive oil. Toss thoroughly, taste, and adjust seasonings. Hold for a few hours at cool room temperature or refrigerated. About an hour before serving, toss with remaining fresh herbs and olive oil. After standing for several hours, the salad may need perking up with a bit more fresh lemon juice and some freshly ground pepper.

Note: This salad can be served as a side salad on a buffet or used as a dip with crisp romaine leaves or fresh or toasted pita for scooping. Some chefs add minced garlic to the salad.

Main Dishes

Buttermilk Fried Chicken

Yield: 40–50 pieces

Ingredients:

40–50	chicken pieces*	40–50
12	whole eggs, beaten	12
1 qt	buttermilk	1 L
3 tbls	paprika	3 tbls
2 tbls	dry mustard	2 tbls
2 tbls	ground black pepper	2 tbls
1 tbls	Worcestershire sauce	1 tbls
dash	hot pepper sauce	dash
4 oz	dry bread crumbs	115 g
2 tsp	chicken bouillon powder	2 tsp
	oil for frying	

*Frying chickens can be cut in standard eight parts, however, you might want to adjust to offer more breast, wings, and drumsticks, which are usually most popular with fried chicken.

1. Combine the eggs, buttermilk, paprika, mustard, pepper, Worcestershire, and hot sauce. Soak the chicken pieces in this marinade for at least 12 hours or 1 day. Keep covered and refrigerated while marinating and turn once or twice.
2. Combine the flour, bread crumbs, and bouillon powder in a dredging pan. Remove the chicken from the marinade, letting the excess drip away, then coat the chicken pieces thoroughly in the flour mixture. Pat firmly to help the crumbs adhere, and set the pieces on a rack over a shallow pan. If time permits, the coated chicken can rest on the rack, refrigerated for about 45 minutes or more, or fry right away.
3. Preheat the oven to 350° F (180° C). Heat about 1 in. (2½ cm) oil in a deep skillet and begin to fry the chicken pieces. Begin with the thighs, then drumsticks, then wings, and lastly breasts. Turn the pieces as they cook, until golden brown and crusty on all sides. Remove from the skillet to absorbent paper to drain for a minute or two, then place in a single layer in baking pans or sheet pans and place in the oven to complete cooking.
4. As you continue to fry the pieces, you may need to replace or replenish the frying oil. Be sure to bring it back to frying temperature before proceeding. Check the chicken pieces baking in the oven, and as they are cooked through (but not dry), remove to paper-lined pans to remove excess grease. Either serve hot, or hold to serve at room temperature. Do not cover while hot, or the chicken will steam and the crust will soften. This is best eaten the day it is made. If holding and transporting, keep cool but do not refrigerate or it will become greasy.

Variations: To serve hot with pan gravy: Remove all but a few spoons of fat from the pan, sprinkle with a handful of flour and cook for a few minutes, scraping all the brown bits from the pan and coloring the roux. Add milk, half-and-half, or buttermilk, season with a bit of seasonings as used in the marinade, and cook down to a nicely thickened gravy.

"Barbecued" Chicken Breasts

Serves: 8

	Ingredients:	
4 large or 8 small	whole chicken breasts, skin on, bone in	4 large or 8 small
	For basting sauce:	
	salt and pepper	
1 cup	Barbecue Sauce (see in recipe index)	¼ L
	or	
	Maple-Mint Basting Sauce:	
½ cup	pure maple syrup	125 ml
¼ cup	each olive oil and balsamic vinegar	60 ml

10 sprigs	**fresh mint**	10 sprigs
	or	
	Orange-Mustard Basting Sauce:	
½ cup	**orange juice**	125 ml
¼ cup	**melted butter**	60 ml
¼ cup	**Dijon mustard**	60 ml

1. Remove the wishbones from the chicken breasts, bend each one inside out to pop the breastbone free (on the larger breasts, slit the connective tissue above the breastbone), remove the breast bone and cartilage. Flatten the breasts: Leave the small ones whole, split the large breasts in two.
2. Preheat the broiler to its highest setting, place the grill pan about 3 in. (8 cm) from the flame.
3. If using Maple-Mint Basting Sauce, combine the syrup, oil, and vinegar, bruise the mint thoroughly and steep it for at least 30 minutes in the liquid. For Orange-Mustard Basting Sauce, combine all ingredients until well blended.
4. To "barbecue" the chicken. Place the breast, skin-side up on the broiler pan, and broil until the skin blisters and begins to blacken in spots. Season the skin with some salt and pepper, turn over and broil for two minutes on the underside. Transfer the chicken to a shallow pan, discard all the rendered chicken fat, lower the oven to 400° F (205° C), and continue to cook the chicken, skin side up for 10 to 15 minutes (depending on size).
5. Turn the chicken over, baste liberally with chosen sauce (either Barbecue, Maple-Mint, or Orange-Mustard), cook 5 minutes. Turn breast side up again, baste again, cook another 5 to 10 minutes, or until the chicken is cooked (just until no longer pink at the bone). Do not overcook: The chicken should be moist and juicy.
6. Remove the chicken to an ovenproof serving platter, discard all the fat in the pan. If cooking juices remain, they can be added to remaining basting sauce, heated, strained, and served on the side with the chicken. The chicken may be held, loosely covered, in a very low oven for about 20 minutes. Or cool and serve at room temperature.

Note: Of course, this same preparation can actually be barbecued on an outdoor grill, but since the flame will now be below rather than above the chicken, reverse all the "skin side up and down" directions accordingly. This preparation, while very good served hot, is an excellent choice for a cold lunch, picnic, or boxed meal, instead of fried chicken.

Variations: Other chicken parts may be prepared in this manner, however, cooking and turning times for thighs, drumsticks, and wings, will have to be altered to achieve the same crusty skin-moist meat result.

Lemony Grilled Chicken

Serves: 8–10

Ingredients:

2	whole chickens or equivalent serving pieces	2
½ cup	dry white wine or vermouth	125 ml
½ cup	olive oil	125 ml
½ cup	lemon juice	125 ml
6 sprigs	fresh thyme or oregano	6 sprigs
4 sprigs	Italian parsley	4 sprigs
2	whole garlic cloves	2
4	peppercorns, cracked	4

Small whole chickens may be split open and flattened, left whole, or cut in half or quarters; Cornish hens may be split open and flattened; or a combination of chicken parts may be used.

1. Prepare the chickens, removing excess fatty skin. Combine the other ingredients to make a marinade, coat the chickens, and refrigerate covered for several hours or overnight.
2. Heat a grill or barbecue until coals are well covered with ash. Set the grill 4 or 5 in. (10 or 13 cm) from the coals or flame.
3. Remove the chicken from the marinade, pat dry and place on grill, skin side down. When skin firms up and begins to color, turn and continue cooking on underside. Adjust the rack or fire so the chicken cooks slowly, basting and turning frequently to color on all sides. (If the grill has a cover, close it once the chicken is colored on both sides, then open at the end of cooking so the skin crisps.) Cooking time will depend on the size of the pieces, the intensity of the grill, and the outdoor wind and temperature, so you must determine proper cooking time by checking the pieces by feel and the color of juices near the bone. As pieces cook, remove to another pan and keep warm while finishing others. Salt and pepper lightly after cooking.
4. Serve hot with more lemon juice squeezed over the pieces. If serving cold, or at room temperature, serve plain or with a mayonnaise, for example, Lemon Caper Mayonnaise (see in recipe index) if desired.

Note: This chicken may be cooked using an indoor broiler. See "Barbecued" Chicken Breasts (see in recipe index) for method.

Chicken Ballottine with Sausage

Yield: about 20 slices

	Ingredients:	
1	large roaster or capon, about 7 lb (3kg)	1
	For meat stuffing:	
2 oz	golden raisins	56 g
¼ cup	brandy	60 ml
3 tbls	minced shallots	3 tbls
1 tbls	grated lemon zest	1 tbls
2 oz	pignoli	56 g
3 oz	diced baked ham	84 g
⅓ cup	sharp Italian grated cheese	5 tbls
2 lb	Italian sausage meat*	900 g
	For spinach stuffing:	
10 oz	frozen chopped spinach	280 g
1	egg yolk	1
2 oz	cream cheese, softened	56 g
1 slice	sandwich bread, crumbled	1 slice
pinch	nutmeg	pinch
	salt and pepper (to taste)	
	For wrapping: needle and thread†, cheesecloth,	
8 oz	melted butter or margarine	224 g

*If you wish to prepare this without pork, combine ground veal and/or chicken or turkey, and about 6 oz (180 g) of chicken or veal fat. Substitute for the sausage meat and eliminate the ham. The sausage should be sweet, rather than hot, preferably without fennel or cheese flavoring.
†The fine, strong string sold as kite twine is excellent for this purpose, or select a smooth butcher's twine or heavy duty thread. Use a large upholstery needle.

1. Bone the bird: Lift the neck skin and scrape the flesh from the wishbone. Remove and discard. Lay the bird breast down and split the chicken along the backbone, cut along other side of backbone and discard. Keeping the knife close to the bones, scrape along carcass moving down to the wing and thigh joints. Cut around the wing joint to separate from the carcass. Wiggle the leg to find the place where the thigh joins the carcass, bend back the leg to pop the joint and cut free with the point of the knife. Scrape around the thigh bone to the knee, and cut around the joint to remove the bone.

If you stop at this point, you will be able to reshape the chicken to something resembling its original shape, with drumsticks and wings intact (you may remove the wing tips if you like). Or you can completely bone the chicken and, when stuffed, form it into an even cylinder. Although either method is fine, the second yields more equal slices. To completely bone: Remove the wing tips and the second joint. Use the knife to scrape along the remaining bone from both inside and outside. Discard the bone. Use your finger to push the boned wing inside out, so the skin and flesh are on the inside of the boned bird.

To remove the drumstick bone, first chop off the knobby outside end. Find the knee joint on the inside and scrape along the bone freeing the drumstick flesh. Discard the bone. Remove any prominent tendons in the drumstick flesh and discard.

2. Prepare the meat stuffing: Soak the raisins in brandy to plump. Mix the other ingredients together with the sausage meat. Add the raisins, reserving the brandy. Set the meat stuffing aside.

3. Squeeze the spinach dry of excess moisture and combine with egg yolk, softened cream cheese, crumbled sandwich bread, nutmeg, salt and pepper. Mix well and set aside.

4. Lay the boned bird flat on a work surface. Sprinkle with the reserved brandy. If there are bare areas of skin, use the filets of the breasts to cover them, so the skin is evenly lined with flesh. Using about two-thirds of the meat stuffing, pat the stuffing over the chicken flesh evenly. If you have boned the legs, push a little stuffing into those cavities.

5. Place the spinach stuffing in a thick strip down the center of the bird, mounding it slightly. Pat the remaining meat stuffing over the mound to enclose it.

6. Draw up the sides of the chicken to meet at the center, and stitch closed from vent to vent. Preheat the oven to 350°F (180°C).

7. Wash a piece of cheesecloth a bit wider than the chicken is long, enough to wrap the bird at least twice. Wring out, dip in melted butter or margarine, and lay out on a clean work surface.

8. Place the stuffed chicken on the cheesecloth, patting it into either a chickenlike shape or cylinder, depending on boning method. Wrap securely in the cheesecloth, rolling it over once or twice, and tie or stitch the two ends snugly.

9. Place the wrapped chicken on a rack in a shallow roasting pan, stitched side down. Brush with more melted butter. Bake for 30 minutes, then turn seam side up, baste again and continue to cook, basting every 30 minutes, for a total of about 2½ hours, or until the internal temperature is 140°F (60°C).

10. Remove from the oven and let the ballottine rest for about 20 minutes before carefully peeling off the cheesecloth. If serving hot, let rest at least another 15 minutes before removing the sewing twine and attempting to slice. The chicken can also be wrapped and refrigerated for 2 to 3 days before serving. When cool, it is possible to slice the chicken into neat, thin slices. It is very flavorful when served at cool room temperature, as well as when warm. If desired, you may degrease the pan juices and serve over the chicken.

Note: The double stuffing forms a pretty three-color bulls-eye in each slice.

Variation: This stuffing and procedure may also be used for a boned turkey breast. Turkey breast is much simpler to bone. Be sure to redistribute the turkey flesh over the thin parts of the breast to create an even wrapper of meat and skin. The boned turkey breast will produce a wider cylinder, so the slices will be larger in diameter than the chicken or capon.

Italian Stuffing for Poultry

Yield: 3 qt		3 L
	Ingredients:	
1 lb	ground beef	450 g
8 oz	chopped onion	224 g
4 tbls	pignoli	4 tbls
4 tbls	chopped parsley	4 tbls
½ cup	soaked and drained dried Italian mushrooms*	125 ml
2 cups	cooked white rice	500 ml
3 tbls	golden raisins	3 tbls
5 tbls	Italian grated cheese (to taste)	5 tbls
6	whole eggs, beaten	6
	salt and pepper (to taste)	
	dry bread crumbs (as needed)	

* You may use another dried imported mushroom if you like, but porcini have a particularly woodsy and distinctive taste. Whatever type you use, soak to soften, trim any hard bits and woody stems and discard. Strain the soaking liquid through a fine cloth to remove grit and add to the stuffing mixture. Chop the mushrooms into small pieces.

1. In a nonstick skillet, brown the beef, add the onions, and cook until limp. Add the pignoli, parsley, and dried mushrooms and cook for another 5 minutes stirring or until mushrooms are tender. Transfer the cooked mixture to a large bowl.
2. To the meat mixture add the rice, raisins, and some of the grated cheese. Add the beaten eggs and mix thoroughly to combine. Season with salt and pepper. Taste and add more grated cheese if needed. The mixture should be soft but not too runny. If it seems very wet, add a bit of dry bread crumbs. Cool and refrigerate the mixture. The mixture can be prepared up to two days ahead.
3. Stuff cold, cleaned poultry with cold stuffing. Pack body cavity loosely and tie or truss. Roast as desired allowing extra cooking time for stuffing. This recipe yields ample stuffing for a 20-lb (9 kg) turkey, several roasting chickens, or 10 to 12 squab or Cornish hens.

Note: If you choose to cook the stuffing separately, place in a buttered ovenproof dish and bake covered until heated through. Since this stuffing bakes up firm, it is a good choice for a stuffed boned roaster or turkey breast as it will slice neatly. It is also good for stuffing squab or large Cornish hens that will be halved for serving. The birds should be semiboneless (rib cage, breast, and backbone removed) and split neatly after roasting. The meat stuffing is substantial so half a stuffed bird is a good portion.

Chicken Cacciatore

Serves: 8–10

	Ingredients:	
2	fryers, plus two breasts, cut into pieces	2
	seasoned flour for dredging	
3 tbls	olive oil	
20 oz	thin-sliced onion	560 g
1 lb	mushrooms, sliced	450 g
14 oz	canned plum tomatoes	400 g
2 fl oz	dry red wine	60 ml
2 fl oz	brandy	60 ml
	salt and pepper (to taste)	
pinch each	dried basil and oregano	pinch each
½ cup	chopped Italian parsley	120 ml

For volume yield, this recipe may be straight multiplied up to five times. For larger amounts, reduce the tomatoes, wine, and brandy by 15%.

1. Trim any excess fatty skin from the chicken pieces. Heat the oil in a large skillet or heavy pot, dredge the chicken pieces in the seasoned flour, and brown in batches in the hot oil. Adjust the heat so the chicken colors on all sides, but does not burn. As the chicken pieces are browned, remove to a pan and keep warm.
2. Remove all but 2 or 3 tbls fat from the pan and discard. Add the onions and mushrooms and cook stirring over moderate heat until the onions are lightly browned and the mushrooms have begun to dry and brown.
3. While the vegetables are browning, drain the tomatoes, remove the hard cores and most of the seeds. Add to the browned onion and mushroom mixture and continue to cook, stirring to break the tomatoes into chunks, for 2 or 3 minutes. Add the basil and oregano.
4. Return the chicken to the pot, with its accumulated juices. Add the wine and the brandy and adjust the heat so the liquid just simmers. Cook for about 20 to 25 minutes, or until the chicken is cooked through and tender. Check a thigh near the bone to test correct doneness. Do not overcook, especially if planning to hold and reheat. Adjust seasoning with salt and pepper. If serving within a few hours, add the parsley. If storing for later service, add the parsley when reheating.

Note: This holds well refrigerated for 2 to 3 days or it can be frozen. Chilling also allows you to remove excess fat that will congeal on top of the sauce.

Variation: Rabbit, although underused in the United States, is a delectable meat. It is widely available frozen, cut into pieces, and is very good as a substitute for chicken in this recipe. To enhance the flavor of rabbit, add some minced garlic when sautéeing the onions, and pepper the finished sauce more generously.

Supreme of Chicken with Wild Mushroom Cream

Serves: 8

Ingredients:

8	boneless, skinless chicken breast halves	8
	seasoned flour for dredging	
	clarified butter	
½ cup	minced shallots	125 ml
2 tbls	minced garlic	2 tbls
1 lb	wild mushrooms, trimmed*	450 g
3 tbls	cognac	45 ml
½ cup	All-Purpose Demi-glace (see in recipe index)	125 ml
1 cup	cream	240 ml
4 tbls	fresh minced herbs, such as chives, chervil, tarragon, or parsley	4 tbls

*Depending on availability, you may use all of one type mushroom, all chanterelles, shiitakes, or morels, for example, or a combination of several types. If economy dictates, you may substitute one-third to one-half domestic mushrooms. Brush or wipe all the mushrooms clean, trim off any tough stem ends. Leave whole or cut into pieces, but do not chop small or you will lose the visual effect of the dish and deprive the diner of the tactile pleasure of biting into meaty pieces of mushrooms.

1. Have all the sauce ingredients measured and ready. Dredge the chicken breasts in seasoned flour.
2. Heat a heavy skillet and add about 2 tbls clarified butter to the pan. Add the breasts, presentation side (what was the skin side) down. Adjust the heat so that the chicken colors nicely but does not burn. Cook for about 2 minutes or until halfway done. Turn to cook and color underside. When the chicken is barely done, remove to a baking pan and hold in a very low oven while preparing sauce.
3. Add the shallots and garlic to the sauté pan with a bit more clarified butter. Sauté for one minute, then add the mushrooms and sauté, tossing or stirring once or twice until the mushrooms are well colored and almost dry.
4. Add the cognac, flame or burn off, add the demi-glace, reduce the heat, and simmer for about 2 minutes. Add the cream and continue to simmer until the sauce is thick enough to coat a spoon. Season with salt and pepper to taste.

5. Place each of the chicken supremes on warm plates (they should be hot and completely cooked by this time). Whisk any pan juices into the sauce and spoon the sauce over the chicken, leaving some of the meat exposed. Be sure to distribute the mushrooms evenly over each portion. Sprinkle with a pinch of the fresh herbs.

Note: As an alternate method of preparation, prepare the sauce and hold. Sauté the dredged chicken pieces just to color on each side, then cover with sauce and continue to cook either over low flame (or in a low oven) until the chicken is cooked through.

Supreme of Chicken with Tart Cherry Sauce

Serves: 8

	Ingredients:	
8	boneless, skinless chicken breast halves	8
	seasoned flour for dredging	
	clarified butter	
8 oz	dried tart (or sour) cherries*	225 g
½ cup	bourbon	125 ml
4 tbls	minced shallots	4 tbls
2 tbls	minced gingerroot	2 tbls
½ cup	All-Purpose Demi-glace (see in recipe index)	125 ml
	salt and pepper (to taste)	
6 tbls	butter	85 g

*Dried sour or tart cherries are available in specialty shops, health food stores, and through nut distributors or bakers' suppliers.

1. Soak the dried cherries in the bourbon until plumped. You may leave whole or snip some into smaller pieces. Have all the other sauce ingredients ready before cooking the chicken. Have warmed serving plates ready.
2. Dredge the chicken pieces in seasoned flour. Heat some clarified butter in a sauté pan and add the chicken pieces presentation side (what was the skin side) down. Adjust the heat so that the chicken colors nicely but does not burn. Cook for about 2 minutes on that side or until halfway done. Turn over and cook other side, just until lightly colored. Transfer to a baking dish and hold in a very low oven while preparing sauce.
3. Add the shallots and gingerroot to the pan with a bit more clarified butter and sauté for a minute. Add the demi-glace and the cherries with the bourbon, lower the heat and simmer for about 3 or 4 minutes, until the mixture is slightly reduced and the bourbon has lost its raw taste. Season with a little salt and generously with pepper. Reduce the heat to a bare simmer and swirl in the butter bit by bit until the sauce has a glossy finish. Remove from heat so the sauce does not break or separate.
4. To serve: Place one supreme on each warmed plate. Add any collected juices to the sauce, whisk briefly, and spoon some of the sauce in a band across (or alongside) each portion. Wild rice or root vegetable puree is a good accompaniment to this dish.

Oven-Poached Chicken Breasts

Yield: 10 lb		*4½ kg*

	Ingredients:	
10 lb	**boneless, skinless chicken breasts**	4½ kg
10 fl oz	**clarified butter**	300 ml
	salt and white pepper	
few sprigs	**herbs (if desired)**	few sprigs
10 fl oz	**either chicken broth, white wine, or apple juice**	300 ml

This method is excellent for cooking chicken breasts in volume resulting in an attractive, tender, and juicy product for a variety of uses.

1. You may remove the tenderloins before cooking and reserve for another use. If you leave them attached, the tendons can be easily stripped from the tenderloin after cooking.
2. Preheat the oven to 500°F (260°C). Film a shallow baking pan with some of the clarified butter. Lay the chicken breasts in the pan, presentation side up. Pour over the rest of the clarified butter and season lightly with salt and white pepper. Add herbs if desired. Pour the wine or other liquid into the pan.
3. Cover pan tightly with foil and place in the oven. The chicken will be cooked in 5 to 8 minutes, depending on the size and thickness of the breasts. If serving cold, allow the breasts to cool in the broth, where they will continue to cook from residual heat so that when you remove them from the oven they should be slightly undercooked. However, if you are plating and serving immediately, then add an extra minute cooking time.

Peasant Chicken Ragout

Serves: 8	*50*		*8*	*50*
		Ingredients:		
24	120	**chicken fryer pieces**	24	120
3 tbls	½ cup	**olive or vegetable oil**	45 ml	125 ml
1 lb	5 lb	**coarsely chopped onion**	450 g	2 kg 250 g
2	5	**garlic cloves, minced**	2	5
12 oz	4 lb	**coarsely chopped leeks**	336 g	1 kg 800 g
12 oz	4 lb	**bulb fennel, sliced**	336 g	1 kg 800 g
1	3	**whole orange**	1	3
2 cups	2 qt	**dry white wine**	500 ml	2 L
1 cup	1 qt	**chicken broth**	¼ L	1 L
12 oz	2 lb	**tomato paste**	336 g	900 g

4 tbls	1½ cups	**chopped Italian parsley**	60 ml	370 ml
½ cup	2 cups	**shredded basil leaves**	125 ml	500 ml
		salt (if needed)		
1 tsp	1½ tbls	**ground black pepper (or to taste)**	1 tsp	1½ tbls
1 cup	1 qt	**Pesto alla Genovese (see in recipe index)**	¼ L	1 L

To serve 8, use two whole fryers, cut into eight pieces each, and two large breasts, cut into four pieces each. To serve 50, use twelve fryers and twelve large breasts. This will yield slightly more than two pieces of chicken per person, as well as providing extra white meat.

1. Use a vegetable peeler to remove the orange zest. Chop coarsely and set aside, adding the juice from the orange(s).
2. Trim excess fatty skin from the chicken, pat the pieces dry, but do not salt. Heat the oil in a large skillet or heavy pot, place the dark meat pieces in the pan and brown, turning to color on all sides and render as much of the fat from the skin as possible. After about 5 minutes, remove from the pan and place in a roasting pan. Place the pan in a low oven, where it will continue to cook while you brown the white meat. (If working with large volumes, be sure not to let the chicken pieces bake longer than 15 to 20 minutes or they will overcook.)
3. When all the chicken has been browned, drain off all but a few spoons of chicken fat and discard. Add the onion, garlic, and leeks to the pan and cook in the chicken fat until lightly browned and wilted, about 5 minutes. Add the fennel and the orange zest and juice. Continue to cook the vegetables over moderate heat for about 5 more minutes or until the fennel has begun to soften.
4. Add the wine, stirring and scraping any browned bits that may still cling to the pan, add the broth and the tomato paste, and stir until the paste is diluted. Lower the heat and simmer for 10 to 15 minutes, stirring occasionally, or until the tomato has lost its raw taste. Add the parsley, the basil leaves, and the pepper. Taste for seasoning. You may wish to add more pepper for a spicier dish. It is unlikely that you will need more salt (remember that the pesto is salty with cheese).
5. When the sauce is cooked sufficiently to have blended its flavors, add the chicken, stir to coat with the sauce and simmer just until the chicken is cooked through (check a thigh near the bone).
6. Gently stir in the pesto, lower the heat and simmer until the sauce is hot. Adjust seasonings one final time. Remove from heat and serve with rice on the side.

Note: May be prepared ahead and refrigerated or frozen if care is taken not to overcook the chicken when reheating or it will break apart. Reheat in hotel pans, covered, in a slow oven for best results.

Variation: Duckling may be substituted. Be sure to render and remove excess fat. A good use for legs and thighs of ducks left from other uses.

Turkey Breast With Vegetable Stuffing

Serves: 20–24

Ingredients:

1	whole turkey breast (approx. 7 lb [3¼ kg])	1
3 tbls	marsala wine	45 ml
	For stuffing:	
4 slices	stale Italian or French bread	4 slices
½ cup	milk	125 ml
1 lb	ground turkey	450 g
10 oz	frozen chopped spinach, thawed and squeezed dry	280 g
1 lb	Swiss chard	450 g
4 oz	chopped shallots	112 g
4 oz	chopped onion	112 g
4 oz	chopped carrot	112 g
2 tbls	sweet butter	30 g
4 tbls	chopped parsley	4 tbls
3 oz	grated Gruyère	84 g
4 oz	shelled pistachio nuts	112 g
4	whole eggs	4
	salt and pepper (to taste)	
	dry bread crumbs (if needed)	
	Also: cheesecloth, needle and thread, melted margarine	

1. Bone the turkey breast: With the point of a boning knife, find the wishbone, scrape and pry it free and discard. Turn the breast over and scrape against the rib cage with the knife on each side to free the meat from the bones. Pull the bones away from the flesh and scrape carefully along the edge of the breastbone to separate from the meat. Reserve the bones for stock. Sprinkle the breast meat with a few drops of marsala and set aside refrigerated until ready to stuff.
2. Soak the bread in the milk to soften, then shred apart with a fork. Trim the leaves from the Swiss chard stalks, blanch the leaves, and cook the stalks in salted water until tender. Chop the leaves and stems and drain well.
3. Heat the butter in a pan, and sweat the shallots, onions, and carrot until tender. Add the spinach, chard, ground turkey, soaked bread, and parsley, stir over heat for 1 minute, then set aside to cool to lukewarm. Then add the eggs, cheese, nuts, and the remaining marsala. Season with salt and pepper. Sauté a bit of the stuffing to check seasonings, then adjust to taste. Refrigerate the stuffing until completely cold. Now, or just before stuffing, if the filling seems too runny, add a bit of dry bread crumbs to make a manageable mixture.

4. To Stuff and Roll: Wash the cheesecloth, wring dry and dip in melted margarine. Lay flat on waxed paper on a work surface. Lay the turkey breast on the cheesecloth, stretching the skin flat into a rough rectangle. Make an even layer of meat by removing the tenderloins from the breast and placing them in bare areas of skin. Cut horizontal slices from the thickest part of the breast, lay them on thin or bare areas as well. If the meat extends beyond the skin onto the cheesecloth, it's OK. Pat the stuffing over the meat as evenly as possible. Use the waxed paper and cheesecloth to shape the stuffed meat into a thick cylinder. The turkey skin and the cheesecloth will be the wrapper. Tie both ends with thread or twine, and either stitch or tie closed. Tie pieces of twine around the roll to keep the cylindrical shape. If not roasting immediately, refrigerate.

5. Preheat the oven to 350°F (180°C). Place the turkey on a rack, seam side down, brush with more melted margarine, roast for 30 minutes. Turn seam side up, baste again, and roast, turning and basting now and then for another 2 hours, to an internal temperature of 140°F (60°C). Remove to a rack to cool for about 20 minutes before attempting to peel off the cheesecloth. Let rest at least another 30 minutes before slicing, or cool completely, slice and serve at room temperature.

Note: For more detail on stuffing, wrapping and roasting see Chicken Ballottine with Sausage recipe.

Variation: The stuffed turkey may be braised rather than roasted. Prepare according to recipe, then braise in butter in a heavy pot or dutch oven until browned on all sides. Add enough combined stock and wine to cover, and braise or simmer gently until cooked through. Cool in broth, unwrap and slice. Such a preparation, called a galantine, is usually served cold, masked with a decorative chaud-froid sauce (see a culinary text for details).

Sweet and Sour Turkey Roulades

Serves: 8

	Ingredients:	
2 lb	turkey breast cutlets	1 kg
2 tbls	lemon juice	30 ml
2 tbls	dry white wine	30 ml
1	clove garlic	1
2	peppercorns, cracked	2
	flour for dredging	

1 bunch	parsley, tops only	1 bunch
4 oz	golden raisins	115 g
4 oz	pignoli	115 g
1	clove garlic	1
2 tsp	grated lemon zest	2 tsp
1 cup	dry bread crumbs	¼ L
1 cup	olive oil	¼ L
8 oz	chopped onion	225 g
6 oz	chopped carrot	180 g
6 oz	chopped celery	180 g
½ cup	chopped parsley	125 ml
½ cup	chicken broth	125 ml
½ cup	white wine	125 ml
	salt and pepper (to taste)	

1. Pound the cutlets lightly to even their thickness. Place in a dish and add lemon juice, wine, one garlic clove and peppercorns. Turn to coat the meat. Cover and refrigerate to marinate for about 30 minutes.
2. Prepare the stuffing: In a food processor combine the parsley tops, raisins, pignoli, the remaining garlic, and lemon zest. Pulse on and off, scraping down the sides of the bowl, until the mixture is finely chopped. Add the dry bread crumbs and process to mix. Add just enough olive oil to make a spreadable paste.
3. Remove the turkey from the marinade. Pat dry and lay flat on a work surface. Spread the stuffing evenly on the pieces of meat. Roll up the turkey and either tie with kitchen string or secure with toothpicks.
4. Heat some of the remaining oil in a heavy pot or Dutch oven. Dredge the filled turkey rolls in flour, shake off the excess and brown on all sides in the oil. Add the chopped onion, carrot, and celery, and cook over low heat until wilted and lightly colored.
5. Add some salt and pepper, then add the wine and the broth. If there is any olive oil left over, add it to the pot as well. Adjust the heat to a bare simmer, cover the pot and braise the meat for about 40 minutes, or until it is tender but not falling apart.
6. When the turkey is tender, remove from the pot and set aside. Either keep warm or refrigerate, depending on planned usage.
7. Cook down the broth and vegetables until very little liquid remains. Adjust seasonings and set aside.
8. The roulades may be served hot or at cool room temperature. They can be prepared ahead. Store in the vegetables to keep moist for 2 to 3 days. They may also be frozen and reheated gently so as not to overcook the turkey or dry it out.
9. When ready to serve, remove the strings or picks from the roulades, and use a sharp knife to cut them into pinwheel slices. At whatever temperature you serve them, the vegetables provide a sauce or accompaniment to the slices. To finish the sauce, just before serving stir in the parsley.

Game Birds with Fruit and Cornbread Stuffing

Serves: 8

Ingredients:

4	Cornish hens, poussins, squab, partridge or 8 quail	4
1½ cups	crumbled cornbread	370 ml
½ cup	dried cranberries (craisins)	125 ml
½ cup	cored chopped apple	125 ml
½ cup	broken toasted cashews	125 ml
4 tbls	chopped parsley	60 ml
1 tsp	crumbled thyme	1 tsp
1 tsp	crumbled sage	1 tsp
½ tsp	salt	½ tsp
¼ tsp	ground black pepper	¼ tsp
½ cup	chopped scallion	125 ml
½ cup	chopped celery	125 ml
3 tbls	bourbon	45 ml
1	egg, lightly beaten	1
	melted butter and/or vegetable oil (as needed)	
	flour for dredging	

For a moderate-sized portion, half of each of the larger stuffed birds is sufficient, as are two stuffed quail per person. For heartier portions, serve each person a whole stuffed bird, or three quail each. It is more elegant to partially bone the birds (remove the wishbone, rib cage and backbone), but it is not necessary. Be sure to clean the cavities well.

1. Prepare the birds as described above, pat dry, and set aside.
2. Combine the crumbled cornbread with the craisins, chopped apple, nuts, parsley, herbs, and seasonings. Set aside.
3. Heat a bit of butter or oil in a sauté pan and cook the scallion and celery until wilted. Add to the cornbread mixture, stir to combine, add the bourbon and beaten egg and mix thoroughly. Taste and add salt if needed and quite a bit of pepper to make a well-flavored mixture. When the stuffing is completely cool, stuff loosely into the birds and truss (or stitch closed if boned).
4. Preheat the oven to 425°F (220°C) for quail, 450°F (230°C) for other birds. Rub or brush the birds liberally with melted butter and/or oil, then dredge in flour seasoned with salt and pepper. Place on a rack in a roasting pan on their sides. Roast on one side for 3 to 5 minutes, then turn to color other side for another 3 to 5 minutes, then finish roasting breast side up. The quail will be cooked after a total roasting time of 12 to 15 minutes; partridge in 25 to 30 minutes; Cornish hens or poussins in 30 to 35 minutes; and squab 35 to 40 minutes. Cooking times may vary slightly depending on size of the birds: test the thigh juices to determine exact doneness. If the birds are not browning as you like, remove from oven a few minutes before they are completely done and brown in butter in a sauté pan. Set the roasted birds aside and keep warm.

5. Skim the pan juices to serve over birds. If you desire a sauce, add game or poultry stock and brandy to the juices, and thicken slightly with buerre manie.

6. Serve the birds hot, with the trussing removed and neatly split in two if required. If the stuffing falls out of the cavities, serve under or alongside each portion. These birds are best served with a simple steamed or sautéed vegetable, such as snow peas or green beans, and with a portion of shoestring sweet potatoes or root vegetables, if desired.

Note: You can eliminate the dredging if desired and instead wrap the stuffed birds in buttered foil and roast until almost done, finishing by browning in butter to crisp the skin. This method is good for advance preparation, since the birds stay very moist, and the skin is crisped just before serving. This method is preferred to full roasting and reheating, since the skin will not shrivel or the flesh dry out. Of course, any of the birds can be stuffed ahead and roasted on site, provided that both the birds and stuffing are ice-cold when filled and kept cold during transport. Quail cook so quickly that they are best cooked entirely on site just before serving.

Variations: White and/or wild rice may be substituted for the cornbread for a different but equally tasty stuffing. Pecans or pistachios may be substituted for cashews. Other stuffings may be used for the birds, but if you choose a very dense meat or sausage stuffing, cooking time will have to be increased proportionate to the size of the bird.

Herb Roasted Cornish Hens

Serves: 8

Ingredients:

8	**Cornish hens or poussins**	8
1 lb	**Herb and Shallot Butter (see Compound or Flavored Butters in recipe index)**	500 g
½ cup	**fresh white bread crumbs**	60 g
	vegetable oil, paprika, salt and pepper (as needed)	

1. Soften the herb butter and stir in the bread crumbs. Set aside.

2. Partially bone the hens, that is, split down and remove the backbone, and remove the entire rib cage and wishbone. Flatten the hens, flesh side down on work surface and loosen the skin as much as possible. Stuff the herb butter mixture between the skin and the flesh, covering the whole breast and working it into the leg area as far as possible without tearing the skin.

3. Pat the hens flat again, make little slits near the tail vent and secure the tips of the drumsticks under the skin. Alternately, you can run skewers through the hen to keep it flat, one between the knee joints, the other through both wings.

4. Preheat the oven to 475°F (245°C). Rub or brush the hens all over with oil. Sprinkle with paprika, salt, and pepper on top and underside. Place on a rack in a shallow pan skin side up and roast for about 5 minutes. Turn over carefully and cook 5 minutes longer. Turn right side up again, brush with more oil (or melted butter) and cook an additional 10 to 15 minutes, depending on size. As soon as the thigh juices are clear, they are done. Serve hot, with pan juices drizzled over each hen.

Boneless Duck Breast (Maigret)

Serves: 8

Ingredients:

8	boneless duck breast halves	8
1 cup	Marinade for Beef, Lamb, or Game (see in recipe index)	¼ L
	clarified butter or oil for sautéeing	
	For peppercorn sauce:	
¼ cup	brandy	60 ml
½ cup	All-Purpose Demi-glace (see in recipe index)	125 ml
3 tbls	green peppercorns	3 tbls
1 tbls	cracked white peppercorns	1 tbls
10 fl oz	heavy cream	310 ml
	salt (to taste)	
	For port and mustard sauce:	
¼ cup	port	60 ml
½ cup	All-Purpose Demi-glace (see in recipe index)	125 ml
¼ cup	orange juice	60 ml
3 tbls	Pommery mustard	45 ml
4 tbls	minced shallots	4 tbls
	salt and pepper (to taste)	
4 tbls	butter	60 g

It is sometime possible to order filet of duck breast directly from your supplier. Otherwise, bone the breasts from four ducks. You will have eight filets or breast halves. Leave the skin on, trimming the edges of skin neatly to match the size of the filets. Reserve the thighs and legs for another use, such as a ragout, pâté, or salad. Use the carcasses for stock.

1. Marinate the prepared and trimmed duck breast pieces for several hours or overnight.
2. Have ready all the ingredients for chosen sauce before cooking the duck. Have warm plates ready for serving.

3. Just before service, remove the duck breasts from the marinade and pat dry. Strain the marinade and reduce to ⅓ cup (80 ml). Set aside and have ready to add to either sauce.

4. Heat a heavy skillet or sauté pan until very hot, brush with clarified butter or oil, and immediately add the duck pieces, skin side down. Cook over high heat for about 3 or 4 minutes, until the skin has started to crisp and brown. Brush the top (meaty parts) of the duck with more clarified butter, turn over, lower the heat to moderate and cook for 2 more minutes. Transfer to a pan, cover loosely with foil, and place in a barely warm oven.

5. For Peppercorn Sauce: Pour the excess fat from the sauté pan, deglaze with brandy, add the reduced marinade and the demi-glace, and bring to the simmer. Add the green peppercorns and the cracked pepper and simmer for 2 or 3 minutes. Add the cream and reduce until the mixture just coats a spoon. Season with a bit of salt to taste.

6. For Port and Mustard Sauce: Pour the fat from the sauté pan, deglaze with port, add the reduced marinade, the demi-glace, and the orange juice and bring to the simmer. Add the mustard and shallots and reduce over high heat for about 4 or 5 minutes. The sauce should have thickened slightly. Add salt and pepper to taste. Lower the heat so the mixture barely simmers, and whisk in the butter bit by bit to finish and thicken the sauce. Remove from heat immediately so sauce does not break (so the butter does not separate).

7. To serve, use a very sharp knife to slice the breasts into thin diagonal slices. Nap each of the warm plates with sauce, and fan out the slices of breast meat over the sauce.

Roast Duckling with Mustard Fruits

Serves: 12

	Ingredients:	
6	dressed ducks	6
2	lemons, seeded and chopped	2
3 cups	mostarda*	750 ml
6	whole garlic cloves	6
	salt and pepper	
¼ cup	soy sauce	60 ml
¼ cup	All-Purpose Demi-glace (see in recipe index)	60 ml
½ cup	port	125 ml
¼ cup	orange marmalade or peach jam	60 ml
	game or poultry stock (as needed)	
	To thicken sauce: cornstarch or buerre manie	

*Mostarda is an Italian conserve of fruits flavored with mustard seeds and hot pepper flakes. It is available in Italian specialty markets.

1. Remove any large lumps of fat from the vents of the ducks, and trim excess fatty skin from the neck. Rinse inside and out with salted water, drain and pat dry. Carefully pierce the very fatty parts of the skin (but not the flesh) of the ducks, especially around the thighs. Salt and pepper the cavities of the ducks.
2. Preheat the oven to 500° F (260° C). Combine the chopped lemon with 1 cup (¼ L) of the mostarda, place some in the cavity of each of the ducks along with one garlic clove. Truss the ducks loosely with twine or skewers. Place the ducks on their sides on a rack in a roasting pan. Put a little water in the bottom of the pan.
3. Roast the duck for about 5 minutes on each side, then lower the heat to 400° F (205° C) and continue to roast, turning and basting the birds for another hour. Rotate the position of the birds in the pan so they color evenly.
4. In a saucepan, combine and heat the soy sauce, demi-glace, port, and jam. Use this mixture to baste the ducks, while they roast for an additional 30 minutes to one hour. The ducks are done when the thigh juices are no longer pink. Remove from the oven to another pan. Empty the fruit and juices from the cavities into a strainer, press to extract the juices, and discard the solids. Cover the ducks and keep warm.
5. Skim as much fat as possible from the pan juices and the internal juices from the ducks. Add any of the soy sauce mixture that remains to the degreased juices, add enough game or poultry stock to make 3 cups (¾ L). Reduce over high heat by one-third. Strain and thicken slightly as desired with either buerre manie or a cornstarch slurry. Adjust seasonings to taste.
6. To serve: Split the ducks in half with a sharp knife or poultry shears. Place a portion of the remaining mostarda on each of 12 hot plates, place half a duck on each. Spoon some of the hot sauce over and serve the remaining sauce on the side.

VEAL, BEEF, AND VENISON
Breaded Cutlets with Sauces

Serves: 8

Ingredients:

8	veal cutlets, turkey scallops, or skinned boneless chicken breasts (each about 6 oz [180 g])	8
	seasoned flour for dredging	
	egg wash	
	dry bread crumbs	
	vegetable or olive oil for frying	

1. Prepare the meats by pounding lightly to flatten and even their thickness. Very thick chicken breasts should be butterflied.
2. Dredge the cutlets in seasoned flour, then in egg wash. Let excess egg drip away, then place in bread crumbs and coat both sides evenly, patting the crumbs to help them adhere. Place the breaded cutlets on a rack and refrigerate for at least 20 minutes to firm the coating. Let come to room temperature before frying.
3. Heat about 1 in. (2½ cm) of oil in a deep-sided skillet. Fry the cutlets a few at a time, until evenly browned on both sides. Transfer to absorbent paper to drain, then set aside until ready to sauce and serve. If cutlets are to be served plain, they are best fried just before serving, then held in a warm oven, uncovered, to keep warm.

Variations: Most of the variations that follow can be prepared ahead, and held covered, in a warm oven; or can be prepared ahead and gently reheated before service. Their moist sauces prevent them from drying out, so they can hold well on a buffet. Those that are best served at once are indicated.

With Fresh Tomato Salad: See the recipe for Pasta with Fresh Tomato Salad (see in recipe index). Top the hot cutlet with the room temperature salad and serve at once.

For Parmigiana: Top each cutlet with a slice of mozzarella cheese and a few table-spoons of tomato sauce, sprinkle with grated Italian cheese. Bake covered before service to heat through and melt the cheese. A second variation of Parmigiana is to layer the cutlet with a slice of fried eggplant followed by the cheese and sauce.

For Piccata: Combine ½ cup (125 ml) each stock, white wine, and lemon juice. Simmer for 3 minutes, swirl in 4 tbls each butter and minced parsley and pour over cutlets. (This is sometime prepared with sautéed rather than breaded cutlets).

For Holstein: Just before service top a hot cutlet with a fried egg, garnish with one or two drained anchovies.

With Garlic, Anchovies, and Capers: Heat 3 tbls butter in a skillet, add garlic, sauté for 30 seconds just to wilt, add ¼ cup (60 ml) each dry vermouth and lemon juice, simmer for 1 minute, add eight chopped anchovies and 4 tbls capers. Swirl together and pour over cutlets. Keep warm until ready to serve.

With Prosciutto and Mushrooms: See recipe for Prosciutto and Mushrooms Scallopine (see in recipe index).

For Prosciutto and Fontina: Heat ½ cup (125 ml) each of marsala and stock in a deep skillet, boil for 1 minute. Lower heat to simmer, add the cutlets to the pan (or place cutlets in a baking pan or chafer and pour sauce over). Cover each cutlet with a slice of prosciutto and Italian fontina cheese. Cover pan and keep over very low heat. Serve as soon as cheese melts.

Variation for Preparation: Omit the flour and the bread crumbs. Instead combine about four beaten eggs with ½ cup (125 ml) each grated Parmesan and minced parsley. Dip cutlets in egg mixture, then fry as for cutlets. These are very good served plain, either freshly fried or held drizzled with a little melted butter.

Herb-Grilled Veal Chops

Serves: 8

Ingredients:

8	loin veal chops, cut about 1-in. (2½ cm) thick	8
4 tbls	flavorful olive oil	60 ml
2 tbls	lemon juice	30 ml
3 sprigs each	rosemary, thyme, parsley	3 sprigs each
2	shallots, sliced	2
2	sage leaves	2
	coarsely ground pepper	
	more olive oil (as needed)	
8 tbls	Herb and Shallot Butter (see Compound or Flavored Butters in recipe index)	112 g

1. Trim the chops so that only a thin band of fat surrounds them. You may remove the tails or leave attached as desired.
2. Combine the olive oil and lemon juice in shallow dish large enough to hold the chops. Crumble or chop the herbs coarsely and add to the dish. Scatter half the sliced shallots, place the chops in the dish, turning them over in the marinade to coat with the oil and herbs. Grind pepper generously over both sides of the chops, scatter the rest of the shallots on top. Cover and marinate for about an hour at cool room temperature or 3 hours refrigerated. Let come to room temperature before broiling.
3. Preheat a broiler to its highest setting. Place the broiler rack about 3 in. (8 cm) from the flame. Remove the chops from the marinade, brushing off the shallot slices (it's OK if some of the herbs and pepper cling to the chops). Place some olive oil on a flat plate.
4. When the broiler is very hot, brush the rack with oil. Dip each chop into the plate of oil and place, oiled side down, on the rack. Cook for about 3 or 4 minutes, until the fat on the edges begins to brown and the chop takes on color. Brush the top surface of the chops with a bit more oil and turn to cook other side, again for 3 or 4 minutes. The chops should take a total of about 10 minutes to cook to medium rare (barely pink inside and very juicy). You may need to turn or change their positions for even cooking. They should have good golden brown color, crusty edges, but still yield to the touch.
5. Transfer immediately to warmed serving plates, top with a pat of herb and shallot butter and serve.

Note: These may be prepared on a grill as well. If using a salamander, set further from the flame to prevent burning. Rib chops may be substituted for the loin if desired.

Variations: Other compound butters may be used, or the chops may be served plain with no embellishment since they are well flavored by the marinade.

Medallions of Veal Normande

Serves: 8

Ingredients:

3 lb	boneless veal loin, cut into medallions*	1350 g
	salt and pepper (as needed)	
3 tbls	butter	40 g
4 tbls	minced shallots	4 tbls
2	apples, cored and thin-sliced	2
1 cup	fermented apple cider, or half apple juice and half hard cider†	¼ L
3 tbls	All-Purpose Demi-glace (see in recipe index)	3 tbls
½ cup	cream	125 ml
2 tbls	calvados or applejack	2 tbls

* Cut the loin into slices of desired thickness, about ½ to ¾ in. (1½ to 2½ cm), depending on the planned portion size. Don't cut thinner or they will not cook properly.

†If you can get unpasteurized fresh cider, store it in bottles or jars, allowing plenty of head space, for a few weeks. It will get fizzy (take care in opening the bottles) and acquire a slightly sour taste. If not, the combination of juice and hard cider has a similar balance of fruit and acid.

1. Heat the butter in a deep-sided sauté pan, pat the veal slices dry, season with salt and pepper, and sauté a few at a time over moderately high heat. Cook for only 1 to 2 minutes per side, depending on thickness, transfer to a pan to keep warm.
2. Drain all but a film of butter from the pan, add the shallots and the apple slices and sauté until lightly colored. Remove the apples from the pan, set aside, and keep warm.
3. Add the cider and demi-glace and boil for a minute or two, scraping any browned bits from the pan. Add the cream and lower the heat to a simmer. Cook until the sauce thickens. Return the veal and accumulated juices to the pan, turning the veal to coat on all sides. Add the calvados and simmer for just a minute until the sauce thickens again.
4. Serve on warm plates, placing a few apple slices on top of or alongside each portion.

Note: The sauce may be prepared ahead and held, and the veal and apples sautéed just prior to service. Finish cooking the veal in the sauce and serve as above. Can be held, partially covered in a chafer for about 30 minutes.

Variations: Veal medallions can also be sautéed as above and served with other sauces, for example, Gorgonzola Sauce (see recipe for Scallopine with Gorgonzola Sauce), with the Peppercorn Sauce used in the recipe for Boneless Duck Breast (Maigret), or with Wild Mushroom Cream (see in recipe index for Supreme of Chicken with Wild Mushroom Cream).

Loin of Pork can be cut into medallions and served with this sauce. However, for pork, first brown the pork on both sides, then add some stock or the cider, lower the heat, and braise gently until the pork is tender and cooked through.

Osso Buco

Serves: 8

	Ingredients:	
2	veal hind shanks, cut in 8 2-in. (5 cm) long pieces	2
	seasoned flour for dredging	
6 tbls	combined olive oil and butter	45 ml + 40 g
1 tbls	minced garlic	1 tbls
10 oz	chopped onion	285 g
8 oz	chopped carrot	225 g
8 oz	chopped celery	225 g
1 cup	dry white wine	¼ L
1 cup	veal stock (or as needed)	¼ L
¼ cup	crushed canned tomatoes	60 ml
¼ tsp each	dried thyme and marjoram	¼ tsp each
4	basil leaves	4
4 tbls	minced parsley	4 tbls
	salt and pepper to taste	
	Optional Gremolada:	
1 tbls	grated lemon peel	1 tbls
1 tbls	minced garlic	1 tbls
3 tbls	minced parsley	3 tbls

1. Heat the oil and butter in a heavy casserole or Dutch oven. Dredge the veal shanks in seasoned flour, add to the pot, and brown on all sides. Remove and set aside. To the pan add the garlic, onion, carrot, and celery and cook over low heat, stirring occasionally, until the vegetables have begun to soften and color.
2. Add the wine to the pan, stirring to loosen the bits on the sides and bottom of the pan. Return the veal to the pan, standing all the pieces upright side by side. Cook for 5 minutes until the wine has reduced somewhat, then add just enough stock to cover the veal. Add the tomatoes, the thyme, and the marjoram. Cover the casserole and lower the heat to a bare simmer. Cook for about 1 hour, basting and turning the shanks once or twice.
3. After an hour's cooking, add the basil and parsley. Grind some pepper over the meat, but hold off on salt until the very end. Cook for at least another 30 minutes or an hour, until the meat is very tender. If there is not enough liquid in the pan, add a bit of stock as you go along. Once the veal is cooked tender, it can be held for 2 or 3 days, then reheated and served.
4. To serve: Reheat gently, transfer the shanks to a platter and keep warm. If necessary, reduce the liquid in the pan until the sauce is concentrated and spoonable. Adjust seasonings to taste. Serve each person a shank and a generous portion of sauce. Osso Buco is traditionally served with risotto (see recipes in recipe index), the plain butter or saffron version being most appropriate.

5. Gremolada: This mixture is traditionally added to the casserole a few minutes before serving, with a little bit of the mixture sprinkled on each bone. If you are not sure of its universal appeal, prepare a little dish of the mixture and offer to guests as they are served.

Note: If the preparation of risotto as an accompaniment is not feasible, little rounds of sautéed polenta are a good alternative.

Scallopine with Gorgonzola Sauce

Serves: 8–10

Ingredients:

2½ lb	**veal scallops**	1¼ kg
	seasoned flour for dredging	
	clarified butter or oil for sautéeing	
4 oz	**broken walnut pieces**	115 g
2 tbls	**minced shallots**	2 tbls
4 tbls	**cognac or brandy**	4 tbls
½ cup	**strong veal or brown stock**	125 ml
1 cup	**cream**	¼ L
4 oz	**gorgonzola, crumbled**	115 g

1. If the scallops are not evenly thin, pound gently to flatten.
2. Dredge the veal in seasoned flour. Heat some of the clarified butter in a sauté pan, and add the scallops a few at a time. Sauté just to color on both sides. Remove to a pan as they are finished and keep warm, loosely covered.
3. Add the walnuts and shallots to the sauté pan. Toss briefly, just enough to toast the nuts. Use a slotted spoon to remove the nuts from the pan. Add them to the reserved veal.
4. Deglaze the pan with the cognac, flame or burn off for a few seconds. Add the stock and cream and reduce until the sauce is just thick enough to coat a spoon. Return the veal and the nuts to the pan and turn to coat veal with sauce. Just before serving add the crumbled cheese and remove pan from heat. As you are serving, the cheese will begin to melt into the sauce. If plating individually, be sure to include some walnuts, and cheese in each portion. Serve with a plain steamed green vegetable: broccoli florets go especially well with this sauce.

Note: To prepare ahead: Begin the sauce with sautéed shallots, then add stock and cream and reduce. Hold for service. Just before serving, sauté the veal, add the walnuts, deglaze with cognac, then add to prepared sauce, stir in cheese and serve.

Variations: As in most recipes that call for veal scallops, turkey scallops (slices cut cross-grain from the breast) may be substituted. They work very well here, as they would with other vividly flavored sauces. The sauce may be prepared ahead as above and used to coat oven-poached chicken breasts. This variation is good for advance preparation, since the chicken may be cooked ahead until barely done, then reheated in some poaching liquid, drained, and coated with hot sauce. The chicken breast version will also hold up better on the buffet since the thicker pieces will remain moist and tender longer than the thinner scallops.

Scallopine with Prosciutto and Mushrooms

Serves: 8–10

	Ingredients:	
2½ lb	veal scallops	1 kg 124 g
	seasoned flour for dredging	
	clarified butter and/or oil for sautéeing	
1 lb	mushrooms, sliced	450 g
¼ lb	prosciutto, cut into bits	112 g
2 cups	muscatel*	500 ml
3 tbls	butter	40 g

*In spite of its low-class reputation, muscatel has a sweet fruity flavor that enhances this dish.

1. Pound the veal gently to flatten slightly. Do not tear or make too thin. Set aside until sauce is prepared.
2. Heat some of the clarified butter in a pan and sauté the mushrooms until evenly browned. In a separate saucepan, simmer the muscatel until reduced by about half. Add the prosciutto and the mushrooms and simmer for another 10 minutes.
3. Dredge the veal scallops in seasoned flour. Heat a bit more clarified butter or oil in a sauté pan, add the scallops a few at a time, sear on one side, quickly turn and cook other side. Transfer the scallops as they are browned to a pan, cover loosely with foil, and keep warm.
4. Whisk the butter bit by bit into the wine mixture to finish the sauce (this is sometimes called "montee au buerre"). Either return the veal scallops to the sauce, or plate the scallops and spoon some sauce over each portion.

Note: To prepare ahead: Prepare the sauce as indicated, except omit the mounting with butter. Instead, place the sautéed scallops in the sauce and hold. When ready to serve, reheat the veal in a bit of the sauce, thicken the rest of the sauce with buerre manie, spoon over veal and serve.

Veal Burgers

Serves: 8

Ingredients:

2 lb	ground veal	1 kg
2 slices	white sandwich bread	2 slices
½ cup	milk	125 ml
4 oz	blanched chopped spinach	115 g
4 tbls	chopped parsley	4 tbls
2 tbls	minced chives	2 tbls
½ cup	minced onion	125 ml
2 tsp	dry mustard	2 tsp
2	whole eggs, lightly beaten	2
	salt and pepper (to taste)	
	dry bread crumbs (as needed)	
2 tbls	butter or vegetable oil for sautéeing	30 g or 30 ml

1. Soak the bread in the milk. Squeeze the spinach very dry.
2. Combine all the ingredients, except the salt, pepper, and bread crumbs, to make a light but thoroughly combined mixture. Sauté a bit of the mixture to taste for seasonings, adding salt and pepper as needed. Keep well chilled until ready to shape and sauté. (You may shape into patties ahead, but they are soft and must be well-protected in transport.)
3. Dust your hands with dry breadcrumbs and shape the meat mixture into patties. Set on paper towels while holding for frying.
4. Heat the butter or oil in a sauté pan, add the veal burgers and cook over medium heat until browned on one side, then turn over and continue to cook until they begin to firm to the touch. They should be cooked through, but not overcooked or they will be dry. If more convenient, they can be quickly browned on both sides and transferred to a parchment lined baking sheet and completed in the oven. Serve while hot and juicy.

Note: These burgers can be served plain, on a plate or bun as you would any burger, or deglaze the pan with a bit of stock, mustard, and/or cream to make a sauce.

Variations: Eliminate the chives and mustard, add Italian grated cheese, and serve with a light marinara sauce.

Ground turkey may be substituted for veal in any version.

Veal with Winter Fruits

Serves: 10	50		10	50
		Ingredients:		
5 lb	25 lb	boneless veal for stew	2 kg 250 g	11¼ kg
1 lb	5 lb	dried apricots	450 g	2¼ kg
1 lb	5 lb	mixed dried fruits*	450 g	2¼ kg
1 cup	3 cups	bourbon	¼ L	¾ L
4 oz	1 lb	butter or margarine	112 g	450 g
3 lb	15 lb	coarsely chopped onion	1 kg 350 g	6¾ kg
½ cup	1½ cups	bourbon liqueur or brandy	125 ml	350 ml
3 cups	1 gal	veal or poultry stock	750 ml	3¾ L
2 oz	8 oz	all-purpose flour (or mochiko)†	56 g	225 g
2 tsp	3 tbls	dry mustard	2 tsp	3 tbls
2 tbls	½ cup	Dijon mustard	2 tbls	125 ml
1 tsp	1 tbls	Worcestershire sauce	1 tsp	1 tbls
dash	1 tsp	hot pepper sauce (or to taste)	dash	1 tsp
		salt and pepper (to taste)		
		Garnish: chopped parsley		

*Use a combination of dried apples, pears, and pitted prunes.
†Use mochiko, or sweet rice flour, instead of flour for thickening if planning to freeze. It does not lose its thickening power.

1. A day ahead, prepare the fruit. Cut large pieces such as apples and pears into two or three pieces each. Halve apricots if they are very large. Be sure all the prunes are pitted. Soak the fruits in the bourbon.
2. Cut the veal into good sized chunks, about 1½ in. (4 cm), at least. Remove any heavy connective tissue or very fatty pieces (they can be used for stock at another time). Blanch the veal by placing in a large pot of cold water. Place over heat and stir as the liquid comes to a simmer. Skim off the scum that rises to the top. As soon as the water is simmering, drain.
3. Heat half the butter in a heavy skillet or Dutch oven (depending on volume of stew), add the onion, cover and sweat for 10 minutes or until wilted. Remove the pot lid, increase the heat and cook rapidly to reduce the liquid and brown the onion. Meanwhile, heat the stock in a separate pot.
4. Add the bourbon liqueur or brandy to the onions and cook or flame off. Put the onion in a bowl with the veal.
5. Add the remaining butter to the pan, heat to foaming and add the flour. Cook, stirring for about 3 minutes, until the roux is golden brown. Gradually add some of the stock to the roux, stirring to blend smoothly, then add the balance of the stock and simmer until thickened. Adjust the heat so the sauce does not scorch.

6. Add the drained fruits, with their soaking bourbon, the veal and the onions to the sauce. Stir to combine. Add the mustards and other seasonings, taste and adjust with pepper. The fruits contribute a lot of sweetness, so after the final simmering, you may need to add additional pepper or mustard to balance to a pleasantly zesty flavor.

7. Simmer the stew, either on the stovetop, or in a low oven, for about 30 to 40 minutes, until the veal is fork tender. If planning to freeze or store refrigerated for up to 2 days, you may stop the cooking process halfway through the simmering time, then complete cooking before serving.

8. Serve hot, garnished with chopped parsley if desired. Rice, couscous, or noodles are a good accompaniment, along with a plain steamed vegetable such as broccoli or green beans.

Note: If preparing in volume, turn out into large hotel pans to cool quickly before storing. This reheats very well, provided you protect from scorching, and holds up well on a buffet.

Marinade for Beef, Lamb, or Game

Yield: 1 pt		½ L
	Ingredients:	
1 cup	olive oil	¼ L
½ cup	dry red or white wine	125 ml
3 oz	brown sugar	85 g
2 tbls	soy sauce	2 tbls
1 tbls	Worcestershire sauce	1 tbls
1 tbls	tarragon vinegar	1 tbls
1	garlic clove, smashed	1
3	halved shallots	3
6	parsley stems	6
6	cracked peppercorns	6
½	bay leaf	½
1 sprig	fresh thyme (or pinch dry)	1 sprig
	For game add:	
1 cup	burgundy	¼ L
6	juniper berries, crushed	6
1 sprig	rosemary	1 sprig
3	whole cloves	3
1	celery heart, with leaves, coarsely chopped	1

1. Combine the first set of ingredients for basic meat marinade, then add additional ingredients for game marinade, if required. Pour over meat and rub on all surfaces. Marinate meat for appropriate time, then drain, pat dry, and cook according to chosen recipe. A used marinade can be boiled, strained, and stored to use in a sauce or to use again as a marinade, enhanced with more fresh herbs and spices. Keep refrigerated.

Note: Most meats gain flavor and tenderness from marinades. Beef tenderloin, for example, while already tender, has little flavor of its own. Many chefs rub the surface with pepper and seasonings, some sear it in butter before roasting, others grill it wrapped in bacon or other fat. The basic marinade flavors the beef and provides a tasty crust to the surface of the meat. It is also useful to flavor a top or bottom round of beef before roasting or braising and is very good as a marinade for boned and butterflied leg of lamb to be grilled. This recipe is sufficient to marinate two or three whole tenderloins, a whole top or bottom round, or two or three boned legs of lamb.

The game marinade should be used for venison, boar, buffalo, rabbit or other game meats. It is also good to use for beef for sauerbraten, muscovy or mallard ducks, or for other game birds when a highly seasoned flavor is desirable. Where extra volume is needed, as when the marinade will be used as the braising liquid or for sauce, the recipe may be factored up at will.

Marinating Time: As a general rule, the more tender and smaller the cut, the shorter the marinating time. Tenderloin of beef or small rabbit loins, for example, will take only a few hours, or at most, overnight. Sauerbraten, or large cuts of wild game will benefit from several days (some up to 2 weeks) of marinating. Obviously, the longer the time, the more pervasive the flavor and tenderizing effect. In addition, a red wine marinade will color the meat, so if you wish a more natural lighter color, use white wine.

Marinating Techniques: It is always safer to marinate meats under refrigeration. This retards the process somewhat but eliminates any risk of contamination. Always use a glass or nonreactive container, or, better, place the meat and its marinade in a large plastic bag, seal well, and place in a pan or dish. This allows you to turn the meat, massaging in the marinade through the plastic, without any mess.

Country Beef Stew

Serves: 10	50		10	50
		Ingredients:		
3 lb	15 lb	boneless chuck or rump	1 kg 350 g	6¾ kg
2 oz	8 oz	all-purpose flour*	60 g	225 g
1 tsp	1 tbls	salt	1 tsp	1 tbls
1½ tsp	3 tsp	ground black pepper	1½ tsp	3 tsp

4 tbls	1 cup	corn or vegetable oil	60 ml	¼ L
10 oz	3 lb	diced onion	300 g	1½ kg
6 oz	2 lb	diced carrot	180 g	900 g
6 oz	2 lb	diced celery	180 g	900 g
4 tbls	1 cup	all-purpose flour*	4 tbls	140 g
8 fl oz	4 cups	dry red wine	¼ L	1 L
12 fl oz	6 cups	beef stock	370 ml	1½ L
2 tbls	½ cup	All-Purpose Demi-glace (see in recipe index	2 tbls	6 tbls
1 cup	3 cups	chopped parsley	¼ L	¾ L
		Garnish vegetables:		
12 oz	4 lb	cubed carrots	350 g	1 kg 750 g
1 lb	5 lb	cubed potatoes	500 g	2½ kg
12 oz	4 lb	pearl onions	350 g	1 kg 750 g
10 oz	3 lb	frozen green peas	285 g	1¼ kg

*If planning to freeze the stew, use mochiko (sweet rice flour) instead of all-purpose flour. It does not lose its thickening power upon freezing.

1. Closely trim the meat of obvious fat and cut into 2-in. (5 cm) cubes.
2. Combine the flour with the salt and pepper, dredge the cubed meat. Heat some of the oil in a heavy pot or Dutch oven and brown the meat, a few pieces at a time. Remove the meat when it is nicely browned on all sides and continue with the balance, adding a bit more oil as needed. Set the meat aside.
3. Add the onions, carrots, and celery to the Dutch oven and cook, stirring occasionally, until the onions begin to soften and the vegetables are lightly colored.
4. Sprinkle the flour over the vegetables in the pan and cook stirring for 3 or 4 minutes until the roux has taken on a light brown color.
5. Stir in the wine and broth and cook for about 10 minutes. Add the demi-glace. Return the meat to the pan, stir well to coat the meat with the sauce. The liquid should just cover the meat. Add a bit more broth if necessary. Simmer on the stovetop or in the oven for about 1½ hours or until the meat is tender. Taste and add more salt and pepper to taste.
6. At this point, the stew may be cooled and held. (For large quantities, cool rapidly in a water bath or by turning out into hotel pans.) Store refrigerated for up to three days or freeze.
7. To finish and serve: Boil or steam the carrots, potatoes, and pearl onions separately until tender. Drain and add to the stew. Thaw the frozen peas and stir into the stew, reserving some for portion garnish if desired.

Note: If preferred, you may eliminate the potatoes and serve buttered noodles or spaetzel as an accompaniment to the stew. If serving as a buffet dish, make the meat cubes smaller, and reduce the simmering time accordingly. Since the peas will overcook on holding, refill chafers frequently, adding a new batch of peas just before serving. Consult a good cookbook or culinary text for a wide selection of beef stews.

Selected Variations: **For Boeuf Bourguignon:** Render lardons (little strips) of salt pork. Use the fat in place of the oil, reserve the lardons to return to the stew with the browned meat. Add a bouquet garni of thyme, bay leaf, and parsley stems to the onions, carrots, and celery, remove when finishing the stew. Use a good Burgundy as the wine. For garnish vegetables, substitute small whole mushrooms and pearl onions, sautéed in butter and flamed with ¼ cup (60 ml) brandy or cognac. Add the vegetables and cognac to the stew.

Carbonnades Flamandes: Render a few bacon slices, chop and reserve the bacon to return to the stew with the meat, and use the bacon fat in place of the oil. Substitute a flavorful dark beer for the wine, add about a tablespoon of sugar to mellow the flavor, finish the sauce with a dash of tarragon vinegar and some minced tarragon. Eliminate the garnish vegetables, serve with steamed and buttered new potatoes instead.

Carbonnada Criolla: Use olive oil for browning; add a cup of diced green pepper and 2 tsp minced garlic to the carrots, celery, and onions; substitute white wine for red; add 1 tsp dried oregano and 2 tbls tomato puree to the sauce before adding the meat. Add a touch of sugar and more pepper to the seasonings. For garnish vegetables, use ½ lb (225 g) each yam (yellow flesh sweet potato) and white potato in small cubes; 2 cups (500 ml) cubed pumpkin or butternut squash, and, at the very end, 2 cubed zucchini and 2 cups (500 ml) corn kernels. This is very dramatic served in a hollowed-out, partially baked pumpkin or a giant, multicolored winter squash. Optional garnish: fresh peach slices.

Tzimmes: To carrots, celery, and onion, add 1 tsp cinnamon, ¼ tsp ground cloves, pinch mace; substitute orange juice for wine; during last half hour of simmering time, add 1 cup (¼ L) each plumped dried apricots and pitted prunes. Simmer over very low heat to avoid scorching, or preferably, oven-braise. If desired, add 1 tbls honey, 2 tbls lemon juice, and more ground pepper to balance sauce flavor. For garnish vegetables, use 12 oz (350 g) each of cubed sweet potatoes, carrots, and pearl onions. Garnish top of stew with a bit of grated rind of lemon, lime, and orange. This stew is traditionally made with beef brisket, but whether you use brisket or chuck, cubed meat makes service easier, especially for buffet.

Hungarian Goulash: Add 2 tsp of minced garlic to the carrots, celery, and onions, along with 1 tsp each marjoram and thyme, and up to 2 tbls Hungarian paprika (hot or sweet, to your taste); add 3 tbls tomato puree to the sauce. The Viennese add a bit of grated lemon rind for piquancy. Or, you may finish the sauce, just before serving with a touch of sugar, more cracked pepper or paprika, and about a cup of sour cream. Remember not to boil after adding the sour cream, or the sauce will curdle. Usually, no garnish vegetables are served with goulash, but you may add butter-sautéed mushrooms and diced green pepper, if you like. Goulash is traditionally served with buttered noodles (you can sprinkle with caraway seeds) or parsleyed boiled potatoes. Boneless pork or veal can be substituted for the beef to make other types of goulash, but be sure to substitute white wine and diluted stock so the beef flavor does not overpower the flavors of the other meats. Since veal has a more delicate flavor, cut back on seasonings accordingly and adjust to taste.

Stifado: Use well-flavored olive oil for browning; add 2 tsp minced garlic, ½ tsp each cinnamon, cumin seed, allspice, oregano, ¼ tsp ground cloves to onion, carrot, and celery; reduce liquid to 1 cup (¼ L) total wine and broth, add 1 cup (¼ L) crushed tomatoes and ¼ cup (60 ml) red wine vinegar; reduce roux flour to 2½ tbls. For garnish vegetables, use 3 lb (1¼ kg) pearl onions only. Garnish top with more chopped parsley. Offer Greek olives and crumbled feta cheese on the side. Serve with orzo, a tiny rice-shaped pasta.

Harvest Beef Stew: Add proportionate amounts of parsnip, white turnip, rutabaga, and celery to the garnish vegetables. Serve with herbed biscuits.

Beef Pot Pie: Top individual portions, or deep-dish casserole with pastry or biscuit crust.

Gravy Variation: Omit the roux flour, instead, thicken the gravy during the last ten minutes cooking time with gingersnap crumbs.

Important: When you vary the garnish vegetables in any of the above versions, you alter the ultimate volume yield. Gauge portions accordingly.

Filet of Beef in a Vegetable Pasta Nest

Serves: 8

	Ingredients:	
8	beef filet mignon steaks or tournedos (3–4 oz [85–115g] each)	8
3 oz	clarified butter	85 g
4 tbls	minced shallots	4 tbls
4 tbls	cognac	60 ml
½ cup	All-Purpose Demi-glace (see in recipe index)	125 ml
	salt and pepper (to taste)	
3 tbls	sweet butter	40 g
	For pasta nest:	
3 tbls	herb butter	40 g
1 lb	fresh angel hair pasta	450 g
1	large carrot	1
1	large zucchini	1
1	large leek	1
1 each	red and yellow bell pepper	1 each
3	large portobello mushrooms	3
4 tbls	minced parsley	4 tbls
4 tbls	minced chives	4 tbls
2 tbls	minced basil leaves	2 tbls

1. Rub the filets all over with cracked black pepper. Let rest at room temperature while preparing vegetables.
2. Scrape the carrot clean, then cut into the finest julienne. Scrub the zucchini, cut into fine julienne. Trim the leek, use the tender white only and cut into fine julienne. Wash the leek pieces in several changes of water to remove grit. Core and seed the peppers. Use a vegetable scraper to make thin slices of pepper flesh, cut those pieces into julienne strips. Clean and trim the mushrooms, reserve stems for another use. Cut the caps into strips. Set all the vegetables aside.
3. Place a large pot of salted water to boil. Fresh egg pasta (especially a thin cut such as angel hair) can cook in less than 1 minute. Therefore, the water should be boiling by the time the steaks are cooked.
4. Heat the clarified butter in a sauté pan, add the steaks and cook over medium heat until well browned on one side, turn and cook on other side until desired degree of doneness, either rare or medium rare. Remove from pan, cover loosely with foil and keep warm.
5. Add the shallots, cognac, and demi-glace to the pan and simmer for several seconds. Remove the pan from the burner but keep warm while preparing the pasta and vegetables.
6. In another sauté pan, heat the herb butter, add the vegetables and sauté until just barely tender. Sprinkle with the fresh herbs and remove from heat.
7. Plunge the fresh pasta into the pot of boiling water. Drain when al dente, toss with vegetables, and hold warm while finishing sauce.
8. Finish the sauce by swirling in the butter. Season with salt and pepper to taste.
9. To plate: Portion pasta and vegetables on each plate, making a space in the center for the beef. Swirl each piece of beef into sauce, and place in center of plate. Spoon more sauce over each beef portion. Serve immediately.

Note: Obviously, this dish cannot be prepared ahead. It is best offered at a seated dinner, with at least two people working the stove and servers ready to rush hot plates to the table.

Norwegian Pot Roast

Serves: 20–25

	Ingredients:	
10 lb	beef top round or venison*	4½ kg
6 tbls	butter and oil	40 g + 45 ml
2 lb	chopped onion	1 kg
1 lb	chopped carrot	450 g
12 oz	chopped celery	340 g
12 oz	chopped parsnip	340 g
2 cups	Marinade for Beef, Lamb, or Game (see in recipe index)	½ L
1 cup	dry red wine	¼ L

6 cups	beef or veal stock	1½ L
1 sachet bag†	bay leaf, 10 peppercorns, 8 parsley stems, thyme, 6 juniper berries, 1 garlic clove	1 sachet bag†
6 oz	tomato paste	180 g
	To finish sauce:	
3 oz	flour	85 g
1 cup	All-Purpose Demi-glace (see in recipe index)	¼ L
6 oz	gjetost (brown Norwegian goat cheese) shredded salt and pepper (to taste)	180 g

Optional: sour cream

*Venison roasts, such as boneless shoulder, are ideal for braising. The roasts should be wrapped with leaf lard and tied. The beef top round needs no larding. Either meat can be marinated for several hours or overnight if you desire a gamier taste to the finished pot roast.
†To assemble the sachet bag, wrap all the items in double cheesecloth and tie securely with string.

1. Pat the roast dry. Heat the oil in a Dutch oven and brown the roasts over medium heat until well browned on all sides. Remove from the pan and set aside.
2. Add the chopped vegetables to the fat in the pan and brown well. Add marinade and wine and simmer and stir for about 10 minutes. Scrape the sides and bottom of the pan well to loosen any browned bits.
3. Return the meat to the pan, add stock to cover, the sachet, and the tomato paste. Stir to blend the paste. Lower the heat to a bare simmer and braise for 2 to 3 hours until the meat is very tender. (You may place the covered casserole in a 300°F (150°C) degree oven, if preferred.) In both cases, check the roast occasionally, turning over, add more stock if needed.
4. When the meat is tender, remove from pan, either set aside to cool for later service or keep warm. Discard the sachet.
5. Degrease the pan juices. Place a few spoons of the fat in a small saucepan, add the flour, and cook to a medium roux.
6. Beat the roux into the pan juices, add the demi-glace, and simmer until reduced by about one-third (you should have about 6–7 cups [1600 ml] sauce).
7. Stir the shredded gjetost into the sauce; it will thicken further. Taste and adjust seasonings. If desired, just before serving stir sour cream into the sauce.
8. Slice the meat and serve with a bit of sauce over the slices. Additional sauce may be served on the side. Serve with roast potatoes, spaetzle, or noodles.

Note: This roast is very good after standing for several hours or overnight. If preparing ahead, add the gjetost to the sauce when reheating. If using the sour cream, do not boil after adding to the sauce. Advance preparation is much more convenient for buffet service. When the roast is well chilled, slice the meat on an electric slicer. Place slices overlapped in hotel or chafing pans, cover with sauce and reheat.

This recipe can be halved, doubled, or otherwise multiplied. The only adjustments to be made are in the amounts of liquid, which should be sufficient to cover the meat in a snug-fitting pot.

Peppered Flank Steak

Serves: 5–6

Ingredients:

2 lb	flank steak	1 kg
½ cup	Marinade for Beef, Lamb, or Game (see in recipe index)	125 ml
2 tbls	cracked black pepper	2 tbls

1. Marinate the flank steak for 2 to 3 hours. Remove from marinade, pat dry, sprinkle pepper on both sides. Let rest at room temperature for about 30 minutes.
2. Preheat a grill or broiler. Broil the meat about 3 or 4 minutes on each side. Flank steak should be cooked rare or it will not be tender and juicy.
3. Rest for at least 5 minutes before slicing if using immediately. For later use, let rest until cool, then wrap well and refrigerate for up to 2 or 3 days. Slice on a sharp diagonal across the grain to make wide, tender slices.

Note: This beef is good sliced and served hot as an entree or for hot beef sandwiches, either in its own juice or with barbecue sauce. Cold, it can be used in sandwiches, for hors d'oeuvre, or in meat salads.

Variations: Other cuts of beefsteak can be marinated and grilled in the same manner to the desired degree of doneness. A thick cut porterhouse, for example, can be marinated (or not) and grilled, cut into thick slices and served with herb butters or béarnaise sauce.

Roast Beef with Vegetable Sauce

Serves: 8–10

Ingredients:

5 lb	boneless roast beef, such as rib eye, strip loin, silver tip, or sirloin	2¼ kg
	ground black pepper	
10 oz	chopped onion	285 g
6 oz	chopped carrot	180 g
6 oz	chopped celery	180 g
½ cup	chopped parsley	125 ml
2	garlic cloves	2
14 oz	crushed tomato	400 g
1 cup	burgundy	¼ L
⅓ cup	All-Purpose Demi-glace (see in recipe index)	80 ml
	salt and pepper (to taste)	

Choose a tender cut that will dry roast well. Be sure to have it wrapped and tied with a layer of fat.

1. Preheat the oven to 500° F (260° C). Rub the surface of the roast with ground black pepper and place on a rack in a shallow roasting pan.
2. Place the roast in the oven and immediately lower the heat to 350° F (180° C). Roast undisturbed for 50 minutes. By that time the surface of the roast should be browned and some fat and juices should have run off into the pan.
3. Remove from the oven, add the vegetables to the pan, seasoning them with a bit of salt and pepper. Remove the rack to add the vegetables if necessary. Place the beef back on the rack, return to the oven and cook for another 20 to 30 minutes or until the internal temperature of the roast is about 125° F to 130° F (52° C to 54° C) for rare to medium rare. Transfer the roast to a platter, tent with foil, and keep warm.
4. Remove the rack and place the roasting pan on the top burners of the stove. Cook over moderately high heat until the vegetables are well cooked and colored. In a separate sauce pan, reduce the wine and demi-glace by one-third. Remove most of the excess fat from the roasting pan and discard. Add the hot wine mixture to the pan and deglaze, scraping all the brown bits from the pan.
5. Transfer the vegetable mixture to a food mill and puree into a thick sauce. Season with salt and pepper.
6. Slice the beef (be sure to let it rest for about 20 minutes to redistribute juices), and serve with the sauce on the side.

Note: This preparation makes very good hot roast beef sandwiches. Use small crusty heros or kaiser rolls, slice the beef paper thin, layer on rolls along with sauce.

Roast Beef Tenderloin

Yield: about 25 slices

Ingredients:

1	whole beef tenderloin, trimmed and tied	1	
1 cup	Marinade for Beef, Lamb, or Game (see in recipe index)	¼ L	
4 tbls	clarified butter for searing	60 ml	

A whole tenderloin of beef, stripped down, usually weighs 3½ to 4 lbs (1500 to 1800 g). Regular trim, which leaves a thin layer of fat and the chain attached, is ordinarily used for dinner cuts, whether the filet is roasted whole or in individual filet mignons. For hors d'oeuvre, or the most pristine appearance for buffet slices, all the fat, the silverskin and chain is removed in what is generally referred to as special trim. Fold the thin tail back on itself and tie so filet has a more even thickness. Tie the whole filet at 1-in. (3 cm) intervals to maintain shape. Or cut off the tail to use separately. A filet of this size, chain removed and tail folded in, will yield at least 25 nice-size slices. Steer filets are preferred.

1. Place the beef in the marinade. Let rest, covered and refrigerated, for several hours or overnight, turning once or twice.
2. Heat the oven to 450°F (230°C). Remove the filet from the marinade and pat dry. Allow to come to room temperature. Heat a heavy roasting pan or fish skillet on the stovetop and add the clarified butter. Sear the filet on all sides for about 5 minutes, then place in the oven and continue to cook, basting and turning two or three times, for about 20 minutes until a meat thermometer registers 120°F to 125°F (49°C to 52°C) at the thick end of the meat. Do not pierce the meat; handle with tongs rather than a meat fork.
3. Remove the meat to a platter to rest for at least 10 minutes before slicing. If serving hot or warm, collect the meat juices to serve over the slices. If serving cold or at room temperature, let the meat cool completely for easiest slicing. Serve with Horseradish Cream (see Smoked Trout with Horseradish Cream in recipe index), with a flavored mayonnaise, or with Barbecue Sauce (see in recipe index). If you are planning to serve the whole filets cold sliced, they can be cooked up to 2 days before use, provided they are well wrapped after roasting and held chilled.

Note: The top of the stove searing gives the meat a nice crust and flavor, but it is a smoky business requiring a well-ventilated kitchen, so this recipe is best prepared ahead in your own space. Or, you can roast totally, allowing about 35 to 40 minutes cooking time. The results will also be very good and the technique is more manageable for an on-site kitchen.

Stir-Fried Beef and Vegetables

Serves: 8–10

Ingredients:

1 oz	mei fun, or rice stick noodles	30 g
1	Peppered Flank Steak (see in recipe index)	1
3 tbls	peanut oil	45 ml
1 tbls	minced garlic	1 tbls
2 tbls	minced gingerroot	2 tbls
1 bunch	scallions, thin sliced	1 bunch
1 each	red and green pepper, cored, seeded, and cut into triangles	1 each
½ lb	trimmed snow peas	225 g
8	water chestnuts, sliced	8
1 cup	cashews or peanuts	¼ L
2 tbls	soy sauce	30 ml

2 tbls	oyster sauce	30 ml
dash	hot chili oil	dash
1 tbls	cornstarch, dissolved in water	1 tbls

1. The mei fun can be prepared ahead. Heat oil in a wok or skillet and add the noodles. As soon as they puff up and crisp, remove to absorbent paper to drain. Set aside.
2. Cut the flank steak into three lengthwise pieces, slice each piece into thin diagonal slices. Set aside.
3. Heat the oil in a wok or skillet, add the garlic and ginger and stir fry until fragrant and barely colored. Add the other vegetables and stir fry or toss until brightly colored. Add the meat and stir fry to heat.
4. Add the soy sauce, oyster sauce and chili oil, toss once or twice, then push the vegetables up the sides of the wok to make a pool of the juices. Add the stirred cornstarch mixture to cook for a few seconds until it turns glossy. Toss all the ingredients together to coat with sauce. Remove from heat and serve with broken mei fun on top.

Note: For volume production, cook in successive batches. Or stir fry batches of vegetables, thicken the sauce, and toss with cooked meat.

Variations: You may substitute shredded cooked chicken, diced ham, strips of cooked pork, or cooked shrimp for the beef.

Stuffed Cabbages

Serves: 6–8

	Ingredients:	
1 head	green cabbage	1 head
2 lbs	ground beef (or beef and pork)	900 g
1	egg, lightly beaten	1
4 tbls	raw rice	4 tbls
1	onion, grated	1
1 tsp	salt	1 tsp
½ tsp	black pepper	½ tsp
1	apple, peeled and thinly-sliced	1
4 tbls	golden raisins	4 tbls
3 tbls	brown sugar	3 tbls
½ cup	water	125 ml
⅓ cup	lemon juice	80 ml
14 oz	canned crushed tomatoes	400 g

1. Rinse the cabbage, cut out the core, and cook in boiling water for about 10 to 15 minutes until leaves are soft enough to loosen. Set aside to drain and cool. When cool enough to handle, peel off the leaves until you reach the tightly curled center. Strip the large outer leaves into two, removing the hard core. Set the leaves aside. Chop up the remains of the cabbage and place in the bottom of a casserole or Dutch oven. Set aside.
2. Combine the ground meat with the egg, rice, grated onion, salt, and pepper. Place a portion of filling on each cabbage leaf (or half leaf), roll up neatly, tucking the edges in to make little pillow or roll shapes.
3. To the casserole, add the sliced apple, the raisins, and the brown sugar. Place the rolled cabbages over the vegetable base. Pour water, lemon juice, and tomatoes over the cabbage rolls.
4. To cook on stovetop, heat Dutch oven until mixture just begins to boil, then lower the heat, and simmer for about 50 minutes to 1 hour until the cabbages are tender and the sauce reduced. If baking in oven, cover and place in a preheated 350°F (180°C) oven. Cook for about 1 hour. In both cases, remove lid during the last few minutes cooking time to reduce excess liquid. Serve the cabbages hot, over some of the base. These may be prepared ahead, refrigerated or frozen, then reheated for service.

Black Bean Chili

Serves: 15–20

Ingredients:

3 tbls	vegetable oil	45 ml
5 lb	chopped or ground beef	2¼ kg
3 lb	chopped onion	1350 g
3 tbls	minced garlic	3 tbls
4 tbls	chili powder	4 tbls
2 tbls	paprika	2 tbls
2 tsp	cayenne powder	2 tsp
2 tsp	salt	2 tsp
1 tsp	cumin	1 tsp
1 tsp	oregano	1 tsp
14 oz	canned crushed tomatoes	400 g
6 oz	tomato paste	180 g
3 lb	cooked, drained black beans*	1350 g
	Garnish: shredded jack cheese, sour cream, salsa, minced pickled jalapeños	

* You may use canned, but better flavor results if you soak and cook the beans with a ham hock and bouquet garni of garlic cloves, bay leaf, parsley stems, thyme, oregano, and cumin.

1. Heat the oil and brown the meat. Add the onions and garlic, and cook until lightly colored. Drain much of the accumulated fat from the pan.
2. Add the spices and cook over medium heat for about 3 minutes. Add the crushed tomatoes and simmer for about 20 minutes. Taste and adjust seasoning.
3. If holding or freezing for later use, cool and store at this point. If preparing for use within 3 days, add the black beans, simmer for another 15 to 20 minutes. Adjust seasonings one final time.
4. Serve with your choice of garnishes.

Venison Scallops with Wild Game Sauce

Serves: 8

Ingredients:

2 lbs	venison, cut into scallops	1 kg
	seasoned flour for dredging	
	butter for sautéeing	
1½ cups	All-Purpose Demi-glace (see in recipe index)	350 ml
2 cups	Marinade for Beef, Lamb, or Game (see in recipe index)	½ L
3 tbls	Dijon mustard	3 tbls
1 tsp	grated unsweetened chocolate	1 tsp
4 tbls	butter to finish sauce	60 g

Slices, each weighing about 2 oz (60 g) can be cut from the saddle, or smaller scallops can be cut from the leg, as one would veal. Either way, they should be thick enough so that, even after pounding lightly, they can be sautéed and still remain medium rare and juicy. This recipe assumes farm-raised venison. If using wild game, marinate in the game marinade for at least 3 days, or up to 2 weeks, then pat dry and slice. Use the marinade in the sauce.

1. Cut or trim the scallops as needed, pound gently to flatten to a thickness of about ¾ in. (2 cm). Wrap and set aside, refrigerated, while preparing sauce.
2. Combine the marinade and the demi-glace in a saucepan and reduce by one-half, skimming during the first few minutes if any scum rises to the top. Set aside, warm, as you prepare the scallops. The sauce will be finished just before serving.
3. Bring the venison to room temperature. Pat dry, dredge in well-seasoned flour. Heat the butter to foaming and sauté the scallops over moderate heat until nicely browned on both sides. Remove to a plate to keep warm.

4. Pour the butter from the pan and discard. Deglaze the pan with the sauce, simmer and scrape all the bits from the pan. Add the mustard and the chocolate. Simmer for 1 or 2 minutes, taste and season with salt and pepper. Add any juices that have accumulated from the venison. Remove the sauce from the heat and swirl in the butter to finish the sauce.

5. Nap warm plate with the sauce and portion the venison. Serve at once with Sautéed Forest Mushrooms (see in recipe index).

Note: This dish, especially if served with the mushrooms, makes a very luxurious entrée for a dinner party. Accompaniments can be shoestring sweet potatoes and parsnips or steamed and buttered fiddlehead ferns or asparagus.

LAMB AND PORK
Grilled Butterfly of Lamb

Serves: 12–14

Ingredients:

1	leg of lamb, boned and butterflied (6 to 7 lb [approx. 3 kg])	1
1 cup	basic Marinade for Beef, Lamb, or Game (see in recipe index)	¼ L
4 tbls	olive oil	60 ml
	salt and pepper (to taste)	

1. Check the lamb to see that the butcher has removed all large pieces of interior fat. You may slash through the thickest portions of meat for even grilling, or separate the thick muscles from the thin for even grilling. Alternately, you may grill the lamb in one piece, resulting in some slices rare, others medium, according to thickness. Rub marinade on lamb, and let rest, covered and refrigerated, for several hours or overnight, turning once or twice.

2. Preheat a grill or broiler. Remove the lamb from the marinade, pat dry, and let come to room temperature. Just before grilling, brush or rub the surface of the meat with the olive oil.

3. Place on the hot grill, and cook, turning frequently to brown evenly until the thick part of the meat reaches 125°F (52°C) for rare. If you grill on an open barbecue, this could take about 40 minutes; if cooked in a closed oven broiler, about 25 to 30 minutes. Toward the end of cooking time, or just before the last turn, sprinkle the cooked side with salt and pepper if desired.

4. Transfer the cooked meat to a cutting board or platter to rest for 15 to 20 minutes before slicing. Slice on a slant across the grain, as one would for flank steak. For the most attractive slices, it is better to cut the meat apart at its natural separations and slice each section. Serve hot plain or with a sauce of your own choosing. Lamb prepared this way is also quite good served at room temperature, as part of a cold meat plate, for sandwiches, or in strips on a salad.

Note: The lamb should be cooked rare, or at least medium rare, for best flavor. People who generally don't like lamb enjoy its flavor served in this way. Lamb prepared according to this recipe makes a good choice for a buffet, served as one would a sliced tenderloin of beef. Or as hearty hors d'oeuvre, with slices served on herb toasts, or strips wrapped in pita bread, or even bite-sized slices served with Horseradish Cream (see Smoked Trout with Horseradish Cream in recipe index) or Lemon-Caper Mayonnaise (see Mayonnaise and Variations in recipe index). Prepared and served as an hors d'oeuvre, one leg of lamb will yield 3–4 dozen pieces.

Lamb Curry

Serves: 12–14

Ingredients:

5 lb	boneless lamb for stew, cut into 1½-in. (4 cm) cubes	2¼ kg
1 lb	diced onion	450 g
4 tbls	minced garlic	4 tbls
3 tbls	curry powder	3 tbls
1 tsp	ground coriander	1 tsp
½ tsp	cumin	½ tsp
2 tsp	ground black pepper	2 tsp
3 tbls	flour	3 tbls
2 cups	dilute meat stock	½ L
3 oz	tomato paste	85 g
1 cup	coconut milk*	¼ L
½ cup	poppy seeds	125 ml
2 oz	finely chopped almonds	60 g
	salt (to taste)	
	Garnishes: rice, slivered almonds, cashews, raisins, chutney, sliced scallions	

*Unsweetened coconut milk, not the sweetened coconut cream used in making piña coladas.

1. Pat the lamb pieces dry. Brown in hot oil, add the onions and garlic, and cook over moderate heat until the vegetables are lightly colored. Add the spices, mix thoroughly and simmer for about 10 minutes.
2. Sprinkle the flour over the meat and vegetables and stir and cook for about 3 minutes until the flour is well absorbed and lightly colored. Add the stock and tomato paste and stir to mix well. Lower the heat and simmer, covered, for about an hour and a half until the meat is very tender.
3. Uncover the curry, degrease, and add the coconut milk, poppy seeds, and almonds. Cook, stirring, for 10 to 15 minutes until the curry is thickened. Taste and add salt and adjust other seasonings as needed.
4. Serve with rice and your choice of accompaniments.

Variations: This recipe may be used for curries of beef or veal as well. The seasonings may need to be adjusted slightly to enhance the flavor of the meats.

Lamb Wrapped in Phyllo with Cabernet Sauce

Serves: 8

	Ingredients:	
3 lb	boneless lamb loin, cut into 16 even slices	1350 g
1 cup	Marinade for Beef, Lamb, or Game (see in recipe index)	¼ L
1 lb	chopped fresh mushrooms	450 g
1 lb	chopped white of leek	450 g
1 cup	minced parsley	¼ L
3 tbls	minced fresh thyme	3 tbls
2 tbls	fresh ground black pepper	2 tbls
½ lb	phyllo leaves	225 g
	butter for sautéeing	
	melted butter and oil	
	For sauce:	
1 qt	cabernet sauvignon	1 L
2	carrots, chopped	2
4	whole garlic cloves	4
8	whole shallots	8
1 cup	All-Purpose Demi-glace (see in recipe index)	¼ L
	salt and pepper (to taste)	
6 tbls	butter	80 g

1. The meat should be well trimmed of any fat. Place the lamb in the marinade and let rest at room temperature for about an hour.
2. Place the chopped mushrooms in a clean cloth, wrap, and wring out tightly to remove excess moisture. Heat some butter in a sauté pan, add the mushrooms and the leeks and sauté until both are browned and reduced. Remove from heat, stir in the herbs and pepper, and set aside.

3. Remove the meat from the marinade, pat the slices dry. Reserve the marinade. Heat butter in a sauté pan, sear the lamb medallions on both sides. Immediately remove to a plate. Stir the marinade into the sauté pan and cook for about a minute to deglaze the pan.

4. Add the marinade to the cabernet sauvignon in a saucepan. Add the carrot, garlic, and shallots. Simmer for about an hour until the vegetables are soft, then add the demi-glace and the accumulated juices from the lamb. Simmer for 10 more minutes. Then remove from heat and hold until ready to finish.

5. To wrap the lamb: Working with one phyllo sheet at a time, lay the phyllo on the work surface, brush with combined melted butter and oil. Spread some of the mushroom leek mixture on each side of the lamb medallion, place in the center of the phyllo, and fold and wrap into a neat package, brushing with some of the melted butter and oil to seal all the folds. Place on a buttered baking sheet, brush with more butter. Continue with all the lamb pieces and the filling until you have 16 neat little bundles. These can rest at cool room temperature for about an hour or be refrigerated for several hours before baking.

6. Preheat the oven to 375°F (190°C). If the lamb has been refrigerated, return to room temperature. Reheat the sauce.

7. Bake the phyllo wrapped lamb for about 10–12 minutes, just until the pastry is golden brown.

8. While the lamb is baking, strain the sauce, pressing gently on the solids, into a clean saucepan, simmer until the sauce is reduced and thick enough to coat a spoon. Season with salt and pepper to taste.

9. When the lamb is done, remove the pan from the oven. Remove the sauce from the heat and swirl in the butter to finish. Nap warm plates with sauce and place two lamb bundles on each plate.

Leg of Lamb with Parsley Mustard Stuffing

Serves: 10–12

	Ingredients:	
1	semiboneless leg of lamb (7 lb [3¼ kg])	1
2 cups	minced parsley	½ L
6 oz	Dijon mustard	180 g
4 tbls	minced shallots	4 tbls
2 tbls	minced garlic	2 tbls
4 tbls	softened butter	60 g
1 cup	dry bread crumbs	¼ L
½ tsp	salt	½ tsp
1 tsp	ground black pepper	1 tsp
3 tbls	olive oil (or as needed)	45 ml
	ground black pepper (as needed)	

The aitch (or hip) bone is removed from the leg, up to the ball joint that connects with the shank bone at the narrow end, forming a pocket or cavity in the wide end of the leg where the flavorful stuffing is inserted. It also makes the lamb very easy to carve. The fell and all but a thin layer of fat should be trimmed from the leg as well.

1. In a food processor or blender, combine the parsley with the mustard, shallots, garlic, softened butter, and bread crumbs to make a paste. Drizzle in a bit of olive oil to moisten the mixture slightly. It should be just spreadable. Stir in the salt and pepper, and set aside.
2. Preheat the oven to 475°F (245°C). Have ready a roasting pan and rack for the lamb.
3. Rub all the surfaces of the lamb with a bit of olive oil. Place about half of the parsley mixture into the cavity and crevices of the lamb. Tie the leg to hold its shape. Place on the rack, sprinkle with pepper, and roast for about 75 to 90 minutes or until it reaches an internal temperature of 135°–140°F (57°–60°C) for rare to medium rare.
4. About 30 minutes before roasting is complete, remove the lamb from the oven to a platter. Quickly pour out all the juices and fat from the roasting pan, using a bit of hot water to deglaze the pan. Set the juices aside. Spread the remaining parsley mixture over the top surface of the leg, replace on the rack in the pan, place in the oven, and continue to cook. If any juices have run from the lamb into the platter, add to the collected pan juices.
5. While the lamb continues to cook, degrease the juices as thoroughly as possible, taste and season with salt and pepper if needed. Keep warm until ready to serve the lamb.
6. When the lamb is properly done, remove from the oven and transfer to a platter to rest for at least 10 minutes before carving.
7. Carve into thin slices. Serve every portion with a bit of stuffing or crust and some of the hot pan juices.

Note: The lamb can be stuffed and prepared for roasting up to one day ahead. Keep well covered and refrigerated. Return to room temperature before roasting (or allow more cooking time).

Milanese and Other Baby Lamb Chops

Yield: 24

Ingredients:

24	small rib lamb chops	24
	salt and pepper	
	flour for dredging	
	egg wash	

1 cup	**dry bread crumbs**	¼ L
1 cup	**grated Parmesan cheese**	¼ L
	olive oil for frying	

1. Trim the chops of all fat. Ideally, you should remove the backbone and the little bone at the corner, leaving the meat attached only to the narrow rib bone. French the rib bone; that is, use a sharp knife to scrape the bone clean from the point where the meat is to the end. Use a meat pounder to gently flatten the meat.
2. Combine the crumbs with the cheese and place in a dish or pan. Put flour in another dredging pan. Prepare a pan of egg wash as well.
3. Salt and pepper the chops on both sides and dredge in flour. Dip into the egg wash and then coat with the cheese and crumb mixture. Pat the crumbs on firmly. Refrigerate the coated chops, loosely covered, for at least an hour. Remove from refrigerator about 20 minutes before cooking.
4. Heat the oil in a skillet. Fry the chops, turning to cook crusty brown on both sides (it should take about 5 minutes total). Transfer to absorbent paper to drain for a minute. Serve hot with lemon wedges. Depending on the balance of the meal, two or three chops makes a generous portion. Serve with a simple hot side dish, such as sautéed spinach or oven roasted potatoes, or with a cold side dish such as Roasted Peppers or Tomato and Basil Salad (see in recipe index).

Note: Baby lamb chops are best for this purpose, but larger chops can be treated in the same way with a slightly longer cooking time. The chops should be cooked rare or medium rare, not well done.

Variations: **Mustard-Coated Lamb Chops:** Prepare the chops as above, but do not flatten too much. Combine Pommery or whole mustard seed mustard with minced parsley and set aside. Place some seasoned bread crumbs in a dredging plate. Preheat the oven to 450° F (230° C) degrees, have ready shallow roasting pans with racks. Coat the chops with the mustard and parsley, dredge in crumbs, patting firmly on each side. Oil the roasting racks, place the coated chops on the rack in the pan. Bake, turning once, for about 6 minutes, until the crust is browned and the meat is rare to medium rare. Serve at once, while piping hot. Serve with grilled tomato or eggplant slices.
Broiled Baby Lamb Chops: Trim the chops and french the bones, as above. Do not flatten the meat. Rub the chops with olive oil, seasoned with garlic or rosemary if you like. Broil or grill the chops quickly to sear and brown on both sides. They should be rare. These make elegant and irresistible hors d'oeuvre, served hot from the grill and seasoned with a bit of salt and pepper. Serve with mint sauce if desired. For this preparation, seek out the tiniest chops you can find and allow at least two per person.

Pastitsio

Serves: 10–12

	Ingredients:	
4 tbls	olive oil	60 ml
12 oz	chopped onion	340 g
2 lb	ground lamb	1 kg
2 tbls	cinnamon	2 tbls
1 tsp	oregano	1 tsp
1 tsp	salt	1 tsp
2 tsp	pepper	2 tsp
14 oz	can crushed tomatoes	400 g
3 tbls	parsley	3 tbls
	For cheese sauce:	
3 cups	milk, scalded	¾ L
4 oz	butter	115 g
2 oz	flour	60 g
2 tbls	farina	2 tbls
6	eggs, lightly beaten	6
1 cup	grated Romano cheese	¼ L
2 cups	shredded cheddar or muenster	½ L
1 lb	cut ziti or elbow macaroni	450 g
	softened butter (as needed)	
	dry bread crumbs for pan	

1. Heat the oil in a large sauté pan, add the onion, cook until wilted, then add the ground lamb and cook until browned. Season with the cinnamon, oregano, salt, and pepper. Add the crushed tomatoes, lower the heat and simmer for at least an hour, until the flavor has mellowed. The completed sauce should be thick rather than liquid. Stir in the parsley and set aside.
2. Prepare the cheese sauce. Heat the butter in a saucepan until foaming. Sprinkle in the flour and the farina, and cook, stirring, over low heat for 2 to 3 minutes. Begin to add the scalded milk, and cook, stirring for about 5 minutes, until thickened. Stir in the grated Romano cheese and remove from heat. Beat in the eggs, until the sauce is smooth. Rub a little softened butter over the top of the sauce and set aside.
3. Preheat the oven to 300°F (150°C). Butter a 2-qt (2 L) shallow ovenproof dish or casserole. Dust the sides and bottom generously with bread crumbs.
4. Cook the pasta until just tender, drain, and toss with a bit of softened butter to prevent sticking.

5. Combine the pasta with some cheese sauce. Spread half the pasta in the bottom of the prepared pan. Sprinkle with one-fourth of the shredded cheese. Spoon all the meat sauce over the pasta layer, sprinkle with another fourth of the shredded cheese. Spread the remaining pasta in the pan, add a fourth more shredded cheese, then top with the remaining cheese sauce. Sprinkle the remaining shredded cheese over the top of the casserole. The prepared pastitsio may be held, covered and refrigerated, for up to 2 days before baking.

6. Bake at 300° F (150° C) for at least 1 hour, until heated through and golden brown on top. Let rest out of the oven for about 15 minutes before cutting into serving portions.

Spinach Stuffed Lamb Chops

Serves: 8

	Ingredients:	
8	**double thick loin lamb chops**	8
3 tbls	**olive oil**	45 ml
2	**cut cloves garlic**	2
	coarsely ground black pepper	
½ recipe	**filling for Spinach Phyllo Triangles (see in recipe index)**	½ recipe

1. Rub the chops with cut garlic cloves and olive oil. Grind black pepper over both sides of chops. Set aside at room temperature for 1 hour.

2. Prepare the spinach and feta filling. Set aside, refrigerated.

3. After the chops have marinated, prepare them for stuffing. Trim all but a thin rim of fat from the chops, leaving the tails attached. With a sharp narrow knife, make a pocket in the loin (larger) side of the chop. Place a portion of stuffing into each pocket, pinching to close the slit. Wrap the tails up to the t-bone of the chop, secure with a toothpick. Force a bit of stuffing between the tail and the chop. Refrigerate until very well chilled. Press excess stuffing into a greased shallow pan, bake to heat through when broiling the chops.

4. When ready to cook, preheat a broiler to its highest setting, position the rack about 3 in. (8 cm) from the flame. Let the chops rest at room temperature for about 20 minutes. Brush the chops with oil, place on the broiler rack and cook for about 4 to 5 minutes on each side, for rare, 6 to 7 minutes for medium rare. Remove the toothpicks, place the chops on hot plates with a portion of extra stuffing and serve.

Note: Grilled tomatoes and garlic roasted potatoes are good accompaniments to this dish.

Drunken Pork

Serves: 6–8

Ingredients:

1	whole loin of pork, boned and tied	1
2 tbls	olive oil	30 ml
2	garlic cloves, smashed	2
3 sprigs	rosemary, or 1 tbls dried	3 sprigs
1	onion, cut in half	1
2 cups	milk	½ L
1 cup	bourbon	¼ L
2 tbls	all-purpose flour	25 g
2 tsp	dry mustard	2 tsp
2 tbls	honey mustard	2 tbls
	salt and pepper (to taste)	
4 tbls	cream (or as needed)	60 ml
	rosemary sprigs for garnish	

1. Heat the oil in a Dutch oven just large enough to hold the pork. Add the garlic, the rosemary, and the onion, cut side down. Cook over moderate heat until the garlic is golden. Remove the garlic. Allow the onion to cook for one or two more minutes until the cut surfaces are browned. Add the pork roast and cook over moderate heat to brown on all sides.

2. When the roast is evenly colored, add the milk, lower the heat to a simmer, cover, and braise for about an hour. The liquid should only approach the simmer but should not boil, so adjust the heat accordingly. Turn the roast once or twice.

3. Add the bourbon, return to the bare simmer, and continue to cook for another 30 to 40 minutes. The pork should be tender and cooked through to 160°–165° F (71°–74° C) internal temperature.

4. When the pork roast is cooked, remove to a platter and keep covered and warm while preparing the sauce.

5. Use a slotted spoon or tongs to remove the rosemary sprigs and onion from the braising liquid. Degrease as much as possible. Discard all but 2 tbls of the fat. Use that fat to prepare a roux with the flour in another saucepan. Cook the roux for 2 to 3 minutes until golden brown. Slowly whisk in the degreased hot pan juices and simmer until the sauce begins to thicken.

6. Stir in both mustards, whisking vigorously to combine. Add as much of the cream as desired, taste and adjust seasonings. Set the sauce aside covered. Keep warm but do not continue to cook.

7. Slice the pork into slices (about ¼ to ½-in. [¾–1 cm] thick) and place on plates or in a hot serving platter. Nap with some of the sauce, pass the rest on the side. Garnish with rosemary sprigs if desired.

Note: While the meat cooks in the milk, it will separate and curdle, forming lots of little brown bits. This is fine, they add color and an interesting taste to the sauce. To prepare ahead, roast the pork, let rest at room temperature for at least 20 minutes, then slice, arrange in a heatproof serving dish, wrap well and refrigerate. Prepare the sauce up to the point of adding the cream and final seasonings. On site, reheat the pork gently in a microwave or a low oven. Keep covered so it stays moist. Reheat the sauce, finish with cream, and serve as above.

Cooking Note: As pork is bred leaner, there is a greater danger of a dry finished product, so be very sure to cook gently. Don't overbrown at the start and braise over the gentlest possible heat for best results.

Glazed Pork Loin with Sauerkraut

Serves: 8

Ingredients:

1	loin of pork, bone in	1
½ cup	tomato ketchup or chili sauce	125 ml
¾ cup	deli mustard (for example, Gulden's)	180 ml
2 tbls	dried rosemary	2 tbls
1 tbls	ground pepper	1 tbls
1 cup	apple juice	¼ L
1 lb	drained sauerkraut	500 g
1	large onion, thinly sliced	1
1 cup	savoy cabbage, thinly sliced	¼ L
2 tbls	brown sugar (or to taste)	2 tbls
2 tbls	cider vinegar (or to taste)	30 ml

The center cut is preferred, yielding thick uniform chops when sliced into portions, but the entire loin is succulent. Determine the required number of cuts or slices per person and order accordingly. Be sure to remove, or have the butcher remove, the chine bone and crack the bones so the roast can be easily and evenly carved.

1. Preheat the oven to 325°F (165°C). Combine the ketchup, mustard, rosemary, and pepper. Score the fat on the top of the roast, and rub in the coating, smearing over the ends of the meat as well. If any of the mixture is left over, spoon over top.
2. Place the roast on a rack (or use the chine bone in place of a rack). Place in the preheated oven and roast, undisturbed and uncovered for 1 hour.
3. Remove some of the fat from the roasting pan to a saucepan. Heat the fat, add the onion and cook over moderately high heat until medium brown. Add the savoy cabbage and cook, stirring, until the cabbage wilts and becomes tender. Remove from heat and stir in the sauerkraut.

4. After about 1 hour's cooking time, the roast will have begun to brown. Remove from oven, remove the roast and rack from the pan, add the prepared vegetables, and replace the roast over the vegetables. Return to the oven and continue to cook for another 1 to 1½ hours. The internal temperature of the roast should reach 160° F (71° C). At that point, remove the roast from the pan, cover and keep warm while finishing the vegetables.

5. Place the roasting pan on the stove top, skim off some excess fat, add the apple juice and cook over high heat, scraping all the browned bits from the bottom and sides of the pan. Taste the vegetables, season with a bit of pepper, if needed, and a bit of brown sugar and/or vinegar to achieve a pleasant sweet-sour taste.

6. Carve the roast, either into thick full chops, or into alternating thin chops and boneless slices. Serve with sauerkraut mixture on the side. Accompany with oven roasted potatoes, mashed potatoes, root vegetable puree or applesauce.

Variation: Prepare a coating of honey mustard and applesauce, sprinkle with mustard seeds or rosemary. Use sliced apples and onions along with the sauerkraut, eliminate the savoy cabbage.

Loin of Pork with Onion Fruit Sauce

Serves: 8

	Ingredients:	
6 lb	boneless pork loin	2¾ k
	For marinade:	
2	minced garlic cloves	2
3 tbls	applejack (or sauterne)	45 ml
2 tbls	minced parsley	2 tbls
1 tsp	powdered thyme	1 tsp
1 tsp	allspice	1 tsp
2 tbls	cracked pepper	2 tbls
4 tbls	vegetable oil	60 ml
	For stuffing:	
½ cup	each: chopped apple, shallots, parsley, plumped currants, whole shelled pistachios	125 ml
2 tbls	butter, softened	30 g
½ tsp	salt	½ tsp
1 tsp	ground black pepper	1 tsp

	For sauce:	
8	dried apricots	8
½ cup	dry white wine	125 ml
12 fl oz	Sweet and Sour Onion Jam (see in recipe index)	350 ml
3 tbls	All-Purpose Demi-glace (see in recipe index)	3 tbls

1. Combine the marinade ingredients and rub into all the surfaces of the roast. Place in a plastic bag in a pan and marinate overnight, turning once or twice.
2. Prepare the stuffing: Mix the chopped apple, shallots, and parsley into the softened butter to make a lumpy paste. Stir in the pistachios and currants. Set aside, refrigerated until ready to use.
3. Preheat the oven to 325°F (165°C). Remove the roast from the marinade and pat dry.
4. To stuff the roast: Use a larding needle or a clean sharpening steel to make three tunnels lengthwise in the roast. Force the stuffing into the tunnels. If any extra remains, stuff it into any crevices in the roast. Tie the roast securely and place, fat side up, on a rack in a shallow roasting pan. Total roasting time will be between 2 and 2½ hours, until the roast reaches an internal temperature of 160°F (71°C).
5. Begin the sauce: Simmer the apricots in the wine until plumped and very soft. Puree in a processor or food mill. Either process with or stir in the onion jam. Just before the roast is done, spread a thin coating of this mixture over the top of the roast. When the roast is cooked, remove to a platter, cover and keep warm.
6. Degrease the pan juices as much as possible. Place the pan on the stovetop burners, add the demi-glace and a bit of water, and deglaze over moderately high heat. Add the liquid to the apricot and onion puree. Season with salt and pepper to taste. (If the sauce seems too sweet, add a splash of balsamic vinegar to balance flavor.)
7. Carve the roast into medium thick slices, placing a portion of sauce under the slices if serving on individual plates. If serving plattered, slice the roast arranging the slices attractively around the perimeter of the platter. Place a mound of sauce in the center and serve the remainder in a sauceboat.

Note: This roast can be served at cool room temperature as follows: Omit the sauce glazing step in final stage of roasting. After the roast has cooled completely, trim off the external fat cover, roll the outside of the roast in a mixture of chopped parsley and pistachios. Slice thin. The sauce may be served warm or at cool room temperature. If planning to serve cool, prepare ahead, cooking it down to thicken. Chill and remove any grease that forms on the top. Adjust seasonings: Cold, the sauce will need additional salt and pepper.

Variation: A boned fresh ham can be prepared in the same manner. One weighing about 15 lb (6¾ kg) will serve about 25 people. Multiply the stuffing and sauce ingredients by three, double the marinade ingredients. Marinate the ham for at least 1 day, preferably 36 hours. After stuffing, roll the ham into shape, score the skin or fat, and tie securely. Begin roasting in a 400°F (205°C) oven for the first hour, then reduce heat to 350°F (180°C) and continue to cook for about 2 to 3 hours until proper internal temperature, 160°F (71°C), is reached.

Pork Tenderloin with Mustard Currant Glaze

Serves: 4–6

Ingredients:

2	whole pork tenderloins	2
	seasoned flour for dredging	
3 tbls	butter and oil combined	3 tbls
4 tbls	minced shallots	4 tbls
4 tbls	sherry vinegar	60 ml
3 tbls	currants	3 tbls
½ cup	All-Purpose Demi-glace (see in recipe index)	125 ml
4 tbls	Dijon mustard	4 tbls
	salt and pepper (to taste)	

Whole pork tenderloins are the tenderloin, or filet, of the loin, about 1 in. (2½ cm) in diameter, about 8- to 10-in. (20 to 23 cm) long. They usually weigh slightly less than 1 pound (450 g). They are very tender and juicy if properly cooked. About 6 to 7 minutes total cooking time will result in a succulent and safe product.

1. Cut the tenderloins into slices about 1½-in. (4 cm) thick. Pat each slice to flatten slightly. Set aside. Place the currants in the vinegar to plump.
2. Heat the butter and oil in a sauté pan. Dredge the pork pieces in seasoned flour, and sauté over medium heat, just until browned on both sides, about 2 to 3 minutes. Remove to a plate and keep warm.
3. Add the shallots to the pan. Add the demi-glace, the mustard, and the currants to deglaze the pan. Cook, stirring, until well blended. Return the pork and accumulated juices to the pan, lower the heat, and simmer for 3 to 4 minutes, turning the pork over once or twice in the sauce. Be sure that the heat is low enough so that the pork has time to cook without drying out. Portion the pork and sauce onto hot plates (two or three slices per person).

Note: Good accompaniments for this dish are Spinach with Pears and Port (see in recipe index) and either mashed potatoes or Root Vegetable Puree (see in recipe index).

Sweet and Sour Spareribs

Serves: 10

Ingredients:

6 lb	**pork spareribs (or baby backs)**	2 kg 700 g
10 oz	**bottled chili sauce**	280 g
12 oz	**crushed pineapple**	336 g
1	**garlic clove, smashed**	1
1 tbls	**dry mustard**	1 tbls
3 tbls	**cider vinegar (or to taste)**	45 ml
4 oz	**dark brown sugar**	112 g

If serving as an hors d'oeuvre or at a buffet, have the butcher saw the ribs crosswise for smaller pieces. You can then split them into manageable pieces. For clients who choose not to eat pork, you may use beef ribs (these are very large and must be cut on a bandsaw), veal ribs, or lamb riblets. The beef and veal will require less precooking than pork. The lamb should be baked to reduce fat. The lamb fat must be discarded, then continue with recipe in a clean pan.

1. Cut the ribs into pieces or portions, if desired. For table service, whole racks of baby backs, split but not completely severed, should be served.
2. Combine the other ingredients to make a pasty sauce. Taste and adjust for seasonings. Set aside.
3. Place the ribs in open roasting pans and bake at 300° F (150° C) for about 1 hour, turning once or twice. Drain fat from pan, brush with a little of the sauce, add about ½ cup (125 ml) water to pan, cover and continue to bake for another hour. Turn once or twice, add a splash more water to prevent sticking if necessary.
4. At this point, the ribs should be almost completely cooked and tender. Remove the pan cover, brush lavishly with sauce, and cook for 30 to 45 minutes. When the ribs are browned and tender, and the sauce has crisped the edges, they are ready. Remove from pan, leaving behind excess grease, and serve hot.
5. Ribs may be prepared and then stored, covered and refrigerated up to 3 days ahead. Reheat gently to avoid scorching. After cooking or reheating, hold covered in a moderate oven.
6. Serve plain, or with an oriental dipping sauce such as Spicy Plum Sauce, Szechuan Chili Sauce, or Chutney Dipping Sauce (see in recipe index).

Note: For grill or barbecue, precook almost completely and finish on grill.

About yield: This recipe will serve 10 when ribs are served as one of a selection of hot hors d'oeuvre or as part of a buffet. When serving ribs to young people in general (young men in particular), all bets are off! Such guests can consume prodigious amounts of ribs, so plan accordingly.

Variations: This sauce is a generalized "Polynesian" type. A more sophisticated audience might enjoy ribs that have been marinated as for Pork Sate or Curried Lamb Sate (see in recipe index). For a more American style barbecue, use Barbecue Sauce (see in recipe index) as the basting sauce. Serve additional sauce, some mild, some hot, some hotter, for dipping on the side.

FISH AND SHELLFISH
Paella

Serves: 16–20

Ingredients:

3 lb	**Italian or Spanish sausage***	1350 g
3	**frying chickens, cut up**	3
2 tbls	**minced garlic**	2 tbls
1 cup	**chopped onion**	¼ L
3 pkg	**Sason accent†**	3 pkg
2 tsp	**chicken bouillon powder**	2 tsp
2 cups	**raw converted rice**	½ L
4½ cups	**diluted chicken broth**	1¼ L

For seafood:
30 medium shrimp, 30 mussels, 30 clams

½ cup	**white wine**	125 ml

Garnish: 1 lb (450 g) frozen peas, 3 roasted peppers or pimientos, cut
in strips

*Select a combination of sweet and hot sausages according to taste.
†Goya distributes Sason accent, a flavoring powder for Spanish dishes.

1. Shell and devein the shrimp. Scrub the clams and mussels. Set all the seafood aside, refrigerated, until ready to cook.
2. In a large Dutch oven or heavy pot, brown the sausages, then lower heat and prick here and there to render fat. Fry gently until cooked through, or brown and finish cooking in oven. Set sausages aside. When they cool slightly, slice into thick chunks.
3. Brown the chicken pieces in the rendered sausage fat, turning to color on all sides. Lower the heat and cover. Simmer gently until cooked through or finish cooking in the oven. Set aside when cooked.
4. Remove all but 4 tbls (60 ml) of fat from the pan and discard. Add the onion and the garlic and cook over medium heat until soft and lightly colored. Stir in the Sason and the bouillon powder, cook to dissolve.
5. Add the rice to the pot, sauté for 2 or 3 minutes. Add the stock, lower the heat to a simmer, cover the pot and cook for 20 to 25 minutes until the rice is just tender. Remove from heat while preparing the seafood.
6. In a separate pot, steam the seafood with the wine until the shrimp turn pink and the mussels and clams open. Pick over and discard any unopened shells.
7. When the rice has cooked and absorbed most of the liquid in the pot, return the cut sausages and chicken pieces to the rice. Turn carefully to submerge most of the items in the rice. Cover the pot and simmer gently just to heat through.

8. Add the seafood, again cover the pot for a few minutes and simmer until all ingredients are heated through. Just before serving, heat the peas, stir some of the peas and the peppers into the paella. Garnish the top with the rest.

Note: To prepare ahead, take recipe through step 5. Pack and transport all components chilled. On site, turn the prepared rice into hotel pans, add a bit more broth and the sausage and chicken. Reheat gently, covered. Just before serving, prepare the seafood, add to paella along with garnish vegetables, and serve.

Seafood Terrine Mosaic

Serves: 12–14

Ingredients:

For plain mousse:

20 oz	**boneless scrod or flounder**	560 g
12 oz	**sea scallops**	340 g
2	**whole eggs**	2
1 tbls	**minced shallot**	1 tbls
1½ tsp	**salt**	1½ tsp
½ tsp	**white pepper**	½ tsp
pinch	**nutmeg**	pinch
2 tbls	**lemon juice**	30 ml
2 tbls	**cognac**	30 ml
2–3 cups	**heavy cream**	½–¾ L

For herb mousse: 3 tbls (45 ml) white wine; 2 tbls each minced dill, parsley, chives, shallots; few leaves spinach and watercress

For Mosaic: ½ lb (225 g) salmon filet, 5–6 large sea scallops, few leaves blanched spinach, softened butter (as needed)

1. Carefully pick over the fish for any bones; if using flounder, remove the bone seam if any. Puree the fish in a food processor until smooth. Transfer to a sieve and press through to remove any fibers. Set aside, well chilled.
2. Rinse the scallops, pat dry, remove the tiny side muscle or sinew and discard. Set aside, well chilled.
3. Prepare the herb mixture: Simmer the herbs, shallots, spinach, and watercress leaves in the wine until the liquid is completely reduced. Puree to liquefy. Set aside, chilled. Wash the processor bowl thoroughly.

4. Pick over the salmon to remove any fine bones, slice as you would smoked salmon to make the largest possible slices, and discard the skin. Place the salmon slices between sheets of waxed paper or plastic wrap and pound gently to flatten. Refrigerate. Remove the tiny side muscles from the large sea scallops, rinse and pat dry. Strip the stems from the spinach leaves, and wrap each scallop in spinach. Set aside, well wrapped. Chill.

5. Prepare a pan or terrine mold, with a capacity of at least 6 cups (1½ L). Butter well, line with parchment or waxed paper, and butter the paper. Cut another piece of paper just large enough to cover the top of the pan, butter and set aside. Cut a piece of aluminum foil large enough to cover the top of the pan and set aside. You will also need a larger pan to serve as a water bath for the terrine. Preheat the oven to 325°F (165°C).

6. In the bowl of the processor, place the pureed fish and the 12 oz. (340 g) of sea scallops, and pulse a few times. Add the eggs, shallots, salt, white pepper, nutmeg, lemon juice, and cognac, and pulse to puree. Scrape down the bowl repeatedly to achieve a homogenous texture.

7. With the machine motor running, add the cream. Add up to 2 cups (500 ml) and check the texture of the mousse and the seasonings. Add more salt and pepper if needed. Continue to add cream while pureeing until the mousse has the consistency of softly whipped cream. It should just hold its shape in a spoon. Remove about half the mixture from the processor, and set aside, chilled. Add the herb mixture to the remaining mousse, pulse once or twice to combine, and set aside. Taste and stir in some salt, pepper, and nutmeg if desired.

8. Assemble the terrine as follows: Place half of the herb mousse in the bottom of the mold, smooth even and thump the pan to remove air pockets. Place half the pounded salmon slices to cover the layer of mousse, piecing if necessary. Add half of the plain mousse over the salmon, then position the spinach-wrapped scallops in a row down the center of the pan. Carefully cover the scallops with the rest of the plain mousse, then layer with salmon slices, and cover with the rest of the herb mousse. Smooth with a wet spatula to even the top. Thump the pan again to release air pockets.

9. Cover the top of the mousse with the prepared paper, buttered side down, then cover with foil. Do not make the foil tight over the top, just crimp the foil to the edges of the pan. The mousse will expand when baking, so you want a sealed, but loose, covering. Place the terrine in the larger pan, place in the preheated oven, and pour in water to reach to at least half the depth of the terrine. Bake for about 70 minutes, then check the mousse. When properly done, it will have puffed slightly and just appear to separate from the edges of the mold. Its internal temperature will be 160°F (71°C). It may need 10 to 20 minutes more baking time.

10. When done, remove from the oven and the water bath and allow to rest for at least 20 minutes before unmolding. It may be served warm or chilled.

11. Before unmolding, remove the foil, and pressing gently on the top of the terrine, tip the pan to collect cooking juices. This will make a delicious base for a sauce for the warm mousse. Place in a saucepan, add more white wine or champagne, boil down for a few minutes, reseason with salt and white pepper, add a touch of tomato paste and some reduced heavy cream.

12. To unmold, invert on a serving platter or board, carefully peel off the paper liner, and blot any excess moisture from the surface. Use a thin, sharp knife to slice.
13. If serving cold, serve with herb or green mayonnaise.

Note: This basic mousse recipe and procedure is referred to in different recipes calling for such a basic preparation, as in Paupiettes of Sole (see in recipe index).

Stuffed Jumbo Shrimp

Yield: 12 shrimp

Ingredients:

12	jumbo shrimp (U-8s or U-10s)	12
6 oz	butter or margarine	180 g
4 fl oz	olive oil	125 ml
½ cup	lemon juice	125 ml
2 tbls	minced shallots	2 tbls
1 cup	chopped parsley	¼ L
2 cups	dry bread crumbs (or as needed)	350 g
	salt and pepper (to taste)	
1 cup	dry white wine	¼ L

1. Rinse the shrimp. Use a shears or sharp knife to split the shell along the curved edge, almost to the tail. Split the shrimp almost through to butterfly. Open and flatten out.
2. Melt the butter with the olive oil. Brush some on the bottom of a baking pan just large enough to hold the shrimp.
3. Combine all but 2 tbls of the butter and oil with the lemon juice, shallots, and parsley. Add just enough bread crumbs to make a loose paste. Season with salt and pepper to taste.
4. Place some of the bread mixture on each of the shrimp to stuff. They may be set aside, covered and refrigerated for up to a day at this point. Remove from the refrigerator about 30 minutes before baking.
5. Preheat the oven to 375°F (190°C). Sprinkle some of the wine over each of the shrimp, pour the remaining wine into the pan. Drizzle a bit of the melted butter mixture over the shrimp. Bake for about 10 to 15 minutes, just until the shrimp begin to turn pink. Run under a broiler to brown the crumbs for a minute or two if desired. Serve hot, moistened with some of the pan juices.

Note: Two of these make a substantial serving.

Variation: You may add chopped raw shrimp or flaked crabmeat to the filling.

Salmon and Sole Paupiettes

Serves: 12

Ingredients:

6	sole or flounder fillets	6
6–8 slices	smoked salmon or gravlax (enough to cover sole)	6–8
	For spinach mousse:	
4 oz	blanched chopped spinach	115 g
10 oz	scallops	285 g
1	egg	1
1 tsp	salt	1 tsp
½ tsp	white pepper	½ tsp
¼ tsp	nutmeg	¼ tsp
2 tbls	lemon juice	30 ml
1 cup	heavy cream	¼ L
	softened butter (as needed)	
4 oz	minced mushrooms	115 g
3 tbls	minced shallots	3 tbls
½ cup	white wine	¼ L
2 tbls	cognac	30 ml
3 tbls	heavy cream	45 ml
2	egg yolks	2
	salt and white pepper (to taste)	

1. Split the sole or flounder fillet in half, removing the bone seam. Set aside.
2. Rinse the scallops, pat dry, and remove side muscle. Place the spinach, scallops, egg, salt, pepper, nutmeg, and lemon juice in a food processor and puree until smooth. Gradually add the heavy cream and pulse until the mousse is a soft, spoonable consistency. Set aside, chilled.
3. Prepare a baking pan by smearing with melted butter. Scatter the shallots and mushrooms over the surface of the pan.
4. Prepare the paupiettes as follows: Lay the fillets, skin side up, on a work surface. Cover evenly and neatly with pieces of smoked salmon or gravlax. Divide the spinach mousse among the fish pieces, placing a mound of mousse at the wide end of the fillets. Roll closed and stand upright in the prepared pan. The paupiettes can be held refrigerated for several hours or up to one day before baking. Pour the wine over before baking.
5. To bake: preheat the oven to 350°F (180°C). Cover the paupiettes with a sheet of buttered parchment, then cover the pan loosely with foil. Bake for 20 to 25 minutes until the mousse has puffed and firmed slightly. Remove from the oven and carefully transfer the paupiettes to a plate or pan. Cover loosely and keep warm.

6. Empty the contents of the baking pan into a saucepan. Add the cognac and cook down for 1 or 2 minutes. In a small bowl, beat the yolks with the cream, add a bit of the hot juices, return to the saucepan, and simmer stirring for a minute or two until sauce has thickened. Season with salt and pepper. Serve under or alongside the paupiettes.

Variation: The paupiettes may be filled with plain or herb mousse (see in recipe index for Paupiettes of Sole) if desired.

Paupiettes of Sole

Serves: 12

Ingredients:

6	sole or flounder fillets	6
½ recipe	plain fish mousse*	½ recipe

For herb mousse: See Seafood Terrine Mosaic (see in recipe index)
   or

For salmon mousse: 2 slices smoked salmon
   or

For creole filling: 2 slices stale sandwich bread, 2 tbls each minced onion, scallion, green pepper, celery, parsley, pinch of thyme, dash hot sauce, 2 tbls (30 ml) olive oil, 1 egg yolk

salt and pepper (to taste)
softened butter (as needed)

	For pan sauces:	
1 cup	dry white wine	¼ L
1 cup	mussel or fish stock	¼ L
3	shallots, chopped	3
1 cup	cream	¼ L
4 tbls combined	minced dill, parsley, chives	4 tbls combined
1 cup	Spicy Tomato Sauce (see in recipe index)	¼ L

*The recipe for Seafood Terrine Mosaic contains a plain white mousse recipe, as well as the additions to convert that to an herb mousse. The same basic procedure is used here. Select your choice of filling from either herb, salmon, or creole. For salmon, puree smoked salmon and stir into plain mousse.

1. Prepare the fillets as follows: Split in half lengthwise, removing the bone seam. Determine the outside (or what was the skin side of the fish), stack skin side up in a plate or pan, cover, and keep cold while preparing your choice of filling.
2. If using the mousse recipes, prepare and set aside, chilled.
3. To prepare creole filling: Cut the bread slices into small cubes. Heat the olive oil in a sauté pan, toss in the bread cubes and brown lightly, remove and set aside. Sauté the onion, scallion, green pepper, and celery. Cook stirring until the vegetables begin to soften and color slightly. Add the parsley and other seasoning and salt and pepper to taste. Remove from heat. After a few minutes, stir in the egg yolk, mixing thoroughly. Stir in the bread cubes. Set aside.
4. To stuff and roll paupiettes: Lay the fish, skin side up, on a work surface. Divide the selected filling among the pieces, placing a mound of filling at the wide end of each fillet half. Roll up to enclose filling and stand upright.
5. Preheat the oven to 350° F (180° C). Select a baking pan just large enough to hold the paupiettes, and grease generously with the melted butter. Scatter about half of the shallots over the bottom of the pan. Place the paupiettes in the pan, close together but not crowded. Pour half the wine and half the fish stock into the pan. Place a sheet of buttered parchment lightly on the top of the paupiettes. Cover pan loosely with foil.
6. Bake covered for 15 to 20 minutes. Cooking time will vary according to the size and thickness of the fish. The paupiettes are done when they puff slightly and have firmed up a bit. Do not overcook. Remove from the oven and drain the cooking juices into a saucepan. Keep the paupiettes warm while preparing appropriate sauce.
7. To prepare sauces: Add the remaining wine, fish stock, and shallots to the cooking juices. Reduce by half. To make Cream Sauce for herbed paupiettes, add reduced cream, season with salt and pepper. To make Herb Sauce for salmon paupiettes, add minced herbs, cream, and salt and pepper. For creole-filled paupiettes, combine reduced wine and fish stock with Spicy Tomato Sauce.
8. Serve sauce under or alongside paupiettes.

Note: To portion, serve one or two as a first or fish course; two or three as a main course. For volume or buffet service, adopt the following procedure: Prepare and fill the paupiettes a few hours or up to 1 day ahead. Keep covered and well chilled at all times, especially during transport, as raw fish and egg are subject to spoilage. On site, prepare a selected sauce from scratch, using increased amounts of shallots, wine, and fish stock. Bake pans of paupiettes in sequence to supply buffet, setting aside the cooking juices for another use or adding them to the sauce as you go along. The mousse-filled paupiettes can be cooked ahead, refrigerated, and then reheated in a water bath, until they are heated through. If you are careful not to overcook during the first baking, they will repuff and reheat nicely. Do not attempt to freeze as the fish will lose texture.

Salmon with Horseradish Mustard Crust

Serves: 8

Ingredients:

8	centercut salmon fillets (each about 8 oz [225 g])	8
1½ cup	strong prepared horseradish	350 ml
1 cup	Pommery mustard	¼ L
½ cup	heavy cream	125 ml
2 tbls	dry bread crumbs	2 tbls
	olive oil (as needed)	

Select portion size you desire depending on whether this recipe is being served as a lunch or dinner main course, as a first course, or a fish course. The center cuts are preferred for their even thickness, but the thinner end cuts will taste just as good if the cooking time is reduced.

1. Trim any excess fat or skin from the outside edges of the salmon pieces. Rub your fingers carefully over the salmon flesh to find small bones. Remove these with tweezers or needle-nose pliers. Keep the fish cold until ready to cook.
2. Preheat a broiler, set the rack about 4 in. (10 cm) from the flame.
3. Mix the horseradish, mustard, and cream. Add just a bit of bread crumbs, stir and rest for a few minutes until the crumbs have had time to absorb moisture. The mixture should be a thick spread, not watery, but not stiff and dry. If still too wet after a few minutes, add a bit more crumb; if too dry, add a few drops of cream or water.
4. Rub a baking sheet or shallow pan with oil. Spread the horseradish mixture evenly on the fleshy surface of the salmon fillets. Be sure to completely cover all the flesh. (If using end cuts, spread the mixture a bit thicker on the thin ends to protect them from overcooking.) Place the coated fish on the oiled pan, placing the thicker pieces toward the center of the pan, directly under the flame, the thinner pieces along the side of the pan where they will receive less direct heat.
5. Broil for 3 to 4 minutes, until the crust has firmed up and become lightly speckled with brown, and the flesh has firmed up somewhat. Very thick cuts may require a minute or two more cooking but check carefully, so as not to overcook the salmon. Do not turn the fish.
6. Serve at once on hot plates. These need no sauce. If properly cooked, the salmon flesh will still be very moist and juicy beneath the crisp crust. Garnish plates, if desired, with a sprig of dill or lemon wedge.

Note: Individual filleted small Coho salmon or salmon trout may be prepared in the same manner. The flesh will be much thinner, so will require less cooking time, possibly only two minutes total.

Variations: You may substitute any whole-mustard-seed mustard in this recipe. Some of these mustards are flavored with different herbs, some are slightly sweetened — each will lend its own distinction.

Dill Mustard Crust: Eliminate the horseradish, add about 1 cup (¼ L) of minced fresh dill to the mustard and cream, adjust crumbs for proper consistency. Salt and pepper the salmon before coating. Cook as above.

About Fish Steaks

This is not a recipe but a reminder that steak cuts of fish, such as salmon, tuna, halibut, shark, and swordfish, are both well received and easy to prepare. All respond well to simple broiling, grilling, or oven baking. Brush the fish with oil or melted butter before grilling and be sure not to overcook. Tuna, in particular, is most delicious when served rare or medium rare. Use thick cuts for the best results. These preparations need little more than a pat of seasoned compound butter to make a finished dish. Salmon, halibut, and swordfish are also very good poached in a flavorful court bouillon (basically wine and herbs, see a culinary text). Served hot, they are enhanced by a simple wine and butter sauce, a hollandaise, or a bearnaise. Chilled poached fish is very good with a green or other flavored mayonnaise, or, in the case of swordfish, Sesame Soy Dipping Sauce (see in recipe index).

Lobster with Ginger Cream

Serves: 8

Ingredients:

4	live lobsters (about 1¼ lb [560 g] each)	4
2 cups	fish, mussel, or shellfish stock	½ L
1 cup	dry white wine	¼ L
1	bay leaf	1
few	parsley stems	few
1	clove garlic	1
4	cracked peppercorns	4
2 tbls	fresh white breadcrumbs	2 tbls
2 oz	chopped gingerroot	56 g
1 cup	heavy cream	¼ L
2	egg yolks	2
½ cup	dry sherry	125 ml
pinch	sugar	pinch
	salt and white pepper (to taste)	
	Garnish: few pieces pickled ginger, few sprigs cilantro	

1. Combine the fish stock, wine, bay leaf, parsley stem, garlic, and peppercorns in a large pot, and bring to the boil. Add the lobster, cover, and cook for about 10 minutes. Remove from heat.

2. As soon as the lobsters are cool enough to handle, carefully split in two. Remove the sand sac at the head and the intestinal vein and discard. Scoop out the coral and liver and place in a small bowl. Remove the feelers and add to the stock. Separate the claws from the body. Carefully crack the claws to remove the meat in one piece. Crack the knuckle joints and pick out any meat. Add the shells to the stock pot and the bits of knuckle meat to the bowl holding the coral and liver. Pour a bit of stock over the claw meat to moisten and set aside. Cover and keep warm in an ovenproof dish or pan.

3. To the stock pot, add the gingerroot and boil down to reduce by one-third. Puree, shells and all, in a food processor, and pass through a fine sieve or food mill to extract all the juice. Add a little water if needed to get all the flavor from the solids. Put the strained liquid in a clean saucepan, add the sherry and reduce to 1½ cups (350 ml).

4. In a separate bowl, combine the cream with the yolks, mix in hot stock to warm, return to the saucepan and simmer for a minute or two to thicken. Taste, add the pinch of sugar if needed and salt and white pepper to taste.

5. Add the bread crumbs to the coral, liver, and knuckle meat. Moisten with a bit of cream sauce. Place some of this mixture in the body cavities of the reserved lobster halves. Reheat the lobster halves and claw pieces for 1 or 2 minutes.

6. To serve: Mask each of eight hot plates with sauce. On each, place one lobster half and the meat of one claw in an attractive arrangement. Place a curl of pickled ginger and a cilantro leaf as an accent on the plate. If you have extra sauce, you may place some on the tail meat, or serve on the side. Serve hot.

Note: To prepare ahead: Cook the lobsters, prepare as above, but do not stuff until ready to serve. Reheat the bodies and claw meat over a steamer or in a water bath on site. Prepare the sauce using prepared shellfish stock and wine, but do not add liason of yolks and cream until just before serving. Then warm the stuffing mixture in a small saucepan in a bit of butter, add the ginger cream sauce, and proceed as above.

Mussels in Saffron Cream

Serves: 8

Ingredients:

6 lb	**fresh mussels, in their shells**	2 kg 700 g
3 cups	**dry white wine**	¾ L
6 oz	**chopped shallots**	180 g
3	**garlic cloves**	3
1 cup	**chopped parsley**	¼ L

1 tsp each	salt and pepper	1 tsp each
pinch	thyme	pinch
1	bay leaf	1
	For sauce:	
2 pinches	saffron threads	2 pinches
4 tbls	minced parsley	4 tbls
1½ cups	cream	370 ml
2 cups	combined fine julienne of leek, carrot, zucchini, and red pepper	½ L

1. Clean the mussels: First, scrub or scrape with a stiff brush or sharp paring knife to remove exterior grit or barnacles and to detach the fibrous threads (or beard) that may connect them to each other. Run under fresh water while scrubbing, then place in a large bowl with a handful of kosher salt, cover with cold water, and allow to soak for about 10 minutes. Lift the mussels from the water into a colander or another bowl, empty the soaking bowl, rinse thoroughly and soak the mussels again. Repeat for a few times or until no trace of grit remains in the soaking water. Discard any mussels that are open (and remain open when tapped) or have broken shells. Any mussels that float easily or that are excessively heavy for their size are either dead or filled with mud. Discard. Drain the cleaned mussels, cover with a damp cloth and keep refrigerated until ready to cook. They should not be cleaned more than several hours before using.
2. To steam mussels, place in a large pot with a well-fitting lid. Add the wine, shallots, garlic, parsley, and other seasonings. Cook over high heat, covered, for about 10 minutes, until mussels open. Stir, or shake the pot once or twice during cooking time.
3. Once the mussels have opened, remove from heat. Scoop the mussels from the pot, leaving the broth behind. Place the broth back over high heat and reduce by half. Meanwhile, pick over the mussels to remove any bits of beard or tiny crabs. Leave the mussels in their shells, cover, and set aside.
4. When the broth has reduced, strain, pressing on solids to extract their flavor. Discard the solids and put the broth in a clean saucepan, adding the saffron threads, parsley, and cream. Simmer for about 5 minutes. Taste and adjust seasonings, if needed.
5. Blanch the julienne of vegetables and drain well.
6. To serve, arrange the mussels in a large shallow serving bowl (or individual portions). Scatter the vegetables among the mussels, pour over hot cream sauce and serve piping hot.

Note: Since mussels look so pretty in their black shells, it is a shame not to serve them that way. However, for a bit more elegance, you can remove one shell and place the mussels on a platter on their half-shells. Combine the vegetables with the sauce and spoon some over each mussel. Top with a bit of fresh minced parsley if desired.

For a lighter version of the recipe above, either eliminate or significantly reduce the cream in the sauce.

The yield of this recipe is approximate, depending on type of service and on the size of the mussels, but 6 lbs (2 kg 700 g) of mussels will serve eight people nicely, if served as an appetizer or for a light lunch. Serve crusty bread or focaccia on the side for dunking in the sauce.

Variations: If you stop the recipe after step 3, you will, of course, simply have steamed mussels and mussel broth, both of which can be used in other recipes.

For Mussel Salad: Remove the mussels from their shells, toss with a flavored mayonnaise (Lemon-Caper Mayonnaise or Green Mayonnaise, see Mayonnaise and Variations in recipe index), chill and serve for a buffet dish, or as an appetizer on lettuce leaf. Or toss with a vinaigrette of your choice.

For Hors d'Oeuvre: Leave mussels on half shell and either drizzle with vinaigrette or mask with mayonnaise.

Clams with Basil, Garlic, and Chiles

Serves: 6

Ingredients:

36	hard-shell clams	36
2 tbls	peanut oil	30 ml
1 cup	beer	¼ L
4	garlic cloves, smashed	4
6	scallions, thinly sliced	6
2	dried hot chiles or hot red pepper flakes (to taste)	2
1 cup	basil leaves, coarsely chopped	½ L
1 tbls	nam pla, or fish sauce*	15 ml

*This dark sauce, made from fermented fish, is available in Oriental markets.

1. Scrub the clams thoroughly with a stiff brush. Rinse in a few changes of water, then soak in salted water for several hours until they disgorge their sand. (Some cooks purge the clams by adding some cornmeal to the soaking water.) Rinse after purging, discard any clams with badly broken shells or shells that remain open.
2. Place the clams and all the other ingredients in a heavy pot with a tight-fitting lid. Reserve a handful of basil leaves for later garnish. Cook the clams over high heat for about 10 minutes until all the clams have opened. Remove the clams to a platter or bowl, reduce the broth for a few minutes, taste and add salt or pepper if needed.
3. Pour broth over clams, scatter with reserved basil, and serve hot.

Note: If you prefer, you can remove one shell from each clam, arrange on a platter and top with broth and basil.

Provencal Seafood Stew

Serves: 8

Ingredients:

16	cherrystone clams	16
2 lb	mussels	900 g
1 lb	medium shrimp	450 g
2 lb	haddock, sea bass, or scrod*	900 g
2 or 3	large ripe tomatoes, or 2 cups (500 ml) canned plum tomatoes	2 or 3
4 tbls	chopped shallots	4 tbls
3	garlic cloves, minced	3
3	leeks, trimmed, washed, and chopped	3
1 lb	chopped onion	450 g
1 head	bulb fennel, trimmed and thinly sliced	1 head
6 oz	red bell pepper, chopped	168 g
1 cup combined	chopped parsley, dill, and basil	¼ L combined
4 tbls	flavorful olive oil	60 ml
1 tsp	salt	1 tsp
1 tsp	ground black pepper	1 tsp
1 cup	dry white wine	¼ L
	Optional: hot pepper flakes, 2 lobster tails, saffron	

*Use a firm-fleshed thick cut of fish, whatever is seasonal and plentiful.

1. Clean the clams and mussels (see recipes for Mussels in Saffron Cream and Clams with Basil, Garlic, and Chiles for cleaning instructions). Wash the shrimp, then, using a narrow-pointed scissors, snip open the shell of the shrimp about halfway along outside curve of shell. This will allow diners to get to the meat easily but still allow the shell to flavor the stew. If using the optional lobster tails, separate into segments, but leave in their shells. Trim the fish, fillet if necessary, pick over for any bones. Skin may be left on, or not, as desired. Cut the fish into eight to ten portions. Store all the cleaned fish, wrapped and refrigerated, until ready to cook.

2. Prepare the vegetables: If using fresh tomato, peel, seed, and chop coarsely; if using canned tomatoes, remove hard cores and seeds and chop. Place the tomatoes in a bowl with the fennel and red bell pepper and set aside.

3. In a large heavy pot or kettle, heat the olive oil and add the shallots, garlic, leeks, and onions. Sauté, stirring briskly, until the vegetables are wilted and lightly colored. Add the tomato mixture and cook over moderate heat for 2 minutes.

4. Add the clams and the mussels to the pot, layer herbs in between. Stir carefully to combine vegetables with shellfish, cook for 3 minutes.

5. Add the salt and pepper, the shrimp, the optional lobster and pour the wine over all. Cover the kettle and cook over moderate heat for about 5 minutes. As soon as the shrimp begin to turn pink and the shells of the clams and mussels start to open, lay the fish over the stew. Cover and cook for a few more minutes, until the fish loses its translucent look. Remove from heat and keep covered while preparing to serve.

6. Have ready either warm individual deep bowls or one deep platter. Carefully remove the fish and various shellfish from the kettle. If serving individual portions, be sure each diner gets some of each variety. Cover and keep warm.
7. Boil down the broth over high heat, tasting for seasoning. Add hot pepper flakes and saffron, if desired.
8. Pour a bit of the reduced broth over the fish, place some more in a sauceboat, or store for another use.

Note: Crusty bread or garlic bread can be served alongside. Or, if you have hardtack or pepper biscotti, place one or two in the bottom of each bowl before filling with fish and broth.

Variation: Segments of king crab legs can be substituted for the lobster tails.

Thai Green Curry of Shrimp and Mussels

Serves: 10–12

Ingredients:

1½ lb	medium shrimp	675 g
3 cups	steamed shelled mussels	¾ L
3 cups	coconut milk, divided*	¾ L
2 tbls	peanut oil	30 ml
2	garlic cloves, minced	2
4 tbls	minced shallots	4 tbls
2 tsp	grated lemon zest	2 tsp
1 tsp	salt	1 tsp
2 tbls	madras curry powder (to taste)†	2 tbls
2 tbls	nam pla**	30 ml
1 tbls	minced cilantro	1 tbls
2 tbls	minced parsley	2 tbls
½ cup	shredded basil leaves	125 ml
	minced hot green chiles (to taste)‡	
8	scallions, trimmed and cut into 2-in. (5 cm) lengths	8

*This is unsweetened coconut milk, not the sweetened coconut cream used in preparing piña coladas.

†The Thais prepare their own green curry paste, with green rather than red chiles, and no paprika. I use an English brand of madras curry that is medium hot and lends a green color to the sauce.

**Nam pla, fish sauce or fish's gravy, is a fermented liquid used as a condiment or seasoning. Available in ethnic specialty markets.

‡Fresh green chiles will vary in hotness, so use accordingly. Be sure to exercise caution in handling chiles, as they can burn the skin, mouth, and eyes. In the case of very hot specimens, remove the seeds, which contain most of the firepower.

1. Rinse, shell, and devein the shrimp. Set aside, refrigerated. Pick over the cooked mussel meats to remove any debris. Set aside, refrigerated.
2. Place half of the coconut milk in a small saucepan and boil it down until thick and oily and reduced by half. Set aside.
3. Heat the peanut oil in a heavy pot, add the garlic, shallots, and lemon zest. Cook, stirring, until the garlic is golden but not burned.
4. Add the salt, the reduced coconut milk, and some of the curry powder, and simmer for about 3 minutes. Add the nam pla, some of the minced chiles, and the rest of the coconut milk. When the mixture returns to the simmer, taste and adjust seasonings. Remember that you will be adding some additional green chiles at the very end (or serving them on the side for guests to add as they please), but the curry should have a pleasantly hot sting.
5. Simmer for several more minutes or until the coconut milk has thickened the curry. If not serving immediately, remove from heat.
6. About 5 minutes before serving, add the shrimp and cook just until they begin to turn pink. Stir in the mussels just to heat through. Stir in the scallions. Add most of the fresh herbs, reserving some for top garnish. Add more green chiles or serve on the side. Serve piping hot with lots of steamed rice.

Note:　The curry, up to the point of adding the shrimp, can be prepared ahead and stored, covered and refrigerated. Reheat slowly, to allow the fat from the coconut milk to liquefy without scorching the mixture. Standing will alter the seasonings, so adjust accordingly.

Variations:　Lump crabmeat or shucked clams may be substituted or added to the curry if desired.

Cajun-Fried Fish

Yield: 1½ lb		675 g
	Ingredients:	
1½ lb	fish fillets*	675 g
1 cup	buttermilk	¼ L
1 tsp	Worcestershire sauce	1 tsp
dash	hot pepper sauce	dash
6 oz	cornmeal	180 g
2 oz	all-purpose flour	60 g
1½ tbls	celery salt	1½ tbls
½ tsp	cayenne pepper	½ tsp
1 tsp	dry mustard	1 tsp
2 tbls	paprika	2 tbls

1 tsp	**ground black pepper**	1 tsp
2 tsp	**ground thyme**	2 tsp
	oil for frying	

*Any mild, white-fleshed fish can be used. Try flounder, perch, haddock, or scrod. Catfish is especially good, but its firmer texture requires a bit more cooking time.

1. Prepare the fish: The fillets should be skinless and checked for any small bones. Cut into ¼-in. (¾ cm) strips, fingers, or small pieces of your own choosing.
2. Combine the buttermilk with the Worcestershire and hot pepper sauces. Pour over the pieces of fish and toss to coat. Set aside, covered and refrigerated, if not using immediately.
3. Combine the cornmeal, flour, and spices, and place in a shallow pan.
4. Heat frying oil in a deep fryer or skillet to 350° F (180° C).
5. Drain the fish pieces, dredge pieces in prepared cornmeal mixture, turning to coat on all sides. Transfer to a strainer to shake off excess crumbs.
6. Fry the fish pieces in batches until golden brown. Cooking time will vary depending on size and thickness of pieces and firmness of fish. Adjust accordingly. Transfer to clean absorbent paper. Serve immediately with lemon and lime wedges or with tartar sauce.

Note: The fried fish can be held in a warm oven but are best fresh-fried.

Variation: Boneless chicken breast may be prepared in the same manner. Shrimp, clams, or oysters may be prepared with the same coating. They may be served individually or combined with fish strips for a mixed fish fry.

Small Meals and Light Fare

French Fruit Toast

Serves: 8

Ingredients:

8 thick slices	Egg Bread (see in recipe index) or challah or brioche	8 thick slices
6	eggs, well beaten	6
1 cup	milk	¼ L
1 cup	either mashed ripe banana, grated apple, pureed peaches	¼ L
1 tsp	cinnamon or sugar (optional)	1 tsp
2 tbls	brandy or orange juice (optional)	2 tbls
	For frying: butter and oil	
	Optional garnish and sauces: confectioners' sugar, cinnamon sugar, pure maple syrup, fresh fruit sauces of choice, or creme anglaise	

1. Mix the eggs with the milk and beat in the fruit. Bananas are sweet enough on their own; the grated apple will need a bit of sugar and/or cinnamon; the peaches might need a bit of sugar depending on ripeness. Add brandy, orange juice, vanilla extract, maple syrup, or a liqueur of your choice as a flavoring.
2. Soak the bread in the egg and fruit mixture, turning to moisten evenly. Let the bread rest in the mixture until all the liquid is absorbed.
3. Preheat the oven to 350°F (180°C). Heat the oil and butter in a pan (or use a well-seasoned griddle) to cook the toast. You may cook totally in the pan or (especially if preparing in volume) just to fry golden brown on each side. Finish cooking on a baking sheet in the oven. If preparing a very large volume, lower the oven heat so the first slices do not overcook or burn while holding.
4. Serve hot, sprinkled with either sugar, or with the sauces or toppings as desired.

Note: This is a good brunch dish or late night supper snack/dessert. If the bread slices are very large, you can cut them in half before soaking, but keep the slices thick for best results. Smaller portions are the better choice when these toasts are parts of a large brunch menu, since they are very rich, especially when sauced. In addition, the smaller pieces cook faster, and it is easier to keep fresh batches coming, especially when feeding a large crowd.

Variation: Pannetone, an Italian yeast bread with candied fruits, makes an interesting version prepared with peach puree and rum. It can be served as a dessert with creme anglaise as a sauce.

Eggs Baked in Tomatoes

Yield: **12 tomatoes**

Ingredients:

12	ripe tomatoes, each about 4- or 5-in. (10 to 13 cm) diam.	12
4 tbls	olive oil	60 ml
2 tbls	minced shallots	2 tbls
2 tbls	minced chives	2 tbls
4 tbls	minced ham	4 tbls
3 slices	white sandwich bread	3 slices
2 tbls	softened butter	2 tbls
1 cup	grated Gruyère	¼ L
1 cup	fresh white breadcrumbs	¼ L
12	extra large eggs	12
	salt and pepper (to taste)	

1. Wash tomatoes. Cut a thick slice from the stem end of each. Using a grapefruit knife, scoop out as much of the tomato pulp as possible. Salt the inside lightly and turn upside down on paper towel to drain. Chop the usable pulp, minus the seeds and stem from the tomato trimmings.
2. Heat 2 tbls of the olive oil in a skillet, add the shallots, chives, and ham. Sauté for 2 or 3 minutes just until the vegetables are wilted. Add the chopped tomatoes and simmer until the juices are reduced. Remove from heat, adjust seasoning with salt and pepper, and set aside.
3. Trim the crusts from the bread slices. Cut each into four pieces. Toast lightly and spread with butter.
4. Preheat the oven to 375° F (190° C). Prepare an ovenproof dish just large enough to hold the tomatoes. Rub with 1 tbls of oil.

5. Place the tomatoes in the pan. Place one buttered bread square in the bottom of each tomato. Divide the prepared filling among the tomatoes.
6. Crack an egg into each tomato, sprinkle with cheese, then with bread crumbs. Drizzle a few drops of oil on each tomato. Bake for 10 to 13 minutes until the cheese is bubbly. Serve immediately with extra hot buttered toast on the side.

Note: Tomatoes may be prepared ahead to the point where the egg is added.

Creamed Eggs with Smoked Salmon and Caviar

Serves: 10

	Ingredients:	
6 oz	butter	180 g
1 cup	chopped onion	¼ L
1 cup	chopped boiled potatoes	¼ L
12 oz	smoked salmon	340 g
	salt and white pepper (to taste)	
	For sauce:	
6 tbls	butter	85 g
6 tbls	flour	60 g
2 cups	milk	½ L
1 cup	cream	¼ L
pinch	nutmeg	pinch
16	eggs, lightly beaten	16
4 tbls	minced dill	4 tbls
	buttered bread crumbs for topping	
	Optional topping:	
12 oz	sour cream	340 g
2 tbls	lemon juice	30 ml
1 cup	salmon caviar	¼ L

1. Butter a 2-qt (2 L) ovenproof casserole or gratin dish. Set aside. Heat half the butter in a sauté pan, add the onion and cook until wilted and lightly colored. Add the cooked potatoes, sauté until golden brown. Sprinkle with a little salt and pepper. Set aside.
2. Prepare the sauce: Heat the milk and cream just to scald and set aside. Heat the butter in a saucepan, add the flour and cook for 2 to 3 minutes, stirring, until the mixture is frothy but not colored. Gradually whisk in some of the hot milk and cream until the mixture is smooth and thickened. Continue adding milk and cream until the sauce coats a spoon. Stir in the nutmeg and some salt and white pepper to taste.

3. Heat 2 tbls of the remaining butter in a sauté pan, add the beaten eggs and cook over low heat, until the eggs just begin to thicken. Use a wooden spoon or spatula to stir the eggs into soft curds. Remove from the heat as soon as the curds take shape. The eggs should be very, very soft and wet, they will finish cooking later. As soon as you remove from the heat add the remaining butter and the dill and stir into the curds.

4. Spoon a layer of sauce into the bottom of the casserole, spoon in some of the onion and potato mixture. Place half of the salmon over the surface, then spoon in the eggs, spreading them evenly over the salmon. Cover with a layer of sauce, then more potato and onion, then the remaining salmon. Coat the casserole completely with the remaining sauce. Sprinkle the top of the casserole with buttered bread crumbs. Hold at room temperature for about 30 minutes or refrigerate for a few hours. Let come to room temperature again before final heating.

5. Just before serving, cover the casserole and place in a very hot oven for 5 to 7 minutes, just until heated through. Brown under a broiler if desired for just a minute before serving.

6. To prepare optional sauce, stir the lemon juice into the sour cream, fold in the salmon caviar. Offer a dollop of caviar cream with each portion of eggs.

Note: These eggs are at their very best when prepared close to serving time. Holding under refrigeration does not really hurt the dish, but be sure it is not too cold when reheating or it will need to be in the oven too long, and the eggs will harden.

Variation: The salmon can be eliminated, and sautéed mushrooms, spinach, or shredded mixed cheeses can be substituted.

Ham and Onion Brunch Muffins

Yield: 12 muffins

	Ingredients:	
10 oz	self-rising flour	285 g
2 tbls each	minced parsley and chives	2 tbls each
4 tbls	chopped ham	4 tbls
3 tbls	minced onion	80 ml
1 cup	milk (approx.)	¼ L
⅓ cup	prepared mayonnaise	80 ml

1. Preheat the oven to 425°F (220°C). Grease standard 12-cup muffin pans.
2. Combine the flour with the ham, herbs, and onion. Mix together the mayonnaise and melted butter. Quickly stir wet into dry, just to moisten. Spoon into prepared muffin tins. Bake 10 to 12 minutes. If not serving at once, wrap tightly. When reheating, sprinkle with a few drops of water, rewrap, and heat in a moderate oven.

Bacon, Liver, and Onion Custard

Serves: 12

Ingredients:

1 lb	fresh chicken livers	450 g
1 cup	milk	¼ L
10 slices	bacon	10 slices
1 lb	onion, thinly sliced	450 g
	salt and pepper to taste	
2 tbls	brandy	30 ml
12	eggs, beaten	12
2½ cups	half-and-half	600 ml
pinch	nutmeg	pinch
	softened butter (as needed)	

1. Trim the chicken livers of fat and connective membranes. Soak in milk for at least 30 minutes.
2. Preheat the oven to 300° F (150° C). Butter a 2-qt (2 L) shallow ovenproof dish, serving casserole, or gratin pan. Set aside.
3. Chop the bacon into small pieces. Fry until cooked but not crisp. Remove all but one-third of the bacon to absorbent paper. Continue to fry the remaining bacon until crisp. Drain and reserve separately.
4. Remove most of the bacon fat from the pan and reserve. Add the onion to the pan, cover and sweat for about 10 minutes or until wilted. Raise the heat and cook the onion, stirring, until golden brown. Remove with a slotted spoon to a bowl.
5. Remove the livers from the milk. Pat very dry on paper towels. Sprinkle with salt and pepper. If more fat is needed in the pan, add more bacon fat (or use some vegetable oil or margarine if preferred), get the oil very hot and add the livers, a few at a time, until well seared on both sides. The livers should be cooked rare. Remove from pan with slotted spoon, add to bowl of onions. Continue searing the livers. When done, pour the fat from the pan, deglaze with brandy, and add the juices to the liver and onion. Taste the mixture and add salt and pepper until well seasoned.
6. Combine the eggs, half-and-half, and nutmeg. Pour the egg mixture over the liver and onions, add the soft-cooked bacon, stir to combine, and turn into the prepared pan.
7. Place in the oven and bake for 20 minutes. Sprinkle the crisp crumbled bacon over the top, and continue to bake for 40 to 50 minutes, until set and golden brown. Let rest for 10 to 15 minutes out of the oven before cutting into squares.

Note: This custard is similar to a frittata or crustless quiche. If you prefer a more tender custard, bake in a water bath, increasing the oven heat to 350° F (180° C), for about an hour and a half or until set. About halfway through baking time, sprinkle the top not only with bacon but with bread crumbs that have been mixed with melted butter and paprika to provide a nice top crust.

Blintzes

Yield: *12 blintzes*

	Ingredients:	
	Batter:*	
4 oz	all-purpose flour	112 g
2	whole eggs, beaten	2
6 fl oz	water	180 ml
pinch	salt	pinch
1 tsp	granulated sugar	1 tsp
	For filling:	
1 lb	pot cheese	450 g
1	egg	1
2 tsp	granulated sugar	2 tsp
½ tsp	cinnamon	½ tsp
pinch	salt	pinch
½ tsp	vanilla extract	½ tsp
	clarified butter for frying	

*You may use 12 Basic Crepes (see in recipe index) for the wrappers, adding a bit of sugar to the batter, and frying the crepes on one side only. Stack as they are made and cover to keep moist.

1. Prepare the batter. Stir the eggs into the flour to make a smooth paste. Add the salt and sugar and gradually add the water. Mix gently until smooth. Cook in a 5- or 6-in. (13 or 15 cm) crepe pan. Cook as for basic crepes, browning lightly on one side only. Leave the top side uncooked. Remove from pan; cover to keep moist.
2. Prepare the filling by combining all the ingredients. The mixture will be a little lumpy and dry.
3. Place the wrappers, cooked side up, on a work surface. Place a generous tablespoon of filling in the center of each wrapper. Fold like an envelope or egg roll to make neat little packets. (If they do not seal themselves, you can use a touch of egg wash to seal. Usually the moisture of the crepe is sufficient to seal them.) Place seam side down in a pan or plate. The filled blintzes may be prepared up to a day ahead if kept well wrapped and refrigerated.
4. Heat clarified butter (or a neutral vegetable oil) in a skillet. Add the blintzes, seam side down. Cook for 1 or 2 minutes, then turn to brown other side. Serve soon after frying or keep warm in a 300° F (150° C) oven.
5. Traditionally, blintzes are served with sour cream on the side. They may be dusted with confectioners' sugar or cinnamon sugar, if you like.

Note: Blintzes are a good choice for brunch, in place of other crepe dishes or omelets. They are also wonderful as the main course for a late night supper after theater or a dance, when guests will have an appetite for something substantial and a bit sweet.

Since they can be prepared in advance except for their final browning in butter, fresh, bubbly hot blintzes are relatively easy to serve to a crowd. Often blintzes are filled with fruit (see a good cookbook), but it is very nice (and simpler) to offer these blintzes with an array of fruit toppings. Simply prepare bowls of whole or sliced berries or fruit, macerated in a bit of sugar and liqueur, along with bowls of sour cream, and allow guests to choose their own garnish.

Variations: Baked Blintzes: Place the filled and rolled blintzes in a buttered oven-proof dish. Hold, refrigerated and well wrapped until ready to bake. Brush the blintzes with melted butter and place uncovered in a 425° F (220° C) oven for about 10 minutes until nicely browned.

Vegetable Blintzes: Eliminate sugar, cinnamon, and vanilla from filling. Add ½ cup (125 ml) combined minced scallions, red pepper, parsley, salt, and pepper.

Basic Crepes and Variations

Yield: 24–30 crepes

	Ingredients:	
4 oz	all-purpose flour*	112 g
pinch	salt	pinch
6	eggs, beaten	6
1 cup	milk (approx.)	¼ L
¼ cup	melted butter	60 ml

*You may use instant-blending flour (such as Wondra). In that case, the weight of the flour will be 4½ oz (130 g). The batter will not require any resting time; it can be used immediately.

1. Combine the flour with the salt. Mix the eggs with the milk and stir into the flour until completely mixed. Allow mixture to rest at least 1 hour to relax gluten.
2. Let the rested batter come to room temperature. Stir gently. If there are any lumps, strain. Add the melted butter.
3. Heat a crepe pan (about 5 to 6 in. [13 to 15 cm] is standard, but you may use any size you require). The pan should be well seasoned or have a good nonstick surface.
4. When the pan is hot, rub with buttered paper towel. Immediately pour in a bit of batter, swirling the pan to coat the surface with the thinnest possible film of batter. If you have added too much, quickly pour off the excess. Allow the crepe to cook for about a minute, just until speckled on bottom side. Lift one edge of the crepe with a thin spatula and turn to cook other side for 5 seconds. Slide crepe out onto waxed paper.

5. Hint: Test one crepe, and if it seems too thick, add a bit more milk and test another. Flour tends to vary in its absorbency, so this adjustment may be necessary to achieve ideal consistency. With only a bit of practice, crepe making will become very easy. Usually, the pan will not need repeated greasing, but if you find crepes sticking as you proceed, rub the pan again with the buttered paper towel. When the individual crepes have cooled, you can stack them and store refrigerated or frozen, until needed.

Note: This recipe varies from the standard: It uses more eggs and butter. It yields a thin, tender, but still durable crepe that makes up easily and stores well. The yield will vary according to the size of the pan and thickness of the crepe. I prefer very thin crepes for delicate hors d'oeuvre uses, a bit thicker for Manicotti (see in recipe index), or for dessert or entree crepe recipes that utilize substantial fillings, such as Turkey Mushroom Crepes Gratinée or Blintzes (see in recipe index). This recipe yields a crepe with a neutral, all-purpose flavor. The variations that follow offer other choices.

Variations: **Sweet Crepes:** Add 1 tbls sugar, 1 tbls flavoring or liqueur.
Herb Crepes: Add 1 tsp each finely minced dill, parsley, chives, ¼ tsp salt.
Parmesan Crepes: Add 2 tbls grated Parmesan, bit more milk.
Confetti Crepes: Add 1 tsp each finely minced red and yellow bell pepper, chives and parsley, ¼ tsp salt, dash hot pepper sauce. Stir between crepes as solids may settle. Add 1 tbls melted butter for consistency.

Turkey Mushroom Crepes Gratinée

Serves: 24

	Ingredients:	
24	**Basic Crepes** (see in recipe index)	24
5 lb	turkey parts, bone in	2 kg 250 g
1 cup	dry white wine	250 ml
4 cups	chicken broth	1 L
8 oz	butter, divided	224 g
2 lb	sliced fresh mushrooms	900 g
1 lb	chopped onion	450 g
3 oz	all-purpose flour	84 g
2 tbls	dry mustard	2 tbls
2 tbls	dry sherry	30 ml
3 cups	combined shredded Swiss, Gruyère, and mozzarella cheese	750 ml
	salt and pepper (to taste)	

For topping:

| 5 tbls | dry bread crumbs | 40 g |
| 1 tbls | paprika | 1 tbls |

1. Either light or dark meat turkey parts, or a combination of both, may be used. Poach the turkey parts in the wine and chicken broth, removing pieces as they are tender and cooked through. Remove to a platter or bowl to cool. Reserve the poaching liquid separately.
2. Use half the butter to sauté the mushrooms until golden brown. Remove to a large bowl. Add the onion to the pan and cook until wilted and lightly colored. Use a slotted spoon to transfer the onion into the bowl holding the mushrooms. Leave the pan unwashed to use for the sauce.
3. When the turkey is cool enough to handle, skin and debone carefully, discarding any tendons, bits of cartilage, or fat. Cut the turkey meat into fairly large dice and add to the mushrooms and onions. Add any juices from the turkey to the chicken broth and set aside.
4. Use about 1 tbls of butter to grease a shallow baking pan or ovenproof casserole just large enough to hold the 24 rolled crepes. Set aside. If baking immediately, preheat the oven to 325°F (165°C).
5. Prepare the sauce. Add the remaining butter to the pot, add the flour and cook, stirring for at least two minutes to cook and lightly color the roux. Gradually add the poaching liquid, stirring over medium heat until the sauce thickens. Simmer for 10 minutes.
6. Add the mustard and sherry to the sauce, and about two-thirds of the cheese. Lower the heat and stir until the sauce is smooth and thick. Taste for seasoning and add salt and pepper.
7. Add about a cup of the sauce to the turkey and mushrooms. Stir to coat. Add a bit more sauce if needed to evenly moisten the mixture, but do not make it runny.
8. Lay the prepared crepes on a work surface. Spoon some filling in a band down the center of each crepe and roll up. Place the crepes, seam side down in the prepared pan. When all the crepes have been filled and rolled, spoon sauce over them. Cover generously, but leave the ends of the crepes exposed.
9. Sprinkle the balance of the shredded cheese over the sauce, and top with a mixture of bread crumbs and paprika. Crepes can be prepared ahead to this point and held, covered and refrigerated, for up to 2 days.
10. When ready to bake, oil or spray a sheet of foil, cover the pan and bake for 20 minutes. Remove the foil and continue to bake for another 10 minutes or until the crepes are heated through and the cheese is bubbly and beginning to brown in spots. Don't overcook or they will dry out. These crepes will hold in a chafer if oven time is shortened (but includes browning). They will continue to cook through while holding.

Old-Fashioned Turkey Hash

Serves: 12–16

Ingredients:

	For sauce:	
4 tbls	butter	56 g
⅓ cup	minced shallots	80 ml
4 tbls	flour	50 g
1 qt	milk	1 L
2 tbls	dry sherry	30 ml
dash	hot pepper sauce	dash
dash	Worcestershire sauce	dash
	salt and pepper (to taste)	
	For turkey mixture:	
1 tbls	butter or oil	15 g or 15 ml
3 tbls each	diced red and green pepper	3 tbls each
3 tbls	scallion, thinly sliced	3 tbls
1 cup	chopped baked ham	¼ L
1 qt	cooked turkey chunks	1 L
	pepper (to taste)	
4 tbls	snipped chives	4 tbls

Optional: buttered croutons, toasted English muffins, baked potato shells, steamed rice

1. Prepare the sauce: Heat the butter and sauté the shallots until wilted but not browned. Add the flour and cook, stirring for 2 to 3 minutes, until barely colored. Gradually add milk a bit at a time, stirring to form a smooth sauce. Add the seasonings and simmer for about 5 minutes. Set aside.
2. Heat the oil and sauté the peppers and scallions for a minute or two. Remove from heat, stir in the ham and sprinkle generously with freshly ground black pepper.
3. In a large bowl, combine the turkey with the sautéed vegetables and ham. Add just enough sauce to make a moist, but not too loose, mixture. May be held, covered and refrigerated, for 1 to 2 days. Reserve any remaining sauce as well.
4. Preheat the oven to 350°F (180°C). Butter a 2- to 3-qt (2–3 L) ovenproof shallow casserole or gratin dish.
5. Place the hash in the dish, mask with a bit more sauce if desired, and bake for about 20 to 25 minutes, until heated through and bubbly. Sprinkle with chives before serving.
6. May be served garnished with freshly made buttered croutons or served over English muffins, rice, or in heated baked potato shells.

Note: Dark meat turkey (or, for that matter, chicken) is particularly good in this dish.

Chef's Spinach Salad

Serves: 10

Ingredients:

5 cups	fresh spinach, washed, stemmed, and crisped	1¼ L
1 cup each	3 or more of the following: shredded Swiss cheese, carrot, ham, chicken, turkey, or beef; alfalfa sprouts, red onion rings, sliced raw mushrooms	¼ L each
½ cup each	crumbled bacon, blue cheese, chopped radishes, and red pepper	125 ml each
5	hard-boiled eggs, halved	5
2 cups	orange vinaigrette (see Vinaigrette Basics in recipe index)	½ L

1. Present as a buffet salad or salad bar arrangement, or arrange on individual plates, serving dressing on the side. The only additions that need to be dressed are the carrots and mushrooms, which should be moistened with a bit of vinaigrette.

Note: This is a good choice for an informal brunch or luncheon. It can also be offered as a casual office lunch where no cooking facilities are available, as a welcome alternative to sandwiches.

Thai Noodle Salad

Yield: 4 lb   **2 kg**

Ingredients:

½ recipe	Hot Peanut Sauce (see in recipe index)	½ recipe
1 lb	spaghetti	450 g
	vegetable oil (as needed)	
2 oz	grated carrots	56 g
1 tbls	rice wine vinegar	1 tbls
pinch	sugar	pinch
2	red peppers, diced	2
1 bunch	scallions, thin sliced	1 bunch
1 lb	diced cooked chicken	450 g
	Optional garnish: blanched broccoli florets, scallion brushes	

1. Boil the spaghetti in salted boiling water until al dente. Drain, rinse with cold water, and drain again. Place in a large bowl and toss with sufficient vegetable oil to prevent sticking. Set aside.
2. Sprinkle the vinegar on the shredded carrots and add a pinch of sugar. Set aside.

3. Toss the noodles with most of the sauce and about two-thirds of the peppers, scallions, and chicken.
4. If serving as a buffet dish, turn into a large shallow bowl or serving platter and scatter the remaining peppers, scallions, and chicken over the top. Just before serving, drizzle some of the remaining sauce over the top of the salad. Drain the shredded carrots and arrange here and there on the edge of the salad.
5. If preparing individual servings, place a portion of salad on each plate and arrange extra vegetables and chicken over the top.
6. Add desired optional garnish.

Note: If preparing salad a day or two before service, cover and keep refrigerated. It will tend to congeal on standing. Let come to room temperature, then toss again with additional sauce and add toppings and garnish just before serving.

Curried Rice Salad

Serves: 25

Ingredients:

2 cups	raw long-grain rice	½ L
2 tbls	vegetable oil	2 tbls
1 cup	chopped onion	¼ L
2 tbls	curry powder	2 tbls
1 tbls	minced garlic	1 tbls
2 tbls	minced gingerroot	2 tbls
2 cups	orange vinaigrette (or as needed) (see Vinaigrette Basics in recipe index)	¼ L
dash	hot pepper sauce	dash
¾ cup	each of the following: finely chopped celery, carrots, red bell pepper, zucchini, thinly sliced scallions, drained and rinsed corn niblets, thawed tiny peas	180 ml
2 cups	minced cooked chicken, shrimp, or ham	½ L
6 tbls each	minced parsley and chives	6 tbls each
	salt and pepper (to taste)	
1 cup	chopped almonds or cashews	¼ L
1 cup	golden raisins, plumped	¼ L

1. Cook the rice in a large quantity of salted boiling water for 15 to 20 minutes just until tender. Drain, place in a large bowl, and moisten with vinaigrette. Let stand to cool to lukewarm.
2. Heat the oil in a sauté pan, add the onion and sauté until barely softened. Add the curry powder, garlic, and gingerroot, cook stirring for a minute. Remove from heat and let cool.

3. Combine the rice, onion mixture, all the vegetables, and meat. Let stand for 1 hour to mellow flavors.
4. Add the nuts, raisins, salt and pepper to taste, and the herbs. Add more vinaigrette if needed to moisten thoroughly. Can be held for 2 days, refrigerated. Serve at cool room temperature.

Note: For best color and flavor if planning to hold more than a day, add the peas and herbs shortly before serving.

Chunky Tarragon Chicken Salad with Apple

Serves: 12–14

Ingredients:

5 lb	cooked boneless chicken	2¼ kg
3	Granny Smith apples, cored and coarsely chopped	3
2	red bell peppers, seeded and coarsely chopped	2
4	celery stalks, coarsely chopped	4
6 oz	pecans, lightly toasted	180 g
2–3 cups	Grainy Mustard Mayonnaise (see Mayonnaise and Variations in recipe index)	½–¾ L
½ cup	apple juice or chicken broth	125 ml
½ cup	tarragon leaves, chopped	125 ml
	salt and pepper (to taste)	
	Optional garnish: lemon juice, apple slices, tarragon sprigs	

You may use Oven-Poached Chicken Breast (see in recipe index) or chicken meat cooked tender in broth (or a combination of broth and apple juice). The very best results come from freshly cooked meat that has not been refrigerated to harden or dry out. Cut the meat into good size chunks, do not chop or mince. Turkey meat may be substituted, provided it is moist.

1. Prepare the fruit and vegetables just before combining the salad. The pecans may be broken into pieces or left in perfect halves.
2. Thin the mayonnaise with broth or juice. Fold in the chicken or turkey, the apples, vegetables, and most of the nuts and tarragon, using just enough mayonnaise mixture to coat. Taste and adjust seasonings.
3. If serving buffet style, turn into an attractive bowl or platter, sprinkle with the remaining nuts and tarragon, and garnish with apple slices dipped in lemon juice and sprigs of tarragon. If serving individual plates, sprinkle each portion with remaining nuts and tarragon with a bit of extra mayo on the side. Or use mayonnaise as a spread for a crusty baguette or croissant if serving the salad in a sandwich.

Note: This salad may be made ahead and refrigerated for 2 or 3 days but is at its best freshly made while the chicken is still soft and moist.

Walnut-Yogurt Chicken

Serves: 12

	Ingredients:	
5 lb	boiled chicken or fowl	2 kg 250 g
	For sauce:	
8 oz	chopped walnuts	224 g
6 oz	chopped onion	168 g
1 cup	shredded Italian or French bread	¼ L
1½ cup	plain yogurt, drained	370 ml
2 tsp	sweet paprika	2 tsp
	salt and pepper (to taste)	
1 cup	chopped parsley	¼ L
	chicken broth (as needed)	

1. If necessary, remove the skin and bones from the chicken. Pull the meat into shreds, discarding any fat or sinew. Cover and set aside.
2. Reserve about one-fourth of the walnuts and parsley for garnish before preparing the sauce.
3. In a food processor or blender, combine the walnuts with the onion and shredded bread to make a thick paste. Add the yogurt and paprika, blend to a sauce consistency, adding a bit of chicken broth to thin the mixture. Turn into a bowl, stir in the parsley and season with salt and pepper to taste.
4. Combine the chicken with some of the sauce and arrange in a shallow platter or serving dish. Mask the surface with more sauce. Wrap airtight, hold covered and refrigerated for several hours or 1 to 2 days.
5. Just before serving, sprinkle the top with the remaining parsley and chopped walnuts.

Creamy Shrimp Salad

Serves: 8–10

	Ingredients:	
3 lb	medium shrimp, cooked, peeled, and deveined	1 kg 350 g
8 oz	finely sliced red onion	224 g
8 oz	cucumber, sliced wafer thin	224 g
1 tsp	salt	1 tsp
2 tbls	sugar	2 tbls
2 tbls	white vinegar	30 ml

1½ cups	Lemon-Caper Mayonnaise (see in recipe index)	370 ml
4 oz	sour cream	112 g
	salt and pepper (to taste)	
	Garnish: 2 tbls each minced red bell pepper and chives	

1. Combine onion, cucumber, salt, sugar, and vinegar. Let marinate until the vegetables are softened and have a sweet-sour taste. Drain well to remove excess marinade.
2. Combine the Lemon-Caper Mayonnaise and the sour cream, fold in the shrimp and the marinated, drained vegetables. Taste and adjust seasonings. Hold, covered and refrigerated, for 1 to 2 days. Garnish with red pepper and chives just before serving.

Note: If the shrimp are chopped before being added to the salad, this recipe makes a delicious sandwich filling, especially on a crusty club roll or flaky croissant. With the shrimp minced very fine, it becomes a filling for hors d'oeuvre choux puffs, bouchées, croustades, or tiny tart shells.

Variation: **Creamy Pasta and Shrimp Salad:** Combine the salad with 1 pound (500 g) or more of cooked pasta shells (conchiglie). You may need a bit more mayonnaise to coat completely.

Squid Salad

Serves: 20

	Ingredients:	
5 lb	squid, cleaned and cut*	2 kg 250 g
½ cup	dry white wine	125 ml
1 tsp	dried oregano	1 tsp
1 tsp	dried basil	1 tsp
1	bay leaf	1
½ cup	fruity olive oil	125 ml
2 tbls	red wine vinegar	30 ml
3 tbls	lemon juice	45 ml
2	garlic cloves, smashed	2
½ tsp	hot red pepper flakes	½ tsp
½ cup	minced red onion	125 ml
¼ cup	minced red bell pepper	60 ml
¼ cup	minced green bell pepper	60 ml
¼ cup	minced yellow bell pepper	60 ml
1 cup	minced parsley	¼ L
2 tsp	salt (or to taste)	2 tsp
1 tsp	ground black pepper (or to taste)	1 tsp

*See recipe for Crisp Calamari (see in recipe index) for instructions on cleaning squid.

1. Place the cleaned and cut squid in a saucepan along with the white wine, oregano, basil, and bay leaf. Add water to cover. Bring to the boil, covered. Squid will become tender in 1 to 2 minutes of cooking time. (Ironically, they then become very tough and require an hour or more of cooking to become tender again, so watch carefully.)
2. Drain quickly as soon as the squid are tender. Cover and refrigerate while preparing the dressing.
3. Combine all the other ingredients, add the cooled squid, stir, and taste for seasonings. Allow to mellow, covered and refrigerated for at least a few hours or up to 3 days. Taste just before serving and adjust seasoning if necessary. The mixture may require more salt or a bit more vinegar or lemon to sharpen the flavor. Remove the garlic cloves.
4. Serve as an appetizer on a lettuce-lined plate. If serving at a cocktail party, provide small plates and forks. Serve crisp bread or herb toasts on the side.

Variation: **Italian Seafood Salad:** Small shelled, cooked shrimp, poached scallops, pieces of crab legs (or sea legs) may be combined with the squid. Diced celery may also be added to either version.

Ceviche (Marinated Fish)

Yield: 3 lb		**1 kg 350 g**
Ingredients:	
1 cup	fresh lime juice	¼ L
½ cup	fresh lemon juice	125 ml
¼ cup	white vinegar	60 ml
4	white peppercorns, cracked	4
1	small red hot dried chile*	1
2	small fresh green chiles*	2
1 tsp	salt	1 tsp
6 oz	thinly sliced red onion	168 g
2 tbls	minced dill	2 tbls
1 tbls	minced cilantro	1 tbls
1 lb	medium shrimp	450 g
1 lb	sea scallops	450 g
1 lb	firm, white-fleshed fish fillet	450 g
Garnish: thinly sliced scallions, fine julienne of red and green bell pepper, cherry tomatoes	

*The hotness of chiles will vary, so select according to taste or substitute red hot pepper flakes for the dried chile. Take care in handling fresh chiles: Use gloves to protect your skin and be careful not to touch your skin or eyes while handling the chiles, especially the hot seeds. To prepare the green chiles for this recipe, remove their tops, split them, and remove and discard the seeds and thick inner ribs.

1. Combine the juices with the vinegar, peppercorns, dried chile, and split green chiles. Add the salt, the red onion, and the herbs and set aside.
2. Rinse the shrimp and poach them in a bit of boiling water until just pink. Drain, shell, and devein, splitting the shrimp in two lengthwise. Rinse the scallops and cut into two or three crosswise slices. Check the fish for any tiny bones and cut into bite-size slices or pieces.
3. Place all the prepared seafood in the marinade, stir to coat thoroughly, and set aside, refrigerated and covered, for a few hours or overnight.
4. After a few hours, taste the fish to see if it is tender (the acid will have "cooked" the raw fish), add additional salt if needed. If the mixture seems hot enough, remove the chiles.
5. No more than 1 or 2 hours before serving, drain excess marinade and add the garnish vegetables of your choice.
6. Serve on lettuce-lined plates or in hollowed-out tomatoes, if desired, for plated service, or in an attractive glass bowl with slotted serving spoon on a buffet.

Note: About ½ cup (125 ml) olive oil may be added to marinade, if desired.

Seafood and Fennel Salad

Serves: 10–12

	Ingredients:	
3 lb	sea legs (imitation crab)*	1350 g
1 lb	medium shrimp	450 g
1 cup	fresh lemon juice	¼ L
2	fennel bulbs	2
½ cup	each minced parsley and dill	125 ml
½ cup	flavorful olive oil	125 ml
	salt and pepper (to taste)	

*Surimi, fish that has been colored, flavored, and shaped to look like seafood is either welcomed or disparaged by chefs. It appears in many forms of varying quality. To my taste, the best is the type that is softer and looser packed. Prepared as it is here, it is tasty and provides an economical way to present a seafood salad, when the cost of crabmeat would be prohibitive to a client. (Remember to be honest in your approach, don't label it or price it as crabmeat!) Taste samples from your supplier before using in a recipe: The less salty and sweet, the better.

1. Wash the sea legs in several changes of cold water. Shred or break apart into bite-size pieces. Rinse again and drain well, pressing out excess water. This procedure will remove some of the excess salt and sugar in the product. Place in a shallow dish, cover with half the lemon juice, tossing to coat and refrigerate while preparing shrimp.
2. Cook the shrimp, then shell, devein, and split lengthwise in two.

3. Trim the fennel of its core, stem, and tough outside stalks. Cut into quarters or sixths and slice very thin or chop medium fine.
4. Combine the herbs and olive oil. Add the sea legs, shrimp, and fennel and as much more lemon juice as suited to your taste. The salad will probably not need any additional salt, but pepper generously.
5. Hold covered and refrigerated for up to two days. If prepared ahead, you might want to improve the flavor of the salad by draining off some of the excess juice and adding fresh lemon juice and olive oil to taste.

Note: You can prepare this salad using only sea legs and eliminate shrimp if desired.

Variations: If preferred, when using as a sandwich or tartlet filling, you may drain the salad of excess liquid and bind with a bit of herb mayonnaise instead. However, don't eliminate the lemon and oil dressing as it greatly improves the flavor of the salad. Chopped celery or chopped sweet onion or scallions may be added to the salad if desired.

Herring and Beet Salad (Sildesalat)

Serves: 10–12

Ingredients:

1 lb	pickled herring fillets	450 g
1 cup	cubed boiled potato	240 ml
2 cups	sliced pickled beets, reserve juice	½ L
1 cup	chopped tart apple	240 ml
6 tbls	minced onion	6 tbls
2 tbls	Dijon mustard	2 tbls
12 oz	sour cream	340 g
1 tbls	granulated sugar or as needed	1 tbls
1 tbls	white vinegar or as needed	1 tbls
	white pepper to taste	
	minced dill for garnish	

1. Drain the herring of its juice, if any. Cut the fillets into bite-size pieces or smaller if desired.
2. Combine the herring with the potatoes, beets, apple, and onion.
3. Mix the dressing by combining the mustard, sour cream, a bit of sugar, and vinegar. Add enough of the reserved beet juice to color the dressing a light pink. Fold into the salad ingredients until all the pieces are coated. You may not need all the dressing. Taste and adjust seasonings with pepper and additional sugar and vinegar to taste. Cover and refrigerate for at least several hours to blend flavors.
4. When ready to serve, mix the salad again, transfer to a serving bowl, and sprinkle with minced dill.

Pan Bagna

This is more a method than a recipe for these moist, filled sandwiches that must be prepared several hours or a day or two ahead. You may prepare individual servings, using small heros or round crusty rolls, or large sandwiches, using extra-long heros or great round breads that are cut into portions and served at a buffet. They are easy to make, messy (but very tasty) to eat, and an imaginative solution for a casual meal that must be prepared ahead. They can be eaten out of hand (with plenty of good napkins), but plates, forks, and knives will be appreciated by well-dressed hungry guests.

For fillings, use any of the tomato or roasted pepper salads (see in recipe index) as they are or combined with sliced salamis, prosciutto, mortadella, or other Italian cold cuts. Use thinly sliced or finely cut vegetables that have been marinated in zesty vinaigrettes; or prepare a nicoise filling with tuna, red onion, tomato, pitted bitter olives, feta cheese, anchovies, and shredded romaine, all dressed with Herb and Caper Vinaigrette (see Vinaigrette Basics in recipe index).

Procedure: Split the rolls or bread in two. Moisten the insides with olive oil or the appropriate vinaigrette or dressing. Layer with chosen filling, wrap tightly in plastic wrap. Place the filled sandwiches in a deep pan to catch any drips, cover with a baking sheet and weight. Store refrigerated for several hours at least. You may remove the weight after 2 or 3 hours, but keep wrapped until ready to serve. The bread crust will soften somewhat as it is supposed to. The whole sandwich will be moist and very flavorful.

Note: See Chapter 18 (The Tea Party) for suggestions about other sandwiches. For additional Small Meal ideas, see the recipes for Chewy Crust Pizza, Focaccia, Stuffed Pizza Slices, Antipasto Crepe Torta, Potato Leek Torta, and Spanokopita. Miniature Calzone, Mini Empanadas, and Shrimp and Feta Turnovers can also be made in larger sizes. (Refer to the recipe index.)

Baked Goods and Desserts

PIES AND TARTS

Lattice Crust Apple Crumb Tart

Serves: 12

Ingredients:

1 lb	Sweet Nut Pastry, made with walnuts (see in recipe index)	450 g
3 lbs	baking apples	1 kg 350 g
2 tbls	lemon juice	2 tbls
2 tbls	sweet butter	28 g
4 tbls	granulated sugar (or to taste)	35 g
2 tbls	calvados or applejack	30 ml
½ tsp	cinnamon	½ tsp
	For topping:	
1	egg white	1
1 tsp	cinnamon	1 tsp
2 tbls	sugar	2 tbls
3 tbls	chopped walnuts	3 tbls

1. Preheat the oven to 450° F (230° C).
2. Roll or press the pastry into a 10-in. (25 cm) loose-bottom tart shell. Save about one-fourth of the dough trimmings for the lattice crust. Bake for about 20 minutes, until lightly browned and firm. Set aside on a rack.

3. Peel, core, and slice the apples thickly. Place the lemon juice, butter, and sugar in a saucepan over very low heat. Add the apples as you peel them and simmer until the apples are just tender. Add a very small amount of water if needed to prevent scorching. Stir in the calvados and cinnamon. Taste and add a touch more sugar, if needed.
4. Roll the remaining pieces of dough out to form lattice strips. If the dough is too difficult to roll, shape into narrow ropes. Pour the filling into the tart, and criss-cross with the crust strips.
5. Mix the egg white with a few drops of water and stir to liquefy. Brush over surface of tart. Sprinkle with a mixture of the cinnamon, sugar, and nuts.
6. Lower the oven heat to 375°F (190°C). Bake the tart for about 40 minutes until set and nicely browned. Cool on a rack. When cool enough to handle, remove from tart ring and transfer to serving plate or cake round. Can be served warm or at room temperature. Whipped cream or creme fraiche can be served alongside, if desired.

Creamy Pumpkin Pie

Serves: 8

Ingredients:

1	8- or 9-in. (20–23 cm) pie shell	1
12 fl oz	cooked pumpkin puree	370 ml
5 oz	light brown sugar	140 g
2	eggs, lightly beaten	2
16 fl oz	heavy cream	500 ml
½ tsp	ground ginger	½ tsp
1 tsp	cinnamon	1 tsp
½ tsp	salt	½ tsp

The puree is best made fresh from "cheese pumpkin," a lighter skinned variety. Alternately, butternut squash may be used. The flesh may be prepared by paring and steaming the fruit, or baking halved fruits and scooping out the cooked flesh. It should be passed through a mill or sieved to remove fibers and then drained well to remove excess moisture. Cooked butternut squash is available already pureed or canned pumpkin may be used, although some brands are darker and stronger flavored. Be certain to drain either product, since excess moisture will ruin the consistency of the custard. Do not use pumpkin pie *filling*, which is already highly seasoned.

1. Preheat the oven to 425°F (220°C).
2. Egg wash the pie shell and blind bake* for 10 minutes. Set aside.
3. Combine the pumpkin, sugar, and spice. Mix well.
4. Add the eggs and the cream, beating at low speed until well combined but not frothy.

*To blind bake: Line the shell with foil or waxed paper, and weight it with pie weights, dried beans, or a second pie pan.

5. Pour into the prebaked crust. Bake at 425° F (220° C) for 10 minutes. Lower the heat to 375° F (190° C) and bake an additional 20 minutes. Remove to a rack to cool.

Note: Although the pie is best served the day it is baked, it can be held in a cool place or under refrigeration for 2 days. The egg wash helps to protect the crust from sogginess. As an alternative, bake the pie in a short nut crust or crumb crust, either of which will hold well under refrigeration.

Italian Ricotta Pie

Serves: 14

Ingredients:

For crust:

8 oz	all-purpose flour	224 g
1 tsp	baking powder	1 tsp
pinch	salt	pinch
4 oz	granulated sugar	112 g
grated rind of	1 orange	grated rind of
grated rind of	2 lemons	grated rind of
3 oz	sweet butter, chilled	84 g
2	eggs, beaten	2
	milk (as needed)	

For filling:

3 lb	ricotta cheese, drained	1 kg 350 g
6 oz	granulated sugar	180 g
4	eggs	4
1 tbls	grated orange rind	1 tbls
1 tbls	grated lemon rind	1 tbls
1 tbls	minced citron	1 tbls
2 oz	bittersweet chocolate, coarsely grated*	56 g

*Use a fine quality eating chocolate, such as Lindt's Excellence or Tobler's Tradition.

1. Prepare the crust: Combine the flour, baking powder, salt, sugar, and grated citrus rinds. Set aside.
2. Cut the butter into bits and cut into the dry ingredients until the consistency of coarse meal. Add the beaten eggs and just enough milk to form a soft, smooth dough.
3. Select an extra-deep 10-in. (25 cm) diameter pie pan. Set aside a scant one-fourth of the dough for the lattice-strip top.
4. Roll out the remaining dough on a lightly floured surface into a generous round. Line the pie plate with the dough, leaving the overhang in place.
5. Preheat the oven to 375° F (190° C).

6. Prepare the filling: Combine the drained ricotta with the sugar and 4 eggs and beat well to combine. Stir in the remaining ingredients and pour the filling into the shell.
7. Roll out the remaining dough and cut appropriate strips to form a lattice crust. Seal the strips to the crust with a few drops of water, trim the excess overhang, and crimp or flute the edge.
8. Bake at 375°F (190°C) for 20 minutes, then lower the oven heat to 350°F (180°C) and continue to bake for about 30 minutes more, until the crust is lightly browned and the filling is set. Remove to a rack to cool completely.
9. This pie is best eaten within 2 to 3 days. Keep in a cool place or refrigerated. Serve at cool room temperature.

Fruit Galettes

Serves: 8–10

	Ingredients:	
1 lb	puff pastry, cream cheese pastry, or plain pie crust pastry	450 g
4 or 5	baking apples or medium ripe pears, or both	4 or 5
2 tbls	sweet butter	28 g
5 tbls	granulated sugar	65 g
1 tbls	lemon juice	15 ml

This rustic-looking and crunchy dessert can be eaten out of hand, so it is a good choice for a casual buffet, picnic, or box lunch. Good quality puff pastry is preferred, but any unsweetened pie dough is fine to use.

1. Preheat the oven to 400°F (205°C). You will need a large flat baking sheet or shallow pizza pan for the galette.
2. Peel, core, and slice the fruits. Melt the butter and combine with 2 tbls (28 g) of the sugar and lemon juice. Moisten the fruit slices with this mixture. Set aside.
3. On a lightly floured work surface, roll out the dough very thin (even the puff pastry must be rolled thin). Transfer the dough to the baking sheet or pan and roll or pinch up a little rim around the edge. (You may shape the dough in a round or oblong, whatever you choose.)
4. Arrange the fruit slices attractively on the crust. If using both apples and pears, mix them or alternate rows of each. Sprinkle half the remaining sugar over the top of the fruit.
5. Bake for 35 minutes, then sprinkle with the remaining sugar and bake for an additional 25 to 35 minutes until the galette is very crisp and well browned. It should be very well cooked and crispy, but if you think it is actually burning, lower the oven heat a bit.
6. Remove to a rack or serving board or tray. The galette may be served very warm or may stand for several hours at room temperature. Use a very sharp knife or pizza cutter to slice into portions.

Note: If you want a glazed top, melt and strain apricot jam, thin with a bit of syrup or brandy, and brush over the tart after you take it from the oven.

Variation: For a fancier look, trim the dough to a perfect round and place the fruit slices in alternating concentric circles on the dough. At the center of the galette, use very thin slices of fruit as petals of a "rose." Bake as above; glaze carefully so as not to disturb the fruit slices. Individual rose galettes can be made by cutting 5 or 6 in. (13 or 15 cm) of dough and layering as above. These will take a little less cooking time and should be moved around in the oven for even cooking.

Lemon Meringue Pie or Tarts

Serves: 8

	Ingredients:	
1	**9-in. (23 cm) baked pie shell**	1
12 oz	**granulated sugar**	336 g
4 tbls	**cornstarch**	35 g
5 tbls	**cake flour**	40 g
¼ tsp	**salt**	¼ tsp
14 fl oz	**boiling water**	430 ml
3	**eggs, separated**	3
1½ tsp	**grated lemon rind**	2
6 tbls	**lemon juice**	90 ml
2 tbls	**sweet butter**	28 g
6 tbls	**confectioners' sugar**	50 g

1. Combine the granulated sugar, cornstarch, flour, and salt. Add a bit of the boiling water and stir to make a smooth paste. Add the rest of the water, stirring. Put mixture into a saucepan and cook, stirring until mixture thickens (about 3 minutes). Lower heat and continue to cook, stirring occasionally for a total of 15 minutes. Remove from heat.
2. In a separate bowl, combine the egg yolks, lemon rind, and juice. Mix thoroughly. Add a bit of the hot sugar water mixture to the eggs. Stir briskly and add more until the yolk mixture is warmed through. Now add the warm yolk mixture to the rest of the sugar water mixture in the saucepan. Cook over low heat, stirring, for 2 more minutes.
3. Remove from heat, stir in the butter until the mixture is smooth, and set aside to cool. You may refrigerate mixture at this point for 1 or 2 days until ready to bake the pie.
4. Just before baking, preheat the oven to 400° F (205° C). Whip the egg whites until thick, sprinkle with confectioners' sugar, and continue to beat until stiff and glossy, but not too dry.

5. Spread the cooled filling into the baked pie shell, spread with a layer of meringue, being sure to seal the edges of the pie with meringue. Pile or pipe the balance of the meringue on top in an attractive pattern or swirls.
6. Immediately bake the prepared pie until the meringue sets and the peaks are lightly browned. This pie is best served the day it is baked.

Note: You may use the same procedure to bake lemon meringue tarts, using a large tart shell or small shells of your choice. You may also use the filling for small tarts, eliminate the meringue and pipe with rosettes of whipped cream, garnished with candied mimosa or violets.

Variation: Use lime juice and lime rind in place of lemon. Key Lime juice, available bottled or frozen in specialty stores, is especially nice.

Macadamia Fudge Tartlets

Yield: about 70 tartlets

	Ingredients:	
1 recipe	Flaky Cream Cheese Pastry (see in recipe index)	1 recipe
6 oz	sweet chocolate (German's)	180 g
1 oz	sweet butter	30 g
3 oz	granulated sugar	85 g
2 tbls	cream	30 ml
2	whole eggs	2
7 oz	macadamia nuts, chopped	200 g

1. Prepare a single recipe of Flaky Cream Cheese Pastry. After the dough has rested sufficiently, prepare 1-in. (2½ cm) tartlet shells as follows: press a small piece of dough into each shell and press to fill, using floured fingers or a suitable object, such as a wooden pestle. Trim any excess dough from the edges. Refrigerate prepared shells while making filling.
2. Preheat the oven to 350° F (180° C).
3. Melt the chocolate and butter over hot water. Stir in sugar until dissolved and remove from heat. Add the cream. Let cool to lukewarm.
4. Beat the eggs lightly and gradually stir into the chocolate mixture.
5. Stir in the macadamia nuts, mixing well to distribute the nuts.
6. Place prepared tartlet shells on jelly roll pan. Fill each tartlet with a scant teaspoon of filling. They should be about half full.

7. Bake for 20 to 25 minutes. The filling will have puffed up and the pastry just begun to color. Do not overbake or the tartlets will taste too dry when cooled.
8. Remove the tartlet shells to a rack to cool for about 5 minutes. When cool enough to handle, carefully remove tartlets from shells and allow to cool completely. Store airtight.

Note: See recipe for Tiny Pecan Tarts (see in recipe index) for note about tartlet shells.

Peaches and Cream Tart

Serves: 8–10

	Ingredients:	
1 lb	Sweet Nut Pastry (see in recipe index)	
1½ lb	ripe peaches (approx.)	675 g
8 oz	granulated sugar	225 g
2 cups	water	½ L
4 tbls	lemon juice	60 ml
1 tsp	cinnamon	1 tsp
⅛ tsp each	ground ginger and cloves	⅛ tsp each
	For custard:	
1	egg	1
1	egg yolk	1
1 cup	light cream	¼ L
2 oz	granulated sugar	60 g
1 tbls	peach or plain brandy	15 ml

1. Preheat the oven to 400°F (205°C). Have ready a 10-in. (25 cm) loose-bottom tart pan and a baking sheet.
2. Line the tart pan with the dough, being sure to form a nice rim. Bake blind as follows: Line with foil or parchment, weight with beans or pie weights, and bake for 5 to 10 minutes, just until set up and barely colored. Set aside.
3. Combine the sugar, water, lemon juice, and spices. Bring to the simmer in a deep saucepan large enough to hold the peaches. If the peaches are very ripe, drop into the syrup, remove from heat and let stand about 3 minutes. If the peaches are only slightly ripe, simmer in the syrup for 3 to 5 minutes. Whether just soaking or poaching the fruit, soak a linen or paper towel in syrup and cover the fruit in the pot.

4. Remove the towel and the peaches from the syrup. Slip off the skins, halve and remove the pits. Cut into even sections (about six or eight slices per half). Place in the tart shell, beginning at the outside edge. Place the slices with their outside curves facing the rim of the tart, continuing in smaller and smaller circles until you reach the center. Trim the center pieces to fit into a little pinwheel design.
5. Place the filled tart pan on the baking sheet. Bake for 20 minutes.
6. While the tart is having its first baking, prepare the custard by stirring together the egg, yolk, light cream, sugar, and brandy. When the tart has baked for 20 minutes, carefully pull out the oven rack and pour the custard evenly over the tart. Depending on the exact quantity of fruit, you may have some custard left over; don't overfill the tart, or it will spill over. Carefully slide the oven rack back into place and bake the tart for an additional 25 to 30 minutes until the custard is set and evenly colored. Remove to a rack to cool. This will hold for a few hours at room temperature. It may be refrigerated if necessary; the nut crust is sturdy and will not get soggy.

Red, White, and Blue Ribbon Fruit Tart

Serves: 12

Ingredients:

1 recipe	**Flaky Cream Cheese Pastry (see in recipe index)**	1 recipe
1	**whole egg**	1
2 tbls	**light cream**	30 ml
1 pt	**Pastry Cream (see Pastry Cream and Variations in recipe index)**	½ L
2 pt	**strawberries**	1 L
2 pt	**blueberries**	1 L
6 oz	**fruit glaze***	168 g
8 oz	**heavy cream**	224 g
1 tbls	**confectioners' sugar**	15 g
1 tbls	**kirsch**	15 ml

*Commercial fruit glaze can be purchased, or you can melt some apple or strawberry jelly, add a bit of corn syrup, and use the sauce as a glaze.

1. Prepare a single recipe (1½ lb [675 g]) of Flaky Cream Cheese Pastry. After the dough has rested sufficiently, roll the dough out on a lightly floured surface to a rough rectangle (at least 15 × 18 in. [38–45 cm]). Gently fold the dough and unfold onto a lightly floured or parchment-lined baking sheet (15 × 13 in. [38 × 30 cm]). Use a sharp knife or a pastry wheel to trim the dough to fit the baking sheet. Reserve the trimmings, unrolled.

2. Beat the egg and light cream together. Use this egg wash to brush over the surface of the pastry sheet. Cut 1-in. (2½ cm) strips from the trimmings and lay on the edges of the pastry as a border. (Unbroken strips give the best result. Shorter strips should be butted end to end and the joint covered by a decorative piece of dough, attached with egg wash.) Make the design as symmetrical as possible and the borders even. With a fingertip, press along the center of the strips along the border to help them adhere. Do not squash the edges. Dock all along the outside edge. Carefully egg wash the tops of the border strips. If not baking immediately, refrigerate prepared dough.
3. To bake: Preheat the oven to 425°F (220°C). Prick the inner surface of the dough. Bake 12 to 15 minutes or until golden brown. If the center of the tart puffs while baking, gently flatten with a spatula. Cool on sheet.
4. About 1 hour before serving, prepare the fruit by picking over and rinsing the blueberries. Drain on paper towel. Rinse and hull the strawberries. If tiny, they may be left whole. If large, slice lengthwise. If the strawberries are not perfectly ripe, discard any slices that are too white or cottony looking.
5. Whip the heavy cream with the sugar and kirsch until of piping consistency. Chill. Prepare a pastry bag with a rosette or star tip.
6. Spread a thin layer of pastry cream on the tart. The cream should only be half the depth of the crust border. You may not need all the pastry cream. Slide the filled tart onto a sturdy cake cardboard.
7. Use a bench scraper to score guidelines in the pastry cream for the placement of the berries. Diagonal or lengthwise bands are most attractive. Beginning at one end or corner carefully place the berries in alternating sections (overlap the strawberry slices). Gently brush the fruit with glaze.
8. Pipe rosettes of cream evenly between the sections of berries.

Note: For a Fourth of July celebration, this dessert is spectacular, if corny, especially if it is made in the design of a flag.

Variations: Other fruits or berries may be used and arranged in a design of one's choosing. Or a large round tart can be decorated with concentric patterns of fruit.

Tiny Pecan Tarts

Yield: 80 tarts

	Ingredients:	
1 recipe	**Flaky Cream Cheese Pastry (see in recipe index)**	1 recipe
	For filling:	
2	**eggs, lightly beaten**	2
7 oz	**dark brown sugar**	196 g
3 fl oz	**light corn syrup**	90 ml

½ oz	sweet butter, softened	15 g
1 tbls	bourbon	15 ml
pinch	salt	pinch
8 oz	pecans, finely chopped	224 g

1. Prepare a single recipe of Flaky Cream Cheese Pastry. After the dough has rested sufficiently, prepare 1-in. (2½ cm) tartlet shells as follows: Press a small piece of dough into each shell and press to fill, using floured fingers or a suitable object, such as a wooden pestle. Trim any excess dough from the edges. Refrigerate prepared shells while making filling.
2. Preheat the oven to 350° F (180° C). Combine all the filling ingredients. Mix well.
3. Place prepared tartlet shells on jelly roll pan. Fill each tartlet with a scant teaspoon of filling.
4. Bake for 25 to 30 minutes, until the filling has puffed and set and the tartlets are lightly browned. If they appear to be burning, lower the oven heat.
5. Remove to a rack to cool slightly. Remove tartlets from tins, cool completely, and pack airtight for storage. If desired, dust lightly with confectioners' sugar just before serving.

Note: Obviously the size of the tartlet shells determines accurate yield. Good quality tartlet tins should be wiped clean or very gently hand washed in mild soap suds and dried thoroughly. Never scour or they will stick! If only a small number of tartlet shells are available, they can be baked in batches. The filling can rest at room temperature, but keep the pastry chilled for easy handling.

Variations: **Tiny Walnut Tarts:** Walnuts may be substituted for economy; add a bit more butter to the filling to improve texture. Eliminate the bourbon, add vanilla extract and a dash of cinnamon.

Flaky Cream Cheese Pastry

Yield: 1½ lb		*674 g*
	Ingredients:	
8 oz	sweet butter, chilled	224 g
8 oz	brick cream cheese	224 g
6 oz	all-purpose flour	168 g
2 oz	cake flour	56 g
¼ tsp	salt	1 ml

1. Cut the chilled butter and the cream cheese into bits.
2. Combine the salt with the flours. Rub or cut in the butter until mixture resembles coarse crumbs. Rub in cream cheese to form a soft, streak-free dough. Processor method: Put flours and salt in a bowl, add the bits of butter and cream cheese, toss to coat with flour. Place the entire mixture into the processor workbowl and pulse until the dough begins to mass into a ball.

3. Pat the dough into a disc, dust lightly with flour, and wrap in plastic wrap or waxed paper. Chill several hours or overnight.
4. After resting, dough is ready to use, or it may be frozen for later use. Thaw wrapped, under refrigeration.

Note: This recipe makes sufficient dough for a large rectangular freestanding tart, 15 × 13 in. (38 × 30 cm); two 9- or 10-in. (23 or 25 cm) tarts; or about 80 miniature tartlets. Weight or prick dough if baking blind.

This dough has a flaky consistency that makes it suitable for hors d'oeuvre or dessert pastries, reminiscent of, but not equal to doughs made with puff pastry. In this regard, appropriate seasonings, such as pepper or cheese, or sugar can be added in small quantities (up to 2 oz) to the dry ingredients as the dough is being prepared.

Sweet Nut Pastry

Yield: 2 lb		900 g
	Ingredients:	
8 oz	all-purpose flour	224 g
4 oz	cake flour	112 g
5 oz	ground almonds, walnuts, pecans, or hazelnuts	140 g
6 oz	granulated sugar	168 g
¼ tsp	salt	¼ tsp
8 oz	sweet butter, cold, in bits	224 g
1	egg, lightly beaten	1
1 tbls	cream	15 ml

1. Combine the dry ingredients, tossing with a fork a few times to evenly distribute the nuts and sugar. Cut in the butter until the mixture resembles coarse meal. Stir the cream into the egg yolk and add to the flour and butter mixture a bit at a time. Stir with a fork and add only enough until the mixture forms a soft dough that pulls away from the bowl.
2. Turn the dough out onto floured plastic wrap. Divide into two or four pieces. Pat into discs, wrap, and refrigerate for at least 1 hour. Freeze for more than 2-day storage.
3. This is a short crust and a bit more difficult to handle than regular pie crust. Always roll on a lightly floured surface or on waxed paper. Work with cold dough. Rather than rolling, this dough can simply be pressed into small tart shells.

BREADS AND MUFFINS

Egg Bread

Yield: Five 1-pound (450 g) loaves or approx. 4 dozen rolls

Ingredients:

1 pt	milk	½ L
8 oz	sweet butter	224 g
1 tsp	salt	1 tsp
8 oz	granulated sugar	224 g
4	eggs, lightly beaten	4
1¼ oz	dry yeast (4 pkg.)	28 g
⅔ cup	warm water, 115°F (46°C)	158 ml
40 oz	all-purpose flour (approx.)	1 kg 124 g
	egg wash	

1. Scald the milk, add the butter, and allow to melt. Stir in the salt and sugar, and, when the mixture has cooled to lukewarm, add the beaten eggs. Set aside.
2. Dissolve the yeast in the warm water. Set aside.
3. Place about 1 lb (450 g) flour in a bowl, make a well and add the milk and egg mixture and the dissolved yeast. Beat well to combine thoroughly.
4. Add more flour gradually, beating and/or kneading after each addition. Continue to add flour until the mixture forms a soft, smooth dough that is moist but not sticky. Turn out onto a lightly floured board to complete kneading. The dough is easy to handle and does not require vigorous kneading. Cover and let rise until double in bulk.
5. Shape into loaves, rolls, braids, coils, or any shapes you desire (see a baking text or recipes for Pumpkin Bread dough for other ideas. Once shaped, the dough should be set on baking pans and allow to rise almost double before baking.
6. To bake: Preheat oven to 350°F (180°C). Brush risen bread with egg wash and bake until deep golden brown and hollow sounding.

Note: This bread is similar to, but not quite as eggy or buttery as a brioche or challah bread. This sweetened version has been Grandma Serra's Easter Bread in our family for years. The Greeks make a similar bread, often flavoring theirs with ground cardamom. It has a delicious taste, especially when warmed as a dinner roll or shaped into cloverleaf or parkerhouse rolls and served with tea. It is good to serve for brunch and wonderful toasted, whether with foie gras or butter and preserves.

Variations: Convert to a plain bread by reducing the sugar to 1 tbls (15 g). This version makes an excellent dough for wrapping sausages, franks, or whole cheeses, for example Brie or Camembert. For wrapping cocktail franks or sausages, spread dough with mustard, wrap, and egg glaze. Sprinkle with poppy or sesame seeds if you like. This recipe will prepare 4 to 5 dozen wrapped hors d'oeuvre.

Cinnamon Bread: Scale dough to 1 lb (450 g) portions. Roll each piece flat, brush with melted butter and sprinkle generously with cinnamon sugar (and raisins, if you like). Roll up firmly and place seam side down in a buttered loaf pan. Brush with melted butter. Allow to rise to double in size. Bake for about 40 minutes or until loaf makes a hollow sound when tapped.

Pumpkin Bread Dough

Yield: 10 lb		4½ kg
	Ingredients:	
	Sponge:	
1¼ oz	dry yeast (4 pkg)	28 g
1 cup	warm water 115°F (46°C)	¼ L
1 tbls	granulated sugar	15 g
2 oz	all-purpose flour	56 g
	Bread:	
2 cups	milk	½ L
4 to 5 lb	all-purpose flour (total)	2 kg (approx.)
12 oz	granulated sugar	340 g
1½ tsp	salt	1½ tsp
2½ cups	pumpkin puree	600 ml
1 lb	sweet butter, softened	450 g

1. Prepare the sponge. Dissolve the yeast in warm water, stir in the small amounts of 1 tbls (15 g) sugar and 2 oz (56 g) flour. Let proof for about 10 minutes.
2. Scald the milk and set aside to cool to lukewarm.
3. In a large bowl or in a mixer fitted with a dough hook, place 2 lb (900 g) of the flour, 12 oz (340 g) sugar and the salt. Mix to combine.
4. Add the pumpkin puree, the lukewarm milk, the softened butter, and the proofed sponge. Stir or beat until all the ingredients are thoroughly combined.

5. Gradually add most of the remaining flour, beating or kneading until a soft, moist (but not sticky), dough forms.
6. Turn the dough out onto a floured board or work surface. Knead by hand for a few minutes until the dough is smooth and moist.
7. Place the dough in a buttered bowl, turn over to butter the surface. Set smooth side up in the bowl, cover, and set aside to rise to double its volume.
8. When the dough has doubled in bulk, turn out, punch down and shape into desired form (see below). Once shaped, allow the dough to rise almost double. Bake in a 450° F (230° C) oven until light textured and golden brown. Bake small rolls or buns for 10 to 15 minutes, large loaves or cakes an hour or more.

Note: This dough can be shaped in any way appropriate for sweet doughs (see a good culinary text or baking manual). A few ideas are listed below.

Variations: **Monkey Bread:** Generously butter two 10-in. (25 cm) bundt pans, or use the volume equivalent of other pans, such as ovenproof pudding basins, deep cake pans, or charlotte molds (you can even use clean, soaked flower pots if you wrap the bottom in double foil to seal the drain hole. Melt about 1 lb (500 g) of butter, cool to lukewarm. Break off irregular knobs of dough, dip in melted butter and layer randomly into pan until half to two-thirds full. Let rise about 20 minutes. Bake for at least 1 hour, depending on pan size. Let bread rest about 15 minutes after baking, then unmold. Guests break off pieces of dough as portions. Serve warm.

Pumpkin Cloverleaf Rolls: Scale out about 1½ lb (680 g) dough for each muffin tin. Shape dough into balls, three for each muffin depression, dip in butter, place in muffin tin, let rise 15 minutes, brush with melted butter or egg wash and bake for about 20 minutes. Can be reheated, well wrapped.

Tiny Buns: Roll dough flat, cut out with a 1- to 1½-in. (2½ to 4 cm) biscuit cutter. Brush tops with melted butter. Bake on greased baking sheet for about 10 minutes. These tiny buns are wonderful for hors d'oeuvre, split and filled with slivers of smoked meat, with herb butter, or onion jam.

Pumpkin Coffee Cake Wreaths: Divide dough into three or four parts. Roll each piece flat into a rectangle. Brush with melted butter, sprinkle with cinnamon sugar, currants or raisins, and chopped nuts. Roll dough up jelly-roll style, overlap ends of the roll to form a circle. At 1-in. (2½ cm) intervals, make deep slashes all along outer edge of circle, fan out slices, all in one direction. Brush with melted butter or egg wash, sprinkle with more cinnamon sugar and chopped nuts.

Sticky Buns: Follow similar procedure as for wreaths, that is, roll dough flat, fill (use brown sugar and honey), and roll. Slice rolls into 2-in. (6 cm) pieces. Prepare cake pans: butter, spread with brown sugar, cinnamon, and/or honey, and coarsely chopped pecans or walnuts. Dip slices into melted butter, fit slices into pan, bake and unmold to serve.

Oatmeal Applesauce Muffins

Yield: 12 muffins

	Ingredients:	
4 oz	rolled oats	112 g
5 oz	whole wheat flour	140 g
6 oz	all-purpose flour	168 g
¾ tsp	cinnamon	¾ tsp
1½ tsp	baking powder	1½ tsp
¾ tsp	baking soda	¾ tsp
1 cup	applesauce	¼ L
4 fl oz	buttermilk	125 ml
3½ oz	brown sugar	84 g
1 oz	granulated sugar	28 g
3 tbls	vegetable oil	45 ml
1	egg	1
2 oz	raisins	60 g
2 oz	chopped walnuts	60 g

1. Preheat the oven to 400°F (205°C). Prepare muffin tins by greasing and flouring or use paper liners.
2. Combine the oats, flours, cinnamon, baking powder, and baking soda in a large bowl. Set aside.
3. Mix together the applesauce, buttermilk, sugars, vegetable oil, and egg.
4. Mix the wet ingredients into the dry in a few strokes, just to moisten the ingredients. Do not overmix. Stir in the raisins and nuts.
5. Spoon the batter into the prepared tins. Each muffin cup should be about three-quarters full.
6. Bake for 25 to 30 minutes. Remove to rack to cool. Wrap airtight to store. Freeze, if desired. Reheat wrapped to serve warm.

Variation: **Oatmeal Pineapple Muffins:** Substitute well-drained crushed pineapple for the applesauce, reduce granulated sugar by ½ oz (15 g).

Banana Nut Loaf

Yield: 12–14 slices

Ingredients:

4 oz	sweet butter, softened	115 g
8 oz	granulated sugar	225 g
2	eggs	2
2 tbls	orange juice	30 ml
12 oz	mashed ripe banana	340 g
6 oz	all-purpose flour	180 g
2 oz	quick-cooking oats	60 g
1 tbls + 1 tsp	baking powder	1 tbls + 1 tsp
½ tsp	salt	½ tsp
1 tsp	cinnamon	1 tsp
¼ tsp	ground ginger	¼ tsp
3 oz	pecans, coarsely chopped	85 g

1. Preheat oven to 350°F (180°C) degrees. Prepare a standard loaf pan by greasing and dusting with fine dry bread crumbs.
2. Cream the butter with the sugar. Add the eggs, orange juice, and banana.
3. Add the dry ingredients and stir only to mix.
4. Pour batter into prepared pan. If desired, extra nuts and oats may be sprinkled on top before baking. Bake for 1 hour or until tester comes out clean.
5. Cool in pan for 30 minutes, then turn out and cool completely before wrapping. Best made at least 1 day ahead. Will keep, well wrapped for several days. Freezes well. Thaw wrapped. Very good sliced and lightly toasted as a breakfast or brunch bread.

Cranberry Walnut Bread

Yield: about 30 slices

Ingredients:

12 oz	all-purpose flour	350 g
4 oz	whole wheat flour	112 g
1½ tsp	salt	1½ tsp
3 tsp	baking powder	3 tsp
1 tsp	baking soda	1 tsp
12 oz	granulated sugar	350 g
2	eggs	2
2 oz	sweet butter, melted	56 g

4 oz	orange juice	125 ml
1 oz	brandy	30 ml
3 tbls	grated orange rind	3 tbls
3 oz	walnuts, coarsely chopped	85 g
6 oz	cranberries, coarsely chopped	180 g
3 oz	golden raisins	85 g

1. Preheat the oven to 350°F (180°C). Prepare two standard loaf or bread pans by greasing and dusting with dry bread crumbs. Set aside.
2. Sift together the dry ingredients. Set aside.
3. Combine the eggs, melted butter, juice, and brandy and mix to combine.
4. Add the liquid ingredients to the sifted dry ingredients and mix just until moistened.
5. Fold in the nuts, cranberries, orange rind, and raisins.
6. Turn the batter into the prepared pans and bake for 1 hour 10 minutes or until the top just begins to crack and the bread begins to shrink from the sides of the pan.
7. Cool in the pans for 15 minutes. Turn out on rack and cool completely before wrapping. Well wrapped, this bread keeps fresh for a week or more. It freezes very well. Thaw wrapped.

Note: The yield assumes that the bread will be thinly sliced, as for tea sandwiches or canapes.

CAKES
Chocolate Tart Cherry Torte

Serves: 8–10

Ingredients:

¼ cup	dried tart cherries	60 ml
2 tbls	kirsch	30 ml
3 tbls	cornstarch	20 g
4 tbls	cake flour	35 g
8 oz	sweet butter	225 g
4 oz	unsweetened chocolate	115 g
4 oz	semisweet chocolate	115 g
6	eggs, separated	6
5 oz	granulated sugar	140 g

1. Preheat the oven to 350°F (180°C). Grease a 10-in. (25 cm) round cake pan with butter, dust with cocoa, and set aside. Put the dried tart cherries in the kirsch to plump. Sift the cornstarch and flour together twice. Have the sifter handy for use.
2. Melt the chocolates and the butter over low heat. When they are almost melted, remove from heat and stir smooth. Set aside.

3. Beat the egg whites until soft peaks form. Gradually add the sugar and beat to combine. The egg whites should be fairly stiff, but not dry, or they will break down. Beat the yolks lightly, then add to the whites and beat for 3 to 4 minutes.
4. Sift some of the cornstarch and flour mixture over the eggs then add some of the chocolate mixture to the eggs. Fold and make more additions of both until the batter is even colored and well combined. Fold gently but thoroughly.
5. Pour about two-thirds of the batter into the prepared pan, place the plumped cherries evenly over the batter. Cover with the remaining batter.
6. Bake for 30 to 35 minutes. The edges will be set but the middle of the cake will still test moist. Remove to a rack to cool for about 20 minutes. Free the edges of the cake from the pan with a thin spatula. Jerk the pan to loosen the cake but do not remove until completely cooled.
7. Unmold the cake when cooled, placing it upside down on a serving plate. Leave plain and serve with whipped cream or sprinkle with confectioners' sugar.

Note: This cake is not glamorous looking but is very rich and luxurious in taste.

Chocolate Chip Rum Cake

Serves: 8–10

	Ingredients:	
4 oz	unsweetened chocolate	115 g
4 oz	sweet butter	115 g
½ cup	boiling water	125 ml
½ cup	dark rum	125 ml
12 oz	granulated sugar	340 g
4 oz	light brown sugar	115 g
1½ tsp	baking soda	1½ tsp
4 oz	sour cream	115 g
2	eggs	2
1 tbls	pure vanilla extract	15 ml
8 oz	flour	225 g
pinch	salt	pinch
6 oz	semisweet chocolate, grated or minichips	180 g
	softened butter and cocoa for pans	
	For frosting:	
1 cup	heavy cream	¼ L
3 tbls	confectioners' sugar	20 g
1 tbls	dark rum	15 ml

1. Preheat the oven to 375°F (190°C). Grease two 8-in. (20 cm) round baking pans and dust with cocoa. Set aside.
2. Melt the chocolate and butter together in a saucepan: Do not overheat. Add the boiling water, the rum, and the sugars and stir over low heat until the sugars are completely dissolved. Scrape the mixture into a mixing bowl. Let cool to lukewarm, stirring once or twice.
3. Stir the baking soda into the sour cream and stir into the chocolate mixture. Add the eggs and vanilla and beat until blended. Combine the flour with the salt and add to the batter. Mix, scraping the bowl to combine evenly. Stir in the grated chocolate. Turn into the two prepared pans and bake for 40 to 45 minutes until the cake just begins to pull away from the sides of the pan.
4. Remove to a rack to cool for 15 minutes, then unmold the cakes to a rack and let cool completely. When cooled the layers may be wrapped and frozen for later use.
5. When the cakes are cool, prepare the frosting by whipping the cream and adding the sugar and rum. Use a sharp serrated knife to split each layer in two. Spread cream between the layers and on top. Chill until 30 minutes before serving.

Variation: This cake may be frosted with Chocolate Ganache or Brown Sugar Cream (see in recipe index). For an elegant torte, spread single whole layers with strained raspberry or apricot jam and glaze cake with liquid Chocolate Ganache.

Hazelnut Chiffon Cake

Serves: 14

	Ingredients:	
8½ oz	cake flour	224 g
8 oz	granulated sugar	224 g
3½ oz	light brown sugar	84 g
3 tsp	baking powder	3 tsp
1 tsp	salt	1 tsp
5	egg yolks	5
4 fl oz	water	125 ml
4 fl oz	hazelnut oil	125 ml
2 tbls	Frangelico (hazelnut liqueur)	30 ml
8	egg whites	8
½ tsp	cream of tartar	½ tsp
5 oz	hazelnuts, toasted and ground	140 g

For years, my mother and I made this cake with flavorless vegetable oil, and it was quite delicious. However, Rose Levy Berenbaum's magnificent book, *The Cake Bible* (William Morrow and Company, 1988), suggests using nut oils to enhance the flavor of chocolate genoise. I tried the substitution in this cake and was delighted with the result.

1. Preheat the oven to 325° F (165° C). Have ready a 10-in. loose-bottom tube pan, clean, dry, and free of grease.
2. Sift together the flour, sugars, baking powder, and salt. Set aside.
3. Combine the egg yolks, water, hazelnut oil, and Frangelico.
4. Add the egg yolk mixture to the dry ingredients and mix to combine.
5. Whip the egg whites with the cream of tartar to soft peaks.
6. Fold the beaten whites into the yolk mixture. Carefully fold in the nuts.
7. Turn into the tube pan and bake for 55 minutes at 325° F (165° C). Raise the oven heat to 350° F (180° C) for another 10 to 15 minutes, until the cake is lightly browned and slightly springy to the touch.
8. Remove from the oven and invert the pan, balancing the tube over a funnel or other suitable prop. Let the cake remain in this position until completely cooled.
9. To remove the cake from the pan, use a sharp, thin knife to free the cake sides, remove the outer pan, and rest the cake on the tube bottom. Slide the knife under the bottom of the cake, pressing against the pan and rotating the tube. Free the cake from the central core by carefully working the knife between the cake and the core. Invert the tube and gently lower the freed cake to the work surface. Keep covered until ready to fill and frost.
10. Fill and frost with Brown Sugar Cream (see in recipe index) or with lightly sweetened whipped cream flavored with more Frangelico, as follows: Prepare the cream filling. Split the cake (use a finely serrated knife and a gentle sawing motion) into three or four layers. Fill and reassemble the layers, and frost the top, sides, and center core. Keep refrigerated with a protective cover for several hours until ready to serve. Use the serrated knife to cut portions.

Variations: Other nuts, corresponding nut oils, and complementary liqueurs can be substituted. Brown Sugar Cream (see in recipe index) is quite delicious with any nut flavor, but liqueur or brandy flavored whipped creams can be used for specific flavor effects.

Blueberry Brunch Cake

Serves: 12

	Ingredients:	
1 lb	all-purpose flour	450 g
2½ tsp	baking powder	2½ tsp
½ tsp	salt	½ tsp
1 tsp	cinnamon	1 tsp
½ tsp	ground ginger	½ tsp
8 oz	sweet butter, softened	225 g
8 oz	granulated sugar	225 g

4	eggs	4
1 cup	milk	¼ L
1 tsp	vanilla extract or rum	5 ml
1 tbls	orange juice	15 ml
1 tsp	grated orange zest	1 tsp
3 cups	blueberries	¾ L
	For streusel crumbs:	
4 oz	granulated sugar	112 g
4 oz	brown sugar	112 g
2 oz	all-purpose flour	56 g
1 tsp	cinnamon	1 tsp
pinch	salt	⅛ tsp
4 oz	cold butter	112 g

1. Preheat the oven to 375° F (190° C). Butter an 8 × 12 in. (20 × 30 cm) baking dish.
2. Prepare the streusel crumbs: Combine the sugars, flour, cinnamon, and salt. Cut the cold butter into the dry ingredients until the mixture is crumbly. Do not cut too fine. Refrigerate while preparing cake.
3. Wash and pick over the blueberries. Drain well and set aside.
4. Combine the flour, baking powder, salt, cinnamon, and ground ginger. Set aside.
5. Cream the butter with the sugar until fluffy. Add the eggs and beat 2 or 3 minutes. Add the milk and flavorings alternately with the flour mixture and beat just until smooth.
6. Pour the batter into the prepared pan. Distribute the blueberries over the surface of the batter. Top with the streusel crumbs.
7. Bake for 40 to 45 minutes. Serve warm or at room temperature, sprinkled with confectioners' sugar.

New England Maple Log

Serves: 10

	Ingredients:	
6	eggs, separated	6
3 oz	light brown sugar	84 g
2 oz	granulated sugar	56 g
2 tbls	pure maple syrup	30 ml
6 oz	finely ground pecans	168 g
1 tsp	baking powder	1 tsp
pinch	salt	pinch

	For filling:	
12 fl oz	**heavy cream**	370 ml
2 tsp	**superfine granulated sugar**	10 g
1 tbls	**pure maple syrup**	15 ml

	For nut brittle:	
4 fl oz	**light corn syrup**	125 ml
2 fl oz	**pure maple syrup**	60 ml
4 oz	**pecan halves**	112 g

For optional garnish: maple leaves, coating chocolate

1. Preheat the oven to 375°F (190°C). Prepare a 15½ × 10½ × 1 in. (39 × 25 cm) jelly roll pan by greasing, lining with waxed paper or parchment, and greasing the paper.
2. Beat the egg yolks until pale yellow, then gradually add the sugars and syrup. Continue to beat until the mixture forms a ribbon.
3. Toss the nuts with the baking powder and stir them into the yolk mixture. Set aside.
4. In a separate bowl, beat the egg whites and salt until the white forms soft peaks. Do not beat dry.
5. Fold the whites into the yolk mixture carefully. Combine thoroughly without deflating.
6. Spread the batter evenly in the prepared pan. Bake for 18 to 19 minutes. The surface of the cake will spring back lightly when touched.
7. Remove the pan from the oven and immediately cover the surface of the cake with a dampened flat-weave towel (a side towel or tea towel): Do not use anything with a nubby terrycloth weave because it will ruin the surface of the cake. Set aside to cool covered. If holding for later filling, cover the whole with plastic wrap to prevent drying out.
8. Prepare filling: Whip the chilled cream with the sugar and syrup until stiff. (To hold the cream or filled cake for several hours, add a stabilizer.)
9. Invert the towel-covered cake onto a flat surface. Carefully peel off the paper. Spread about half of the filling evenly over the surface of the cake. Use the towel to gently nudge the cake into a jelly roll shape.
10. Ease the rolled cake onto a serving platter or board. Spread the remaining cream evenly over the roll. Leave the ends exposed. Cut a diagonal slice off one or both ends. Use the trimmings to form a "knot" to place decoratively on the cake.
11. To prepare brittle: Boil the syrups down to the hard crack stage. Mix in the nuts and immediately turn out onto an oiled pan. When cooled, break into odd-size pieces for garnish. Or alternately, dip single nuts into the syrup to make more perfect pieces.

12. To garnish: Comb or ridge the cream to simulate bark. Chocolate may be piped on to enhance this effect. Place pieces of the brittle attractively on and around the log. Crush bits of brittle into crumbs to sprinkle over the log. If desired, maple leaves of chocolate or colored coating can decorate the serving board. For a centerpiece dessert, several logs can be joined to resemble a fallen tree branch. Roll some cakes lengthwise to form thinner branches.

Cheesecake

Serves: 12

Ingredients:

16 oz	whipped cream cheese	450 g
1 tsp	vanilla extract	5 ml
1 oz	granulated sugar	28 g
pinch	salt	pinch
1 oz	all-purpose flour	28 g
4	egg yolks	4
1 tbls	lemon juice	15 ml
8 fl oz	heavy cream	¼ L
4	egg whites	4
2 oz	sugar, granulated	56 g
3 oz	sweet butter	84 g
6 oz	gingersnap crumbs	168 g

1. Prepare a 9-in. (23 cm) springform pan for water-bath baking by overwrapping with foil or tape to prevent leakage from the bottom seal. Lightly butter the sides of the pan or spray with a nonstick coating. Melt the 3 oz (84 g) of butter and combine with the gingersnap crumbs. Place the mixture in the pan, press to bottom and slightly up sides to form crust. Refrigerate while preparing batter.
2. Preheat oven to 325° F (165° C).
3. Combine the cream cheese, vanilla, 1 oz (28 g) of sugar, flour, and salt. Cream until fluffy.
4. Add the egg yolks. Beat to combine. Add the lemon juice and the cream and beat until smooth and creamy.
5. In a separate bowl beat the egg whites with the additional 2 oz (56 g) of sugar until the whites form soft peaks.

6. Fold the whites into the cream cheese mixture.
7. Pour batter into prepared pan. Set pan in a water bath and bake for 1 hour and 20 minutes. To test for doneness: The center of the cake will wiggle slightly when the cake is tapped.
8. Let cake cool in the turned-off open oven for about an hour. Refrigerate, well wrapped. Remove from pan and transfer to serving plate when cake is well chilled and firm.

Note: The cake may be baked without a water bath if desired. The cooking time will be shorter and the end product less creamy with browner sides but still quite good.

Variations: Zwieback crumbs or dry bread crumbs mixed with sugar can be substituted for the gingersnap crumbs.
Marble Cheesecake: Substitute chocolate cookie crumbs for gingersnap crumbs. Eliminate the lemon juice. Set aside about two-thirds of the prepared batter. Add 4 oz (120 ml) melted and cooled semisweet chocolate to the remaining one-third batter. Place batter in pan in alternating cupsful, creating a random pattern of both colors. When all the batter has been used, drag a spatula through the batter in a curving motion in three or four places for a marbleized effect. Bake this variation in the water bath for best results.

Pumpkin Cheesecake

Serves: 12

	Ingredients:	
1	**crumb crust (see Cheesecake recipe)**	1
16 oz	**whipped cream cheese**	450 g
6 oz	**granulated sugar**	180 g
2 oz	**light brown sugar**	60 g
1 tbls	**all-purpose flour**	7 g
5	**eggs**	5
4 oz	**pumpkin puree**	115 g
4 fl oz	**heavy cream**	125 ml
½ tsp	**cinnamon**	½ tsp
¼ tsp	**ground ginger**	¼ tsp
⅛ tsp	**ground cloves**	⅛ tsp
pinch	**nutmeg**	pinch
	Optional garnish:	
2 oz	**pecans, finely chopped**	60 g
1 tbls	**granulated sugar**	15 g
½ tsp	**cinnamon**	½ tsp

3 tbls	simple syrup, corn syrup, or fruit glaze	45 ml
8 fl oz	heavy cream	¼ L
1 tbls	brandy	15 ml
1 tbls	confectioners' sugar	15 g

1. Preheat the oven to 400°F (205°C). Prepare a crumb crust (either zweiback or gingersnap is good) in a 9-in. springform pan.
2. Blend the cream cheese with the sugars and flour, add the eggs, beating well.
3. Beat in the pumpkin puree, cream, and spices. When well combined turn into the prepared pan.
4. Bake at 400°F (205°C) for 10 minutes, then turn the oven down to 250°F (120°C) and bake an additional 40 to 50 minutes, or until the cheesecake appears almost set. It will still seem soft at the center.
5. Let the cake cool, either in the turned off, open oven, or at room temperature. Refrigerate in its pan to store. Unmold when completely cold.
6. If using the optional garnish, toss the nuts with the granulated sugar and cinnamon. Lightly brush the top of the cooled cake with syrup or glaze and sprinkle the nut mixture over the top. Cover the whole top, or create a design of your choosing. Just before serving, whip the cream with the sugar and brandy, and pipe a border of rosettes around the unmolded cake. If preferred, the flavored whipped cream may be served alongside each slice.

Lemon Cheesecake Squares

Yield: 48 squares

	Ingredients:	
32 oz	whipped cream cheese	900 g
14 oz	granulated sugar	400 g
4	eggs	4
1 tbls plus 1 tsp	vanilla extract	20 ml
1 tbls	lemon juice	15 ml
1 tbls	grated lemon zest	15 ml
4 tbls	sour cream	60 ml
2½ oz	all-purpose flour	56 g
	crumb crust (see Cheesecake in recipe index)	

1. Preheat oven to 350°F (180°C). For this recipe use two 12 × 8 × 1¼ in. (30 × 20 × 4 cm) disposable foil pans. Prepare pan by spraying with nonstick spray or greasing very lightly. Prepare a crust as in the recipe for Cheesecake, using 3 cups (675 g) crumbs and 12 oz (350 g) butter. Line pans with crust and refrigerate while preparing filling.
2. Beat the cream cheese with the sugar. Add the eggs and beat until fluffy.

3. Add the vanilla, lemon juice and zest, and sour cream. Beat smooth.
4. Add flour and beat to combine.
5. Spoon filling into prepared crust, smoothing with a spatula to level.
6. Bake for 20 to 25 minutes. Filling will puff up during baking and then sink.
7. Cool completely in pans. Refrigerate for several hours or overnight before cutting into portions. When the cakes are well chilled, they can be turned out onto a baking sheet and then set right side up on another sheet for cutting. Use a sharp wet knife to cut into even 2-in. (6 cm) squares, wiping the blade as needed between cuts.

Note: These freeze very well and transport is easiest when they are frozen solid, either in sheets or squares. They need little thawing time before serving (less than 30 minutes) and are best served well chilled.

Variations: **Amaretto Squares:** Prepare a chocolate cookie crumb crust, eliminate the lemon juice and zest from filling, add a tablespoon of amaretto liqueur. Just before serving, sprinkle tops of squares with crushed amaretto cookies or finely chopped toasted almonds.
Spiced Cheesecake Squares: Eliminate lemon juice and zest, substitute 1 tbls (15 ml) dark rum, ¼ tsp ground ginger, a pinch of nutmeg, and ½ tsp cinnamon. Use a gingersnap crust.

Peach and Pecan Pound Cake

Serves: 12

	Ingredients:	
8 oz	canned peaches, drained	224 g
5 oz	peach jam	140 g
3 fl oz	peach schnapps	90 ml
1 tsp	vanilla extract	5 ml
6 oz	sweet butter, softened	180 g
6 oz	granulated sugar	180 g
2	eggs	2
8 oz	all-purpose flour	224 g
½ tsp	salt	½ tsp
1 tsp	baking powder	1 tsp
1 tsp	baking soda	1 tsp
2 oz	shelled pecans, chopped	60 g

1. Preheat the oven to 350°F (180°C). Prepare a standard loaf pan by greasing and dusting with dry bread crumbs or flour.
2. Puree the canned peaches, and combine with the peach jam, peach schnapps, and vanilla. Set aside.

3. Cream the butter with the sugar until light and fluffy. Add the two eggs and beat well.
4. Add the peach mixture and beat thoroughly.
5. Combine the flour, salt, baking powder, and soda. Add to the batter in two portions, mixing well and scraping down the bowl if needed.
6. Fold in the nuts.
7. Pour the batter into the prepared pan and bake at 350°F (180°C) for 1 hour. Lower the heat to 325°F (165°C) and continue to bake for 10 to 15 more minutes. Cake is done when it appears to shrink from sides of pan.
8. Cool in the pan for 10 minutes before unmolding. Set on a rack to cool completely before wrapping. Well wrapped, this cake will remain fresh and moist for 2 to 3 days. It freezes well. Thaw wrapped.

Mocha Walnut Loaf Cake

Serves: 12

	Ingredients:	
4 oz	sweet butter, softened	112 g
10 oz	granulated sugar	280 g
2	eggs	2
1 tsp	vanilla extract	5 ml
3 fl oz	Kahlua (or coffee liqueur)	80 ml
8 oz	sour cream	224 g
8 oz	all-purpose flour	224 g
1 tsp	baking powder	1 tsp
1 tsp	baking soda	1 tsp
¼ tsp	salt	¼ tsp
	For coffee flavoring:	
1 tbls	instant espresso powder	1 tbls
2 fl oz	boiling water	60 ml
	or	
2 fl oz	very strong brewed coffee	60 ml
2 oz	shelled walnuts, finely grated	60 g
½ oz	unsweetened chocolate, grated	15 g

1. Prepare a standard loaf pan by greasing well and dusting with a combination of flour and cocoa powder. Shake out excess and set pan aside.
2. If using espresso powder, dissolve in boiling water and set aside to cool.
3. Combine the grated nuts and chocolate, fluff with a fork, and set aside in a cool place.

4. Preheat the oven to 350° F (180° C).
5. Cream the butter with the sugar until light and fluffy.
6. Add the eggs. Beat well. Add the vanilla, Kahlua, coffee flavoring, and sour cream. Beat to combine.
7. Combine the flour with the baking powder, soda, and salt. Add one half at a time to batter. Beat just to mix, scraping the bowl as needed.
8. Fold in the grated nuts and chocolate. Turn batter into prepared pan.
9. Bake for 50 to 55 minutes. Cake is done when top crack has formed and it springs back lightly when touched. It will just begin to shrink from sides of pan.
10. Set the pan on a rack to cool for about 15 minutes before unmolding. Unmold and set upright on rack to cool completely before wrapping.

Note: Well wrapped, this cake will remain moist and fresh for 3 days. It freezes well. Thaw wrapped.

Sour Cream Bourbon Cake

Serves: 20

	Ingredients:	
8 oz	sweet butter, softened	224 g
16 oz	granulated sugar	450 g
4	eggs	4
2 tsp	vanilla extract	10 ml
1 fl oz	bourbon	30 ml
16 oz	sour cream	450 g
16 oz	all-purpose flour	450 g
2 tsp	baking powder	2 tsp
2 tsp	baking soda	2 tsp
¼ tsp	salt	¼ tsp
	For filling:	
4 oz	shelled walnuts, chopped	112 g
3 tsp	cinnamon	3 tsp
4 oz	granulated sugar	112 g

1. Preheat oven to 350° F (180° C).
2. Grease and flour two 8-in. (20 cm) loaf pans or one 10-in. (25 cm) tube or bundt pan.
3. Cream butter with sugar. Add eggs and beat to combine.
4. Add vanilla, bourbon, and sour cream.

5. Combine remaining dry ingredients and add, in two portions, to egg mixture. Scrape bowl down to insure even mixing. Do not overbeat.
6. Spoon half the batter into prepared pan(s). Combine the filling ingredients and sprinkle about two-thirds over batter.
7. Add remaining batter, sprinkle with remaining filling. Cut through batter lightly so top filling will adhere.
8. Baking time: 50 to 60 minutes for loaf pans; 1 hour 10 minutes for tube. Top should rise and crack slightly. Cake should be almost firm to the touch.
9. Cool upright in pans on rack for at least 15 minutes. Unmold and cool completely right side up before wrapping.

Note: If well wrapped in foil, cake will remain moist and fresh for up to 3 days. Cake freezes very well. Thaw wrapped.

Variation: Add ⅓ cup (80 ml) miniature chocolate chips to filling if desired.

Tropical Cake

Serves: 12

	Ingredients:	
14 oz	all-purpose flour	392 g
1 tsp	baking powder	1 tsp
1 tsp	baking soda	1 tsp
¼ tsp	salt	¼ tsp
10 oz	sweet butter	280 g
8 oz	granulated sugar	224 g
4 oz	light brown sugar	112 g
4	eggs	4
2 fl oz	dark rum	60 ml
1 cup	mashed ripe banana	¼ L
1 cup	crushed pineapple	¼ L
4 fl oz	milk	125 ml
7 oz	chopped shredded coconut*	196 g
4 oz	chopped toasted macadamia nuts	112 g
8	pitted dates, chopped	8
1 tbls	orange zest	1 tbls

*Since the long strings of shredded coconut will spoil the texture of the cake, either purchase flaked coconut in a health food store (or nut and spice shop), or grind regular shredded coconut in a food processor until you have tiny short bits. You may use toasted or not as you like, but don't use the very moist sweetened kind.

1. Preheat the oven to 350°F (180°C). Prepare pans by greasing well. Use either a 10-in. (25 cm) diameter ring or bundt pan or a standard loaf. Doubling the recipe will produce two loaves or a double height bundt cake. The single recipe will produce a ring about 3-in. (8 cm) high.
2. Combine the flour with the baking powder, soda, and salt. Set aside.
3. Cream the butter with the sugars until fluffy. Add the eggs and beat for about 5 minutes.
4. Add the rum, banana, and pineapple. Mix until well combined.
5. In a separate bowl, combine the coconut, nuts, dates, and orange zest. Toss with a spoonful of the flour mixture to coat and set aside.
6. To the egg batter, alternately add the flour mixture and the milk, beating to combine. Stir in the coconut mixture until the ingredients are well distributed. Pour into pan and bake for 1 hour until the cake just begins to shrink from the sides of the pan. Let rest, right side up, for 15 minutes.
7. Unmold the cake on a rack and let cool completely. Wrap airtight and store. The cake will keep for 2 to 3 days at room temperature or may be frozen for longer storage. Thaw wrapped.

Note: You may use chopped pecans in place of macadamia nuts, raisins or dried currants instead of dates.

COOKIES
Applesauce Raisin Cookies

Yield: about 36 large cookies

	Ingredients:	
4 oz	sweet butter, softened	112 g
8 oz	granulated sugar	224 g
1	egg	1
¼ tsp	ground cloves	¼ tsp
½ tsp	cinnamon	½ tsp
pinch	nutmeg	pinch
1 tsp	baking soda	1 tsp
1 cup	applesauce	¼ L
8 oz	all-purpose flour	224 g
4 oz	chopped walnuts	112 g
4 oz	raisins	112 g

1. Preheat the oven to 400°F (205°C). Grease baking sheets. Set aside.
2. Cream the butter with the sugar, add the egg and spices. Beat well.
3. Dissolve the baking soda in the applesauce and add to the mixture.

4. Stir in the flour until well combined. Add the nuts and raisins and mix to distribute throughout.
5. Drop by tablespoons onto the prepared sheets. Space about 1 in. (2½ cm) apart.
6. Bake for 13 to 15 minutes. Transfer to racks to cool. Store airtight.

Note: This recipe may be quadrupled to yield a gross of cookies.

Brown Sugar Tuiles

Yield: 36

Ingredients:

4 oz	**sweet butter, softened**	112 g
7 oz	**light brown sugar**	196 g
2	**eggs**	2
1 tsp	**vanilla extract**	5 ml
pinch	**salt**	pinch
1½ oz	**all-purpose flour***	28 g

*Because of the variations in flour, a slight adjustment in this amount may be necessary. Bake one test cookie to establish perfect dough consistency, adding either a bit more flour or a few drops of water as necessary.

1. Prepare two nonstick baking sheets by greasing lightly. Keep a greased paper towel handy for wiping and regreasing sheets between batches. Have a rolling pin (or baguette mold) ready for cooling the cookies in the traditional curved roof-tile shape. You will also need a broad, thin-bladed spatula to remove the baked cookies from the sheet.
2. Preheat the oven to 400°F (205°C).
3. Cream the butter with the sugar, add the eggs, vanilla, salt, and flour.
4. Drop the batter by scant tablespoons onto the baking sheet, spacing widely, only two or three to a sheet. The batter will spread when placed and spread further while baking, to form a very thin cookie.
5. Bake for 7 to 8 minutes. Remove the sheet from the oven, count to ten, then carefully slip the spatula under one edge of the cookie. If the dough is the right consistency and the cookie properly baked, it will be possible to peel the cookie from the sheet by this edge. If the spatula causes the cookie to wrinkle up, it is underbaked and will need a few seconds more oven heat.
6. Immediately place the cookie over the curved mold to shape. It will harden in seconds. If the other cookies on the sheet should stiffen up, return to the oven for a few seconds to soften. When the cookies are completely cool store carefully, airtight and well protected. They are somewhat fragile, so always allow for some breakage during transport.

Note: The directions for this cookie may seem intimidating and tedious but after test baking a few, you can easily establish a working rhythm that will allow you to bake these more quickly by preparing several baking sheets and staggering the baking time by a few minutes. The cookies are delicate, delicious, and impressive to guests, so well worth the effort.

Variations: These cookies can be shaped as cigarettes russes as follows: Remove from baking sheet, lay on a board, place the handle of a wooden spoon on one edge, roll the cookie up around the handle, and slide off. They may be decorated by dipping one or both ends in melted chocolate (and ground nuts, if desired) and drying on a rack. Prepared in this manner, the cookies are especially festive and, as a bonus, transport more easily.

This same recipe can be used to create edible dessert cups as follows: Bake as usual, but invert the warm cookie over a custard cup or small bowl. Fill with mousse, sherbet, or ice cream just before serving.

Coconut Meringues

Yield: approx. 48

	Ingredients:	
2	egg whites	2
6 oz	granulated sugar	168 g
12 oz	shredded coconut	336 g

1. Prepare baking sheets by greasing and flouring. Set aside. Preheat oven to 350°F (180°C).
2. Beat egg whites until foamy. Gradually add the sugar and continue to beat until the whites form soft mounds. Do not beat stiff.
3. Stir in the coconut.
4. Mound by tablespoons onto prepared baking sheets. Bake for 12 minutes. They will have set up, but will be barely colored, with just a touch of gold at the edges.
5. Immediately remove from pan and cool on parchment or waxed paper. When thoroughly cooled, pack airtight to keep the cookies moist and chewy.

Note: These cookies are ridiculously easy to make and very popular. Make in large batches, quadrupling the above recipe if desired, if sufficient oven space is available to bake all the batches within an hour. If the batter stands longer than that in a warm room, the meringue has a tendency to weep.

Maple Walnut Icebox Cookies

Yield: 60

	Ingredients:	
4 oz	sweet butter, softened	112 g
7 oz	light brown sugar	196 g
1	egg, lightly beaten	1
1 tbls	pure maple syrup	15 ml
5 oz	all-purpose flour	140 g
¼ tsp	baking soda	¼ tsp
¼ tsp	salt	¼ tsp
2 oz	walnuts, finely chopped	56 g

1. Cream butter with sugar until light and fluffy.
2. Add the egg and maple syrup and beat well.
3. Sift together the flour, soda, and salt and add to the butter mixture.
4. Add the nuts and mix well to distribute throughout the dough.
5. Turn the dough out onto lightly floured plastic wrap or waxed paper. Shape into a roll or oblong, wrap tightly, and refrigerate for several hours or overnight.
6. To bake: Preheat oven to 350° F (180° C). Slice the dough as thin as possible (less than ¼ in. [¾ cm]) and place on ungreased baking sheets. Bake for 7 to 9 minutes until browned and firm enough to handle. Remove to racks to cool. Pack airtight.

Note: These cookies keep well and transport easily. They can be shaped as desired to yield either round or square cookies. The thickness of the slice will determine the baking time, and, of course, the exact yield.

Rugelach (Sweet Crescents)

Yield: 24

	Ingredients:	
8 oz	all-purpose flour	224 g
8 oz	sweet butter, softened	224 g
8 oz	sour cream	224 g
1	egg yolk	1

	For filling:	
8 oz	granulated sugar	224 g
4 oz	shelled walnuts, finely chopped	112 g
2 tsp	cinnamon	2 tsp
	egg wash	

1. Preheat oven to 350°F (180°C). Prepare baking sheets by greasing lightly or by coating with nonstick spray.
2. Combine flour and butter, then add sour cream and egg yolk. Mix until a smooth, soft dough forms.
3. Wrap ball of dough in lightly floured plastic wrap and refrigerate for at least 1 hour.
4. Combine the filling ingredients and set aside. Prepare an egg wash.
5. Divide the chilled dough into thirds. Place every third on a lightly floured surface and roll out to a circle about 10-in. (25 cm) in diameter.
6. Sprinkle one-third of the filling on the circle of dough. Lay a piece of parchment or wax paper over the filling and roll lightly.
7. Using a sharp knife or pastry wheel, cut the circle into eight pielike wedges. Roll up each section from rim to point, sealing the point with a bit of egg wash. Shape each roll into a crescent shape and place, point side down, on the prepared baking sheet. Repeat procedure with remaining dough and filling.
8. If desired, shaped pastries may be brushed with egg wash and sprinkled with cinnamon sugar before baking.
9. Bake for 20–30 minutes, until lightly browned. Cool on rack and store airtight.

Note: The pastries may be prepared and frozen, unbaked. This recipe may be made in quantity: It doubles or quadruples successfully.

Variations: To make a variety of pastries, other fillings may be used, such as seedless raspberry or blackberry jam, strained apricot jam, or prune butter. Be sure the fillings are not too liquid and are scantly applied.

Sinful Chocolate Oatmeal Cookies

Yield: 100

	Ingredients:	
4 oz	all-purpose flour	112 g
1 tsp	baking soda	1 tsp
1 tsp	salt	1 tsp
8 oz	sweet butter, softened	224 g
7 oz	brown sugar	196 g
8 oz	granulated sugar	224 g
2	eggs	2

1 tsp	vanilla extract	5 ml
6 oz	semisweet chocolate, melted	168 g
8 oz	rolled oats	224 g
5 oz	semisweet chocolate minichips	140 g
2 oz	shelled walnuts, chopped	56 g
7 oz	shredded coconut	196 g

1. Preheat oven to 350°F (180°C). Prepare cookie sheets by lining with parchment or greasing lightly. Use heavy gauge pans or double pan to prevent scorching.
2. Sift the flour, soda, and salt together and set aside.
3. Cream the butter with the sugars until light and fluffy.
4. Add the eggs and vanilla. Mix well, then mix in the cooled melted chocolate.
5. Combine the oats, chips, walnuts, and coconut. Set aside.
6. Alternately add the flour and oat mixture to the batter, stirring well and scraping the bowl to insure that the additions are well distributed.
7. Place heaping tablespoons of dough about 2 in. (6 cm) apart on prepared pans.
8. Bake 13 to 15 minutes. The cookies will still appear slightly soft.
9. Remove from the oven and let rest about one minute. Then, using a thin spatula, carefully remove the cookies to a rack to cool completely. Store in an airtight tin or container, using bits of crumpled waxed paper or serving tissue to protect them from rough handling.

Note: Depending on the accuracy of the oven and the placement of pans, these cookies can scorch easily. Check periodically and rotate pans for best results.

Swirled Brownies

Yield: 16–20

	Ingredients:	
6 oz	butter	180 g
3 oz	unsweetened chocolate	85 g
3	eggs	3
12 oz	granulated sugar	340 g
6 oz	all-purpose flour	180 g
½ tsp	salt	½ tsp
1 tbls	pure vanilla extract	15 ml
	For Marble Cheese Brownies:	
8 oz	cream cheese	225 g
1	egg	1
4 tbls	flour	35 g

2 tbls	granulated sugar	25 g
2 tbls	lemon juice	30 ml
	For Peanut Swirl Brownies:	
½ cup	chunky peanut butter	125 ml
1	egg	1
4 tbls	flour	35 g
2 tbls	melted butter	30 ml
2 oz	chopped peanuts (optional)	60 g

1. Preheat the oven to 350° F (180° C). Grease and flour a 13 × 9 × 2 in. (33 × 23 × 5 cm) baking pan.
2. Melt the chocolate and butter until smooth. Cool to lukewarm.
3. Beat the eggs with the sugar until light and fluffy. Add the chocolate mixture and combine thoroughly. Stir in the flour, salt, and vanilla. Set batter aside and prepare either cheese or peanut mixture.
4. For cheese: Beat the cream cheese with the egg until thoroughly mixed, then mix in the flour, sugar, and lemon juice. For peanut: Beat the peanut butter with the egg until blended, add the flour, and stir in the melted butter.
5. Place the chocolate batter in the prepared pan. Drop spoonsful of the marbling mixture over the batter. Drag a spatula or blunt knife through the mixture to swirl together. If using the peanuts, scatter over the top of the batter and press in lightly.
6. Bake for 25 to 30 minutes, until the surface looks shiny and cracked. The brownies will still appear soft, but not liquid. Remove to a rack. Cut into squares in pan. Cool completely before removing squares.

Note: Store airtight for 3 days or freeze for longer storage. The recipe may be multiplied at will for desired volume.

Triple Chocolate Brownies

Yield: *32*

	Ingredients:	
4 oz	unsweetened chocolate	112 g
4 oz	semisweet chocolate	112 g
8 oz	sweet butter	225 g
5	eggs	5
16 oz	granulated sugar	450 g
3½ oz	light brown sugar	84 g
1 tbls	vanilla extract (or rum)	15 ml
6 oz	all-purpose flour	168 g

¼ tsp	salt	¼ tsp
2 tbls	cocoa	15 g
8 oz	**coarsely chopped pecans or walnuts**	

1. Preheat oven to 425°F (220°C). Prepare a 9 × 13 × 2 in. (23 × 35 × 5 cm) pan by greasing generously.
2. Melt the chocolates with the butter over low heat. Stir to combine. Set aside to cool.
3. Beat the eggs, sugars, and vanilla (or rum) for about ten minutes until pale and thickened.
4. Add the chocolate and butter mixture and beat to combine.
5. Add the dry ingredients and beat only until well mixed.
6. Add about two-thirds of the nuts and stir in by hand.
7. Turn batter into the prepared pan. Distribute the remaining nuts evenly over batter and press lightly so they stay in place.
8. Bake for 10 minutes at 425°F (220°C). Lower oven to 400°F (205°C) and bake an additional 25 minutes. The surface of the brownies will be glossy. They will seem underdone. Remove the pan to a rack and cool completely.
9. When the brownies are completely cooled, use two baking sheets to unmold and then invert (so they are right side up). Let the brownies stand, right side up and uncovered, for 6 to 12 hours before cutting. Use a thin, sharp knife, wiping the blade with a damp paper towel if necessary between cuts. Cut in four lengthwise strips, then cut each strip into eight bars.

Note: These brownies are extremely rich and chocolatey, more like candy than cake, so even smaller portions can be cut for a dessert buffet. They keep well for two to three days if well wrapped. They may be refrigerated or frozen. Thaw wrapped. In very hot weather, keep in a cool place or refrigerate before long transport.

Walnut Puffs

Yield: *48*

	Ingredients:	
4 oz	**sweet butter, softened**	112 g
2 tbls	**granulated sugar**	28 g
1 tsp	**vanilla extract**	5 ml
4 oz	**shelled walnuts, finely chopped**	112 g
4 oz	**all-purpose flour**	112 g
	For coating:	
8 oz	**confectioners' sugar (approx.)**	224 g

1. Preheat the oven to 300° F (150° C). Prepare baking sheets by greasing lightly.
2. Cream the sugar with the butter. Add the vanilla, walnuts, and flour and combine thoroughly into a soft dough.
3. Shape the dough into small balls no more than 1-in. (2½ cm) diameter. Roll gently between palms to round and place on the baking sheets about 1 in. (2½ cm) apart.
4. Bake for 25 to 30 minutes. The cookies will firm up but barely color.
5. Remove from baking sheet. Roll in confectioners' sugar while still hot. Roll in the sugar a second time when cool. Store airtight. These cookies will keep very well for at least a week. If a snow-white appearance is desired, dust with additional confectioners' sugar just before serving.

Note: The dough may be prepared ahead and refrigerated or frozen. If frozen, thaw under refrigeration. Remove from the refrigerator and let stand at room temperature for about 40 minutes or until soft enough to roll. This recipe may be doubled or quadrupled (or more) with no difficulty, except be certain that the dough is well mixed and the nuts are well distributed. In larger batches, it is preferable to rest the dough after prolonged and strenuous mixing for a more tender result.

PUDDINGS, CUSTARDS, SAUCES, AND CREAMS
Zuppa Inglese

Yield: 2 qt		2 L

	Ingredients:	
48–60	good quality ladyfingers	48–60
⅓ cup	light rum or kirsch	80 ml
⅓ cup	other flavoring (see below)	80 ml
2 qt	Pastry Cream (see Pastry Cream and Variations in recipe index)	2 L
	For topping:	
1 cup	heavy cream	¼ L
2 tbls	confectioners' sugar	15 g
1 tsp	pure vanilla extract	1 tsp

Garnish: chopped pistachios, crushed amaretti cookies, or chocolate curls

There are a lot of options in making this dessert, which is very close to being the "soup" of its name, comprised of moistened ladyfingers and flavored pastry cream. In its simplest form, the ladyfingers can be moistened with just rum, or rum and brandy, or anisette, and layered with vanilla pastry cream. Or the pastry cream can be of two or three different flavors, perhaps chocolate, mocha, and vanilla in three distinct layers, with the ladyfingers flavored with rum, creme de cacao, kahlua, or even strong coffee.

1. Have ready a 2-qt (2 L) clear glass serving dish, either a bowl, soufflé dish, or footed trifle bowl. Place the combined liquors or flavorings in a platter or shallow bowl, dip strips of the ladyfingers into the liquor on both sides, and transfer to another plate. Don't let them soak too long or they will fall apart.
2. Line the serving bowl with ladyfingers, good side out all along the sides. Place a layer of ladyfingers in the bottom of the bowl. They don't need to be cut to shape as for a charlotte, since no one will see the bottom of the bowl. Reserve 10 or 12 perfect ladyfingers for the top.
3. Spoon about one-third of the pastry cream into the bowl, cover the surface with more ladyfingers (broken pieces are OK), then add another third of the cream, then ladyfingers, then the last third of the pastry cream. If there is extra soaking liquid left, you can spoon it in as you proceed with the layering.
4. Place the top layer of reserved ladyfingers in a spoke pattern, trimming edges as necessary. If serving the following day, cover and refrigerate.
5. On the day you plan to serve, decorate the top of the zuppa with the flavored whipped cream. If desired, sprinkle the top with one of the garnishes.
6. Serve in deep dessert bowls with spoons. Extra whipped cream may be offered with each portion.

Note: You may cover the entire top surface with cream, in which case, the final layer of ladyfingers can be placed any which way. Remember that this dessert is both very rich and very perishable, so serve small portions, and always keep well chilled.

Variations: Take a look at all the possible variations suggested in the recipes for both Pastry Cream and Creme Anglaise, for ideas on your own flavor combinations. Use compatible liqueurs or flavorings and suitable garnish.

A Zuppa Inglese is similar to an English trifle, but does not include fruit. If you like, however, you may combine a fruit puree, for example raspberry, with one-third of the pastry cream to use for one of the layers.

Pastry Cream and Variations

Yield: 1½ qt   *1 L 500 ml*

	Ingredients:	
2 cups	milk	½ L
2 cups	light cream or half-and-half	½ L
12	egg yolks	12
12 oz	granulated sugar	336 g
2 tsp	vanilla extract (or 1 tsp [5 ml] each vanilla and rum or brandy)	10 ml
4 oz	all-purpose flour	112 g

1. Combine the milk and cream, scald, and set aside.
2. Combine the sugar, yolks, and flavorings. Beat until thick enough to form a ribbon. Sprinkle on the flour and beat to combine.

3. Temper the egg mixture with some of the hot milk, beating vigorously. When egg mixture is quite warm, return to saucepan holding the balance of the hot milk mixture.

4. Cook over medium heat, stirring until mixture reaches the boil and thickens. Continue to cook, stirring for 2 to 3 minutes. Turn into a clean, shallow container to cool rapidly. Cover closely with plastic wrap pressed onto the surface of the cream. Refrigerate and use within 2 to 3 days. Always keep pastry cream (or any tarts or pastries filled with it) well chilled.

Note: Some chefs add a bit of butter to the finished cream, others float a film of butter over the surface of the cream to prevent a skin from forming, which is the purpose the plastic wrap serves. You may always add a spoon or so of other liqueurs or flavorings to cream when completed. Do not use too much or you will dilute the cream. You may fold whipped cream into pastry cream to lighten texture just before using. Pastry cream is sometime combined with whipped cream and/or beaten egg whites for mousselike desserts.

Variations: **Chocolate Pastry Cream:** Blend up to 4 oz (115 g) chocolate, melted, into the hot pastry cream. Or blend in finely grated chocolate, stir until melted.
Mocha Pastry Cream: Combine 2 tbls (30 ml) strong espresso, 2 tbls (30 ml) Kahlua, and 1 oz (30 g) melted chocolate with the hot pastry cream.
Orange Pastry Cream: Add 3 tbls (45 ml) grated orange zest to milk and cream before scalding. Let steep for about 20 minutes, then strain. Reheat cream to bring to temperature before proceeding with recipe. Add 2 tbls (30 ml) orange liqueur (Triple Sec or Grand Marnier) to pastry cream as flavoring.
Pistachio Pastry Cream: Lightly toast and skin 1 cup (¼ L) pistachio nuts, chop coarsely, and add to milk and cream mixture as above. Add cognac to pastry cream as flavoring.
Hazelnut Pastry Cream: Treat hazelnuts as pistachios, above. Add Frangelico (a hazelnut-flavored liqueur) as flavoring to pastry cream.

Creme Anglaise (Custard Sauce)

Yield: 1 qt   **1 L**

	Ingredients:	
1 pt	milk	½ L
½ pt	light cream	¼ L
8 oz	granulated sugar	225 g
1	vanilla bean, split	1
10	egg yolks	10
2 tbls	optional flavoring*	30 ml

*Rum, brandy, or any fruit liqueur or extract may be added according to planned use. If using a concentrated extract, add few drops gradually until desired flavoring is achieved.

1. Combine the milk, cream, sugar, and vanilla bean in a heavy gauge saucepan. Stir to dissolve the sugar completely and heat to scalding.
2. In a bowl, stir the egg yolks to liquefy. Slowly add some of the hot milk mixture, stirring to combine. Add about half the milk to temper or warm the yolks thoroughly.
3. Return the yolk mixture to the remaining hot milk in the saucepan and cook over medium heat, stirring constantly, until the custard begins to thicken and will coat a spoon. The temperature of the mixture will be 185° F (85° C) degrees.
4. Immediately remove from the heat and strain into a cold, clean container. Stir for a few minutes to hasten cooling, or set the bowl in a bowl of ice water and stir to cool down. Retrieve the vanilla bean from the strainer and return to the custard. It will continue to flavor the custard as it cools. Add optional flavoring if desired.

Note: Custard Sauce is very perishable. Keep cold at all times, well covered and in clean containers, to protect from contamination. Do not add old cream to a new batch. Prepare what can be used within three days.

Variations: **Chocolate Custard Sauce:** Add a few ounces of finely grated semisweet or bittersweet chocolate to the warm custard and stir to melt and combine.
Mocha Custard Sauce: Make a paste of 1 tbls (15 ml) of cocoa, 1 tbls (15 ml) of strong coffee, and 1 tbls (15 ml) of coffee liqueur. Combine with a bit of custard sauce until smooth, then add to the whole.
Orange Custard Sauce: Rub a few sugar cubes over the rind of an orange to capture the oil, dissolve in the hot cream and milk before proceeding with the rest of the recipe. Add 2 tbls (30 ml) Grand Marnier or other orange liqueur to the completed custard. Slivered candied orange rind may be used as a garnish on this sauce.
Mint Custard Sauce: Bruise a few leaves of fragrant mint with the sugar. Steep in the hot milk mixture, discard the leaves, and proceed with recipe. Flavor the finished custard with a good creme de menthe.
Ginger Custard Sauce: Add 1 tsp powdered ginger to the milk and sugar mixture. Garnish with slivered candied ginger.
Pistachio Custard Sauce: Lightly toast 6 oz (180 g) shelled pistachios. While they are still warm, rub off as much of their inner skins as you can with a rough towel. Chop the nuts coarsely, and simmer in 1 cup (¼ L) of the milk required for the recipe. Let steep for about 20 minutes, then either strain, or puree in a blender. Use the milk to prepare the custard, adding brandy as flavoring. If desired, you may add the tiniest drop of green food coloring to the finished custard. Garnish with, or blend in, an additional few spoons of ground pistachios.
Hazelnut Custard Sauce: Treat hazelnuts as pistachios above, toasting, skinning, and steeping in milk. Add 2 tbls (30 ml) Frangelico (a hazelnut-flavored liqueur) to the finished custard.

Chocolate Clouds

Yield: 24

Ingredients:

16	egg whites	16
1 lb	granulated sugar	500 g
½ lb	confectioners' sugar	250 g
4 oz	cocoa powder	115 g
1 qt	milk	1 L
1 qt	flavored Custard Sauce (see directions)	1 L

This dessert is really a chocolate Oeufs a la Niege, so the Chocolate Clouds are served in a pool of harmonious custard sauce. You can use the poaching milk to prepare a custard sauce of your choice. Some suggestions are a sauce flavored with orange liqueur, mocha, mint, or a nut-flavored custard made with pistachios or pecans. Appropriate garnish would be candied orange rind, chocolate leaves, mint leaves, or chopped nuts. Of course, spun sugar is always glamorous as a topping.

1. Beat the egg whites until they begin to form soft peaks. Gradually add the granulated sugar, a little at a time, and continue to beat until the meringue is stiff, smooth, and glossy.
2. Sift together the confectioners' sugar and cocoa. Fold gently but thoroughly into the meringue.
3. Heat the milk in a wide pan and keep simmering at about 170° F (77° C). Use two moistened kitchen spoons to shape the chocolate meringue into egglike shapes. Drop gently into the simmering milk. Poach for about 2 minutes, rolling them over in the milk. Remove with a slotted spoon to a parchment-lined baking sheet or tray. Cool and refrigerate until ready to serve. Reserve the poaching milk to prepare a custard sauce if desired.
4. To serve, pour custard into a shallow glass bowl or individual bowls, float chocolate clouds on top of custard. Garnish. Serve cold.

Lemon Curd

Yield: 1½ qt   *1½ L*

Ingredients:

30 oz	granulated sugar	900 g
2½ cups	fresh lemon juice	590 ml
4 tbls	grated lemon rind	4 tbls
10 oz	sweet butter	285 g
13	eggs	13

1. Combine all the ingredients in the order given in a saucepan or double broiler. Whisk vigorously to combine. Cook, first over moderate heat, and then over lower heat, stirring constantly until the mixture thickens into a custard. Immediately turn into a chilled clean bowl and continue to stir to hasten cooling. The curd will thicken further when cool.
2. Lemon curd may be strained if desired, not to remove the zest, but the little bits of coagulated egg white that may form while cooking. Straining, however, is not necessary for most uses.
3. Store refrigerated and covered, for 2 to 3 weeks.

Note: Lemon, or other curds, are very useful to have on hand. Fill tiny tarts with curd, decorate with sugared zest or candied violets or mimosa. Use as a cake filling, swirl into whipped cream or parfaits for quick desserts. Lemon curd is delicious as a topping for cheesecake. Curds can be used in place of pastry cream to line fresh fruit tarts, for example, lemon with raspberry or orange with blueberries.

Variations: **Lime Curd:** Proceed as above, but use about 4 oz (115 g) less zest if you prefer a more tart flavor.
Orange Curd: Use up to twice the amount of zest to intensify the orange flavor.

Chocolate Ganache

Yield: *1 qt*	*1 L*

	Ingredients:	
1 lb	semisweet, bittersweet, or sweet chocolate*	500 g
1 pt	heavy cream	½ L

*The choice of chocolate will determine the flavor of the ganache. Use a chocolate of very good quality. You may combine the chocolates, some semisweet with some extra-bittersweet, for example to achieve the color and flavor you like best for a specific purpose.

1. Grate or shave the chocolate into fine pieces.
2. Place cream in a large saucepan and bring to a full boil. Add the chocolate and, beating constantly, bring to the boil again until the chocolate is melted and the mixture is smooth. Strain into a clean bowl and allow to cool. At this point the ganache can be used as a glaze, as explained in the Note below.
3. When the mixture has cooled, beat until light-colored and lightened in texture to a spreading consistency. Use as a filling or frosting for cakes or a filling for small pastries, such as tiny choux (cream puffs). Always keep cakes and pastries with ganache well chilled.

Note: To use ganache as a glaze, let cool until it thickens slightly; stir carefully, trying not to create bubbles. Place cake to be glazed on a rack set over a pan. The cake surface should be smooth and free of crumbs. Pour ganache over, beginning at the center of the cake and allowing the ganache to flow over the sides. If any spots are uncovered, or unevenly covered, quickly use a spatula to smooth over and spread the glaze. This must be done within seconds of pouring the glaze or the finish will not be glossy and smooth.

Brown Sugar Cream

Yield: *1 qt*		*1 L*

	Ingredients:	
1 pt	**heavy cream**	½ L
6 oz	**brown sugar**	180 g

1. Place the brown sugar in a bowl. Pour the cream over. Do not stir. Let rest, covered and refrigerated for several hours or overnight.
2. Whip with chilled beaters until the cream holds stiff peaks. Use to frost and fill cakes, especially Hazelnut Chiffon Cake (see in recipe index).

Note: This cream is very good on other sponge cakes, chocolate sponge rolls, or piped as a garnish on chilled baked apples.

Fruit Dessert Sauces

Sauces made from fresh or dried fruits lend color and flavor to desserts such as mousses, ices, dessert fruit salads, or plain pound, sponge, or angel cakes. They can also be used with such preparations as coeur à la crème, molded yogurt cheeses, or fromage blanc, and are nice to offer as toppings for crepes, pancakes, and waffles at brunches.

For fresh fruit, such as strawberries or raspberries, simply sieve the fruit through a food mill to remove seeds. Add only as much superfine sugar as needed to sweeten and add liqueur—for the raspberries, chambord, for the strawberries, kirsch. Keep cold, use within two days.

For dried fruit, such as pitted prunes or apricots, simmer the fruit in water or dry white wine. Puree and sieve as above, adding some of the poaching liquid to bring to consistency. Liqueurs may be added, if desired, for example, armagnac to prunes, brandy to apricots. Lemon juice can be added to cut sweetness.

Chocolate Rum Sauce

Yield: 1 pt		½ L

	Ingredients:	
8 oz	bittersweet chocolate	225 g
6 oz	sweet butter	180 g
2–4 tbls	rum	30–60 ml
	simple syrup, or corn syrup (as needed)	

1. Melt the chocolate and butter over gentle heat, stir smooth. Add rum and use as is, or add syrup as needed to bring sauce to desired consistency.

Note: Other flavorings such as orange liqueur, kahlua, or kirsch may be used.

Raspberry-Strawberry Mousse

Yield: 2 qt		2 L

	Ingredients:	
1 qt	fresh sweet raspberries	1 L
4–5 tbls	verifine sugar	50–60 g
1 tbls	lemon juice	15 ml
4 tbls	chambord or framboise*	60 ml
½ oz	gelatin	15 g
4 tbls	water	60 ml
12 oz	frozen strawberries in syrup	340 g
1 tbls	kirsch	15 ml
1 pt	heavy cream	½ L

*Chambord is a black raspberry liqueur, framboise a red raspberry liqueur. Chambord is a bit sweeter, darker, and stronger.

1. Mash the raspberries with half the sugar. Let stand for about 20 minutes. Puree in a blender and pass through a fine sieve to remove seeds. Add the chambord or framboise, and the lemon juice. If the berries are extremely tart, add a bit more sugar.
2. Soften the gelatin in the water. Puree the frozen strawberries, add the kirsch, and set aside. Do not strain.
3. Whip the cream until it holds soft peaks. Warm the softened gelatin to liquefy, then stir into the raspberry puree.

4. Fold together the whipped cream and the raspberry-gelatin mixture until evenly colored. Place large spoonsful of the mixture into a 2-qt (2 L) glass trifle bowl or serving dish. Pour some of the strawberry puree here and there in the bowl. Add more of the mousse, more puree and so on until both are used up. Gently cut a spatula through the mousse to swirl the mixtures. Don't overdo or the contrast will be lost.

5. Refrigerate for several hours until set.

Note: This may be made in individual glass bowls or stemmed glasses. Top with a few fresh berries if desired.

Gingered Pear Mousse

Yield: 1 qt		1 L
	Ingredients:	
1 tsp	gelatin	1 tsp
1 tbls	dark rum	15 ml
3 tbls	Poire William (or pear brandy)	45 ml
2	large ripe pears	2
2 inch	piece peeled gingerroot	5 cm
1 tbls	pure vanilla extract	15 ml
1 tsp	ground ginger	1 tsp
¼ tsp	cinnamon	¼ tsp
pinch each	nutmeg and ground cloves	pinch each
4	eggs, separated	4
4 oz	light brown sugar	115 g
1 cup	heavy cream	¼ L
pinch	salt	pinch

1. Combine the rum and the Poire William. Sprinkle the gelatin over to soften.
2. Peel and core the pears, puree, and add the vanilla and spices. Smash the gingerroot slightly and add to the pear puree. Set aside.
3. Combine the yolks and sugar in the top of a double boiler and heat, beating with a whisk, until the mixture begins to thicken. Do not overheat or the yolks will scramble. Remove from heat, stir in the pear puree, removing and discarding the smashed ginger.
4. Stir the gelatin smooth. If it seems lumpy, set the container in hot water and stir to liquefy. When the pear custard is just warm to the touch, stir in the gelatin and set aside.
5. Beat the cream until soft peaks form. Beat the whites with a pinch of salt until peaks form. It should not be too stiff or grainy or it will break down.

6. When the pear mixture is cool, add scoops of the cream and the egg whites and fold until all three mixtures are well combined. Proceed gently, do not overmix, or the mousse will deflate. Turn the mixture either into a serving bowl or individual dishes and freeze.

7. Can be served directly from the freezer, or tempered in the refrigerator for 1 or 2 hours.

Note: This mousse is very good served in cookie cups made from Brown Sugar Tuiles (see in recipe index). If planning to use in this way, freeze in a container that will make it easy to portion with a small ice cream scoop. Do not freeze the mousse in the tuiles.

Variations: **Apple Mousse:** Substitute calvados or applejack for the liquor, eliminate the gingerroot, add more cinnamon, and a bit more sugar to taste. Simmer the puree for 1 minute, then allow to cool before adding to the yolks.
Brandied Peach Mousse: Use very ripe sweet peaches (or first quality canned), substitute peach brandy for the Poire William. Add a bit more ground cloves and 2 tbls (30 ml) lemon juice to the puree. The gingerroot is optional.

Chestnut Charlotte

Serves: 10–12

Ingredients:

48	ladyfingers	48
4 tbls	creme de cacao	60 ml
4 tbls	dark rum	60 ml
3 cups	whipped Chocolate Ganache (see in recipe index)	¾ L
2 cups	chestnut puree*	½ L
2 tbls	brandy	30 ml
2 cups	heavy cream	½ L
	optional confectioners' sugar for chestnut puree*	
2 oz	grated unsweetened chocolate	60 g
	Garnish:	
1 cup	heavy cream	¼ L
2 tbls	confectioners' sugar	15 g
14	marrons glacés†	14
	dark coating chocolate	

*Select an imported chestnut puree that is not heavily sweetened, or make your own by stewing dried chestnuts until very tender, pureeing in a food mill or ricer, and adding confectioners' sugar to taste.
†Marrons glacés are whole French chestnuts in syrup and are available in specialty gourmet shops.

1. Combine the creme de cacao and rum in a shallow bowl. Dip the flat side of the ladyfingers in the bowl just to moisten slightly. Lay round (or good) side down on waxed paper.
2. Select a 10-in. (25 cm) springform pan. Set strips of ladyfingers, round side out around the rim to line the pan completely. Trim individual ladyfingers to completely line the bottom of the pan. Cover the remaining ladyfingers with plastic wrap.
3. Rewhip the ganache to soften slightly. With a spoon (or a pastry bag with an open tip), place a layer of ganache on the ladyfingers on the bottom of the pan. Smooth out as much as possible. Spread a layer of ganache on the ladyfingers lining the sides of the pan as well, so that the entire charlotte is now lined with ganache. Set the remaining ganache aside.
4. Beat the 2 cups (½ L) of cream until fairly stiff. Beat the chestnut puree with the brandy, beat in some of the whipped cream to lighten the texture. Fold the chestnut puree, the grated chocolate, and the whipped cream together gently: A little streakiness is OK.
5. Spoon half the chestnut cream into the charlotte then add another layer of ladyfingers, being sure to reserve about 12 for the top. Pipe another layer of chocolate ganache over the ladyfingers, then add the balance of the chestnut cream.
6. Top the charlotte with a layer of carefully trimmed ladyfingers (trim one end of each to a point so that they fit in the center. Press lightly on the ladyfingers to settle the mixture. Pipe remaining chocolate ganache on the top of the charlotte. Wet a spatula and smooth the top carefully, but try not to run the chocolate over the ladyfinger border. Cover and refrigerate for several hours until firm.
7. Prepare the garnish: Remove the marrons glacés from their syrup and allow to dry on absorbent paper. Melt the coating chocolate and dip each marron in the chocolate (either part or all the way). Prop on toothpicks to dry. Whip the cream with the sugar to a stiff piping consistency.
8. Unmold the charlotte onto a serving dish or cake stand. Pipe the cream decoratively on the charlotte, either with a border of large rosettes or make rows of fluted cream from the center to the edges. Leave some of the chocolate ganache showing on the top for contrast. Place the dipped marrons all around the edge of the charlotte and one or two in the center.

Chocolate-Hazelnut Parfaits

Serves: 12–16

Ingredients:

For hazelnut mixture:

8	egg yolks	8
10 oz	granulated sugar	285 g
2 tbls	water	30 ml

1 pt	heavy cream	½ L
4 oz	chopped toasted hazelnuts	115 g
2 tbls	Frangelico liqueur	30 ml
	For chocolate mixture:	
8	egg yolks	8
10 oz	granulated sugar	285 g
2 tbls	water	30 ml
½ tsp	instant espresso powder	½ tsp
3 oz	grated bittersweet chocolate	85 g
1 pt	heavy cream	½ L

Garnish: chopped toasted hazelnuts

1. Place the yolks in the bowl of a mixer and begin to beat until foamy. Meanwhile, combine the sugar with the water and heat until a clear syrup forms and the syrup has reached the soft ball stage, about 240° F (115° C).
2. Pour the hot syrup over the yolks while they are being beaten, continue to beat until the entire mixture is cold and fluffy.
3. When the eggs are almost done, whip the cream to soft peaks. Fold into the yolk mixture, add the liqueur, and fold in the nuts. Set aside, refrigerated, while preparing the chocolate mixture.
4. Beat the eggs and prepare the syrup as above. When the syrup has reached temperature, stir in the grated chocolate and the espresso powder. Add the syrup to the yolks and beat until cool as above. Whip the cream and fold into the chocolate mixture.
5. Select parfait glasses, wine goblets, or small timbale molds. Spoon the two mixtures into the containers in an attractive swirled pattern. Sprinkle the tops with chopped hazelnuts if desired. Freeze for at least 3 hours. For longer storage (1 week or more), be sure to wrap airtight to protect flavor.
6. Temper in the refrigerator for about 1 hour if desired before serving. To unmold, dip in hot water or wrap in a hot wet cloth and place on a serving dish, napped with chocolate sauce or creme anglaise.

Bourbon Bread Pudding

Serves: 24

	Ingredients:	
3 oz	golden raisins	84 g
3 oz	dried currants	84 g
4 fl oz	bourbon	125 ml
2 lb	dense white sandwich bread	900 g
½ lb	sweet butter, softened	224 g

1 tbls	**cinnamon**	1 tbls
1 lb	**granulated sugar**	450 g
2 qt	**milk**	2 L
1 pt	**light cream**	½ L
12	**eggs, lightly beaten**	12
1 tbls	**vanilla extract**	15 ml
½ tsp	**salt**	½ tsp

1. Soak the raisins and currants in bourbon to plump. Set aside.
2. Combine half the sugar with the cinnamon. Reserve the rest separately.
3. Lightly butter the bottom and sides of a hotel pan, 20 × 12 in. (50 × 30 cm). Set aside.
4. Spread the bread slices with the remaining butter. Trim the crusts, stack, and cut in halves or quarters.
5. Place the bread, in a neat pattern, buttered side up, in the pan to form one layer. Reserve about 2 tbls (25 g) of cinnamon sugar. Sprinkle with some of the remaining cinnamon sugar and some of the plumped fruit and bourbon. Continue to layer bread and fruit. The top layer should be only bread sprinkled with cinnamon sugar.
6. Prepare the custard: Scald the milk and cream and mix with the remaining plain sugar. Slowly add the hot milk to the eggs, stirring, then return the heated egg mixture to the balance of the milk and cream. Stir in the vanilla and salt.
7. Carefully pour the custard mixture around the edges of the layered bread, mostly into the corner and sides of the pan. Add a little at a time, allow to absorb, then add more. Try not to wet the top bread slices. Press down on the bread to help it absorb the custard. Let stand about 30 minutes. Sprinkle the reserved cinnamon sugar over the top.
8. While the bread pudding is soaking, preheat the oven to 350° F (180° C).
9. Place the bread pudding pan into a larger pan and place in oven. Pour hot water into the outer pan, until the level is at least halfway up the sides of the inner pan. Bake for 45 minutes or until just set.
10. Let cool slightly before cutting into portions if serving warm. Serve with cold Creme Anglaise (Custard Sauce) (see in recipe index) on the side. Or refrigerate covered for up to 3 days. Serve cold with lightly sweetened whipped cream if desired. Bread Pudding may be baked and frozen, well wrapped. Thaw covered and heat covered with foil. Remove foil for the last 5 minutes to crisp top. To reheat in the microwave (which works very well) heat at half power, uncovered.

Variations: Substitute other breads—French, Italian, challah, brioche, or Egg Bread (see in recipe index). If so, leave the crusts on for a more rustic effect. In the case of round bread slices, a round or oval baking dish, with the slices laid in concentric circles, makes a very attractive buffet presentation. Rum or orange juice may be substituted for bourbon. Other dried fruits or chocolate or butterscotch chips may be layered in.

Spiced Fruit Clafouti

Serves: 24

Ingredients:

4 oz	cake flour	112 g
4 oz	granulated sugar	112 g
3 oz	light brown sugar	84 g
1 tsp	salt	1 tsp
1 tsp	cinnamon	1 tsp
pinch	nutmeg	pinch
pinch	ground cloves	pinch
5	eggs	5
1 pt	milk	½ L
1 tsp	vanilla extract	5 ml
2 tbls	rum, brandy, or fruit liqueur	30 ml
3 to 4 lb	fruit, such as pitted cherries, sautéed apples, poached pears, sliced peaches, apricots, plums, or blueberries	1350 g to 2 kg

1. Prepare fruit of your choice as follows: If cherries are canned, drain; If cherries are fresh, halve and macerate in a bit of sugar and kirsch. Apples can be thinly sliced or chopped and sautéed in a bit of butter and sugar. If you have leftover poached pears, simply cut the fruit into small chunks. Very ripe peaches or apricots can simply be peeled, stoned, and sliced or diced; if they are not ripe and soft, they may be simmered in a bit of butter, sugar, and lemon juice. Ripe purple plums can be stoned and sliced with the skin intact. Blueberries should simply be picked over, rinsed and well drained, then tossed in a bit of flour and a pinch of sugar.

2. Preheat the oven to 400°F (205°C). Prepare pan(s) by buttering generously. Use one 12 × 18-in. (30 × 45 cm) or three 8- or 9-in. (20 or 23 cm) round or square pans. The pans should be at least 2-in. (5 cm) high. If planning to serve directly from a buffet, choose attractive ceramic or glass ovenproof dishes.

3. Sift together the flour, sugars, salt, and spices. Set aside.

4. Beat the milk with the eggs, vanilla, and spirits. Stir into dry ingredients and beat until smooth. Pour half the batter into the prepared pan. Arrange the fruit over the batter, distributing evenly in the pan. Add the rest of the batter.

5. Bake for about 30 minutes, until golden. Check one corner to see that the clafouti is set well enough to have crusted a bit on the sides. Serve warm or at room temperature. If serving warm, slightly sweetened whipped cream or ice cream served alongside makes a lavish dessert. Or simply sprinkle with a little confectioners' sugar before serving.

Note: To prevent scorching, set the baking pans on a heavy baking sheet.

Strawberry Rhubarb Crisp

Serves: 10

Ingredients:

6 cups	trimmed, sliced rhubarb	1½ L
8 oz	granulated sugar, or to taste	225 g
	water as needed	
2 pt	ripe strawberries, washed, hulled, and sliced	1 L
3 tbls	sweet butter	40 g

For topping:

6 oz	cold butter	180 g
8 oz	brown sugar	225 g
3 oz	all-purpose flour	85 g
½ cup	quick-cooking rolled oats	125 ml
4 oz	chopped walnuts	115 g
1 tsp	cinnamon	1 tsp
1 tsp	ground ginger	1 tsp

Garnish:

1 cup	heavy cream	¼ L
2 tsp	confectioners' sugar	2 tsp
1 tbls	kirsch or rum	15 ml

1. Simmer the rhubarb in a saucepan with some of the sugar and a bit of water until the rhubarb is close to being tender. Add the strawberries and continue to cook down, adding a bit more water only if needed to prevent scorching and sugar to taste. The mixture should not be too liquid. If it is, cook down over higher heat until it is reduced. Spoon the fruit into a shallow baking dish or casserole with a 2-quart (2 L) capacity, and dot with the 3 tbls (40 g) of butter. Let cool. Preheat the oven to 350°F (180°C).
2. Combine the remaining dry ingredients in a bowl and cut in the butter. Place the topping over the cooled fruit. Bake for about 40 minutes until the fruit is bubbly and the topping crisp. Let settle for at least 10 minutes before serving.
3. May be served hot or at room temperature. As a garnish, whip the cream, flavor with the sugar and liquor. Place some cream on or alongside each portion or offer to guests on the side.

Note: May be prepared ahead and refrigerated or frozen for later use.

Variations: Rhubarb alone may be used but more sugar will be needed. Other fruits, alone or in combination, can be substituted and used with this topping.

OTHER HAPPY ENDINGS

Amaretto Pears

Serves: 8

Ingredients:

4	large ripe pears*	4
2 cups	dry white wine	½ L
½ cup	amaretto	125 ml
3 oz	light brown sugar	85 g
2 tsp	pure vanilla extract	10 ml
	For sauce and garnish:	
8	whole cloves	8
8	chocolate leaves	8
12	amaretti cookies	12
2 tbls	creme de cacao	30 ml
2 cups	**Creme Anglaise (see in recipe index), flavored with amaretto**	½ L

*See the recipe for Vanilla Poached Pears for detailed instructions on poaching pears. In this recipe, the pears may be halved and cored after poaching.

1. Prepare the poaching syrup by combining the wine, amaretto, sugar, and vanilla. Simmer for about 5 minutes. More sugar may be added to taste. Peel the pears, add to the syrup (you may add water to cover if needed) and poach until barely tender. Let the pears cool in the syrup. Hold, covered and refrigerated, in the syrup until ready to use.
2. Sprinkle eight of the amaretti cookies with the creme de cacao. Let stand to soften slightly. Crush the remaining cookies and set the crumbs aside.
3. Carefully halve the pears and spoon out their cores. Place a soaked cookie in the hollow of the pear. Remove the stems and replace with cloves.
4. Spoon about ¼ cup (60 ml) of creme anglaise onto the eight chilled rimmed dessert plates to coat the surface completely. On each plate, carefully place a filled pear half, cookie side down, on the custard. Place a chocolate leaf at the clove "stem" and sprinkle the cookie crumbs over the custard. Serve cold.

Note: May be preplated, except for the chocolate leaf and crumbs. Hold, covered and refrigerated. Be careful moving the plates around or the creme anglaise will run over the rim of the plates.

Vanilla Poached Pears

Serves: 10

Ingredients:

10	**ripe, firm pears, any type**	10
4 cups	**dry white wine**	1 L
1 cup	**water**	¼ L
1½ cups	**brown sugar**	370 ml
1	**vanilla bean, split**	1
3	**whole cloves**	3
3 strips	**fresh lemon peel**	3 strips

1. Prepare the syrup by combining the wine, water, brown sugar, spices, and lemon peel. Place in a pot large enough to hold the pears submerged in the syrup. Stir to dissolve sugar. Simmer for about 10 minutes while preparing pears.
2. The pears should be perfect specimens, beautifully shaped and even in size, especially if planning to serve whole as part of a fancy dessert. Use a very sharp swivel-bladed peeler to remove the thinnest possible peel from pears. Peel carefully, leaving the pears in their perfect shape. Leave the stems intact, but make a shallow gouge to remove the blossom end. The Europeans have no objection to the core left in a whole poached pear, but if you prefer, you may carefully core from the bottom, using a small paring knife or apple corer. If you are serving the poached pears halved, it is much easier to core neatly after poaching.
3. If you have prepared the syrup ahead and it had been removed from heat, place the pears in the syrup as you peel them. Otherwise, drop peeled pears into acidulated water as they are peeled.
4. Place the peeled pears in the poaching syrup, heat just to the simmer and poach at a bare simmer for about 10 to 15 minutes or just until pears are tender throughout. Test with a hat pin or long needle at the widest part of the pear. Remove from heat and let pears stand in syrup for about an hour to fully absorb flavor. Refrigerate to hold more than 1 day. You may remove the vanilla bean, lemon peel, and cloves after the first several hours.
5. Poached pears can simply be served, chilled, in their syrup as part of a dessert buffet. Or, you may boil down some of the syrup to a thicker glaze and serve over the drained pears. They are very good served with Chocolate Rum Sauce (see in recipe index) or raspberry puree.
6. Reserve the syrup, refrigerated, to use again for pears, to poach other fruits, to enhance a fruit compote, or drizzle over a winter fruit salad. It is good used as a glaze for grapefruit halves or sections, lightly broiled.

Note: Take care removing the pears from the syrup, so as not to cut into their delicate flesh. A broad, shallow plastic kitchen spoon works better than a sharp-edged metal one.

Variations: Poached pears are used in many ways for desserts (see recipe index). They may also be sliced and used for a pear tart, pureed for mousse or custard desserts, or diced and tossed with lightly sautéed spinach for an unusual vegetable dish.

Chocolate Chestnut Ravioli

Yield: **48**

Ingredients:

For filling:

3 cups	cooked, riced chestnuts	750 ml
4 oz	bittersweet chocolate	112 g
6 fl oz	honey	180 ml
3 fl oz	orange juice	90 ml
1½ tsp	grated orange rind	1½ tsp
1 oz	citron, minced	28 g

For dough:

12 oz	all-purpose flour	336 g
¼ tsp	salt	¼ tsp
2 tbls	hot olive oil	30 ml
5	eggs, lightly beaten	5
	egg wash	
	oil for frying	

Dried chestnuts are sold in Italian and Chinese specialty stores. Boil them until they are tender, drain, and pass through a food mill or potato ricer. Do a large batch at one time, measure out what is needed for this recipe and store the balance of the puree in the freezer for use in desserts or vegetable side dishes. These dried chestnuts can also be boiled and chopped for use in stuffings, a satisfactory and far easier solution to roasting and hand-peeling and skinning raw chestnuts. The Italian variety are the best quality.

1. Prepare the filling: Melt the chocolate, stir in the honey, orange juice, orange rind, and minced citron. Stir vigorously to combine. Set aside at room temperature to cool.
2. Prepare the dough: Combine the flour and salt, make a well and add the oil and the eggs, mix well. Turn out onto a lightly floured board and knead as for pasta or bread dough. If the dough is too dry, sprinkle on a few drops of water or white wine. Rest the dough, covered, for an hour or two.

3. Cut the dough into three or four pieces. Work with one piece at a time, keeping the remainder moist under an overturned bowl. With a lightly floured rolling pin, roll the dough to a ⅛-in. (½ cm) thickness. Cut into two equal pieces and prepare to shape ravioli. You may use a ravioli form if you like, or simply shape by hand, using a ravioli stamper or fluted pastry wheel.

4. Place a generous tablespoon of filling on the dough at evenly spaced intervals on one sheet of dough. Brush egg wash on the edges and around each mound of filling. Carefully lay the second sheet of dough over the first, press down to seal between each mound and all around edges. Cut into ravioli, being certain the edges are well crimped. Set aside and continue with the rest of the dough until all the ravioli are made.

5. Heat the oil in a deep fryer or in a skillet to a depth of 3 in. (8 cm). Fry the ravioli, a batch at a time, turning to color golden brown on both sides. Transfer to clean absorbent paper to drain. Sprinkle with confectioners' sugar before serving.

Note: This traditional Southern Italian Christmas dessert is unusual and delicious to serve during any winter month. Leftover strips of dough may be shaped into rings or bows, fried, and served sprinkled with confectioners' sugar or brushed with honey.

Puffed Apple Pancake

Serves: 8–10

Ingredients:

1 lb	baking apples	450 g
2 tsp	lemon juice	10 ml
4 tbls	butter or margarine	60 g
4 tbls	light brown sugar	55 g
2 tsp	cinnamon	2 tsp
4	eggs, separated	4
4 tbls	granulated sugar	50 g
6 tbls	milk	90 ml
6 tbls	flour	60 g
1 tsp	baking powder	1 tsp
	confectioners sugar or cinnamon sugar (as needed)	

Optional topping:

1 cup	whipped cream	¼ L
4 oz	sour cream	115 g

1. This pancake may be prepared in a cast-iron or other ovenproof 10-in. (25 cm) skillet and unmolded or served in the skillet, rustic-style. It may also be prepared in a flameproof casserole and served as it comes from the oven, puffy side up. The recipe may be multiplied for volume up to 3 ×: Increase the proportion of fruit by 10%. Preheat the oven to 400°F (205°C).
2. Peel and slice the apples, sprinkle with lemon juice. Heat the butter or margarine in the skillet or pan. Spread the cinnamon and light brown sugar over the butter. Add the apples (if planning to unmold, arrange the slices attractively), simmer over low heat, undisturbed, for 10 minutes.
3. While the apples cook, beat the egg whites until thick and foamy, add the granulated sugar and beat until stiff but not dry. Combine the eggs and milk and mix in the flour and baking powder. Pour over the whites and fold in.
4. Add the egg mixture to the skillet once the apples have cooked for 10 minutes. If planning to serve from the pan, sprinkle the top with confectioners' sugar or cinnamon sugar. Place in the oven and bake for 15 to 20 minutes until puffed and golden.
5. Serve as is or unmold by loosening the sides and inverting onto a serving plate. Sprinkle the top with confectioners' sugar.
6. Good served hot or warm. If held, it will begin to collapse, but will still taste good. Combine the whipped cream with the sour cream and serve a dollop on each piece. Or offer ice cream on the side.

Variation: Pears may be substituted for apples: Add some ground ginger and a pinch of nutmeg to the sugar mixture.

Candied Eggplants

Yield: 50

	Ingredients:	
50	**baby eggplants (about 2 in. [5 cm])**	50
16 oz	**sugar**	450 g
8 fl oz	**water**	¼ L
8 fl oz	**light corn syrup**	¼ L
4 tbls	**lemon juice**	60 ml
2	**cinnamon sticks**	2
6	**whole cloves**	6

1. Begin eggplant preparation 2 days ahead. Wash and carefully trim the stems and caps from the eggplant. Make a slit in the side of each one. Soak in cold water for one day. Drain, replace with fresh water, and soak one more day.
2. Dissolve the sugar in water and boil to make a clear syrup. Put the drained eggplants in the syrup and boil for 6 minutes. Turn off the heat and let rest in the syrup for 1 hour. Turn on the burner and boil for 5 minutes.
3. Remove the eggplants from the sugar syrup, add corn syrup, the lemon juice, cinnamon sticks, and cloves. Boil this mixture for 5 minutes.
4. Return eggplants to syrup. Store refrigerated for a few months. You may pack in smaller containers, covering the eggplant with syrup and distributing the spices among the containers.

Note: This Greek recipe produces a surprising confection that can be served as one would poached or glazed fruits. The candied eggplants are very sweet and are set off nicely by the bland creaminess of a coeur à la crème, a mascarpone, or drained yogurt cheese. These are obviously best prepared when baby eggplants are plentiful at farm or market stands.

Appendix

PURVEYORS

Foodstuff

Beef

Kohler Beef
Kohler Farms
Kohler, Wisconsin 53044
   Grass- and grain-fed beef, hormone- and
   drug-free

Brae Beef
Stamford Town Center
Third Level
Stamford, Connecticut 06901
800–323–4484 (in CT 203–323–4482)
   Grass- and beer-fed beef, hormone- and
   drug-free

Bread

Fleischmann's Hot Line
800–932–7800
Monday–Friday, 9 A.M.–9 P.M. (EST)
   Croissants not crisp enough? Bread won't
   rise? Call in!

Cajun Ingredients

K-PAUL'S
501 Elysian Fields
P. O. Box 770034
New Orleans, Louisiana 70177–0034
800–4KPAULS
   Spices, jambalaya mix, etouffee mix,
   andouille sausage, pork tasso, red beans
   and rice mix (and Cajun music on cassette!)

Cheeses

Mozzarella Company
2944 Elm Street
Dallas, Texas 75226
214–741–4072
   Fresh mozzarella, mozzarella rolls (with
   herbed fillings), goat cheese, ancho chili
   cheese, caciotta (semi-soft, buttery), crème
   fraîche

Pollio Dairy Products Corp.
120 Mineola Boulevard
Mineola, New York 11501
800–632–3356 (in NY 800–545–1245)
  The POLLY-O brand of Italian dairy products is always reliable. Their new line, Fior di Latte, is a fresh, water-packed mozzarella in a variety of sizes. The ⅓- and ½-ounce sizes are especially good for hors d'oeuvre. These products are available in many supermarkets, or call the 800 number for a nearby distributor.

Chiles and Mexican-Type Ingredients

Los Chileros de Nuevo Mexico
P.O. Box 6215
Santa Fe, New Mexico 87502
  Pod and ground chiles (nine kinds); blue, yellow, and white corn meal and chips; pine nuts; raw Mexican sugar; corn husks

Tia Mia, Inc.
720 North Walnut
El Paso, Texas 79903
800–854–2003 (24 hours)
  Salsas, chili sauces, whole green chiles, jalapeño mustard, marinade mixes

La Cantina
6140 Brockton Road
Hatboro, Pennsylvania 19040
215–487–1360
  Chiles, salsas, fresh southwestern/Mexican produce, spices such as epazote, beans, corn products, frozen hors d'oeuvre, and entrees

Fish and Shellfish, Fresh

East Coast Fisheries
360 West Flagler Street
Miami, Florida 33130
305–377–2529
  Florida rock lobster and stone crab claws are a specialty along with Florida-fished grouper, snapper, pompano, sea trout, and mahi-mahi, wild Alaskan salmon, farmed Norwegian salmon, kiwa shrimp, among other varieties according to season. The company maintains its own fleet and processing facility along with an open-kitchen restaurant, and exercises strict quality control. They will ship any size order overnight via Federal Express. Fish will be shipped either whole gutted or filleted as requested. Speak to Ron Goldstein for further information or special requests.

Pike Place Fish
86 Pike Place
Seattle, Washington 98101
206–682–7181
  Will ship (fin and shellfish) anywhere in the United States in 48 hours.

Triple M Seafood
2821 East Atlantic Boulevard
Pompano Beach, Florida 33062
800–722–0073 (in Florida 800–323–0073)
  Hard-to-find varieties (fin and shellfish), shipped overnight

The Great Eastern Mussel Farms
P.O. Box 141
Tenanats Harbor, Maine 04860
207–372–6217
  Plump, evenly-sized farm-raised mussels

Dodge Cove Marine Farm, Inc.
P.O. Box 211
Newcastle, Maine 04553
207–563–8168
  Belon oysters, caraquet oysters, blue mussels, mahogany littleneck quahogs, sea urchins with roe

Lusty Lobster, Inc.
167 Rumery Street
South Portland, Maine 04106
207–767–5537
  Fresh lobsters

Fish, Smoked

Ducktrap River Fish Farm
RFD 2, Box 378
Lincolnville, Maine 04849
207–763–3960
    Smoked salmon, trout, scallops, mussels

Totem Smokehouse
1906 Pike Place
Seattle, Washington 98101
800–9–SALMON
    Northwest alder-smoked salmon

Flour

Great Valley Mills
687 Mill Road
Telford, Pennsylvania 18969
215–256–6648
    Superior-grown and -milled bread flour,
    pastry flour, cornmeal

Walnut Acres
Penns Creek, Pennsylvania 17862
717–837–0601 (24 hours)
    Organically grown flours and grains

Game

D'Angelo Bros. Products, Inc.
909 South 9th Street
Philadelphia, Pennsylvania 19147
215–923–5637
    Frozen venison (imported), boar, bear,
    alligator, eland, moose, elk, lion, buffalo,
    rattlesnake, quail, partridge, goose, wild
    turkey, Muscovy duck, mallard

Manchester Farms
P.O. Box 97
Dalzell, South Carolina 29040
803–469–2588
    Quail, complete with grill pins

The National Buffalo Association
10 Main Street
Fort Pierre, South Dakota 57532
605–223–2829
    There are over 500 buffalo ranchers in the
    United States. The association will direct
    you to the one nearest you.

Texas Wild Game Cooperative
P.O. Box 530
Ingram, Texas 78025
512–367–5875
    Farm-raised axis venison, blackbuck
    antelope, wild boar

D'Artagnan, Inc.
399–419 St. Paul Avenue
Jersey City, New Jersey 07306
800–DARTAGN (in NJ 201–792–0748)
    Game birds and free-range chickens, redtail
    and fallow venison, buffalo, baby lamb
    and goat, rabbit, Russian boar

Herbs, Fresh

Fox Hill Farm
440 West Michigan Avenue
Box 7
Parma, Michigan 49269–0007
517–531–3179
MCI Mail: HERBS 175–3505
    Year-round availability on almost 30 kinds,
    seasonal availability on an additional 20
    kinds; also herbed vinegars

Patty's Herbs
Route 1, Box 31J
Pearsall, Texas 78061
512–334–3944
    Year-round availability of a very large
    number of fresh herbs. Patty's also carries
    a full range of edible flowers, some baby
    vegetables, and other specialty produce.
    They will ship overnight UPS and no
    minimum order is required.

The Mushroom Man
800–441–7017
 Year-round, six-day delivery of popular
herb varieties

Balducci's
Mail order address:
11–02 Queen's Plaza South
Long Island City, New York 11101–4908
800–822–1444 (in NY 800–247–2450)
 Seasonal availability on popular varieties

Herbs, Dried

San Francisco Herb and Natural Foods Co.
4543 Horton Street
Emeryville, California 94608
415–547–6345
 More than 350 bulk herbs, teas, and spices

Penn Herb Co. Ltd.
603 North 2nd Street
Philadelphia, Pennsylvania 19123–3098
800–523–9971, orders only
215–925–3336 for information
 Huge selection

Ice Cream

St. Clair Ice Cream Co.
One Hanford Place
South Norwalk, Connecticut 06854
203–853–4774
 This company produces exquisite little
lifelike fruit-shaped ice creams that are as
delicious as they are beautiful. They will
ship any size order in dry ice. The shipping
fee is about $15, but it's practical to place a
large order because the little ice creams
keep well in a good freezer.

Oriental Ingredients

De Wildt Imports, Inc.
Fox Gap Road
RD 3
Bangor, Pennsylvania 18013
800–338–3433
 Ingredients from Indonesia, Malaysia,
Singapore, Philippines, India, Japan, Korea,
Taiwan, China, Thailand, Vietnam, and
Mongolia (oriental cookware, too)

Pasta

Gaston Dupre, Inc.
7904 Hopi Place
Tampa, Florida 33634
813–885–9445 or 800–937–9445
 Frozen or dried hand-cut pasta. Flavors
include chili, curry, lemon-basil, squid ink,
tomato, whole wheat, and confetti. Many
shapes from which to choose. Call 800
number for catalogue or mail order.

Pâtés, Sausages

D'Angelo Bros. Products, Inc.
909 South 9th Street
Philadelphia, Pennsylvania 19147
215–923–5637
 Sausage varieties include Italian, Boudin
Blanc, French Summer, Sicilian, Bratwurst,
Chorizo, Andouillettes, English Breakfast,
and Tuscanno; pâtés include Pheasant,
Country, Madeira, Rabbit, and Boar

D'Artagnan, Inc.
399–419 St. Paul Avenue
Jersey City, New Jersey 07306
800–DARTAGN (in NJ 201–792–0748)
 Sausages include duck and foie gras,
venison with juniper, wild boar with sage;

also foie gras au natural, fois gras au Sauternes, and bloc de foie gras

Michel's Magnifique, Ltd.
34 North Moore Street
New York, New York 10013
212–431–1070

An assortment of vegetable, meat, fish, and game pâtés that are attractive and well-flavored. Call for the names of regional distributors or to arrange for ground or air express delivery.

Produce and Other Specialty Products

American Spoon Foods
1688 Clarion Avenue
P.O. Box 566
Petoskey, Michigan 49770
616–347–5030

Chef Larry Forgione and forager Justin Rashid provide a varied selection of wild and cultivated berries, wild mushrooms, nuts, varietal honeys, jams, and preserves, including No-sugar Spoon Fruits, a line of Larry Forgione's Sauces, and dried tart cherries.

A.L. Bazzini Company, Inc.
339 Greenwich Street
New York, New York 10013
212–227–6241 or 800–288–0172

Nuts of every description, first-quality dried fruits and confections. Small orders can be picked up locally, They service primarily wholesalers, but call to inquire about bulk mail order.

Bel Canto Fancy Foods
555 Second Avenue
New York, New York 10016
212–689–4433

Features a variety of domestic and imported Italian products including arborio rice,

pastas, oils, vinegars, etc. Bel Aria (the company's import label) Olive Oil is truly delicious and well-priced. Call to inquire about mail orders.

De Choix Specialty Foods Company
58–25 52nd Avenue
Woodside, New York 11377
718–507–8080 or 800–DE–CHOIX

A great source for specialty baked goods, baking products, fruit spreads and filling, and Callebaut chocolate, along with a line of gourmet specialty products. Call for either a direct shipment or the name of a distributor in your area.

Todaro Bros.
555 Second Avenue
New York, New York 10016
212–532–0633

A food specialty shop with an excellent variety of imported and domestic products, as well as fresh pasta, Italian sauces, extensive cheese selection (including fresh mozzarella made on the premises), first-quality fresh and cured meats, homemade sausages, smoked fish, and caviar. They will express mail orders on request and have a free catalog.

Paprikas Weiss, Importer
1546 Second Avenue
New York, New York 10028
212–288–6117

Send for a free catalog of the many specialty spices, flours, grains, and difficult-to-find ingredients available in this marvelous shop. The staff is both helpful and knowledgeable: If they don't carry an item, they can probably tell you who does.

The Mushroom Man
800–441–7017

Year-round six-day delivery of 15–20 varieties of fresh and dried mushrooms, exotic fruit, and baby vegetables

Delftree Corporation
234 Union Street
North Adams, Massachusetts 01247
413–663–5680
   Exotic fresh mushrooms

Folsom Farms
Route 3, Box 249
Glennville, Georgia 30427
800–634–4878
   Vidalia onions

Balducci's
11–02 Queens Plaza South (mail order address)
Long Island City, New York 11101–4908
800–822–1444 (in NY 800–247–2450)
   Exotic fruits and vegetables

Seaside Banana Garden
6823 Santa Barbara Avenue
La Conchita, California 93001
805–643–4061
   Exotic, organically grown bananas. They arrive green, so allow a week for ripening.

Kitchen Needs

Cookware

A Cook's Wares
3270 37th Street
Beaver Falls, Pennsylvania 15010
412–846–9490
   Work tables, serving carts, cutlery, molds, pots, pans, ingredients. Call for a catalog, it's worth the $1.50.

Bridge Kitchenware Corp.
214 East 52nd Street
New York, New York 10022
212–688–4220
   This shop, and its well-informed staff, is a great source for quality equipment and kitchen wisdom.

Doylestown Supply Company
P.O. Box 1206
Doylestown, Pennsylvania 18901
   Professional discounts on cookware and cutlery. Write, don't call.

Chocolate, Baking, and Candy-Making Supplies

Assouline and Ting, Inc.
926 West Allegheny Avenue
Philadelphia, Pennsylvania 19133
800–521–4491

The Chocolate Gallery
34 West 22nd Street
New York, New York 10010
212–675–2253
   If you're in the area, visit, or call for a catalogue. The shop carries a wide assortment of cake decorating and candy supplies, along with pans, parchment, cake boards, edible glitter and leaf, and coating chocolates. Courses are also given. Mail orders are handled promptly.

Maid of Scandinavia
3244 Raleigh Avenue
Minneapolis, Minnesota 55416
800–328–6722
   Call for their catalogue ($1.00). They carry a vast array of cake pans, cookie and candy molds, and all baking and cake decorating accessories as well as specialty ingredients and supplies.

Madame Chocolate
1940-C Lehigh Avenue
Glenview, Illinois 60025
312–729–3330

Wilton Enterprises
2240 West 75th Street
Woodridge, Illinois 60517
708–963–7100 or 800–772–7111
   Call the 800 number for a catalogue ($4.95) of a mind-boggling line of baking pans and equipment, as well as equipment

and materials for cake decorating, sugarwork, and candy and chocolate making. The Wilton Method of cake decorating is taught in courses offered in department and specialty stores that carry Wilton products. Call 800–323–1717 (operator 440) for information.

RESOURCES IN PRINT

Books

No one can be expected to read or own every book or periodical that might apply to the hospitality trade in general, or to off-premise catering in particular. A first, and most useful, step would be occasional visits to the local library, where a scan of *Books in Print* and a chat with the librarian will keep you apprised of publications that might be of interest.

One or two general cookbooks should be on hand in every kitchen. Among others, *Joy of Cooking* (Bobbs-Merrill) and *The Fannie Farmer Cookbook* (Little, Brown & Co.) are useful general reference books. The recipes included may not necessarily be on the cutting edge of modern taste, but the books have a broad scope in terms of regional recipes and historical perspective, and offer good advice and sound cooking principles.

The *Larousse Gastronomique* (Crown) is an illustrated encyclopedia of food, wine, traditional recipes, and cooking techniques and equipment. As such it is a very useful reference and resource book.

All of the Julia Child cookbooks are worthwhile for their good explanations of culinary techniques, and a solid, common-sense approach to cooking. Julia Child has earned her position as a leading cooking authority and as a culinary pioneer who demystified the complexities of French cuisine for her readers (and TV viewers). Her sense of humor and enjoyment of both cooking and eating come through in all her books. If you can choose only one, pick either *Mastering the Art of French Cook-*

ing (with Beck and Bertholle), or her latest, *The Way to Cook* (Knopf).

Nicholas Malgieri's *Perfect Pastry* (Macmillan) is one book I consider a necessity for anyone interested in the art and craft of baking. The author is both a Master Pastry Chef and a superb teacher. The book has the well-organized approach of a complete baking course, with explanations of the basic techniques and components from which great desserts are made. Years back, I was one of his students, and this book comes close to the marvelous experience of being in his classes.

Maida Heatter's books on baking are all excellent. The recipes are foolproof and the instructions carefully detailed so results are good at the first try. Rose Levy Berenbaum's *The Cake Bible* (Morrow) is amazingly detailed and complete. It is especially good for its explanation of the chemistry of baking, which can help you make alterations and improvements in recipes of your own.

Jacques Pepin's *La Technique* and *La Methode* (Quadrangle, The New York Times Co.) amount to private lessons with a talented chef. The instructions, along with step-by-step demonstration photographs, reveal many of the trucs (culinary tricks of the trade) that will make you feel confident attempting even complex procedures.

Kosher Cuisine, by Helen Nash (Schapolsky, 1989), is a good source for guidelines to the kosher kitchen even though the recipes are designed for the home.

Two of Judith Benn Hurley's cookbooks, *Garden-Fresh Cooking* (Rodale Press, 1987) and *The Healthy Gourmet* (Penguin, 1989), are excellent choices for guidelines and inspiration in developing recipes and menus for a health-conscious clientele. The recipes are designed for small-scale cooking, but they can be easily expanded and produce dishes that are delicious and beautifully presented, as well as healthful.

Martha Stewart's books on entertaining, weddings, and so on are full of imaginative ideas and beautiful photographs of plating and serving concepts that can be inspirational to a caterer aspiring to a sophisticated country style.

These and the rest of the books listed in this section have been of interest and use to me and provide a suggested starting point for building a reference library.

The Food Professional's Guide
Compiled by Irena Chalmers
Wiley

An excellent sourcebook for anyone involved in the food industry. It lists an extensive variety of food sources (from markets to mail order), public and private information agencies, trade associations, culinary schools and cooking courses, and food authorities and professionals of every description.

The Chefs' Source Book
Chefs in America Publishing
109 Minna Street
Suite 555
San Francisco, California 94105

A directory of food distributors, specialty producers, and gourmet product manufacturers that can be useful when searching out unusual ingredients. Some of the companies listed offer direct mail or phone service; others provide the names of wholesalers or brokers that carry their lines.

The Professional Chef Book Guild
Attention: Karen Carter
Van Nostrand Reinhold
P.O. Box 668
Florence, Kentucky 41022–0668

At the risk of sounding biased, I recommend exploring membership in the Professional Chef Book Guild, a book club offered by Van Nostrand Reinhold. A wide selection of excellent culinary and hospitality titles are available at significant savings. Bulletins describing the books are mailed to members throughout the year.

The Professional Caterer Series
Volumes 1–4
Denis Ruffel
Van Nostrand Reinhold

Lavishly illustrated, and containing detailed instructions and recipes, this four volume series is literally a soup-to-nuts library for the caterer. There is great emphasis on presentation, the exercise of culinary showmanship that every caterer can use to increase profits.

Special Events, The Art and Science of Celebration
Joe Jeff Goldblatt
Van Nostrand Reinhold

The first book to address the emerging industry of special events planning and managing, a growing field that is sometimes merged with, or at least goes hand-in-hand with, the off-premise catering business. It is a real nuts-and-bolts guide by a seasoned professional, with in-depth explanations of various types of functions, helpful diagrams and floor plans, and a useful resource list of support services.

Places, Seventh Edition
Tenth House Enterprises, Inc.
Caller Box 810, Gracie Station
New York, New York 10028
212–737–7536

An interesting directory of spaces and places available for parties and special events. All of the locations are unique, many with either architectural or historical interest. While many are located in the greater metropolitan New York City area, there are listings for areas around the country as well. The book is carried in some bookstores, but for information or to order by mail, write to or call Tenth House Enterprises.

Successful Catering
Bernard Splaver
Revised and updated third edition edited by

William Reynolds and Michael Roman
Van Nostrand Reinhold

Gives a good general overview of the on-premise catering business, with a chapter on off-premise catering. The overall information and recipes are useful for menu planning, service, and function management.

Successful Buffet Management
Ronald A. Yudd
Van Nostrand Reinhold

While not specifically designed for off-premise catering, this book, with its focus on menu planning, cost control, service, equipment, and creative presentation of buffets, make it useful to the off-premise caterer.

The Book of Great Hors d'Oeuvre
Terence Janericco
Van Nostrand Reinhold

Indispensible to a caterer. It is very thorough and well-organized, with good recipes and careful instructions.

The New Professional Chef
Culinary Institute of America
Van Nostrand Reinhold

An excellent text, complete and well-structured, from basic principles and procedures, through complex techniques and completed recipes and menus. It should be considered a basic culinary text, important to have in every working kitchen.

Professional Cooking
Wayne Gisslen
Wiley

An excellent basic text, well-organized and with instructional photographs, that teaches culinary fundamentals. Another book by Gisslen, *Professional Baking* (Wiley), is also a good basic baking text.

The Professional Pastry Chef, Second Edition
Bo Friberg
Van Nostrand Reinhold

A complete professional baking text that teaches baking skills in a logical order, with clear explanations, and includes a wide range of recipes.

Escoffier Le Guide Culinaire
Translated by H. L. Cracknell and
   R. J. Kaufman
Van Nostrand Reinhold

The classic sourcebook of French cuisine, with a useful guide to measurement and conversion for modern day usage.

La Repertoire de la Cuisine
Louis Saulnier
Barron's Educational Series

Another approach to Escoffier's classic codification of French cuisine. Both this and the preceding book are really expanded dictionaries or glossaries. The recipes, which are shorthand descriptions of classic dishes, techniques, and terminology, should be part of an accomplished food professional's body of knowledge.

Classic and Contemporary Italian Cooking
Bruno H. Ellmer
Van Nostrand Reinhold

A beautiful and well-detailed work that explores the whole of Italian cuisine, with hundreds of recipes for traditional, regional, and specialty dishes. Its emphasis on fresh, quality ingredients and light, healthful preparations (always the hallmark of authentic Italian cuisine), make it especially suitable to today's modern tastes.

The Classic Italian Cook Book
More Classic Italian Cooking
Marcella Hazan
Knopf

Excellent sources of recipes for Italian dishes as native Italians prepare and enjoy them. The introductions to the books, and to the recipes themselves, give the reader a real understanding of each dish, its ingredients, and its place as part of a meal.

Uncommon Fruits and Vegetables
Elizabeth Schneider Colchie
Harper & Row

A good source book for learning about the unusual and new (to some of us) produce appearing in more and more markets.

Bookstores

Kitchen Arts & Letters, Inc.
1435 Lexington Avenue
New York, New York 10128
212–876–5550

A bookstore with an incredible inventory of books on food and wine and with knowledgeable and helpful staff. Mail and phone inquiries and orders are handled promptly.

Season to Taste Books, Ltd.
91 West School Street
Chicago, Illinois 60657
312–327–0210

In addition to having an extensive inventory, this shop also provides recipe searches.

Trade Publications

There is a great deal of printed material in the marketplace: In addition to consumer magazines devoted to food, entertaining, and the culinary arts, many professional culinary associations and networking groups publish journals and bulletins. Almost all food producers' groups and specialty growers have information bureaus or promotional organizations that publish newsletters and recipe booklets about their products. Refer to the *Food Professional's Guide* for listings that will give you a broad selection. The following publications may be of particular interest.

Catering Today
P.O. Box 222
Santa Claus, Indiana 47579
812–937–4464

Special Events Magazine
Miramar Publishing
P.O. Box 3640
Culver City, California 90231
213–337–9717

Fancy Foods Magazine
1414 Merchandise Mart
Chicago, Illinois 60654
312–670–0800

COMPUTER SOFTWARE

Today, professionals in most businesses feel that computers are a basic part of any office set-up. The decision to purchase and the selection of a computer must be an individual's own responsibility, as is the choice of software that may be suited to one's own business. Having said all that, I can give the following recommendations, based on personal usage.

The Recipe Writer Pro™ Version 3.0 is a program that assists with the preparation of standardized recipes, costing, yield conversions, and the like. One can list ingredients, along with their current market prices; print out recipes for kitchen use; change costs, selling prices, and portion sizes; create market lists for ordering; convert from English to metric equivalents; and cross-reference recipes to suit. I used this program to write, factor, and convert the recipes for this book, and found it easy and efficient to use.

Cater Pro™ is a wonderful system designed just for caterers. I had the opportunity to give it a trial run just as this book's manuscript was being completed. It has remarkable capabilities to create all sorts of forms, lists, menus, customer files, invoices, order sheets, and so on. In short, it can handle almost everything one would need to run an efficient catering operation. It can also be merged with the previously discussed Recipe Writer Pro to synthesize all the costing and planning aspects of one's business.

At-Your-Service Software (450 Bronxville Road, Bronxville, New York 10708) is a company that markets, sells, and services both programs. Call them (914–337–9030) for information about these and other programs. The company is very knowledgeable about the food business and very user-friendly. I'm no "techno-whiz," and made extensive use of their telephone support, which was excellent.

SCHOOLS AND ORGANIZATIONS

Cooking Schools and Courses

Recommending a cooking school to an individual is similar to playing matchmaker: tempting to do when you are familiar with the pleasures and satisfactions of a successful marriage, but fraught with peril. Even combinations that seem perfect may not flourish if the match does not suit personal tastes or need. The following list is in no way intended to be complete; instead, it includes the schools or courses of which I have personal knowledge, those that are the recommendations of associates, or those that are so world-renowned as to be "sure things."

Any omissions should not be interpreted as disapproval on my part, but rather a reflection of the enormous variety of training available both nation- and worldwide. Often, local courses may be offered that are not listed in any national directory, and they can still be very worthwhile: A talented instructor in whatever setting can provide excellent training. Keep in mind as well that local cooking schools can be a good forum for an off-premise caterer to offer courses or demonstrations, an endeavor that enhances both the profession at large and the caterer's own exposure.

The *Guide to Cooking Schools*, Second Edition (Shaw Associates, Publishers, 625 Biltmore Way, Suite 1406, Coral Gables, Florida 33134, 305–446–8888) is a good place to start for a thorough international listing of cooking schools, courses, culinary programs in technical schools and universities, as well as travel and cooking tours. The listings are filled with useful information, including the scope of courses, descriptions of the faculty, and approximate costs or tuition fees, along with mail and phone contacts.

The *International Directory of IACP Cooking Schools* is a listing of the organization's accredited schools and instructors, which is a guarantee that the schools meet a high professional standard. Contact the International Association of Cooking Professionals, 304 West Liberty Street, Suite 301, Louisville, Kentucky 40202 (502–583–3783).

The American Culinary Federation, has, in addition to its other programs, a system of accreditation for culinary schools. For information, contact The Educational Institute, American Culinary Federation, P.O. Box 3466, St. Augustine, Florida 32084 (904–824–4468).

California Culinary Academy
625 Polk Street
San Francisco, California 94102
415–771–3555

The French Culinary Institute
462 Broadway
New York, New York 10013
212–219–8890

Johnson & Wales University
Culinary Arts Division
1 Washington Avenue
Providence, Rhode Island 02905
401–456–1130

The New York Restaurant School
27 West 34th Street
New York, New York 10001
212–947–7097

The Restaurant School
2129 Walnut Street
Philadelphia, Pennsylvania 19103
215–561–3446

The Culinary Institute of America
North Road
P.O. Box 53
Hyde Park, New York 12538
914–452–9430

Culinary Arts at the New School
100 Greenwich Avenue
New York, New York 10011
212–255–4141

Peter Kump's New York Cooking School
307 East 92d Street
New York, New York 10128
212–410–4601

Cornell University
School of Hotel Administration
Statler Hall
Ithaca, New York 14853
607–256–5106

Culinary Arts Program
Department of the Arts, Room 414
UCLA Extension
10995 Le Conte Avenue
Los Angeles, California 90024
213–206–8120

Western Culinary Institute
1316 S.W. 13th Avenue
Portland, Oregon 97201
503–223–2245 or 800–666–0312

Professional Associations

Many professionals find membership in one or more peer organizations worthwhile and supportive. Such groups, many of which are local and regional, are certainly worth exploring as you begin or expand your business. Again, I have selected only a few of the major established organizations for inclusion here. All of them will send information about their groups to interested parties or potential members. In general, the groups listed here have at least annual meetings, send newsletters or bulletins to members, and some have certification programs, either for individuals or schools, to maintain the standards of their membership.

National Institute for Off-Premise Catering
2555 North Clark Street
Suite 302
Chicago, Illinois 60614
312–525–6800

International Special Events Society
7080 Hollywood Boulevard
Suite 410
Los Angeles, California 90028
800–344–ISES
  (in CA and Canada 213–469–4500)

International Caterer's Association
220 South State Street
Suite 1416
Chicago, Illinois 60604
312–922–1271

American Culinary Foundation
P.O. Box 3466
St. Augustine, Florida 32085
904–824–4468

International Association of Cooking
  Professionals
304 West Liberty Street
Suite 301
Louisville, Kentucky 40202
502–583–3783

American Institute of Wine and Food
1550 Bryant Street
Suite 700
San Francisco, California 94103
415–255–3000

The Educational Foundation of the National
  Restaurant Association
250 South Wacker Drive
Suite 1400
Chicago, Illinois 60606
312–715–1010

Council on Hotel, Restaurant, and
  Institutional Education
1200 17th Street N.W.
Washington, D.C. 20036
202–331–5990

Recipe Index

Subject Index